Lecture Notes in Computer Science 15417

The series Lecture Notes in Computer Science (LNCS), including its subseries Lecture Notes in Artificial Intelligence (LNAI) and Lecture Notes in Bioinformatics (LNBI), has established itself as a medium for the publication of new developments in computer science and information technology research, teaching, and education.

LNCS enjoys close cooperation with the computer science R & D community, the series counts many renowned academics among its volume editors and paper authors, and collaborates with prestigious societies. Its mission is to serve this international community by providing an invaluable service, mainly focused on the publication of conference and workshop proceedings and postproceedings. LNCS commenced publication in 1973.

Janos Kertesz · Bo Li · Thepchai Supnithi ·
Akkharawoot Takhom
Editors

Computational Data and Social Networks

13th International Conference, CSoNet 2024 Bangkok, Thailand, December 16–18, 2024 Proceedings

Springer

Editors
Janos Kertesz
Central European University
Vienna, Austria

Bo Li
The Hong Kong Polytechnic University
Hong Kong, China

Thepchai Supnithi
National Electronics and Computer
Technology Center
Khlong Nueng, Thailand

Akkharawoot Takhom
Thammasat University
Bangkok, Thailand

ISSN 0302-9743 ISSN 1611-3349 (electronic)
Lecture Notes in Computer Science
ISBN 978-981-96-6388-0 ISBN 978-981-96-6389-7 (eBook)
https://doi.org/10.1007/978-981-96-6389-7

This Springer imprint is published by the registered company Springer Nature Singapore Pte Ltd.
The registered company address is: 152 Beach Road, #21-01/04 Gateway East, Singapore 189721, Singapore

Preface

We are delighted to present the proceedings of the 13th International Conference on Computational Data and Social Networks (CSoNet 2024), held in the Bangkok Metropolitan Region (Pathum Thani), Thailand, from December 16 to 18, 2024. This volume includes all contributed papers from the main track of CSoNet 2024, as well as the special track of the International Workshop on Artificial Intelligence for Signal, Image Processing, and Multimedia (AI-SIPM2 2024). The conference served as a premier interdisciplinary platform, bringing together researchers and practitioners from diverse fields related to big data networks, including large-scale network computing, data network analysis, mining, security and privacy, optimization, and learning. CSoNet 2024 not only featured original research presentations but also encouraged the exchange of innovative ideas and real-world development experiences. The conference topics spanned foundational theories, technological advancements, and practical applications in these areas.

The Program Committee for the main track, consisting of 29 active researchers, selected 18 regular papers, 17 short papers, and 4 extended abstracts for presentation. Each submission underwent a rigorous single-blind peer review process, with at least two reviews per paper, and additional reviews were solicited as needed. Furthermore, AI-SIPM2 2024 accepted 9 submissions for presentation. Besides the regular talks, CSoNet 2024 had keynote talks from Joongheon Kim (Korea University), Minming Li (City University of Hong Kong) and Alexis Drogoul (French National Research Institute for Sustainable Development, IRD). We extend our sincere appreciation to everyone who contributed to the success of CSoNet 2024: the authors, whose research advances the field; the Program Committee members, whose expertise guided the selection process; and the reviewers, whose valuable feedback helped maintain the scientific quality of the conference.

We are also grateful to Springer for publishing the CSoNet 2024 proceedings in the Lecture Notes in Computer Science (LNCS) series. A special thanks goes to the general chairs, Sabrina Gaito and Sanya Mitaim, as well as the local organizing team, for their dedication and exceptional efforts in making this event a success.

December 2024

Janos Kertesz
Bo Li
Thepchai Supnithi
Akkharawoot Takhom

Organization

Steering Committee

My T. Thai	University of Florida, USA
Kim-Kwang Raymond Choo	University of Texas at San Antonio, USA
Weili Wu	University of Texas at Dallas, USA
Zhi-Li Zhang	University of Minnesota, USA

General Co-chairs

Sabrina Gaito	University of Milan, Italy
Sanya Mitaim	Thammasat University, Thailand

Program Committee Co-chairs

Janos Kertesz	Central European University, Austria
Bo Li	Hong Kong Polytechnic University, China
Thepchai Supnithi	National Electronics and Computer Technology Center, Thailand

Program Committee

Son Ha	Royal Melbourne Institute of Technology, Australia
Min Shi	University of Louisiana at Lafayette, USA
Mohammed Abuhama	Loyola University Chicago, USA
Canh V. Pham	Phenikaa University, Vietnam
Vincenzo Moscato	University of Naples "Federico II", Italy
Xin Huang	Hong Kong Baptist University, China
Ankang Sun	Hong Kong Polytechnic University, China
Yu Zhou	Pennsylvania State University, Pennsylvania
Jinyoung Han	Sungkyunkwan University, South Korea
Wenjing Liu	Ocean University of China, China
Bin Liu	Ocean University of China, China
Hoang Long Nguyen	Meharry Medical College

Weian Li	Shandong University, China
Houyu Zhou	University of New South Wales, Australia
Viet Hung Nguyen	Clermont Auvergne University, France
Duy Dung Le	Vin University, Vietnam
Thu Dang	Lancaster University, UK
Thuy Nguyen	Royal Melbourne Institute of Technology, Australia
Weizhi Meng	Technical University of Denmark, Denmark
Seba Hamida	Claude Bernard University Lyon 1, France
Alexander Lam	City University of Hong Kong, China
Yi He	William and Mary, Virginia
Guangmo Tong	University of Delaware, Delaware
Jianxiong Guo	Beijing Normal University, China
Rosa Maria Benito	Universidad Politécnica de Madrid, Spain
Laura Ricci	University of Pisa, Italy

Special Track Program Co-chairs

Phisan Kaewprapha	Thammasat University, Thailand
Akkharawoot Takhom	Thammasat University, Thailand

Local Organizing Co-chairs

Phisan Kaewprapha	Thammasat University, Thailand
Thanatchapan Petcharat	Thammasat University, Thailand
Kanyalag Phodong	Phranakhon Si Ayutthaya Rajabhat University, Thailand
Thidarat Pinthong	Phetchaburi Rajabhat University, Thailand
Patiyuth Pramkeaw	King Mongkut's University of Technology Thonburi, Thailand

Web Chair

Tre' R. Jeter	University of Florida

Publicity Co-chairs

Teeradaj Racharak	Japan Advanced Institute of Science and Technology, Japan
Kwanrutai Saclim	Yala Rajabhat University, Thailand

Extended Abstracts

Approximate Core Allocations for Vertex Cover Games

Haitao Wang, Han Xiao, and Qizhi Fang

School of Mathematical Sciences, Ocean University of China, Qingdao, China
haitao_w@stu.ouc.edu.cn, {hxiao,qfang}@ouc.edu.cn

Abstract. We examine approximate core allocations for the minimum weight vertex cover (MWVC) game in this paper. The MWVC game is a class of combinatorial optimization game [1, 2] derived from the MWVC problem. The core of a cooperative game is a set of stable allocations where no coalition can improve their payoffs by deviating from the grand coalition. However, the core can be empty in many games, including the MWVC game. To address this issue, the concept of the approximate core is introduced, which offers a relaxation of the core constraints. Among various definitions of the approximate core, we study the α-core [3]. This is the set of allocations where the cost allocated to every coalition does not exceed α $(0 < \alpha \leq 1)$ times the cost of the coalition that it would incur if it worked on its own. Clearly, the α-core is always non-empty when α is small enough.

A key question in studying the α-core is finding the smallest α such that the α-core is non-empty [4–6]. We show that the smallest α for the MWVC game is equal to the integrality gap of the linear programming (LP) relaxation of the corresponding MWVC problem. We remark that the integrality gap is the ratio between the optimal solutions of the integer program and its LP relaxation. We also present an allocation scheme that always returns an allocation in the α-core with the smallest α. Our allocation scheme relies on the dual optimal solution of the LP relaxation of the MWVC problem.

Another key question in studying the α-core is finding allocations in the α-core with the smallest [4–6]. Since the MWVC problem is NP-hard, it is computationally challenging to use our allocation scheme with the integrality gap. Hence we introduce a polynomial-time algorithm that returns allocations within the $\frac{2d}{1+d}$-core of the MWVC game, where d is the maximum degree of the vertices in the underlying graph. Our algorithm leverages the fact that a half-integral optimal solution for the LP relaxation of the MWVC problem can be computed in polynomial time. We also show that this approximation ratio of $\frac{2d}{1+d}$ cannot be improved with parameter d.

This work provides valuable insights into the stability and computational aspects of the MWVC game. The findings highlight the connection between approximate core allocations and the integrality gap of the underlying optimization problem. Additionally, the proposed polynomial-time algorithm offers a practical method for computing

Supported in part by the National Natural Science Foundation of China (Nos. 12001507 and 12171444) and Natural Science Foundation of Shandong (No. ZR2020QA024)

approximate core allocations, particularly in scenarios where finding the exact core is computationally challenging.

Keywords: Approximate core · Vertex cover game · Integrality gap

References

1. Deng, X., Ibaraki, T., Nagamochi, H.: Algorithmic aspects of the core of combinatorial optimization games. Math. Oper. Res. **24**(3), 751–766 (1999)
2. Deng, X., Ibaraki, T., Nagamochi, H., Zang, W.: Totally balanced combinatorial optimization games. Math. Program. **87**(3), 441–452 (2000)
3. Faigle, U., Kern, W.: On some approximately balanced combinatorial cooperative games. ZOR - Methods Models Oper. Res. **38**(2), 141–152 (1993)
4. Lu, T., Xiao, H., Fang, Q.: Approximate core allocations for edge cover games. Theor. Comput. Sci. **991**, 114433 (2024)
5. Vazirani, V.V.: The general graph matching game: approximate core. Games Econ. Behav. **132**, 478–486 (2022)
6. Xiao, H., Lu, T., Fang, Q.: Approximate core allocations for multiple partners matching games. arXiv:2107.01442 (2021)

Multivariate Distribution Modeling via Multidimensional Conditional Cross-Entropy Loss Functions in Neural Networks

Alexander Semenov[1], Vladimir Boginski[2], and Eduardo L. Pasiliao[3]

[1] University of Florida, Gainesville, FL, 32611 USA
asemenov@ufl.edu
[2] University of Central Florida, Orlando, FL, 32816 USA
vladimir.boginski@ucf.edu
[3] Air Force Research Laboratory, Eglin AFB, FL, 32542 USA
eduardo.pasiliao@us.af.mil

Abstract. We introduce a new artificial neural network architecture that efficiently models and trains multivariate distribution functions using conditional and marginal distributions. Our approach computes an output layer from the last hidden layer directly, without having to optimize weights between them. By reshaping the network's last hidden layer into a multidimensional tensor with equal dimensions that match the length of its one-hot label, we are able to interpret the hidden layer tensor as a multivariate distribution function on which we apply standard multivariate statistical techniques to produce several uni-variate distribution functions. We compute the marginal distributions and measure the difference between them and the target distribution function. We also investigate the use of conditional distribution functions to predict the target distribution. Although conditional distributions are computationally less demanding, marginal distributions are able to generate better estimates. Finally we can add the marginal distributions to produce a single distribution function estimate. This approach reduces computational complexity typically associated with high-dimensional data by eliminating the need for explicit loops when summing over dimensions. Additionally, we explore training methods based on marginal distributions, providing alternative techniques to capture complex data structures. The novelty of the proposed architecture is in integrating multidimensional conditional probabilities directly into the learning process, potentially paving the way for enhanced performance in tasks involving multivariate probability estimations.

Keywords: Neural Networks · Cross-Entropy Loss Functions · Multivariate Distribution Modeling

Extended Abstract

In neural network architectures, particularly in classification tasks, the output layer typically provides a probability distribution over the possible classes. Traditional methods often use a softmax layer to achieve this. However, modeling the output as a multivariate

N-dimensional distribution allows us to capture complex interactions between multiple variables, potentially improving performance in tasks where such interactions are significant.

In this work, we propose an approach to generate the output function by interpreting the neural network's outputs as representing a joint distribution over multiple random variables. We compute the final class scores using marginal and conditional distributions derived from this joint distribution. This work extends our previous approach presented in [2]. Other related research also includes [1].

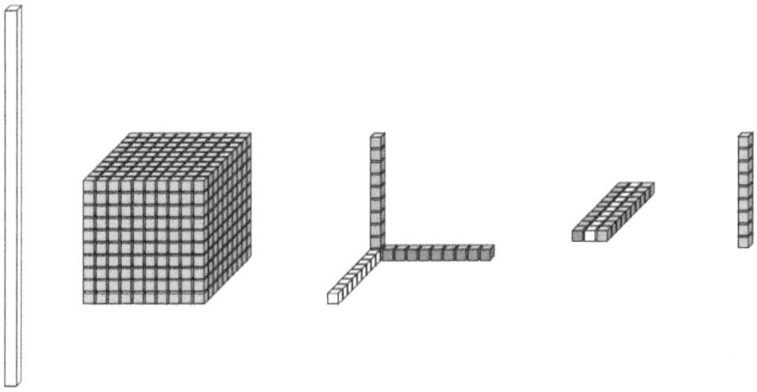

Fig. 1. Graphical representation of the transformation from a high-dimensional tensor into its marginal distributions along each axis. From left to right: original input, tensor, marginals along each dimension, and subsequent aggregation steps.

Marginalization Over Each Dimension. Consider an N-dimensional hypercube where the tensor $\mathbf{T}$ represents the joint distribution of N discrete random variables, each taking values from a discrete set of size K. This means that the tensor $\mathbf{T}$ has the shape $(K, K, \ldots, K)$, with N dimensions in total. For example, if $N = 3$ and $K = 10$, the tensor $\mathbf{T}$ would have the shape (10, 10, 10), which is a 3-dimensional cube with 10 discrete entries per dimension, and represents the joint distribution of three discrete random variables X, Y, and Z, each taking values from 0 to 9 (see Fig. 1).

For each dimension $d = 1, 2, \ldots, N$, we compute the marginal distribution by summing over all dimensions except X_d. This can be expressed mathematically as:

$$S_d(n) = \sum_{\substack{i_1,\ldots,i_N \\ i_d \neq n}} \mathbf{T}_{i_1,i_2,\ldots,i_N}, \tag{1}$$

for $n = 0, 1, \ldots, K - 1$. This operation marginalizes over all dimensions except for X_d, resulting in a vector of length K representing the marginal distribution for that dimension.
Cross-Entropy Calculation. After computing the marginal distributions for each dimension, we calculate the cross-entropy between the predicted marginal distribution and the true distribution for each dimension d. Let $\mathbf{P}(X_d = n)$ be the predicted marginal distribution ($\mathbf{P}(X_d = n) = S_d(n)$) and $\mathbf{Q}(X_d = n)$ be the true distribution. The cross-entropy

for each dimension is defined as:

$$H(\mathbf{Q}_d, \mathbf{P}_d) = -\sum_{n=0}^{K-1} \mathbf{Q}(X_d = n) \log \mathbf{P}(X_d = n). \tag{2}$$

The total cross-entropy over all dimensions is the sum of the individual cross-entropies:

$$H_{\text{total}}(\mathbf{Q}, \mathbf{P}) = \sum_{d=1}^{N} H(\mathbf{Q}_d, \mathbf{P}_d), \tag{3}$$

for $n = 0, 1, \ldots, K-1$. This accounts for the contributions of each variable individually, while retaining the interactions captured by the joint distribution.

The marginalization for each variable proceeds as follows:

1. Sum over Y and Z to obtain marginal for X:

$$S_1(n) = \sum_{j=0}^{K-1} \sum_{k=0}^{K-1} \mathbf{T}_{n,j,k}, \tag{4}$$

for $n = 0, 1, \ldots, K-1$.

2. Sum over X and Z to obtain marginal for Y:

$$S_2(n) = \sum_{i=0}^{K-1} \sum_{k=0}^{K-1} \mathbf{T}_{i,n,k}, \tag{5}$$

for $n = 0, 1, \ldots, K-1$.

3. Sum over X and Y to obtain marginal for Z:

$$S_3(n) = \sum_{i=0}^{K-1} \sum_{j=0}^{K-1} \mathbf{T}_{i,j,n}, \tag{6}$$

for $n = 0, 1, \ldots, K-1$.

The final loss is obtained by aggregating the contributions of each dimension through cross-entropy.

Implementation in Neural Networks. This approach can be implemented in a neural network as follows. The network first outputs a vector $\mathbf{x}$ of length K^N, representing the joint distribution of N discrete random variables across all possible combinations of values. This vector is then reshaped into an N-dimensional tensor $\mathbf{T}$ of shape $(K, K, \ldots, K)$, which represents the joint distribution of the random variables in an N-dimensional space. Next, the marginal sums $S_d(n)$ are computed for each dimension d by summing over all dimensions except X_d, effectively reducing the dimensionality and obtaining the marginal distributions for each random variable. These marginal distributions are then aggregated across all dimensions to compute the final prediction scores.

Concluding Remarks. The proposed approach demonstrates several advantages. By modeling the output as a joint distribution, it captures complex interactions between random variables, enhancing the model's representation of dependencies in the data. It is also flexible, adaptable to any number of dimensions N, and computationally efficient due to the use of tensor operations, which avoid explicit loops. In conclusion, the proposed method provides a robust framework for capturing both individual and joint behaviors of multiple variables, making it suitable for applications requiring high-dimensional modeling.

References

1. Acharya, D., Siddiqui, H., Pasiliao, E., Banerjee, C.: Mutually exclusive learning for generators with multi-label classifiers. In: 2023 IEEE International Conference on Big Data (BigData), pp. 4258–4267. IEEE (2023)
2. Semenov, A., Boginski, V., Pasiliao, E.L.: Neural Networks with multidimensional cross-entropy loss functions. In: Tagarelli, A., Tong, H. (eds.) CSoNet 2019. LNCS, vol. 11917, pages 57–62. Springer, Cham (2019). https://doi.org/10.1007/978-3-030-34980-6_5

Distributed Facility Location Games with Candidate Locations

Feiyue Sun

School of Mathematical Sciences, Ocean University of China, Qingdao, China
1127327435@qq.com

Abstract. In mechanism design problems for facility location games with incomplete information [3], a set of strategic agents report their private information (e.g., locations) and a mechanism maps the reported information into the locations of several facilities. Considering that agents may misreport to decrease their costs, the social planner aims to design mechanisms that can incentivize agents to report truthfully (referred to as strategyproofness or group strategyproofness) while guaranteeing optimizing some social objective approximately.

Recently, a variant of facility location games called *distributed* facility location has been studied, where all the agents are divided into several groups, and a mechanism is carried out in two steps: first select a representative for each group based on reports from the agents in this group, then choose the facility locations based on all the groups' representatives [1]. In distributed facility location games, *distortion* was introduced to measure the performance of a mechanism, which is defined as the worst-case ratio between the social objective value of the mechanism and the optimal social objective value and can be seen as a distributed version of approximation ratio [2]. In this paper, we study the distributed single facility location games with candidate locations, where each agent is located on a line and has location as her private information. Both desirable and obnoxious facility location games are discussed. For the former, we consider the problem in the discrete candidate locations setting where the facility location can be selected from a finite subset of $\mathbb{R}$ [4], compared with the continuous setting where the facility can be located at any point in an interval of $\mathbb{R}$ [1]. For the latter, we consider the problem both in a discrete setting and in a continuous setting where the candidate location set is a finite interval.

In the desirable facility location game, we propose three strategyproof distributed mechanisms. Under the social objective of the sum of the maximum cost of the agents in each group (abbreviated as Sum-Max), we give a strategyproof mechanism (called Median-of-Rightmost) with 5-distortion as follows: For each group d, select the candidate z_d as the representative in d such that $z_d := \arg\min_{z \in C} \delta(r_d, z)$ where C is the candidate location set and r_d is the rightmost agent's location in d, and the final winner is the median of all the groups' representatives; and prove that no strategyproof mechanism can have a distortion better than $\frac{\sqrt{5}+1}{2}$. Under the maximum of the sum cost of all the agents in each group (Max-Sum), we propose a strategyproof mechanism (called Rightmost-of-Median) with 5-distortion and prove that no strategyproof mechanism can have a distortion better than $\sqrt{2}+1$. Under the maximum of the maximum cost of the agents in each group (Max-Max), we give a strategyproof mechanism (called Median-of-Median) with 3-distortion, and prove that no strategyproof mechanism can have a distortion better than $\frac{\sqrt{5}+1}{2}$.

In the obnoxious facility location game, we consider the problem under three corresponding social objectives, which are the sum of the minimum utility of the agents in each group, and the minimum of the sum utility of all the agents in each group, the minimum of the minimum utility of the agents in each group, respectively. We prove that there is no strategy proof mechanism with bounded distortion in the discrete setting, and no group strategyproof mechanism with bounded distortion in the continuous setting.

Keywords: Distributed facility location · Mechanism design · Distortion · Strategyproofness

References

1. Filos-Ratsikas, A., Kanellopoulos, P., Voudouris, A.A., Zhang, R.: The distortion of distributed facility location. Artif. Intell. **328**, 104066 (2024)
2. Filos-Ratsikas, A., Micha, E., Voudouris, A.A.: The distortion of distributed voting. Artif. Intell. **286**, 103343 (2020)
3. Procaccia, A.D., Tennenholtz, M.: Approximate mechanism design without money. ACM Trans. Econ. Comput. **1**(4), 1–26 (2013)
4. Tang, Z., Wang, C., Zhang, M., Zhao, Y.: Mechanism design for facility location games with candidate locations. In: Proceedings of the 14th International Conference on Combinatorial Optimization and Applications (COCOA), pp. 440–452 (2020)

Influence Maximization Considering Stochastic Network Topology

Zhecheng Qiang[1], Eduardo L. Pasiliao[2], and Qipeng P. Zheng[1]

[1] Industrial Engineering and Management Systems, University of Central Florida, Orlando, FL, 32765 USA
[2] Air Force Research Lab, Eglin, FL, USA
qipeng.zheng@gmail.com

Abstract. Influence Maximization, one of the most important problems in social media, aims to find the seed nodes representing users or organizations to help achieve the maximum influence within the whole network. It can be applied in a great variety of areas, such as viral marketing, cybersecurity, and many others. In this extended abstract, we study the influence maximization problem within networks of stochastic topology. We formulate the problem as a two-stage stochastic optimization problem, and solve it via the Sample Average Approximation, hoping to shed light on decision making for influence maximization under uncertainty.

Keywords: Influence Maximization · Social Media · Stochastic · Network Topology · Optimization

1 Introduction

Social media has become a critically important platform for people to spread their influence and get influenced. Recognizing influential users is essential for all applications of social media. The problem of recognizing influential users in social media is called the influence maximization problem (IM), which refers to selecting the seed nodes (e.g., users) at the beginning so that they can help spread the most influence. Most of the past research has focused on solving the influence maximization problem in a deterministic way [1–3].

However, network topology is rarely deterministic especially in the social network setting. Incorporating the randomness of the network topology, user behaviors, and costs and benefits is very necessary in real-world applications [4, 5]. Hence, in this research, we introduce a two-stage stochastic programming model addressing the stochastic topology of the network. In the following sections, we will first introduce the mathematical formulation and then discuss how numerical experiments were conducted and their results before concluding this extended abstract.

2 Two-Stage Stochastic Optimization Models

The influence maximization problem refers to finding a set of k seed nodes to start a cascade process so that the total number of nodes being activated at the end is maximized. In the real world, social media networks are dynamic and random in some sense, which means there's rapid evolution between nodes and the structure of the network. In social media, users may add new friends or remove people from their friends everyday. Therefore, we assume that uncertainty exists in network topology in social media. Here we consider a variant of the Influence Maximization Problem: instead of just selecting the seed nodes to activate at the beginning, here we're solving a two stage stochastic programming problem. Firstly, we select the seed nodes to activate at the beginning when the uncertainties are unknown. Then we activate some nodes after the uncertainty is known to maximize the influence in social media networks. The two-stage stochastic programming model for influence maximization in a network with random topology is presented as follows,

$$\max \quad \sum_{\omega} \sum_{i=1}^{n} \rho_{\omega}(z_i^{\omega} + y_i^{\omega}) \tag{OBJ}$$

$$s.t. \quad \sum_{i=1}^{n} c_i x_i + d_i^{\omega} y_i^{\omega} \leq B \tag{1}$$

$$\frac{1}{|N(i)^{\omega}|} \sum_{j \in N(i)^{\omega}} x_j + \theta x_i \geq \theta z_i^{\omega} \tag{2}$$

$$z_i^{\omega} + y_i^{\omega} \leq 1 \tag{3}$$

$$x, y \in \{0, 1\}^n \tag{4}$$

Here ρ_{ω} represents the probabilities of different network topologies. x_i refers to the initial status of node i. y_i^{ω} refers to whether to activate the node i under scenario ω. z_i^{ω} refers to the final status of node i under scenario ω. θ represents the threshold in our experiment. $N(i)^{\omega}$ represents the neighbors of user i under scenario ω. $c_i = c|N(i)|$ and $d_i = d|N(i)^{\omega}|$, and B represents the total budget. In numerical experiments, if user i and user j are not connected, then their probability to be connected at the next time step is 0.1. If user i and user j are already connected, then their probability to disconnect at the next time step is 0.01.

3 Numerical Experiments

Here we use two different networks to test our stochastic influence maximization models, i.e., Watts-Strogatz, and Erdos-Renyi networks. The Watts-Strogatz model generates a random graph with small-world properties, including short average path lengths and high clustering. We generate a Watts-Strogatz graph with 20 nodes and each node is connected to 6 nearest neighbors in a ring topology with a 0.1 probability of rewiring. The Erdos-Renyi model also has the property of having short average path lengths but with low clustering. We generate an Erdos-Renyi graph with 20 nodes where we choose each of the possible edges with probability $p = 0.1$.

For the influence maximization model considering stochastic network topology, the scenarios of network topology could be very large, which is $2^{\frac{|V|(|V|-1)}{2}}$, where $|V|$ refers to the total number of nodes. Therefore, we utilize the sample average approximation (SAA) to reformulate the influence maximization model considering stochastic network topology with a limited number of scenarios. M samples (each containing N scenarios) were generated to obtain an approximation of the optimal objective value, $\bar{f}_{N,M}$. In addition, we also compute the sample variances and related gaps.

For the influence maximization model considering stochastic network topology, we set the budget as 30% of total edges, and the activation threshold as 0.3. The cost of node i at time 0 is the total number of neighbors of node i and the cost of node i at time 1 is 80% of the total number of neighbors of node i. To generate the stochastic network topology, we assume there's a 10% probability to create an edge and 1% probability to delete an edge. The computational results of different networks are shown in Table 1.

Table 1. Computational Results for Stochastic Network Topology Model

Network	$\bar{f}_{N,M}$	$\bar{f}_{N'}(\bar{x})$	$gap_{N,M,N'}$	$\sigma^2_{\bar{f}_{N,M}}$	$\sigma^2_{N'}(\bar{x})$	σ^2_{gap}
ER-20	9.6370	9.2775	0.3595	0.0007	0.0007	0.0014
Watts-20	6.6610	6.2415	0.4195	0.0008	0.0006	0.0014

4 Conclusions

This research tackles the influence maximization problem considering the randomness of network topology. The problem can be formulated as a two-stage stochastic optimization problem. We implement a Sample Average Approximation method to estimate the optimal objective values, which all show gains when using stochastic solutions.

References

1. Qiang, Z., Pasiliao, E.L., Semenov, A., Zheng, Q.P.: Incorporating neighborhood information and sentence embedding similarity into a repost prediction model in social media networks. In: Dinh, T.N., Li, M. (eds.) CSoNet 2022. LNCS, vol. 13831, pp. 3–14. Springer, Cham (2023). https://doi.org/10.1007/978-3-031-26303-3_1

2. Qiang, Z., Pasiliao, E.L., Zheng, Q.P.: Target set selection in social networks with influence and activation thresholds. In: Mohaisen, D., Jin, R. (eds.) CSoNet 2021. LNCS, vol. 13116, pp. 371–380. Springer, Cham (2021). https://doi.org/10.1007/978-3-030-91434-9_32
3. Qiang, Z., Pasiliao, E.L., Zheng, Q.P.: Target set selection in social networks with tiered influence and activation thresholds. J. Comb. Optim. **45**, Article No. 117 (2023)
4. Tanınmış, K., Aras, N., Altınel, I.: Influence maximization with deactivation in social networks. Eur. J. Oper. Res. **278**(1), 105–119 (2019)
5. Zheng, Q.P., Shen, S., Shi, Y.: Loss-constrained minimum cost flow under arc failure uncertainty with applications in risk-aware kidney exchange. IIE Trans. **47**(9), 961–977 (2015). https://doi.org/10.1080/0740817X.2014.991476

Contents

Navigating Trustworthiness in LLMs: An Examination of Privacy, Security, and Robustness

Kieu Dang(✉) and Phung Lai

State University of New York at Albany, Albany, NY 12222, USA
{vdang,lai}@albany.edu

Abstract. Large Language Models (LLMs) have transformed natural language processing, demonstrating remarkable capabilities across diverse tasks. However, deploying these models in real-world applications need to ensure their trustworthiness. This paper explores three critical dimensions of trustworthiness: privacy, security, and robustness. We examine privacy concerns related to data handling and user confidentiality, highlighting the need for transparent practices and robust data protection measures. Security issues, including adversarial attacks and model vulnerabilities, are analyzed to underscore the potential risks and necessary countermeasures. Furthermore, we address robustness challenges, focusing on bias, overfitting, and the impact of noisy inputs on model performance. By systematically synthesizing existing research and strategies for improvement, this study aims to provide a comprehensive framework for enhancing the trustworthiness of LLMs, ultimately fostering their safe and effective deployment in real-world scenarios.

Keywords: Trustworthiness · LLMs · Privacy · Security · Robustness

1 Introduction

Large Language Models (LLMs) have revolutionized natural language processing, demonstrating remarkable capabilities across various tasks and applications [62,83]. Despite their impressive capabilities, deploying LLMs in the real-world, especially in sensitive domains like healthcare and finance raises serious concerns about trustworthiness and reliability. Models that expose private data, produce harmful outputs, or are vulnerable to attacks can lead to privacy and security violations, and compromised systems. Therefore, addressing privacy, security, and robustness challenges is crucial for the safe and responsible use of LLMs.

This paper explores the core issues related to the trustworthiness of LLMs and the current state of solutions addressing these challenges. The focus will be on three key areas: privacy, security, and robustness. In terms of privacy, we examine the risks associated with training data exposure, inference attacks, and user data vulnerability during deployment. Security issues are addressed through an analysis of adversarial attacks, model stealing, and backdoor attacks,

J. Kertesz et al. (Eds.): CSoNet 2024, LNCS 15417, pp. 1–13, 2025.
https://doi.org/10.1007/978-981-96-6389-7_1

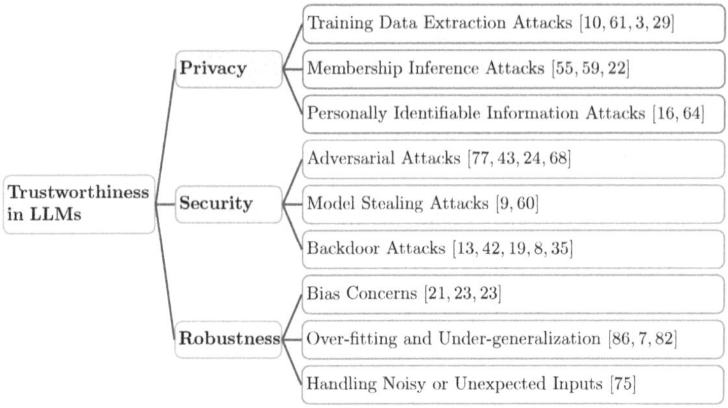

Fig. 1. Taxonomy of Primary Concerns of Trustworthiness in LLMs.

highlighting the weaknesses that threaten LLM integrity. Finally, we discuss the robustness challenges related to bias, generalization, and the handling of noisy or unexpected inputs, which affect the fairness and reliability of LLMs.

This paper is structured as follows: Sect. 2 examines trustworthiness issues in LLMs, including privacy, security, and robustness challenges. Section 3 reviews existing solutions, covering privacy-preserving techniques, security mechanisms, and robustness enhancements. Section 4 proposes future directions for improving LLM trustworthiness, focusing on advanced privacy methods, enhanced security measures, and robustness solutions. Finally, Sect. 5 summarizes key insights and reflects on the future of trustworthy LLM development.

2 Trustworthiness Problems in LLMs

In this section, we will outline problems related to different components of trustworthiness in LLMs, focusing on privacy, security, and robustness (Figure 1).

2.1 Privacy Problems

LLMs pose significant privacy problems, including risks from different attacks aimed at revealing training data and model information. These problems stem from how LLMs are trained, particularly when using sensitive datasets or interacting with real-time user data, leading to models that can memorize user inputs and behave differently with varying data samples. Several significant attacks exploit the vulnerabilities of LLMs. First, ***training data extraction attacks*** refers to situations where models unintentionally reveal sensitive information embedded in their training datasets and adversaries can reconstruct portions of the training data from the model's outputs. In [10] and [61], the authors show that GPT-2 can generate verbatim sequences from its training data, including sensitive details such as personal significant and contract information, with high confidence. In addition, we can exploit the co-occurrence of special characters and raw text during training [3], and backdooring models for controlled extraction of specific training data [29] to extract training data. Second, ***membership inference attacks*** (MIAs) [55,70] allow adversaries to infer whether a data sample was used in training. For instance, [55] exploits the differences in model behaviors to distinguish training and non-training data samples. [59] improves attack performance by analyzing semantic content of both training and non-training data samples, while SPV-MIA [22] leverages probabilistic variation using self-prompt calibration to provide a more reliable membership signal. Third, recent studies [16,64] demonstrate that even well-designed language models can be vulnerable to privacy breaches. During deployment, as seen in chatbots or virtual assistants, adversaries can exploit system vulnerabilities to ***extract personally identifiable information*** (PII) by inserting benign sentences into training datasets. Addressing these privacy challenges is crucial, and implementing effective mitigation strategies throughout the model's lifecycle is essential to safeguarding sensitive information and ensuring user trust.

2.2 Security Problems

Security issues in LLMs involve vulnerabilities that can compromise model integrity, with key threats including adversarial attacks, model stealing, and backdoor attacks. First, ***adversarial attacks*** involve inputs crafted to appear legitimate but cause LLMs to generate incorrect or harmful responses. Attackers introduce small perturbations, such as altering word order or substituting characters, to mislead the model [68]. These attacks can be classified into two main categories: Unimodal and Multimodal attacks. Unimodal attacks focus solely on text-based manipulations to bypass model's safety constraints or alignment mechanisms or cause the model to prioritize the injected prompt over its intended instructions [43,77]. Similar purposes with unimodal attacks, but multimodal attacks manipulate inputs across different modalities such as text, image, audio, etc. [24,68]. Second, ***model stealing attacks*** occur when attackers mimic an LLM's behavior by querying it and using that data to train their own model. This can involve extracting detailed information from black-box LLMs or stealing decoding algorithms and hyperparameters at low cost [9,60]. Third, ***backdoor attacks*** embed hidden triggers, such as specific phrases, into training data, leading to misbehavior when activated [26]. Backdoor attacks pose a severe threat, as they can remain dormant until triggered, making them challenging to detect during standard testing. A common method involves data poisoning, where attackers introduce compromised data during training. Techniques include data poisoning [13,42], where compromised data is introduced during training, and methods like Poisoned Prompt Tuning (PPT) [19] and Bad-Prompt [8], which embed triggers while maintaining performance on clean data. The Composite Backdoor Attack (CBA) [35] complicates detection by distributing multiple triggers across prompts, activating only when all components are present. Other approaches involve semantic-preserving modifications, data-free

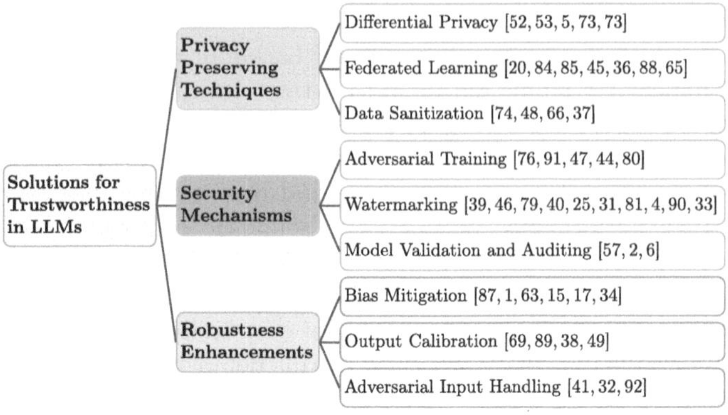

Fig. 2. Taxonomy of Existing Solutions for Trustworthiness in LLMs.

methods, and weight poisoning, which embeds backdoors directly into model weights.

2.3 Robustness Problems

Robustness challenges in LLMs refer to the difficulties in ensuring reliable and fair performance under various real-world conditions. Key issues include managing biased data that can result in unfair outcomes, preventing overfitting to specific training data for better generalization, and maintaining performance against noisy or adversarial inputs. First, ***bias*** issues are the most pressing robustness challenges for LLMs [21], as these models are trained on large text corpora that may contain historical and societal biases, leading to outputs that reflect these unfair tendencies [23]. Even subtle linguistic biases can be amplified, perpetuating existing inequalities [23]. In addition, the model itself such as loss functions, attention mechanisms, embeddings, can introduce or exacerbate biases by unevenly prioritizing certain features. Users contribute to bias through interactions, as confirmation bias leads them to favor outputs that align with their beliefs, while automation bias can result in uncritical trust in LLM outputs. Second, ***overfitting*** is another significant robustness issue in LLMs, as it prevents the model from generalizing to new and unseen data [7,86]. This problem arises from two main factors: dataset size and quality, and model complexity [82]. Smaller, low-quality datasets are more easily memorized when reused across epochs, while complex LLMs with many parameters tend to overfit, particularly when training objectives misalign with data characteristics. Third, ***noisy or unexpected inputs***, including Automatic Speech Recognition and Optical Character Recognition errors, grammatical or typographical mistakes [75], can significantly impact model performance, therefore, affecting the robustness.

3 Existing Solutions for Improving Trustworthiness

To address the trustworthiness challenges outlined above, we present existing solutions as shown in Fig. 2.

3.1 Privacy-Preserving Techniques

Several techniques have been developed to protect privacy for LLMs.

Differential Privacy (DP). DP is a key technique for privacy preservation in LLMs, ensuring models do not reveal specific data details. DP methods vary by application timing: data modification approaches, like the Split-and-Denoise [52], add noise to embeddings during inference, while lightweight perturbation mechanisms enhance privacy during decoding [53]. In fine-tuning, methods such as EW-Tune [5] improve both privacy and performance. DP also supports model alignment and in-context learning [73]. Although DP may introduce noise that impacts accuracy, careful tuning can help balance privacy and performance [56].

Federated Learning (FL). Federated learning (FL) offers a privacy-preserving method for training LLMs on decentralized devices, keeping data localized. Each device trains a local model and sends updates to a central server for aggregation. Frameworks like FATE-LLM [20] and OpenFedLLM [84] enable collaborative training on private data while maintaining performance through instruction tuning. Efficiency improvements to reduce communication costs include FedJudge [85], Federated Zeroth-Order Optimization [45] and Low-Parameter FL [36]. FedPepTAO [11] enhances prompt tuning, while FedsLLM [88] and FDLoRA [65] optimize computation. Federated pre-training shows promise, but challenges like communication overhead and device heterogeneity remain [30].

Data Sanitization. Data sanitization is vital in LLMs for removing sensitive or personally identifiable information (PII) from training datasets, preventing unintended data exposure. Recent techniques address privacy concerns, such as pre-training sanitization to avoid memorization of sensitive data and anonymization for call transcripts [74]. Curating clean text can enhance safety and robustness against adversarial manipulation [48]. Advanced methods include data purification using benign language models and unlearning frameworks for selective removal of specific data points without full retraining [66]. Emerging frameworks for remote systems also focus on user privacy [37]. While essential, overly aggressive sanitization can degrade model performance, requiring a balance between retaining useful information and minimizing privacy risks.

3.2 Security Mechanisms

To address security challenges, various mechanisms have been developed to enhance resilience, improve model security, and maintain integrity.

Adversarial Training. Adversarial training enhances robustness by incorporating adversarial examples into training data, helping models resist attacks. Methods vary in perturbation techniques. For instance, [76] adds noise to the output embedding layer, while [91] applies perturbations to word embeddings. ALUM [47] uses embedding-space perturbations during pre-training and fine-tuning, and TextAT [44] introduces token-level perturbations. Recent methods like C-AdvUL and C-AdvIPO [80] compute adversarial examples in continuous embedding space. While adversarial training improves resilience, it can be computationally intensive and may reduce performance on benign inputs, creating a trade-off between robustness and accuracy [51].

Watermarking. Recently, watermarking has become an emerging technique for detecting and preventing model stealing or unauthorized use of LLMs. It involves embedding a unique pattern within the model that does not affect its normal behavior but can verify ownership under specific conditions [39]. Watermarking methods are categorized by when the watermark is embedded: logits generation methods, such as KGW [39], SIR [46], and DiPmark [79]; sampling process methods, including EXP [40], EDRW [25], and SemStamp [31]; training phase methods like Hufu [81] and Cross-Attention Watermark [4]; and mixed-method approaches such as Duwak [90] and Waterpool [33]. Key challenges include ensuring robustness against removal attacks and minimizing the impact on model utility, particularly in perplexity and accuracy in downstream tasks.

Model Validation and Auditing. Model validation and auditing are crucial for the security and integrity of LLMs. Validation ensures models function correctly, while auditing monitors for abnormalities and hidden backdoors. For instance, [57] propose a three-layered auditing framework, and LLMAuditor [2] provides a human-in-the-loop method to identify inconsistencies. In applications, [6] examine LLMs for automated regulatory compliance in finance industries, comparing open-source and proprietary models. These processes are vital in sensitive domains like law, finance and healthcare, where security lapses may lead to serious consequences.

3.3 Robustness Enhancements

Ensuring LLM robustness is essential for reliability and fairness. Techniques have been developed to enhance resilience and defend against adversaries.

Bias Mitigation Strategies. Bias mitigation in LLMs is vital to prevent unfair outcomes, especially in sensitive areas like hiring and legal decisions. Key strategies include: Pre-processing to correct biases in training data; In-processing methods that incorporate fairness constraints during training; and Post-processing to debias outputs after inference. For example, [87] addresses gender bias in embeddings. Techniques like Direct Preference Optimization (DPO) significantly reduce bias in language generation [1]. Innovative approaches include using biased instances as few-shot examples [63], multi-role debates [15], and prompt-based methods [17]. For code generation, one-shot and few-shot learning can reduce bias by up to 90% [34]. However, these strategies may create trade-offs, as addressing bias in one area can lead to issues in others.

Calibration of Model Outputs. Proper calibration of LLM outputs is crucial for ensuring that confidence scores accurately reflect the likelihood of correct predictions. Several approaches have been proposed recently. For instance, THERMOMETER [69] uses an auxiliary model for task calibration. Another method employing Pareto optimal self-supervision generates risk scores to aid error detection [89]. Calibration-tuning fine-tunes LLMs to produce well-calibrated probabilities, enhancing performance on question-answering tasks [38]. In another work, AutoCalibrate aligns LLM evaluators with human preferences through a multi-stage process [49]. Regular calibration is essential to ensure LLMs are accurate and trustworthy, especially in some critical applications.

Adversarial Input Handling. Enhancing robustness to adversarial inputs is vital, as LLMs are vulnerable to crafted prompts. In [41], the authors introduce "erase-and-check" for certifiable safety against adversarial prompts, while [32] developed a token-level detection method using perplexity and context. In addition, PromptBench [92] assesses LLM robustness against attacks, providing insights for prompt composition. LLM providers should also rigorously check data inputs. While these strategies improve generalization, anticipating evolving adversarial attacks remains challenging. Continuous efforts in defense and optimization are crucial for maintaining performance and security.

4 Future Directions for Trustworthy LLMs

This section outlines potential directions to enhance LLM trustworthiness (Fig. 3).

Homomorphic Encryption. Homomorphic encryption enhances LLM privacy by enabling computations on encrypted data without decryption, securing sensitive information during training and inference. Recent advancements have improved its efficiency. Studies include BasedAI's decentralized zero-knowledge LLM network using Fully Homomorphic Encryption (FHE) and "Cerberus Squeezing" [78], while there are other works of dual approach combining cryptographic techniques and secure mutual authentication [28], and FHE framework for secure disease diagnosis [54]. These efforts demonstrate the potential of homomorphic encryption to protect data privacy for future research, especially in healthcare.

Zero-Knowledge Proofs. Zero-knowledge proofs (ZKPs) offer a promising method for enhancing LLM privacy. ZKPs allow a prover to confirm a statement's truth to a verifier without revealing additional information, enabling private

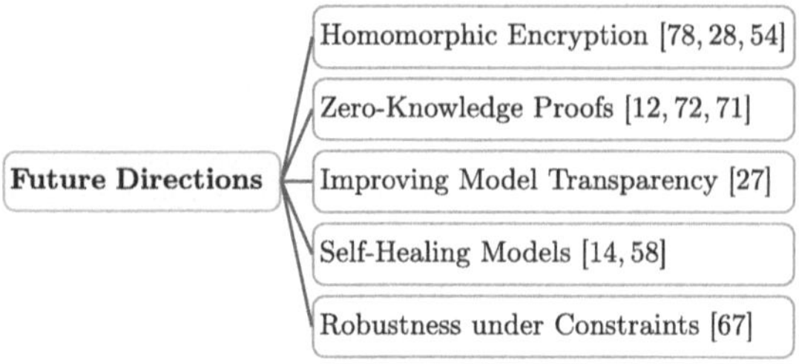

Fig. 3. Taxonomy of Potential Future Directions for Trustworthiness in LLMs.

inference where models compute on encrypted data while keeping the data and model details confidential. Research in this area has been growing as a potential direction. For example, the ZKML framework supports zero-knowledge proofs for LLMs [12]. [72] introduced zkLLM, a system that generates correctness proofs while preserving parameter privacy, whereas [71] proposed a method using ZKPs for data validation and malicious prompt filtering. These advancements address challenges in LLM authenticity and integrity, but further research is needed to integrate ZKPs into LLM pipelines without significant computational costs.

Improving Model Transparency. Model transparency is crucial for enhancing the security and trustworthiness of LLMs. By improving explainability, users can better understand decision-making processes, helping to identify vulnerabilities. Explainable AI (XAI) techniques make complex models more interpretable, allowing security experts to assess whether a model is functioning as intended [18]. Increased transparency not only uncovers adversarial manipulations but also builds user trust. Furthermore, transparent models facilitate easier auditing for potential backdoors [27]. Future research should focus on balancing performance with interpretability to ensure transparency does not compromise accuracy.

Self-healing Models. Self-healing models enhance LLM resilience by autonomously detecting and recovering from adversarial attacks. By continuously monitoring for anomalies, these models can revert to stable states or adjust parameters when issues arise. Recent research includes a PID control method [14] that corrects behavior during inference, or N-Critics [58], which refines outputs to address toxicity and fact hallucination. These strategies significantly improve LLM performance and reliability, fostering more trustworthy AI systems.

Robustness Under Constraints. Ensuring LLM reliability in low-resource languages and constrained environments is crucial for future research. While LLMs perform well in high-resource settings, they often struggle with limited data. Developing language-agnostic techniques and transfer learning can help adapt models for low-resource contexts. Additionally, compression methods like pruning, quantization, and knowledge distillation can reduce the computational footprint, enabling deployment in resource-limited areas while maintaining robustness [67]. Addressing these issues is essential for global accessibility of LLMs.

5 Conclusion

In conclusion, as LLM continue to evolve and integrate into various real-world applications, ensuring their trustworthiness across privacy, security, and robustness remains paramount. This paper has outlined key challenges in these areas, emphasizing the critical nature of addressing bias, adversarial vulnerabilities, and transparency to foster user trust and secure responsible deployments. Notably, other studies, such as the work by [50], have expanded the discourse on LLM alignment, focusing on evaluating alignment across seven major trustworthiness categories. While their findings underline the variability in effectiveness across trustworthiness measures, our survey reinforces the importance of innovative strategies to improve LLM resilience, such as homomorphic encryption, zero-knowledge proofs, and self-healing models. Future research should strive to balance efficiency, interpretability, and inclusivity to adapt LLMs for diverse environments and languages. Ultimately, advancing these areas will ensure that LLMs meet ethical standards and perform reliably, supporting their integration into society.

References

1. Allam, A.: BiasDPO: mitigating bias in language models through direct preference optimization. arXiv preprint arXiv:2407.13928 (2024)
2. Amirizaniani, M., Yao, J., Lavergne, A., Okada, E.S., Chadha, A., et al.: Llmauditor: a framework for auditing LLMS using human-in-the-loop. arXiv (2024)
3. Bai, Y., Pei, G., Jindong, G., Yang, Y., Ma, X.: Special characters attack: toward scalable training data extraction from LLMS. arXiv (2024)
4. Baldassini, F.B., et al.: Cross-attention watermarking of LLMS. In: ICASSP (2024)
5. Behnia, R., Ebrahimi, M.R., Pacheco, J., Padmanabhan, B.: Ew-tune: a framework for privately fine-tuning LLMS with differential privacy. In: ICDMW (2022)
6. Berger, A., Hillebrand, L., Leonhard, D., et al.: Towards automated regulatory compliance verification in financial auditing with LLMS. In: IEEE BigData (2023)
7. Bordt, S., Nori, H., Rodrigues, V., Nushi, B., Caruana, R.: Elephants never forget: memorization and learning of tabular data in large language models. arXiv (2024)
8. Cai, X., Haidong, X., Sihan, X., Zhang, Y., et al.: Badprompt: backdoor attacks on continuous prompts. In: NeurIPS, vol. 35, pp. 37068–37080 (2022)
9. Carlini, N., et al.: Stealing part of a production language model. arXiv (2024)
10. Carlini, N., et al.: Extracting training data from LLMS. In: USENIX Security 21 (2021)
11. Che, T., Liu, J., Zhou, Y., Ren, J., Zhou, J., et al.: Federated learning of LLMS with parameter-efficient prompt tuning and adaptive optimization. arXiv (2023)
12. Chen, B.-J., Waiwitlikhit, S., Stoica, I., Kang, D.: An optimizing system for ml inference in zero-knowledge proofs. In: EuroSys, Zkml (2024)

13. Chen, X., Salem, A., Chen, D., Backes, M., Ma, S., et al.: BADNL: backdoor attacks against NLP models with semantic-preserving improvements. In: ACSAC (2021)
14. Chen, Z., Wang, Z., Yang, Y., Li, Q., Zhang, Z.: PID control-based self-healing to improve the robustness of LLMS. arXiv (2024)
15. Cheng, R., Ma, H., Cao, S., Shi, T.: RLDF: reinforcement learning from multi-role debates as feedback for bias mitigation in LLMS (2024)
16. Das, B.C., Hadi Amini, M., Wu, Y.: Security and privacy challenges of large language models: a survey. arXiv (2024)
17. Dong, X., Wang, Y., Yu, P.S., Caverlee, J.: Disclosure and mitigation of gender bias in LLMS. arXiv preprint arXiv:2402.11190 (2024)
18. Doshi-Velez, F., Kim, B.: Towards a rigorous science of interpretable machine learning. arXiv (2017)
19. Wei, D., Zhao, Y., Li, B., Liu, G., Wang, S.: PPT: backdoor attacks on pre-trained models via poisoned prompt tuning. In: IJCAI (2022)
20. Fan, T., et al.: Fate-LLM: a industrial grade federated learning framework for LLMS. arXiv (2023)
21. Ferdaus, M.M., et al.: Towards trustworthy AI: a review of ethical and robust LLMS. arXiv (2024)
22. Fu, W., Wang, H., Gao, C., Liu, G., Li, Y., Jiang, T.: Practical membership inference attacks against fine-tuned LLMS via self-prompt calibration. arXiv (2023)
23. Gallegos, I.O., Rossi, R.A., Barrow, J., Tanjim, M., Kim, S., et al.: Bias and fairness in large language models: a survey. Computational Linguistics (2024)
24. Gao, K., Bai, Y., Bai, J., Yang, Y., Xia, S.-T.: Adversarial robustness for visual grounding of multimodal LLMS. arXiv (2024)
25. Golowich, N., Moitra, A.: Edit distance robust watermarks for language models. arXiv (2024)
26. Gu, T., Dolan-Gavitt, B., Garg, S.: BadNets: identifying vulnerabilities in the machine learning model supply chain. In: MLCS Workshop (2017)
27. Guidotti, R., Monreale, A., Ruggieri, S., Turini, F., Giannotti, F., Pedreschi, D.: A survey of methods for explaining black box models. In: ACM CSUR (2018)
28. Gupta, B.B., Gaurav, A., Arya, V., et al.: Enhancing user prompt confidentiality in LLMS through advanced differential encryption. Comput. Electr. Eng. (2024)
29. He, J., et al.: Data stealing attacks against LLMS via backdooring. Electronics **13**(14), 2858 (2024)
30. Hilmkil, A., Callh, S., Barbieri, M., Sütfeld, L.R., Zec, E.L., Mogren, O.: Scaling federated learning for fine-tuning of LLMS. In: NLDP, pp. 15–23 (2021)
31. Hou, A.B., Zhang, J., He, T., Wang, Y., Chuang, Y.S., et al.: Semstamp: a semantic watermark with paraphrastic robustness for text generation. In: NAACL (2024)
32. Hu, Z., Wu, G., Mitra, S., Zhang, R., et al.: Token-level adversarial prompt detection based on perplexity measures and contextual information. arXiv (2023)
33. Huang, B., Wan, X.: Waterpool: a watermark mitigating trade-offs among imperceptibility, efficacy and robustness. arXiv (2024)
34. Huang, D., et al.: Bias testing and mitigation in LLM-based code generation (2024)
35. Huang, H., Zhao, Z., et al.: Composite backdoor attacks against LLMS. arXiv (2023)
36. Jiang, J., et al.: Low-parameter federated learning with LLMS. In: WISA (2024)
37. Kan, Z., Qiao, L., Yu, H., et al.: Protecting user privacy in remote conversational systems: a privacy-preserving framework based on text sanitization. arXiv (2023)
38. Kapoor, S., Gruver, N., Roberts, M., Pal, A., et al.: Calibration-tuning: Teaching large language models to know what they don't know. In: UncertaiNLP 2024 (2024)

39. Kirchenbauer, J., Geiping, J., Wen, Y., Katz, J., Miers, I., Goldstein, T.: A watermark for large language models. In: ICML (2023)
40. Kuditipudi, R., Thickstun, J., Hashimoto, T., Liang, P.: Robust distortion-free watermarks for language models. TMLR (2023)
41. Kumar, A., Agarwal, C., Srinivas, S., Li, A.J., Feizi, S., Lakkaraju, H.: Certifying LLM safety against adversarial prompting. arXiv (2023)
42. Kurita, K., Michel, P., Neubig, G.: Weight poisoning attacks on pre-trained models. arXiv preprint arXiv:2004.06660 (2020)
43. Li, B., Xing, H., Huang, C., Qian, J., et al.: Structuralsleight: automated jailbreak attacks on LLMS utilizing uncommon text-encoded structure. arXiv (2024)
44. Li, L., Qiu, X.: Textat: adversarial training for natural language understanding with token-level perturbation. arXiv (2020)
45. Ling, Z., Chen, D., Yao, L., Li, Y., Shen, Y.: On the convergence of zeroth-order federated tuning for LLMS. In: ACM SIGKDD (2024)
46. Liu, A., Pan, L., Hu, X., Meng, S., Wen, L.: A semantic invariant robust watermark for LLMS. In: ICLR (2024)
47. Liu, X., et al.: Adversarial training for large neural LMS. arxiv (2020)
48. Liu, X., Liang, J., Ye, M., Xi, Z.: Robustifying safety-aligned large language models through clean data curation. arXiv (2024)
49. Liu, Y., et al.: Calibrating LLM-based evaluator. arXiv (2023)
50. Liu, Y., Yao, Y., Ton, J.-F. et al.: Trustworthy LLMS: a survey and guideline for evaluating large language models' alignment. arXiv (2023)
51. Madry, A., Makelov, A., Schmidt, L., Tsipras, D., Vladu, A.: Towards deep learning models resistant to adversarial attacks. STAT **1050**(9) (2017)
52. Mai, P., Yan, R., Huang, Z., Yang, Y., Pang, Y.: Split-and-denoise: protect LLM inference with local differential privacy. arXiv (2023)
53. Majmudar, J., Dupuy, C., Peris, C., Smaili, S., Gupta, R., Zemel, R.: Differentially private decoding in LLMS. arXiv (2022)
54. Malik, A., Ratha, N., Yalavarthi, B., Sharma, T., Kaushik, A., Jutla, C.: Confidential and protected disease classifier using fully homomorphic encryption. arXiv (2024)
55. Mattern, J., Mireshghallah, F., Jin, Z., et al.: Membership inference attacks against language models via neighbourhood comparison. ArXiv (2023)
56. McMahan, H.B., Ramage, D., Talwar, K., Zhang, L.: Learning differentially private language models without losing accuracy. ArXiv (2017)
57. Mökander, J., Schuett, J., Kirk, H.R., Floridi, L.: Auditing large language models: a three-layered approach. AI and Ethics (2023)
58. Mousavi, S., et al.: N-critics: self-refinement of LLMS with ensemble of critics. arXiv (2023)
59. Mozaffari, H., Marathe, V.J.: Semantic membership inference attack against large language models. arXiv (2024)
60. Naseh, A., Krishna, K., Iyyer, M., Houmansadr, A.: Stealing the decoding algorithms of language models. In: ACM CCS, pp. 1835–1849 (2023)
61. Nasr, M., et al.: Scalable extraction of training data from (production) language models. arXiv (2023)
62. Naveed, H., et al.: A comprehensive overview of LLMS. ArXiv (2023)
63. Ohi, M., Kaneko, M., Koike, R., Loem, M., Okazaki, N.: Likelihood-based mitigation of evaluation bias in LLMS. arXiv (2024)
64. Panda, A., Choquette-Choo, C.A., Zhang, Z., Yang, Y., Mittal, P.: Teach LLMS to phish: stealing private information from language models. arXiv (2024)

65. Qi, J., Luan, Z., Huang, S., Fung, C., Yang, H., Qian, D.: FDLoRA: personalized federated learning of large language model via dual Lora tuning. arXiv (2024)
66. Qu, Y., Ding, M., Sun, N., Thilakarathna, K., Zhu, T., Niyato, D.: The frontier of data erasure: machine unlearning for large language models. arXiv (2024)
67. Sanh, V.: Distilbert, a distilled version of Bert: smaller, faster, cheaper and lighter. arXiv preprint arXiv:1910.01108 (2019)
68. Shayegani, E., Mamun, M., Fu, Y., Zaree, P., Dong,Y., Abu-Ghazaleh, N.: Survey of vulnerabilities in LLMS revealed by adversarial attacks. arXiv (2023)
69. Shen, M., Das,S., Greenewald, K., Sattigeri, P., Wornell, G., Ghosh, S.: Thermometer: towards universal calibration for large language models. arXiv (2024)
70. Shokri, R., Stronati, M., Song, C., Shmatikov, V.: Membership inference attacks against machine learning models. In: IEEE S& P (2017)
71. Singh, S.: Enhancing privacy and security in large-language models: a zero-knowledge proof approach. In: ICCWS, vol. 19, pp. 574–582 (2024)
72. Sun, H., Li, J., Zhang, H.: ZKLLM: zero knowledge proofs for large language models. arXiv preprint arXiv:2404.16109 (2024)
73. Tang, X., Shin, R., Inan, H.A., Manoel, A., et al.: Privacy-preserving in-context learning with differentially private few-shot generation. arXiv (2023)
74. Thomas, A., Adelani, D.I., Davody, A., et al.: Investigating the impact of pre-trained word embeddings on memorization in neural networks. In: TSD (2020)
75. Wang, B., Wei, C., Liu, Z., Lin, G., Chen, N.F.: Resilience of large language models for noisy instructions. arXiv (2024)
76. Wang, D., Gong, C., Liu, Q.: Improving neural language modeling via adversarial training. In: ICML, pp. 6555–6565. PMLR (2019)
77. Wang, Z., et al.: Poisoned langchain: Jailbreak LLMS by langchain. arXiv (2024)
78. Wellington, S.: Basedai: a decentralized p2p network for zero knowledge LLMS (2024)
79. Yihan, W., Zhengmian, H., Zhang, H., Huang, H.: A stealthy, efficient and resilient watermark for large language models, Dipmark (2024)
80. Xhonneux, S., Sordoni, Al., Günnemann, S., Gidel, G., Schwinn, L.: Efficient adversarial training in LLMS with continuous attacks. arXiv (2024)
81. Xu, H., Xiang, L., Ma, X., et al.: HUFU: a modality-agnositc watermarking system for pre-trained transformers via permutation equivariance. arXiv (2024)
82. Xue, F., Fu, Y., Zhou, W., Zheng, Z., You, Y.: To repeat or not to repeat: insights from scaling LLM under token-crisis. In: NeurIPS, vol. 36 (2024)
83. Xue, Q.: Unlocking the potential: a comprehensive exploration of large language models in natural language processing. ACE (2024)
84. Ye, R., et al.: Openfedllm: training LLMS on decentralized private data via federated learning. In: SIGKDD (2024)
85. Yue, L., Liu, Q., et al.: Fedjudge: federated legal large language model. arXiv (2023)
86. Zhang, H., Da, J., Lee, D., Robinson, V., et al.: A careful examination of large language model performance on grade school arithmetic. arXiv (2024)
87. Zhao, J., Wang, T., Yatskar, M., Ordonez, V., Chang, K.W.: Gender bias in coreference resolution: evaluation and debiasing methods. arXiv (2018)
88. Zhao, K., Yang, Z., Huang, C., Chen, X., Zhang, Z.: FedsLLM: federated split learning for large language models over communication networks. In: Ucom (2024)
89. Zhao, T., Wei, M., Preston, S., Poon, H.: Automatic calibration and error correction for large language models via pareto optimal self-supervision. arXiv (2023)
90. Zhu, C., Galjaard, J., Chen, P.Y., Chen, L.Y.: Duwak: dual watermarks in large language models. arXiv (2024)

91. Zhu, C., Cheng, Y., Gan, Z., Sun, S., Goldstein, T., Liu, J.: Freelb: enhanced adversarial training for natural language understanding. arXiv (2019)
92. Zhu, K., Wang, J., Zhou, J., Wang, Z., et al.: Promptbench: towards evaluating the robustness of LLMS on adversarial prompts. arXiv (2023)

Multiscale Bernstein Copula with Bayesian Model Averaging

Martin Burda[1] and Artem Prokhorov[2,3,4](✉)

[1] University of Toronto, 150 St. George St., Toronto, ON M5S 3G7, Canada
martin.burda@utoronto.ca

[2] University of Sydney, H70 Abercrombie Building, Sydney, NSW 2006, Australia
artem.prokhorov@sydney.edu.au

[3] HSE University, Moscow, Russia

[4] CIREQ, Montreal, Canada

Abstract. Multiscale random Bernstein polynomial (msBP) priors exhibit many favorable properties for nonparametric Bayesian inference. In msBP, an infinite tree of probability weights is generated from a generalization of the stick-breaking process representation of the Dirichlet process, with each tree scale featuring a weighted random Bernstein polynomial. The prior can generate densities with locally varying smoothness, accommodating abrupt local changes. The degree of smoothness of the resulting function approximation is determined by a hyperparameter that controls the decline in probabilities over the scales. In this paper we extend the multiscale Bernstein polynomial prior from $[0, 1]$ analyzed in the previous literature to the unit hypercube $[0, 1]^d$ for the link function in copula dependence modeling, accounting for the uncertainty inherent in the degree of approximation smoothness by Bayesian Model Averaging over the smoothness hyperparameter. The favorable properties of the resulting non-parametric copula model are attained at the cost of an increased computational burden in practical implementation. We provide details of the implementation algorithm that is based on large-scale parallelization tailored to the internal model structure. We implement the algorithm on distributed nodes of a Unix High Performance Computing system with Graphical Processing Units (GPU) acceleration via a Message Passing Interface (MPI) in Modern Fortran. The algorithm scales well across MPI ranks. The routines can be pre-compiled into numerical libraries and invoked from high-level languages such as Python or R.

Keywords: Copula dependence modeling · Heterogeneous computing · GPU acceleration

1 Introduction

Most traditional models of the copula dependence structure assume a parametric specification, such as the Gaussian, Clayton, Gumbel, or Frank copulas [11]. Parametric copula link functions are often computationally efficient and easy

J. Kertesz et al. (Eds.): CSoNet 2024, LNCS 15417, pp. 14–22, 2025.
https://doi.org/10.1007/978-981-96-6389-7_2

to interpret, but their functional form assumptions can lead to model misspecification issues if the true dependence structure deviates significantly from the assumed model. Nonparametric approaches in copula modeling provide more flexibility and adaptability to complex dependence relationships. However, nonparametric copula modeling methods can be computationally intensive.

In particular, the random Bernstein polynomial (BP), approximating the Dirichlet process, has been proposed as a non-parametric prior on the space of distribution functions on the unit interval [13,14]. The prior has full support, selects absolutely continuous distribution functions with continuous derivatives, and has been shown to possess desirable asymptotic properties [15]. In the copula literature, a multivariate non-parametric prior for the copula link function based on the BP on the unit cube was analyzed in [2].

A multiscale extension of the random BP on the unit interval was proposed in [4]. The prior is based on a sequence of scales $s = 0, 1, \ldots$, using 2^s Bernstein polynomial basis densities at scale s with smaller variances for higher s. Stochastically decreasing weights are allocated to higher scales using a stick-breaking characterization of an infinite binary tree. The resulting multiscale Bernstein polynomial (msBP) prior is locally adaptable and can accommodate abrupt local density changes. The degree of smoothness of the resulting density approximation is determined by a hyperparameter a that controls the decline in probabilities over the scales.

In this paper, we extend the msBp prior from the unit interval to the unit hypercube for use in copula dependence modeling. We further account for the uncertainty inherent in the degree of approximation smoothness by Bayesian Model Averaging (BMA) over a varying smoothness hyperparameter. The resulting non-parametric copula model inherits the desirable features of multiscale function representation.

However, its multiscale structure over the unit cube presents a heavy computational burden in practical implementation. We devise and provide details of a feasible implementation algorithm that benefits from large-scale parallelization tailored to the internal model structure. We implement the algorithm on distributed nodes of Graphical Processing Unit (GPU) clusters at a Unix server system [9,16] via a Message Passing Interface (MPI) in Modern Fortran [10]. The algorithm is scalable both across GPU cores and server nodes. It can be seamlessly ported to any readily available commercial cloud computing services such as AWS or IBM Cloud.

2 Multivariate Multiscale Random Bernstein Polynomial

Let $\boldsymbol{y}$ denote a random vector defined over a unit hypercube $[0, 1]^d$ with density $f(\boldsymbol{y})$, which is assumed to follow a multivariate multiscale mixture of Bernstein polynomials (mmBp) process

$$f(\boldsymbol{y}) = \sum_{s=0}^{\infty} \sum_{\boldsymbol{h}=(1,\ldots 1)}^{(2^s,\ldots,2^s)} \pi_{s,\boldsymbol{h}} \prod_{j=1}^{d} Be(y_j; h_j, 2^s - h_j + 1) \tag{1}$$

where y_j is the jth coordinate of $\boldsymbol{y} \in [0,1]^d$ and h_j is the node index within each scale s along the dimension j, with $\boldsymbol{h} = (h_1, \ldots, h_d)$. $\boldsymbol{h}$ is implicitly indexed by its corresponding s but we omit this indexing for notational convenience.

Progressing through the levels $s = 0, \ldots, \infty$ of the multivariate tree, conditionally on reaching node $(s, \boldsymbol{h})$ the random variable $S_{s,\boldsymbol{h}} \sim Be(1, a)$ defines the prior probability of stopping at $(s, \boldsymbol{h})$. Conditionally on not stopping at $(s, \boldsymbol{h})$ the 2^d–dimensional random vector $\boldsymbol{H}_{s,\boldsymbol{h}} \sim Dir(\boldsymbol{b})$ with $\boldsymbol{H}_{s,\boldsymbol{h}} = (H_{s,\boldsymbol{h}_1}, \ldots, H_{s,\boldsymbol{h}_{2^d}})$ denotes the prior probabilities of advancing at level $s+1$ to any one of the 2^d daughter nodes of the node $(s, \boldsymbol{h})$, and $Dir(\boldsymbol{b})$ denotes the Dirichlet distribution with $\boldsymbol{b} = (b_1, \ldots, b_{2^d})$.

The unconditional tree node prior weights are given by

$$\pi_{s,\boldsymbol{h}} = S_{s,\boldsymbol{h}} \prod_{r=0}^{s-1} \left(1 - S_{r,\boldsymbol{g}_{shr}}\right) H_{r,\boldsymbol{g}_{shr}} \tag{2}$$

where $\boldsymbol{g}_{shr} = (g_{sh_1r}, \ldots, g_{sh_dr})$ with $g_{sh_jr} = \lceil h_j/2^{s-r} \rceil$ is the node traveled through at scale r on the way to node $\boldsymbol{h}$ at scale s. The scale s_{max} approximation of (1) takes the form

$$f_{s_{max}}(\boldsymbol{y}) = \sum_{s=0}^{s_{max}} \sum_{\boldsymbol{h}=(1,\ldots 1)}^{(2^s,\ldots,2^s)} \widetilde{\pi}_{s,\boldsymbol{h}} \prod_{j=1}^{d} Be(y_j; h_j, 2^s - h_j + 1) \tag{3}$$

where $\widetilde{\pi}_{s,\boldsymbol{h}}$ is identical to $\pi_{s,\boldsymbol{h}}$ except that all the stopping probabilities at scale s_{max} are set to equal to one so that the weights $\widetilde{\pi}_{s,\boldsymbol{h}}$ in (3) sum to one.

3 Implementation Algorithm

The implementation algorithm consists of two key steps that are iterated to obtain a Markov chain (MC) of parameter draws:

(a) Conditionally on the current values of the probabilities $\{\pi\}$, allocate each observation $\boldsymbol{y}_i$ to a node $(s, \boldsymbol{h})$.
(b) Conditionally on the node allocations, update the probabilities $\{\pi\}$.

In the node allocation step (a) of the full tree, for each i, new MC update s_i is drawn from a multinomial with probabilities proportional to total posterior probability mass associated with the given s,

$$Pr(s_i = s|\boldsymbol{y}_i) = \sum_{\boldsymbol{h}=(1,\ldots,1)}^{(2^s,\ldots,2^s)} \bar{\pi}_{s,\boldsymbol{h}} \prod_{j=1}^{d} Be(y_{ij}; h_j, 2^s - h_j + 1) \tag{4}$$

where $\bar{\pi}_{s,\boldsymbol{h}} = \pi_{s,\boldsymbol{h}}/\pi_s$ with

$$\pi_s = \sum_{\boldsymbol{h}=(1,\ldots 1)}^{(2^s,\ldots,2^s)} \pi_{s,\boldsymbol{h}} \tag{5}$$

if π_s exceeds a threshold $u_i \sim U(0, \pi_{s_i})$ from the previous MC draw. A new MC update of $\boldsymbol{h}$, for each i and the corresponding s_i, requires a draw from a multinomial over the support $\boldsymbol{h} = (1, \ldots, 1), \ldots, (2^{s_i}, \ldots, 2^{s_i})$ with posterior probability

$$Pr(\boldsymbol{h}_i = \boldsymbol{h} | \boldsymbol{y}_i, s_i) = \bar{\pi}_{s_i, \boldsymbol{h}} \prod_{j=1}^{d} Be(y_{ij}; h_j, 2^{s_i} - h_j + 1)$$

In the tree weights update step (b) of the full tree, conditionally on the node allocations the posterior MC draws of $S_{s,\boldsymbol{h}}$ and $H_{s,\boldsymbol{h}}$ are taken from their posteriors

$$S_{s,\boldsymbol{h}} \sim Be(1 + n_{s,\boldsymbol{h}}, a + v_{s,\boldsymbol{h}} - n_{s,\boldsymbol{h}}) \quad (6)$$

$$\boldsymbol{H}_{s,\boldsymbol{h}} \sim Dir(b_1 + v_{s+1,\boldsymbol{h}_1}, \ldots, b_{2^d} + v_{s+1,\boldsymbol{h}_{2^d}}) \quad (7)$$

where $n_{s,\boldsymbol{h}}$ is the number of subjects i allocated to node $(s, \boldsymbol{h})$, i.e. "stopping" at node $(s, \boldsymbol{h})$, $v_{s,\boldsymbol{h}}$ is the number of subjects i allocated either to $(s, \boldsymbol{h})$ or to any of the daughter nodes of $(s, \boldsymbol{h})$ so that $v_{s,\boldsymbol{h}} - n_{s,\boldsymbol{h}}$ is the number of subjects "passing through" node $(s, \boldsymbol{h})$, and $v_{s+1,\boldsymbol{h}_k}$ is the number of subjects turning to node $(s+1, \boldsymbol{h}_k)$ having passed through $(s, \boldsymbol{h})$. The posterior weights $\{\pi_{s,\boldsymbol{h}}\}$ are then updated according to (2). The weights $\{\tilde{\pi}_{s,\boldsymbol{h}}\}_{s=0}^{s_{max}}$ for the scale s_{max} approximation (3) are obtained by capping s at s_{max} and setting $S_{s_{max},\cdot} = 1$.

4 Bayesian Model Averaging for Random Bernstein Polynomials

The prior $\pi_{s,\boldsymbol{h}}$ in (2) is implicitly parametrized by the smoothness hyperparameter a via $S_{s,\boldsymbol{h}} \sim Be(1, a)$, with larger values of a inducing a-priori more variability to $f_{s_{max}}(\boldsymbol{y})$ in (3).

The analyst can choose a value for a that reflects their prior expectation about the smoothness of the posterior approximation. However, this would ignore the informational content of the data about the variation in the posterior. One way to incorporate data-driven learning about a is to specify a hierarchical prior over a, but this would necessitate sequential sampling from the posterior of a during the MC run, resulting in a substantial increase in implementation time.

An alternative approach that we take here accounts for the uncertainty inherent in a via Bayesian Model Averaging (BMA) [7,18]. Within a set of models indexed by $m = 1, \ldots, M$, BMA treats each model as a hypothesis about the data-generating process and uses its posterior probability as the model weight, based on how well the model explains the data. The BMA of the quantity of interest is then calculated as the corresponding weighted average outcome of each model. In the Bayesian sense, model averaging provides a natural reflection of model uncertainty.

We implement BMA for the posterior draws in (6) over a set $\{a_m\}_{m=1}^{M}$ of admissible values of a chosen by the analyst. Denote by $S_{s,\boldsymbol{h}}(a_m)$ the posterior draws in (6) for a given hyperparameter value a_m. Conditional on a_m, the posterior draws of $S_{s,\boldsymbol{h}}(a_m)$ are independent over $m = 1, \ldots, M$ and can therefore be taken concurrently in M parallel draws using distributed computing. The implementation time is thus comparable to one model with a given degree of prior smoothness a. The draws are averaged to yield

$$\overline{S}_{s,\boldsymbol{h}} = \sum_{m=1}^{M} S_{s,\boldsymbol{h}}(a_m) \times p(S_{s,\boldsymbol{h}}(a_m)|\boldsymbol{y}_{i=1}^{N}) \tag{8}$$

where $p(S_{s,\boldsymbol{h}}(a_m)|\boldsymbol{y}_{i=1}^{N})$ is the posterior probability of $S_{s,\boldsymbol{h}}(a_m)$. The model-averaged $\overline{S}_{s,\boldsymbol{h}}$ is then used in place of $S_{s,\boldsymbol{h}}$ in the posterior counterpart of (2).

5 Application to Risk Management

Due to its desirable local adaptability properties on the unit hypercube, the mmBp prior is highly suitable for flexible modeling of the copula link function in nonlinear dependence structure analysis. In this context, we apply our approach to capturing dependence patterns between equity and bonds in the Canadian stock market.

The relationship between equity and bonds has been characterized as highly non-linear in the empirical finance literature [5,6,8]. Equity and bonds often exhibit a negative correlation during periods of economic downturn or financial market stress, as investors tend to rebalance their portfolios towards safer assets (bonds) away from riskier assets (equity). In times of economic expansion or periods of inflation, equities tend to perform well as corporate profits grow and consumer demand rises. However, bonds may underperform because interest rates tend to rise in such environments, reducing bond prices. In these periods, the correlation may be low or even positive depending on the specific dynamics such as the speed of interest rate changes or inflation.

The relationship between equity and bonds can change rapidly during periods of extreme volatility. For example, in the initial stages of a crisis, both stocks and bonds can fall together due to a general loss of appetite for risk. Later, bonds may rebound as investors seek safe-haven assets, while stocks may continue to decline or recover. Market sentiment and investor behavior can further alter the strength and direction of the correlation between these two asset classes.

In our empirical analysis, for equity we utilize the iShares S&P/TSX Capped Composite Index ETF (XIC), a Canadian Exchange Traded Fund (ETF) that provides broad exposure to all Canadian equities, representing companies across all sectors of the Canadian economy. Key holdings include major Canadian companies across industries such as financials, energy, materials, and utilities. For bonds, we use the BMO Aggregate Bond Index ETF (ZAG), which tracks the FTSE Canada Universe Bond Index that includes a wide range of Canadian government and corporate bonds. Both XIC and ZAG are listed and traded on the Toronto Stock Exchange (TSE).

We calculated the log returns of XIC and ZAG based on their close prices obtained from yahoo finance for trading days between January 1, 2020, and

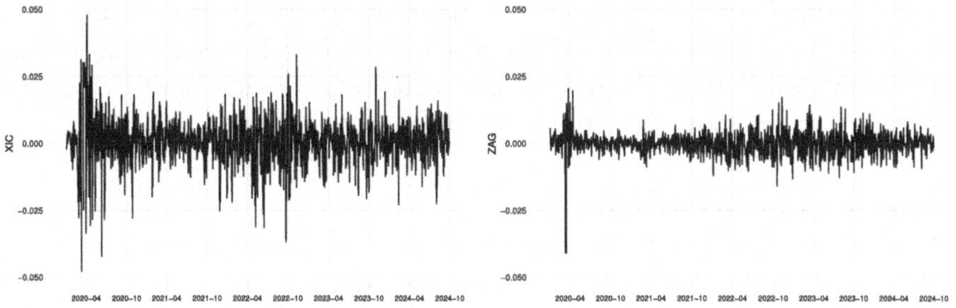

Fig. 1. Daily log-returns of XIC and ZAG

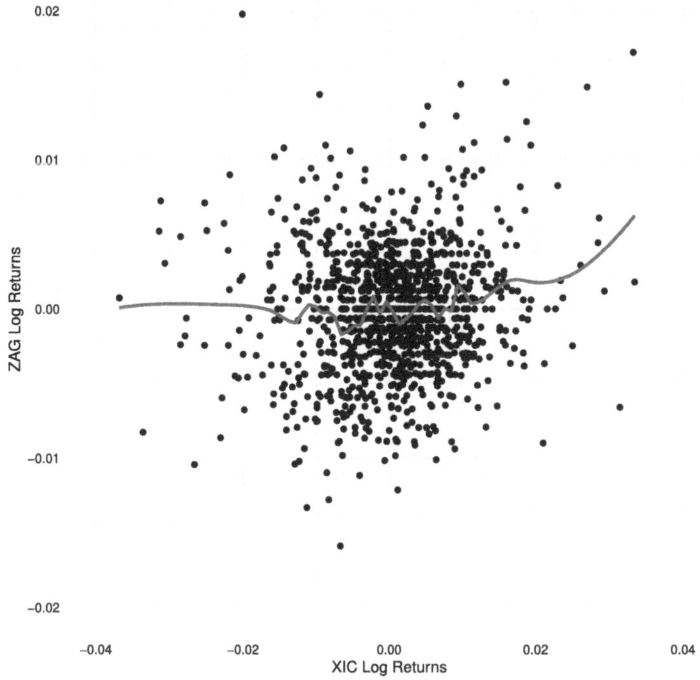

Fig. 2. Scatterplot log-returns of XIC and ZAG

October 1, 2024. Close prices refer to the final price of a financial asset at the end of the trading day, and are typically used to determine the asset's daily performance as well as a benchmark for identifying trends. Our data, consisting of 1,191 log returns observations, is plotted in Fig. 1. A scatter plot of log returns for the two series is shown in Fig. 2.

A portfolio consisting of two separate asset classes with different risk and return profiles, such as XIC and ZAG, is of interest to retail investors who benefit from its simplicity and cost-efficiency, but still seek to rebalance their asset class holdings based on current economic outlook and their personal risk preferences. In order to assess the risk profile and performance metrics of such portfolio, we calculate its Value at Risk (VaR) using a copula with Gaussian marginals and posterior draws from the mmBp copula density (3).

6 Implementation Details

We ran out implementation algorithm at the Niagara Unix server system of SciNet HPC Consortium at the University of Toronto, Canada, using the nvfortran compiler in the NVidia High-Performance Computing Software Development Kit (HPC SDK), version 23.11. The Message Passing Interface (MPI) communication library of this SDK is optimized for GPU acceleration, and we linked each rank to a Mist GPU device (NVidia V100-SMX2-32GB) for offloading of parallelized code regions using OpenACC directives. The implementation code is provided in a GitHub repository [1] along with references to invoked external routines [3,12,17].

We set the number of MCMC iterations to 21,000 with 1,000 burnin, with $s_{max} = 5$. Judging by several robustness checks on its length, the chain converged well within the burnin section. As the model prior we use 0.8^a reflecting a preference for model parsimony. We specified a range of prior values for the smoothness hyperparameter a on an equispaced grid from 1 to 10, corresponding to the expected stopping scale within the tree. We implemented these in parallel with one value per MPI rank, ensuring run time comparable to a single-value implementation.

The number of ranks `-np` is provided as a runtime option. For the serial `-np=1` the MCMC wallclock run time was 146s while for the parallel `-np=10` the time was 184s, yielding an 8× efficiency increase per rank that indicates close to linear scalability.

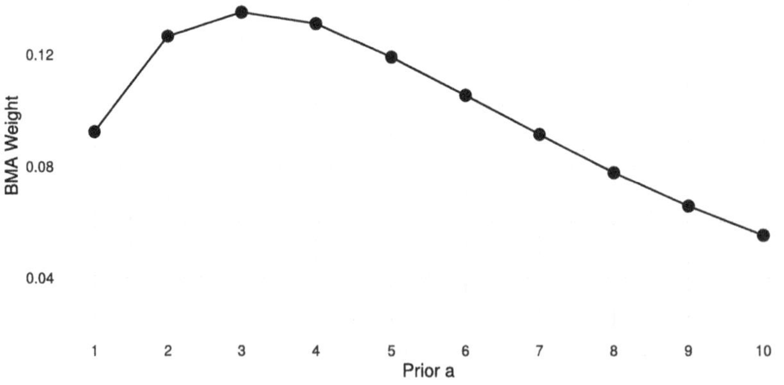

Fig. 3. BMA Model Weights

Figure 3 shows the smoothness hyperparameter grid along with the resulting BMA model weights. The corresponding VaR values (in % terms) ranged from −1.052 to −1.122, indicating a relatively high degree of robustness to changes in the smoothness hyperparameter. The resulting BMA VaR was evaluated at −1.084.

7 Conclusions

In this paper, we extend the multiscale Bernstein polynomial prior from the unit interval to the unit hypercube and utilize it as a flexible link function in a copula dependence structure. We account for the uncertainty inherent in the model approximation by Bayesian Model Averaging (BMA) over a varying smoothness hyperparameter. We implement a parallelized version of the BMA algorithm via distributed computing using MPI communication and GPU acceleration with a near-linear efficiency improvement factor, indicating a high degree of scalability.

References

1. Burda, M.: mmBp implementation code (2024). https://github.com/martin-burda/mmBp
2. Burda, M., Prokhorov, A.: Copula based factorization in Bayesian multivariate infinite mixture models. J. Multivar. Anal. **127**, 200–213 (2014). https://doi.org/10.1016/j.jmva.2014.02.011
3. Burkardt, J.: PROB: Fortran code for random number generation and probability distributions. https://people.math.sc.edu/Burkardt/f_src/prob/prob.f90
4. Canale, A., Dunson, D.B.: Multiscale Bernstein polynomials for densities. Stat. Sin. **26**, 1175–1195 (2016)
5. David, A., Veronesi, P.: The Economics of the Comovement of Stocks and Bonds, chap. 15, pp. 313–326. Wiley (2016). https://doi.org/10.1002/9781118709207.ch15, https://onlinelibrary.wiley.com/doi/abs/10.1002/9781118709207.ch15
6. Garcia, R., Tsafack, G.: Dependence structure and extreme comovements in international equity and bond markets. J. Banking Finance **35**(8), 1954–1970 (2011). https://doi.org/10.1016/j.jbankfin.2011.01.003, https://www.sciencedirect.com/science/article/pii/S0378426611000240
7. Hoeting, J.A., Madigan, D., Raftery, A.E., Volinsky, C.T.: Bayesian model averaging: a tutorial. Stat. Sci. **14**(4), 382–401 (1999). http://www.jstor.org/stable/2676803
8. Jorion, P., of Risk Professionals), G.G.A.: Financial Risk Manager Handbook. Wiley Finance, Wiley (2009). https://books.google.ca/books?id=bGQxlDjujmMC
9. Loken, C., et al.: Scinet: lessons learned from building a power-efficient top-20 system and data centre. J. Phys: Conf. Ser. **256**(1), 012026 (2010). https://doi.org/10.1088/1742-6596/256/1/012026, http://stacks.iop.org/1742-6596/256/i=1/a=012026
10. Metcalf, M., Reid, J., Cohen, M.: Modern Fortran Explained: Incorporating Fortran 2023. Oxford University Press, Oxford (2024)
11. Nelsen, R.B.: An Introduction to Copulas. Springer Series in Statistics, Springer, 2nd edn. (2006). https://doi.org/10.1007/0-387-28678-0

12. Netlib: Random number generation routines. https://www.netlib.org/random/random.f90
13. Petrone, S.: Bayesian density estimation using Bernstein polynomials. Can. J. Stat. **27**(1), 105–126 (1999)
14. Petrone, S.: Random Bernstein polynomials. Scand. J. Stat. **26**(3), 373–393 (1999)
15. Petrone, S., Wasserman, L.: Consistency of Bernstein polynomial posteriors. Journal of the Royal Statistical Society. Series B (Statistical Methodology) **64**(1), 79–100 (2002)
16. Ponce, M., et al.: Deploying a top-100 supercomputer for large parallel workloads: The Niagara supercomputer. In: Proceedings of the Practice and Experience in Advanced Research Computing on Rise of the Machines (Learning). PEARC '19, New York, NY, USA. Association for Computing Machinery (2019). https://doi.org/10.1145/3332186.3332195
17. Rutter, M.J.: Fortran code for sorting algorithms. https://www.mjr19.org.uk/IT/sorts/sorts.f90
18. Steel, M.F.: Model averaging and its use in economics. J. Econ. Literat. **58**(3), 644–719 (2020)

Facility Location Under Nonlinear Customer Demand: A Fully Polynomial-Time Approximation Scheme

Ba Luat Le[1], Thuy Anh Ta[1(✉)], Ngoc Anh Vu Thi[1], and Minh Hoàng Hà[2]

[1] ORLab, Faculty of Computer Science, Phenikaa University, Hanoi, Vietnam
anh.tathuy@phenikaa-uni.edu.vn

[2] ORLab-SLSCM and CADA, Faculty of Data Science and Artificial Intelligence, College of Technology, National Economics University, Hai Ba Trung, Hanoi, Vietnam

Abstract. This work addresses the facility location problem, a key area of research in Operations Research and Artificial Intelligence. Specifically, we examine a competitive facility location problem where a firm seeks to establish new facilities in a market already served by existing competitors. To predict customer demand, we utilize a general class of customer behavior models, known as the nested-logit model, which is widely recognized as one of the most popular demand models in the literature. The facility location problem under the nested-logit model is characterized by its high nonlinearity and complexity. Existing methods either do not operate within polynomial time or fail to guarantee near-optimal solutions at any desired level of precision. In this study, by leveraging the unique structure of the nested logit choice model, we propose a Fully Polynomial-Time Approximation Scheme (FPTAS) to efficiently solve the problem. To the best of our knowledge, this is the first FPTAS developed for this type of competitive facility location problem.

Keywords: Facility Location · Nested logit · Dynamic Programming · Cutting plane

1 Introduction

This paper considers the facility location problem in the competitive market, which has long been an essential problem in decision-making for modern transportation, logistics, and service systems. This problem traditionally involves selecting the optimal facilities from a set of candidates while considering the competitive dynamics of customer choice among available options. These facilities aim to maximize their market shares and profits, which are significantly influenced by the selection of their locations. In this study, we address the competitive facility location problem (CFLP), where customer demand is forecasted using a random utility maximization (RUM) model [2,4,10]. Customers are assumed to select facilities by maximizing their perceived utility, influenced by factors such as facility attributes (e.g., price, quality) and customer characteristics (e.g.,

J. Kertesz et al. (Eds.): CSoNet 2024, LNCS 15417, pp. 23–34, 2025.
https://doi.org/10.1007/978-981-96-6389-7_3

income, proximity). We consider a simplified problem by focusing only on the CFLP with a single customer type.

Prior works primarily proposed exact methods for solving CFLP under the multinomial logit (MNL) model [2,9,10], which is one of the most popular choice models in demand modeling. A limitation of the MNL model, known as the Independence of Irrelevant Alternatives (IIA) property, is that it assumes proportional substitution patterns. This means that when a new facility is introduced, the probability of choosing each existing option decreases by the same proportion across all alternatives, which can lead to unrealistic demand representations. To address this, several studies have explored more advanced models, such as the nested-logit (NL) model [1], Generalized Extreme Value (GEV) [11], and mixed-logit models [12]. The NL model groups options into distinct subsets or "nests," based on the similarities between facility options, which is essential in competitive markets where facilities may offer comparable services. However, the IIA property still applies between options in different nests.

In this paper, we propose a Fully Polynomial-Time Approximation Scheme (FPTAS) for the CFLP under the NL model. To the best of our knowledge, this is the first time that an FPTAS approach has been examined in the context of CFLP. This approach is well-suited to handle the computational complexity of the problem, balancing solution quality and efficiency in large-scale competitive scenarios. FPTAS always guarantees an error margin (ϵ) while maintaining polynomial time complexity. Current state-of-the-art exact methods for the CFLP [8], such as cutting plane (CP) [7,10] and branch-and-cut (B and C) [9], relies on outer-approximation and submodular cuts. However, they can become computationally prohibitive for large-scale problems. In contrast, FPTAS offers a practical trade-off between solution accuracy and computational efficiency. By applying FPTAS, we ensure that near-optimal solutions are obtained efficiently, allowing us to handle large problem instances while balancing accuracy and runtime, which is crucial for decision-making in competitive markets.

Literature Review: In the context of the CFLP under RUM models, most existing studies employ the MNL model to capture customer demand. [2] appears to be the first to propose the CFLP under the MNL model. Their solution method involves a Mixed-Integer Linear Programming (MILP) approach based on a branch-and-bound procedure for small instances and a simple variable neighborhood search for larger instances. Two state-of-the-art exact methods currently exist for solving CFLP under the MNL model. [9] proposed a B and C method that integrates outer-approximation and submodular cuts, while [10] developed a multicut outer-approximation algorithm for efficiently solving large instances. Regarding the NL model, [13] explicitly studied the CFLP under the NL model and proposed exact methods based on outer-approximation and submodular cuts within a B and C procedure. However, the work of [13] assumes that the competitor's facilities are separated from the new ones within the cross-nested structure, which is limited in capturing the correlation between competitors' and opening facilities [7]. Our work builds on the more general configuration introduced by [7], where competitor and opening facilities can belong to the same nests. [7] also showed that, in this configuration, the objective function is not necessarily concave, meaning previous state-of-the-art methods cannot be directly applied. To address this, they proposed a reformulation that transforms the problem into one with a concave objective and convex constraints, allowing the use of CP and B and C methods with outer-approximation and submodular cuts to find optimal solutions. In our study, we will implement FPTAS and compare its performance with the cutting plane method from [7] to evaluate the efficiency of FPTAS in this configuration for the CFLP under NL model.

Paper Outline: The paper is organized as follows. Section 2 discusses the problem formulation. Section 3 presents the FPTAS approach and its complexity. Section 4 presents our experimental results, and finally, Sect. 5 concludes the paper. Additional experiments are included in the appendix.

Notation: Boldface characters represent matrices (or vectors), and a_i denotes the i-th element of vector $\mathbf{a}$ if it is indexable. We use $[m]$, for any $m \in \mathbb{N}$, to denote the set $\{1, \ldots, m\}$.

2 Problem Formulation

In this section, we present the problem formulation of the CFLP under the NL model. We begin by discussing the theoretical foundation of CFLP under a customer choice model. Then, we will provide a detailed explanation of the formulation for the CFLP under the NL model.

In the classic facility location problem, decision-makers aim to establish new facilities in a way that optimizes the demand fulfilled by customers. However, accurately assessing customer demand in real-world scenarios is challenging and inherently uncertain. In this work, we explore a facility location problem where discrete choice models [14] are used to estimate and predict customer demand. Among the various approaches discussed in the demand modeling literature, the RUM framework [14] stands out as the most prevalent method for modeling discrete choice behaviors. This method is grounded in random utility theory, positing that a decision-maker's preference for an option is represented through a random utility. Consequently, the customer tends to choose the alternative offering the highest utility. According to the RUM framework [6,11], the likelihood of an individual choosing an option i from a given choice set S is determined by $P(u_i \geq u_j, \; \forall j \in S)$, implying that the individual will select the option providing the highest utility. Here, the random utilities are typically defined as $u_i = v_i + \epsilon_i$, where v_i represents the deterministic component, which can be calculated based on the characteristics of the alternative and/or the decision-maker and some parameters to be estimated, and ϵ_i represents random components that are unknown to the analyst.

Let $[m] = \{1, 2, ..., m\}$ represent the set of all potential locations, and let $\mathcal{C}$ denote the set of competitors' existing facilities. Under the NL model, these locations can be grouped into distinct disjoint subsets, also known as nests. Specifically, we assume that the set $[m] \cup \mathcal{C}$ can be partitioned into N disjoint subsets (nests) $\mathcal{N}_1, \mathcal{N}_2, \ldots, \mathcal{N}_N$, based on their attributes or characteristics.

The choice process in the NL model can viewed as a two-stage process where a customer would first select a nest and then select a location/facility within this nest. Consider the set of available locations $S \subseteq [m]$, the probability that a customer would select a nest $\mathcal{N}_n$, for any $n \in [N]$ can be computed as

$$P(\mathcal{N}_n|S) = \frac{W_n^{\sigma_n}}{\sum_{n' \in [N]} W_{n'}^{\sigma_{n'}}},$$

where $W_n = \sum_{i \in \mathcal{N}_n \cap (S \cup C)} e^{v_i/\sigma_n}$ is the total preference utilities of all facilities in $\mathcal{N}_n \cap S$, σ_n is the dissimilarity parameter of nest $\mathcal{N}_n$. It is typically assumed that the value of σ_n varies in the unit interval for all nests to guarantee that the model is consistent with the RUM framework [3,11].

In the second stage, the customer decides to select a location/facility $i \in S$ from the chosen nest $\mathcal{N}_n$ with probabilities:

$$P(i|\mathcal{N}_n) = \frac{\alpha_{in} e^{v_i/\sigma_n}}{W_n}, \forall i \in S.$$

where α_{in} is a binary parameter such that α_{in} is equal to 1 if the facility i is is in nest n, 0 otherwise. Then, the probability that a customer select a facility in S can be computed as:

$$\begin{aligned} P(i|S) = \sum_{n \in [N]} P(\mathcal{N}_n|S)P(i|\mathcal{N}_n) &= \sum_{n \in [N]} \frac{W_n^{\sigma_n}}{\sum_{n' \in [N]} W_{n'}^{\sigma_{n'}}} \times \frac{\alpha_{in} e^{v_i/\sigma_n}}{W_n} \\ &= \frac{\sum_{n \in [N]} {W_n}^{\sigma_n - 1} \alpha_{in} e^{v_i/\sigma_n}}{\sum_{n \in [N]} W_n^{\sigma_n}}, \ \forall i \in S. \end{aligned}$$

Now, by the law of total expectation, the expected captured market share given by the selected locations S can be computed as

$$F(S) = Q \cdot \frac{\sum_{n \in [N]} {W_n}^{\sigma_n - 1} (\sum_{i \in S} \alpha_{in} e^{v_i/\sigma_n})}{\sum_{n \in [N]} W_n^{\sigma_n}},$$

where Q is the number of customers. With the objective of maximizing total expected demand, the competitive facility location problem under the NL model can be formulated as:

$$\max_{S:|S| \leq r} F(S).$$

where r is the maximum number of facilities to be opened. It is also convenient to formulate the problem as a binary nonlinear program. To this end, let $\mathbf{x} = (x_1, x_2, \ldots, x_m) \in \{0,1\}^m$ be a binary vector representing a location choice decision where $x_i = 1$ if, and only if, the location i is chosen. We can formulate the CFLP under the NL model as the following binary nonlinear program:

$$\max_{\mathbf{x}} \quad \left\{ F(\mathbf{x}) = Q \cdot \frac{\sum_{n\in[N]} {W_n}^{\sigma_n - 1}\left(\sum_{i\in[m]} \alpha_{in} e^{v_i/\sigma_n} x_i\right)}{\sum_{n\in[N]} W_n^{\sigma_n}} \right\} \tag{CFLP-NL}$$

$$\text{subject to} \quad \sum_{i\in[m]} x_i \leq r$$

$$\mathbf{x} \in \{0,1\}^m$$

where $W_n = \sum_{i\in[m]\cup\mathcal{C}} \alpha_{in} e^{v_i/\sigma_n} x_i, \forall t \in [T], n \in [N]$.

3 Fully Polynomial-Time Approximation Scheme

The primary contribution of this work is the introduction of an FPTAS for solving the binary nonlinear program in (CFLP-NL). In this section, we will present the structure of FPTAS algorithm for solving (CFLP-NL), along with its time complexity. Our FPTAS approach involves transforming (CFLP-NL) into a sequence of simpler subproblems and demonstrating that each subproblem can be solved in polynomial time.

Given any $\epsilon > 0$, we will prove that the problem (CFLP-NL) can be solved to an ϵ-optimal solution in $\mathcal{O}(m \log m + r^2 N \log(1/\epsilon))$ time. Specifically, this means that a solution $\hat{\mathbf{x}}$ can be found such that $F(\hat{\mathbf{x}}) \geq \max_{\mathbf{x}\in\mathcal{X}} F(\mathbf{x}) - \epsilon$, within $\mathcal{O}(m \log m + r^2 N \log(1/\epsilon))$ computational steps. To prove that the problem $\{\max_{\mathbf{x}} F(\mathbf{x}) \mid \mathbf{x} \in \{0,1\}^m, \sum_{i\in[m]} x_i \leq r\}$ can be solved in polynomial time, we will construct a two-step approach. In the first step, we convert the problem into a bisection procedure, where each iteration involves solving a sub-problem with a simpler structure. In the second step, we demonstrate that each sub-problem can be solved in polynomial time.

Due to the disjoint of all nests, it implies that each facility belongs to only one nest, i.e., for each $i \in [m] \cup \mathcal{C}$, there is only one nest $n \in [N]$ such that the membership values $\alpha_{in} = 1$, and $\alpha_{in'} = 0$ for all $n' \neq n$. For ease of notation, we can denote that $V_{in} = e^{v_i/\sigma_n}, \forall n \in [N], i \in \mathcal{N}_n$. Then, we can rewrite the total preference utilities W_n as $W_n = \sum_{i\in\mathcal{N}_n\cap[m]} V_{in} x_i + \sum_{i\in\mathcal{N}_n\cap\mathcal{C}} V_{in}$. Then, we can reformulate the objective function as follows

$$\begin{aligned} F(\mathbf{x}) &= Q \cdot \frac{\sum_{n\in[N]} {W_n}^{\sigma_n - 1}\left(\sum_{i\in[m]} \alpha_{in} e^{v_i/\sigma_n} x_i\right)}{\sum_{n\in[N]} W_n^{\sigma_n}} \\ &= Q \cdot \frac{\sum_{n\in[N]} {W_n}^{\sigma_n - 1}\left(\sum_{i\in\mathcal{N}_n\cap[m]} V_{in} x_i\right)}{\sum_{n\in[N]} W_n^{\sigma_n}} \\ &= Q - Q \cdot \frac{\sum_{n\in[N]} W_n^{\sigma_n - 1} U_n^c}{\sum_{n\in[N]} W_n^{\sigma_n}} \end{aligned}$$

where $U_n^c = \sum_{i\in\mathcal{N}_n\cap\mathcal{C}} V_{in}$.

For ease of notation, we denote that $\mathcal{X}_k = \{\mathbf{x} \in \{0,1\}^m \mid \sum_{i\in[m]} x_i \leq k\}, \forall k \in [r]$. In the first step, we convert the maximization problem into a minimization one as

$$\min_{\mathbf{x}\in\mathcal{X}_r} \left\{ \frac{\sum_{n\in[N]} W_n^{\sigma_n - 1} U_n^c}{\sum_{n\in[N]} W_n^{\sigma_n}} \right\} \tag{1}$$

which is equivalent to:

$$\min \left\{ \delta > 0 \mid \exists \mathbf{x} \in \mathcal{X}_r \text{ s.t. } \mathcal{G}(\mathbf{x}, \delta) = \sum_{n\in[N]} W_n^{\sigma_n - 1} U_n^c - \delta \sum_{n\in[N]} W_n^{\sigma_n} \leq 0 \right\} \tag{2}$$

We can solve (2) by performing a binary search over δ, where at each iteration we determine whether there is a binary solution $\mathbf{x}$ such that $\sum_{i\in[m]} x_i \leq r$ and $\mathcal{G}(\mathbf{x}, \delta) \leq 0$. If this is not the case, we increase δ; otherwise, we decrease it. At each iteration, to answer this question, we need to solve the following sub-problem:

$$\min_{\mathbf{x}\in\mathcal{X}_r} \{\mathcal{G}(\mathbf{x}, \delta)\} \tag{3}$$

Using dynamic programming techniques, the following lemma demonstrates that we can solve (3) in polynomial time for any non-negative δ.

Lemma 1. *The problem* $\min_{\boldsymbol{x}\in\mathcal{X}_r} \{\mathcal{G}(\boldsymbol{x}, \delta)\}$ *can be solve to optimality in* $\mathcal{O}(r^2 N)$ *for any* $\delta \geq 0$.

Proof. We write the objective function as

$$\mathcal{G}(\mathbf{x}, \delta) = \sum_{n\in[N]} \phi_n(W_n, \delta)$$

where $\phi_n(W_n, \delta) = U_n^c W_n^{\sigma_n - 1} - \delta W_n^{\sigma_n}$. Since $\sigma_n \leq 1$ and $\delta \geq 0$, we see that $\phi_n(W_n, \delta)$ is decreasing in W_n. Given the constraint $\sum_{i\in[m]} x_i \leq r$, we will formulate the sub-problem as the following dynamic program. Let N be the number of stages, where at each stage $n \in [N]$ we need to select locations for nest n. For each stage $n \in [N]$, let us define the following value function:

$$\mathcal{V}(n, k) = \min \left\{ \sum_{l=1}^{n} \phi_l(W_l, \delta) \middle| \sum_{l=1}^{n} \sum_{i\in\mathcal{N}_l\cap[m]} x_i \leq k \right\}$$

In other words, the value function $\mathcal{V}(n, k)$ represents the minimum value from nest 1 to nest n where there are at most k locations remaining to be selected. It can be seen that

$$\mathcal{V}(N, r) = \min_{\mathbf{x}\in\mathcal{X}_r} \left\{ \sum_{n\in[N]} \phi_n(W_n, \delta) \right\} = \min_{\mathbf{x}\in\mathcal{X}_r} \{\mathcal{G}(\mathbf{x}, \delta)\}.$$

Moreover, the value function $\mathcal{V}(n,k)$ satisfies the following Bellman equation:

$$\mathcal{V}(n,k) = \begin{cases} \min\limits_{0\le u\le k} \left\{ \min\limits_{\substack{x_i|i\in\mathcal{N}_n\cap[m] \\ \sum_{i\in\mathcal{N}_n\cap[m]} x_i\le u}} \Phi_n(W_n,\delta) + \mathcal{V}(n-1,k-u) \right\} & \forall n\in[N], k\ge 0 \\ 0 & \text{if} n=0 \end{cases}$$

Moreover, the subproblem

$$\min_{\substack{x_i|i\in\mathcal{N}_n\cap[m] \\ \sum_{i\in\mathcal{N}_n\cap[m]} x_i\le u}} \Phi_n(W_n,\delta) \tag{4}$$

is equivalent to finding the maximum value of W_n such that $W_n = \sum_{i\in\mathcal{N}_n\cap[m]} V_{in}x_i + U_n^c$ and $\sum_{i\in\mathcal{N}_n\cap[m]} x_i \le u$. This can be done easily by sorting V_{in} for all $i\in\mathcal{N}_n\cap[m]$ in decreasing order and selecting the top u highest values. It can be easily observed that this property does not depend on delta. Therefore, we can perform these sortings before binary search procedure in $\mathcal{O}(\sum_{n\in[N]} |\mathcal{N}_n\backslash\mathcal{C}|\log|\mathcal{N}_n\backslash\mathcal{C}|)$. For each nest $\mathcal{N}_n$, let $V_{i_1n}, V_{i_2n},\ldots$ be the array after sorting, and $\omega(n,u) = U_n^c + \sum_{l=1}^{u} V_{i_ln}$. Then, we have

$$\min_{\substack{x_i|i\in\mathcal{N}_n\cap[m] \\ \sum_{i\in\mathcal{N}_n\cap[m]} x_i\le u}} \Phi_n(W_n,\delta) = \Phi_n(\omega(n,u),\delta), \forall n\in[N], u\le\min(r,|\mathcal{N}_n\cap[m]|)$$

Since $|\mathcal{N}_n\backslash\mathcal{C}|\log|\mathcal{N}_n\backslash\mathcal{C}|$ can be bounded from above by $\sum_{n\in[N]}|\mathcal{N}_n\backslash\mathcal{C}|\log|\mathcal{N}_n\backslash\mathcal{C}| \le m\log m$, the subproblems (4) can be solved in $\mathcal{O}(m\log m)$ in the preprocessing procedure. Then, we can utilize the results of the subproblems (4) during the Bellman system in $\mathcal{O}(1)$. Thus, if the value function is given at stage $n-1$, computing $\mathcal{V}(n,k)$ will take $\mathcal{O}(k)$. Consequently, the computation of $\mathcal{V}(n,k)$ for all $k\le r$ takes $\mathcal{O}(\sum_{k=0}^{r}\mathcal{O}(k))$, which means it can be solved in about $\mathcal{O}(r^2)$.

To compute $\mathcal{V}(N,r)$, we need to calculate $\mathcal{V}(n,k)$ backwards from $\mathcal{V}(l,u),\forall l\le n, u\le k$. At each stage, the computation can be done in $\mathcal{O}(r^2)$, implying that solving the Bellman system will take about $\mathcal{O}\left(\sum_{n\in[N]}\mathcal{O}(r^2)\right)$. Consequently, the Bellman equation can be solved in $\mathcal{O}(r^2N)$. This completes the proof.

We now return to the main proof. The binary search guarantees that, given any $\epsilon>0$, after $\log(1/\epsilon)$ iterations, it can find a $\widehat{\delta}$ such that $|\widehat{\delta}-\delta^*|\le\epsilon$ and

$$\min_{\mathbf{x}\in\mathcal{X}_r} \mathcal{G}(\mathbf{x},\widehat{\delta}) \le 0$$

where δ^* is the optimal solution to (2), which is also the optimal value of the main problem (1). This implies that there exists $\widehat{\mathbf{x}}\in\mathcal{X}_r$ such that $G(\widehat{\mathbf{x}},\widehat{\delta})\le 0$, or

$$\delta^* \le \frac{\sum_{n\in[N]} W_n(\widehat{\mathbf{x}})^{\sigma_n-1}U_n^c}{\sum_{n\in[N]} W_n(\widehat{\mathbf{x}})^{\sigma_n}} \le \widehat{\delta} \le \delta^*+\epsilon$$

which directly implies that

$$\left| \frac{\sum_{n\in[N]} W_n(\widehat{\mathbf{x}})^{\sigma_n - 1} U_n^c}{\sum_{n\in[N]} W_n(\widehat{\mathbf{x}})^{\sigma_n}} - \delta^* \right| \leq \epsilon.$$

As a result, $\widehat{\mathbf{x}}$ is a (ϵ)-optimal solution of the maximization problem $\max_{\mathbf{x}\in\mathcal{X}_r} F(\mathbf{x})$, i.e.,

$$F(\widehat{\mathbf{x}}) \geq \max_{\mathbf{x}\in\mathcal{X}_r} F(\mathbf{x}) - \epsilon$$

as desired. In addition, we also need preprocessing for subproblems (4) with a complexity of $\mathcal{O}(m\log m)$. This implies that we can find an ϵ-optimal solution to (CFLP-NL) in $\mathcal{O}(m\log m + r^2 N\log(1/\epsilon))$ computational steps.

Algorithm 1: Fully Polynomial-Time Approximation Scheme

Input: $\epsilon > 0$
For each nest $\mathcal{N}_n$, sort V_{in} in decreasing order for all $i \in \mathcal{N}_n \cap [m]$.
Let $V_{i_1 n}, V_{i_2 n}, \ldots$ be the array after sorting.
for $n \in [N]$ **do**
    $\omega(n,0) \leftarrow U_n^c$;
    for $u = 1 \rightarrow \min(r, |\mathcal{N}_n \cap [m]|)$ **do**
        $\omega(n,u) \leftarrow \omega(n,u-1) + V_{i_u n}$;
$UB \leftarrow 1 - F(\mathbf{0})/Q$;
$LB \leftarrow 1 - F(\mathbf{1})/Q$;
$\delta \leftarrow UB$;
while $Q(UB - LB) > \epsilon$ **do**
    $mid \leftarrow (UB + LB)/2$;
    for $k = 0 \rightarrow r$ **do**
        $\mathcal{V}(0,k) \leftarrow 0$;
        for $n \in [N]$ **do**
            $\mathcal{V}(n,k) \leftarrow \infty$;
            for $u = 0 \rightarrow \min(k, |\mathcal{N}_n \cap [m]|)$ **do**
                $\mathcal{V}(n,k) \leftarrow \min(\mathcal{V}(n,k), \Phi_n(\omega(n,u), mid) + \mathcal{V}(n-1, k-u))$;
    if $\mathcal{V}(N,r) \leq 0$ **then**
        $\delta \leftarrow mid$;
        $UB \leftarrow mid$;
    else
        $LB \leftarrow mid$;
return $Q - Q\delta$.

The entire FPTAS algorithm is presented in Algorithm 1. Before implementing the binary search procedure, we can easily observe that the lower bound of the objective function of (CFLP-NL) can be obtained by not opening any locations, meaning $\mathbf{x} = \mathbf{0}$. Similarly, a simple upper bound of the objective function is obtained by opening all locations, which means $\mathbf{x} = \mathbf{1}$. From this, we can derive an initial upper and lower bound for δ during the binary search process. After finding optimal δ for (2), the resulting objective function will be $Q - Q\delta$.

4 Numerical Experiments

In this section, we present numerical results to evaluate the performance of our proposed methods for solving the competitive facility location problem under the NL model. We first present the settings of the experiment, followed by a comparison of performance between the FPTAS approach and the state-of-the-art cutting plane approach proposed by [7].

4.1 Experimental Settings

In this experiment, we utilize three benchmark datasets commonly used in previous CFLP studies [4,9,10]. We flatten these data by considering locations in different customer zones as distinct. As a result, each problem instance in the dataset will have $m = T \times m'$ locations, where T is the number of customers and m' is the number of locations in these datasets.

- **ORlib**: This dataset comprises 11 problem instances, including four instances with $(T, m') = (50, 25)$, four instances with $(T, m') = (50, 50)$, and three instances with $(T, m') = (1000, 100)$. Instances from this dataset are labeled with the prefix "cap".
- **HM14**: This dataset consists of 15 problem instances with $T \in \{50, 100, 200, 400, 800\}$ and $m' \in \{25, 50, 100\}$. Instances from this dataset are labeled with the prefix "OUR".
- **NYC**: This dataset comes from a large-scale park-and-ride location problem in New York City, featuring $T = 82341$ and $m' = 59$.

The maximum number of facilities to be opened, r, varies in $\{25, 50, 100\}$. The deterministic part of the utility is calculated as $v_i = -\beta c_i$ for a location $i \in S$, and $v_{i'} = -\beta c_{i'}$ for any competitor $i' \in \mathcal{C}$, where $c_{i'}$ is the cost of location $i' \in \mathcal{C}$. The parameter β, representing customer sensitivity to perceived utilities, is set to 0.01. Consequently, each problem has 9 different instances. The NL parameters are randomly generated as follows. The dissimilarity parameter σ_n for nest $\mathcal{N}_n$ is randomly generated in range from 0.5 to 1. Moreover, the number of nests, N, is chosen in $\{25, 50, 100\}$. We randomly assign the m locations to the N nests, ensuring that each location is assigned no more than once per nest and each nest contains at least two distinct locations.

We will compare our approach, particularly the FPTAS, in solving (CFLP-NL). For comparison, we also include a state-of-the-art method from prior work [7] that solves the non-convex problem in (CFLP-NL). Specifically, this approach formulates (CFLP-NL) as a nonlinear optimization problem with a linear objective and convex constraints, and then applies a cutting-plane method with outer-approximation cuts. Additionally, we include a Greedy Heuristic (GH), which starts with an empty solution and iteratively selects locations to maximize the objective value as the initial solution for CP. Recent studies on the CFLP have shown that greedy and local search procedures can achieve state-of-the-art performance in terms of returning the best solutions within short computation times, compared to other methods [4,5]. By integrating GH, we aim to benchmark the performance of this state-of-the-art method against our exact approaches. It is important to note that $F(\mathbf{x})$ is not concave in $\mathbf{x}$ [7], meaning the traditional direct cutting-plane method cannot guarantee optimal solutions.

The algorithms were written in C++, and the MILP models were solved by IBM ILOG CPLEX 22.1.1, where the number of CPUs is set to 8 cores. All experiments were run on 13th Gen Intel(R) Core(TM) i5-13500 @ 4.8 GHz, and 64 GB of RAM. The CP algorithm terminates when it reaches the maximum number of iterations $nb_{iter} = 10000$ or the running time exceeds 600 seconds. The ϵ in FPTAS and cutting plane method are both set to 10^{-6}.

4.2 Numerical Results

In this section, we provide comparison results for the CFLP under the NL model between our approach, FPTAS, and outer-approximation, the state-of-the-art method for this problem. To evaluate the performance of our approach compared to the CP, we report the number of times that CP returns the optimal solution (# Opt) or the best objective values (# Best). We also report the average computing time for all approaches. It is important to note that FPTAS ensures ϵ-optimal solutions in $\mathcal{O}(m \log m + r^2 N \log(1/\epsilon))$. Consequently, we only report the average computing time (Avg. Time) in seconds for the FPTAS approach. All comparison results are reported in Table 1.

We first observe that the FPTAS approach outperforms the outer-approximation in all problem instances. Table 1 shows that our approach consistently returns ϵ-optimal solutions in less than 1 second for most problem instances. Even for large-scale cases, such as the NYC dataset with over 4 million locations, FPTAS still delivers near optimal solutions with an average computation time of 1.02 seconds. In contrast, the outer-approximation method struggles with these instances. For example, in small-sized instances with $m = 1250$, the state-of-the-art method is unable to guarantee optimal solutions for all problem instances within the time budget of 600 seconds. Although the CP algorithm often finds the best solution, thanks to the strong lower bound provided by the GH, it cannot always prove that these solutions are truly optimal. Specifically, in larger problems with $M \geq 80000$, the CP algorithm fails to solve any instance to optimality. It leads to the higher average computing time of outer-approximation (more than 300 seconds) in all problem instances.

This experiment demonstrates that the FPTAS consistently guarantees an ϵ-optimal solution within polynomial time, as outlined in Sect. 3. Our approach offers flexibility in balancing solution quality and computation time, outperforming current state-of-the-art algorithms applied to the CFLP under the NL model.

Table 1. Numerical results for competitive facility location problem under nested-logit model, average computing times are given in seconds.

Dataset	Instance	m	Outer-Approximation			FPTAS
			# Opt	# Best	Avg. Time	Avg. Time
ORLib	cap101	1250	3	6	403.18	0.07
	cap102	1250	4	6	374.54	0.07
	cap103	1250	3	6	402.40	0.07
	cap104	1250	4	6	338.58	0.07
	cap131	2500	1	6	538.36	0.10
	cap132	2500	2	6	471.48	0.10
	cap133	2500	1	6	537.77	0.10
	cap134	2500	2	5	470.13	0.10
	capa	100000	0	6	609.26	0.17
	capb	100000	0	6	609.52	0.17
	capc	100000	0	5	609.29	0.17
HM14	OUR_50_25	1250	3	6	415.51	0.05
	OUR_50_50	2500	3	6	410.13	0.08
	OUR_50_100	5000	3	6	402.03	0.10
	OUR_100_25	2500	3	5	400.74	0.08
	OUR_100_50	5000	3	6	405.52	0.10
	OUR_100_100	10000	3	6	414.80	0.12
	OUR_200_25	5000	3	6	402.96	0.11
	OUR_200_50	10000	3	6	408.29	0.12
	OUR_200_100	20000	0	6	603.43	0.12
	OUR_400_25	10000	3	6	402.18	0.12
	OUR_400_50	20000	1	6	478.14	0.13
	OUR_400_100	40000	0	6	605.14	0.13
	OUR_800_25	20000	3	6	404.96	0.13
	OUR_800_50	40000	3	6	408.27	0.13
	OUR_800_100	80000	0	6	608.29	0.14
NYC	NYC	4858119	0	6	603.81	1.02

It achieves ϵ-optimal solutions with significantly smaller computing times, making it both efficient and highly competitive compared to other methods.

5 Conclusion

In this paper, we studied the competitive facility location problem with a single customer type, where customer behavior is predicted using the NL choice model. To handle the nonlinearity and complexity of this problem, we proposed an FPTAS approach that guarantees an ϵ-optimal solution with a time complexity of $\mathcal{O}(m \log m + r^2 N \log(1/\epsilon))$. In contrast, existing exact methods either do not operate within polynomial time or cannot guarantee near-optimal solutions. Our numerical experiments demonstrate that our approach outperforms the current state-of-the-art exact method for CFLP under the NL model in terms of computing time, while still ensuring an ϵ-optimal solution. Future work will extend this approach to tackle the facility cost optimization problem, more general competitive facility location problems with multiple customer types, or more advanced models such as the cross-nested logit models.

Acknowledgment. This research was funded by Vingroup Innovation Foundation (VINIF), Vietnam under project code VINIF.2024.DA072.

References

1. Ben-Akiva, M.: The Structure of Travel Demand Models. Ph.D. thesis, MIT (1973)
2. Benati, S., Hansen, P.: The maximum capture problem with random utilities: problem formulation and algorithms. Eur. J. Oper. Res. **143**(3), 518–530 (2002)
3. Bierlaire, M.: A theoretical analysis of the cross-nested logit model. Ann. Oper. Res. **144**, 287–300 (2006)
4. Dam, T.T., Ta, T.A., Mai, T.: Submodularity and local search approaches for maximum capture problems under generalized extreme value models. Eur. J. Oper. Res. **300**(3), 953–965 (2022)
5. Dam, T.T., Ta, T.A., Mai, T.: Robust maximum capture facility location under random utility maximization models. Eur. J. Oper. Res. **310**(3), 1128–1150 (2023)
6. Fosgerau, M., Bierlaire, M.: Discrete choice models with multiplicative error terms. Transp. Res. Part B **43**(5), 494–505 (2009)
7. Le, B.L., Mai, T., Ta, T.A., Ha, M.H., Vu, D.M.: Competitive facility location under cross-nested logit customer choice model: hardness and exact approaches (2024). https://arxiv.org/abs/2408.02925
8. Legault, R., Frejinger, E.: A model-free approach for solving choice-based competitive facility location problems using simulation and submodularity. INFORMS J. Comput. (2024)
9. Ljubić, I., Moreno, E.: Outer approximation and submodular cuts for maximum capture facility location problems with random utilities. Eur. J. Oper. Res. **266**(1), 46–56 (2018)
10. Mai, T., Lodi, A.: A multicut outer-approximation approach for competitive facility location under random utilities. Eur. J. Oper. Res. **284**(3), 874–881 (2020)
11. McFadden, D.: Modelling the choice of residential location. Transportation Research Record (1978)
12. McFadden, D., Train, K.: Mixed MNL models for discrete response. J. Appl. Econometrics **15**(5), 447–470 (2000)
13. Méndez-Vogel, G., Marianov, V., Lüer-Villagra, A.: The follower competitive facility location problem under the nested logit choice rule. Eur. J. Oper. Res. **310**(2), 834–846 (2023)
14. Train, K.E.: Discrete Choice Methods with Simulation. Cambridge University Press (2009)

Leveraging Auto-distillation and Generative Self-supervised Learning in Residual Graph Transformers for Enhanced Recommender Systems

Eya Mhedhbi[1], Youssef Mourchid[2(✉)], and Alice Othmani[1,3]

[1] Declic AI Research, Melbourne, Australia
[2] CESI LINEACT Laboratory, 7527 Dijon, UR, France
ymourchid@cesi.fr
[3] Université Paris-Est, LISSI, UPEC, 94400 Vitry sur Seine, France
alice.othmani@u-pec.fr

Abstract. This paper introduces a cutting-edge method for enhancing recommender systems through the integration of generative self-supervised learning (SSL) with a Residual Graph Transformer. Our approach emphasizes the importance of superior data enhancement through the use of pertinent pretext tasks, automated through rationale-aware SSL to distill clear ways of how users and items interact. The Residual Graph Transformer incorporates a topology-aware transformer for global context and employs residual connections to improve graph representation learning. Additionally, an auto-distillation process refines self-supervised signals to uncover consistent collaborative rationales. Experimental evaluations on multiple datasets demonstrate that our approach consistently outperforms baseline methods.

Keywords: Recommender Systems · Generative Self-supervised learning · Residual Graph Transformer · Masked Autoencoder · Representation Learning

1 Introduction

In today's age of information overload, recommender systems are essential for offering personalized suggestions for items that users might find appealing, such as products on e-commerce platforms [1] and social media [2]. These systems are integral to enhancing user engagement and facilitating discovery amid vast content repositories like Amazon, Alibaba, Facebook, YouTube, and TikTok.

Collaborative filtering (CF) is widely employed within these systems, it generates suggestions by leveraging the preferences of similar users or items to recommend new items for a given user [3]. In recent years, graphs have been extensively utilized in a variety of applications [4,5], with Graph Neural Networks (GNNs) enhancing collaborative filtering by modeling users and items as connected nodes. Models like PinSage [6], NGCF [7], and LightGCN [8] use GCNs for better embeddings and accuracy. LightGCN [8] focuses on structural

J. Kertesz et al. (Eds.): CSoNet 2024, LNCS 15417, pp. 35–47, 2025.
https://doi.org/10.1007/978-981-96-6389-7_4

signals, while GNNs face challenges with sparse and noisy data. Self-supervised learning (SSL), a powerful technique that trains models using unlabeled data, has emerged as a valuable approach in recommender systems by learning from unlabeled data. SSL methods are either contrastive, like SGL [9], which creates varied views of interaction graphs, or generative, like GFormer [10], which reconstructs masked interactions. Graph Contrastive Learning (GCL) is useful but struggles with noise. Traditional methods, such as hypergraph-based passing (HCCF) [11] and node clustering (NCL) [12], address some issues but are also noise-prone.

Generative Learning in recommendation systems involves generating new data instances from existing ones. Self-supervised collaborative filtering leverages this approach through several advanced techniques: (1) Variational Autoencoders (VAE): Methods like CaD-VAE [13] enhance modeling by integrating item content, optimizing hyperparameters, and using advanced frameworks to improve efficiency. (2) Masked Autoencoders: Techniques such as AutoCF [14] and GFormer [10] reconstruct data by focusing on significant user-item interactions. GFormer emphasizes autonomous edge detection and reconstruction using user and item representations. (3) Denoised Diffusion Models: Approaches like DiffRec [15] use diffusion models to reduce noise from user ratings or latent variables, enhancing prediction accuracy and efficiency.

To overcome the limitations of the different approaches and in order to leverage the strengths of various techniques, we propose a novel recommender system called Residual Graph Transformer. It automatically extracts self-supervised signals, improves the graph autoencoder with adaptive methods, and uses Transformers to capture relationships and collaborative patterns for better recommendations. Auto-distillation is also used to improve the performance. Our main contributions can be summarized as follows:

- We introduce automated ways to enhance data through self-supervised learning (SSL) and explain how these methods can make recommendations more robust.
- We use graph transformer models with residual connections and light self-attention to identify consistent data patterns. Auto-distillation boosts recommendation performance, and a graph autoencoder enhances the representation of user-item interactions.
- We evaluate our proposed model on multiple datasets and find it consistently outperforms other methods in various scenarios.

The organization of the rest of this paper is as follows. Section 2 comprehensively details different components of our proposed model. Section 3 outlines the experimental setup and presents the results. Finally, concluding remarks are presented in Sect. 4.

2 Proposed Approach

2.1 Problem Formulation

In this work, we consider a recommendation system with I users $U = \{u_1, u_2, ..., u_I\}$ and J items $P = \{p_1, p_2, ..., p_J\}$. The user interactions are captured by an interaction matrix $A \in R^{I \times J}$, where $a_{i,j} = 1$ indicates an interaction between user u_i and item p_j, and $a_{i,j} = 0$ otherwise. To convert the interaction matrix into an interaction graph for graph-based CF, we define a graph $G = \{V, E\}$, where $V = U \cup P$ represents the set of nodes, and $E = \{e_{i,j} | a_{i,j} = 1\}$ denotes the set of edges corresponding to user-item interactions. With these definitions, the graph-based CF can be represented as a prediction function for user-item interactions: $\hat{y}_{i,j} = f(G; \Theta)$, where $\hat{y}_{i,j}$ is the predicted score for the unknown interaction between user u_i and item p_j, and Θ represents the model parameters.

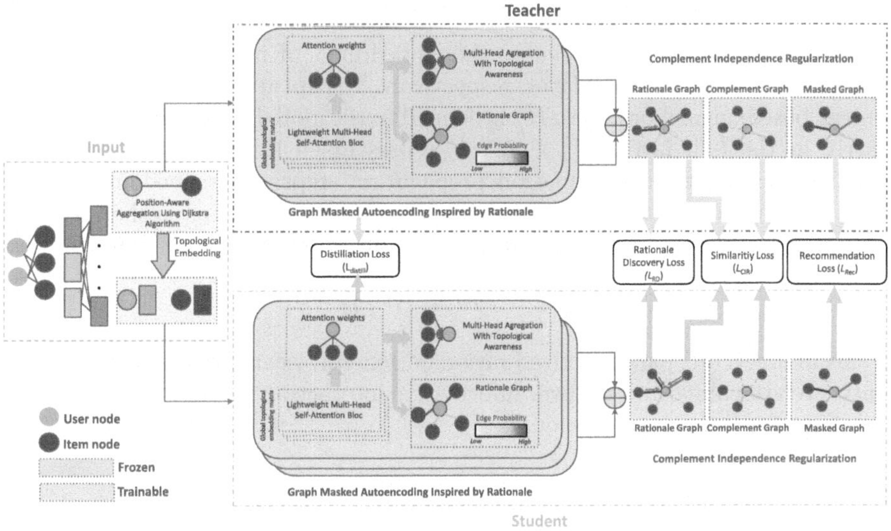

Fig. 1. Overall framework illustration of our proposed approach. The figure is better seen zoomed in the digital version of the document.

2.2 Integration of Global Topology Information

Inspired by the efficiency of position-aware graph neural networks(P-GNNs) [16] in capturing comprehensive relational information on a global scale, we initially select a subset of anchor nodes $V_A \subset V$ from the user-item interaction graph $G = \{V, E\}$. We then compute the distance between a target node v_k and the anchor sets v_a using Dijkstra's algorithm. Given the calculated distances, we compute the correlation weight, denoted as $\omega_{k,a}$, for each pair of target-anchor nodes (k, a). The correlation weight is defined as follows:

$$\omega_{k,a} = \begin{cases} \frac{1}{d_{k,a}+1} & \text{if } d_{k,a} \leq q \\ 0 & \text{otherwise.} \end{cases} \tag{1}$$

q is the upper limit for the correlation weight between any target and anchor node. This method ensures that only nodes within a certain distance contribute to the target node's embedding, effectively capturing the positional relationships within the graph. Dijkstra's algorithm is used for a more accurate representation of these relationships, resulting in more informative node embeddings. This holds true even when edge weights are binary, Dijkstra's algorithm can provide a more nuanced understanding of the graph structure, which can lead to improved performance. The correlation weights of the nodes are normalized to a range of [0, 1]. Using the weight $\omega_{k,a}$, the target node embedding is refined by considering the correlation weights between the target node k and each anchor node $v_a \in V_A$: $\tilde{h}_k^l = \sum_{v_a \in V_A} W^l \cdot \omega_{k,a} \cdot [\tilde{h}_k^{l-1} || \tilde{h}_a^{l-1}]/|V_A|$

Here, $\tilde{h}_k^l$ and $\tilde{h}_k^{l-1} \in R^d$ denote the embeddings of node v_k in the l-th and $(l-1)$-th graph propagation layer, respectively. To capture the global topological context based on anchor nodes, H_T^l is defined as the global topological embedding matrix in the l-th layer. $W^l \in R^{d \times 2d}$ represents a learnable transformation matrix. After L graph information propagation steps, the embeddings in $\tilde{H}^L$ retain the high-order topological information. This information is then injected into the id-corresponding embeddings to produce the topological embeddings:

$$\bar{H} = TE(H; \{W_T^l\}) \tag{2}$$

In this manner, our parameterized rationale generator can capture global collaborative relationships and uncover informative interaction patterns between users and items for SSL augmentation.

2.3 Residual Graph Transformer-Based Collaborative Rationale Discovery

Rational discovery helps to find useful patterns in how users interact with items. These patterns can help improve recommendation systems in changing environments, even when there are few labels for supervision. We propose an advanced method for extracting these rationales using our Graph Transformer model with residual connections. Our method is inspired by the core self-attention mechanisms of the Transformer architecture, focusing on invariant user preference information for robust generative self-supervision. This approach mitigates noise and biases in observational behavior data, enhancing recommendation performance. The core of our method is a rationale discovery module within a graph transformer framework, encoding node-wise relations as selected rationales and incorporating the positional information of user and item nodes. We leverage global topology-aware node embeddings, $\bar{H}$, in a multi-head self-attention mechanism for the rationalization process. The correlation between nodes v_k and $v_{k'}$ for the h-th attention head is computed as:

$$\alpha_{k,k'}^h = \frac{\exp(\tilde{\alpha}_{k,k'}^h)}{\sum_{k'} \exp(\tilde{\alpha}_{k,k'}^h)}; \tilde{\alpha}_{k,k'}^h = \frac{(W_Q^h \cdot \bar{h}_k)^T \cdot (W_K^h \cdot \bar{h}_{k'})}{\sqrt{d/H}} \tag{3}$$

Here, $\alpha_{k,k'}^h$ represents the normalized attention score between nodes v_k and $v_{k'}$ for the h-th attention head, and $\tilde{\alpha}_{k,k'}^h$ is the raw attention score before normalization. W_Q^h and W_K^h in $\mathbb{R}^{d_H \times d}$ are the transformations used to derive the query and key embeddings for calculating the attention scores. As the attention scores encoded by our graph transformer reflect the strength of node-wise dependencies, we aggregate the multi-head scores to obtain the probability scores, $p((v_k, v_{k'})|G)$, of graph edges, such as $(v_k - v_{k'})$, being selected as rationales. These rationales represent a subset of crucial user-item interaction patterns that most effectively highlight the user preference learning process with consistent representations, as shown:

$$\bar{p}((v_k, v_{k'})|G) = \frac{\bar{\alpha}_{k,k'}}{\sum_{(v_k, v_{k'}) \in E} \bar{\alpha}_{k,k'}}; \bar{\alpha}_{k,k'} = \frac{\sum_{h=1}^{H} \alpha_{k,k'}^h}{H} \tag{4}$$

To sample a rationale estimated by our topology-aware graph transformer, we individually select $\rho_R \cdot |E|$ edges from the edge set E based on their probability scores, $p((v_k, v_{k'})|G)$. Here, the hyperparameter $\rho_R \in R$ determines the proportion of important edges chosen for rationalization. To improve our model, we added a residual operation to our residual graph transformer. This upgrade builds on the basic graph transformer by repeatedly applying it and combining the results through a residual link. This helps maintain the flow of gradients during training, making learning more efficient and improving the model's performance. This residual modification significantly boosts the model's ability to find and understand important patterns in user-item interactions, enhancing recommendation effectiveness in changing environments with limited supervised data. In addition to the above, we have also incorporated a streamlined version of self-attention, into our model. This version employs linear layers for transforming the input vectors, which facilitates easier initialization and improved gradient propagation. An output projection layer has been integrated to transform the resulting embeddings back to the original dimensionality. This makes the Light Self-Attention particularly suitable for large datasets and deep architectures, while being more computationally and memory efficient.

2.4 Self-augmentation with Rationale Awareness

Integrating Rationales into Graph Masked Autoencoding. The approach uses a graph-masked autoencoder for self-augmentation, leveraging collaborative rationales. The rationale-aware mask autoencoder masks identified rationales from the interaction graph, allowing for effective reconstruction. The masked graph structure $G_M = \{V, E_M\}$ is created by inverting the rationale scores. The masked graph maintains a higher edge density than the rationale graph, ensuring only the most significant rationale edges are removed, promoting noise-resistant autoencoding. The process begins with the following operation:

$$S = GT(G_M, TE(\bar{S}_L)); \bar{s}_l = \sum_{(v_k, v_{k'}) \in E_M} \beta_{k,k'} \cdot \bar{s}_{l1_{k'}} \tag{5}$$

Here, $GT(\cdot)$ and $TE(\cdot)$ represent the graph transformer network and the topological information encoder, respectively. $\bar{s}_l$ is the sum of the product of $\beta_{k,k'}$ and $\bar{s}_{l1_{k'}}$ for all edges in E_M. This equation is used to enhance the initial embeddings with L-order local node embeddings $\bar{S}_L$, encoded from LightGCN. The embeddings S are then used to train the reconstruction of the masked user-item interactions. The final embeddings $S \in R^{(I+J) \times d}$ in the autoencoder are utilized for training the reconstruction of the masked user-item interactions, and for computing the masked autoencoder loss L_{MAE}, which is defined as follows:

$$L_{MAE} = \sum_{(v_k, v'_k) \in E \setminus E_M} -\tilde{y}_{k,k'}; \tilde{y}_{k,k'} = s_k^{\top} s_{k'} \tag{6}$$

This loss is specifically designed for reconstructing masked interaction patterns, $\tilde{y}_{k,k'}$ represents the predicted scores for the edge $(v_k, v_{k'})$ on graph G. The reconstruction process is enhanced by encoding local node embeddings from LightGCN into the initial embeddings, ensuring effective reconstruction of key interaction patterns adaptable to downstream recommendation tasks. This approach helps prevent noise in the generative self-supervised learning process.

Modeling Complement Independence. To make the rationale discovery process more independent and reduce redundancy, we use a learning technique called contrastive regularization. This minimizes the mutual information between the rationale graphG_R and a complement graph G_C. We create the complement graphG_C by sampling edges with a low rate $\rho_C << \rho_M$ to focus on noisy edges. The edges of the complement graph (E_C) are generated as follows:

$$E_C \sim p_C(E_C|G) = \rho_M(E_C|G); |E_C| = \rho_C \cdot |E| \tag{7}$$

This is similar to graph masking but with a smaller sampling rate. Then, we used the loss function $\mathcal{L}_{CIR}$, to reduce the similarities between the rationale graph G_R and the complement graph G_C in high-order representations, which can be defined as follows:

$$\mathcal{L}_{CIR} = \log \sum_{v_k \in V} \exp\left(\frac{\cos(e_k^R, e_k^C)}{\tau}\right) \tag{8}$$

Here, e_k^R and e_k^C are the embeddings of node k in the rationale graph and complement graph, respectively. The cosine similarity between these embeddings is divided by a temperature coefficient τ, and the exponential sum of these values across all nodes is taken. This loss function ensures that the embeddings of the rationale graph and the complement graph are pushed apart, enhancing the model's ability to separate useful information from noise.

SSL-Augmented Model Optimization. During training, we use embeddings $S \in R^{(I+J)\times d}$ to predict interactions for training the recommender system. The point-wise loss function L_{Rec} is minimized as follows:

$$L_{Rec} = \sum_{i,j=1}^{A} -\log\left(\frac{\exp(s_i^T s_j)}{\sum_{p' \in P}\exp(s_i^T s_{p'})}\right) \quad (9)$$

Our Model maximizes predictions for all positive user-item interactions and contrasts by minimizing predictions for negative interactions. During testing, we substitute the masked graph G_M with the observed interaction graph G and predict user u_i's relation to item p_j as $\hat{y}_{i,j} = s_i^T s_j$.

2.5 Auto Distillation Graph

Auto-distillation improves model training by using a single model as both teacher and student. After steps like negative sampling and embedding generation, the model's embeddings (user, item, and graph structure) are used to train a second model, the distillation model. The distillation model learns to mimic the main model's outputs, guided by a loss function, Mean Squared Error (MSE), which reduces differences between the outputs of the main model and the distillation model. This process can be expressed as:

$$\begin{aligned} L_{\text{distill}} = &\text{MSE}(h_u^{\text{student}}, h_u^{\text{teacher}}) + \text{MSE}(h_i^{\text{student}}, h_i^{\text{teacher}}) \\ &+ \text{MSE}(h_c^{\text{student}}, h_c^{\text{teacher}}) + \text{MSE}(h_s^{\text{student}}, h_s^{\text{teacher}}) \end{aligned} \quad (10)$$

where $h_u^{student}$ and $h_u^{teacher}$ represent the user embeddings generated by the student and teacher models, respectively, $h_i^{student}$ and $h_i^{teacher}$ represent the item embeddings, $h_c^{student}$ and $h_c^{teacher}$ represent the contrastive list embeddings, and $h_s^{student}$ and $h_s^{teacher}$ represent the subgraph list embeddings.

2.6 Our Objective Loss

The BPR loss, L_{RD}, guides rationale discovery by optimizing the model's objective for the downstream task:

$$L_{RD} = \sum_{(u_i, p_j^+, p_j^-)} -\log \text{sigm}(\bar{y}_{i,j+} - \bar{y}_{i,j-}) \quad (11)$$

Here, a triplet of user u_i and items p_j^+, p_j^- is sampled such that $(u_i, p_j^+) \in E$ and $(u_i, p_j^-) \notin E$. The sigmoid function, $\text{sigm}(\cdot)$, models the probability that the positive interaction p_j^+ is preferred over p_j^-.

In our model, the total loss function L integrates several key objectives: L_{Rec}, L_{RCS}, L_{RD}, L_{CIR}, and the Frobenius norm regularization $||\Theta||_F^2$. Additionally, the distillation loss L_{distill} refines the model's internal representations over training epochs, enhancing the accuracy of recommendations. The overall objective L to be minimized during training consolidates these components:

$$L = L_{\text{Rec}} + \lambda_{\text{distill}} L_{\text{distill}} + \lambda_1 \cdot L_{\text{RD}} + \lambda_2 \cdot L_{\text{CIR}} + \lambda_3 \cdot ||\Theta||_F^2 \tag{12}$$

Here, λ_1, λ_2, λ_3, and λ_{distill} are hyperparameters balancing the impact of each loss term. The Frobenius norm regularization $||\Theta||_F^2$ helps keep the model stable by limiting parameter values. This approach balances reconstruction, rationale discovery, and regularization for better optimization in recommendation systems.

3 Experiments and Results

3.1 Experimental Settings

Datasets. We use three real-world datasets to assess the performance of our proposed model. These include the Yelp dataset, which focuses on recommending business venues from the renowned Yelp platform; the Ifashion dataset, a collection of fashion outfit data gathered by Alibaba, and the LastFM dataset, which records user interactions within music applications and internet radio platforms. The characteristics and statistics of these datasets are detailed in Table 1.

Table 1. Statistics of the experimental datasets

Dataset	Users	Items	Interactions	Density
Yelp	42,712	26,822	182,357	$1.6e^{-4}$
Ifashion	31,668	38,048	618,629	$5.1e^{-4}$
LastFM	1,889	15,376	51,987	$1.8e^{-3}$

Evaluation Protocols. For each dataset, interactions are split into training, validation, and test sets with a division ratio of 70%, 5%, and 25%, respectively. To evaluate the effectiveness of our proposed model, we employ a comprehensive all-rank evaluation method that mitigates potential biases from negative sampling. The performance of the models is assessed using two key metrics: Recall Ratio (Recall@K) and Normalized Discounted Cumulative Gain (NDCG@K) for $K = 10, 20, 40$. NDCG is calculated using the formula:

$$NDCG@k = \frac{DCG@k}{IDCG@k} \tag{13}$$

where $DCG@k$ is the Discounted Cumulative Gain at position k, calculated by summing the gains of the recommendations up to position k and giving more weight to higher-ranked recommendations, and $IDCG@k$ is the Ideal Discounted Cumulative Gain at position k, representing the optimal possible DCG when the recommendations are perfectly ranked.

3.2 Hyperparameter Settings

We used Weights & Biases (W&B)[1] for hyperparameter tuning to maximize Recall and NDCG values. Table 2 presents the best hyperparameter combinations for the different datasets.

Table 2. The best hyperparameter combinations used across various datasets in our model.

Dataset	anchor_set	reg	lr	ssl_reg	GCN	B2	PNN	Batch	ctra	GT	GTW	Head	latdim
Yelp	16	0.0001	0.001	0.5	3	0.5	2	4096	0.005	2	0.05	2	64
Ifashion	64	0.00001	0.001	1.5	3	1	1	4096	0.0005	1	0.05	2	32
LastFM	32	0.0001	0.001	0.5	1	1	2	4096	0.005	1	0.1	8	64

3.3 Ablation Study

To validate the effectiveness of our contributions, we conducted an ablation study comparing three versions of our model using the LastFM dataset. The first version, Graph Transformer, served as our baseline model. We then added Dijkstra's algorithm and the Residual Graph Transformer(RGT) with light attention(LA) in the second version, followed by the application of auto-distillation in the third version(AD). As shown in Fig. 2, each enhancement led to progressive improvements in Recall@40 and NDCG@40 metrics, underscoring the effectiveness of our proposed methods.

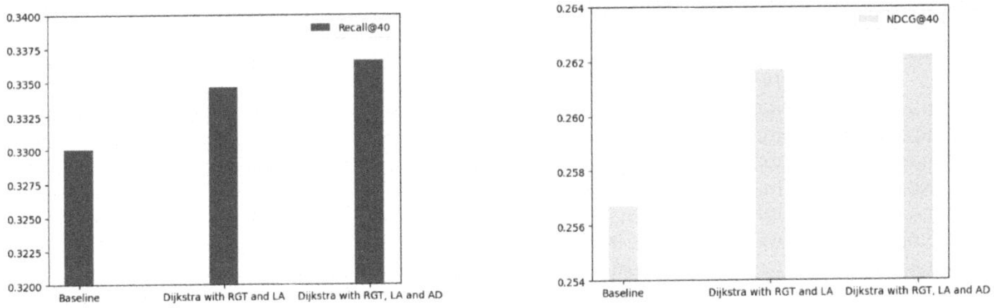

(a) LastFM Dataset - Recall@40 (b) LastFM Dataset - NDCG@40

Fig. 2. Effect of different components of our proposed models on LastFM dataset in terms of Recall@40 and NDCG@40

[1] https://wandb.ai/site.

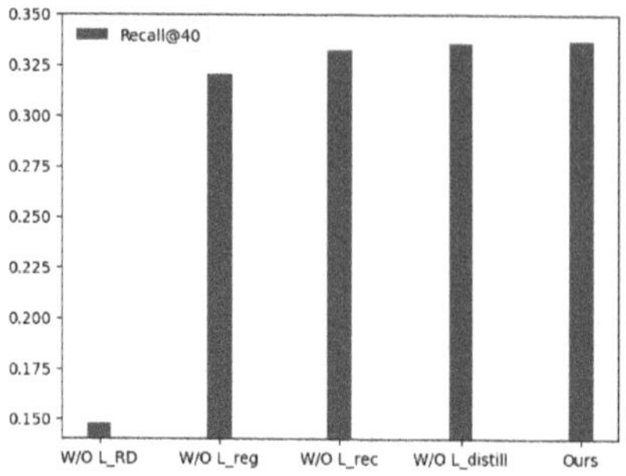

(a) LastFM Dataset - Recall@40

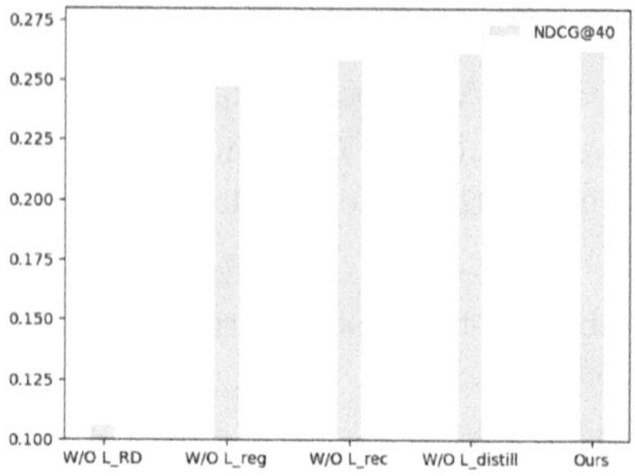

(b) LastFM Dataset - NDCG@40

Fig. 3. Effect of different losses used in our model on the Recall@40 and NDCG@40 metrics for the LastFM dataset

Additionally, as mentioned in Fig. 3, we assess the impact of individual loss compo-nents on model performance, we conducted an ablation study by sequentially removing each component and measuring changes in Recall@40 and NDCG@40. Results show that the L_RD component is crucial for guiding rationale discovery and optimizing the model, with its removal leading to significant drops in both metrics. The L_rec component is also vital, as its absence results in a major performance decline. The L_distill component, while less critical, still provides a positive but modest contribution. The L_reg component is essential for preventing overfitting, as indicated by the performance decrease when it is removed. Overall, the full model with all loss components included demon-

Table 3. Performance comparison between our proposed approach and all baselines on Ifashion, Yelp, LastFM datasets.

Datasets	Metric	BiasMF	NCF	AutoRec	PinSage	NGCF	GCCF	LightGCN	EGLN	SLRec	NCL	HCCF	SGL	GFormer	Ours
Ref	--	[17]	[3]	[18]	[6]	[7]	[19]	[8]	[20]	[21]	[12]	[11]	[9]	[10]	--
Yelp	Recall@10	0.0122	0.0166	0.0230	0.0278	0.0438	0.0484	0.0422	0.0458	0.0418	0.0493	0.0518	0.0522	0.0562	**0.0583**
	NDCG@10	0.0070	0.0101	0.0133	0.0171	0.0269	0.0296	0.0254	0.0278	0.0258	0.0301	0.0318	0.0319	0.0350	**0.0363**
	Recall@20	0.0198	0.0292	0.0410	0.0454	0.0678	0.0754	0.0761	0.0726	0.0650	0.0806	0.0789	0.0815	0.0878	**0.0911**
	NDCG@20	0.0090	0.0138	0.0186	0.0224	0.0340	0.0378	0.0373	0.0360	0.0327	0.0402	0.0391	0.0410	0.0442	**0.0458**
	Recall@40	0.0303	0.0442	0.0678	0.0712	0.1047	0.1163	0.1031	0.1121	0.1026	0.1192	0.1244	0.1249	0.1328	**0.1377**
	NDCG@40	0.0117	0.0167	0.0253	0.0287	0.0430	0.0475	0.0413	0.0456	0.0418	0.0485	0.0510	0.0517	0.0551	**0.0572**
Ifashion	Recall@10	0.0302	0.0268	0.0309	0.0291	0.0375	0.0373	0.0437	0.0473	0.0373	0.0474	0.0489	0.0512	0.0542	**0.0555**
	NDCG@10	0.0281	0.0253	0.0264	0.0276	0.0350	0.0352	0.0416	0.0438	0.0353	0.0446	0.0464	0.0487	0.0520	**0.0526**
	Recall@20	0.0523	0.0451	0.0537	0.0505	0.0636	0.0639	0.0751	0.0787	0.0633	0.0797	0.0815	0.0845	0.0894	**0.0910**
	NDCG@20	0.0360	0.0306	0.0351	0.0352	0.0442	0.0445	0.0528	0.0549	0.0444	0.0558	0.0578	0.0603	0.0635	**0.0650**
	Recall@40	0.0858	0.0785	0.0921	0.0851	0.1062	0.1047	0.1207	0.1277	0.1043	0.1283	0.1306	0.1354	0.1424	**0.1435**
	NDCG@40	0.0474	0.0423	0.0483	0.0470	0.0585	0.0584	0.0677	0.0715	0.0582	0.0723	0.0744	0.0773	0.0818	**0.0826**
LastFM	Recall@10	0.0609	0.0574	0.0543	0.0899	0.1257	0.1230	0.1490	0.1133	0.1175	0.1491	0.1502	0.1496	0.1573	**0.1610**
	NDCG@10	0.0696	0.0645	0.0599	0.1046	0.1489	0.1452	0.1739	0.1263	0.1384	0.1745	0.1773	0.1775	0.1831	**0.1886**
	Recall@20	0.0980	0.0956	0.0887	0.1343	0.1918	0.1816	0.2188	0.1823	0.1747	0.2196	0.2210	0.2236	0.2352	**0.2385**
	NDCG@20	0.0860	0.0800	0.0769	0.1229	0.1759	0.1681	0.2018	0.1557	0.1613	0.2021	0.2047	0.2070	0.2145	**0.2180**
	Recall@40	0.1450	0.1439	0.1550	0.1990	0.2794	0.2649	0.3156	0.2747	0.2533	0.3130	0.3184	0.3194	0.3300	**0.3366**
	NDCG@40	0.1067	0.1055	0.1031	0.1515	0.2146	0.2049	0.2444	0.1966	0.1960	0.2437	0.2458	0.2498	0.2567	**0.2622**

strates the highest performance, underscoring the effectiveness of the combined loss strategy.

3.4 Comparison with Existing Methods

We present the performance comparison between our proposed approach and several baseline methods on the Ifashion, Yelp, and LastFM datasets in Table 3. Our approach consistently surpasses the baselines across all datasets and metrics. For instance, on the Yelp dataset, our approach achieves the highest Recall@10 (0.0583) and NDCG@10 (0.0363), significantly surpassing the other models. Similar trends are observed in the Ifashion and LastFM datasets, where our model attains the best results in Recall and NDCG at various K values, with notable improvements in Recall@40 and NDCG@40. These results demonstrate the efficacy of our model, particularly the residual graph transformer and the automatic distillation strategies, which contribute to superior performance by efficient mining and leveraging collaborative rationales. Among these components, the topological graph position encoding and the multi-head self-attention mechanism are crucial, as they capture global context and enhance the understanding of user-item interactions

4 Conclusion

This paper highlights how discovering meaningful user-item interaction patterns can improve collaborative filtering techniques through self-supervised learning. For that, we propose in this work a recommendation system that uses a residual graph transformer to automatically find hidden signals and coherent patterns. Our method includes topological graph position encoding for a global context and uses automatic distillation strategies to boost performance. Experiments show that our model outperforms several literature approaches across multiple datasets. In future work, we plan to explore advanced data augmentation techniques and expand our model to handle larger datasets and more diverse recommendation scenarios.

Acknowledgement. This work was supported by Declic, a deep tech startup. Declic is a social network for outings, meetings, and events, fostering genuine connections and shared activities in the real world (https://declic.net/).

References

1. Wang, J., Louca, R., Hu, D., Cellier, C., Caverlee, J., Hong, L.: Time to shop for valentine's day: shopping occasions and sequential recommendation in e-commerce. In: Proceedings of the 13th International Conference on Web Search and Data Mining, pp. 645–653 (2020)
2. Zhang, F., et al.: Understanding wechat user preferences and "wow" diffusion. IEEE Trans. Knowl. Data Eng. **34**(12), 6033–6046 (2021)

3. He, X., Liao, L., Zhang, H., Nie, L., Hu, X., Chua, T.S.: Neural collaborative filtering. In: Proceedings of the 26th International Conference on World Wide Web. International World Wide Web Conferences Steering Committee, 173–182 (2017)
4. Cherifi, C., Cherifi, H., Karsai, M., Musolesi, M.: Complex networks and their applications vi. In: Proceedings of Complex Networks 2017 The Sixth International Conference on Complex Networks and Their Applications. Springer, Berlin(2017)
5. Mourchid, Y., Slama, R.: D-STGCNT: a dense spatio-temporal graph conv-GRU network based on transformer for assessment of patient physical rehabilitation. Comput. Biol. Med. **165**, 107420 (2023)
6. Ying, R., He, R., Chen, K., Eksombatchai, P., Hamilton, W.L., Leskovec, J.: Graph convolutional neural networks for web-scale recommender systems. In: Proceedings of the 24th ACM SIGKDD International Conference on Knowledge Discovery & Data Mining, pp. 974–983 (2018)
7. Wang, X., He, X., Wang, M., Feng, F., Chua, T.-S.: Neural graph collaborative filtering. In: Proceedings of the 42nd International ACM SIGIR Conference on Research and Development in Information Retrieval, pp. 165–174 (2019)
8. He, X., Deng, K., Wang, X., Li, Y., Zhang, Y., Wang, M.: LightGCN: simplifying and powering graph convolution network for recommendation. In: Proceedings of the 43rd International ACM SIGIR Conference on Research and Development in Information Retrieval, pp. 639–648 (2020)
9. Wu, J., et al.: Self-supervised graph learning for recommendation. In: Proceedings of the 44th International ACM SIGIR Conference on Research and Development in Information Retrieval, pp. 726–735 (2021)
10. Li, C., Xia, L., Ren, X., Ye, Y., Xu, Y., Huang, C.: Graph transformer for recommendation. In: Proceedings of the 46th International ACM SIGIR Conference on Research and Development in Information Retrieval, pp. 1680–1689 (2023)
11. Xia, L., Huang, C., Xu, Y., Zhao, J., Yin, D., Huang, J.: Hypergraph contrastive collaborative filtering. In: Proceedings of the 45th International ACM SIGIR Conference on Research and Development in Information Retrieval, pp. 70–79 (2022)
12. Lin, Z., Tian, C., Hou, Y., Zhao, W.X.: Improving graph collaborative filtering with neighborhood-enriched contrastive learning. In: Proceedings of the ACM Web Conference 2022, pp. 2320–2329 (2022)
13. Wang, S., Chen, X., Sheng, Q.Z., Zhang, Y., Yao, L.: Causal disentangled variational auto-encoder for preference understanding in recommendation. In: Proceedings of the 46th International ACM SIGIR Conference on Research and Development in Information Retrieval, pp. 1874–1878 (2023)
14. Xia, L., Huang, C., Huang, C., Lin, K., Tao, Yu., Kao, B.: Automated self-supervised learning for recommendation. In: Proceedings of the ACM Web Conference 2023, pp. 992–1002 (2023)
15. Wang, W., Xu, Y., Feng, F., Lin, X., He, X., Chua, T.-S.: Diffusion recommender model. In: Proceedings of the 46th International ACM SIGIR Conference on Research and Development in Information Retrieval, pp. 832–841 (2023)
16. You, J., Ying, R., Leskovec, J.: Position-aware graph neural networks. In: International Conference on Machine Learning, pp. 7134–7143. PMLR (2019)
17. Koren, Y., Bell, R., Volinsky, C.: Matrix factorization techniques for recommender systems. Computer **42**(8), 30–37 (2009)
18. Sedhain, S., Menon, A.K., Sanner, S., Xie, L.: Autorec: autoencoders meet collaborative filtering. In: Proceedings of the 24th International Conference on World Wide Web, pp. 111–112 (2015)

19. Chen, L., Wu, L., Hong, R.: Revisiting graph based collaborative filtering: a linear residual graph convolutional network approach. In: Proceedings of the AAAI Conference on Artificial Intelligence, pp. 27–34 (2020)
20. Yang, Y., Wu, L., Hong, R., Zhang, K., Wang, M.: Enhanced graph learning for collaborative filtering via mutual information maximization. In: Proceedings of the 44th international ACM SIGIR Conference on Research and Development in Information Retrieval, pp. 71–80 (2021)
21. Yao, T., et al.: Self-supervised learning for large-scale item recommendations. In: Proceedings of the 30th ACM International Conference on Information & Knowledge Management, pp. 4321–4330 (2021)

Query-Decision Regression for Misinformation Prevention in Social Networks

Siqi Wang, Jiahao Xie, Yifan Wang, and Guangmo Tong(✉)

University of Delaware, Newark De 19711, USA
{wsqbit,jiahaox,yifanw,amotong}@udel.edu

Abstract. Misinformation prevention is a crucial research topic in the social network community, which aims to identify, mitigate, and ultimately prevent the spread of false or misleading information across the social network. Traditional methods typically rely on detailed information on underlying networks and propagation mechanisms. However, these approaches can be impractical due to privacy concerns and restrictions on data accessibility. To overcome this challenge, we propose MetaLearner, a novel framework that leverages historical pairs containing queries and their high-quality decisions. This approach enables us to derive effective decisions for new queries without requiring complete network and diffusion information. We evaluate the performance of MetaLearner by comparing it with existing methods. The results show significant improvements in both accuracy and computational efficiency, demonstrating MetaLearner as a scalable and effective solution for misinformation prevention.

Keywords: Misinformation Prevention · Social Network · Data-driven Learning

1 Introduction

Social networks can connect people worldwide and enable rapid information exchange, but they also facilitate the spread of misinformation, which refers to false, inaccurate, or misleading information [4,16]. Preventing misinformation on social media is essential to avoid distorting perceptions, public opinion impact, and harmful consequences [1]. Additionally, disseminating accurate information is important for informed decision-making [11], public safety [2], and maintaining trust in institutions [14].

An effective strategy for preventing misinformation is to select influential users in social networks to disseminate accurate information before others encounter false content [3,13,23]. This approach selects key individuals to spread truthful information, thereby minimizing the number of users affected by misinformation. The spread of information within networks can be captured by various diffusion models [7,9,12], which indicate that the number of users

J. Kertesz et al. (Eds.): CSoNet 2024, LNCS 15417, pp. 48–60, 2025.
https://doi.org/10.1007/978-981-96-6389-7_5

unaffected by misinformation can be represented by a monotone-increasing submodular function [3]. Previous works leverage this property to design greedy algorithms for misinformation prevention in social networks [3,6,8]. However, these methods typically require comprehensive information of social networks and diffusion models, which is usually inaccessible in real-world scenarios due to privacy concerns [17]. This constraint leads to an unknown objective function for misinformation prevention, limiting the practical application of such methods.

Recently, Tong proposed StratLearner [18], an effective method for estimating the objective function using randomly sampled subgraphs and historical query-decision pairs, without requiring complete diffusion model information. In each query-decision pair, the query represents users initially affected by misinformation and the decision refers to users selected to minimize misinformation spread. However, StratLearner has two main limitations: 1) Its performance depends on the number of sampled subgraphs, with more subgraphs improving accuracy but increasing training time and memory cost; 2) It shows limited performance gains even with larger training datasets, similar to the findings in Model Soup [22], often converging to the same sub-optimal region with identical hyperparameters.

To address above limitations, we propose MetaLearner, a two-step framework for misinformation prevention in social networks with restricted access to the underlying diffusion model. In the first step, we refine the sampling method by leveraging historical query-decision pairs. Multiple models are trained on distinct subsets of training data and randomly sampled subgraphs, producing estimations of the objective function. Since we cannot directly select the most accurate model due to limited access to the true objective function, we draw inspiration from Multi-head Attention [21] and Model Soup [22], considering each estimation as a representation of the social network graph. Ideally, we would train numerous models, with each providing a representation to replace a randomly sampled subgraph, thereby enhancing the accuracy of objective function estimation in the second step. However, this approach is computationally infeasible. To address this, in the second step, we introduce an importance sampling method that reduces the number of required models while still generating high-quality subgraphs for objective function estimation. Once the objective function is estimated, traditional misinformation prevention algorithms can be employed to optimize it to generate solutions for new queries.

Overall, our contributions are summarized: 1) We propose MetaLearner, a novel framework inspired by model ensemble techniques, enhancing the accuracy of objective function estimation by a two-step learning process; 2) We introduce an importance sampling strategy to reduce the number of required models to $\frac{1}{10}$, $\frac{1}{40}$, $\frac{1}{80}$, and $\frac{1}{160}$ of the original amount. This reduction significantly decreases computational cost and memory usage, making the approach practical for applications with limited data access; 3) We conduct extensive experiments, showing that MetaLearner consistently outperforms the state-of-the-art methods in accuracy and computational efficiency across various social network structures, demonstrating its robustness and scalability for large-scale applications.

The rest of the paper is organized as follows. Section 2 introduces the problem, Sect. 3 describes the proposed method, Sect. 4 presents the experimental results, and Sect. 5 concludes the paper.

2 Problem Setting

A social network can be modeled as a directed graph $G = (V, E, T)$, where V represents the user set and E represents the connections between users. Specifically, a directed edge $(u, v) \in E$ with $u, v \in V$, indicates that the user u can spread information to user v. T is a function that maps each edge (u, v) to a real value $T(u, v) \in (0, +\infty)$ which represents the time cost for spreading information from u to v. In addition, for each node $v \in V$, its out-neighbor set and in-neighbor set are denoted as $N_{out}(v) \subseteq V$ and $N_{in}(v) \subseteq V$, respectively.

The considered diffusion model follows the mechanism in triggering model [12]. Given a social graph G, two types of cascades are disseminated simultaneously: the misinformation cascade $\mathcal{M}$ and the positive information cascade $\mathcal{P}$. Each node in the graph can be in one of three activation states: $\mathcal{M}$-active state, $\mathcal{P}$-active state, and inactive state. Initially, a set of nodes $M \subseteq V$ is $\mathcal{M}$-active, while another set of nodes $P \subseteq V$ is selected to be $\mathcal{P}$-active. The remaining nodes are inactive. The diffusion process can be defined as follows.

- **Timestep** 0: Nodes in the $\mathcal{M}$-active and $\mathcal{P}$-active states begin attempting to activate their neighbors.
- **Timestep** t: When a node u becomes $\mathcal{M}$-active at time t, it attempts to activate all its inactive out-neighbors $N_{out}(u)$. Each neighbor $v \in N_{out}(u)$ will become $\mathcal{M}$-active at time $t + T(u, v)$. Similarly, if a node u becomes $\mathcal{P}$-active at time t, it attempts to activate all its inactive out-neighbors to become $\mathcal{P}$-active, following the same process. A node can only be activated by the first attempt from any in-neighbors and will not switch states afterward. If a node is activated by multiple in-neighbors in different states simultaneously, it will become $\mathcal{M}$-active.
- **Termination**: The diffusion process terminates when no more nodes can be activated.

Given a social network $G = (V, E, T)$, a diffusion model described above, a node set $M \subseteq V$, and a budget $r \in \mathbb{Z}^+$, the objective of misinformation prevention problem is to select a set of nodes $P \subseteq V$ with $|P| \leq r$ and $P \cap M = \emptyset$ such that the number of nodes that are not $\mathcal{M}$-active after the diffusion process can be maximized. Let $F(M, P, G)$ represent the number of nodes that are not $\mathcal{M}$-active after the diffusion process. The objective function $f(M, P, G)$ is defined as follows.

$$f(M, P, G) = F(M, P, G) - F(M, \emptyset, G)$$

where $F(M, \emptyset, G)$ represents the number of nodes that are not $\mathcal{M}$-active when no positive nodes are initially selected. Formally, the misinformation prevention problem aims to find a node set P such that the objective function is maximized.

$$\underset{P \subseteq V, P \cap M = \emptyset, |P| \leq r}{\arg\max} \quad f(M, P, G). \tag{1}$$

Algorithm 1. MetaLearner

1: Input: $N, n, K \in \mathbb{Z}^+, \phi, D$;
2: Update the sampling method ϕ to a set of sampling methods ϕ' with Algorithm 2;
3: Estimate the objective function through Algorithm 3;
4: Return an estimation of the objective function $f^*(M, P, G)$;

In this paper, the collected data is represented as $D = \{M_i, P_i\}_{i=1}^m$ where each P_i is an approximate decision for $M_i \in \mathcal{X}$ with its corresponding objective function using some traditional misinformation prevention methods, where $\mathcal{X}$ denotes the query space. Our goal is to learn a framework $\mathcal{A}$ for the misinformation prevention problem based on the historical query-decision data such that it can obtain a good decision $\hat{P} = \mathcal{A}(M)$ for a new given query $M \in \mathcal{X}$. We use l to measure the performance of $\mathcal{A}$.

$$l(M, \mathcal{A}(M)) = 1 - \frac{f(M, \hat{P}, G)}{f(M, P', G)},$$

where P' is an approximate decision for the new query M, obtained using the same method applied to compute the decisions in the collected data. We prefer lower values of l, as they indicate higher quality in the predicted decision $\hat{P}$. Formally, given the training data D, we aim to develop a framework $\mathcal{A}$ such that the following loss function is minimized.

$$\mathcal{L}(\mathcal{A}) = \mathbb{E}_{M \in \mathcal{X}}[l(M, \mathcal{A}(M))].$$

3 Method

In this section, we introduce our proposed framework MetaLearner. The main challenge stems from the unknown objective function $f(M, P, G)$ due to the lack of information about the underlying diffusion models. To overcome this challenge, we follow the idea in [18] that the objective function can be approximated by using the subgraphs randomly drawn from some fixed distribution. We assume that the objective function lies in the following space parameterized by some learnable $w \in \mathbb{R}$.

$$\left\{ \sum_{i=1}^{K} w_i \cdot f(M, P, g_i) \,\middle|\, w_i \in \mathbb{R}, g_i \in S, k \in \mathbb{Z}^+ \right\}, \tag{2}$$

where S indicates a set of subgraphs with size K that are sampled from the true graph structure $G = (V, E)$. Specifically, $S = \{g_1, \cdots, g_K\}$ and $g_i = (V_i, E_i, T_i)$ where $V_i \subseteq V$, $E_i \subseteq E$, and T_i is a function that assigns each edge in g a non-negative weight. Therefore, our approach focuses on accurately estimating $f(M, P, G)$ via searching from the above space by using the historical query-decision data. We can then apply traditional optimization algorithms to infer a

Algorithm 2. Sampling modification

Input: $N, n, K \in \mathbb{Z}^+, \phi, D$;
for $j = 1, 2, \cdots, N$ **do**:
  Sample K subgraphs with the sampling method ϕ to construct $S^j = \{g_1^j, \cdots, g_K^j\}, g_i^j = G(V_i^j, E_i^j, T_i^j)$;
  Sample n training pairs from the dataset D to construct D^j;
  Calculate $\mathbf{w}^j = \{w_1^j, \cdots, w_K^j\}$ for D^j, S^j by applying cutting plane algorithm [10] to solve Equation 3;
  Construct an edge set $E^j = \bigcup_{i=1}^K E_i^j$, where E_i^j is the edge set of subgraph g_i^j;
  for $e \in E_i^j$ **do**:
    Calculate the weighted weight $T^j(e) = \sum_{i=1}^K w_i^j \cdot T_i^j(e)$, $T_i^j(e) = 0$ if $e \notin g_i^j$;
    Sample a from a uniform distribution $[A, B]$, with positive integers A, B;
    Calculate b by solving $\mathbb{E}[\text{Weibull}(a, b)] = T^j(e)$;
    $\phi^j(e) = \text{Weibull}(a, b)$;
  end for
  $\phi^j = \{\phi^j(e)\}, e \in E^j$;
end for
Return a set of sampling method $\phi' = \{\phi^1, \cdots, \phi^N\}$;

decision P when given a new query M by solving Eq. 1. In general, the overall framework is composed of two main steps: in the sampling modification step, we train $N \in \mathbb{Z}^+$ different models using $n \in \mathbb{Z}^+$ training pairs to learn an effective sampling method that approximates the true graph structure. In objective function estimation step, we estimate the objective function using the learned sampling method, yielding the final approximation $f^*(M, P, G)$. The overall algorithm is summarized in Algorithm 1.

Sampling Modification. We summarize this step in Algorithm 2. Following the idea of the multi-head attention mechanism, this approach estimates the social network graph by analyzing different groups of weighted subgraphs across various subsets of training data, resulting in a diverse set of sampling methods. Specifically, we use ϕ to denote the initial sampling method, which is a function that samples a weighted subgraph $g = (V', E', T')$ from a graph structure $G = (V, E)$, where $V' \subseteq V, E' \subseteq E$, and T' is a function that assigns a non-negative weight to each edge in g. Given an initial sampling method ϕ and the training dataset D, MetaLearner samples $N \in \mathbb{Z}^+$ groups of different weighted subgraphs $\{S^1, \cdots, S^N\}$ using ϕ and N subsets of training datasets $\{D^1, \cdots, D^N\}$ from D. The size of each subgraph group is denoted by $K \in \mathbb{Z}^+$, and the size of each training data subset by $n \in \mathbb{Z}^+$. Using each dataset D^j and subgraph group S^j, we obtain estimated objective functions from the search space following the margin-based maximization strategy by training N Structured Support Vector

Machines (SSVM) [20] as follows.

$$
\begin{aligned}
&\min \frac{1}{2}\|\mathbf{w}^j\|_2^2 + \frac{C}{2n}\sum_{i=1}^{n}\xi_i \\
&\text{s.t.} \sum_{k=1}^{K} w_k^j \cdot f(M_i, P_i, g_k) - \sum_{k=1}^{K} w_k^j \cdot f(M_i, P^*, g_k) \geq \alpha \cdot H(P_i, P^*) - \xi_i, \\
&\forall i \in [n], j \in [N], \forall (M_i, P_i) \in D^j, \forall P^* : |P^*| < r, P^* \neq P_i,
\end{aligned} \tag{3}
$$

where $C, \alpha \in \mathbb{R}^+$ are hyperparameters. The function $H(P_i, P^*)$ measures the similarity between two decisions. Specifically, $H(P_i, P^*) = h(P_i, P_i) - h(P_i, P^*)$, where $h(P_i, P^*) = |N_{P_i} \cap N_{P^*}|$ with N_P denoting the set of nodes directly connected to any of the nodes in P, including P itself.

After training the N SSVMs, MetaLearner obtain a group of weight vectors $\{\mathbf{w}^1, \cdots, \mathbf{w}^N\}$ with size N, where $\mathbf{w}^j = \{w_1^j, \cdots, w_K^j\}$ and $j \in [N]$. Each SSVM searches for an objective function that is most suitable for the given dataset D^j from the search space in Eq. 2. After obtaining the weights $\mathbf{w}^j$, MetaLearner estimates the objective function as follows.

$$
f^*(M, P, G) = \sum_{i=1}^{K} w_i^j \cdot f(M, P, g_i^j), w_i^j \in \mathbf{w}^j, g_i^j \in S^j.
$$

MetaLearner then updates the sampling method based on each trained SSVM. For each group of subgraphs S^j, a corresponding edge set $E^j = \bigcup_{i=1}^{K} E_i^j$ is generated, where E_i^j is the edge set of subgraph g_i^j. The diffusion time $T^j(e)$ for each edge $e \in E^j$ is then calculated as follows.

$$
T^j(e) = \sum_{i=1}^{K} w_i^j \cdot T_i^j(e),
$$

where $T_i^j(e)$ represents the diffusion time of edge e in subgraph g_i^j. If edge e is absent from subgraph g_i^j, then $T_i^j(e) = 0$. Given these $T^j(e)$, MetaLearner updates the sampling methods. The distribution of the weight on each edge is modeled as a Weibull distribution, denoted by $\phi^j(e) = \text{Weibull}(a, b)$, where $a, b \in \mathbb{R}$ are the distribution parameters. By setting the expectation equal to $T^j(e)$, a new sampling method $\phi^j = \{\phi^j(e)\}, e \in E^j$, is obtained.

Objective Function Estimation. Given the N learned sampling methods $\{\phi^1, \ldots, \phi^N\}$ and the dataset D, MetaLearner proceeds to estimate the final objective function. We outline the objective function estimation process in Algorithm 3. The key challenge is effectively combining the outputs of the multiple SSVMs. Given that each SSVM provides an estimated objective function along with a corresponding social network graph, we explore two strategies for integration. One approach is to uniformly average the learned social network graphs, similar to the uniform soup. The other approach involves training a final SSVM

Algorithm 3. Function estimation

1: Input: $n, K \in \mathbb{Z}^+$, $\{\phi^1, \cdots, \phi^N\}$, D;
2: Sample $\frac{K}{N}$ subgraphs from each new sampling method and combine them as a new group of subgraphs S';
3: Sample n training data from D as training dataset D';
4: Calculate $\mathbf{w}' = \{w_1', \cdots, w_K'\}$ for D', S' by applying cutting plane algorithm [10] to solve problem 3;
5: Return the final estimation of objective function as $f^*(M, P, G) = \sum_{i=1}^{K} w_i' \cdot f(M, P, g_i'), w_i' \in \mathbf{w}', g_i' \in S'$;

based on the learned social network graphs from the previous SSVMs. Specifically, we can train $N = K$ different SSVMs, and the resulting K subgraphs are used to train the final SSVM, which can estimate the final objective function. However, as the value of K increases, the computational resources and time required also grow, making it infeasible to train a large number of SSVMs.

To address the challenge of scaling, we employ importance sampling, which allows us to balance effectiveness and efficiency by estimating a sampling method from the learned social network graphs and sampling subgraphs accordingly. MetaLearner samples $\frac{K}{N}$ subgraphs from each sampling method ϕ^j to obtain a group of subgraphs S'. Then, another SSVM is trained on a new dataset D', sampled from D, to optimize the final weight vector $\mathbf{w}'$. Altogether, the final objective function is calculated by the following equation.

$$f^*(M, P, G) = \sum_{i=1}^{K} w_i' \cdot f(M, P, g_i'), w_i' \in \mathbf{w}', g_i' \in S'.$$

4 Experiment

In this section, we present empirical studies on our proposed method for the misinformation prevention task across various graph datasets.

4.1 Experiment Setting

Graph Data. Our approach is evaluated on three graph datasets which are generated from classic graph models, i.e., Erdős-Rényi graph (ER) [5], power-law graph (Pow) and Kronecker graph (Kro) [15]. For each generated graph $G(V, E, T)$, we assume that each edge weight follows a Weibull distribution Weibull(a, b) with parameters a and b sampled from the set $\{1, \cdots, 10\}$ independently, and the weight set to the expected value of this distribution.

Sample Generation. The size of the set M is determined by random sampling from a power-law distribution with a parameter of 2.5. Subsequently, we randomly select $|M|$ nodes from the set V to form M. For each query M, we employ the HMP algorithm [19] to compute the approximated decision P on the graph $G(V, E, T)$, with the budget $r = |M|$. A sample pool with a total of 2,500 such pairs (M, P) is generated for each graph dataset.

Baseline Method. We select the state-of-the-art method, StratLearner, as the baseline for our comparisons. We also compare our method with a random algorithm that randomly selects the decision P.

Training Settings. In the experiment evaluating StratLearner, we use $n' = \{270, 540, 1080, 2160\}$ samples for training and 270 samples for testing, reporting the ratio $\frac{f(M,\hat{P},G)}{f(M,P,G)}$, where $\hat{P}$ is the decision made by StratLearner. Each $f(M, P, G)$ is calculated through 10,000 simulations. The number of weighted graphs K' is set to $\{100, 400, 800, 1600\}$. In the experiment of MetaLearner, we set $N = 10$ and use $n = \{27, 54, 108, 216\}$ samples for training each model and 270 samples for testing, also reporting the ratio $\frac{f(M,\hat{P},G)}{f(M,P,G)}$. The number of weighted graphs K is set to $\{10, 40, 80, 160\}$. This ensures that the total number of training samples and weighted graphs remain consistent across experiments, such that $N \times n = n'$, $N \times K = K'$. For each (n, K) pair, we repeat the experiment five times and report the mean ratio and corresponding variance. The hyperparameter α in Eq. 3 is set to 1,000, and C is set to 0.01. In the StratLearner, each subgraph is generated by selecting each edge independently at random with a probability of 0.01 and assigning a fixed weight of 1.0 to each selected edge. We denote such distribution as $\phi_{1.0}^{0.01}$. In the MetaLearner approach, subgraphs are also generated with a 0.01 probability for selecting each edge, but the edge weights are sampled from a different Weibull(c, d) distribution, with c and d independently sampled from $\{1, \cdots, 10\}$ for each edge during each sampling process. We denote such distribution as $\phi_{WR}^{0.01}$.

4.2 Analysis

Table 1. Results for the Misinformation Prevention on Kro Graph. Each cell shows the average ratio compared with the sample decision, together with the standard deviation (std). The total number of sampled graphs K' are 100, 400, 800 and 1600 respectively.

	Training Size n'	Number of sampled grpah 100	400	800	1600
Strat-Learner	270	0.699 (8E−3)	0.759 (7E−3)	0.785 (1E−2)	0.810 (9E−3)
	540	0.707 (5E−3)	0.743 (8E−3)	0.780 (9E−3)	0.813 (7E−3)
	1080	0.708 (2E−2)	0.760 (1E−2)	0.782 (8E−3)	0.817 (5E−3)
	2160	0.701 (1E−2)	0.756 (1E−2)	0.792 (5E−3)	0.821 (8E−3)
Meta-Learner	270	0.698 (5E−3)	0.777 (8E−3)	0.807 (1E−2)	0.819 (9E−2)
	540	0.694 (1E−2)	0.772 (8E−3)	0.805 (5E−3)	0.827 (8E−2)
	1080	0.704 (8E−3)	0.773 (6E−3)	0.807 (9E−3)	0.831 (8E−2)
	2160	0.710 (1E−2)	0.773 (1E−2)	0.811 (9E−3)	0.834 (9E−2)
Other Method		**Random**	0.190 (5E−3)		

Table 2. Results for the Misinformation Prevention on ER Graph. Each cell shows the average ratio compared with the sample decision, together with the standard deviation (std). The total number of sampled graphs K' are 100, 400, 800 and 1600 respectively.

	Training	Number of sampled grpah			
	Size n'	100	400	800	1600
Strat-Learner	270	0.661 (2E−2)	0.853 (6E−3)	0.873 (1E−2)	0.892 (3E−3)
	540	0.673 (2E−2)	0.861 (1E−2)	0.876 (6E−3)	0.897 (1E−2)
	1080	0.688 (3E−2)	0.844 (9E−3)	0.870 (1E−2)	0.899 (8E−3)
	2160	0.674 (2E−2)	0.857 (2E−2)	0.873 (5E−3)	0.903 (3E−3)
Meta-Learner	270	0.678 (2E−2)	0.853 (2E−2)	0.913 (7E−4)	0.941 (3E−3)
	540	0.645 (2E−2)	0.862 (6E−3)	0.917 (1E−3)	0.938 (5E−3)
	1080	0.669 (3E−2)	0.858 (2E−2)	0.913 (1E−2)	0.936 (3E−3)
	2160	0.660 (3E−2)	0.868 (1E−2)	0.910 (6E−3)	0.937 (4E−3)
Other Method		**Random**	0.052 (2E−2)		

The main results of the StratLearner and the MetaLearner are shown in Table 1. We observe that when the number of sampled graphs is small, the MetaLearner achieves a similar performance compared to StratLearner. As the number of sampled graphs increases, MetaLearner consistently outperforms StratLearner across all three graph datasets. The magnitude of the performance gap between StratLearner and MetaLearner varies across different social network graphs, with additional results provided in Table 2. We believe this is because the function estimation step requires a sufficient number of subgraphs to gain adequate prior knowledge about the social network.

Table 3. Results for Memory and Time Costs on ER Graph. The memory cost is measured in MB, and the time cost is measured in seconds. The total number of sampled graphs K' are 100, 400, 800 and 1600 respectively.

	Training	Memory Cost (MB)				Time Cost (S)			
	Size n'	100	400	800	1600	100	400	800	1600
Strat-Learner	270	51.1	195.5	387.2	772.0	111.0	435.31	987.3	2070.4
	540	53.1	197.9	390.1	776.4	665.2	197.9	1378.1	2677.3
	1080	56.8	202.7	396.4	784.9	294.4	1154.5	2331.5	3848.5
	2160	64.4	212.2	408.5	802.2	518.5	2177.4	4356.2	6819.1
Meta-Learner	270	8.9	26.5	52.8	144.9	94.1	364.9	691.6	1493.9
	540	9.0	26.6	52.9	145.4	154.4	479.1	954.1	2069.4
	1080	9.4	27.1	53.2	145.4	222.8	609.6	1437.6	3260.7
	2160	10.1	27.7	54.2	146.0	358.5	1153.1	2301.4	4764.6

We also report the time and memory cost of the StratLearner and MetaLearner in Table 3. It is not surprising that the memory cost of MetaLearner is less than that of StratLearner since MetaLearner trains models with less training data and fewer sampled subgraphs. However, we are pleased to find that the time cost of MetaLearner is also less than that of StratLearner, even though MetaLearner trains multiple small models while StratLearner trains a single model. These results demonstrate that MetaLearner is more efficient than StratLearner. Additionally, we observe that the number of sampled graphs has a greater impact on time cost than the amount of training data. Increasing the number of sampled graphs significantly improves performance but also increases time cost. Therefore, a trade-off between effectiveness and efficiency must be considered.

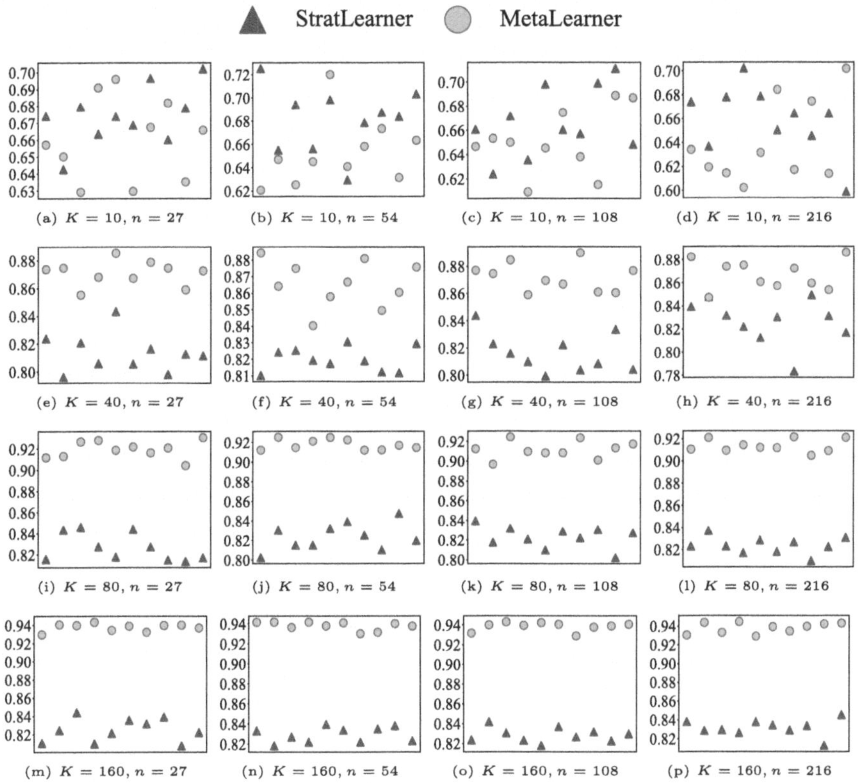

Fig. 1. The results on the ER graph without training. Each subgraph is labeled by the value of K and n and displays the results of 10 repeated experiments without training for StratLearner and MetaLearner. The result indicates the ratio $\frac{f(M,\hat{P},G)}{f(M,P,G)}$.

To evaluate the effectiveness of function estimation step, we conduct experiments to test the performance of StratLearner and MetaLearner without training using the sampling method $\phi_{WR}^{0.01}$ on the ER graph. The results are displayed in

Fig. 1. It is clear that when the number of sampled graphs is insufficient, the sampling method refined by MetaLearner does not necessarily perform better than the initial sampling method $\phi_{WR}^{0.01}$. However, with an increased number of sampled graphs, the quality of the sampling method refined by MetaLearner is improved significantly over the initial sampling method. Moreover, as the number of sampled graphs increases, the performance gap between MetaLearner and the initial method becomes larger. Another interesting observation is that increasing the number of sampled graphs from 100 to 400 significantly improves StratLearner's performance without training. However, further increasing the number of sampled graphs beyond this point results in less noticeable performance gains. This suggests that both StratLearner and MetaLearner require a sufficient number of samples to reach optimal performance levels.

It is worth noting that although we train the models sequentially in the function estimation step of MetaLearner, these models can be trained concurrently. This parallel training approach would significantly reduce the training time but would also increase memory cost. Thus, MetaLearner provides an option to balance between memory cost and time efficiency.

5 Conclusion

In this paper, we introduce MetaLearner, a novel two-step framework designed to enhance the accuracy and efficiency of misinformation prevention in social networks. MetaLearner addresses the challenge of limited access to the complete diffusion model by leveraging historical query-decision pairs and employing refined sampling methods. Our approach combines the strengths of the StratLearner framework with the robustness of ensemble methods, specifically incorporating the concepts of Model Soup and importance sampling. Extensive experiments on various graph structures demonstrate that MetaLearner consistently outperforms the state-of-the-art methods in terms of accuracy. Furthermore, MetaLearner exhibits significant improvements in computational efficiency, reducing both memory usage and training time compared to those of the state-of-the-art methods. This makes MetaLearner a more practical solution for large-scale social network applications. Overall, MetaLearner represents a significant advancement in misinformation prevention techniques for social networks, providing a scalable and efficient solution that can adapt to various network structures and constraints.

Acknowledgments. This project is supported in part by the National Science Foundation under IIS-2414308 and Career IIS-214428.

References

1. Aïmeur, E., Amri, S., Brassard, G.: Fake news, disinformation and misinformation in social media: a review. Soc. Netw. Anal. Min. **13**(1), 30 (2023)

2. Amoruso, M., Anello, D., Auletta, V., Cerulli, R., Ferraioli, D., Raiconi, A.: Contrasting the spread of misinformation in online social networks. J. Artif. Intell. Res. **69**, 847–879 (2020)
3. Budak, C., Agrawal, D., El Abbadi, A.: Limiting the spread of misinformation in social networks. In: Proceedings of the 20th International Conference on World Wide Web, pp. 665–674 (2011)
4. Del Vicario, M., et al.: The spreading of misinformation online. Proc. Natl. Acad. Sci. **113**(3), 554–559 (2016)
5. Erdos, P., Renyi, A.: On random graphs I. Publ. Math. Debrecen **6**, 290–297 (1959)
6. Fan, L., Lu, Z., Wu, W., Thuraisingham, B., Ma, H., Bi, Y.: Least cost rumor blocking in social networks. In: 2013 IEEE 33rd International Conference on Distributed Computing Systems, pp. 540–549. IEEE (2013)
7. Gruhl, D., Guha, R., Liben-Nowell, D., Tomkins, A.: Information diffusion through blogspace. In: Proceedings of the 13th International Conference on World Wide Web, pp. 491–501 (2004)
8. He, X., Song, G., Chen, W., Jiang, Q.: Influence blocking maximization in social networks under the competitive linear threshold model. In: Proceedings of the 2012 SIAM International Conference on Data Mining, pp. 463–474. SIAM (2012)
9. Jiang, Y., Jiang, J.: Diffusion in social networks: a multiagent perspective. IEEE Trans. Syst. Man Cybern. Syst. **45**(2), 198–213 (2014)
10. Joachims, T., Finley, T., Yu, C.: Cutting-plane training of structural SVMs. Mach. Learn. **77**, 27–59 (2009)
11. Karduni, A., et al.: Can you verifi this? Studying uncertainty and decision-making about misinformation using visual analytics. In: Proceedings of AAAI, vol. 12 (2018)
12. Kempe, D., Kleinberg, J., Tardos, É.: Maximizing the spread of influence through a social network. In: Proceedings of the ninth ACM SIGKDD International Conference on Knowledge Discovery and Data Mining, pp. 137–146 (2003)
13. Kumar, K., Geethakumari, G.: Detecting misinformation in online social networks using cognitive psychology. HCIS **4**(1), 1–22 (2014). https://doi.org/10.1186/s13673-014-0014-x
14. Lee, S.J., Lee, C.J., Hwang, H.: The impact of COVID-19 misinformation and trust in institutions on preventive behaviors. Health Educ. Res. **38**(1), 95–105 (2023)
15. Leskovec, J., Chakrabarti, D., Kleinberg, J., Faloutsos, C., Ghahramani, Z.: Kronecker graphs: an approach to modeling networks. J. Mach. Learn. Res. **11**(2) (2010)
16. Lewandowsky, S., Ecker, U.K., Cook, J.: Beyond misinformation: understanding and coping with the "post-truth" era. J. Appl. Res. Mem. Cogn. **6**(4), 353–369 (2017)
17. Pham, V., Yu, S., Sood, K., Cui, L.: Privacy issues in social networks and analysis: a comprehensive survey. IET Networks **7**(2), 74–84 (2018)
18. Tong, G.: Stratlearner: learning a strategy for misinformation prevention in social networks. Adv. Neural. Inf. Process. Syst. **33**, 15546–15555 (2020)
19. Tong, G.A., Du, D.Z.: Beyond uniform reverse sampling: a hybrid sampling technique for misinformation prevention. In: IEEE INFOCOM 2019-IEEE Conference on Computer Communications, pp. 1711–1719. IEEE (2019)
20. Tsochantaridis, I., Joachims, T., Hofmann, T., Altun, Y., Singer, Y.: Large margin methods for structured and interdependent output variables. J. Mach. Learn. Res. **6**(9) (2005)
21. Vaswani, A., : Attention is all you need. In: Advances in Neural Information Processing Systems, vol. 30 (2017)

22. Wortsman, M., et al.: Model soups: averaging weights of multiple fine-tuned models improves accuracy without increasing inference time. In: International Conference on Machine Learning, pp. 23965–23998. PMLR (2022)
23. Zubiaga, A., Aker, A., Bontcheva, K., Liakata, M., Procter, R.: Detection and resolution of Rumours in social media: a survey. ACM Comput. Surv. (CSUR) **51**(2), 1–36 (2018)

Energy Distance-Based EBM for Skin Lesion Classification: A Novel Approach

Quyen Van Vo[1,2] and Hiep Xuan Huynh[1(✉)]

[1] Can Tho University, Can Tho, Vietnam
hxhiep@ctu.edu.vn
[2] Can Tho University of Medicine and Pharmacy, Can Tho, Vietnam

Abstract. Skin lesion classification is a significant challenge in the medical field, particularly in the early detection of malignant skin lesions. Traditional methods require large amounts of data and often struggle to handle heterogeneous datasets, especially in medical datasets where there is an uneven distribution of disease types. A novel approach has been proposed that integrates Energy-Based Models (EBM) with an Energy Distance (ED) approach. This method aims to incorporate ED into the training process of the EBM model. The experimental results on the ISIC_2019 dataset achieved classification accuracy of 74.19%, a sensitivity of 60.29%, and a specificity of 95.46%. This shows that the proposed model is capable of classifying skin lesions with expected results, particularly showing better handling of imbalanced datasets. With the achieved results, along with the desire to contribute a new approach to skin lesion classification in particular and medical image classification in general, this method also provides an effective diagnostic support tool.

Keyword: Energy-Based Models (EBM) · Energy Distance (ED) · Skin Lesion Classification · ISIC Dataset

1 Introduction

Skin lesions are among the most common dermatological conditions, particularly skin cancer, which has a high mortality rate if not detected early and treated promptly. According to the World Health Organization (WHO), approximately 132,000 new cases of melanoma are diagnosed globally each year [8]. Early detection and accurate diagnosis of skin lesions play a crucial role in improving patient survival rates. However, diagnosis based on traditional methods, such as visual observation by dermatologists, relies heavily on experience and can lead to errors.

In recent years, disease classification methods through medical image processing, particularly dermatological images, have garnered significant attention from the scientific community, aiming to support diagnosis and classification of diseases in general, and skin lesion classification in particular. The development of Artificial Intelligence (AI) [16], especially machine learning, has opened new opportunities for building diagnostic support systems and skin lesion classification. Deep learning models, such as

J. Kertesz et al. (Eds.): CSoNet 2024, LNCS 15417, pp. 61–72, 2025.
https://doi.org/10.1007/978-981-96-6389-7_6

Convolutional Neural Networks (CNNs) [17], have achieved high performance in the medical field, especially in various tasks related to automatic diagnosis and disease classification [7, 9, 10, 12–14]. However, these models require sufficiently large datasets and often face difficulties in handling medical datasets with uneven distribution among disease types. Moreover, the issue of class imbalance (CI) [6] is a common challenge in medical datasets [6] specifically, and large datasets in general. Rare lesions, such as melanoma, typically have fewer samples compared to benign lesions, leading to biased models and inaccurate results.

We propose a new approach for skin lesion classification using Energy-Based Models (EBM) [1] with an Energy Distance approach. This model focuses on leveraging the characteristics of ED while utilizing the Energy Distance Loss (L_{ED}) function. The aim is to optimize the model by minimizing the energy distance between samples of the same class and increasing the distance between samples of different classes.

We hope that the proposed method will improve accuracy in skin lesion classification, particularly in detecting types of skin cancer. Moreover, it aims to provide an efficient solution that relies less on large datasets, enhancing the feasibility of implementation in clinical practice.

The paper is structured as follows: Sect. 1 provides an overview of the research, explores the context, and evaluates the current state, leading to the proposed study. Section 2 presents the theoretical foundation of skin lesion classification using EBM. Section 3 introduces the functionality and algorithm of the proposal. Section 4 describes the experiments on skin lesion classification with EBM. Finally, summarizes the study's findings, discusses the contributions to the field of skin lesion classification, and suggests potential future directions to further improve the proposed.

2 Skin Lesion Image Representation

2.1 Skin Lesion Image

Skin lesion images, from a mathematical and machine learning perspective, can be represented in a way that allows computer models to process and analyze them. Skin lesion images can be expressed as a matrix of weights or as feature vectors, with each element in the matrix or vector representing a specific attribute of the image.

Representation of Skin Lesion Images as a Pixel Matrix
The skin lesion image is represented as a three-dimensional matrix A.

$A \in R^{h \times w \times c}$, with h is the image height; w is the width of the image and c is the number of color channels (RGB has 3 channels, c = 3) (Fig. 1).

$$\rightarrow A = \begin{pmatrix} a_{h1} & a_{12} & \dots & a_{1w} \\ a_{h1} & a_{22} & \dots & a_{2w} \\ \vdots & \vdots & \ddots & \vdots \\ a_{h1} & a_{h2} & \cdots & a_{hw} \end{pmatrix}$$

Fig. 1. Skin lesion image [5] → Weight matrix A with a_{ij} being the pixel value at coordinates (*i*, *j*)

Skin images are represented as a matrix of weights, where each value represents the brightness intensity of a pixel at the corresponding position. Suppose there is a skin image with dimensions m x n, where m is the number of rows (horizontal) and n is the number of columns (vertical):

- A grayscale image can be represented as a brightness intensity matrix with values ranging from 0 to 255 (with 0 being completely black and 255 being completely white).

$$A(x, y) \in R^{m \times n} \tag{2}$$

With $A(x, y)$ is the light intensity value at pixel position (x, y).

- A color image can be represented by three matrices, each corresponding to one of the three color channels: R (Red), G (Green), and B (Blue). Each matrix contains the brightness intensity values for its respective color channel at each pixel.

$$A_{RGB}(x, y) = (R(x, y)\, G(x, y)\, B(x, y)) \tag{3}$$

Where R (x, y), G (x, y), B (x, y) ∈ R represent the intensity values of the red, green, and blue colors at the pixel position (x, y), with values ranging from 0 to 255.

Representation of Skin Lesion Images Using Feature Vectors

To represent a skin image as a general feature vector, it is necessary to extract important features from the image and represent them by a mathematical vector. Suppose there is a skin image A, the features of the image can be represented by a vector F, where each element of the vector represents a specific feature of the image.

$$F = \begin{bmatrix} f_1 \\ f_2 \\ \vdots \\ f_k \end{bmatrix} \tag{4}$$

F is a feature vector with k elements, each element fi represents a feature extracted from the skin image.

2.2 Loss Function According to ED (Energy Distance Loss - L_{ED})

Energy Distance (ED) [4, 15] is a distance measure based on the gap between probability distributions, and it is used to compare two probability distributions or to assess the differences between groups of samples. ED is a useful tool in statistics and machine learning, especially in the EBM model.

Suppose we have two distributions P and Q with feature vectors sampled from two different probability distributions, the ED between these two distributions can be calculated using the following formula:

$$D_E(P, Q) = 2 \cdot Ex_p \sim P, x_q \sim Q[d(x_p, x_q)] - Ex_p, x'_p \sim P\left[d\left(x_p, x'_p\right)\right] - Ex_q, x'_q \sim Q\left[d\left(x_q, x'_q\right)\right] \tag{5}$$

Where: D_E *(P, Q)* is the energy distance between two distributions *P* and *Q*; *E* denotes the mathematical expectation; *d* (x_p, x_q) is a distance function between two data points x_p and x_q. The Euclidean distance (L2 norm) is a common choice:

$$d\left(x_p, x_q\right) = \|x_p - x_q\|_2 = \sqrt{\sum_{i=1}^{d}\left(x_p^{(i)} - x_q^{(i)}\right)^2} \quad (6)$$

$x_p, x_p' \sim P$ are two data points sampled independently from distribution *P*; $x_q, x_q' \sim Q$ are two data points sampled independently from distribution *Q*.

Loss Function [3] in EBM: Designing and analyzing loss functions help train the EBM model effectively, ensuring that correct states (training data) have lower energy compared to incorrect states (invalid data or wrong labels). This enables the model to learn to distinguish between different data classes more clearly, thereby improving the model's classification ability and generalization performance [2].

Energy Distance Loss (L_{ED}): The proposal uses L_{ED} to train the model, based on the idea that samples of the same classification class will have similar energy and samples of different classes will have different energy.

Loss Function L_{ED} is defined as follows:

$$L_{ED}(\theta) = 2E[d\left(X_i, X_j; \theta\right)|y_i = y_j] - E[d(X_i, X_k; \theta)|y_i \neq y_k] \quad (7)$$

Where:

- $d\left(X_i, X_j; \theta\right) = \|X_i - X_j\|_2$ is the energy distance between the data points X_i và X_j.
- y_i và y_j are the classification labels corresponding to the data points X_i và X_j.

The L_{ED} function ensures that samples within the same class have a smaller energy distance, while samples from different classes will have a larger energy distance.

2.3 EBM Model for Skin Lesion Classification

The EBM model uses the energy function $E\,(X;\ \theta)$ to assess the suitability of the skin image features *X* with a classification label, represented as a feature vector.

The energy function: $E(X, y; \theta)$ is constructed based on the conditional probability of the classification label *y* given the input features *X*, as follows:

$$E\,(X,\ y;\ \theta) = -\,logP\,(y \mid X;\ \theta) \quad (8)$$

Where θ represents the model parameters, with the task of optimizing the energy function to identify the most likely classification label y for each skin lesion image.

The ED calculation function is expressed as a weighted sum of the features:

$$E(X; \theta) = \sum_{i=1}^{n} w_i f_i(X) \quad (9)$$

Where:

- $f_i(X)$ is the specific features extracted.
- w_i are the weights learned during training, reflecting the importance of each feature.

Model parameter update: The parameters θ of the model are updated using the Gradient Descent method [11] to minimize the loss function L_{ED}:

$$\theta \leftarrow \theta - \eta \nabla_\theta L_{ED}(\theta) \tag{10}$$

Where: η is learning rate, $\nabla_\theta L_{ED}(\theta)$ is the gradient of the loss function with respect to the parameters θ.

This process continues until the model converges to the optimal value of the parameters, meaning when the energy difference between samples of the same class and different classes is clearly distinguished.

Classification calculation: After the model is trained, classification for a new skin lesion image X^* is performed by selecting the class y such that the energy function $E(X^*, y; \theta^*)$ is minimized:

$$y^* = \text{argmin} E(X^*, y; \theta^*) \tag{11}$$

The expected outcome is an efficient classification system that utilizes the Loss Function L_{ED} with Energy Distance to achieve high accuracy in classifying different types of skin lesions.

3 Functions and Algorithm

3.1 Overview Diagram

The overview diagram of the system is designed to illustrate the entire process from data input to result evaluation. This diagram is divided into four main functional blocks: Image Acquisition, Image Preprocessing and Feature Extraction, Energy Modeling, and Skin Lesion Classification. The steps in the diagram are sequentially connected, ensuring that the input data is processed, modeled, and ultimately classified accurately and efficiently (Fig. 2).

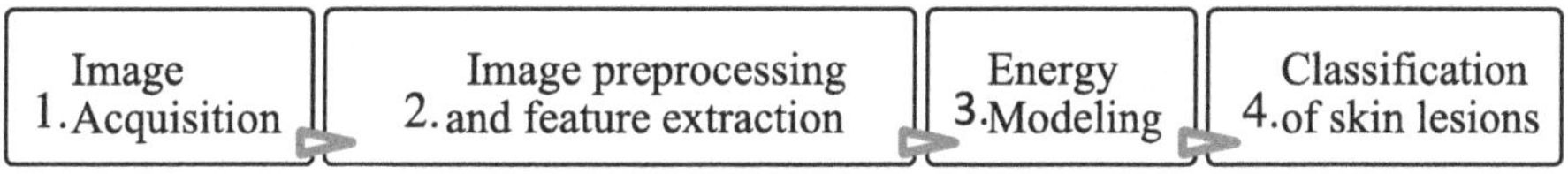

Fig. 2. System overview diagram

3.2 Main Functions and Algorithms

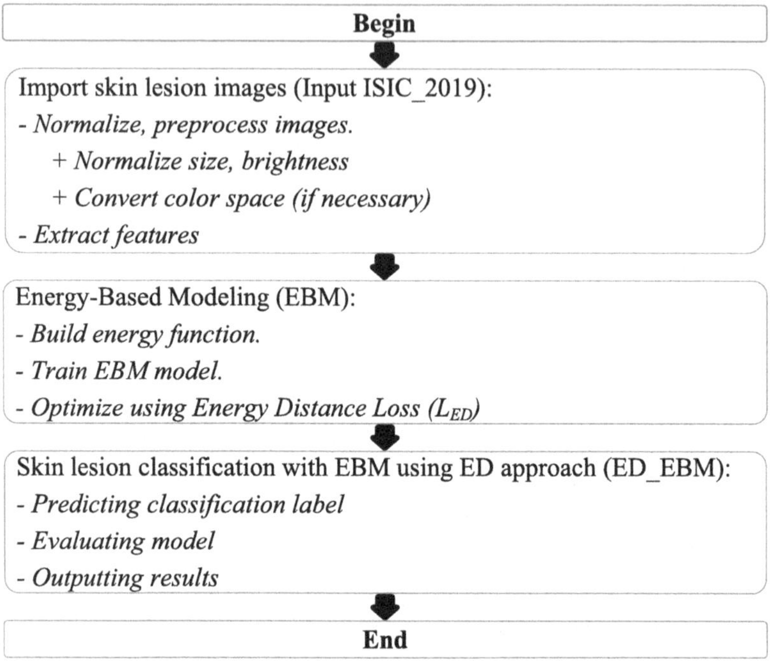

Fig. 3. Main system function diagram

Pre-processing: Prepare input images to ensure consistency in size and quality of the data before feeding it into the model: Normalize the size and brightness of the images and perform color space conversion (if necessary).

Input: Skin lesion images are not standardized.
Output: Images are standardized in size, brightness, and color space uniformity.

```
Begin
CLASS skin lesion data initialization:
    FUNCTION initialize a data object with a list of images and their corresponding labels:
        List of image paths (image_paths)
        List of corresponding labels (labels)
        Transform (if any)
            transform = Transform chain ([
                Perform Resize image to size (128, 128),
                Convert image to Tensor (value from [0, 255] to value [0, 1]),
                Normalize image according to mean and standard deviation:
                    - Mean = [0.485, 0.456, 0.406] cho (R, G, B)
                    - Standard deviation = [0.229, 0.224, 0.225] cho (R, G, B)])
        Returns the pair (transformed image, corresponding label)
End
```

Skin lesion classification with EBM model:

Input: Preprocessed image (128x128x3) from the ISIC 2019 dataset, the feature vector is extracted from the CNN and Label of each image (1 of 8 types of lesions - 8 classes)

Output: - Energy Score: EBM calculates the energy for each input image).
- Label Output: The result is a predicted label (one of 8 lesion types).

```
Begin
   CLASS EnergyDistanceLoss (L_ED):
      FUNCTION initialize function:
         Call the constructor of the class
      FUNCTION returns the value L_ED:
         Calculate true energy (energy_true) = Get the energy value at the posi-
      tion of the correct label for each sample
         Calculate average energy (energy_all) = Calculate average of all labels
         Return average of (energy_all - energy_true)
   # Training function: Train_EBM
   FUNCTION Train EBM with epoch = 100:
      Create an empty list to save loss history
      FOR epoch FROM 1 TO epochs DO:
         Set total_loss = 0 // To save total loss in each epoch
         Set correct = 0 // To save number of correct predictions
         Set total = 0 // To save total number of data samples
      FOR each batch (images, labels) IN dataloader DO:
         Send images and labels to a computer device
         Set optimizer gradient to 0
         features = Extract features from feature_extractor
         output = ebm(features)
         // Calculate loss function with Energy Distance Loss
         loss = Cal EnergyDistanceLoss with output and correct label
         Execute backward () to calculate gradient of loss
         Update model weights via optimizer
         // Calculate total loss
         total_loss += Value of loss
      // Calculate model prediction (predict label with highest probability)
      predicted = Get predicted label with highest energy value from output
      correct += Total number of correct predicted labels compared to actual la-
    bels
      total += Number of labels in current batch
      average_loss = total_loss / Number of batches in dataloader
      accuracy = correct / total * 100
      Add average_loss to loss_history
      Print "Epoch [epoch/epochs], Loss: average_loss, Accuracy: accuracy%"
End
```

Starting with a dataset consisting of feature vectors extracted from skin lesion images of the ISIC 2019 dataset and the corresponding labels for various types of skin lesions. The model calculates the Energy Distance Loss between the feature vectors, which is the ratio of interclass energy to intraclass energy. During training, the model adjusts the parameters to minimize Energy Distance Loss. In the result, the model computes the energy values for each classification label, and the label with the lowest energy value is selected as the predicted label, as it has the highest probability (Fig. 3).

4 Experimental Skin Lesions Classification with EBM

4.1 Dataset Used

The ISIC_2019 skin image dataset [5] is used in model experiments (Table 1).

Table 1. Summary of the ISIC_2019 dataset [5]

Diagnostic Label	Abbreviation	Number of Skin Image
Melanoma	MEL	4,522
Melanocytic Nevus	NV	12,722
Basal Cell Carcinoma	BCC	3,452
Actinic Keratosis/Bowen's Disease	AKIEC	867
Benign Keratosis	BKL	2,694
Dermatofibroma	DF	239
Vascular Lesion	VASC	253
Squamous Cell Carcinoma	SCC	628
Unknown	UNK	954

Characteristics and challenges in the dataset: Imbalanced class distribution, uneven lighting in images, varying angles, noisy images, and multi-class classification.

To prepare the data for training and testing, the dataset is split into two parts: 80% for training and 20% for testing.

4.2 Tools Used

ED_EBM is a tool built on the Python platform, utilizing the PyTorch, TensorFlow/Keras, and Energy libraries. This tool enables efficient model training, experimentation, and deployment of the EBM model, covering processes such as data preprocessing, feature extraction, energy distance calculation, model building, skin lesion classification, and result evaluation.

4.3 Experimental Scenario for Skin Lesion Classification with EBM and Energy Distance

The results of skin lesion classification using the EBM approach with Energy Distance were experimented with the EBM model on the ISIC 2019 dataset.

Training Results and L_{ED} Chart Across Epochs

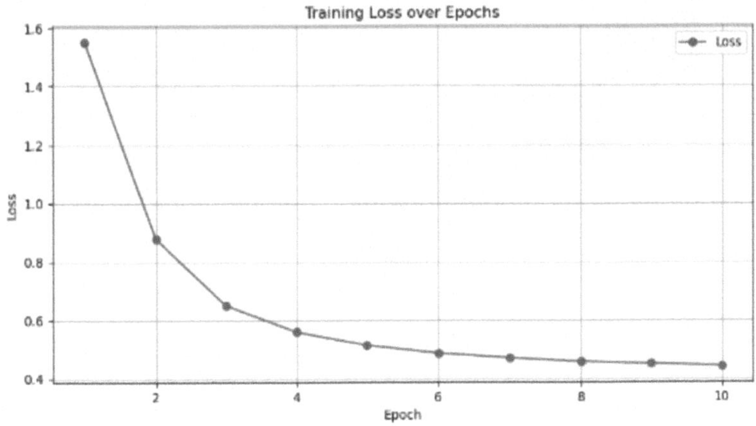

Fig. 4. Training EBM with Energy Distance Loss (L_{ED}), Epoch = 10

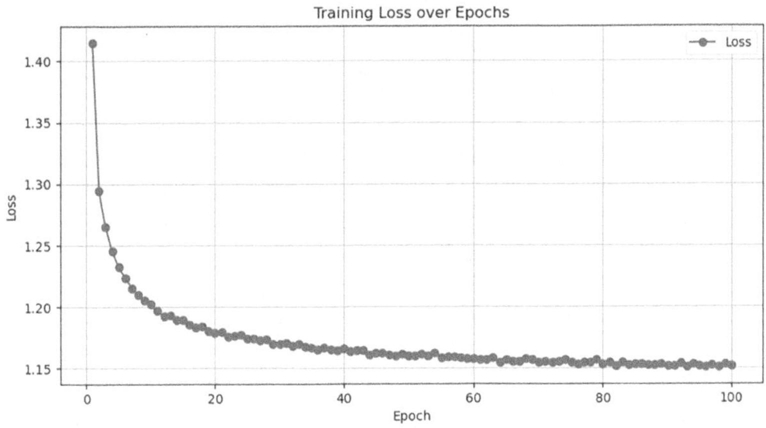

Fig. 5. Training EBM with Energy Distance Loss (L_{ED}), Epoch = 100

During the training of the EBM model on the ISIC_2019 dataset, the value of the loss function (L_{ED}) gradually decreased across epochs, indicating that the model was converging and learning the distinguishing features between different types of skin lesions. In the initial epoch, the loss dropped sharply, showing that the model was learning quickly.

After around the 10th epoch, the loss began to decrease more slowly and stabilized after approximately 50 epochs (Figs. 4 and 5).

Classification Results

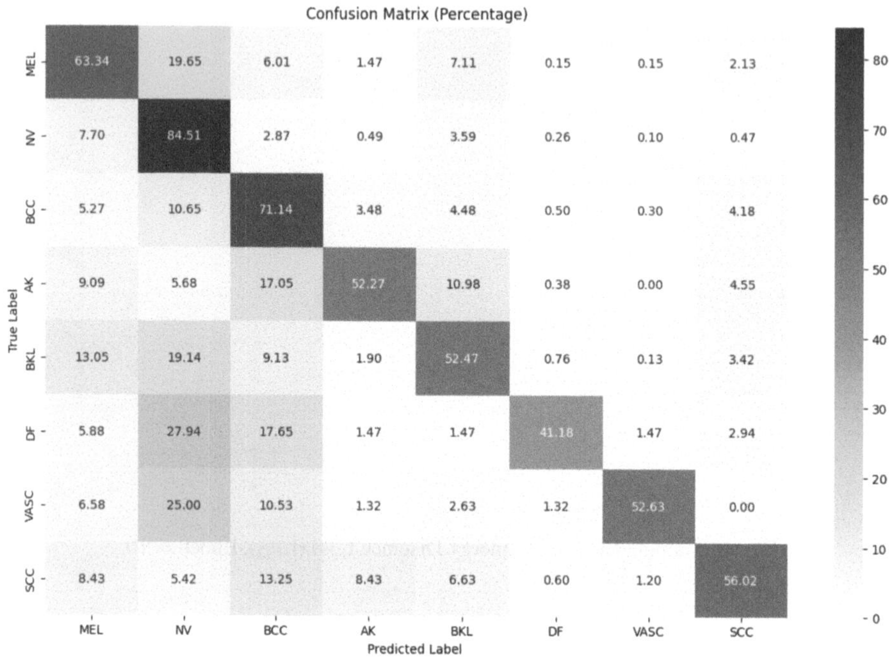

Fig. 6. Confusion Matrix

The result from Fig. 6 indicates that the model was able to classify all diagnostic labels with fairly high accuracy. The achieved classification accuracy, sensitivity and specificity percentages are 74.19%, 60.29%, 95.46%, respectively. Some labels were classified with particularly good results, achieving high accuracy rates, such as Nevus (84.51%) and Basal Cell Carcinoma (71.14%). This suggests that the model accurately learned the distinguishing features for these types of lesions. However, for certain lesions like Dermatofibroma (41.18%) and Benign Keratosis (52.47%), the model encountered more difficulty in accurate classification, showing a high misclassification rate.

MEL (Melanoma): The correct prediction rate is 63.34%, with most errors misclassified as Nevus (19.65%) and Basal Cell Carcinoma (6.01%). This suggests the model struggles to distinguish between Melanoma and Nevus, likely due to the visual similarities between these two types.

NV (Nevus): The highest correct prediction rate at 84.51%. The main misclassification is with Melanoma (7.70%), reflecting the morphological similarities between Nevus and Melanoma.

BCC (Basal Cell Carcinoma): The correct prediction rate is 71.14%, with misclassifications primarily as Nevus (10.65%) and Melanoma (5.27%). This indicates an overlap in features between BCC and these other types, especially Nevus.

AK (Actinic Keratosis): The correct prediction rate is 52.27%, a moderate level. It is often confusing with Basal Cell Carcinoma (17.05%) and Melanoma (9.09%), suggesting a crossover in the image characteristics of AK and these skin cancers.

BKL (Benign Keratosis): The correct prediction rate is 52.47%. Misclassifications largely occur with Nevus (19.14%) and Melanoma (13.05%), indicating that BKL, though benign, shares features with several malignant lesions.

DF (Dermatofibroma): The lowest correct prediction rate at 41.18%, with frequent misclassifications as Nevus (27.94%) and Basal Cell Carcinoma (17.65%). This may be due to the difficulty in clearly differentiating DF from other lesions.

VASC (Vascular Lesion): The correct prediction rate is 52.63%, with most errors being classified as Nevus (25.00%), indicating an overlap between vascular lesions and benign moles in imaging.

SCC (Squamous Cell Carcinoma): The correct prediction rate is 56.02%, with misclassifications into Basal Cell Carcinoma (13.25%) and Melanoma (8.43%), reflecting similarities between these carcinomas.

In summary, the model can classify all labels with relatively high accuracy. However, several labels have visually and feature-wise similar characteristics, which impacts the model's classification performance.

5 Conclusion

The study proposed a new approach for skin lesion classification using the Energy-Based Model (EBM) with an Energy Distance approach. By utilizing the L_{ED} loss function, the model not only achieved multi-class classification performance but also addressed issues related to data imbalance, a common challenge in the medical field. Experiments on the ISIC 2019 dataset demonstrated that the EBM model can effectively distinguish between different types of skin lesions, particularly dangerous types such as skin cancer. In addition, the research opens many avenues for developing medical diagnostic support systems, from expanding datasets to improving modeling techniques, preprocessing, and feature extraction. Deploying the model in real clinical applications to ensure the transparency and accuracy of decisions is also a critical next step for bringing this research into practice.

In conclusion, the proposed method not only contributes to skin lesion classification but also broadens the potential applications of Energy-Based Models (EBM) in medical and machine learning fields.

References

1. Lecun, Y., Chopra, S., Hadsell, R., et al.: A tutorial on energy-based learning. In: Predicting Structured Data, pp. 191–246. MIT Press (2006)

2. LeCun, Y., Huang, F.J.: Loss functions for discriminative training of energy-based models. In: Proceedings of the Tenth International Workshop on Artificial Intelligence and Statistics, vol. R5, pp. 206–213. PMLR (2005). https://proceedings.mlr.press/r5/lecun05a.html
3. Loss Function. https://en.wikipedia.org/wiki/Loss_function
4. Energy Distance. https://en.wikipedia.org/wiki/Energy_distance
5. International Skin Imaging Collaboration (ISIC): ISIC 2019: Skin Lesion Analysis Towards Melanoma Detection (2019). https://www.isic-archive.com/
6. He, H., Garcia, E.A.: Learning from imbalanced data. IEEE Trans. Knowl. Data Eng. **21**(9), 1263–1284 (2009). https://doi.org/10.1109/TKDE.2008.239
7. Pathan, S., Siddalingaswamy, P.C., Prabhu, K.: Techniques and algorithms for computer aided diagnosis of pigmented skin lesions—a review. Biomed. Signal Process. Control **39**, 237–262 (2017). https://doi.org/10.1016/j.bspc.2017.07.010
8. WHO. Skin Cancer Facts. https://www.who.int/news-room/questions-and-answers/item/radiation-ultraviolet-(uv)-radiation-and-skin-cancer
9. Litjens, G., Kooi, T., Bejnordi, B.E., et al.: A survey on deep learning in medical image analysis. Med. Image Anal. **42**, 60–88 (2017). https://doi.org/10.1016/j.media.2017.07.005
10. Shen, D., Wu, G., Suk, H.I.: Deep learning in medical image analysis. Annu. Rev. Biomed. Eng. **19**, 221–248 (2017). https://doi.org/10.1146/annurev-bioeng-071516-044442
11. Gradient descent. https://en.wikipedia.org/wiki/Gradient_descent
12. Jha, A., Ananthanarayana, V.S.: An interpretable deep learning model for skin lesion classification. In: Singh, M., Tyagi, V., Gupta, P., Flusser, J., Ören, T. (eds.) ICACDS 2023. CCIS, vol. 1848, pp. 543–553. Springer, Cham (2023). https://doi.org/10.1007/978-3-031-37940-6_44
13. Subramanian, M., Shobha Rani, P.: Deep learning techniques in skin cancer detection: a survey. In: 2022 1st International Conference on Computational Science and Technology (ICCST), Chennai, India, pp. 378–381 (2022). https://doi.org/10.1109/ICCST55948.2022.10040424
14. Naqvi, M., et al.: Skin cancer detection using deep learning-a review. Diagnostics **13**(11), 1911 (2023). https://doi.org/10.3390/diagnostics13111911
15. Rizzo, M.L., Székely, G.J.: Energy distance. WIREs Comput. Stat. **8**, 27–38 (2016). https://doi.org/10.1002/wics.1375
16. Artificial intelligence. https://en.wikipedia.org/wiki/Artificial_intelligence
17. Convolutional neural network. https://en.wikipedia.org/wiki/Convolutional_neural_network

Trustworthiness in Vision-Language Models

Kiana Vu(✉) and Phung Lai

State University of New York at Albany, Albany, NY 12222, USA
{kvu,lai}@albany.edu

Abstract. As vision-language models (VLMs) are increasingly used in various applications, their trustworthiness becomes critical. This paper explores key dimensions of VLM trustworthiness-accuracy, fairness, safety, and robustness. We review methods to enhance visual-textual alignment and tackle challenges like adversarial attacks, biases, and privacy risks through innovative vulnerability assessment frameworks. Our findings highlight ongoing trustworthiness challenges despite some progress. We propose a research agenda emphasizing interdisciplinary approaches to address these gaps and promote responsible VLM deployment.

Keywords: Trustworthiness · Vision-language models · Privacy · Fairness · Robustness · Safety

1 Introduction

In recent years, vision-language models (VLMs) have made significant progress in understanding and generating multimodal content, excelling in tasks like image captioning, visual question answering, and visual storytelling. State-of-the-art models such as LLaVA [57], Flamingo [3], and GPT-4 [1] showcase enhanced perceptual and semantic capabilities across various datasets. However, despite these advancements, trustworthiness remains a critical issue that can undermine the reliability and societal applicability of these models. Models that expose private data, produce harmful outputs, or are vulnerable to attacks can lead to privacy, security, and fairness violations, and compromised systems. Therefore, addressing privacy, fairness, robustness, safety, and truthfulness challenges is crucial for the safe and responsible use of VLMs.

This work is structured to explore each of these trustworthiness issues in depth. Section 2 addresses privacy, discussing the challenges associated with personal information leakage in different contexts. Section 3 covers fairness, focusing on biases in data and model outputs that may lead to discriminatory or unequal treatment across demographic groups. Section 4 explores robustness, analyzing how VLMs handle out-of-distribution data and withstand adversarial attacks. Section 5 examines safety concerns, emphasizing risks such as harmful content generation and inappropriate responses. Lastly, Sect. 6 provides an overview of visions and proposals for future research. Through this structured approach, we aim to provide a thorough, nuanced perspective on each issue, facilitating both understanding and future research in improving trustworthiness in vision-language systems (Fig. 1).

J. Kertesz et al. (Eds.): CSoNet 2024, LNCS 15417, pp. 73–85, 2025.
https://doi.org/10.1007/978-981-96-6389-7_7

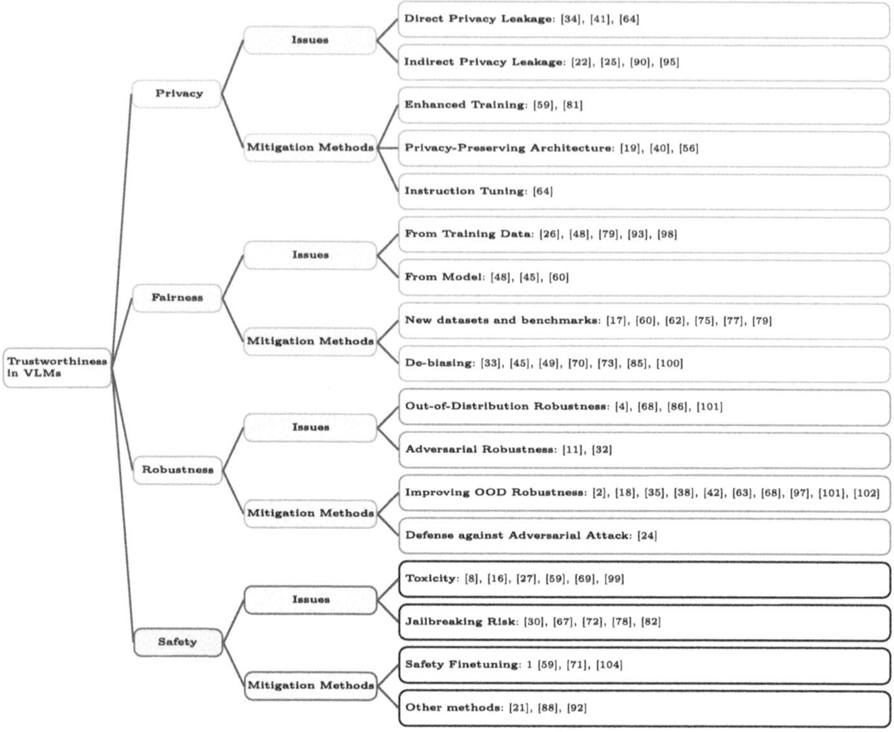

Fig. 1. Taxonomy of Trustworthiness Issues and Current Mitigation Methods.

2 Privacy

As VLMs advance, concerns about privacy exposure grow. These concerns can divide into two main categories as follows.

2.1 Direct Privacy Leakage

Privacy risks arise from training data, particularly when collectors fail to implement adequate safeguards, resulting in non-anonymized information in datasets [34]. This leaves users with less control and a higher risk of leaks, especially since many VLMs use crowd-sourced data. Research indicates that while text-only models are less likely to leak information, the risk escalates significantly with relevant images, as optimizing in the pixel domain is easier than in text [41,72]. Therefore, additional filtering is necessary during training to mitigate these risks, highlighting the importance of careful examination before deployment.

2.2 Indirect Privacy Leakage

Privacy threats from inference attacks remain a concern, even with trusted cloud services. These attacks can reveal if specific data trained a model [95], infer properties of the training data [25], or expose sensitive information [22]. Vulnerabilities in vision-language models (VLMs) highlight the need for better privacy measures. VLMs can unintentionally memorize sensitive data, leading to leaks without knowledge of the model's specifics [9,95]. Overfitting may also cause retention of sensitive attributes during inference [80]. Additionally, threats like gradient-based and backdoor attacks further jeopardize VLM privacy, particularly with open-source data [90].

2.3 Mitigation Methods

To enhance privacy in vision-language models (VLMs), quantifying risks is crucial. New metrics have been created to assess a model's ability to reproduce training instances and facilitate cross-model comparisons [43]. It has also been suggested that models utilizing multiple modalities provide better privacy [12]. Training modifications can improve privacy; for instance, safety modules can be integrated to boost resilience against violations [59], while adversarial training can enhance privacy but risks reducing accuracy [81]. Some researchers propose new architectures, such as differentially private CLIP model [40]. However, others contend that existing methods like data sanitization and differential privacy are inadequate, often failing to protect identifiable information [9]. Furthermore, privacy leakage can still occur with privacy-inducing prompts [64]. These challenges underscore the need for mitigating privacy risks in VLMs.

3 Fairness and Bias

Bias mitigation and fairness are critical concerns, especially since social biases can be present in and propagated by these models [51]. We focus on bias in two key areas: training data and model outputs.

3.1 Bias from Training Data

Bias in training data often goes unnoticed, resulting in unfair model outcomes. This is especially concerning with open-source datasets. For instance, the Google Conceptual Captions dataset disproportionately features men and lighter-skinned individuals [26], while COCO Captions associates gender with context [79]. ImageNet also has issues with outdated vocabulary and imbalanced representation [93]. These biases raise concerns about the performance and benchmarks of many VLMs. State-of-the-art models may excel on test sets but can still show biases in real-world applications, impacting generalizability. Moreover, datasets reflecting real-world biases-like skewed labor demographics-can misrepresent reality [48]. Research indicates that clinical models may favor certain patient groups based on gender, language, etc. [98].

3.2 Bias from Model

Bias in training data often goes unnoticed, yet it significantly affects the outputs of VLMs, especially when datasets are inaccessible. Many pre-trained VLMs exhibit stereotypical biases [45], which can have serious implications in fields like healthcare. Gender biases are common in tasks such as occupation prediction [48]. Moreover, misclassification of race-related elements and biased outputs further highlight these issues [60]. Such biases negatively impact users and reinforce harmful stereotypes, underscoring the urgent need for fairer systems.

3.3 Mitigation Methods

New Datasets and Benchmarks. To tackle bias in VLMs, accurate risk assessment is essential. Existing evaluation datasets like Harvard-FairVLMed [62], PATA [77], and BOLD [17] enhance evaluations but often lack the scale of established benchmarks. Researchers also create synthetic datasets to improve fairness assessments. These datasets include a gender-balanced dataset generated with DALL-E-3 [75] and another consisting of gender-swapped images [79]. Other researchers develop counterfactual image-text pairs that highlight biases in datasets like COCO Captions [60]. New metrics, such as gender polarity and bias distance in embeddings, support these assessments [17]. However, generating multiple counterfactuals can be inefficient, necessitating human evaluation to validate fairness and emphasizing the need for well-constructed benchmarks.

De-biasing. To combat bias in AI models, several strategies are employed, including fine-tuning instructions and post-processing outputs. Some researchers adjust model instructions and architectures for improved fairness [70], while others focus on detecting biased prompts in pre-trained models [33]. Methods like Post-hoc Bias Mitigation (PBM) effectively reduce bias in image retrieval [49]; others maintain accuracy during post-processing [45]. Re-sampling underperforming clusters can enhance fairness [100], and modification of facial features also mitigate biases [73]. Additionally, self-debiasing reduces biased text generation [76], especially when paired with other methods, and fair sampling and feature clipping significantly lower gender bias in image searches [85].

4 Robustness

4.1 Out-of-Distribution (OOD) Robustness

Recent research highlights challenges in foundation models like ChatGPT [86] and multimodal large language models (MLLMs) [101]. ChatGPT excels in adversarial tasks but struggles with OOD robustness and informal medical responses [4]. MLLMs often fail to generalize beyond training domains due to mapping issues, while vision-language models face difficulties with open-domain concepts, especially when overfitting during fine-tuning [68]. Large pre-trained image classifiers show initial robustness, which diminishes over time. Current visual question answering (VQA) models are limited to specific benchmarks, hindering generalization to OOD datasets. Techniques like SDRO can enhance performance [29], but existing prompt learning methods lack robustness for novel classes, and fine-tuning may impair model calibration in OOD contexts.

4.2 Adversarial Attack Robustness

VLMs are vulnerable to malicious attacks that exploit their limitations. Adversaries can introduce small, imperceptible perturbations in image inputs, generating adversarial examples that disrupt model performance [11]. In addition, backdoor attacks use poisoned training data, leading to misbehavior during inference [32]. Studies indicate that open-sourced VLMs show performance gaps in red teaming tasks, highlighting the need for improved safety and security. Additionally, misalignment between language and vision modalities creates a "modality gap," complicating adversarial vulnerability.

4.3 Mitigation Methods

Improving Out-of-Distribution Robustness. Recent research in VLMs aims to enhance OOD detection and generalization. A simple maximum logit detector has been shown to outperform complex methods for anomaly segmentation [38]. In-context learning (ICL) can also improve multimodal generalization [101]. A fine-tuned CLIP excels in unsupervised OOD detection [2], while Denoising ICL enhances vision model performance [42]. The OGEN method synthesizes OOD features [97], while another improves prompt-tuning for OOD detection [18]. Maximum Concept Matching aligns visual and textual features [63], and anchor-based finetuning leads to better domain shifts [35]. Other studies focus on distillation and prompt learning to boost robustness [102].

Defense Against Adversarial Attacks. VILLA is a two-stage framework for adversarial training of VLMs, featuring task-agnostic adversarial pre-training and task-specific finetuning [24]. VILLA conducts adversarial training in the embedding space rather than on raw image pixels and text tokens, improving the model's resilience against adversarial examples. It uses a "free" adversarial training strategy with KL-divergence regularization. When applied to existing VLMs, VILLA sets new state-of-the-art performance across various tasks, highlighting the effectiveness of embedding-space training for enhancing model robustness.

5 Safety

5.1 Toxicity

The LAION-400M dataset contains problematic content, including explicit materials and harmful stereotypes, raising concerns for stakeholders [8]. Pre-trained LLMs exhibit biases and varying toxicity across languages [69]. MLLMs also face safety vulnerabilities that require thorough evaluation [59]. Advanced models like GeminiProVision and GPT-4V show inherent biases, highlighting the need for greater robustness [99]. In addition, pretrained models can generate toxic text from benign prompts, with current methods failing to fully mitigate this issue [27]. Assigning personas to ChatGPT can increase toxicity and reinforce harmful stereotypes against certain groups [16].

5.2 Jailbreaking Risk

Recent studies have exposed vulnerabilities in VLMs to adversarial inputs. Adversarial images have been shown to "jailbreak" VLMs, leading to harmful responses [72, 78]. Perturbation can be performed effectively now [67], while FigStep converts harmful content into images with an 82.5% attack rate across multiple VLMs [30]. Another attack replaces captions with malicious prompts, enabling jailbreaks [82].

5.3 Mitigation Methods

Safety Fine-Tuning. Fine-tuning VLLMs with the VLGuard dataset has been shown to enhance safety while maintaining helpfulness, resulting in better rejection of unsafe instructions and lower adversarial attack success rates [104]. The safety of models like CLIP can also be fine-tuned on synthetic data, reducing sensitivity to NSFW inputs and enhancing performance in cross-modal tasks [71]. Models can also be strengthened against jailbreak attacks through integration of safety modules during training, effectively reducing toxic responses [59].

Other Methods. Analysis of how prompts and training data impact language model toxicity results in an unsupervised method that effectively reduces toxicity without requiring large datasets, outperforming supervised baselines in quality [92]. Meanwhile, the Reinforce-Detoxify approach uses reinforcement learning to mitigate toxicity and bias in transformer models [21]. Other researchers critique toxicity evaluation methods, highlighting that while simple mitigations improve automatic scores, these methods risk over-filtering marginalized texts and create discrepancies between automatic and human judgments [88].

6 Future Research Directions

6.1 Privacy

Cryptography-Based Privacy Preservation. Cryptographic security is a valuable approach to enhancing the privacy and trustworthiness of VLMs. Secure multi-party computation (SMPC) divides secret information into shares among multiple parties, ensuring that individual shares reveal nothing unless combined [94]; SMPC frameworks designed for transformer models have since been proposed [61]. Homomorphic encryption (HE) allows computations on encrypted data without decryption [28], and has also been utilized for privacy preservation in transformers [14] (Fig. 2).

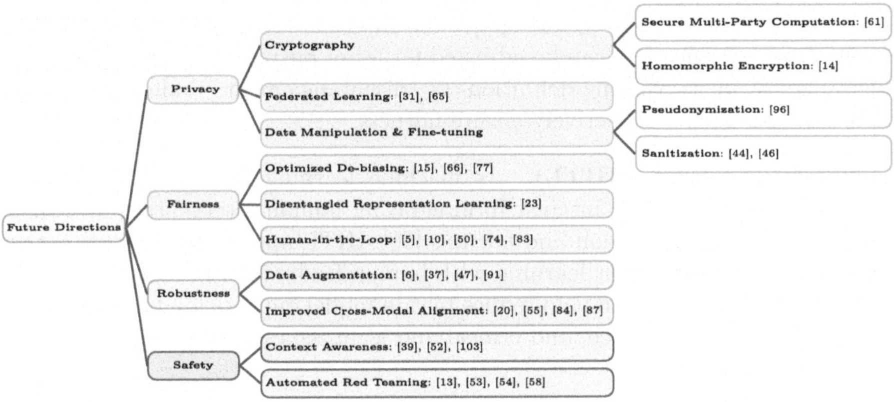

Fig. 2. Taxonomy of Future Research Directions for Improving Trustworthiness.

Federated Learning. Federated learning enhances privacy in vision-language models (VLMs) by localizing model training, which protects training data from leakage. Researchers have adapted prompt-based learning for VLMs in this context [31] and improved training efficiency [65]. However, challenges remain, such as communication overhead among devices and statistical heterogeneity from diverse data distributions [89].

Data Manipulation and Finetuning. Privacy in vision-language models (VLMs) can be improved using techniques like data pseudonymization, which substitutes sensitive information with synthetic alternatives [96]. Data sanitization, which removes duplicates to reduce memorization and privacy risks [46], and knowledge sanitization-fine-tuning models to provide safe responses when leakage risks arise [44]-are also emerging strategies. Further exploration is needed regarding the effectiveness and contextual definitions of"sensitive" information in these approaches.

6.2 Fairness

Optimized De-biasing. Improving fairness in VLMs can be achieved through effective de-biasing methods. Additive residual learning has been proposed as a method for fairer image representations [77]. Calibration loss can also be used to retain semantically similar embeddings [15]. Meanwhile, a counterfactual inference framework has been shown to help models learn correct responses through cause and effect [66]. Additionally, adversarial classifiers that predict image attributes from visual-textual similarities can be combined with instruction tuning to reduce bias [7]. These methods require minimal changes to model architecture, allowing for easier integration into larger VLMs.

Disentangled Representation Learning (DRL). Disentangled representation learning (DRL) simplifies complex data by breaking it into independent feature groups, improving model predictions. Traditional DRL methods use variational autoencoders (VAEs) for feature encoding based on impact or generative adversarial networks (GANs) for separation. In vision-language models (VLMs), attention in text encoders can be adjusted for fairer outputs [23]. However, challenges persist due to varying definitions of "disentanglement," indicating a need for further research to effectively ensure fairness.

Human-in-the-Loop (HITL). As machine learning models become more complex, there is growing interest in integrating human intervention into their training to improve precision and fairness [50]. HITL approaches include active learning [10], reinforcement learning with human feedback [74], and explainable AI [83]. These methods can help reduce bias in model outputs [5], but challenges such as human bias, finance, and ethical and legal issues persist [36].

6.3 Robustness

Data Augmentation. MixGen is a data augmentation method that generates new image-text pairs by interpolating images and concatenating text to preserve semantics [37], and can be further refined to mitigate distribution shifts [47]. Another end-to-end method for creating synthetic images involves extracting text prompts via an image captioning model for use in text-to-image diffusion, then mixing these with real datasets [6]. There is also a bimodal augmentation (BiAug) technique that decouples objects and attributes to synthesize vision-language examples and hard negatives, using LLMs and an object detector to generate detailed descriptions and inpaint corresponding images [91].

Improved Cross-Modal Alignment. Enhancing alignment between the modalities of VLMs can boost accuracy. Techniques include sharing learnable parameters [20], applying bidirectional constraints [55], and adjusting cross-modal projections [87]. These methods have shown promise in basic tasks like image-text matching [55] and retrieval [87]. However, challenges persist in addressing the modality gap, which impacts robustness to OOD data and adversarial examples [78]. Thus, cross-modal alignment remains a valuable research direction.

6.4 Safety

Context Awareness. Methods like fine-tuning on CAER datasets, developing zero-shot and few-shot patterns for limited data, and integrating Chain-of-Thought for improved reasoning can enhance CAER tasks with Large VLMs [52]. Another method, Dual-Aligned Prompt Tuning, combines explicit context from pre-trained LLMs with implicit modeling to create more context-aware prompts [39]. Other researchers propose Visual In-Context Learning, which optimizes image retrieval and summarization to enhance task-specific interactions [103].

Automated Red Teaming (ART). RTVLM is a dataset that benchmarks VLMs across faithfulness, privacy, safety, and fairness [54]. Meanwhile, Arondight automates multi-modal jailbreak attacks using reinforcement learning and uncovers significant security vulnerabilities [58]. Another dataset contains

1,445 harmful questions tested on 11 LLMs and MLLMs [13]. Findings indicate that GPT-4 and GPT-4V are more robust against jailbreaks than open-source models, with Llama2 and Qwen-VL-Chat performing best among them. The study also notes limited transferability of visual jailbreak methods compared to textual ones. A different ART framework connects unsafe outputs to prompts, improving the detection of vulnerabilities in text-to-image models [53].

7 Conclusion

In conclusion, ensuring the trustworthiness of VLMs is essential as their applications grow in fields like healthcare and security. This paper has highlighted critical challenges, including accuracy, fairness, safety, and robustness, alongside vulnerabilities to adversarial attacks and biases. Future research should adopt a multidisciplinary approach, incorporating ethics and social sciences, while emphasizing transparency and accountability in model development. Collaboration among researchers, practitioners, and policymakers is crucial for responsible VLM deployment. Ultimately, enhancing VLM trustworthiness is a societal necessity that balances their benefits with potential risks.

References

1. Achiam, J., Adler, S., et al.: GPT-4 technical report. arXiv (2023)
2. Adaloglou, N., et al.: Adapting CLIP models for OOD detection. arXiv (2023)
3. Alayrac, J.B., et al.: Flamingo: a VLM for few-shot learning. In: NIPS, vol. 35 (2022)
4. Andreassen, A., Bahri, Y., Neyshabur, B., Roelofs, R.: The evolution of out-of-distribution robustness throughout fine-tuning. arXiv (2021)
5. Bai, Y., et al.: Constitutional AI: Harmlessness from AI feedback. arXiv (2022)
6. Bakhtiarnia, A., Zhang, Q., Iosifidis, A.: Promptmix: text-to-image diffusion models enhance the performance of lightweight networks. In: IJCNN (2023)
7. Berg, H., Hall, S.M., Bhalgat, Y., Yang, W., et al.: A prompt array keeps the bias away: debiasing vision-language models with adversarial learning. arXiv (2022)
8. Birhane, A., Prabhu, V.U., Kahembwe, E.: Multimodal datasets: misogyny, pornography, and malignant stereotypes. arXiv (2021)
9. Brown, H., Lee, K., Mireshghallah, F., Shokri, R., Tramèr, F.: What does it mean for a language model to preserve privacy? In: ACM FAccT, pp. 2280–2292 (2022)
10. Brutzkus, A., Globerson, A.: Why do larger models generalize better? a theoretical perspective via the XOR problem. In: ICML, pp. 822–830. PMLR (2019)
11. Carlini, N., et al.: Are aligned neural networks adversarially aligned? In: NIPS (2024)
12. Chen, L., et al.: Are we on the right way for evaluating LVLMs? arXiv (2024)
13. Chen, S., et al.: Red teaming GPT-4V: Are GPT-4V safe against uni/multi-modal jailbreak attacks? arXiv (2024)
14. Chen, T., et al.: The-X: privacy-preserving transformer inference with homomorphic encryption. arXiv (2022)
15. Chuang, C.Y., et al.: Debiasing VLMs via biased prompts. arXiv (2023)

16. Deshpande, A., Murahari, V., Rajpurohit, T., Kalyan, A., Narasimhan, K.: Toxicity in ChatGPT: analyzing persona-assigned language models. arXiv (2023)
17. Dhamala, J., Sun, T., Kumar, V., et al.: Bold: dataset and metrics for measuring biases in open-ended language generation. In: ACM FAccT, pp. 862–872 (2021)
18. Ding, K., Zhang, H., Yu, Q., Wang, Y., et al.: Weak distribution detectors lead to stronger generalizability of vision-language prompt tuning. In: AAAI (2024)
19. Dwork, C.: Differential privacy: a survey of results. In: TAMC, pp. 1–19 (2008)
20. Eslami, S., de Melo, G.: Mitigate the gap: investigating approaches for improving cross-modal alignment in clip. arXiv (2024)
21. Faal, F., Schmitt, K., Yu, J.Y.: Reward modeling for mitigating toxicity in transformer-based language models. Appl. Intell. **53**(7), 8421–8435 (2023)
22. Fredrikson, M., Jha, S., Ristenpart, T.: Model inversion attacks that exploit confidence information and basic countermeasures. In: ACM SIGSAC CCS (2015)
23. Gaci, Y., Benattallah, B., Casati, F., Benabdeslem, K.: Debiasing pretrained text encoders by paying attention to paying attention. In: EMNLP (2022)
24. Gan, Z., Chen, Y.C., Li, L., Zhu, C., Cheng, Y., Liu, J.: Large-scale adversarial training for vision-and-language representation learning. In: NIPS (2020)
25. Ganju, K., et al.: Property inference attacks on fully connected neural networks using permutation invariant representations. In: ACM SIGSAC CCS (2018)
26. Garcia, N., Hirota, Y., Wu, Y., Nakashima, Y.: Uncurated image-text datasets: Shedding light on demographic bias. In: IEEE/CVF CVPR, pp. 6957–6966 (2023)
27. Gehman, S., Gururangan, S., Sap, M., Choi, Y., Smith, N.A.: Realtoxicityprompts: evaluating neural toxic degeneration in language models. arXiv (2020)
28. Gentry, C.: Fully homomorphic encryption using ideal lattices. In: STOC (2009)
29. Gokhale, T., Chaudhary, A., Banerjee, P., Baral, C., Yang, Y.: Semantically distributed robust optimization for vision-and-language inference. arXiv (2021)
30. Gong, Y., Ran, D., Liu, J., Wang, C., Cong, T., et al.: Figstep: jailbreaking large vision-language models via typographic visual prompts. arXiv (2023)
31. Guo, T., Guo, S., Wang, J.: Pfedprompt: learning personalized prompt for vision-language models in federated learning. In: Proceedings of ACM WWW (2023)
32. Guo, W., Tondi, B., Barni, M.: An overview of backdoor attacks against deep neural networks and possible defences. IEEE OJSP **3**, 261–287 (2022)
33. Guo, Y., Yang, Y., Abbasi, A.: Auto-debias: debiasing masked language models with automated biased prompts. In: Proceedings of ACL, pp. 1012–1023 (2022)
34. Gurari, D., Li, Q., Stangl, A.J., Guo, A., Lin, C., et al.: Vizwiz grand challenge: Answering visual questions from blind people. In: IEEE CVPR (2018)
35. Han, J., et al.: Anchor-based robust finetuning of VLMs. In: IEEE CVPR (2024)
36. Han, L.: When the human is in the loop: cost, effort and behavior. In: Proceedings of the 43rd International ACM SIGIR Conference, pp. 2480–2480 (2020)
37. Hao, X., et al.: MixGEN: a new multi-modal data augmentation. In: WACV (2023)
38. Hendrycks, D., et al.: Scaling OOD detection for real-world settings. In: ICML (2022)
39. Hu, H., Lin, T., Wang, J., Sun, Z., Xu, Y.: Context-aware prompt tuning for vision-language model with dual-alignment. arXiv (2023)
40. Huang, A., Liu, P., Nakada, R., Zhang, L., Zhang, W.: Safeguarding data in multimodal AI: a differentially private approach to CLIP training. arXiv (2023)
41. Huang, J., Zhang, J.: A survey on evaluation of multimodal LLMS. arXiv (2024)
42. Huang, Z., Liu, C., Dong, Y., Su, H., et al.: Machine vision therapy: MLLMs can enhance visual robustness via denoising in-context learning. In: ICML (2023)

43. Inan, H.A., et al.: Privacy analysis in language models via training data leakage report. arXiv (2021)
44. Ishibashi, Y., Shimodaira, H.: Knowledge sanitization of LLMS. arXiv (2023)
45. Janghorbani, S., de Melo, G.: Multi-modal bias: Introducing a framework for stereotypical bias assessment beyond gender and race in VLMs. arXiv (2023)
46. Kandpal, N., Wallace, E., Raffel, C.: Deduplicating training data mitigates privacy risks in language models. In: ICML, pp. 10697–10707. PMLR (2022)
47. Kim, S., Im, H., Lee, W., et al.: Robustmixgen: Data augmentation for enhancing robustness of VLMs in the presence of distribution shift. Authorea (2023)
48. Kirk, H.R., et al.: Bias out-of-the-box: an empirical analysis of intersectional occupational biases in popular generative language models. In: NIPS (2021)
49. Kong, F., et al.: Mitigating test-time bias for fair image retrieval. In: NIPS, vol. 36 (2024)
50. Kumar, S., Datta, S., Singh, V., Datta, D., Singh, S.K., et al.: Applications, challenges, and future directions of human-in-the-loop learning. IEEE Access (2024)
51. Lee, N., Bang, Y., Lovenia, H., et al.: Survey of social bias in VLMs. arXiv (2023)
52. Lei, Y., et al.: LVLMs as emotion recognizers in context awareness. arXiv (2024)
53. Li, G., Chen, K., Zhang, S., Zhang, J., Zhang, T.: Art: automatic red-teaming for text-to-image models to protect benign users. arXiv (2024)
54. Li, M., Li, L., Yin, Y., Ahmed, M., et al.: Red teaming VLMs. arXiv (2024)
55. Li, Z., Zhang, L., Zhang, K., Zhang, Y., Mao, Z.: Improving image-text matching with bidirectional consistency of cross-modal alignment. IEEE TCSVT (2024)
56. Lison, P., Pilán, I., Sánchez, D., et al.: Anonymisation models for text data: State of the art, challenges and future directions. In: 59th ACL and 11th IJCNLP (2021)
57. Liu, H., Li, C., Wu, Q., Lee, Y.J.: Visual instruction tuning. In: NIPS, vol. 36 (2024)
58. Liu, Y., Cai, C., Zhang, X., et al.: Arondight: red teaming large vision language models with auto-generated multi-modal jailbreak prompts. arXiv (2024)
59. Liu, Z., Nie, Y., Tan, Y., Yue, X., et al.: Safety alignment for VLMs. arXiv (2024)
60. Lui, N., Chia, B., Berrios, W., Ross, C., Kiela, D.: Leveraging diffusion perturbations for measuring fairness in computer vision. arXiv (2023)
61. Luo, J., Zhang, Y., Zhang, Z., Zhang, J., et al.: Secformer: fast and accurate privacy-preserving inference for transformer models via SMPC. In: ACL (2024)
62. Luo, Y., et al.: Fairclip: harnessing fairness in VL learning. In: CVPR (2024)
63. Ming, Y., Cai, Z., Gu, J., Sun, Y., Li, W., Li, Y.: Delving into out-of-distribution detection with vision-language representations. NIPS **35**, 35087–35102 (2022)
64. Mireshghallah, N., Kim, H., et al.: Can LLMs keep a secret? testing privacy implications of language models via contextual integrity theory. arXiv (2023)
65. Nguyen, D.P., Munoz, J.P., Jannesari, A.: Flora: enhancing vision-language models with parameter-efficient federated learning. arXiv (2024)
66. Niu, Y., Tang, K., Zhang, H., Lu, Z., Hua, X., rong Wen, J.: Counterfactual VQA: a cause-effect look at language bias. In: IEEE/CVF CVPR (2020)
67. Niu, Z., Ren, H., Gao, X., et al.: Jailbreaking attack against MLLM. arXiv (2024)
68. Oh, C., et al.: Towards calibrated robust fine-tuning of VLMs. arXiv (2023)
69. Ousidhoum, N., et al.: Probing toxic content in pre-trained LLMs. In: ACL (2021)
70. Petryk, S., Dunlap, L., Nasseri, K., Gonzalez, J.E., Darrell, T., Rohrbach, A.: On guiding visual attention with language specification. In: IEEE/CVF CVPR (2022)
71. Poppi, S., et al.: Safe-clip: removing NSFW concepts from VLMs. arXiv (2023)
72. Qi, X., et al.: Visual adversarial examples jailbreak aligned LLMs. In: AAAI (2024)

73. Quadrianto, N., Sharmanska, V., Thomas, O.: Discovering fair representations in the data domain. In: IEEE/CVF CVPR, pp. 8227–8236 (2019)
74. Retzlaff, C.O., et al.: Human-in-the-loop reinforcement learning: A survey and position on requirements, challenges, and opportunities. JAIR **79**, 359–415 (2024)
75. Sathe, A., Jain, P., Sitaram, S.: A unified framework and dataset for assessing gender bias in vision-language models. arXiv (2024)
76. Schick, T., Udupa, S., Schütze, H.: Self-diagnosis and self-debiasing: a proposal for reducing corpus-based bias in NLP. ACL **9**, 1408–1424 (2021)
77. Seth, A., et al.: DeAR: debiasing VLMs with additive residuals. In: CVPR (2023)
78. Shayegani, E., Dong, Y., Abu-Ghazaleh, N.: Jailbreak in pieces: Compositional adversarial attacks on multi-modal language models. In: The Twelfth ICLR (2023)
79. Smith, B., Farinha, M., Hall, S.M., Kirk, H.R., et al.: Balancing the picture: debiasing vision-language datasets with synthetic contrast sets. arXiv (2023)
80. Song, C., Shmatikov, V.: Overlearning reveals sensitive attributes. arXiv (2019)
81. Song, C., et al.: Information leakage in embedding models. In: SIGSAC (2020)
82. Tao, X., et al.: ImgTrojan: jailbreaking VLMs with one image. arXiv (2024)
83. Turek, M.: Explainable artificial intelligence (XAI). DARPA (2018)
84. Wang, F., Zhou, Y., Wang, S., et al.: Multi-granularity cross-modal alignment for generalized medical visual representation learning. In: NIPS, vol. 35 (2022)
85. Wang, J., Liu, Y., Wang, X.E.: Are gender-neutral queries really gender-neutral? mitigating gender bias in image search. arXiv (2021)
86. Wang, J., Hu, X., Hou, W., Chen, H., Zheng, R., et al.: On the robustness of ChatGPT: an adversarial and out-of-distribution perspective. arXiv (2023)
87. Wehrmann, J., Kolling, C., Barros, R.C.: Adaptive cross-modal embeddings for image-text alignment. In: Proceedings of AAAI, vol. 34, pp. 12313–12320 (2020)
88. Welbl, J., et al.: Challenges in detoxifying language models. arXiv (2021)
89. Wen, J., et al.: A survey on FL: challenges and applications. IJMLC **14**(2) (2023)
90. Wen, Y., Marchyok, L., Hong, S., Geiping, J., et al.: Privacy backdoors: enhancing membership inference through poisoning pre-trained models. arXiv (2024)
91. Wu, Q., Zhao, M., He, Y., et al.: Towards reporting bias in VL datasets: bimodal augmentation by decoupling object-attribute association. arXiv (2023)
92. Xu, C., He, Z., He, Z., McAuley. J.: Leashing the inner demons: self-detoxification for language models. In: AAAI, vol. 36, pp. 11530–11537 (2022)
93. Yang, K., Qinami, K., et al.: Towards fairer datasets: filtering and balancing the distribution of the people subtree in the ImageNet hierarchy. In: ACM FAccT (2019)
94. Yao, A.C.C.: How to generate and exchange secrets. In: IEEE SFCS (1986)
95. Yeom, S., Giacomelli, I., Fredrikson, M., Jha, S.: Privacy risk in machine learning: analyzing the connection to overfitting. In: IEEE 31st CSF, pp. 268–282 (2018)
96. Yermilov, O., Raheja, V., Chernodub, A.: Privacy-and utility-preserving NLP with anonymized data: a case study of pseudonymization. arXiv (2023)
97. Zang, Y., Goh, H., Susskind, J., Huang, C.: Overcoming the pitfalls of vision-language model finetuning for OOD generalization. arXiv (2024)
98. Zhang, H., Lu, A.X., Abdalla, M., McDermott, M.B.A., et al.: Hurtful words: quantifying biases in clinical contextual word embeddings. In: ACM CHIL (2020)
99. Zhang, H., Shao, W., Liu, H., et al.: Avibench: towards evaluating the robustness of large vision-language model on adversarial visual-instructions. arXiv (2024)
100. Zhang, M., Chunara, R.: Leveraging clip for inferring sensitive information and improving model fairness. arXiv (2024)
101. Zhang, X., et al.: On the OOD generalization of MLLMs. arXiv (2024)

102. Zhou, A., et al.: Distilling OOD robustness from foundation VLMs. In: NIPS (2024)
103. Zhou, Y., Li, X., et al.: Visual in-context learning for LVLMs. arXiv (2024)
104. Zong, Y., Bohdal, O., Yu, T., Yang, Y., Hospedales, T.: Safety fine-tuning at (almost) no cost: a baseline for vision large language models. arXiv (2024)

TIP: Predicting Tipping for User-Centered Misinformation Prevention

Youval Kashuv[1(✉)], Raed Alharbi[2], and My T. Thai[1]

[1] Department of Computer and Information Science and Engineering, University of Florida, Gainesville, FL 32611, USA
youval.kashuv@ufl.edu, mythai@cise.ufl.edu

[2] College of Computing and Informatics, Saudi Electronic University, Riyadh 11673, Saudi Arabia
ri.alharbi@seu.edu.sa

Abstract. Addressing misinformation in the digital age poses a complex challenge with significant societal implications, as it continues to influence critical events such as elections and pandemic responses. Despite extensive research, misinformation remains a pressing threat, largely because current mitigation strategies emphasize detection accuracy without fully addressing the social and behavioral perspectives of users. This paper proposes a novel approach, treating information as a social norm and tracking its evolution at the individual user level. By targeting specific users who are more susceptible to adopting certain norms, this paper offers a more effective approach to combating misinformation. To accomplish this, a temporal graph neural network is trained to predict the tipping points of individual users, equipped with projection operators capable of forecasting user behavior in real time. To our knowledge, this paper represents the first successful attempt to predict individual tipping points in a real-world setting.

Keywords: Deep learning · TGNNs · Social norms · Predicting tipping

1 Introduction

The emergence of social media platforms in the 2000s created unprecedented opportunities for communication and information sharing. However, over the past decade, these platforms have become key channels for the spread of misinformation and disinformation. In fact, research has demonstrated that false information disseminates more rapidly, widely, and deeply than factual content on social media platforms [20]. Because misinformation exerts substantial influence on global politics and economies [2,6], it is crucial to develop proactive measures that counteract the growing threats posed by misinformation.

J. Kertesz et al. (Eds.): CSoNet 2024, LNCS 15417, pp. 86–97, 2025.
https://doi.org/10.1007/978-981-96-6389-7_8

A common approach to addressing these threats, known as pre-bunking, entails preemptively debunking misinformation online before it spreads globally. However, attempting to debunk every inaccurate tweet or comment within an online social network (OSN) is resource-intensive and inefficient, with no assurance that the misinformation being addressed would have reached a wide audience [5,15]. Regardless of the costs, pre-bunking has proven to be a suboptimal strategy. Research indicates that repeated corrections, particularly when poorly timed, can result in user fatigue and reduced overall effectiveness [5]. Moreover, studies show that individuals often ignore corrections that contradict their pre-existing beliefs [22], indicating that even with extensive debunking efforts, misinformation will continue to spread if it aligns with users' biases. In some instances, debunking can backfire, increasing engagement with low-quality or toxic content, suggesting that public corrections may inadvertently reinforce rather than combat misinformation [17]. Another approach focuses on misinformation that has already gained traction, but research has shown that intervening at this stage is often too late to be effective [16].

The findings from these studies suggest an alternative and potentially more effective strategy: targeting individuals. By focusing on *who* is susceptible to believing certain information and *when* to start an intervention at the user-level, increasing the likelihood of that individual building resistance to the misinformation. In fact, a user-centric approach directly address many of the challenges previously mentioned. First, it reduces the need for repeated corrections and allows for optimal timing by identifying when a user is most likely to adopt certain information. Second, personalized messages can address individual biases more effectively and at a timely manner. Third, by targeting misinformation on a personal level, public corrections-and the risk of unintentionally reinforcing false information-can be avoided. Fourth, this approach can reach users who may not have been reached by credible news outlets. Ultimately, addressing misinformation at the individual level could more effectively halt its spread and mitigate its harmful consequences, all while minimizing unintended outcomes. Unfortunately, this approach is complex and under-researched.

This paper aims to tackle the above challenges by treating information as a social norm and predicting the tipping points of individual users. Social norms are shared standards of acceptable behavior within groups. Recent studies have demonstrated that as local social norms spread, they may reach a critical point in time known as a tipping point [3,8] in which the acceptance of a social norm accelerates dramatically. Following this phase, the norm expands beyond local communities and enters the broader societal context [8]. To effectively prevent the spread of misinformation by targeting specific users, it is essential to accurately predict when these users are likely to adopt the norm. If intervention occurs too early or too late, the efforts risk losing effectiveness. Therefore, accurately forecasting users' tipping points ahead of time is of paramount importance for mitigating the spread of misinformation.

While this paper focuses on misinformation as a case study, the proposed approach extends beyond this specific domain. The methodology presented here can be applied to track and predict the adoption of any emerging opinions, beliefs, or social norms within online networks. This broader applicability makes our framework valuable for understanding various social phenomena, from consumer preferences and political opinions to cultural trends and social movements. By treating information adoption as a social norm-forming process, our approach provides insights into how any new ideas or beliefs propagate through social networks, regardless of their nature or content.

The remainder of this paper is structured as follows. Section 2 presents the background information and formally define our problem. Section 3 details our solution, a temporal graph neural network with a novel community-module to predict the tipping point of individual users. The robustness of our model is evaluated in Sect. 4 and finally the paper is concluded in Sect. 5.

2 Preliminaries and Problem Definition

2.1 Predicting Tipping

Identifying the right individuals and the optimal timing is critical for preventing the spread of negative norms at the user level. Goel *et al.* [12] analyzed large-scale communication networks of over 100 million individuals, demonstrating that social data significantly improves the prediction of personal actions. Building on this, Abbasi *et al.* [1] introduced a framework aimed at enhancing prediction accuracy in domains such as marketing and e-commerce. In controlled environments, Andreoni *et al.* [3] conducted large-scale lab experiments using a threshold model, accurately predicting norm changes %96 of the time.

However, real-world networks are far more intricate, and simply predicting a norm change is insufficient. Key to a user-centric approach for mitigating negative norms is identifying both the most susceptible individuals and the critical timing of their behavior. Gao *et al.* [10] successfully predicted susceptibility to norm adoption based on user profiles, but their model overlooked the evolving nature of user characteristics and dynamic network structures, resulting in the loss of essential structural insights. Moreover, while their approach identifies vulnerable users, it does not predict *when* an individual will adopt a norm-equally crucial information for timely intervention. Furthermore, their model is not continuous in time, necessitating retraining with new data.

To our knowledge, this work is the first to predict individual users' tipping points in real-world environments, focusing on social networks and their topology. While previous studies have explored similar concepts of predicting user behavior from online interaction data, our approach is distinct in its focus and methodology. Our work utilizes a temporal graph neural network to deliver a framework that identifies both *who* and *when* in real time.

2.2 Dynamic Graphs and Temporal Graph Neural Networks

A graph $G = (V, E)$ consists of a set of nodes V and a set of edges E. Dynamic graphs, which evolve over time, are typically classified into two main

Table 1. Datasets

M	Nodes	Interactions	proportion of positive labels
3	8,748	42,955	.1121
5	8,996	69,598	.0448
10	9,146	102,779	.0068

categories: Discrete-Time Dynamic Graphs (DTDGs) and Continuous-Time Dynamic Graphs (CTDGs). A DTDG, $G = \{G^{(i)}\}_{i=1}^{n} = \{(V^{(t)}, E^{(t)})\}_{i=1}^{n}$, represents a sequence of n static graph snapshots captured at specific time intervals. In contrast, CTDGs are more flexible and can be modeled as a sequence of timestamped events, which may include node additions/deletions, edge additions or deletions, and transformations of node or edge features. This study focuses on learning from CTDGs, specifically those involving node and edge addition events.

Temporal Graph Neural Networks (TGNNs) are a class of deep learning models designed to learn from dynamic graph data. These models extend traditional Graph Neural Networks (GNNs) by incorporating a recurrent neural network (RNN)-based updater, such as a GRU [9] or LSTM [13], to handle the temporal aspect of the data. In this work, we leverage the Temporal Graph Network (TGN) introduced by Rossi *et al.* [18] as a foundational model for learning from timestamped interactions in CTDGs, building on this architecture to suit our specific objectives.

2.3 Problem Formulation

Definition 1. *(Predicting user tipping) Consider a set of users V and let a timestamped edge $e = (u, v, t, \mathbf{f})$ represent a directed interaction from user u to user v at time t with features $\mathbf{f}$. Given a sequence of timestamped edges $E = \{e_1, e_2, \cdots, e_n\}$, the goal is to approximate a function $\Gamma : V \times [0, \infty] \rightarrow \{0, 1\}$ that determines if a user $u \in V$ will be tipped by time $t \in [0, \infty]$.*

Definition 2. *(User Tipping) A user has tipped if their last $M \in \mathbb{N}$ consecutive interactions have all supported/propagated the information of interest. We assume that once a user has tipped, they cannot untip.*

Challenges. Predicting individual tipping points presents several challenges due to the multifaceted nature of human behavior and the dynamic structure of social networks. Individual actions are influenced by a combination of social, psychological, and contextual factors, making behavioral shifts difficult to anticipate. Furthermore, social norms themselves evolve over time, with interactions between individuals generating complex cascading effects. Accurately modeling these temporal and network-dependent dynamics to predict when a significant behavioral shift will occur remains a significant challenge in this field.

This paper addresses these challenges by developing a TGNN integrated with a novel community module and learnable projection operators. The TGNN captures temporal dependencies in social interactions, allowing the model to learn evolving patterns in user behavior over time. The community module enhances this by identifying and leveraging the influence of tightly-knit user groups, which are critical in shaping social norms. Additionally, the learned projection operators allow for forecasting future behavior by mapping historical interaction dynamics, enabling the model to predict future tipping points with greater precision. This combined approach accounts for both individual interactions and broader community-level dynamics, ensuring more accurate predictions of behavioral shifts.

3 TIP Model Overview

Social norm dynamics are incredibly complex and not clearly understood. However, one thing is clear: since norms spread through interactions, the properties of both the user and their neighbors must be taken into account to learn a robust representation of individual tipping. To successfully achieve such a representation, TIP, our proposed model is composed of a User-Interaction module and a Community module, each of which essential for the model's high performance and are visualized in Fig. 1.

3.1 User-Interaction Module

When a user u initiates an interaction with user v, rich and expressive features must be constructed that take into account both u's information, v's information, and the text in the tweet.

TGN Block Interaction Tracking. A temporal graph network (TGN) designed by [18] is employed with a projection operator introduced by [14] to learn temporal-spatial embeddings for users that are continuous in time. To prevent overfitting, the TGN block is pre-trained on message link prediction [14], and user embeddings are projected into the future via the following formula:

$$\text{emb}_*(u, t) = \langle 1 + \Delta t \mathbf{W}^* \, , z_u^* \rangle$$

where Δt is the time difference since u's last interaction, z_u^* is u's current memory in model component $*$, and W^* is learned during pre-training for the TGN block and during training for the other two model components. To prevent data leakage, projection uses the user's memory only updated up to the current batch. Only after computing the loss is the memory updated with interactions from the current batch. Later in inference, predictions for u are made by first projecting their learned embedding and then concatenating with the other features before feeding into a decoder.

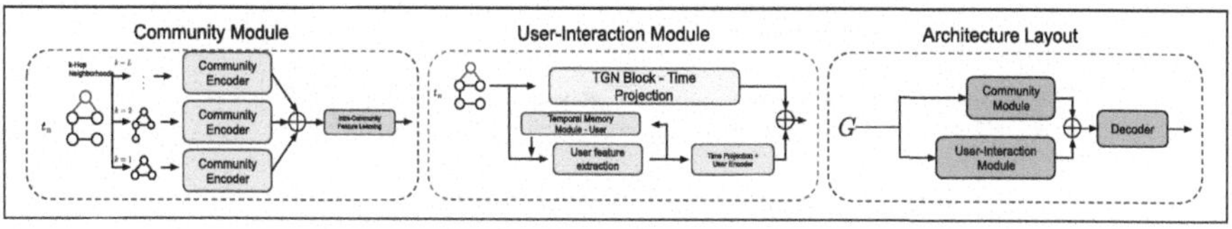

Fig. 1. Visualization of different model components, including the community module (left), user-interaction module (center), and architectural layout (right).

User Feature Extraction. These features encode both the structural attributes of u and its neighbors as well the intensity and timestamp of interactions between u and $N(u)$. The approach introduced by [4] is adopted, beginning by computing the in, out, and total degree of u, and calling the tuple of these features

$$f_u^{deg} = (D_{in}(u), D_{out}(u), D_{total}(u)).$$

Next, the same features for u's immediate neighbors are calculated and fed through a set of aggregation functions to construct structural embeddings of u's neighbors f_u^{neigh}:

$$AGG = \{\bar{x}, \max(x), \min(x), \sum x, \sigma(x)\}$$

where AGG consists of average, maximum, minimum, summation, and standard deviation respectively. AGG is similarly applied on the sets of incoming, outgoing, and total edges between u and $N(u)$, as well as on the actual textual embeddings calculated using a bert model [21], giving us f_u^{edge} and f_u^{text} respectively. Finally, AGG is applied on the timestamps of interactions between u and $N(u)$ to obtain z_u^{time}. These features are all concatenated together to obtain

$$f_u^{user} = [f_u^{deg}||f_u^{neigh}||f_u^{edge}||f_u^{text}||f_u^{time}].$$

Again, to prevent data leakage, prediction uses $f_u^{stats}(t^-)$, the user's extracted features from the previous batch. Afterwards, $\text{MEMORY}_{\text{user}}$ is updated using a GRU,

$$\text{MEMORY}_{\text{user}}(u) = \text{GRU}_{\text{user}}(f_u^{user}(t), f_u^{user}(t^-)).$$

After updating $\text{MEMORY}_{\text{user}}$ and before feeding into the final decoder, the user's features are projected and embeded into a latent space using

$$z_u^{user}(t) = \text{MLP}_{\text{user}}(\text{emb}_{\text{user}}(f_u^{user}, t)).$$

3.2 Community Module

Experimental evidence has demonstrated that community structure can affect an individual's susceptibility to information [7]. To leverage this insight and

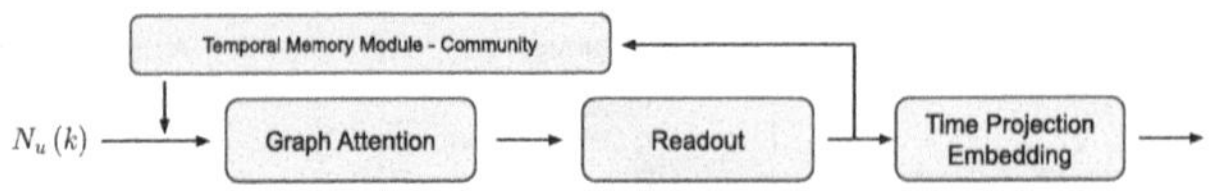

Fig. 2. Visualization of community encoder

enhance predictive accuracy, a novel module is designed to encode community structure at varying depths.

Let $K = (k_1, k_2, \cdots, k_i)$ be a hyperparameter representing the hops of interest, and let $N_u(k,t)$ denote the k-hop neighborhood of user u at time t, i.e., the set of users reachable from u by traversing k edges that occurred before time t. To mitigate sparsity, all edges are treated as undirected when calculating $N_u(k,t)$. Upon observing an interaction $e = (u, v, t)$, $N_u(K,t) = (N_u(k,t))_{\forall k \in K}$ is calculated. For each neighborhood, a subgraph is constructed comprised of interactions between users in the neighborhood that occurred at or before time t. At the time of computation, each node in each subgraph is also given a one-hot encoding of whether they have tipped and a measure of how close the user is to tipping, calculated as:

$$P_{tip} = \max\left(0, \frac{\#\text{positive posts} - \#\text{negative posts}}{M}\right),$$

where positive posts indicate tipping behavior and M is the tipping point threshold. Note that $0 \leq P_{tip} \leq 1$ as users are no longer tracked post tipping.

These subgraphs are each fed into their own GNN block followed by a readout layer to generate embeddings representative of u's local community structure at different depths. These learnable embeddings are denoted as

$$z_u^{comm,k} = \text{Readout}(\text{GNN}(G_u(k,t))), \quad \forall k \in K,$$

with z_u^{comm} representing the concatenation of learned embeddings over K. During testing, we find that using a GAT [19] combined with sum-pooling leads to optimal results. Once again, to prevent data leakage, prediction uses $z_u^{comm}(t^-)$ and afterwards $\text{MEMORY}_{\text{comm}}$ is updated using a GRU.

As before, after updating $\text{MEMORY}_{\text{comm}}$ and before feeding into the final decoder, the user's community embedding are projected and fed through an MLP to extract inter-community features from the intra-community embeddings:

$$z_u^{comm}(t) = \text{MLP}_{\text{comm}}(\text{emb}_{\text{comm}}(z_u^{comm}, t)).$$

MLP_{comm} is essential to restrict the model's attention to community level features before learning their interplay with user-interaction level features. Note that in the community module, each community encoder for different values of k learns is own GRU and projection operator. The layout of a single community encoder can be seen in Fig. 2.

3.3 Training and Inference

To obtain a label for a user u, embeddings learned are first concatenated,

$$z_u = [z_u^{user}||z_u^{TGN}||z_u^{comm}],$$

and then fed it into a MLP while minimizing a cross-entropy loss. The entire system is trained in an end to end fashion with a standard batching algorithm.

During inference for user u, u's memory from each module is projected into the future to the time of interest T before concatenating and feeding into the learned decoder as before. After training, the model can be iteratively queried to obtain the approximate time to tipping of any user given a desired threshold.

Table 2. AUC for Dynamic Node Classification Task

Model	M = 3	M = 5	M = 10
TGN	0.561	0.615	0.555
TGN+user	0.672	0.681	0.667
TGN+comm	0.622	0.698*	0.760*
TIP	0.684*	0.720*	0.823*

* indicates statistically significant improvement when using novel community module. All averages had margins of error for 95% confidence interval < 0.01

4 Experimental Evaluation

Datasets. We begin with raw tweets posted between Nov 1, 2020 and Nov 30, 2020, extracted using Twitter's Streaming API, and filter for tweets related to COVID-19 vaccines as in [11]. Tweets are then classified as pro/anti vaccine using an LSTM. A CTDG is then constructed by making destination nodes users who were mentioned in the tweet itself. Hugging Face's Bert model [21] is then used to generate textual embeddings for each tweet. Operating under the assumption that tipping is irreversible, interactions originating from tipped users are not tracked for boosted efficiency in training. Using values of $M = 3, 5, 10$, we construct three final datasets. For a description of each, see Table 1.

TIP is evaluated experimentally on the three datasets described above, comparing model performance with and without certain components. The TGN Block is used alone as the baseline. For all tasks and datasets, the same 70%-15%-15% chronological split is performed as in Xu et al. (2020), with a patience of 5. Additionally, model performance is compared over different train-val-test splits. For these experiments, the first X% is used as train, the following 15% as val, and the rest as test. As the value of M becomes more refined in defining tipping points (e.g., M=10), positive labels tend to cluster near the dataset's end, leading to fewer positive instances as the training set size decreases. This makes achieving good results exponentially harder. Similarly, smaller values of M (e.g., M=3,5) present their own challenges, as inferring a user's genuine stance from just a few interactions leads to high uncertainty and noise - resulting in increased false positives where brief sequences of supportive interactions may not reflect true conviction (Table 2).

Results demonstrate that the novel community module significantly enhances model robustness across two critical scenarios: (1) when both positive instances and training data become scarce due to larger M values pushing tipping points towards the dataset's end, and (2) when dealing with the inherent noise and uncertainty of smaller M values where genuine ideological shifts must be distinguished from transient interaction patterns. Model robustness is also evaluated across various embedding dimensions and batch sizes.

Performance Evaluation. Table 3 shows results comparing model performance with and without certain components. These experiments were run using an embedding dimension of 64 and a batch size of 100 for $M = 3$ and $M = 5$. For $M = 10$, a batch size of 50 was used to avoid out-of-memory errors. As the value of M increases, the model's performance improves. While it becomes easier to differentiate between tipping and non-tipping characteristics as M becomes more refined, the task grows more difficult due to the reduced percentage of positive labels. For $M = 5$ and $M = 10$, we observe a statistically significant improvement when incorporating the community module, both with and without user-level features.

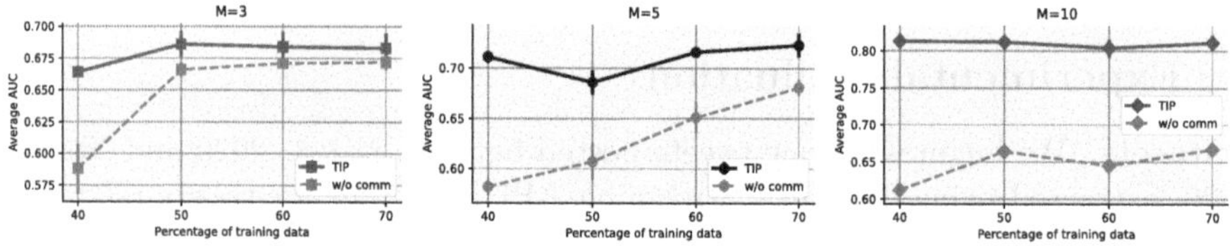

Fig. 3. Robustness to various train-val-test splits.

Figure 3 displays model performance across various train/val/test splits. Observe that the community module proves crucial for maintaining robustness as the training set size and number of positive instances decrease. In real-world scenarios, it is essential to identify emerging norms early to allow enough time for intervention before tipping occurs, making robustness to smaller training sets vital. From left to right, the figure displays performance for $M = 3/5/10$, with the model's performance without the community module shown in grey. The model consistently performs better with the community module, except for the 70-15-15 split with $M = 3$, where the margins of error overlap.

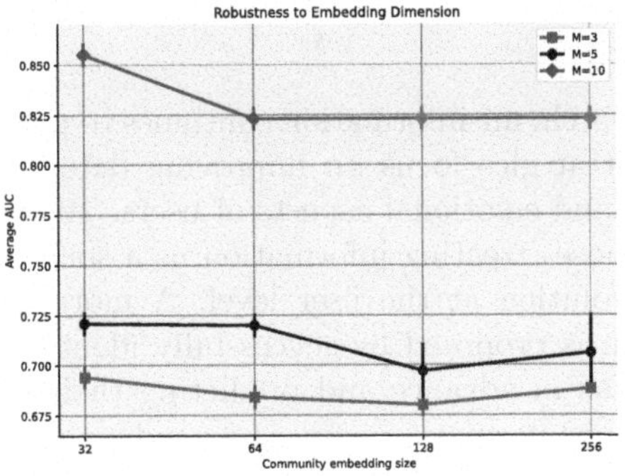

Fig. 4. Robustness to community embedding dimension for $M = 3/5/10$. (Color figure online)

Figure 4 displays the model's performance robustness across different embedding dimensions, a key factor for scalability. For billion-scale graphs, maintaining performance with smaller embedding sizes is crucial for reducing memory usage. The plot shows that TIP remains robust even with community embedding dimensions as small as 32. Grey points in the figure indicate instances where the program ran out of memory and should be disregarded.

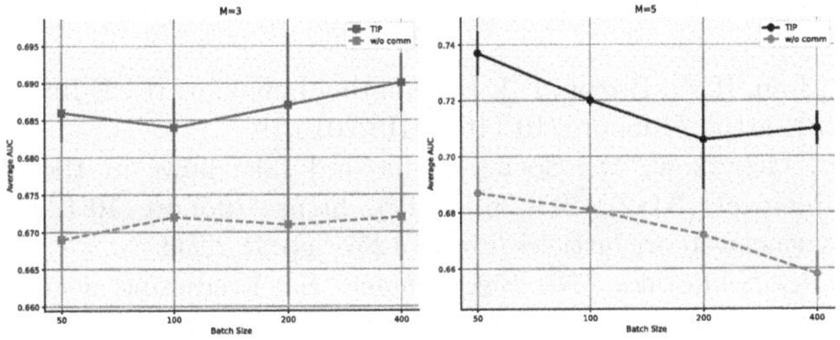

Fig. 5. Robustness to batch sizes of 50/100/200/400. For M=3/5, TIP is robust for batch sizes ≤400.

Finally, Fig. 5 illustrates TIP's performance robustness across batch sizes. Just as smaller embedding dimensions help conserve memory, larger batch sizes reduce computational demands by enabling faster training through parallelization. This can significantly shorten the time between norm identification and user inference. As shown, TIP maintains robustness across various batch sizes, with a batch size of 400 offering a notable 3.8x computational boost with only a marginal performance loss.

5 Conclusion

Despite extensive research, misinformation continues to pose a significant threat, as most mitigation strategies focus on improving detection accuracy without addressing the social and emotional aspects of users. To overcome these limitations, this paper proposes treating information as a social norm while tracking and predicting its evolution at the user level. A more effective way of combating misinformation is proposed by successfully identify users who are likely to adopt certain norms in advance and predicting their tipping points. While demonstrated using misinformation as a case study, this approach generalizes to predicting the adoption of any emerging opinions or social norms in online networks. TIP achieves high performance with M as small as 5 and is robust to train set size, community embedding dimension, and batch size. To our knowledge, this is the first successful attempt at predicting individual tipping points in a real-world setting.

Acknowledgments. This work was supported in part by the National Science Foundation Program under award No. 2323794.

Disclosure of Interests. The authors have no competing interests to declare that are relevant to the content of this article.

References

1. Abbasi, A., Lau, R.Y., Brown, D.E.: Predicting behavior. IEEE Intell. Syst. **30**(3), 35–43 (2015). https://doi.org/10.1109/MIS.2015.19
2. Allcott, H., Gentzkow, M.: Social media and fake news in the 2016 election. J. Econ. Perspect. **31**(2), 211–36 (2017). https://doi.org/10.1257/jep.31.2.211, https://www.aeaweb.org/articles?id=10.1257/jep.31.2.211
3. Andreoni, J., Nikiforakis, N., Siegenthaler, S.: Predicting social tipping and norm change in controlled experiments. Proc. Natl. Acad. Sci. **118**(16), e2014893118 (2021). https://doi.org/10.1073/pnas.2014893118, https://www.pnas.org/doi/abs/10.1073/pnas.2014893118
4. Banerjee, A., Zhou, Z.H., Papalexakis, E.E., Riondato, M.: Proceedings of the 2022 SIAM International Conference on Data Mining (SDM). Society for Industrial and Applied Mathematics, Philadelphia, PA (2022). https://doi.org/10.1137/1.9781611977172, https://epubs.siam.org/doi/abs/10.1137/1.9781611977172
5. Bayiz, Y.E., Topcu, U.: Prebunking design as a defense mechanism against misinformation propagation on social networks (2023). https://arxiv.org/abs/2311.14200
6. Bovet, A., Makse, H.A.: Influence of fake news in twitter during the 2016 us presidential election. Nat. Commun. **10**(1), 7 (2019). https://doi.org/10.1038/s41467-018-07761-2
7. Centola, D.: The spread of behavior in an online social network experiment. Science **329**(5996), 1194–1197 (2010). https://doi.org/10.1126/science.1185231, https://www.science.org/doi/abs/10.1126/science.1185231

8. Centola, D., Becker, J., Brackbill, D., Baronchelli, A.: Experimental evidence for tipping points in social convention. Science **360**, 1116–1119 (2018). https://doi.org/10.1126/science.aas8827
9. Cho, K., van Merrienboer, B., Bahdanau, D., Bengio, Y.: On the properties of neural machine translation: encoder-decoder approaches (2014). https://arxiv.org/abs/1409.1259
10. Gao, S., Wang, Y.: Can user characteristics predict norm adherence on social media? exploring user-centric misinformation interventions. In: Proceedings of the 21st ISCRAM Conference. ISCRAM Proceedings, vol. 21. ISCRAM (2024). https://iscram.org/proceedings/2024/
11. Gao, S., Wang, Y., Thai, M.T.: Investigating the dynamics of social norm emergence within online communities (2023). https://arxiv.org/abs/2301.00453
12. Goel, S., Goldstein, D.: Predicting individual behavior with social networks. Mark. Sci. **33** (2014). https://doi.org/10.1287/mksc.2013.0817
13. Hochreiter, S., Schmidhuber, J.: Long short-term memory. Neural Comput. **9**(8), 1735–1780 (1997). https://doi.org/10.1162/neco.1997.9.8.1735
14. Kumar, S., Zhang, X., Leskovec, J.: Predicting dynamic embedding trajectory in temporal interaction networks. CoRR abs/1908.01207 (2019). http://arxiv.org/abs/1908.01207
15. Lewandowsky, S., van der Linden, S.: Countering misinformation and fake news through inoculation and prebunking. Eur. Rev. Soc. Psychol. **32**, 348–384 (2021). https://doi.org/10.1080/10463283.2021.1876983
16. Lewandowsky, S., Ecker, U., Seifert, C.M., Schwarz, N., Cook, J.: Misinformation and its correction. Psychol. Sci. Public Interest **13**, 106–131 (2012). https://doi.org/10.1177/1529100612451018
17. Mosleh, M., Martel, C., Eckles, D., Rand, D.G.: Perverse downstream consequences of debunking: being corrected by another user for posting false political news increases subsequent sharing of low quality, partisan, and toxic content in a twitter field experiment. In: Proceedings of the 2021 CHI Conference on Human Factors in Computing Systems (2021). https://doi.org/10.1145/3411764.3445642
18. Rossi, E., Chamberlain, B., Frasca, F., Eynard, D., Monti, F., Bronstein, M.M.: Temporal graph networks for deep learning on dynamic graphs. CoRR abs/2006.10637 (2020). https://arxiv.org/abs/2006.10637
19. Veličković, P., Cucurull, G., Casanova, A., Romero, A., Liò, P., Bengio, Y.: Graph attention networks (2018). https://arxiv.org/abs/1710.10903
20. Vosoughi, S., Roy, D., Aral, S.: The spread of true and false news online. Science **359**(6380), 1146–1151 (2018). https://doi.org/10.1126/science.aap9559, https://www.science.org/doi/abs/10.1126/science.aap9559
21. Wolf, T., et al.: Huggingface's transformers: state-of-the-art natural language processing. CoRR abs/1910.03771 (2019). http://arxiv.org/abs/1910.03771
22. Zollo, F., Quattrociocchi, W.: Misinformation spreading on facebook (2017), https://arxiv.org/abs/1706.09494

A One-Dimensional Generative Diffusion Model for Network Traffic Dataset Generation

Hung Le Viet(✉), Khoa Tran Dinh Minh, Nhut Pham Quang, and Danh Nguyen Cong

The University of Danang - University of Science and Technology, Da Nang, Vietnam
hungle.dut@gmail.com

Abstract. Generative AI emerged as a powerful method for generating new data, which is famous for image, video, and text generation. For this inspiration, our study aims to leverage the Generative AI for Network Traffic Dataset Generation. This type of data is very important to cybersecurity, as it is used for detection, prediction, and classification tasks in the network traffic. Recent studies have utilized the variant of Generative AI models for generating Network Traffic Data, gaining considerable achievements. In our study, we proposed a novel approach using the One-Dimensional Generative Diffusion Model to generate the synthetic Network Traffic data. As a result, our proposed model surpasses the previous studies' models on the UNSW-NB15 dataset, with the Chi-Squared Test and Kolmogorov-Smirnov Test values being 0.863 and 0.838 respectively. Moreover, our proposed method considerably improves the performance of detecting attack activities of network traffic in terms of accuracy and F1-score, demonstrating its powers in cybersecurity.

Keywords: Network Traffic Generation · Generative AI · Generative Diffusion Model · 1-D U-Net

1 Introduction

Traditional machine learning and deep learning models have the ability to discriminate or predict the data by learning the existing training dataset [7,9,16]. Therefore, these models are applied to various tasks, such as detection, prediction, and classification tasks. To improve these tasks' performance, the diversity of the dataset as well as the quantity is very important. For this reason, some studies have proposed Generative Network models to generate new data. Generative Network is famous for its ability to generate new data by learning the distribution of existing data. For this motivation, we intend to apply generative models to generate network traffic data. Due to privacy reasons, network traffic data is not allowed to be published, showing the essential of generative data while realistic data is very limited and not diverse. Specifically, Nukavarapu et al. [11], Yukito et al. [12] and Anande et al. [2] have proposed variants of the GAN (Generative Adversarial Network) model to generate the synthetic network traffic data, while Shengzhe et al. [20] apply Autoregressive Model and Kholgh et al.

J. Kertesz et al. (Eds.): CSoNet 2024, LNCS 15417, pp. 98–109, 2025.
https://doi.org/10.1007/978-981-96-6389-7_9

[8] utilize the GPT-3 model to generate the synthetic network traffic data. Most previously mentioned studies just use GAN models for Synthetic Network Traffic Generation. Recently, the Generative Diffusion Model (GDM) has emerged as the Generative Network outperforming the other Generative Network models. GDM surpasses other generative models for tasks related to image, video, and audio generation, inspiring me to investigate and apply GDM for synthetic network data generation. In this study, we proposed a One-Dimensional Diffusion Model which has an architecture different from GAN models' architecture to generate Synthetic Network Traffic data. For the experiment, we use UNSW-NB15 [10] to evaluate models, based on Chi-Squared Test (CS Test) and Kolmogorov-Smirnov Test (KS Test). Both metrics are used to compare 2 independent random variables. The results show that our proposed model (One-Dimensional Generative Diffusion Model) outperforms the other models with the CS Test and KS Test metrics being 0.863 and 0.838 respectively. In the experiment, we evaluate classification models on the dataset with and without data generated by our proposed model in terms of accuracy and F1-score. Our contributions are summarized as follows:

- Propose a novel approach for synthetic network traffic data generation using the Generative Diffusion Model, which is called the One-Dimensional Generative Diffusion Model. Our proposed model surpasses the models previously proposed in recent studies on synthetic network traffic generation.
- Propose a simplified attention-based 1-D U-Net for the model
- Successfully apply the preprocessing method for our proposed model, considerably improving and stabilizing the performance.

2 Related Work

2.1 Generative AI

Unlike the traditional AI models discriminating the existing data, Generative Networks emerged as the ability to generate new data, based on the existing data. A lot of kinds of Generative Models were proposed with different architectures, such as GANs, AutoEncoder, VAE, VQ-VAE, VQ-GAN, Generative Diffusion Model, and other variants. AutoEncoder is one of the first proposed generative models with 2 key components, which includes an Encoder and a Decoder using CNN to compress input into lower-dimensional latent space and decode it from the compressed latent representation. Based on AutoEncoder, VAE (Variational AutoEncoder) [18] is the developed variant of AutoEncoder, which has the encoder outputting the parameters (mean and variance) of a probability distribution (usually a Gaussian) in the latent space. The architecture of VQ-VAE(Vector Quantised-Variational AutoEncoder) is similar to the figure for VAE and AutoEncoder but it uses the vector quantization method to transform continuous latent space into discrete latent space [15]. VQ-GAN [3] applies the Transformer, sequence to sequence model based on attention mechanism [17], in the latent space. Besides, the GAN (Generative Adversarial Network) has the

Discriminator and Generator which are implemented by the Learning Adversarial Mechanism. There are a lot of variants of the GAN model, some of which were applied in Synthetic Network Traffic Generation. Different from previously mentioned models, the Generative Diffusion Model [6] implements a very different architecture which includes Forward and Reverse Processes, surpassing the previous models in image and text generation tasks. For the superior performance of this model, we applied the variant of the Diffusion Model, the One-Dimensional version of the Diffusion Model, with the aim of generating the Network Traffic Data.

2.2 Synthetic Network Traffic Generation

The recent generative models only focus on generating the image [4], audio, text, and video, and a few were proposed to generate tabular data. Therefore, recent studies have utilized the Generative Network to generate the synthetic network traffic data. For example, Nukavarapu et al. [11], Yukito et al. [12] and Anande et al. [2] propose variants of the GANs model to generate the synthetic network traffic data, while Shengzhe et al. [20] apply Autoregressive Model for generating. In addition, Kholgh et al. [8] leverage the GPT-3 model to generate the synthetic network traffic data. These studies have gained considerable results. For this inspiration, we applied the Diffusion Model which hasn't been investigated for Network Traffic Data Generation previously, with the expectation of gaining outstanding performance.

3 Methodology

The GDM (Generative Diffusion Model) is known as a modern Generative model outperforming previously proposed models, which has 2 key processes including Forward Process and Reverse Process. For implementing the One-dimensional Generative Diffusion Model, we define variable x_0 as an input with M features, which means that variable $x_0 \in \mathbb{R}^{1 \times M}$ is a vector with the length of M, before feeding it into the Generative Diffusion Model (GDM).

Firstly, we define the Forward Process to get the gaussian noise x_T by iteratively adding noise $\epsilon_{t\in\{1,2,..,N\}}$to create the sequence of $x_1, x_2, ..., x_T$ as the following equation:

$$x_t = \sqrt{1 - b_t} x_{t-1} + \sqrt{b_t} \epsilon_t \tag{1}$$

ϵ_t is an independent standard Gaussian and b_t is the scalar parameter with the range of $(0, 1)$. This process is represented as:

$$q(\mathbf{x}_t \mid \mathbf{x}_{t-1}) = \mathcal{N}(\mathbf{x}_t; \sqrt{1 - b_t}\mathbf{x}_{t-1}, b_t\mathbf{I}) \tag{2}$$

An approximate posterior can express the Forward Process [6] as below:

$$q\left(\mathbf{x}_{1:T} \mid \mathbf{x}_0\right) = \prod_{t=1}^{T} q\left(\mathbf{x}_t \mid \mathbf{x}_{t-1}\right) \tag{3}$$

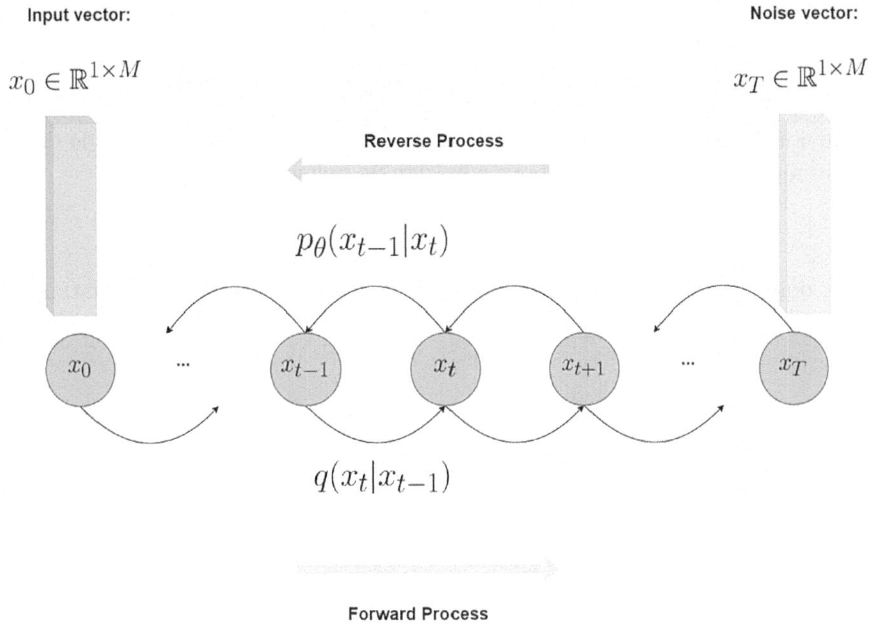

Fig. 1. The visual overview of the Training Algorithm of our proposed model

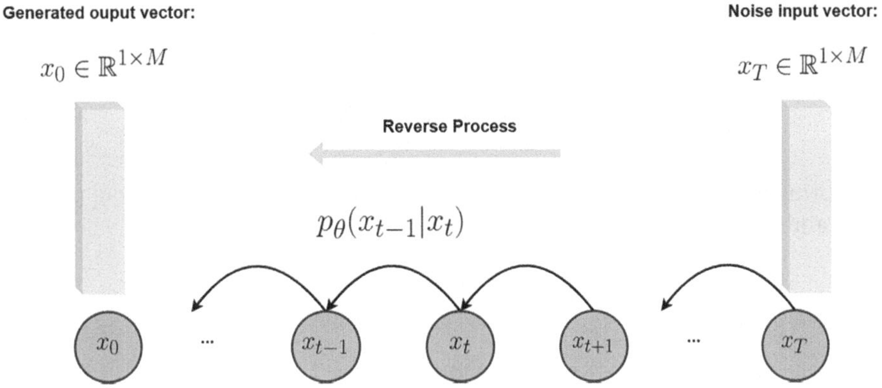

Fig. 2. The visual overview of the Generating Algorithm of our proposed model

We then define $a_t = 1 - b_t$ so the equation (1) can be rewritten as the following equation:

$$x_t = \sqrt{a_t} x_{t-1} + \sqrt{1 - a_t} \epsilon_t \tag{4}$$

Similar to equation (4), x_{t-1} is also calculated by the equation $x_{t-1} = \sqrt{a_{t-1}} \mathbf{x}_{t-2} + \sqrt{1 - a_{t-1}} \epsilon_{t-1}$.Therefore, equation (4) can be expressed as the following:

$$\begin{aligned}\mathbf{x}_t &= \sqrt{a_t}\left(\sqrt{a_{t-1}}\mathbf{x}_{t-2} + \sqrt{1-a_{t-1}}\boldsymbol{\epsilon}_{t-1}\right) + \sqrt{1-a_t}\boldsymbol{\epsilon}_t \\ &= \sqrt{a_t a_{t-1}}\mathbf{x}_{t-2} + \sqrt{a_t}\sqrt{1-a_{t-1}}\boldsymbol{\epsilon}_{t-1} + \sqrt{1-a_t}\boldsymbol{\epsilon}_t\end{aligned} \tag{5}$$

Obviously, we can consider $\sqrt{a_t}\sqrt{1-a_{t-1}}\boldsymbol{\epsilon}_{t-1} + \sqrt{1-a_t}\boldsymbol{\epsilon}_t$ as a single Gaussian [5] and then rewrite the above equation as below:

$$\mathbf{x}_t = \sqrt{a_t a_{t-1}}\mathbf{x}_{t-2} + \sqrt{1-a_t a_{t-1}}\boldsymbol{\epsilon}_{t,t-2} \tag{6}$$

By doing the above rule iteratively, we finally get the following equation:

$$\mathbf{x}_t = \sqrt{a_t a_{t-1}\dots a_{k+1}}\mathbf{x}_k + \sqrt{1-a_t a_{t-1}\dots a_{k+1}}\epsilon_{t,k} \tag{7}$$

For equation (7), we set $k=0$ and $\bar{a}_t = \prod_{i=1}^{t} a_i$. Therefore, equation (7) can be rewritten as the following:

$$\mathbf{x}_t = \sqrt{\bar{a}_t}\mathbf{x}_0 + \sqrt{1-\bar{a}_t}\bar{\boldsymbol{\epsilon}}_t \tag{8}$$

The probability of x_t given x_0 can be expressed by:

$$q(\mathbf{x}_t \mid \mathbf{x}_0) = \mathcal{N}\left(\mathbf{x}_t; \sqrt{\bar{a}_t}\mathbf{x}_0, (1-\bar{a}_t)\mathbf{I}\right) \tag{9}$$

Secondly, we define the Reverse Process to learn how to denoise the noise x_T, with the aim of predicting x_0 from a standard Gaussian x_T, depicted in Fig. 2. This process is represented by the following joint probability:

$$p_\theta(\mathbf{x}_{0:T}) = p(\mathbf{x}_T)\prod_{t=1}^{T} p_\theta(\mathbf{x}_{t-1} \mid \mathbf{x}_t) \tag{10}$$

Optimizing the usual variational bound on negative log-likelihood [6] perform the training process:

$$\mathbb{E}\left[-\log p_\theta(\mathbf{x}_0)\right] \leq \mathbb{E}_q\left[-\log \frac{p_\theta(\mathbf{x}_{0:T})}{q(\mathbf{x}_{1:T} \mid \mathbf{x}_0)}\right] := L \tag{11}$$

where the value of $q(\mathbf{x}_{1:T} \mid \mathbf{x}_0)$ is obviously below 1.

The expression L then can be expressed by the following, which was proved by the Sohl-Dickstein et al. [14]:

$$\begin{aligned}L = \mathbb{E}_q[&\underbrace{D_{\mathrm{KL}}(q(\mathbf{x}_T \mid \mathbf{x}_0) \| p(\mathbf{x}_T))}_{L_T} \\ &+ \sum_{t\geq 2}\underbrace{D_{\mathrm{KL}}(q(\mathbf{x}_{t-1} \mid \mathbf{x}_t, \mathbf{x}_0) \| p_\theta(\mathbf{x}_{t-1} \mid \mathbf{x}_t))}_{L_{t-1}} \underbrace{- \log p_\theta(\mathbf{x}_0 \mid \mathbf{x}_1)}_{L_0}]\end{aligned} \tag{12}$$

where L_T has no learnable parameter and we can get the better result without L_0, which is proved by Jonathan et al. [6]. So our aim is to optimize L_{t-1}. Then, we calculate $q(\mathbf{x}_{t-1} \mid \mathbf{x}_t, \mathbf{x}_0)$ by following steps:

$$q(\mathbf{x}_{t-1} \mid \mathbf{x}_t, \mathbf{x}_0) = \frac{q(\mathbf{x}_t \mid \mathbf{x}_{t-1}, \mathbf{x}_0)\, q(\mathbf{x}_{t-1} \mid \mathbf{x}_0)}{q(\mathbf{x}_t \mid \mathbf{x}_0)} \tag{13}$$

$$q(\mathbf{x}_{t-1} \mid \mathbf{x}_t, \mathbf{x}_0) = \frac{\mathcal{N}\left(\mathbf{x}_t; \sqrt{a_t}\mathbf{x}_{t-1}, (1-a_t)\mathbf{I}\right) \mathcal{N}\left(\mathbf{x}_{t-1}; \sqrt{a_{t-1}}\mathbf{x}_0, (1-\bar{a}_{t-1})\mathbf{I}\right)}{\mathcal{N}\left(\mathbf{x}_t; \sqrt{\bar{a}}\mathbf{x}_t\mathbf{x}_0, (1-\bar{a}_t)\mathbf{I}\right)} \tag{14}$$

Therefore, $q(\mathbf{x}_{t-1} \mid \mathbf{x}_t, \mathbf{x}_0)$ can be expressed by the following equation :

$$q(\mathbf{x}_{t-1} \mid \mathbf{x}_t, \mathbf{x}_0) = \mathcal{N}\left(\mathbf{x}_{t-1}; \tilde{\boldsymbol{\mu}}_t(\mathbf{x}_t, \mathbf{x}_0), \tilde{b}_t\mathbf{I}\right) \tag{15}$$

where $\tilde{\boldsymbol{\mu}}_t(\mathbf{x}_t, \mathbf{x}_0) = \frac{\sqrt{\bar{a}_{t-1}}b_t}{1-\bar{a}_t}\mathbf{x}_0 + \frac{\sqrt{a_t}(1-\bar{a}_{t-1})}{1-\bar{a}_t}\mathbf{x}_t$ and $\tilde{b}_t = \frac{1-\bar{a}_{t-1}}{1-\bar{a}_t}b_t$, the steps of the calculation were explained by Higham et al. [5].

We then introduce $p_\theta(\mathbf{x}_{t-1} \mid \mathbf{x}_t) = \mathcal{N}\left(\mathbf{x}_{t-1}; \boldsymbol{\mu}_\theta(\mathbf{x}_t, t), \sigma_t^2\mathbf{I}\right)$. Therefore, we can rewrite L_{t-1} as below:

$$L_{t-1} = \mathbb{E}_q\left[\frac{1}{2\sigma_t^2}\left\|\tilde{\boldsymbol{\mu}}_t(\mathbf{x}_t, \mathbf{x}_0) - \boldsymbol{\mu}_\theta(\mathbf{x}_t, t)\right\|^2\right] + C \tag{16}$$

$$L_{t-1} - C = \mathbb{E}_{\mathbf{x}_0,\epsilon}\left[\frac{1}{2\sigma_t^2}\left\|\tilde{\boldsymbol{\mu}}_t\left(\mathbf{x}_t(\mathbf{x}_0,\epsilon), \frac{1}{\sqrt{\bar{a}_t}}\left(\mathbf{x}_t(\mathbf{x}_0,\epsilon) - \sqrt{1-\bar{a}_t}\epsilon\right)\right)\right.\right. \\ \left.\left. - \boldsymbol{\mu}_\theta(\mathbf{x}_t(\mathbf{x}_0,\epsilon), t)\right\|\right] \tag{17}$$

$$L_{t-1} - C = \mathbb{E}_{\mathbf{x}_0,\epsilon}\left[\frac{1}{2\sigma_t^2}\left\|\frac{1}{\sqrt{a_t}}\left(\mathbf{x}_t(\mathbf{x}_0,\epsilon) - \frac{b_t}{\sqrt{1-\bar{a}_t}}\epsilon\right) - \boldsymbol{\mu}_\theta(\mathbf{x}_t(\mathbf{x}_0,\epsilon), t)\right\|^2\right] \tag{18}$$

Therefore, we need to satisfy the below equation to find the optimal variational bound, mentioned in equations (11) or (12):

$$\boldsymbol{\mu}_\theta(\mathbf{x}_t, t) = \frac{1}{\sqrt{a_t}}\left(\mathbf{x}_t - \frac{b_t}{\sqrt{1-\bar{a}_t}}\epsilon_\theta(\mathbf{x}_t, t)\right) \tag{19}$$

Subquently, we can calculate the $\mathbf{x}_{t-1} \sim p_\theta(\mathbf{x}_{t-1} \mid \mathbf{x}_t)$ value by the following equation:

$$\mathbf{x}_{t-1} = \frac{1}{\sqrt{a_t}}\left(\mathbf{x}_t - \frac{b_t}{\sqrt{1-\bar{a}_t}}\epsilon_\theta(\mathbf{x}_t, t)\right) + \sigma_t\mathbf{z} \tag{20}$$

where $\mathbf{z} \in N(0,1)$ is a standard gaussian distribution. So $L_{t-1} - C$ expression in equation (18) can be represented by the following equation:

$$L_{t-1} - C = \mathbb{E}_{\mathbf{x}_0,\epsilon}\left[\frac{b_t^2}{2\sigma_t^2 a_t(1-\bar{a}_t)}\left\|\epsilon - \epsilon_\theta\left(\sqrt{\bar{a}_t}\mathbf{x}_0 + \sqrt{1-\bar{a}_t}\epsilon, t\right)\right\|^2\right] \tag{21}$$

Simply because $\frac{b_t^2}{2\sigma_t^2 a_t(1-\bar{a}_t)}$ is supposed to be a constant expression, we now only need to optimize the variational bound by the following:

$$\mathcal{L}_t(\theta) = \mathbb{E}_{\mathbf{x}_0,t,\epsilon}\left[\left|\left|\epsilon - \epsilon_\theta\left(\sqrt{\bar{a}_t}\mathbf{x}_0 + \sqrt{1-\bar{a}_t}\epsilon, t\right)\right|\right|^2\right] \tag{22}$$

Leveraging equation (22), we can implement the training process as the following algorithm:

Training Algorithm
1: repeat
2: $\mathbf{x}_0 \in \mathbb{R}^{1\times M} \sim q(\mathbf{x}_0)$
3: $t \sim$ Uniform $(\{1, 2, \ldots, T\})$
4: $\epsilon \sim \mathrm{N}(\mathbf{0}, \mathbf{I})$
5: Take gradient step on $\left|\left|\epsilon - \epsilon_\theta\left(\sqrt{\bar{a}_t}\mathbf{x}_0 + \sqrt{1-\bar{a}_t}\epsilon, t\right)\right|\right|_2^2$
6: until converged

After training our 1-D GDM model, to generate the sample from noises, we need to implement the following algorithm based on the equation (20):

Generating Algorithm
1: $\mathbf{x}_T \in \mathbb{R}^{1\times M} \sim \mathrm{N}(\mathbf{0}, \mathbf{I})$
2: for $t = T, T-1, \ldots, 1$ do
3: $\mathbf{z} \sim N(0, \mathbf{I})$
4: $\mathbf{x}_{t-1} = \frac{1}{\sqrt{a_t}}\left(\mathbf{x}_t - \frac{1-a_t}{\sqrt{1-\bar{a}}}\epsilon_\theta\right) + \sigma_q(t)\mathbf{z}$
5: end for
6: return $\mathrm{x}_0 \in \mathbb{R}^{1\times M}$

Overall, the GDM model consists of a Training Algorithm and a Generating Algorithm, with certain missions. The Training Algorithm aims to add noises to the input and learn how to denoise its noise version, which includes both Forward and Reverse Processes. Meanwhile, the Generating Algorithm aims to generate a synthetic sample from a noise input by using only the Reverse Process. The Training and Generating Algorithms of our proposed model are depicted in Fig. 1 and Fig. 2 respectively.

Especially, the ϵ_θ is the function with parameter θ, representing the 1-D U-Net model, which means we use 1-D U-Net as a backbone. In this study, we proposed a simplified attention-based 1-D U-Net model [13], receiving the one-dimensional vector input. Our proposed attention-based 1-D U-Net is depicted in Fig. 3.

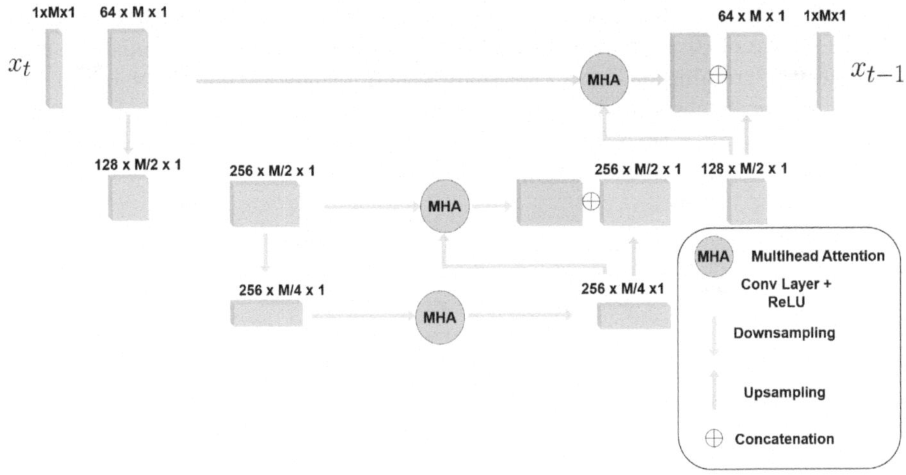

Fig. 3. The architecture of our simplified proposed attention-based 1-D U-Net model

4 Experiments

4.1 Dataset

In the experiment, we applied our model to the part of the UNSW-NB15 dataset [10] including 45 features and 257673 samples (the combination of train data and test data files from the dataset published in Kaggle website [1]). This dataset is depicted in Fig. 4 . The feature of the dataset consists of 2 types of data, numerical and categorical data, 4 features are categorical data and 41 features are numerical data. For the huge and diverse dataset, we can apply and evaluate generative models accurately. Overall, the Network Traffic data is considered tabular data with specific features. The dataset link is available at Kaggle [1]

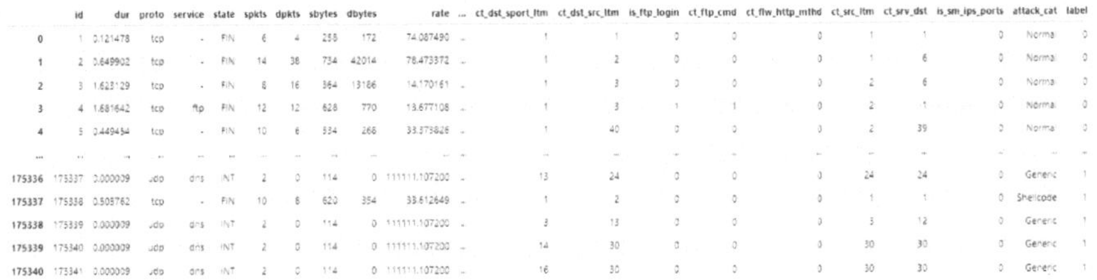

	id	dur	proto	service	state	spkts	dpkts	sbytes	dbytes	rate	...	ct_dst_sport_ltm	ct_dst_src_ltm	is_ftp_login	ct_ftp_cmd	ct_flw_http_mthd	ct_src_ltm	ct_srv_dst	is_sm_ips_ports	attack_cat	label
0	1	0.121478	tcp	-	FIN	6	4	258	172	74.087490	...	1	1	0	0	0	1	1	0	Normal	0
1	2	0.649902	tcp	-	FIN	14	38	734	42014	78.473372	...	1	2	0	0	0	1	6	0	Normal	0
2	3	1.623129	tcp	-	FIN	8	16	364	13186	14.170161	...	1	3	0	0	0	2	6	0	Normal	0
3	4	1.681642	tcp	ftp	FIN	12	12	628	770	13.677108	...	1	3	1	1	0	2	1	0	Normal	0
4	5	0.449454	tcp	-	FIN	10	6	534	268	33.373826	...	1	40	0	0	0	2	39	0	Normal	0
...	...	...	...	...	...	...	...	...	...	...	...	...	...	...	...	...	...	...	...	...	...
175336	175337	0.000009	udp	dns	INT	2	0	114	0	111111.107200	...	13	24	0	0	0	24	24	0	Generic	1
175337	175338	0.505762	tcp	-	FIN	10	8	620	354	33.612649	...	1	2	0	0	0	1	1	0	Shellcode	1
175338	175339	0.000009	udp	dns	INT	2	0	114	0	111111.107200	...	3	13	0	0	0	3	12	0	Generic	1
175339	175340	0.000009	udp	dns	INT	2	0	114	0	111111.107200	...	14	30	0	0	0	30	30	0	Generic	1
175340	175341	0.000009	udp	dns	INT	2	0	114	0	111111.107200	...	16	30	0	0	0	30	30	0	Generic	1

Fig. 4. The overview of UNSW-NB15 dataset

4.2 Data Preprocessing

Because the dataset contains categorical data, we apply the One-hot Encoder, a feature embedding method, to embed it into the one-hot vector, and thus it increases the number of columns in the dataset. This preprocessing method is depicted in Fig. 5. After embedding the categorical data, we normalize the data into the range of $(0, 1)$, which prevents the gradient explosion or vanishing and stabilizes the training process. The main reason for this is that the value in the dataset is sometimes very low around under 0.001, or very high up to 30000–40000. Besides, after the Generating Process, we scale the output and decode it into categorical data to get the final synthetic data.

Categorical data		One-hot vector								
proto		proto_tcp	proto_udp	proto_arp	proto_ospf	proto_icmp	proto_igmp	proto_rtp	proto_ddp	...
tcp		1.0	0.0	0.0	0.0	0.0	0.0	0.0	0.0	...
tcp		1.0	0.0	0.0	0.0	0.0	0.0	0.0	0.0	...
tcp		1.0	0.0	0.0	0.0	0.0	0.0	0.0	0.0	...
tcp		1.0	0.0	0.0	0.0	0.0	0.0	0.0	0.0	...
tcp	Feature Embedding	1.0	0.0	0.0	0.0	0.0	0.0	0.0	0.0	...
...		...	...	...	...	...	...	...	...	...
udp		0.0	1.0	0.0	0.0	0.0	0.0	0.0	0.0	...
tcp		1.0	0.0	0.0	0.0	0.0	0.0	0.0	0.0	...
udp		0.0	1.0	0.0	0.0	0.0	0.0	0.0	0.0	...
udp		0.0	1.0	0.0	0.0	0.0	0.0	0.0	0.0	...
udp		0.0	1.0	0.0	0.0	0.0	0.0	0.0	0.0	...

Fig. 5. The illustration of One-hot Encoder method for categorical data

4.3 Implementation Details

We assign the forward process variances to constant values that increase linearly, starting from $b_1 = 10^{-4}$ and ending at $b_T = 0.02$ and choose $T = 1000$. After applying the preprocessing method which includes one-hot encoding and normalization, the input has 205 features, meaning that the vector input has the shape of 1×205. So we have to add 3 zero variables at the end of the vector input and it then has the shape of 1×208, helping the input fit our proposed 1-D U-Net model. Therefore, the input of our model is $x_0 \in \mathbb{R}^{1 \times M}$ with $M = 208$.

4.4 Experimental Result

To demonstrate the performance of our proposed model, we compared ours to the original GAN, C-GAN, CTGAN, STAN, and Copula GAN. These are models which were utilized in the studies of Nukavarapu et al. [11], Shengzhe et al. [20], Yukito et al. [12] and Anande et al. [2]. Firstly, we use each model to generate 10000 synthetic samples. For the comparison of the performance of generative models, we compute the Chi-Squared Test (CS Test) and Kolmogorov-Smirnov Test (KS Test) of generated data with the real data, which are popularly used to compare the distribution between 2 independent random variables in the Probability Theory. The high CS Test and KS Test values demonstrate the good performance of the model. The higher the output of CSTest and KSTest functions are, the better performance will be. So we aim to compare the distribution of

Table 1. The comparison between our proposed model and other models based on CS Test and KS Test metrics

Model	Chi-Squared Test ↑	Kolmogorov-Smirnov Test ↑
GAN (Nukavarapu et al. [11])	0.289	0.323
C-GAN (Yukito et al. [12])	0.217	0.315
CTGAN (Lei Xu et al. [19])	0.424	0.613
STAN (Shengzhe et al. [20])	0.693	0.602
Copula GAN (Anande et al. [2])	0.814	0.732
Ours	**0.863**	**0.838**

Table 2. The validation accuracy and F1-Score of machine learning and deep learning models with and without generated dataset in two-label classification task (Normal and Attack categories)

Dataset (2 Classes)	Model	Accuracy(%)	F1-Score(%)
Without Generated Samples	Support Vector Machine	84.2	81.4
	K-Nearest Neighbors	82.1	76.2
	Decision Tree	**81.1**	78.2
	Multilayer Perceptron	86.8	84.1
With Generated Samples	Support Vector Machine	**85.4**	**82.9**
	K-Nearest Neighbors	**83.5**	**81.7**
	Decision Tree	80.9	**79.3**
	Multilayer Perceptron	**87.5**	**85.9**

10000 generated samples with the distribution of real data by using CS Test and KS Test metrics.

Depicted in Table 1, our proposed GDM model surpasses the GAN, C-GAN, CTGAN, STAN, and Copula GAN models with the CS Test value being 0.863 and the KS Test value being 0.838. Overall, our proposed model outperforms the other models in recent studies that apply Generative AI for Synthetic Network Traffic Generation.

Moreover, we do one more experiment to detect attack activities of the network traffic on the UNSW-NB15 dataset. Firstly, we aim to classify two classes, consisting of Normal and Attack. Number 0 represents the Normal category, while number 1 represents the Attack category, represented by the 'label' column in the UNSW-NB15 Dataset. To evaluate the performance of generative models, our experiment compares the performance of classification models with and without the dataset which is generated by our proposed model. Besides, we just take 30000 samples from the original dataset, having the same distribution as the original dataset. This aims to highlight the efficiency of 10000 generated samples. Additionally, we also classify 1 Normal category and 9 Attack categories by utilizing machine learning and deep learning models, labeled by

Table 3. The validation accuracy and F1-Score of machine learning and deep learning models with and without generated dataset in multi-label classification task (one Normal and multiple Attack categories)

Dataset (10 Classes)	Model	Accuracy(%)	F1-Score(%)
Without Generated Samples	Support Vector Machine	**81.9**	67.3
	K-Nearest Neighbors	**77.1**	65.2
	Decision Tree	79.1	69.4
	Multilayer Perceptron	80.7	63.3
With Generated Samples	Support Vector Machine	81.5	**70.2**
	K-Nearest Neighbors	76.4	**68.7**
	Decision Tree	**80.2**	**70.2**
	Multilayer Perceptron	**82.1**	**65.3**

the 'attack_cat' column in the UNSW-NB15 Dataset. For the training strategy, we divide the Train and Validation Set with a ratio of 7:3 respectively. The results in Table 2 and Table 3 show that most classification models - applied on Dataset with generated samples - achieve higher Accuracy and F1-Score than those applied on Dataset without generated samples.

5 Conclusion and Future Work

Recognizing the importance of Network Traffic Data, we applied the Generative Diffusion Model (GDM) for generating this data. Compared to previous studies on the Synthetic Network Traffic Generation, our study proposed a novel approach using the One-Dimensional Diffusion Model. This approach gains outstanding results with the CS Test value being 0.863 and the KS Test value being 0.838, outperforming the previous studies' models. This demonstrates its potential for Network Data Generation. Besides, our preprocessing method helps data fit our model well and considerably improves the performance of our proposed model. Our study will help improve the diversity of the Network Traffic Dataset as well as the number of the dataset, which encourages AI models to gain better performance in various tasks, such as detection, prediction, and classification tasks in cybersecurity. In the future, we have a plan to improve our proposed model by adding the conditional mechanism layer to our model.

References

1. Unsw_nb15. https://www.kaggle.com/datasets/mrwellsdavid/unsw-nb15
2. Anande, T.J., Al-Saadi, S., Leeson, M.S.: Generative adversarial networks for network traffic feature generation. Int. J. Comput. Appl. **45**(4), 297–305 (2023)
3. Esser, P., Rombach, R., Ommer, B.: Taming transformers for high-resolution image synthesis. In: Proceedings of the IEEE/CVF Conference on Computer Vision and Pattern Recognition, pp. 12873–12883 (2021)

4. Han, L., Hien, N., Huy, L.V., Hieu, N.V.: A deep learning model for multi-domain MRI synthesis using generative adversarial networks. Informatica **35**(2), 283–309 (2024)
5. Higham, C.F., Higham, D.J., Grindrod, P.: Diffusion models for generative artificial intelligence: an introduction for applied mathematicians. arXiv preprint arXiv:2312.14977 (2023)
6. Ho, J., Jain, A., Abbeel, P.: Denoising diffusion probabilistic models. Adv. Neural. Inf. Process. Syst. **33**, 6840–6851 (2020)
7. Hung, L.V., Binh, P., Minh Nhat, P., Van Hieu, N.: Enhanced attention-based multimodal deep learning for product categorization on e-commerce platform. In: Nguyen, N.T., Huynh, CP., Nguyen, T.T., Le-Khac, NA., Nguyen, QV. (eds.) The 13th Conference on Information Technology and its Applications, pp. 87–98. Springer Nature Switzerland, Cham (2024). https://doi.org/10.1007/978-3-031-74127-2_8
8. Kholgh, D.K., Kostakos, P.: PAC-GPT: a novel approach to generating synthetic network traffic with GPT-3. IEEE Access **11**, 114936–114951 (2023)
9. Le Viet, H., Ngoc, H.L.H., Minh, K.T.D., Van Hong, S.T.: A deep learning framework for gym-gesture recognition using the combination of transformer and 3D pose estimation. Cybern. Phys. **13**(2), 161–167 (2024)
10. Moustafa, N., Slay, J.: UNSW-NB15: a comprehensive data set for network intrusion detection systems (UNSW-NB15 network data set). In: 2015 Military Communications and Information Systems Conference (MilCIS), pp. 1–6. IEEE (2015)
11. Nukavarapu, S.K., Ayyat, M., Nadeem, T.: Miragenet-towards a GAN-based framework for synthetic network traffic generation. In: GLOBECOM 2022-2022 IEEE Global Communications Conference, pp. 3089–3095. IEEE (2022)
12. Onodera, Y., Takeshita, E., Kosugi, T., Suzuki, S.: Proposal of temporal feature layers for network traffic dataset generation using C-GAN. IEICE Commun. Express **13**, 319–322 (2024)
13. Petit, O., Thome, N., Rambour, C., Themyr, L., Collins, T., Soler, L.: U-Net transformer: self and cross attention for medical image segmentation. In: Lian, C., Cao, X., Rekik, I., Xu, X., Yan, P. (eds.) MLMI 2021. LNCS, vol. 12966, pp. 267–276. Springer, Cham (2021). https://doi.org/10.1007/978-3-030-87589-3_28
14. Sohl-Dickstein, J., Weiss, E., Maheswaranathan, N., Ganguli, S.: Deep unsupervised learning using nonequilibrium thermodynamics. In: International Conference on Machine Learning, pp. 2256–2265. PMLR (2015)
15. Van Den Oord, A., Vinyals, O., et al.: Neural discrete representation learning. In: Advances in Neural Information Processing Systems, vol. 30 (2017)
16. Van Huy, L., Tuong, N.H., Van Hieu, N.: Masked autoencoder-based self-supervised learning for forest plant classification. Cybern. Phys. **13**, 32–41 (2024)
17. Vaswani, A.: Attention is all you need. In: Advances in Neural Information Processing Systems (2017)
18. Wang, Y., Blei, D.: Variational bayes under model misspecification. In: Advances in Neural Information Processing Systems, vol. 32 (2019)
19. Xu, L., Skoularidou, M., Cuesta-Infante, A., Veeramachaneni, K.: Modeling tabular data using conditional GAN. In: Advances in Neural Information Processing Systems, vol. 32 (2019)
20. Xu, S., Marwah, M., Arlitt, M., Ramakrishnan, N.: STAN: synthetic network traffic generation with generative neural models. In: Wang, G., Ciptadi, A., Ahmadzadeh, A. (eds.) MLHat 2021. CCIS, vol. 1482, pp. 3–29. Springer, Cham (2021). https://doi.org/10.1007/978-3-030-87839-9_1

Pharmaceuticals Supply Chain Integrity: Ensuring the Authenticity of Drugs and Preventing Counterfeit Medicine by Leveraging Smart Contracts, NFT, IPFS, and Distributed Ledgers Technology

Phat T. Tran-Truong[1,2(✉)], Khanh H. Vo[3], Triet M. N.[3], Hieu M. D.[3], Hung N. N.[3], and Ngan K. T. N.[4]

[1] Department of Software Engineering, Faculty of Computer Science and Engineering, Ho Chi Minh City University of Technology (HCMUT), 268 Ly Thuong Kiet Street, District 10, Ho Chi Minh City, Vietnam
phatttt@hcmut.edu.vn

[2] Vietnam National University Ho Chi Minh City, Linh Trung Ward, Thu Duc District, Ho Chi Minh City, Vietnam

[3] FPT University, Can Tho City, Vietnam

[4] FPT Polytechnic, Can Tho City, Vietnam

Abstract. The pharmaceutical industry faces significant challenges in ensuring supply chain transparency, ethical sourcing, and data integrity. Traditional pharmaceuticals supply chain often falls short in providing the necessary traceability and accountability. This paper proposes a novel supply chain management system that leverages cutting-edge blockchain technologies such as smart contracts, Non-Fungible Tokens (NFTs), and the InterPlanetary File System (IPFS) to address these issues. Our system is specifically designed to meet the unique needs of the pharmaceutical sector, prioritizing traceability, ethical sourcing, and data integrity. We evaluate the system's performance on four EVM-compatible platforms: Binance Smart Chain, Polygon, Fantom, and Celo, demonstrating its adaptability and potential for operational efficiency. Our research highlights the significant potential of blockchain technology in revolutionizing pharmaceutical supply chain management, fostering trust, and ensuring ethical practices.

Keywords: Pharmaceuticals Supply Chain · Supply Chain Integrity · Blockchain · Smart Contracts · Non-Fungible Tokens (NFTs)

1 Introduction

Pharmaceuticals supply chain is a complex network involving multiple stakeholders. As illustrated in Fig. 1, raw material suppliers provide the essential ingredients for drug production. Pharmaceutical manufacturers then formulate, produce, and package these materials into finished drug products. Rigorous quality

J. Kertesz et al. (Eds.): CSoNet 2024, LNCS 15417, pp. 110–121, 2025.
https://doi.org/10.1007/978-981-96-6389-7_10

control and testing are implemented throughout the manufacturing and distribution phases to ensure product safety and efficacy. Wholesalers and distributors play a crucial role in transporting and distributing medications to healthcare providers, such as hospitals and pharmacies. Ultimately, patients rely on the integrity of this supply chain to access reliable and safe medications.

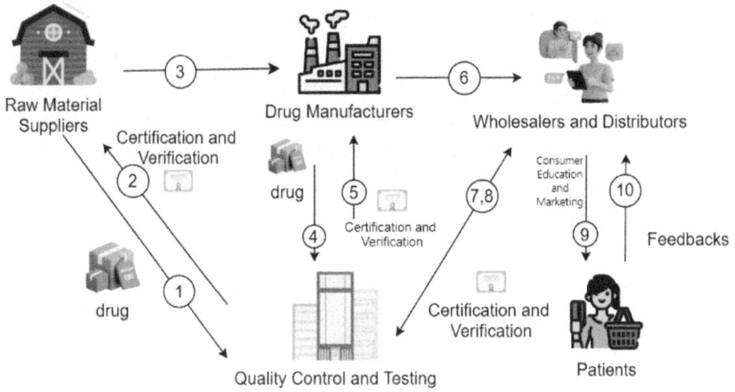

Fig. 1. Traditional Pharmaceuticals Supply Chain: From Raw Material Sourcing to Patient Delivery

Despite its structured approach, the traditional pharmaceutical supply chain faces several challenges: (1) Lack of transparency: Limited visibility into the supply chain can hinder traceability and accountability; (2) Ethical sourcing concerns: Ensuring ethical sourcing practices and fair trade throughout the supply chain can be difficult; (3) Counterfeit drug threat: The rise of counterfeit medications poses a significant risk to public health. To address these challenges, the integration of blockchain technology to the business processes related to pharmaceuticals supply chain rose to promising solutions. In recent advancements within the pharmaceutical supply chain, a variety of blockchain-based solutions have been proposed to combat the prevalence of counterfeit drugs and enhance the traceability and security of drug transactions. Nobly, Uddin (2021) [14] introduced a blockchain-enabled Medledger system utilizing Hyperledger Fabric, which aims for efficient and secure drug supply chain transactions. Another worth-mentioning solution is that Musamih et al. [8] presented an Ethereum blockchain-based system for drug supply chain product traceability, utilizing smart contracts and decentralized storage. Besides, Gebreab et al. (2022) [4] proposed a novel system using NFTs for the traceability and ownership management of medical devices within healthcare supply chains.

In this paper, to address these challenges, we propose a novel comprehensive system that have integration of blockchain technology such as smart contracts, Non-Fungible Tokens (NFTs), and InterPlanetary File System (IPFS) into the pharmaceuticals supply chain. The system then is evaluated across

EVM-compatible blockchain platforms, including Binance Smart Chain, Polygon, Fantom, and Celo to demonstrate the practicality and operationality.

2 Related Work

2.1 Sustainable Supply Chain and Transparency

In recent advancements, a variety of blockchain-based solutions have been proposed to combat the prevalence of counterfeit drugs and enhance the traceability and security of drug transactions. Uddin [14] introduced a blockchain-enabled Medledger system utilizing Hyperledger Fabric, which aims for efficient and secure drug supply chain transactions. Rai, Srivastava, & Arora [11] explored the application of smart contracts on the Ethereum blockchain, alongside IPFS for data storage, to track counterfeit drugs. Comparatively, Lingayat et al. [7] evaluated existing blockchain and IoT-based systems for pharmaceutical supply chain management, highlighting the benefits and challenges of each approach. Amarasinghe et al. [10] discussed SUPPLYDECK, a solution leveraging blockchain technology for improved transparency, traceability, and security in drug supply chains. Musamih et al. [8] presented an Ethereum blockchain-based system for healthcare supply chain product traceability, utilizing smart contracts and decentralized storage. Additionally, Gebreab et al. [4] proposed a novel system using NFTs for the traceability and ownership management of medical devices within healthcare supply chains. These studies collectively underscore the potential of blockchain technology to revolutionize the pharmaceutical supply chain by ensuring drug authenticity, enhancing traceability, and securing transactions.

2.2 Enhancing Pharmaceutical Supply Chain Integrity Through Blockchain Technology

Recent studies underscore the transformative potential of blockchain technology in the pharmaceutical supply chain, aiming to bolster drug traceability, security, and counteract counterfeit medicines. Haq & Muselemu [5] underscore the technology's capability to track pharmaceuticals from production to patient, promising a substantial leap in supply chain transparency. Similarly, Kumar & Tripathi [6] introduce an innovative approach using blockchain and encrypted QR codes, enhancing the traceability of medications to ensure drug safety. Further exploration by Bali et al. [2] reveals how blockchain can curtail drug counterfeiting by facilitating ownership transfer traceability, while Rai, Srivastava, & Arora [12] propose a cost-effective, decentralized tracking solution via smart contracts on the Ethereum blockchain. Dave et al. [3] suggest a permissioned blockchain network for enhanced collaboration and trust among supply chain stakeholders. The work of Saindane et al. [13] leverages blockchain to render the drug supply chain transparent, thus mitigating counterfeit risks, while Pathak et al. [9] and Ali et al. [1] both propose systems that ensure the end-to-end supply of traceable and safe pharmaceuticals through blockchain implementation. Collectively, these studies present a compelling case for blockchain as a linchpin for security, authenticity, and traceability in the pharmaceutical supply chain.

3 Approach

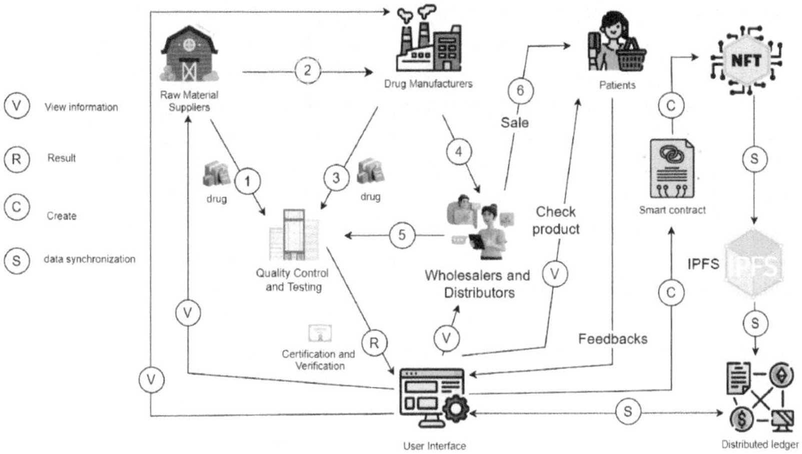

Fig. 2. A Schematic Representation of the Pharmaceuticals Supply Chain Management System Integrating Smart Contracts, NFTs, IPFS, and Distributed Ledgers

To ensure the integrity of pharmaceutical products from source to end-user, we propose a comprehensive supply chain management system that leverages a combination of blockchain technologies, including smart contracts, NFTs, and IPFS. As illustrated in Fig. 2, the process begins with raw material suppliers providing essential ingredients for drug production. Rigorous quality assurance and authentication measures are implemented to verify the quality and authenticity of these materials. Smart contracts automate the transactional elements, ensuring that agreed-upon terms, such as delivery times and quality parameters, are met and recorded on the distributed ledger.

Then, Drug manufacturers receive raw materials and initiate the formulation, production, and packaging processes. Throughout these stages, stringent quality control and testing procedures are implemented to ensure product quality and safety. Certification and verification steps are documented on the distributed ledger, providing a transparent and auditable record. Each drug package or batch is assigned a unique NFT, acting as a digital fingerprint that can be traced throughout the supply chain. This enables stakeholders, including wholesalers, distributors, and patients, to verify the authenticity and origin of the product.

A robust feedback loop is established between patients, healthcare providers, and the supply chain. User interfaces interact with distributed ledgers and IPFS to collect and analyze data on drug efficacy and adverse events. IPFS ensures secure and decentralized storage of this critical data.

4 Implementation

This exposition delves into the practical implementation of a blockchain-based system to enhance pharmaceutical supply chain integrity. By integrating smart contracts, NFTs, and IPFS, this system establishes a transparent and immutable record of drug authenticity and regulatory compliance from production to patient. We explore the system's user interfaces and operational procedures, focusing on the issuance and renewal of certificates. These certificates are indelibly linked to the drug's identity and track its journey through the supply chain. The goal is to elucidate the role of each component within the system and demonstrate how their collective impact fosters a robust and reliable supply chain.

4.1 Transaction/Data Creation

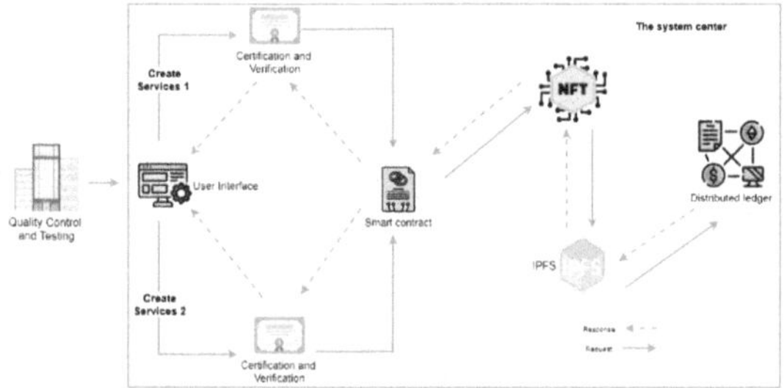

Fig. 3. Creation Framework for Enhanced Certificate Management in the Blockchain-Enabled Supply Chain for Pharmaceuticals Supply Chain

The schematic displays a blockchain-oriented structure aimed at fortifying the pharmaceutical supply chain, centering on steadfast product tracking, authentication, and record-keeping from the initial supplier to the consumer (Fig. 3). Smart contracts at the heart of this system automate pivotal transactions and verify compliance through predefined quality metrics, contributing to uniformity and reducing discrepancies across the supply chain. Inspectors validate products and processes, with their certified outcomes stored on the blockchain to ensure transparency. Digital certificates, represented as NFTs, both affirm the quality and ethical procurement of pharmaceuticals and provide a means for stakeholders to confirm product data along the supply chain. These NFTs are crucial in securing a trustworthy record of compliance, tied to a distributed ledger that meticulously logs each transaction. Additionally, IPFS is deployed for the decentralized preservation of sensitive data, such as sourcing details and transaction records, bolstering the security and retrievability of information, and thus supporting the integrity of the pharmaceutical supply chain.

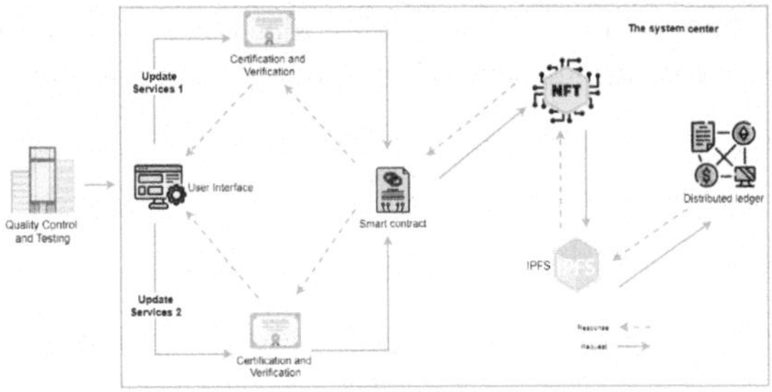

Fig. 4. Updation Framework for Enhanced Certificate Management in the Blockchain-Enabled Supply Chain for Pharmaceuticals Supply Chain

4.2 Data Update

The revised framework for managing the pharmaceutical supply chain employs blockchain technology to enhance the certification process, adapting to the sector's specific requirements (Fig. 4). At its core, the system leverages smart contracts to handle the issuance and updates of certificates, reflecting the variable nature of pharmaceutical production and distribution. This feature allows for real-time adjustments, ensuring certificate accuracy on the blockchain. Inspection agencies are key, validating each stage of production and inputting data into the blockchain, thus marrying real-time accuracy with the system's inherent need for adaptability. NFTs serve as digital stand-ins for certificates, anchoring the product's compliance and journey to an immutable ledger, thereby ensuring transparency in the drug's pathway from manufacture to patient. The use of IPFS further secures data against alteration, maintaining the integrity and permanent accessibility of the supply chain's information, an essential factor for trust and reliability in the system's digital records.

4.3 Data Query Process

The design we present for the pharmaceutical supply chain uses blockchain to streamline data retrieval and certification verification, improving the accessibility of such information throughout the network (Fig. 5). Central to this infrastructure is the deployment of smart contracts that manage and automate transactions in response to supply chain activities. These contracts standardize business operations and ensure consistent practices by executing actions triggered by key supply chain events. Stakeholders access and authenticate data regarding drug origins, quality, and ethical compliance through query services, which translate requests into blockchain actions for efficient data recovery. Inspection entities utilize these capabilities to register and update certificates on the blockchain, which, as NFTs, represent the product's quality assurance. Additionally, incorporating IPFS ensures data security and integrity, preserving the accuracy of information and protecting against unauthorized alterations. This system thus maintains supply chain transparency and fortifies the trustworthiness of the verification processes, assuring all network participants of the data's reliability.

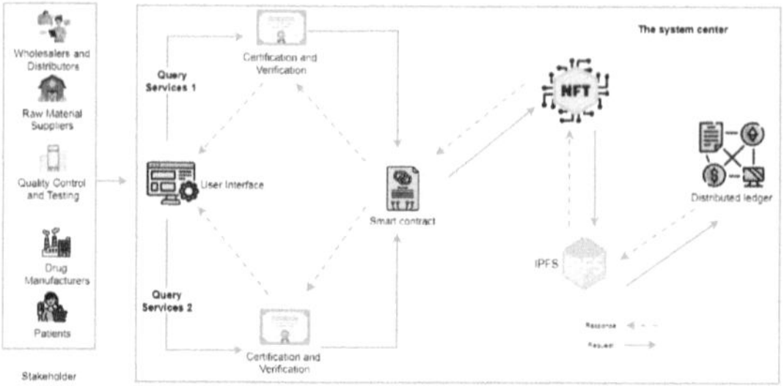

Fig. 5. Query Framework for Enhanced Certificate Management in the Blockchain-Enabled Supply Chain for Pharmaceuticals Supply Chain

5 Evaluation

In our examination of blockchain's role in reinforcing transparency within pharmaceutical supply chains, we have pinpointed four EVM-compatible platforms suitable for executing our smart contracts: Binance Smart Chain (BSC), Polygon, Fantom, and Celo. These platforms were selected based on their unique features and potential effectiveness in managing supply chain processes. Our approach extends beyond the use of blockchain for secure transaction processing and verification; it includes the adoption of decentralized data storage methods. Specifically, we're focusing on employing NFTs to validate key supply chain events. For interfacing with the InterPlanetary File System (IPFS), we will utilize the Pinata platform, which facilitates decentralized file management. This method is expected to improve the handling and transparency of certification and supply chain-related information.

5.1 Environment Simulation

This scenario presents a blockchain network tailored for the pharmaceutical supply chain, integrating NFTs and IPFS to verify and manage supply records. Within this network, nodes represent different supply chain participants-such as quality inspectors, manufacturers, and distributors-each secured through distinct public-private key cryptography. The public keys act as node identifiers for network transactions, while private keys safeguard transaction integrity. These nodes carry out specialized tasks, including the creation of NFTs and the execution of smart contracts. To ensure the network operates without the typical constraints of limited resources, the test environment is provisioned with ample ether. This setup is intended to critically assess how NFTs and IPFS can be

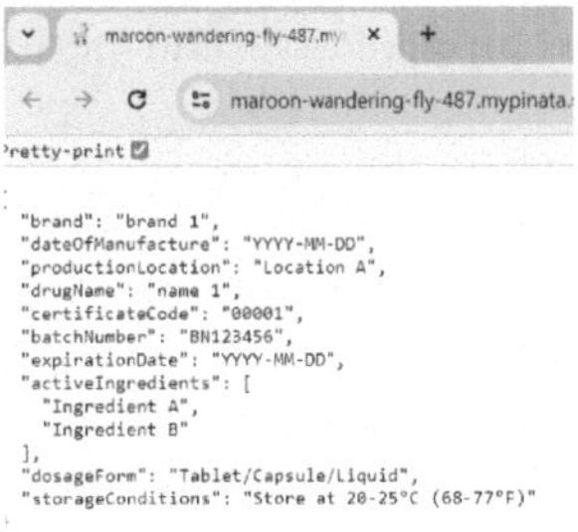

Fig. 6. Generated IPFS Hash for Stored NFT Metadata

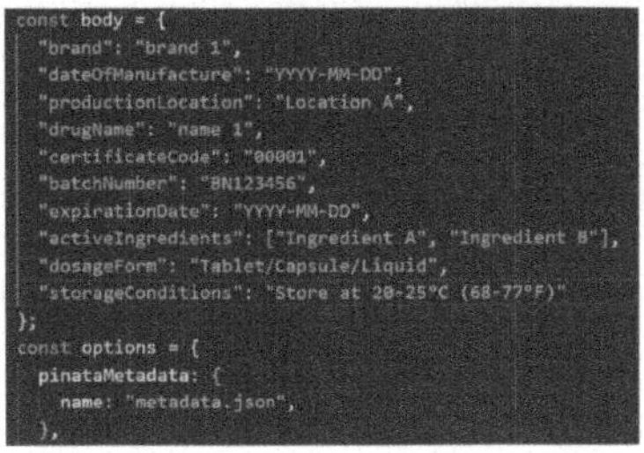

Fig. 7. Defining the Data Structure for Supply Chain Item NFT

applied to authenticate and maintain supply chain documentation, offering a controlled space to evaluate the systems strengths and potential obstacles without real-world risks. The aim is to gather meaningful insights into the practicality and implications of this technology for maintaining the integrity of pharmaceutical supply chains.

5.2 Implementing IPFS for Supply Chain Management Systems

To improve the transparency of the pharmaceutical supply chain, the creation of a NFT starts with developing a structured data format for the pharmaceutical product (depicted in Fig. 7). This involves compiling a JSON object that encapsulates key data points such as drug type, point of origin, manufacturing process, and associated certifications. Serving as the NFT's metadata, this JSON object provides a transparent record of the pharmaceutical's journey through the supply chain, aiming to instill a layer of trust and clarity for all parties involved.

Upon establishing the data framework for the Non-Fungible Token (NFT), attention shifts to confirming the associated smart contract's functionality (Fig. 8). This critical verification stage, evidenced by successful testing, ensures the smart contract is accurately initiated and active, adept at fulfilling its designated parameters, including the management of time-critical operations. This validation step is fundamental, confirming the smart contract's dependability in automating the pharmaceutical supply chain's encoded procedures. Verifying that the smart contract operates correctly is crucial for facilitating a transparent and efficient supply chain, capitalizing on blockchain's capability to enhance and secure pharmaceutical supply chain management.

After confirming the smart contract's efficacy, securing the NFT metadata on a decentralized platform follows, ensuring its preservation and accessibility (Fig. 9). The use of Pinata highlights this process by streamlining the uploading of metadata JSON files to the InterPlanetary File System (IPFS), thus safeguarding the pharmaceutical supply chain item's digital representation. By housing the metadata on IPFS, accessed through a unique IPFS hash, a durable and retrievable record of the supply chain data is established. This approach underpins the transparency and trust in pharmaceutical supply chain management, embracing decentralized storage to maintain a comprehensive and permanent dataset.

The generation of an IPFS hash, documented in the process, signifies an important development in associating the NFT with a steadfast and unalterable record of the pharmaceutical supply chain item's metadata (Fig. 6). This hash functions as a distinct identifier, guaranteeing that the metadata hosted on IPFS remains unchanged and accessible to anyone with the hash. This stage is critical in linking the NFT to a reliable, immutable account of the supply chain item's details, completing the NFT creation process. It highlights the dedication to improving the transparency and trustworthiness of pharmaceutical supply chain management by securely embedding the supply chain information in a decentralized storage facility.

Fig. 8. Test Confirmation of Smart Contract Functionality

Fig. 9. Pinata Cloud Interface for IPFS Metadata Storage

5.3 Testing on EVM-Supported Platforms

Our research utilizes the Ethereum Virtual Machine (EVM) to deploy smart contracts on various EVM-compatible platforms, including BSC, Polygon, Fantom, and Celo, to evaluate their performance in managing a transparent pharmaceutical supply chain. The study focuses on critical processes such as data entry for documenting supply chain activities, generating NFTs for product traceability, and transferring NFTs to ensure secure data exchange across the supply chain. We assessed each platform based on transaction speed, resource efficiency, and the ease of use of their interfaces, which are vital for adoption by supply chain stakeholders. The goal of this analysis is to identify the platforms that best facilitate a transparent and efficient supply chain, highlighting their effectiveness in secure NFT creation and management within the pharmaceutical sector.

Transaction Fee. The table provided delivers a comparative analysis of transaction costs across various blockchain platforms, focusing on their implications for supply chain management costs. These transaction fees are crucial for evaluating the blockchain's operational expenses and play a significant role in determining the system's financial feasibility. Additionally, it includes a current evaluation of the token prices for the platforms in question, recorded on March 27,

2024, at 7:00 AM UTC. This overview is designed to succinctly present the economic landscape of these blockchain networks, aiding in the assessment of their suitability for a pharmaceutical supply chain integrity system that relies on Smart Contracts, NFTs, IPFS, and Distributed Ledgers (Table 1).

Table 1. Transaction fee

	Transaction Creation	Create NFT	Transfer NFT
BNB Smart Chain	0.0273134 BNB ($8.27)	0.00109162 BNB ($0.33)	0.00057003 BNB ($0.17)
Fantom	0.00957754 FTM ($0.00)	0.000405167 FTM ($0.00)	0.0002380105 FTM ($0.00)
Polygon	0.006840710032835408 MATIC ($0.01)	0.000289405001852192 MATIC ($0.00)	0.000170007501088048 MATIC ($0.00)
Celo	0.007097844 CELO ($0.005)	0.0002840812 CELO ($0.000)	0.0001554878 CELO ($0.000)

For the Binance Smart Chain (BSC), creating a blockchain entry, which is comparable to recording a new supply chain event, costs 0.0273134 BNB, equivalent to $8.27. This fee applies to actions such as documenting the arrival of pharmaceutical ingredients at a facility. Minting an NFT on BSC, which digitally represents a physical item or certificate in the supply chain, incurs a fee of 0.00109162 BNB or $0.33. This process involves creating a unique token that details the product's specifics, like its origin and certification status. Transferring an NFT, akin to changing its custody or ownership within the supply chain, is charged at 0.00057003 BNB, or $0.17, showcasing the platform's efficiency in asset transfers.

The Fantom network presents a very low fee structure, with the costs for initiating a transaction, creating an NFT, and transferring an NFT priced at 0.00957754 FTM, 0.000405167 FTM, and 0.0002380105 FTM, respectively. These fees translate to nominal dollar values, indicating a budget-friendly option for supply chain operations such as tracking pharmaceutical shipments or exchanging documentation.

Polygon also offers cost-effectiveness with its transaction fees for recording an entry, minting an NFT, and transferring an NFT set at 0.006840710032835408 MATIC, 0.000289405001852192 MATIC, and 0.000170007501088048 MATIC, respectively. The minimal expenses associated with these actions make Polygon a viable platform for conducting numerous transactions within the pharmaceutical supply chain without incurring substantial costs.

Lastly, Celo's transaction fee structure supports economical operations, with charges for new entries, NFT minting, and NFT transfers at 0.007097844 CELO, 0.0002840812 CELO, and 0.0001554878 CELO, respectively. These rates, amounting to fractions of a cent, underline Celo's capacity to facilitate the high-volume transactions typical of supply chain activities at minimal cost, emphasizing its suitability for pharmaceutical supply chain management tasks involving Smart Contracts, NFTs, IPFS, and Distributed Ledgers.

6 Discussion and Conclusion

Conclusion. This research demonstrates the potential of integrating blockchain technology, smart contracts, NFTs, and IPFS to enhance pharmaceutical supply chain management. By addressing the challenges of transparency, traceability, and ethical sourcing, our proposed system offers a secure, efficient, and transparent solution. The evaluation on various EVM-compatible platforms highlights the system's flexibility and potential for cost savings. This study contributes to the ongoing discourse on improving pharmaceutical supply chain practices, emphasizing the transformative potential of blockchain technology.

Limitation. The validity of the study is subject to several limitations. The dynamic nature of blockchain and cryptocurrency markets, the focus on EVM-compatible platforms, and the narrow scope of economic factors considered may impact the generalizability of the findings. Furthermore, the reliance on simulated environments for performance evaluation may not accurately reflect the complexities of real-world supply chain operations.

Future Work. Future research should explore a wider range of blockchain platforms beyond EVM-compatible ones. Expanding the evaluation criteria to include user adoption, scalability, and cross-chain interoperability would provide a more comprehensive assessment. Longitudinal studies can monitor the long-term impact of market dynamics on the cost-effectiveness and efficiency of blockchain implementations. Finally, pilot programs in real-world supply chain scenarios can validate the practical application of smart contracts, NFTs, and IPFS in improving transparency and integrity.

Acknowledgement. We acknowledge the support of time and facilities from Ho Chi Minh City University of Technology (HCMUT), VNU-HCM for this study.

References

1. Ali, S., Anwar, W., Salem, B.J., Al Dhuhlia, M.: Tracing pharmaceutical products utilizing blockchain technologies. Int. J. Comput. Digit. Syst. **12**(1), 1173–1181 (2022)
2. Bali, V., Khanna, T., Soni, P., Gupta, S., Chauhan, S., Gupta, S.: Combating drug counterfeiting by tracing ownership transfer using blockchain technology. Int. J. E-Health Med. Commun. (IJEHMC) **13**(1), 1–21 (2022)
3. Dave, M., Patil, K., Jaiswal, R., Pawar, R.: Monitoring supply chain of pharmaceutical drugs using blockchain. In: 2022 IEEE Delhi Section Conference (DELCON), pp. 1–5. IEEE (2022)
4. Gebreab, S.A., Hasan, H.R., Salah, K., Jayaraman, R.: NFT-based traceability and ownership management of medical devices. IEEE Access **10**, 126394–126411 (2022)
5. Haq, I., Esuka, O.M.: Blockchain technology in pharmaceutical industry to prevent counterfeit drugs. Int. J. Comput. Appl. **180**(25), 8-12 (2018)

6. Kumar, R., Tripathi, R.: Traceability of counterfeit medicine supply chain through blockchain. In: 2019 11th International Conference on Communication Systems & Networks (COMSNETS), pp. 568–570. IEEE (2019)
7. Lingayat, V., Pardikar, I., Yewalekar, S., Khachane, S., Pande, S.: Securing pharmaceutical supply chain using blockchain technology. In: ITM Web of Conferences, vol. 37, p. 01013. EDP Sciences (2021)
8. Musamih, A., et al.: A blockchain-based approach for drug traceability in healthcare supply chain. IEEE Access **9**, 9728–9743 (2021)
9. Pathak, A., et al.: Blockchain technology in pharmaceutical supply chain management. In: 2022 14th International Conference on Computational Intelligence and Communication Networks (CICN), pp. 723–727. IEEE (2022)
10. Pitigala, K., Abeywardena, K.Y., Yapa, K., et al.: Supplydeck–a blockchain-based pharmaceutical supply chain management. In: 2022 4th International Conference on Advancements in Computing (ICAC), pp. 84–89. IEEE (2022)
11. Rai, B.K., Srivastava, S., Arora, S.: Blockchain-based traceability of counterfeited drugs. Int. J. Reliab. Qual. E-Healthcare (IJRQEH) **12**(2), 1–12 (2023)
12. Rai, B.K., Srivastava, S., Arora, S.: Blockchain-based traceability of counterfeited drugs. Int. J. Reliable Qual. E-Healthcare (IJRQEH) **12**(2), 1–12 (2023)
13. Saindane, P., Jethani, Y., Mahtani, P., Rohra, C., Lund, P.: Blockchain: a solution for improved traceability with reduced counterfeits in supply chain of drugs. In: 2020 International Conference on Electrotechnical Complexes and Systems (ICOECS), pp. 1–5. IEEE (2020)
14. Uddin, M.: Blockchain medledger: hyperledger fabric enabled drug traceability system for counterfeit drugs in pharmaceutical industry. Int. J. Pharm. **597**, 120235 (2021)

Enhancing Poultry Disease Classification with Data Augmentation and Ensemble Learning

Thuan Van Tran(✉)

FPT University, Can Tho, Vietnam
tvthuanit@gmail.com

Abstract. Poultry diseases pose a significant threat to the global poultry industry, impacting both economic profitability and public health. Early and accurate diagnosis is crucial for effective treatment and prevention of these diseases. This study investigates the potential of deep learning for automated classification of four common poultry diseases: Coccidiosis, Healthy, Newcastle Disease, and Salmonella, using fecal images. We propose a novel ensemble model, combining two independently trained EfficientNetB3 and MobileNet architectures, to enhance classification accuracy. Our methodology incorporates a comprehensive preprocessing pipeline, including image resizing, ICA whitening, and image standardization, to optimize the input data for the model. To address the challenge of limited data availability, we employ a data augmentation strategy, effectively expanding the training dataset. The research utilizes a dataset of 8067 annotated poultry fecal images, providing a diverse representation of different disease conditions. The proposed approach achieves a remarkable accuracy of 98.33% in classifying poultry diseases, surpassing the performance of individual CNN models and recent studies in this field.

Keywords: Convolutional Neural Network · Ensemble Learning · Deep Learning · Image Classification · Chicken Diseases

1 Introduction

Poultry diseases, particularly in chickens, pose a significant threat to economic well-being and public health. Gastrointestinal diseases, such as coccidiosis, fowl cholera, Newcastle disease, and salmonellosis, are major causes of mortality and decreased productivity in poultry farming [18].

Poultry diseases have serious negative impacts on the economy, consumer health and food security. A study in Debre Zeit, Ethiopia, showed that coccidiosis in chickens causes significant losses in both small and large farms [11]. The disease causes a variety of losses, including mortality, medication costs, weight loss, reduced market value of affected birds, culling, delayed marketing and reduced egg production. This results in an average profit loss of 11.86% and 8.40% for each small and large farm, respectively. With the main agents being

J. Kertesz et al. (Eds.): CSoNet 2024, LNCS 15417, pp. 122–133, 2025.
https://doi.org/10.1007/978-981-96-6389-7_11

Salmonella, Staphylococcus aureus and Clostridium perfringens, they are often the cause of foodborne diseases. Poor handling and improper storage, especially in food service establishments, are the main causes of these diseases. Salmonella is considered a major pathogen associated with poultry, resulting in high healthcare costs and reduced productivity of affected workers [21]. The study [9] also concluded that although uncontrolled disease outbreaks can cause significant financial losses to poultry producers, effective interventions are available to minimize losses.

Early and accurate diagnosis is crucial for effective control and treatment of poultry diseases. Traditional diagnostic methods often rely on clinical observation, sample analysis, and serological testing. However, these methods can be time-consuming, require specialized expertise, and may not always be accurate. The advent of Machine Learning (ML) [3] and Convolutional Neural Network (CNN) [22] has opened up promising new avenues for poultry disease diagnosis. CNN are renowned for their efficient image analysis capabilities and have found wide application in various fields, including healthcare [13,16]. CNN can automatically learn complex features from images, enabling more accurate and faster disease classification compared to traditional methods.

Ensemble Learning [6] is a powerful technique in ML that enhances the accuracy and stability of predictive models. The principle of ensemble learning involves combining multiple independently trained models to make a final decision. Ensemble Learning has proven effective in various domains, including medical image analysis, particularly in disease diagnosis [7,17].

This study introduces a novel ensemble learning model, combining two independently trained EfficientNetB3 and MobileNet models. This model is trained on a dataset of chicken fecal images, encompassing four disease classes: Coccidiosis, Healthy, Newcastle Disease, and Salmonella. This study makes several significant contributions to the field of poultry disease classification using deep learning:

- We propose a novel parallel ensemble model, combining two independently trained EfficientNetB3 and MobileNet architectures, to achieve higher classification accuracy compared to individual models. This approach leverages the strengths of each model and mitigates the limitations of individual models.
- The research compares the performance of the ensemble model with four popular CNN architectures (EfficientNetV2L, MobileNet, InceptionV3, EfficientNetB3) on a chicken fecal image dataset. The results demonstrate the superior performance of the ensemble model, achieving a remarkable accuracy of 98.33%, highlighting its effectiveness in poultry disease classification.
- The demonstrate the efficacy of data augmentation techniques in mitigating the challenges posed by limited data availability in medical imaging. Our findings highlight the potential of these techniques to enhance model performance and generalization capabilities.
- This research contributes to the growing body of evidence supporting the transformative potential of deep learning in healthcare, particularly in automating and improving the accuracy of poultry disease diagnosis.

2 Related Works

Deep learning is rapidly transforming poultry disease classification, offering a powerful alternative to traditional machine learning methods. This section provides a comprehensive review of recent studies utilizing deep learning for poultry disease classification, highlighting their advantages, drawbacks, and paving the way for our proposed approach.

In 2022, several studies explored the potential of deep learning for poultry disease classification. Moch Kholil et al. [10] investigated the use of deep learning for classifying chicken diseases based on fecal images, achieving an accuracy of 95.28%. Dina Machuve et al. [14] proposed a deep Convolutional Neural Network (CNN) model for classifying poultry diseases, achieving an accuracy of 98.02%. Hope Mbelwa et al. [15] proposed a deep learning solution based on CNN for classifying chicken fecal images, achieving a validation accuracy of 94%.

Building upon these advancements, research in 2023 further explored the potential of deep learning for poultry disease diagnosis. Mizanu Zelalem Degu et al. [5] proposed a system using YOLO-V3 for object detection and ResNet50 for image classification, achieving a mean average precision of 87.48% for ROI detection and a classification accuracy of 98.7%. Suthagar et al. [20] proposed a deep learning model for early detection and classification of poultry diseases using a dataset of 6812 fecal images, achieving a 97% accuracy with the DenseNet model. Mahendra Kumar Gourisaria et al. [8] investigated the use of deep learning for early detection of chicken diseases, achieving an accuracy of 94.49% with the ChicNetV6 model. Khushi Srivastava et al. [19] proposed a CNN based framework for classifying poultry diseases, achieving an accuracy of 93.23% in classifying chicken diseases.

Continuing this momentum, research in 2024 showcased the effectiveness of deep learning for poultry disease classification. Mohammed Al Qatrawi et al. [2] proposed a CNN-based method for classifying chicken images into three disease categories: Newcastle disease, avian influenza, and infectious bursal disease, achieving an impressive F1-score of 99.04%. Luong Huong Hoang et al. [12] investigated the ViT16 model, trained through transfer learning and fine-tuning on an augmented dataset, achieving accuracy ranging from 98.25% to 100% in classifying chicken diseases. Mohd Anif Akhmal Abu Bakar et al. [1] explored the use of image processing and machine learning for early detection of Newcastle disease virus infection in chickens, achieving 79.00% validation accuracy at 36 h post-infection using a hybrid chromaticity-morphology machine learning model.

While promising, the application of deep learning for poultry disease classification faces challenges such as limited data, model interpretability, and generalization to diverse datasets. This study directly addresses these challenges by introducing a novel ensemble learning model that not only achieves state-of-the-art accuracy but also demonstrates significant potential for improving poultry disease diagnosis and management.

3 Methods

This study adheres to a rigorous and systematic eight-step implementation procedure, as detailed in Fig. 1.

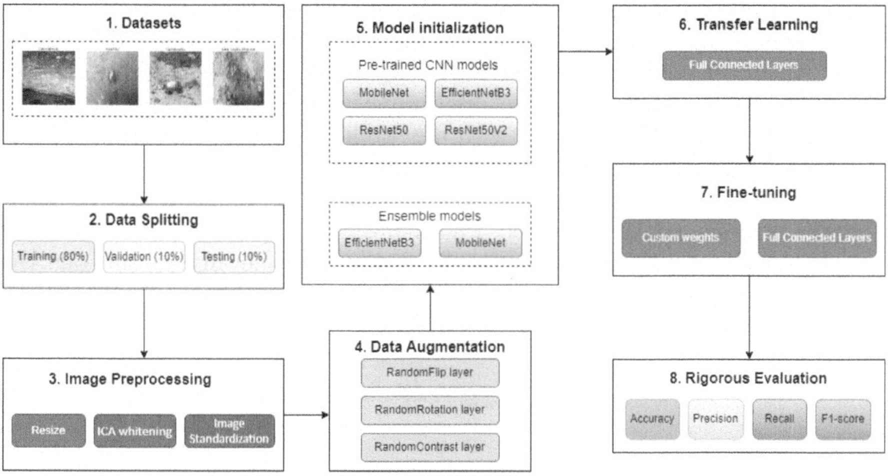

Fig. 1. The Research Implementation Procedure

3.1 Dataset Selection

This study utilizes an annotated dataset for poultry disease diagnostics, focusing on images of poultry feces. Collected between September 2020 and February 2021 in the Arusha and Kilimanjaro regions of Tanzania, the dataset comprises 8067 images is publicly available on Kaggle[1] and categorized into four classes: Coccidiosis (30.4%), Healthy (29.5%), New Castle Disease (7.8%), and Salmonella (32.3%).

3.2 Pre-processing Image

To prepare images for training and evaluation, we implemented a preprocessing pipeline consisting of the following steps:

1. *Image Resizing:* To ensure uniformity and optimal model compatibility, all images underwent a resizing process, standardizing their dimensions to 224×224 pixels. This step guarantees consistent input size, a crucial factor

[1] https://www.kaggle.com/datasets/allandclive/chicken-disease-1.

for achieving optimal model performance. The resizing process can be mathematically represented as Eq. 1, where $I_{resized}$ represents the resized image.:

$$I_{resized}(new_{width}, new_{height}) = I_{resized}(224, 224) \tag{1}$$

2. *ICA Whitening:* To reduce the redundancy and improve the independence of features in the images, we applied Independent Component Analysis (ICA) whitening using the FastICA algorithm from the scikit-learn library in Python. This technique transforms the input data into a new representation where the components are statistically independent, potentially enhancing the model's ability to learn discriminative features [4]. Specifically, we applied the FastICA algorithm with the 'tanh' nonlinearity function and the 'parallel' algorithm for faster computation.
3. *Image Standardization:* To address variations in illumination and optimize model training, we implemented a normalization step. This process involves scaling pixel intensities to a standardized range. Specifically, we subtract the mean (μ) from each pixel intensity and then divide by the standard deviation (σ). This transformation is mathematically represented in Eq. 2:

$$I_{norm} = \frac{I_{in} - \mu}{\sigma} \tag{2}$$

3.3 Customize The CNN Model For Transfer Learning And Fine-Tuning

We employed a fine-tuned pre-trained CNN model to enhance disease classification accuracy from poultry feces images. Figure 2 illustrates the model's architecture, highlighting our modifications aimed at improving feature extraction and mitigating overfitting. To optimize the model for our specific task of classifying poultry diseases from fecal images, we undertook a meticulous fine-tuning

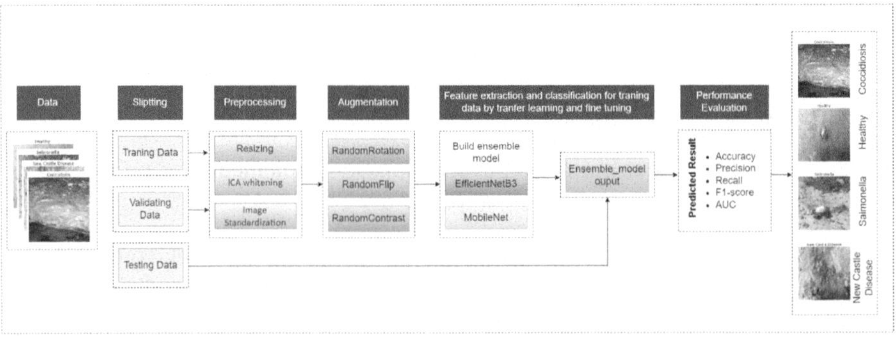

Fig. 2. Proposed architecture framework.

process. This involved two key modifications: adapting the output layer and integrating auxiliary layers. First, we replaced the pre-trained model's original softmax layer with a new one specifically designed to accommodate our four target classes (Coccidiosis, Healthy, New Castle Disease, and Salmonella). This ensured that the model's output directly aligned with our classification objectives.

Second, we introduced eight auxiliary layers before the final softmax layer to enhance the model's capacity for feature learning and classification accuracy. These layers act as specialized filters, refining the extracted features to capture subtle visual cues indicative of different poultry diseases. This enhanced feature representation empowers the model to make more precise and discriminative classifications.

To further maximize performance, we conducted a comprehensive hyperparameter search. This involved systematically experimenting with various training epochs, batch sizes, hidden layer configurations, and learning rates to determine the optimal combination for our dataset. This rigorous optimization process aimed to strike a balance between achieving high training accuracy and ensuring the model's ability to generalize effectively to unseen data, ultimately minimizing overfitting and maximizing its real-world applicability.

3.4 Data Augmentation

To mitigate the risk of overfitting, we employed data augmentation techniques, including random rotation, flipping, and contrast adjustment, to effectively expand the training dataset and expose the model to a wider range of variations. In addition, to address class imbalance, we randomly selected 500 images per class for training, ensuring diverse representation while mitigating overfitting and enhancing model generalizability. Following image preprocessing and augmentation, the final dataset comprised 8000 images. The following augmentation techniques were employed:

- *Random Contrast Adjustment:* To simulate varying lighting conditions, which can significantly impact image appearance, we randomly adjusted the contrast of the images within a factor of 0.1. This helps the model learn to identify key features regardless of lighting variations.
- *Random Rotation:* Images were randomly rotated within a range of $\pm 15^\circ$C. This helps the model generalize to images captured at different orientations, as poultry feces may be photographed from various angles.
- *Random Flipping:* Images were randomly flipped horizontally. This augmentation ensures the model is not biased towards a specific left-right orientation, further enhancing its generalization capabilities.

By incorporating data augmentation techniques such as random rotation, flipping, and contrast adjustment, we effectively expanded our training dataset sixfold. This approach promoted model generalization and robustness, mitigating the risk of overfitting. These techniques help the model adapt to images captured at different orientations and with varying lighting conditions, further enhancing its performance and reducing the likelihood of overfitting.

3.5 Ensemble Model

To enhance the accuracy and robustness of our poultry disease classification system, we implemented a parallel ensemble learning approach, combining the strengths of two independently trained Convolutional Neural Networks (CNNs): EfficientNetB3 and MobileNet. This strategy leverages the unique capabilities of each model while mitigating the limitations of relying on a single model.

Our selection of EfficientNetB3 and MobileNet was driven by their promising performance on our dataset and their efficiency. EfficientNetB3 (12.3M parameters), and MobileNet (4.3M parameters), offer a favorable balance between accuracy and computational efficiency compared to larger models like ResNet50 and ResNet50V2 with 25.6M parameters. This balance is crucial for ensuring the feasibility of deploying the model in real-world settings.

Both EfficientNetB3 (represented as M_1) and MobileNet (M_2) were trained independently on the same augmented poultry feces image dataset. This parallel training allows each model to learn distinct features and patterns, potentially capturing complementary aspects of the image data. Let $F_1(x)$ and $F_2(x)$ represent the feature vectors extracted by EfficientNetB3 and MobileNet, respectively, for an input image x. Instead of combining the models' predictions directly, our ensemble approach merges their learned features through concatenation:

$$F_{ensemble}(x) = Concatenate(F_1(x), F_2(x)) \tag{3}$$

This concatenated feature vector, $F_{ensemble}(x)$, representing a richer representation of the input image, is then passed through additional layers, including global max pooling and dense layers, to produce the final classification output.

This approach, conceptually similar to feature-level stacking in ensemble learning, harnesses the strengths of both models, resulting in a more accurate and robust poultry disease classification system. By combining the unique insights of EfficientNetB3 and MobileNet, the ensemble model reduces the influence of any single model's potential biases and overfitting.

3.6 Performance Metrics

To rigorously evaluate the performance of our poultry disease classification models, we utilize four key metrics: Accuracy (Eq. 4), Precision (Eq. 5), Recall (Eq. 6), and F1-score (Eq. 7). These metrics provide a comprehensive assessment of the model's ability to correctly classify both positive and negative cases, taking into account true positives (TP), true negatives (TN), false positives (FP), and false negatives (FN).

$$\text{Accuracy} = \frac{TP + TN}{TP + TN + FP + FN} \tag{4}$$

$$\text{Precision} = \frac{TP}{TP + FP} \tag{5}$$

$$\text{Recall} = \frac{TP}{TP + FN} \tag{6}$$

$$\text{F1} = 2 * \frac{Precision * Recall}{Precision + Recall} \tag{7}$$

4 Experiments

In this experimental part, we divide into 2 scenarios to test the effectiveness of data augmentation for model training.

4.1 Scenario 1: Evaluating Ensemble Learning Performance Using Unaugmented Datasets

Table 1 presents the performance of the CNN models in classifying four poultry diseases on the original dataset (without augmentation). Overall, Fine-tuning yields better performance than Transfer Learning across all network architectures, indicating that fine-tuning the entire model helps to exploit the data more effectively.

Table 1. CLASSIFICATION PERFORMANCE OF 5 MODELS ON DATASET WITHOUT AUGMENTATION

Model	Transfer Learning				Fine-tuning			
	Acc	Pre	Recall	F1	Acc	Pre	Recall	F1
ResNet50	81.28%	80.75%	81.28%	80.97%	89.09%	88.79%	89.09%	88.82%
ResNet50V2	76.82%	74.49%	74.82%	74.70%	82.89%	82.82%	82.89%	81.64%
EfficientNetB3	81.04%	80.62%	81.04%	80.69%	92.06%	92.02%	92.06%	91.94%
MobileNet	72.98%	71.44%	72.98%	71.08%	83.76%	83.37%	83.76%	83.08%
Ours	**94.42%**	**94.49%**	**94.42%**	**94.35%**	**93.92%**	**94.03%**	**93.92%**	**93.78%**

Among the architectures evaluated, EfficientNetB3 demonstrates promising performance, but the proposed model (Ours) achieves superior performance, reaching an accuracy of 94.42% when using Transfer Learning and 93.92% when using Fine-tuning. This indicates that the ensemble model, combining EfficientNetB3 and MobileNet, has proven effective in classifying poultry diseases, even without using data augmentation.

In contrast, ResNet50 shows the lowest performance in both methods, suggesting that this architecture might not be complex enough to learn features from chicken fecal images. ResNet50V2 performs better than ResNet50, but its performance decreases when Fine-tuning, possibly due to overfitting when fine-tuning the entire model on a limited dataset.

4.2 Scenario 2: Evaluating Ensemble Learning Performance with the Augmented Dataset

Table 2 presents the performance of the CNN models in classifying four poultry diseases on the augmented dataset. Compared to Scenario 1, the application of data augmentation has significantly improved the performance of the models. Fine-tuning continues to yield better performance than Transfer Learning across all models. The proposed model (Ours) achieves the highest accuracy (98.33% with Fine-tuning) among the architectures tested.

Table 2. CLASSIFICATION PERFORMANCE OF 5 MODELS ON AUGMENTED DATASET

Model	Transfer Learning				Fine-tuning			
	Acc	Pre	Recall	F1	Acc	Pre	Recall	F1
ResNet50	86.54%	86.97%	86.54%	86.65%	91.69%	91.90%	91.69%	91.72%
ResNet50V2	68.27%	69.23%	68.27%	68.34%	74.41%	75.08%	74.41%	74.60%
EfficientNetB3	80.73%	81.57%	80.73%	80.93%	94.85%	95.01%	94.85%	94.86%
MobileNet	72.75%	74.09%	72.75%	73.04%	86.21%	86.36%	86.21%	86.20%
Ours	**97.00%**	**97.08%**	**97.00%**	**97.02%**	**98.33%**	**98.33%**	**98.33%**	**98.33%**

This confirms the effectiveness of the ensemble model combining EfficientNetB3 and MobileNet, especially when combined with data augmentation. EfficientNetB3 also performs well, achieving a high accuracy of 94.85% with Fine-tuning, highlighting the effectiveness of this architecture in poultry disease image classification. The two models ResNet50 and ResNet50V2 show promising performance when Fine-tuning, but still fall short of EfficientNetB3 and the proposed model. MobileNet achieves fairly good performance, but still lags behind other models.

Scenario 2 demonstrates the effectiveness of using data augmentation and Fine-tuning in classifying poultry diseases. The proposed model achieves the highest accuracy, confirming the potential of deep learning in supporting poultry disease diagnosis. Data augmentation has significantly improved the performance of the models, especially for the proposed model. However, further research is needed to optimize model performance and improve classification accuracy for each disease class.

5 Comparison with Other State-of-the-Art Methods

Table 3 compares the performance of the proposed model with recent studies on chicken disease classification from chicken feces images. The proposed model achieved an accuracy of 98.33%, ranking high among the compared studies. The compared studies used a variety of methods, including deep learning, traditional machine learning, and a combination of techniques. The datasets used also varied in size and origin.

In terms of comparison with other studies using the same dataset of 8067 chicken droppings images. Our proposed model achieved an accuracy of 98.33%, outperforming the studies of Srivastava et al. [19] (93.23%), Machuve et al. [14] (98.02%), and Huong Hoang Luong et al. [12] (98.25%). The proposed model uses

Table 3. COMPARISON WITH OTHERS STATE-OF-THE-ART METHODS

Ref	Year	Dataset	Approach	Acc(%)
[15]	2021	1590 poultry fecal images	Deep learning based on CNN	94%
[10]	2022	Not specified	Deep learning	95.28%
[14]	2022	8067 poultry fecal images	Deep CNN model	98.02%
[5]	2023	Not specified	YOLO-V3 for object detection and ResNet50	98.7%
[20]	2023	6812 fecal images	Deep learning model using DenseNet	97%
[8]	2023	Not specified	Deep learning using ChicNetV6 model	94.49%
[19]	2023	8067 poultry fecal images	CNN	93.23%
[2]	2024	10,800 chicken images	CNN	99.04%
[12]	2024	8067 poultry fecal images	ViT16	98.25%
[1]	2024	Not specified	Hybrid chromaticity-morphology machine learning model	79.00%
Ours		**8067 poultry fecal images**	**Ensemble learning (EfficientNetB3 + MobileNet)**	**98.33%**

an ensemble learning technique combining EfficientNetB3 and MobileNet, while other studies used single models, demonstrating the effectiveness of ensemble learning in improving classification performance.

Our proposed ensemble model, combining EfficientNetB3 and MobileNet, demonstrates competitive performance in poultry disease classification compared to existing approaches. This strong performance, exceeding that of some previous studies, highlights the effectiveness of ensemble learning in this domain. Notably, our study leverages a larger dataset (8067 images) than some prior work, contributing to enhanced model generalizability and robustness.

6 Conclusion

The proposed model's remarkable accuracy (98.33%) is a result of a combination of strategies designed to enhance model performance and generalization. Firstly, the parallel ensemble model leverages the strengths of two independently trained architectures, EfficientNetB3 and MobileNet. By combining the unique features and capabilities of each model, the ensemble approach leads to a more robust and accurate prediction compared to using either model alone. Secondly, the study utilizes data augmentation techniques to effectively expand the training dataset. These techniques address the challenge of limited data availability in medical imaging by generating synthetic images with variations like random rotation, flipping, and contrast adjustment. This expanded training dataset allows the model to learn from a wider range of image variations, leading to better generalization and contributing to the high accuracy achieved.

While this research showcases the promising potential of deep learning for poultry disease diagnosis, further investigation is needed to address certain limitations. A more in-depth analysis of the performance of each disease class, along with exploring model interpretability using techniques like Integrated Gradients, LIME, or SHAP, is crucial for enhancing the model's reliability and understanding its decision-making process. Finally, evaluating the practical applicability of the model in real-world settings is essential to ensure its successful integration into poultry farming practices.

Acknowledgments. We express our deepest appreciation to Mr. Huong Hoang Luong, Mr. Duy Khanh Nguyen and Mr. Bang Huu Do Dang for their invaluable contributions to this research. Their guidance and support throughout the entire process, from building our foundational knowledge of machine learning to navigating the complexities of experimentation and manuscript preparation, have been instrumental to our success. Their dedication, experience, and unwavering encouragement were essential in helping us overcome challenges and maintain our motivation. We are sincerely grateful for their mentorship and support.

References

1. Abu Bakar, M.A.A., et al.: A hybrid chromaticity-morphological machine learning model to overcome the limit of detecting newcastle disease in chicken within 36 hours. SSRN 4805571 (2024)
2. Al Qatrawi, M., Abu-Naser, S.S.: Classification of chicken diseases using deep learning (2024)
3. Alpaydin, E.: Introduction to Machine Learning. MIT press (2020)
4. Chawla, M.: PCA and ICA processing methods for removal of artifacts and noise in electrocardiograms: a survey and comparison. Appl. Soft Comput. **11**(2), 2216–2226 (2011)
5. Degu, M.Z., Simegn, G.L.: Smartphone based detection and classification of poultry diseases from chicken fecal images using deep learning techniques. Smart Agri. Technol. **4**, 100221 (2023)
6. Dong, X., Yu, Z., Cao, W., Shi, Y., Ma, Q.: A survey on ensemble learning. Front. Comp. Sci. **14**, 241–258 (2020)
7. Ganaie, M.A., Hu, M., Malik, A.K., Tanveer, M., Suganthan, P.N.: Ensemble deep learning: a review. Eng. Appl. Artif. Intell. **115**, 105151 (2022)
8. Gourisaria, M.K., Arora, A., Bilgaiyan, S., Sahni, M.: Chicken disease multiclass classification using deep learning. In: Proceedings of International Conference on Information Technology and Applications: ICITA 2022, pp. 225–238. Springer (2023). https://doi.org/10.1007/978-981-19-9331-2_19
9. Jones, P., Niemi, J., Christensen, J.P., Tranter, R., Bennett, R.: A review of the financial impact of production diseases in poultry production systems. Anim. Prod. Sci. **59**(9), 1585–1597 (2018)
10. Kholil, M., Waspada, H.P., Akhsani, R.: Classification of infectious diseases in chickens based on feces images using deep learning. In: 2022 International Conference on Electrical and Information Technology (IEIT), pp. 362–365. IEEE (2022)
11. Kinung'hi, S.M., et al.: Assessment of economic impact caused by poultry coccidiosis in small and large scale poultry farms in Debre Zeit, Ethiopia. Int. J. Poult. Sci. **3**(11), 715–718 (2004)
12. Luong, H.H., Nguyen, T.M.: Improving chicken disease classification based on vision transformer and combine with integrated gradients explanation. Int. J. Adv. Comput. Sci. Appl. **15**(4), 1229–1235 (2024)

13. Luong, H.H., et al.: Utilising unet3+ for tooth segmentation on x-ray image. In: Nguyen, N.T., et al. (eds.) Asian Conference on Intelligent Information and Database Systems, vol. 1863, pp. 181–192. Springer, Cham (2023). https://doi.org/10.1007/978-3-031-42430-4_15
14. Machuve, D., Nwankwo, E., Mduma, N., Mbelwa, J.: Poultry diseases diagnostics models using deep learning. Front. Artif. Intell. **5**, 733345 (2022)
15. Mbelwa, H., Machuve, D., Mbelwa, J.: Deep convolutional neural network for chicken diseases detection (2021)
16. Nguyen, T.M., Van Tran, T., Lu, Q.T.: FEC-IGE: an efficient approach to classify fracture based on convolutional neural networks and integrated gradients explanation. Int. J. Adv. Comput. Sci. Appl. **15**(6), 1398–1409 (2024)
17. Poonia, R.C., Al-Alshaikh, H.A.: Ensemble approach of transfer learning and vision transformer leveraging explainable ai for disease diagnosis: an advancement towards smart healthcare 5.0. Comput. Biol. Med. **179**, 108874 (2024)
18. Serbessa, T.A., Geleta, Y.G., Terfa, I.O.: Review on diseases and health management of poultry and swine. Int. J. Avian Wildlife Biol. **7**(1), 27–38 (2023)
19. Srivastava, K., Pandey, P.: Deep learning based classification of poultry disease. Int. J. Autom. Smart Technol. **13**(1), 2439 (2023)
20. Suthagar, S., Mageshkumar, G., Ayyadurai, M., Snegha, C., Sureka, M., Velmurugan, S.: Faecal image-based chicken disease classification using deep learning techniques. In: Smys, S., Kamel, K.A., Palanisamy, R. (eds.) Inventive Computation and Information Technologies: Proceedings of ICICIT 2022, pp. 903–917. Springer, Singapore (2023). https://doi.org/10.1007/978-981-19-7402-1_64
21. Todd, E.C.: Poultry-associated foodborne disease-its occurrence, cost, sources and prevention. J. Food Prot. **43**(2), 129–139 (1980)
22. Wu, J.: Introduction to convolutional neural networks. National Key Lab for Novel Software Technology. Nanjing University. China **5**(23), 495 (2017)

Classifying Lexical Variations in Thai Social Media: A Machine Learning and LLMs Approach

Pimmada Chirawat[1], Dhanon Leenoi[3], Akkharawoot Takhom[2](✉), Prachya Boonkwan[3], and Tharathon Utasri[3]

[1] King Mongkut's Institute of Technology Ladkrabang, Bangkok, Thailand
66070135@kmitl.ac.th

[2] Faculty of Engineering, Thammasat School of Engineering, Thammasat University, Bangkok, Pathum Thani, Thailand
takkhara@engr.tu.ac.th

[3] Language and Semantic Technology Research Team National Electronics and Computer Technology Center, Thammasat University, Bangkok, Pathum Thani, Thailand
{dhanon.leenoi,prachya.boonkwan,tharathon.utasri}@nectec.or.th

Abstract. Social media platforms like Facebook, X (formerly Twitter), and TikTok produce large amounts of user content, offering valuable data for Social Media Analytics (SMA). However, analyzing Thai social media presents challenges due to lexical variations, such as spelling changes, semantic shifts, and the creation of new words (lexicogenesis). These features, along with the lack of spaces between words in Thai script, complicate traditional text analysis methods. This study addresses these challenges by using a combination of machine learning (ML) models and large language models (LLMs). We employ Bidirectional Long Short-Term Memory (Bi-LSTM) networks, pretrained models like BERT-base-Thai, and advanced LLMs such as LLaMA-3, Mistral, Gemma, and Phi to classify and analyze Thai social media content. Our research enhances the understanding of lexical variations and improves the processing of Thai language in social media, contributing to the development of more effective natural language processing tools.

Keywords: Lexical Variations · Machine Learning · Large Language Model · Social Media Analytic

1 Introduction

Social media platforms like Facebook, X (formerly Twitter), and TikTok have creates valuable data for Social Media Analytics (SMA), analyzing Thai social media presents specific challenges. Lexical variations, such as spelling changes, shifts in word meanings (semantic shifts), and the creation of new words (lexicogenesis), along with the absence of spaces between words in Thai script, make

J. Kertesz et al. (Eds.): CSoNet 2024, LNCS 15417, pp. 134–147, 2025.
https://doi.org/10.1007/978-981-96-6389-7_12

it difficult for standard text analysis methods and require more specialized solutions.

Previous studies in SMA have provided important insights. Batrinca and Treleaven (2015) discussed key methods for gathering and analyzing large social media data, while Ghania et al. (2019) introduced machine learning techniques, like deep learning, to improve the analysis of online content. However, these studies focused mostly on English and other widely spoken languages. In contrast, research on Thai social media, such as by Singkul et al. (2019), has highlighted the complexity of processing informal Thai language, but more work is needed to address these unique linguistic challenges.

Our research aims to address these challenges by combining machine learning (ML) models and large language models (LLMs) to analyze lexical variation in Thai social media. We will use Bidirectional Long Short-Term Memory (Bi-LSTM) networks and pretrained models such as BERT-base-Thai, alongside newer LLMs like LLaMA-3, Mistral, Gemma, and Phi. The main objective is to classify and analyze variations in Thai social media language, including spelling variations, changes in meaning, and the creation of new words, to improve understanding of language use online. This research will contribute to developing more effective tools for processing the Thai language in social media.

This paper is organized as follows: Sect. 2 reviews related work on SMA and Thai social media analysis. Section 3 outlines our research design, including data collection, labeling, and model implementation. Section 4 presents the results and discusses model performance. Finally, Sect. 5 concludes the study, summarizing key contributions and suggesting areas for future research.

2 Related Work

2.1 Social Media Analytics

Social media analytics has rapidly advanced, offering tools and techniques to extract insights from large-scale, user-generated data. Batrinca and Treleaven (2015) reviewed key methods, including sentiment analysis and data scraping, while highlighting challenges in accessing raw data from platforms like Twitter and Facebook [3].

Ghania et al. (2019) expanded on this by examining big data analytics in social media, classifying data formats and emphasizing the need for real-time analysis. They identified machine learning techniques like clustering, classification, and deep learning as central to extracting actionable insights from diverse content [8]. The integration of Machine Learning (ML) Models and Natural Language Processing (NLP) has enhanced the ability to detect lexical variations and meaning shifts in social media.

Together, these works provide a foundational understanding of the technical developments in social media analytics, supporting the exploration of lexical variations in Thai social media.

2.2 SMA in Thai

Thai data in an social media platforms such as Facebook, X (formerly Twitter), and TikTok present unique challenges for social media analytics (SMA), especially in handling lexical variation. Singkul et al. (2019) explored the complexity of processing informal Thai social media language, where syntax ambiguity are common [18]. These language variations create difficulties for traditional machine learning models, particularly in tasks such as sentiment analysis and opinion mining. The absence of spaces between words in Thai script further complicates tasks like word segmentation, leading to frequent errors in pre-processing steps.

Rojratanavijit and Eiamsithipan (2019) addressed challenges in sentiment analysis by examining how Thai social media content often lacks standardization due to the use of slang words, word usage variation, and code-switching between Thai and English [17]. These characteristics make it difficult to apply standard text mining and natural language processing (NLP) techniques. Their work also highlighted the difficulty in analyzing short-length messages, which frequently contain emotional and informal expressions, complicating the accurate classification of sentiment.

Chansanam et al. (2021) outlined a structured approach to data collection and labeling in their study of Korean popular culture on Thai YouTube channels [4]. The research utilized tools such as the YouTube API to systematically gather streaming data, which was then analyzed for patterns and user interactions. Their method of manually labeling data based on user engagement metrics, such as likes, dislikes, and comments, can be applied to Thai social media platforms like Facebook, X (formerly Twitter), and TikTok. Additionally, they employed deep learning techniques, specifically Long Short-Term Memory (LSTM) networks, to model the time-dependent nature of the data. This technique is particularly useful in detecting trends and variations in Thai social media language over time, such as the emergence of new slang or shifts in semantic meaning.

2.3 Lexical Variation in Social Media

Lexical variation is a linguistic phenomenon frequently observed in social media, reflecting the dynamic nature of language in the digital age. Research on lexical variation in social media was examined, focusing on three main aspects: lexicogenesis, semantic shift, and typing variation.

Lexicogenesis. Lexicogenesis, or the creation of new words, is an important process in language evolution. In social media contexts, it manifests in two primary forms:

1. **New Words for New Concepts**
   As new technologies and platforms emerge, language adapts to accommodate them. Crystal (2006) observed this phenomenon in his study of internet language, noting the rapid emergence of new terms related to digital technology [5]. For instance, words like "คลิ๊ก" /kʰlík/ for "click"; "เฟสบุ๊ก' '/fésbúk/ for

"Facebook," and "โควิด" /kʰo:wìt/ for "COVID" have entered the Thai lexicon to describe new concepts in the digital era. This process expands the vocabulary of a language, reflecting societal changes.

2. **New Words for Existing Concepts**
Social media users, particularly younger generations, often create new words to refer to existing concepts. Androutsopoulos (2011) highlighted this trend in his research on language use in social media [2]. In Thai, words like "กี" /ki:/ or "กีกี้" /ki:kî:/ for 'female genital', and "จูจู๋" /tɕu:tɕû:/ for 'male genital' have emerged as alternative words in Thai. This phenomenon increases lexical variation by providing users with more choices in expression.

Semantic Shift. Another aspect of lexical variation in social media is the use of existing words with new meanings:

1. **Euphemism**
Users often employ euphemisms to soften potentially offensive language. Allan and Burridge (2007) extensively studied this phenomenon in English online communication [1]. In Thai social media, phrases like "นางดอกไม้" /na:ŋ dɔ̀:k má:i/ (flower lady) replace more vulgar terms, while "สะตอ" /sa tɔ:/ is used instead of /tɔ: lǽ:/ (liar). This practice helps maintain politeness in online communication.
2. **Metonymy**
Metonymy, using one term to refer to a related concept, is common in social media language. Lakoff and Johnson (1980) described metonymy as a fundamental cognitive process that shapes language use [12]. Examples in Thai as shown in Table 1. These expressions add creativity and in-group identity to online discourse.

Table 1. The examples of Thai Metonymy

Example (a)	
Thai word	สามใบเทา
Phonetic	/sǎ:m bai tʰaw/
Literal Meaning	Three grey leaves
Meaning	3,000 baht

Example (b)	
Thai word	ขยี้ใบ
Phonetic	/kʰa jî: bai/
Literal Meaning	Leaf rubbing
Meaning	Referring to cannabis use

3. **Semantic and Grammatical Category Shift**
Words often undergo a shift in their grammatical category when used in social media contexts. This phenomenon, known as functional shift or conversion, adds flexibility to language use. Examples in Thai shown as Table 2.

Typing Variation. Typing variation is a distinctive feature of social media communication, manifesting in three main ways:

Table 2. Examples of Semantic Shift in Thai Language

	Example (a)
Thai word	ฉ่ำ
Phonetic	/tɕʰâ:m/
Traditional Meaning	Moist
New Usage	Used as an intensifier
	Example (b)
Thai word	ปัง
Phonetic	/paŋ/
Traditional Meaning	Onomatopoeia for an explosion sound
New Usage	Used as an adjective meaning "excellent" or "impressive"

1. **Reduction**
   Users often shorten words to save time and space. Thurlow and Brown (2003) observed this practice in their study of SMS language [20]. This practice reflects the fast-paced nature of online communication. In Thai, examples are showed in Table 3. These reductions not only save time and space but also create a more informal, conversational tone in digital communication. They demonstrate how users adapt language to suit the rapid, often character-limited nature of online platforms, while still maintaining comprehensibility within their linguistic community. In some cases, like "อุ" for "อุบาทว์", the reduction also serves as a form of euphemism, allowing users to reference potentially offensive concepts in a more socially acceptable manner.

Table 3. Examples of Word Reduction in Thai Language

	Example (a)
Thai Word	เด่ว
Phonetic	/dě:u/
Original Word	เดี๋ยว (/dǐ:au/)
Meaning	"Moment": The diphthong is reduced to a single vowel sound.
	Example (b)
Thai Word	อุ
Phonetic	/ùʔ/
Original Word	อุบาทว์ (/ùʔ bà:t/)
Meaning	"Obscene": Using only the first syllable to represent the entire word, often used to refer to obscene or vulgar content in a subtle way.

2. **Elongation**
   Conversely, users sometimes elongate words for emphasis or to express emotions. This technique helps convey tone and intensity in text-based communication. Examples in Thai shown in Table 4. These elongations not only add emphasis but also help mimic the prosodic features of spoken language, such as intonation and stress, in written form. This practice allows users to inject

more expressiveness and emotional distinction into their digital communications, compensating for the lack of face-to-face cues in online interactions.

Table 4. Examples of Elongation in Thai Language

Example (a)	
Thai Word	จร้า
Phonetic	(chra)
Explanation	An elongated form of ”จ้า” (cha), used to express agreement or acknowledgment with added emphasis.
Example (b)	
Thai Word	ดีย์
Phonetic	(deey)
Explanation	An elongated and stylized form of ”ดี” (dee), meaning ”good,” used to express strong approval or satisfaction.
Example (c)	
Thai Word	เบื่ออออ
Phonetic	(bueaaa)
Explanation	An elongated version of ”เบื่อ” (buea), meaning ”bored,” used to express intense or prolonged boredom.

3. **Character Substitution**
   Character substitution is another common practice in social media, often used to bypass censorship or add novelty. Herring and Danet (2007) discussed this phenomenon in their comprehensive study of internet language [6]. It can be categorized into three types showed in Table 5.

Table 5. Types and Examples of Substitution in Thai Language

Type	**Word**	**Phonetic**	**Explanation**
Similar shape	ควe	/k^huai/	Users replace characters with others that have a similar visual appearance. ”ควe” is used instead of the Thai swear word referring to male genitalia.
Similar sound	kวย	/k^huai/	Characters are replaced with others that produce a similar sound when read. ”kวย” is used in place of the same Thai swear word.
Hybrid	kวe	/k^huai/	This combines both shape and sound substitution techniques. ”kวe” represents the Thai swear word by mixing Roman and Thai characters.

4. **Use of Abbreviations**
   Abbreviations are widely used in social media to save time and space, and sometimes to create in-group language. Thai social media users frequently employ abbreviations, often derived from the initial consonants of phrases or sentences. These abbreviations often carry sexual connotations or vulgar

meanings, allowing users to express taboo concepts in a more covert manner. Examples include in Table 6.

These abbreviations serve multiple purposes: they speed up communication, create a sense of in-group identity, and allow users to express potentially controversial or taboo ideas in a less overt manner. They also demonstrate how social media language evolves to discuss sensitive topics while maintaining a degree of plausible deniability.

It's important to note that the full meanings of these abbreviations are often highly vulgar and not suitable for formal academic writing. Researchers studying this phenomenon must be aware of the cultural and linguistic context to fully understand the implications of these expressions in Thai social media communication.

Table 6. Examples of Abbreviations in Thai Language

Example (a)	
Thai Word	นปจต
Phonetic	(no po jo to)
Explanation	An expression of intense sexual attraction.

Example (b)	
Thai Word	ยนน
Phonetic	(yo no no)
Explanation	Implies the certainty of sexual activity between two individuals on social media.

These variations demonstrate users' creativity in adapting language to the constraints and opportunities of digital platforms.

Lexical variation in social media reflects the dynamic nature of language use in digital contexts. Understanding these phenomena is crucial for linguists, educators, and developers of natural language processing systems. Further research in this area could provide valuable insights into the evolution of language in the digital age and inform the development of more effective communication technologies.

3 Study Design

Figure 1 presents the workflow of Thai Social Media Analytics, which outlines the key stages involved in the process, labeled from **A to F**. The workflow begins with **(A)** data sources, where relevant social media content from platforms like Facebook, X (formerly Twitter), and TikTok is gathered, focusing on posts and comments with lexical variations such as typing variations, semantic shifts, and lexicogenesis. Following this, **(B)** step is data collection and data labeling, where posts are categorized into specific classes of lexical variation. The **(C)** involves data preprocessing, including tasks like word segmentation and cleaning, which prepares the dataset for further analysis. **(D)** consists of model training, where machine learning models, such as Bi-LSTM and BERT-base-Thai, are applied to the labeled data. **(E)** focuses on model enchanment with Thai WordNet and Thai FrameNet, **(F)** involves the classification results.

The details of each step will be further explained in the each subsections of this section.

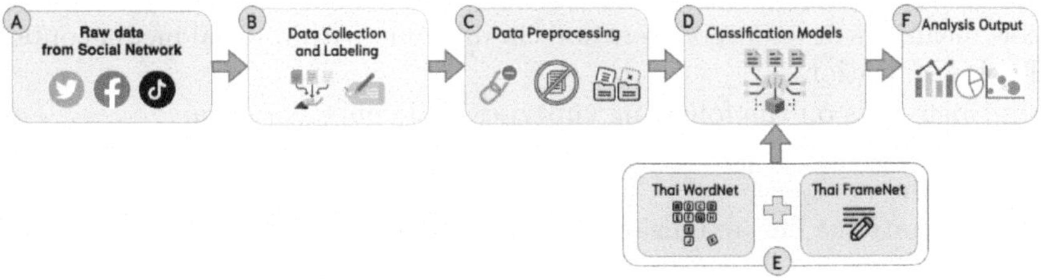

Fig. 1. Workflow of Thai Social Media Analytic

3.1 Dataset Construction

Data Collection. Since the dataset required for this research has not been released yet, we needed to construct our own. We chose to collect data from Twitter, Facebook, and TikTok, as these social platforms are popular among teens for expressing their emotions and opinions. Our data collection method starts by specifying an initial set of relevant keywords, which serve as search terms to retrieve information from the platforms. These form the foundation of our dataset. For instance, we initially scraped data using the keyword "สอบถาม" for 'to ask' and retrieved sentences like "ทักสอบถาม นัดจองQ พรุ่Jนี้นะค๊า" /t^{h}ák sɔ̀:p t^{h}ǎ:m nát tɕɔ:ŋ k^{h}iu p^{h}ûŋ ní:naʔ ká:/ for 'say hi and make an appointment for tomorrow.' After the first compilation, we analyze the data to identify additional keywords within the text. In the example above, we discovered a new keyword "จอง" tɕɔ:ŋ/ for 'to make an appointment' or 'to reserve', "พรุ่Jนี้" /p^{h}ûŋ ní:/ for 'tomorrow', "นะ" /naʔ/ and "ค๊า" /ká:/ (final-particle words used for politeness and firmness of statements or requests). These new keywords are then used to collect additional information, creating an iterative process of keyword identification and data crawling. This cycle continues until we amass a broad and diverse dataset. Once a certain amount of information has been collected We will use large language models (LLM) to add additional data sets. LLM learns and creates additional sentences based on the context and content of the data collected. It increases the volume of the dataset while adding variety and distinction.

Data Labeling. In this study, the data were manually labeled to ensure accuracy and consistency in categorization. The categorization was conducted based on three key linguistic phenomena pertinent to lexical variation in social media:

1. Lexicogenesis
   This category captures New Words for Existing Concepts, where users create novel terms to represent established ideas or concepts. It is important to note that New Words for New Concepts are excluded from the scope of this research.
2. Semantic Shift
   This category captures the semantic changes in which existing words acquire new meanings or undergo alterations in meaning within social media contexts.
3. Typing Variation
   Our focus was on the following subtypes of Typing Variation:
   (a) Reduction: The process of shortening words to enhance communication efficiency.
   (b) Elongation: The extension of words to convey emphasis or emotional expression.
   (c) Character Substitution: Modifications to word characters for creative purposes or to bypass automatic detection systems.
   Abbreviations were not included in the scope of this research.

The examples of data in each class are presented in Table 7.

Table 7. The examples of Thai lexical variation in social media

Classes	Thai Sentence	Keywords	Describe
Typing Variation	ยิJ grab กะข่mขืn dek 1 year old	ยิJ, ข่mขืn	This sentence uses English characters to avoid writing Thai words that may be vulgar or directly offensive, employing English letters that resemble or phonetically correspond to the original terms. This sentence translates into "Shooting a Grab driver and raping a 1-year-old child."
Semantic Shift	สวยตาแตก	ตาแตก	"ตาแตก," in its original meaning, refers to an eye injury. However, in this context, it is used as a slang term among teenagers to express something that is extremely beautiful, implying "very, very beautiful."
Lexicogenesis	สิ่งนี้ดีต่อกีกี้	กีกี้	"กีกี้" is a newly coined term used to refer to the female genitalia. This sentence translates to "This is very good for the female genitalia."

3.2 Data Preprocessing

In the data preprocessing phase, several key steps are undertaken to ensure the dataset is clean and suitable for model training:

- **Removal of URLs**: All URLs are eliminated from the dataset to remove irrelevant or extraneous information.
- **Removal of User Handles**: User handles (e.g., "@username") are deleted to protect user privacy and reduce noise in the data.
- **Elimination of Duplicate Entries**: Duplicate entries are identified and removed to maintain the integrity of the dataset and prevent biases in the analysis.

- **Handling Null or Missing Values**: Any null or missing values are either removed or imputed based on the context to avoid errors in downstream processing.
- **Dataset Split**: The dataset is split into three parts, consisting of 60% for the training set, 20% for the testing set, and 20% for the validation set. This ensures a balanced approach to model training, evaluation, and fine-tuning.

3.3 Classification Models

In this study, we will employ a diverse set of models to enhance our natural language processing tasks, particularly focusing on the Thai language. The models we will utilize include the Bidirectional Long Short-Term Memory (Bi-LSTM) model, a pretrained BERT model specific to Thai, and several large language models (LLMs), namely LLaMA3, Mistral, Gemma and Phi. The selection of these models is based on their distinct capabilities and strengths in handling various aspects of language understanding and generation.

Bi-LSTM Model. The study will employ a Bidirectional Long Short-Term Memory (Bi-LSTM) model for Thai text classification. Bi-LSTM is a variant of recurrent neural networks that processes input sequences in both forward and backward directions, capturing contextual information effectively [9]. This approach is particularly valuable for Thai, a language with complex morphological structures and contextual dependencies.

Pretrained BERT-Base-Thai. The research will utilize the pretrained BERT-base-Thai model, which is an adaptation of the original BERT (Bidirectional Encoder Representations from Transformers) architecture for the Thai language [7]. This model has been pretrained on a large corpus of Thai text, allowing it to capture intricate linguistic patterns and contextual distinctions specific to the Thai language [16].

Large Language Models (LLMs). The study will explore the application of several state-of-the-art LLMs for Thai text classification:

1. **LLaMA 3**
   Building upon the success of its predecessors, LLaMA 3 represents the latest iteration in the LLaMA family of language models developed by Meta AI [21]. Its potential for Thai text classification will be investigated, leveraging its advanced capabilities in understanding and generating human-like text.
2. **Mistral**
   As a high-performance language model, Mistral has shown promising results in various natural language processing tasks [11]. The study will examine its effectiveness in classifying Thai text, particularly focusing on its ability to handle the unique characteristics of the Thai language.

3. **Phi**
   Developed by Microsoft, the Phi model series has demonstrated impressive performance on various language tasks [10]. This study will explore its applicability to Thai text classification, assessing its capacity to understand and categorize Thai linguistic structures.
4. **Gemma**
   As one of the more recent additions to the LLM landscape, Gemma, developed by Google, will be evaluated for its potential in Thai text classification [19]. The study will investigate how well Gemma can be fine-tuned or adapted for the specific distinctions of the Thai language.

4 Result and Discussion

4.1 Statistical Information

Dataset. The dataset for this study was constructed by collecting social media content from popular platforms like Facebook, X (formerly Twitter), and TikTok, focusing on posts and comments containing lexical variations with total 3,296 records. The data collection process involved identifying relevant keywords and iteratively expanding the dataset through keyword refinement.

The final dataset included diverse samples of Thai social media language, categorized into three main classes: Typing Variation with 1,145 records, Semantic Shift with 1,130 records, and Lexicogenesis with 1,021 records. Each class was manually labeled.

Model Performance. The model evaluation focused on comparing the performance of several machine learning models, including Bi-LSTM, BERT-base-Thai, and advanced LLMs like LLaMA-3, Mistral, Gemma, and Phi. Each model was evaluated using standard performance metrics, such as accuracy and F1-score, across the three classes of lexical variation, which calculate by an equations following 1, 2 and 3.

$$\text{Precision} = \frac{\text{True Positive}}{\text{True Positive} + \text{False Positive}} \tag{1}$$

$$\text{Recall} = \frac{\text{True Positive}}{\text{True Positive} + \text{False Negative}} \tag{2}$$

$$\text{F1 Score} = 2 \times \frac{\text{Precision} \times \text{Recall}}{\text{Precision} + \text{Recall}} \tag{3}$$

Results in Table 8 showed that Bi-LSTM performed well in overall accuracy in classifying all of three types, while Gemma demonstrated better accuracy in classifying in Semantic Shift and typing variation. However, the pretrained BERT-base-Thai, Mistral and Llama-3.1 model struggled with certain lexicogenesis, highlighting the need for further refinement. These results emphasize the importance of selecting appropriate models for Thai language processing and reveal potential avenues for improving NLP tools for Thai social media analysis.

Table 8. F1 Score Performance Evaluation of Models: Lexicogenesis, Semantic Shift, and Typing Variation

Model	Lexicogenesis	Semantic Shift	Typing Variation	Accuracy F1 Score
bi-LSTM	**0.72**	**0.70**	**0.75**	**0.72**
monsoon-nlp/bert-base-thai	0.20	0.51	0.54	0.47
unsloth/mistral-7b-instruct-v0.3-bnb-4bit	0.45	0.39	0.07	0.36
unsloth/Meta-Llama-3.1-8B-Instruct-bnb-4bit	0.23	0.45	0.40	0.38
unsloth/gemma-2-9b-bnb-4bit	0.37	0.54	0.05	0.40
unsloth/Phi-3-medium-4k-instruct	0.28	0.54	0.57	0.49

4.2 Discussion

Our study of Thai language use on social media reveals the dynamic and diverse nature of language in the digital age. We can analyze this in three main areas:

New Word Creation (Lexicogenesis). We found that new words are constantly being created on social media. Examples include /bôŋ/ (บ๋ง), /fíaski:/ (เฟียสกี), and /lî:a hû:/ (เลี่ยหู้). This shows how creative and adaptable language is in modern communication. People often create new words to express specific meanings within their groups or to create a unique language identity. We also noticed that new words are sometimes created to avoid detection by content moderation systems. This is especially true for words that might trigger content filters, such as those related to buying and selling or crime. For example, using /tui/ (ตุย) instead of /ta:i/ (ตาย) to mean "die" helps users avoid being flagged.

Meaning Changes (Semantic Shift). Our research shows that existing words often take on new meanings. For instance, /ra: k^ha: mít tra p^hâ:p/ (ราคามิตรภาพ) now means "cheap price" instead of "friendship price", and /ta: tàek/ (ตาแตก) is used to mean "stunning" rather than "eye injury". These changes show how flexible language is and how it adapts to new social contexts. Sometimes, changing a word's meaning is also a way to avoid detection by content moderation systems. Users might use words with innocent original meanings but give them new meanings in specific contexts to communicate sensitive topics.

Spelling Variations (Typing Variation). We found many instances of intentional misspellings on social media. For example, using "ค_ย" instead of /k^huai/ (male private part), or "เง่น" /ŋên/ instead of /ŋî:an/ (horny). This often happens when users want to avoid detection by content filters or to make offensive words less obvious. These variations show how users adapt their language to communicate within the limitations of online platforms.

We also found that spelling variations are an effective way to avoid detection, especially for words that might trigger content filters. For example, using "ตาe" instead of /ta:i/ (ตาย) for "die", or using numbers or symbols to replace certain letters.

Models Performance. Small-scale LLMs require substantial datasets for fine-tuning to achieve optimal performance. In this study, the bi-LSTM model outperformed smaller LLMs due to limited data availability and computational constraints. However, when sufficient data and fine-tuning resources are available, LLMs demonstrate significant advantages, particularly in their ability to learn and adapt to new lexical variations and patterns more effectively. This adaptability makes them highly suitable for processing social media data, which is characterized by frequent lexical changes and the emergence of new terms.

The constraints of this study included limited computational resources and a small dataset, preventing full optimization of models such as BERT or other advanced LLMs. Despite these limitations, the study highlights the potential of leveraging lexical variation detection for broader applications, such as identifying circumvention of automated moderation systems, detecting subtle political or legal discourse avoidance, and monitoring covert advertising strategies. These findings underscore the importance of adaptable models in dynamic and evolving linguistic environments like social media.

5 Conclusion and Future Work

Thai language use on social media is unique and different from language use in other contexts. It involves creating new words, changing word meanings, and varying spellings in many ways. These phenomena show how lively language is and how it adapts to new technology and communication cultures.

Our study also found that these language variations are connected to linguistic concepts like Frame Semantics in FrameNet [14,15] and synonymy in WordNet [13]. Users change words to avoid "evoking words" or "lexical units" that might link to frames that content moderation systems consider inappropriate. Using synonym words from WordNet is another way to avoid using words that might be blocked.

Due to the manual labeling process, the dataset size was limited, as automated classification systems were not yet available. However, future work will focus on expanding the dataset size to improve the quality and generalizability of the results and we will focus on developing adaptable rules and guidelines for real-time scenarios to enhance the efficiency in detecting emerging typing variations.

However, these language changes can make it hard for people of different ages or cultures to understand each other. They also create challenges for developing natural language processing systems for Thai. Therefore, studying and tracking language changes on social media is important for understanding social dynamics and developing language technology. It's also crucial for improving content moderation systems to make them more effective.

References

1. Allan, K., Burridge, K.: Forbidden Words: Taboo and the Censoring of Language. Cambridge University Press, Cambridge (2006)
2. Androutsopoulos, J.: Language change and digital media: a review of conceptions and evidence. Stand. Lang. Lang. Stand. Changing Europe **1**, 145–159 (2011)
3. Batrinca, B., Treleaven, P.C.: Social media analytics: a survey of techniques, tools and platforms. AI Soc. **30**, 89–116 (2015)
4. Chansanam, W., Tuamsuk, K., Kwiecien, K., Oh, S.: Korean popular culture analytics in social media streaming: evidence from Youtube channels in Thailand. Int. J. Adv. Intell. Inf. **7**(3), 329–344 (2021)
5. Crystal, D.: Language and the Internet, 2 edn. Cambridge University Press, Cambridge (2006)
6. Danet, B., Herring, S.C.: The Multilingual Internet: Language, Culture, and Communication Online. Oxford University Press, Cambridge (2007)
7. Devlin, J.: Bert: pre-training of deep bidirectional transformers for language understanding. arXiv preprint arXiv:1810.04805 (2018)
8. Ghani, N.A., Hamid, S., Hashem, I., Ahmed, E.: Social media big data analytics: a survey. Comput. Hum. Behav. **101**, 417–428 (2019)
9. Graves, A., Schmidhuber, J.: Framewise phoneme classification with bidirectional lstm and other neural network architectures. Neural Netw. **18**(5–6), 602–610 (2005)
10. Gunasekar, S., et al.: Textbooks are all you need. arXiv preprint arXiv:2306.11644 (2023)
11. Jiang, A.Q., et al.: Mistral 7b. arXiv preprint arXiv:2310.06825 (2023)
12. Lakoff, G., Johnson, M.: Metaphors We Live By. University of Chicago Press, Chicago (1980)
13. Leenoi, D., Alongkornchai, A., Takhom, A., Boonkwan, P., Sunnithi, T.: A construction of thai wordnet through translation equivalence. In: 2022 17th International Joint Symposium on Artificial Intelligence and Natural Language Processing (iSAI-NLP), pp. 1–4. IEEE (2022)
14. Leenoi, D., Jumpathong, S., Porkaew, P., Supnithi, T.: Thai framenet construction and tools. Int. J. Asian Lang. Process. **21**(2), 71–82 (2011)
15. Leenoi, D., Utasri, T., Kriengket, K., Boonkwan, P., Takhom, A.: Semantic enrichment of thai framenet: generated knowledge graph on pathamasambodhi. Transform. Inf. Libr. Educ. Prof. Next **334** (2023)
16. Lowphansirikul, L., Polpanumas, C., Jantrakulchai, N., Nutanong, S.: Wangchanberta: pretraining transformer-based thai language models. arXiv preprint arXiv:2101.09635 (2021)
17. Rojratanavijit, J., Eiamsithipan, C.: Analysing Thai social media content to improve customer satisfaction (2019)
18. Singkul, S., Khampingyot, B., Maharattamalai, N., Taerungruang, S., Chalothorn, T.: Parsing Thai social data: a new challenge for Thai NLP. In: 2019 14th International Joint Symposium on Artificial Intelligence and Natural Language Processing (iSAI-NLP), pp. 1–7. IEEE (2019)
19. Team, G., et al.: Gemma: open models based on gemini research and technology. arXiv preprint arXiv:2403.08295 (2024)
20. Thurlow, C., Brown, A.: Generation txt? The sociolinguistics of young people's text-messaging. Discourse Anal. Online **1**(1), 30 (2003)
21. Touvron, H., et al.: Llama: open and efficient foundation language models. arXiv preprint arXiv:2302.13971 (2023)

TVGN: Mastering Predictions of Information Transmissibility in Time-Varying Networks

Xinrui Shi and Yupeng Li(✉)

Department of Interactive Media, Hong Kong Baptist University, Hong Kong, China
21482853@life.hkbu.edu.hk, ypengl@hkbu.edu.hk

Abstract. In the era of information overload, various types of information interconnect to form complex networks. To better manage diffusion paths within networks, we propose predicting information transmissibility—the probability of information being transmitted under the influence of other information in the network. Accurate transmissibility prediction has practical applications in recommendation systems and misinformation control, enabling relevant information to reach appropriate audiences while curbing the spread of less useful content. Diverging from existing research that focuses on static networks, our work addresses the more realistic scenario—time-varying networks where the interdependence between information evolves over time. We propose a novel graph neural network model, Temporal Variation Graph Network (TVGN), to predict transmissibility by capturing time-varying features and learning dynamic diffusion patterns. Our proposed model is evaluated on two popular citation networks, Cora [10] and CiteSeer [13]. The results demonstrate that our model outperforms state-of-the-art models, achieving low estimation error.

Keywords: Information network · Transmissibility · Graph neural network

1 Introduction

In today's digital era, diverse data types are interconnected through complex networks, such as social media where posts are linked by retweets, comments, and likes. Understanding the underlying structures and interconnections within these networks is crucial for managing the information diffusion process, which can be applied in real-world applications such as advertising placement [14] and content recommendation [3]. To deploy efficient diffusion paths and control information dissemination efficiently, for improving services, such as maximizing the benefits of targeted advertising traffic and recommending the most relevant content, we propose predicting information transmissibility, i.e., the probability of each information entity being transmitted based on its network relationships. By predicting transmissibility, we can optimize information flow to ensure content

J. Kertesz et al. (Eds.): CSoNet 2024, LNCS 15417, pp. 148–160, 2025.
https://doi.org/10.1007/978-981-96-6389-7_13

reaches the right audience, which enhances resource deployment and improves user engagement.

Our study plays a critical role in information influence spread—estimating the number of affected information entities given a seed information set [2]. This topic has inspired numerous related research questions, including predicting information cascade sizes [8], estimating influence probabilities [4], and identifying key influencers within networks [9]. These studies focus on different components of information networks, laying the foundation for accurately estimating the diffusion path and influence of information. For works that focus on specific entities in network, [18] proposes DeepIS to predict the probability of being influenced for targeted individuals. However, their study predominantly treats networks as static structures, while in reality, networks are dynamic with relationships within entities evolving over time. In this study, we aim to enhance the understanding of information spread by incorporating dynamics of network evolution.

Researchers study information diffusion using classical diffusion models like the widely accepted Independent Cascade (IC) model [9]. This model simulates how information spreads across networks by allowing entities to independently attempt to activate their neighbors. While Monte Carlo (MC) simulations have been used for these studies, they are time-consuming and less suitable for large networks. This has led to the adoption of Graph Neural Networks (GNNs), which efficiently capture the structure and dynamics of social networks. Recent GNN advancements include using snapshots of dynamic graphs and incorporating recurrent mechanisms like RNNs or LSTMs to track changes over time. However, these approaches often lack the detail required for precise, node-specific predictions and struggle to fully capture the evolving nature of diffusion processes. Therefore, there is a growing need for more advanced GNN architectures that can more accurately reflect the probabilistic and dynamic characteristics of information spread across networks.

To address the above challenges, we propose the Temporal Variation Graph Network (TVGN) model. This model estimates the probability that each entity will be transmitted after the seed entity by integrating the seed node vector with an influence probability matrix[1] at each timestep, allowing for the capture of fine-grained variations in the diffusion process for each entity. Specifically, we introduce an aggregation mechanism to characterize the evolving diffusion process. This mechanism aggregates the representations of neighboring entities for more accurate calculations, while also enabling the aggregation of information from multi-hop neighbors through iterative processes. During aggregation, the model captures the exact timestep at which any node may be activated, facilitating access to the corresponding influence probability for accurate prediction. We test the TVGN model using article citation datasets and achieve great performance, proving the model's ability to generalize across different graphs.

[1] Influence probability matrix quantifies the strength of interactions between arbitrary entities in a network.

The rest of this paper is organized as follows: Sect. 2 summarizes related work and Sect. 3 introduces the practical system model. In Sect. 4, we present a detailed description of the proposed framework. Finally, Sect. 5 discusses the experimental details and presents the results.

2 Related Work

2.1 Influence Spread in Time-Varying Networks

Influence spread, a core concept in network analysis, aims to estimate the extent of impact from a specified seed set within a network [2]. There are various problem settings, leading to focused studies on various network scales. At the broad network level, research like [9] seeks to maximize influence by identifying key nodes. More localized studies investigate cascade dynamics, such as cascade size [8] and propagation paths [6]. Further detailed analysis at a fine-grained level explores edge and node attributes, for instance, learning influence probabilities [4] and node activation likelihoods [18]. Our research focuses on granular node-level analysis, specifically investigating the node transmission in evolving network structures, departing from conventional approaches that predominantly examine static networks. We develop a more nuanced understanding of information transmissibility patterns across temporal dimensions. This approach enables us to capture the complex dynamics of real-world networks, where connections and influence patterns continuously evolve, thereby providing more practical insights for information diffusion processes.

2.2 Graph Neural Networks

Graph Neural Networks (GNNs) [12] excel in processing non-Euclidean graph structures by leveraging node and graph characteristics. GNNs typically alternate between transforming node features and aggregating neighboring information. Existing research has explored influence spread using GNNs. For example, [11] predicts an individual's state based on neighbors' states and local subgraphs; [1] focuses on accurately predicting the popularity of online content; [8] develops DeepCas to predict information cascades; and [18] introduces DeepIS to estimate individual susceptibility by combining GNN structures with influence diffusion models. While existing studies predominantly focus on static graph analysis, they often overlook the dynamic nature of networks and their diffusion processes. Our work addresses this limitation by employing GNNs to estimate node transmissibility in information networks characterized by time-varying relationships. Through capturing and learning both the network evolution and the dynamic diffusion processes, our approach aims to achieve more precise and realistic estimations of information propagation behaviors.

Table 1. Symbols in the article

symbol	description
G	Information network
V	Node (information entity) set of G
E	Edge set of G
p_{ij}^t	Influence probability from i to j at time t
P_t	Influence strength at time t
S	Seed node (information entity) set
i, j	Nodes (information entities)
D	An instance of diffusion process
$I_{S,D}^t(i)$	The state of i given S, D at t
$\delta_S^t(i)$	Information transmissibility of i given S at t

3 System Model

In this section, we begin with an introduction to the IC Model that illustrates the diffusion process in our study. We then provide a detailed definition of the prediction problem.

Before formulating the problem, we introduce the concept of influence probability. Within the information network, influence probability quantifies the likelihood that one piece of information will affect another, thereby reflecting the strength of the interaction between two information entities. This probability can vary over time in real-world scenarios. For example, initially, social media posts A and B may have only a weak relationship due to their similar themes. However, when it is later observed that users who like post A are also likely to share post B, the influence probability between them increases significantly. By incorporating this dynamic probability, our framework can accurately model the temporal evolution of network relationships.

The symbols used in this paper are detailed in Table 1.

3.1 Independent Cascade Model

In this study, we consider a graph $G = (V, E)$ where V represents the set of nodes and E denotes the set of edges, with each edge assigned a weight denoting the influence probability between two nodes at a given timestep t, symbolized as p_{ij}^t. This probability p_{ij}^t reflects the likelihood that node i will influence node j in the subsequent timestep, given that node i has been activated in the current timestep. The diffusion process begins from a predefined set of seed nodes S at timestep 0. At each following timestep t (where $t > 0$), every node that is activated in the previous timestep $t-1$ has a single opportunity to activate each of its out-neighbors according to the probability p_{ij}. Once activated, nodes remain active throughout the process. The diffusion ceases when no nodes are activated at a given timestep t, signaling the end of the process.

3.2 The Transmissibility Prediction Problem

In a network, diffusion processes vary significantly based on the choice of seed nodes, and even the identical seed set can lead to multiple diffusion instances. We define a diffusion instance D initiated by a specific seed set S. For such an instance, if node i is activated by seed set S at time t, we denote the state of the node i as $I^t_{S,D}(i) = 1$, and 0 otherwise. Each edge in the network carries a time-dependent influence probability, p^t_{ij}, reflecting the probability that node i influences node j at time t. The probabilities between nodes form an influence strength matrix for each timestep, which we denote as P_t. Our primary objective is to estimate the transmissibility $\delta^t_S(i)$ of node i under seed set S at time t, which is defined as $\delta^t_S(i) = E_{D \sim p(D)}[I^t_{S,D}(i)]$, where $p(D)$ represents the probability distribution over all possible diffusio n instances in the network.

4 TVGN Model

Our model comprises three modules, as illustrated in Fig. 1. The first module constructs features for each node, providing a foundational representation. The second module performs a coarse estimation of the transmissibility for each node. Finally, the third module refines these estimations by diffusing them among neighboring nodes to achieve fine-grained predictions.

4.1 Feature Extraction Module

This module (Fig. 1b) constructs the necessary features. Seed set is one of the most important factors, as information transmission is dependent on seed nodes. We represent the seed nodes using a multi-hot vector x, where $x_{[i]} = 1$ if node $i \in S$, and $x_{[i]} = 0$ otherwise. Another key factor is the influence strength P_t, which maintains the graph's topology and the influence probability between any two nodes at timestep t. According to DeepIS [18], these two factors are sufficient for accurate prediction. Therefore, we use them to form the feature matrix.

$$X = [x, P_1^T x, P_1^T P_2^T x, P_1^T P_2^T P_3^T x, \ldots, P_1^T P_2^T P_3^T \ldots P_t^T x] \tag{1}$$

Each element represents the probability that one seed set affect any target node at a specific time t. For example, $P_1^T P_2^T P_3^T x$ represents the probability of nodes being infected at timestep t=3. $P_1^T P_2^T P_3^T \ldots P_t^T x$ means the upper bound for all nodes being influenced at timestep t under IC model.

4.2 Feature Embedding Module

The feature matrix, derived from time-dependent influence probabilities for each node, is treated as a sequence and embedded into a Transformer [15] encoder, leveraging its proficiency in handling sequential data. The encoder, equipped with positional encoding, self-attention mechanisms, layer normalization, and

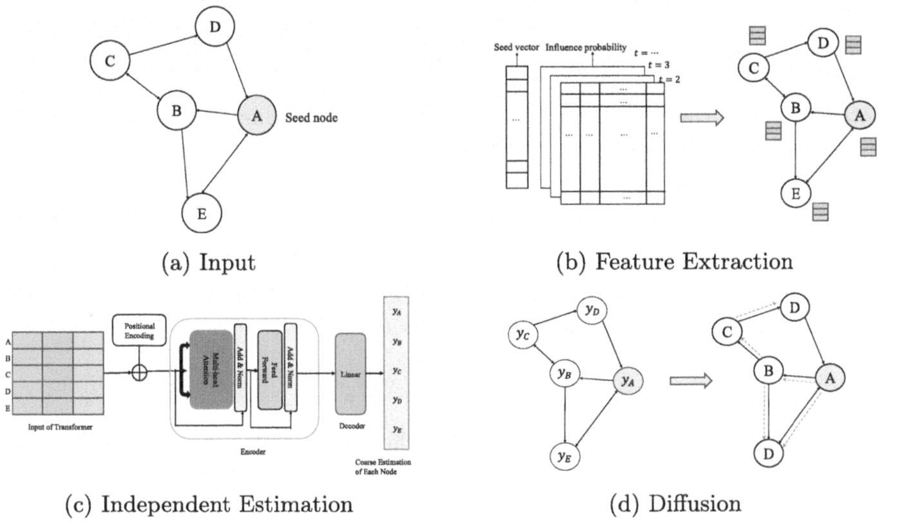

(a) Input (b) Feature Extraction

(c) Independent Estimation (d) Diffusion

Fig. 1. The estimation process of the proposed TVGN model: (a) Input: the input of the TVGN model is a directed graph with nodes A (seed node), B, C, D, and E. (b) Feature Extraction: the model first constructs each node's feature vector based on influence strength at different time and the seed nodes. (c) Independent Estimation: the feature vector is input to the Transformer framework for coarse estimation, mapping each node's representation to a probability in [0, 1]. (d) Diffusion: the coarse estimation of each node is diffused to its neighbors to produce fine-grained estimation, excluding the seed node.

residual connections, processes this sequence. A fully connected neural network then predicts the rough transmissibility of each node (Fig. 1c).

Position encoding: it involves encoding each probability at different timesteps into a d-dimensional space. The sequence data, $x_{embedding}$, is thus composed of t d-dimensional vectors. Position encoding provides the Transformer with location information for each vector in the sequence, ensuring the order is preserved. We achieve this using sine and cosine functions:

$$\begin{cases} PE_{(pos,2i)} = sin(pos/10000^{2i/d_{model}}) \\ PE_{(pos,2i+1)} = cos(pos/10000^{2i/d_{model}}) \end{cases} \tag{2}$$

In the equation, pos represents the position, and i denotes the dimension. Each dimension of the positional encoding corresponds to a sinusoidal wave of different frequencies, where higher dimensions have longer wavelengths. This design allows the model to easily learn relative positions, as for any fixed offset k, PE_{pos+k} can be represented as a linear function of PE_{pos} [15]. The sequence representation can be formulated as $X_{\text{embedding}} = x_{\text{embedding}} + \text{position encoding}$.

Self-attention: The attention mechanism computes an output by using a query vector to calculate weights through a compatibility score with key vectors. These weights are then applied to sum up the corresponding value vectors.

To learn representations with multiple meanings, a linear mapping function is applied to $X_{\text{embedding}}$. Specifically, weights W_Q, W_K, and W_V are assigned to $X_{\text{embedding}}$, resulting in the formation of three matrices: Q, K, and V. These matrices retain the dimensions of the original embedding and serve as query, key, and value weights in processing sequence data.

$$Attention(Q, K, V) = softmax(\frac{QK^T}{\sqrt{d_k}})V \tag{3}$$

Rough Estimation: Once the feature embedding is obtained, we adopt a non-linear neural function to predict each nodes $\delta_S^t(i)$.

$$y_\theta(X) = Sigmoid[XW_1 + b_1] \tag{4}$$

θ is the parameter of the neural network, W_1, W_2 are trainable parameters, and b_1, b_2 are bias.

4.3 Diffusion Module

This module (Fig. 1d) aims to aggregate information from neighbors to make fine-grained estimations. We follow the theoretical formula proposed by DeepIS [18], using the approximate stationary distribution $\widetilde{\delta}$ under the IC model, based on the stationary distribution of random walks. Specifically, each node forms a sub-network with its neighbors that may activate it. The information from these sub-networks enables a more precise determination of the potential timesteps for node activation, facilitating fine-grained estimations.

$$\widetilde{\delta}_i^t = 1 - \prod_{j \in N(i)} (1 - P_{ji}^t \widetilde{\delta}_j^t) \tag{5}$$

In this approach, the information from in-neighbors is aggregated to approximate the transmissibility of node i. Let $N(i)$ represent the in-neighbors of i, and t denote the timestep at which node j activates i. The influence probability that j influences i at timestep t is denoted by P_{ji}^t. To compute the transmissibility of i, it is necessary to identify when j influences i by considering all paths from seed nodes to i. While this process is manageable for small networks, it becomes exceedingly time-consuming for large-scale networks. Thus, we propose a pruning method under the IC model to eliminate unnecessary path branches during the search process, thereby improving algorithm efficiency. By calculating the path length from the seed node to the neighbor node, we can estimate the approximate range of activation steps. We then average obtained P_{ij}^t values and use the formula to calculate transmissibility. It is important to note that for seed nodes, neighbor representations are not aggregated, as their transmissibility is always equal to 1.

4.4 Training

We adopt the loss function of DeepIS [18], as we are focused on a node regression task. Mean Square Error (MSE) is used to compute the estimation error for training cascade m. Each cascade consists of a seed set and ground truth of each node.

$$L_{\text{MSE}} = \frac{1}{M}\sum_{m=1}^{M} \|\hat{y}_{(m)} - y_{(m)}\|_2 \tag{6}$$

Since our task serves as a component of influence spread, assessing graph-level errors is also essential. We use Mean Relative Square Error to evaluate performance across the graph.

$$L_{\text{MRSE}} = \frac{1}{M}\sum_{m=1}^{M} \left(\frac{\|\hat{y}_{(m)}\|_1 - \|y_{(m)}\|_1}{\|y_{(m)}\|_1}\right)^2 \tag{7}$$

The final objective function is:

$$Loss = L_{\text{MSE}} + \lambda L_{\text{MRSE}} + \gamma\|\theta\|_2 \tag{8}$$

5 Evaluation

5.1 Datasets

We use CORA and CITESEER, two popular citation network datasets, due to their widespread use in studying information networks.

CORA [10]: It consists of 2,810 scientific publications and 15,962 links, in which scientific publications are represented by nodes, and links are represented by edges. If one article cites an article, there would be a link between them.

CITESEER [13]: It consists of 2,110 scientific publications and 7,336 links. In CITESEER graph, nodes denote articles, and edges denote citation links.

5.2 Data Preparation

Due to the unavailability of time-varying influence probability for these datasets, we follow the practice of previous literature. First, we initialize influence probability at timestep 0 with values drawn from a uniform distribution over [0,1]. For subsequent timesteps, we use an exponential decay function to model the time-varying influence probability.

$$N(t) = N_0 e^{-\alpha t} \tag{9}$$

where $N(t)$ represents the influence probability at timestep t, with $N(0) = N_0$ being the initial influence probability at $t = 0$. The parameter α, known as the decay constant, is set to ensure the influence probability decays over a sufficiently long period.

Ground truth. For each dataset, we simulate the diffusion process by setting seed sizes ranging from 20 to 500. Nodes are randomly selected according to these sizes to initiate the diffusion based on the IC model. The diffusion process involves a stochastic component where each activated node attempts to activate its neighbors. This is done by comparing a randomly generated threshold (between 0 and 1) to the influence probability at the specific activation timestep of each neighbor. A node is activated (set to 1) if the influence probability exceeds the threshold; otherwise, it remains inactive (set to 0). To address the inherent randomness and ensure robust results, we apply Monte Carlo Simulation algorithms, repeating the diffusion process 10,000 times and averaging the outcomes to determine the transmissibility of each node under various seed sets. The ground truth data includes a seed vector, which is a multi-hot vector indicating seed nodes (1 for seed nodes, 0 otherwise), and the corresponding transmissibility for each node.

Data splitting. For all diffusion instances, we randomly sample 80% of them as training data, 10% as validation data and 10% as test data.

5.3 Baselines

Our model performs node regression tasks. We compare it with classical Graph Neural Networks (GNNs). Additionally, we include DeepIS in our benchmarks, as it is a pioneering model in predicting activation probability within the network for individuals.

GCN [7]: The model aggregates information from neighbor nodes and the node itself in an average manner.

GraphSAGE [5]: A framework that concatenates the node's own features with its neighbors information. This concatenation distinguishes self-information from neighbor information, highlighting the node's own importance.

GAT [16]: The attention mechanism enables nodes to weight the importance of their neighbors. The model learns attention coefficients that determine each neighbor's contribution during feature aggregation, enabling more adaptive and context-aware node representations.

SGC [17]: SGC is proposed to reduce the complexity of GCN-like models. It transforms nonlinear GCNs into simple linear models by eliminating the nonlinearity between GCN layers.

DeepIS-mean: Using the seed node vector and fixed influence probability to form a feature matrix, inputting it to the fully connected neural network for rough estimation, and then aggregating the features of in-neighbor nodes to obtain the final estimation. In response to our problem, we calculate the mean of all timesteps' influence probability between nodes to satisfy DeepIS that only static influence probability can be accepted.

DeepIS-timestep 0: Since the input of DeepIS is static influence probability, we take the influence probability at timestep 0 as input.

DeepIS-exact influence probability: We enhance the diffusion propagation mechanism in this model to calculate the activation probability of any node by its neighbors. Unlike the DeepIS model, where influence probability is constant and derived from the adjacency matrix, our problem emphasizes the dynamic influence probability at each timestep. To achieve this, we integrate an algorithm based on the IC model, enabling precise calculation of influence probabilities that correspond to the specific timestep when a node is activated. This enhancement allows this model to more effectively adapt to changing activation dynamics.

5.4 Implementation Details

To ensure fairness, all models use a feature matrix generated by Eq.(1). Each model uses a 2-layer structure with 64 hidden units. Besides, the GAT model employs 4 attention heads, and the DeepIS model incorporates a 2-layer Multi-layer Perceptron in the GNN stage.

We first set hyper-parameter ranges, then employ five-fold cross-validation to identify optimal parameters based on validation performance. The optimized model is subsequently evaluated across different seed sizes, ranging from 20 to 500 nodes, to comprehensively assess its generalizability and performance stability.

5.5 Evaluation Metrics

Mean Error (ME): It is the average of the absolute differences between the predicted $\hat{y}_i$ and actual y_i transmissibility of each node, averaged over multiple instances M.

$$ME = \frac{1}{M}\sum_{m=1}^{M}\frac{1}{\mid V \mid}\sum_{i=1}^{|V|} \mid \hat{y}_m(i) - y_m(i) \mid \tag{10}$$

Total Error (TE): It quantifies the average absolute difference between the sum of predicted transmissibility $\hat{y}_i$ of all nodes and the sum of ground truth y_i across graph instances M.

$$TE = \frac{1}{M}\sum_{m=1}^{M}\left(\mid \sum_{i=1}^{|V|} \hat{y}_m(i) - \sum_{i=1}^{|V|} y_m(i) \mid \right) \tag{11}$$

5.6 Result

The mean error across all models is depicted in Fig. 2a and 2b. Overall, our model performs the best. Traditional GNNs perform poorly because they treat the upper bound probability at each step as independent features rather than as interdependent elements in the diffusion process. Thereby, GNNs fails to account for the time-varying influence probabilities that characterize the calculation at each step. Moreover, traditional GNNs employ mean, concatenation, and attention mechanisms to aggregate neighbor node information, which do not effectively capture the diffusion dynamics. DeepIS variants such as DeepIS-mean, DeepIS-timestep 0, and DeepIS-exact timestep utilize a 2-layer fully connected

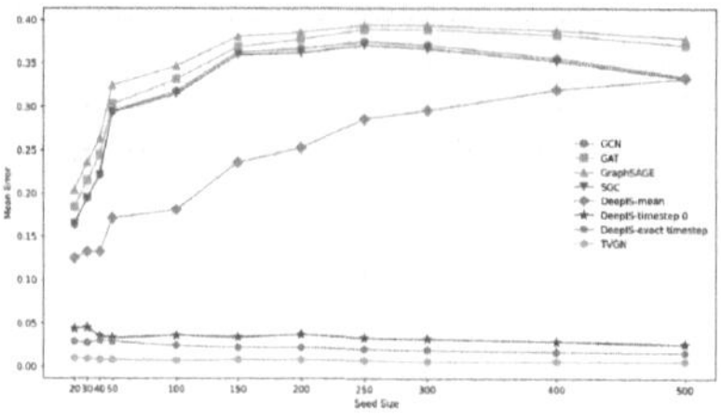

(a) Mean error on Cora dataset

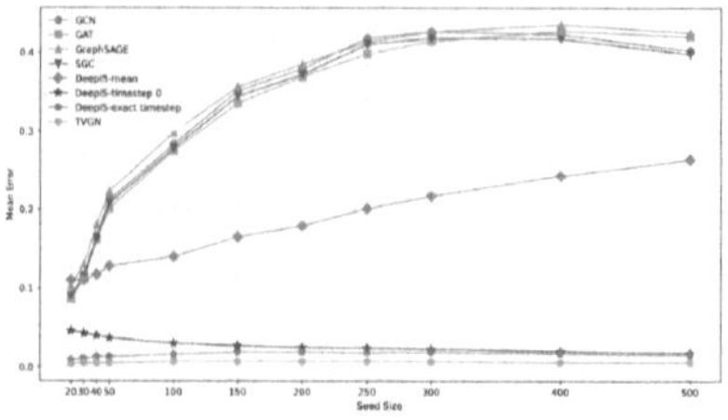

(b) Mean error on Citeseer dataset

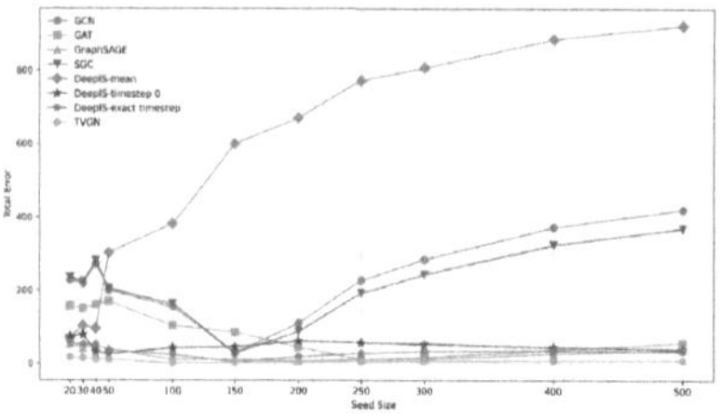

(c) Total error on Cora dataset

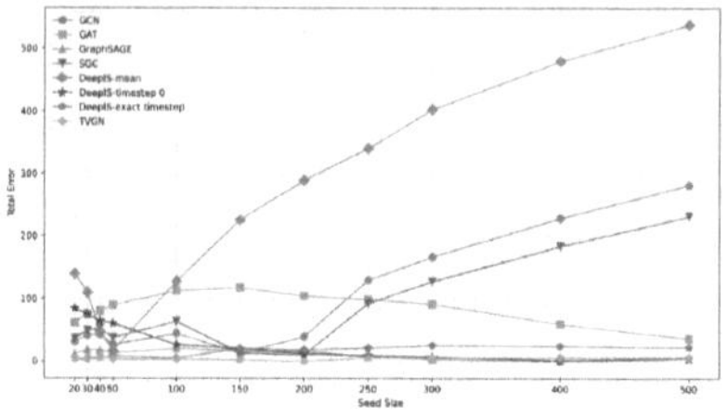

(d) Total error on Citeseer dataset

Fig. 2. The performance comparisons of various graph neural network models on Cora and Citeseer datasets. (a) Mean error on Cora dataset: Line chart comparing performance of traditional GNNs, DeepIS variants, and TVGN across different seed sizes ranging from 20 to 500 on Cora dataset. TVGN demonstrates the best performance. (b) Mean error on Citeseer dataset: Similar comparison for Citeseer dataset, with traditional GNNs showing relatively poorer performance. (c) Total error on Cora dataset: Line chart depicting total error for various models on Cora dataset over increasing seed sizes. TVGN achieves the best performance, maintaining stable results across different seed sets. (d) Total error on Citeseer dataset: Total error trends for Citeseer dataset, with traditional GNNs exhibiting greater fluctuations, and DeepIS variants showing moderate performance.

neural network to approximate transmissibility. While these models do not fully capture time-varying information, they capture diffusion characteristics through its propagation scheme that approximate stationary probabilities under the IC model, leading to better performance than traditional GNNs. Our model, in particular, significantly outperforms others, reducing estimation error by an order of magnitude. With the seed size increases, the mean error of traditional GNNs and DeepIS-mean increases. This is because larger seed sets lead to more complex diffusion patterns, making it more difficult for models to learn and predict accurately. Conversely, the estimation error of DeepIS-timestep 0 and DeepIS-exact timestep remains relatively stable across all seed sizes. This stability is due to the partial capture of time-varying influence probabilities during feature extraction and the approximation of stationary probabilities, which effectively aids prediction accuracy.

The total error of all models is shown in Fig. 2c and 2d. We can see that traditional GNNs typically exhibit irregular fluctuations across different seed sizes. In contrast, the TVGN and DeepIS variants demonstrate relatively minor fluctuations. Combined with the Mean Error, it becomes evident that the total error does not consistently correlate with the mean error for identical seed sizes. This discrepancy arises because the total error is not a direct summation of the absolute errors for all nodes.

6 Conclusion

In this paper, we introduce a practical problem to estimate transmissibility of each information entity within information networks, accounting for time-varying influence probabilities. We develop a GNN model to address the problem. The model operates in three stages: initially, it captures time-varying features for each node; subsequently, it estimates the transmissibility of each entity coarsely and independently; finally, it aggregates neighboring entities information to decode the underlying mechanism of the dynamic diffusion process. Experiments demonstrate that our model outperforms state-of-the-art benchmark methods across all evaluation metrics. However, a limitation of TVGN model is its higher computational cost compared to other models, primarily due to the incorporation of Transformer mechanisms for temporal information processing. Future research will focus on optimizing the model's computational efficiency to enable its application in large-scale real-world networks.

Acknowledgement. This work was supported in part by National Natural Science Foundation of China (No. 62202402), Guangdong Basic and Applied Basic Research Foundation (No. 2023A1515011562 and No. 2022A1515011583), Hong Kong RGC Early Career Scheme (No. 22202423), The Initiation Grant for Faculty Niche Research Areas 2023/24 (No. RC-FNRA-IG/23-24/COMM/01), Startup Grant (Tier 1) for New Academics AY2020/21 of Hong Kong Baptist University.

References

1. Cao, Q., Shen, H., Gao, J., Wei, B., Cheng, X.: Popularity prediction on social platforms with coupled graph neural networks. In: Proceedings of the 13th International Conference on Web Search and Data Mining, pp. 70–78 (2020)
2. Chen, W., Yuan, Y., Zhang, L.: Scalable influence maximization in social networks under the linear threshold model. In: 2010 IEEE International Conference on Data Mining, pp. 88–97 (2010)
3. Cheng, J., Sun, A., Hu, D., Zeng, D.: An information diffusion-based recommendation framework for micro-blogging. J. Assoc. Inf. Syst. **12**(7), 2 (2011)
4. Goyal, A., Bonchi, F., Lakshmanan, L.V.: Learning influence probabilities in social networks. In: Proceedings of the Third ACM International Conference on Web Search and Data Mining, pp. 241–250 (2010)
5. Hamilton, W., Ying, Z., Leskovec, J.: Inductive representation learning on large graphs. In: Advances in Neural Information Processing Systems (2017)

6. Hu, W., Singh, K.K., Xiao, F., Han, J., Chuah, C.N., Lee, Y.J.: Who will share my image? Predicting the content diffusion path in online social networks. In: Proceedings of the eleventh ACM International Conference on Web Search and Data Mining, pp. 252–260 (2018)
7. Kipf, T.N., Welling, M.: Semi-supervised classification with graph convolutional networks. arXiv preprint arXiv:1609.02907 (2016)
8. Li, C., Ma, J., Guo, X., Mei, Q.: DeepCas: an end-to-end predictor of information cascades. In: Proceedings of the 26th International Conference on World Wide Web, pp. 577–586 (2017)
9. Li, Y., Fan, J., Wang, Y., Tan, K.L.: Influence maximization on social graphs: a survey. IEEE Trans. Knowl. Data Eng. **10**, 1852–1872 (2018)
10. McCallum, A.K., Nigam, K., Rennie, J., Seymore, K.: Automating the construction of internet portals with machine learning. Inf. Retrieval **2**, 127–163 (2000)
11. Qiu, J., Tang, J., Ma, H., Dong, Y., Wang, K., Tang, J.: DeepInf: social influence prediction with deep learning. In: Proceedings of the 24th ACM SIGKDD International Conference on Knowledge Discovery & Data Mining, pp. 2110–2119 (2018)
12. Scarselli, F., Gori, M., Tsoi, A.C., Hagenbuchner, M., Monfardini, G.: The graph neural network model. IEEE Trans. Neural Netw. **1**, 61–80 (2008)
13. Sen, P., Namata, G., Bilgic, M., Getoor, L., Galligher, B., Eliassi-Rad, T.: Collective classification in network data. AI Mag. **3**, 93 (2008)
14. Stewart, A., Chen, L., Paiu, R., Nejdl, W.: Discovering information diffusion paths from blogosphere for online advertising. In: Proceedings of the 1st International Workshop on Data Mining and Audience Intelligence for Advertising, pp. 46–54 (2007)
15. Vaswani, A.: Attention is all you need. In: Advances in Neural Information Processing Systems (2017)
16. Velickovic, P., Cucurull, G., Casanova, A., Romero, A., Lio, P., Bengio, Y.: Graph attention networks. stat, p. 20 arXiv:1710.10903 (2017)
17. Wu, F., Souza, A., Zhang, T., Fifty, C., Yu, T., Weinberger, K.: Simplifying graph convolutional networks. In: International Conference on Machine Learning, pp. 6861–6871 (2019)
18. Xia, W., Li, Y., Wu, J., Li, S.: DeepIS: susceptibility estimation on social networks. In: Proceedings of the 14th ACM International Conference on Web Search and Data Mining, pp. 761–769 (2021)

Agent-Based Modelling Approach to Support Strategic Planning for EV Charging Stations in A University Campus

Luca Ambrosino, Linh Do-Bui-Khanh, Khai Nguyen-Manh, Giuseppe Calafiore, Laurent El-Ghaoui, and Doanh Nguyen-Ngoc(✉)

Cosmos Lab, Center of Environmental Intelligence (CEI), VinUniversity, South-East Asia, Vietnam
doanh.nn@vinuni.edu.vn

Abstract. The future of transportation is rapidly transforming with the increasing adoption of electric vehicles (EVs), signifying a global commitment to sustainability. This expansion introduces significant challenges, particularly in the construction and maintenance of EV charging infrastructure. As EV numbers rise, user dissatisfaction due to inadequate charging facilities threatens the adoption of electric mobility. Additionally, the strain on financial and power resources necessitates strategic planning to avoid misallocation. This paper focuses on addressing these challenges within the context of charging stations inside a university campus where these challenges are significantly emerging due to the synchrony of EV users (arrival time, charging time,...) as well as electrical uses with different purposes (charging and other activities) at the same time. To tackle these issues, we propose a Simulation Environment using an Agent-Based Modelling Approach (ABM). We simulate the charging behaviours of EV users, optimize infrastructure deployment, and enhance decision-making for charging station operations thanks to simulations based on real data. The results showed that increasing active charging ports in targeted areas, combined with strict rules banning gasoline vehicles from EV spots, achieved over 90% satisfaction for charged electric vehicles. The performance analysis assessed how parameters like charging port numbers, locations, and policies influenced infrastructure efficiency, helping define an optimal configuration that balances cost while aligning electricity use with the universitys overall consumption.

Keywords: Agent-Based Modelling · Electric Vehicles · Charging Stations · Strategy Planning · University Campus

1 Introduction

The future of transportation is undergoing a significant transformation, driven by the growing adoption of electric vehicles (EVs). This increase does not merely reflect a shift in vehicle preference but shows worldwide commitment to promoting a more sustainable future. In 2020, the global number of electric vehicles

J. Kertesz et al. (Eds.): CSoNet 2024, LNCS 15417, pp. 161–173, 2025.
https://doi.org/10.1007/978-981-96-6389-7_14

(EVs) reached a significant milestone of 10 million, representing a notable 43% increase compared to the previous year [4]. Vietnam is one of the most emerging nations in this sector, where many companies are pushing to expand the EV market in the country. However, overly ambitious plans could place significant strain on Vietnam's critical 500 kV power grid, potentially reaching the limits of voltage fluctuation and power loss by 2030 [8].

EVs, as symbols of cleaner, sustainable transportation, are driving us toward a greener future. Research on EV charging stations has grown, with many located in high-density cities and, more recently, on university campuses at the forefront of this field. On university campuses, managing vehicle arrival times is critical, as students and staff tend to charge during peak periods. This paper focuses on optimizing campus charging station management to address these challenges and prepare for the rising use of EVs.

Extensive research has focused on optimizing EV charging systems. In [12], a capacitated coverage model reallocates stations to maximize charging demand coverage. The authors in [1] optimize EVs charging allocating power to different times during the day, obtaining a cost-saving in the off-peak hours. Genetic algorithms use city data to find optimal locations [5], while a stochastic agent-based framework predicts day-ahead demand based on SOC, traffic, and weather [7]. The lack of infrastructure affects EV owner satisfaction and behavior, with models exploring how policies like incentives and smart charging impact user satisfaction [6]. Studies simulate energy demand, traffic-based electricity needs [11], and forecast demand with spatio-temporal networks [10] or queueing theory [2], though gaps remain between simulations and real behavior.

To address the growing number of EVs and future charging demands, this research project proposes optimizing the university's charging station infrastructure through an agent-based modelling approach, creating a simulation environment with a visual interface. The project has two main objectives: managing charging stations effectively on campus and analyzing EV owners' behaviour to generate optimization insights. This environment allows operational teams, even without technical expertise, to model scenarios, conduct training, and evaluate performance under various conditions without impacting real-time operations, saving both costs and resources. The simulations insights will guide the strategic planning of charging stations, creating efficient and user-focused infrastructure. With an accessible visual interface, the project aims to support sustainable transportation on campuses and potentially expand to other public locations.

2 Case Study

This study examines Vin University (VinUni), located on the outskirts of Hanoi, Vietnam, as the only university in the country with EV charging infrastructure, although the concept behind our work can be applied to any university campus with charging stations. The growing number of EV users has raised concerns about long wait times, lack of real-time availability updates, and service access issues, potentially affecting EV adoption and VinUni's sustainability goals. With projected EV growth due to VinUni's purchase incentives, parking priorities, and

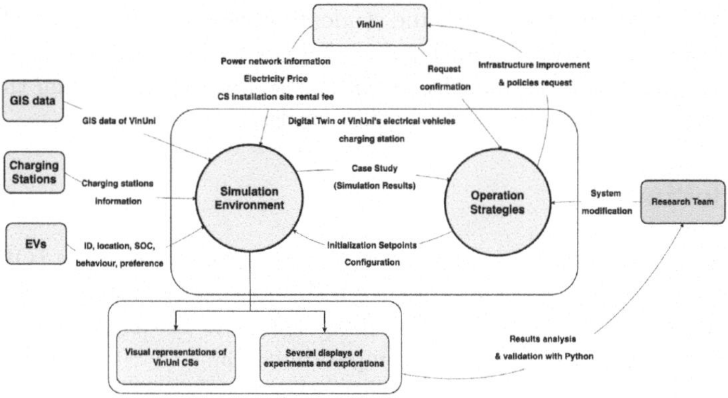

Fig. 1. System diagram

charging access for nearby residents and electric taxis, expanding the infrastructure is essential.

Specifically, VinUni has installed EV charging stations at two campus locations: Building C (Learning Spaces) and Building J (Dormitory). Due to demand and cost, only some ports are active. The charging infrastructure consists of 11kW chargers, described as normal chargers, and 30kW chargers, described as fast chargers. At Building C, 7 of 29 normal ports are operational, while at Building J, 6 of 27 ports are active, including 25 normal ports and 2 fast ports.

Table 1. Information of the presence of the electric car and gasoline car.

Category	Entity	Mon	Tue	Wed	Thu	Fri	Sat
Car	EV	12	11	11	12	8	6
	Gasoline car	24	21	23	27	18	16
	Total vehicle	36	32	34	39	26	22
	Gasoline car parked in active charging parking	3	2	4	3	1	0

We conducted a field study collecting data on vehicle patterns in university parking lots, focusing on electric and gasoline cars, especially those occupying charging spots during peak hours (9:00 AM & 2:00 PM). We used these data to establish typical EV presence and estimate probabilities, such as the likelihood of a gasoline car using a charging spot. This approach models parking and EV occupancy patterns while allowing for random variation. Table 1 summarizes the findings, intended to reflect general trends rather than exact daily counts, with an understanding that schedule and usage patterns may vary.

In addition, a structured online survey using Google Forms, along with qualitative interviews, was conducted to gather insights on drivers' behaviours at VinUni. The survey covered participant demographics, parking and charging behaviour, and suggestions for future improvements. The results serve as a baseline for setting the logic of the decision-making process in vehicle modelling.

The scope of this research focuses on VinUnis charging infrastructure and EV ecosystem, emphasizing geographic information system (GIS) data, charging station details, and university staff and student behaviour. This approach aims to address current and future operational challenges within VinUnis environment. The system context and boundaries are illustrated in Fig. 1, showing the flow of information between the system and other entities.

3 Modelling

This section employs the Overview, Design Concepts, and Details (ODD) protocol to outline our agent-based model (ABM). The ODD protocol offers a clear and standardized framework for describing complex models, enhancing their understandability, replicability, and comparability [3].

3.1 Overview

Purpose. This model aims to replicate EV charging behaviors and assess the impact of strategic policies on EV usage within the campus, especially as EV numbers rise. It evaluates policy effectiveness using three key indicators: (1) the daily percentage of charged EVs, (2) the profit from activating new charging ports, and (3) total monthly energy consumption (kWh).

Entities, State Variables, and Scales. In the model, the following entities are used to replicate the on-campus behaviour of EV owners and the environment.

Table 2. Common state variables of electric and gasoline car.

Variable name	Description	Type
parking_area	Targeted parking area of the car owner	Charging areas
home	Initial location of car owner	residential
start/end_work	Start/end of the car owner's working hours	integer
moving_obj	The car's movement objectives include "resting" (off-campus), "parking", "working", and "leaving" (on-campus), assigned based on context.	string
parking_slot	The status of the car's parking slot: active or inactive charging stations. Cars can park in both active and inactive slot	string
in_parkingArea	The car's current location, checking if it's in a parking area (Building C or J)	bool

- **Vehicles Agent (electric and gasoline cars):** Vehicle agents represent both electric and gasoline-powered cars. State variables representing the behaviours of these two vehicle types are shown in Table 2, while EV agents own unique state variables such as the State of Charge (SoC), the owner satisfaction, the flag to recognize EV in charge, the car model and the preference about which charging station to reach.
- **Charging Areas Agent:** Reflecting VinUni's actual setup, Charging Areas encompass two locations, buildings C and J as introduced before. Three individual agents appear in the model: active charging station ($active_{CS}$), active fast charging station($activeCS_{fast}$) and number of charging stations(num_{CS}).

- **Road Agent:** The Road agent is designed to simulate traffic lanes for the Vehicles agent, with its positioning and details mirroring actual road configurations within and surrounding VinUni. The attributes "type" and "direction" specify the road's location (either inside or outside VinUni) and its traffic flow (one-way or two-way), respectively.
- **Global Environment:** It acts as the overarching setting where all the previously mentioned agents exist and interact. In our simulation, this encompasses the VinUni campus and select adjacent buildings.

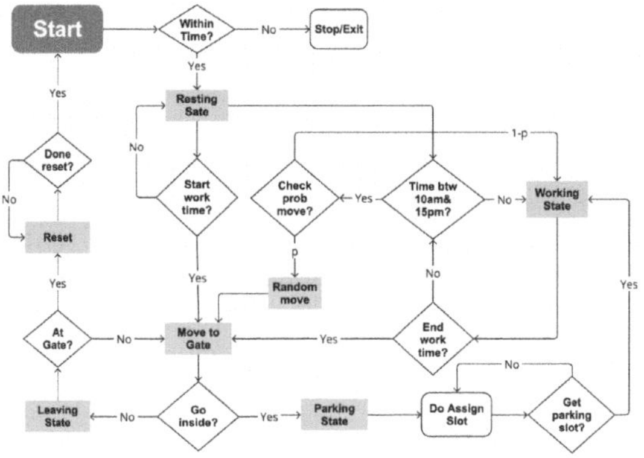

Fig. 2. Vehicles agent decision-making process *(p and 1-p indicate the probability that the agent will move to the state)*

Process Overview and Scheduling. As shown in Fig. 2, agent behaviors and timing are orchestrated through a discrete event simulation framework. At the beginning of a simulation cycle, certain global variables are initialized as introduced in Table. Subsequently, numerous agents are instantiated to simulate the start of a day (12:00 AM). The conduct of primary agents, such as the Vehicles agent, is dictated by a set of pre-defined actions that are triggered upon meeting specific conditions. Additionally, other actions, both scheduled and unconditioned, are executed in alignment with the simulation's timeframe.

3.2 Design Concepts

Next, **"D - Design concepts"** presents Basic Principle, Objective, Adaptation, Sensing, Interaction, Stochasticity, and Emergence in the model.

The VinUni campus EV charging simulation optimizes charging station placement by modelling driving and charging patterns. It focuses on when and where drivers choose to charge, considering station location and simulating competition for limited spots, prompting strategy adjustments when availability is scarce. Adaptive behavior is demonstrated when vehicles, faced with an unavailable charging station, choose either to remain parked at a nearby port without charging or to move to another location. This decision is based on a priority system that balances the availability of charging options against the proximity of a preferred parking spot.

The model maintains a sensing capability that allows vehicle agents to detect the location and type of charging stations but verifies the availability of charging ports only upon arrival. Leadership influences agent behavior by implementing policies and increasing the number of charging ports, while EV owners compete for both charging and parking slots. To ensure impartiality, the model incorporates stochastic elements such as random initial battery levels (20%-90% SoC), randomized arrival and departure times, and randomized prioritized choices with probabilities based on survey data. The core outcomes, including the percentage of EVs charged, revenue/profit, and energy consumption, emerge from the interplay of stochastic factors, agent adaptation, and interactions.

3.3 Details

Finally, **"D - Details"** will explain how the model is initialized and structured via 3 main parts: Initialization, Input data, Submodel.

Model initialization involves several steps. First, GIS shape files are loaded to create the Global Environment agent's geometric boundary, including the VinUni campus map, roads, and charging areas. Next, global variables are initialized based on predefined values, which users can customize via an interactive dashboard. Finally, the created Vehicle agents are triggered by the event "time-to-work" to start their daily journey.

Electric Car's Decision-Making Process. This section outlines the decision-making process and the underlying logic for actions and events within the simulation model, specifically focusing on how EV and gasoline agents decide on their charging ports and parking slots, plus the methodology for calculating charging time at the end. After entering the VinUni campus, the EV agent starts finding a charging/parking slot based on their needs.

The process is named *Assign Slot*, which starts by evaluating the randomly assigned battery level (SoC) of each EV, and consequently checking available charging ports and assigning them prioritizing the EVs with $SoC <= 35\%$. EVs with $SoC >= 70\%$ are instead considered already quite satisfied, therefore they are randomly assigned at an inactive charging port.

Gasoline Car's Decision-Making Process. Gasoline cars check if there is a policy that prohibits them from parking in active charging stations.

- If **Yes**, the car will park at an inactive charging station, thereby freeing up space at active ones for EVs to charge.
- If **No**, the car will enter *Assign Slot* randomly to determine whether it will park at an active or inactive charging station.

4 Simulation Results and Discussion

We use the GAMA platform to implement our simulation setup. GAMA platform is an agent-oriented language tailored for agent-based simulations, drawing

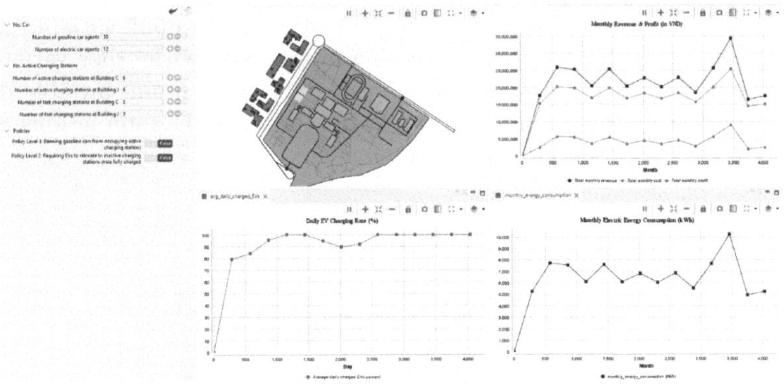

Fig. 3. Simulation dashboard in GAMA

inspiration from object-oriented languages such as Java and Smalltalk. We chose GAMA platform among the others because it is easy to integrate GIS data as the environment for agents. Figure 3 shows the interactive interface of our model.

The left panel features a list of parameters that could change with the evolving VinUni landscape, particularly with an increase in EVs and charging stations. This panel allows users to adjust parameter values for simulations. Currently, there are three parameter groups displayed:

- Number of Cars: Settings for the number of electric and gasoline cars.
- Number of Active Charging Stations: Adjust settings for the active charging stations at Building C and Building J.
- Policies: Two levels of policies currently implemented at VinUni, which may be tightened in the future. Policy level 1: banning gasoline cars from occupying active charging stations, and policy level 2: requiring EVs to relocate to inactive charging stations once fully charged. By toggling these policies on or off, users can alter the simulation's global environment by applying these policies to all agents.

The right panel features a geographical map, generated from GIS data, illustrating the movement of electric cars (green dots) and gasoline cars (red dots) around the VinUni campus. Additionally, three time-series graphs display key indicators relevant to assessing VinUni charging infrastructure's effectiveness. This interactive dashboard provides a dynamic observation of the daily EV charging rate (in percentage), monthly energy consumption (in kWh), and monthly profit (in VND), offering valuable insights to potential end-users.

4.1 Sobol Sensitivity Analysis

We performed a Sobol sensitivity analysis to assess the impact of variations in six input parameters on the 3 key indicators of VinUni's EV infrastructure performance. Sobol analysis gives two important metrics [9]:

- **First-order index** measures the impact of a single input variable on the variance of an output indicator, ignoring interactions with other variables.
- **Total-order index** measures the impact of a single input variable on the variance of an output indicator, taking into account the interactions of this input variable with other input variables.

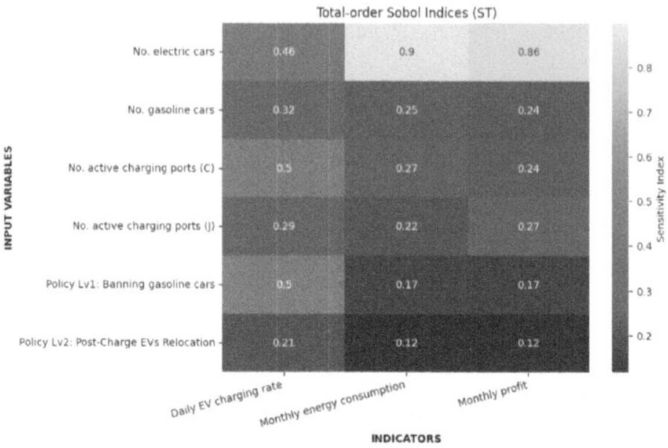

Fig. 4. Sobol analysis on how 6 variables contribute to 3 indicators variance

The Sobol analysis in this paper is conducted using a dataset of 1,400 data points, each randomly selected from the space of input parameters. Every data point represents the average outcome of 20 replicates for each set of inputs and algorithms run directly on the GAMA platform.

Figure 4 summarises the Sobol analysis results. The number of EVs inside the campus is not surprising to be by far the most impacting variable on the energy consumption variance, the charging station profit, and the daily EV charging rate index. However, this first index is mostly influenced by the number of active charging ports at building C and the policy of banning gasoline cars, which exerts instead less impact on both Monthly Energy Consumption and Monthly Profit. These two indices are influenced, other than the number of EVs, by the increasing number of charging ports inside the campus.

The policy of prohibiting gasoline cars from using active charging stations stands out as having the most significant individual influence on the charging rate. This aligns with real-world efforts by VinUni to implement this policy to allocate more space for EVs requiring charging. Furthermore, the Sobol analysis indicates that *Policy Level 1* consistently shows a greater influence on all three indicators than *Policy Level 2*. This analysis provides a valuable recommendation for both the VinUni leadership and EV owners, indicating that relocating EVs to inactive charging ports once fully charged does not significantly enhance the performance of the EV infrastructure at VinUni, compared to banning gasoline cars from occupying charging ports.

4.2 Application of the Simulation Model: Analyzing the Effectiveness of Strategies

VinUni currently considers two main strategies to address the rising EVs number:

- Alternative (1): Activating more charging ports inside the charging stations.
- Alternative (2): Implementing a two-tiered policy approach, with *Policy Level 1* entailing the prohibition of gasoline vehicles from active charging stations, and *Policy Level 2* forcing the relocation of fully charged EVs to inactive charging stations.

While increasing the number of active stations enables more EVs to charge, it also escalates costs and energy consumption. Thus, Alternative (1) suggests the need to find a good tradeoff between charging vehicles and energy consumption. The simulations on the GAMA platform are performed by keeping inactive (set FALSE) both the policies and keeping a fixed reasonable number of 30 gasoline cars inside the VinUni simulated campus.

Several scenarios are tested, with two significant cases: one featuring a lower number of EVs, representing the current situation (10), and another with a higher number (50), reflecting future expected trends. VinFast, a car manufacturer under the same parent company as VinUni, currently supplies the entire charging station network. In alignment with VinUnis green living initiative, a policy has been implemented restricting all gasoline cars, except VinFast, from entering the campus, making this scenario particularly relevant.

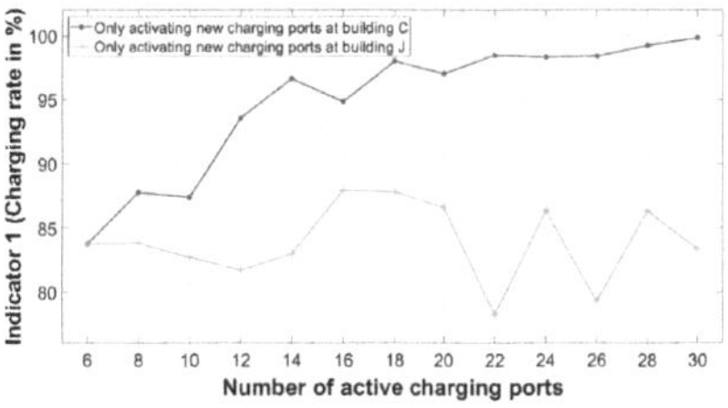

Fig. 5. 10 EVs $<$ 30 Gasoline cars

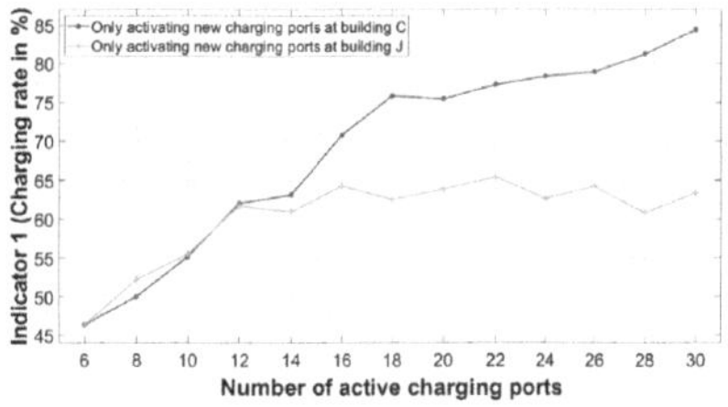

Fig. 6. 50 EVs $>$ 30 Gasoline cars

The plots above in Fig. 5 and Fig. 6 illustrate how the EV Charging Rate reasonably improves with the activation of additional charging ports in each area while keeping fixed six charging ports in the other area. The findings indicate that as the number of EVs rises, introducing more charging ports effectively enables a higher number of EVs to be charged as needed. Notably, adding new charging ports at Building C proves way more efficacious than at Building J, corroborating the insights from the Sobol analysis discussed in Sect. 4.1. Beyond assessing the relative impact of activating new ports in each area, these plots also serve as a resource for the VinUni operations team or VinFast in determining the optimal number of new ports required to achieve a significant enhancement in the percentage of charged EVs.

The monthly electricity consumption is also analyzed to forecast peak usage and ensure that the current electricity grid can handle the load without undue stress. Figure 7 illustrates the impact of activating additional charging ports at VinUni on the percentage of EVs that can be charged. Correspondingly, electricity consumption rises in a similar pattern. The peak electricity consumption reaches approximately 20,000 kWh, representing about 10% of VinUni's current monthly usage, according to data from the VinUni operations department. This analysis aids in understanding how infrastructure enhancements affect overall energy demands.

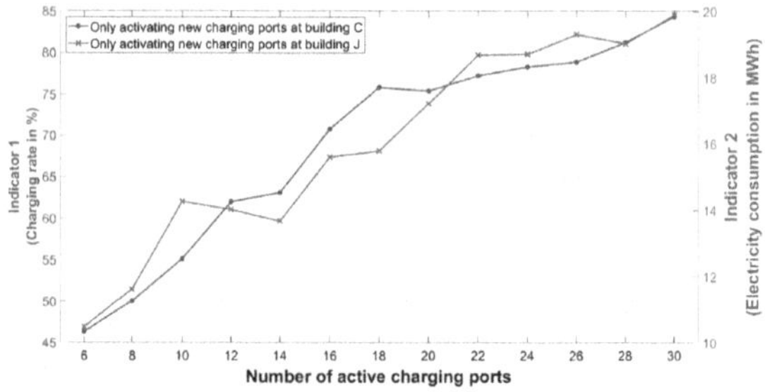

Fig. 7. Grid load management

Other simulations are performed to evaluate the impact of two policy levels on enhancing the ability to charge EVs as needed. Given that *Policy Level 2* is stricter than *Policy Level 1*, there is no case in which *Policy Level 2* is inactive while *Policy Level 1* is active, therefore three cases are investigated. Furthermore, since Fig. 6 highlights that it is more clever to increase the number of charging ports at building C rather than building J, for these simulations we fixed the charging ports at building J while increasing only those at building C.

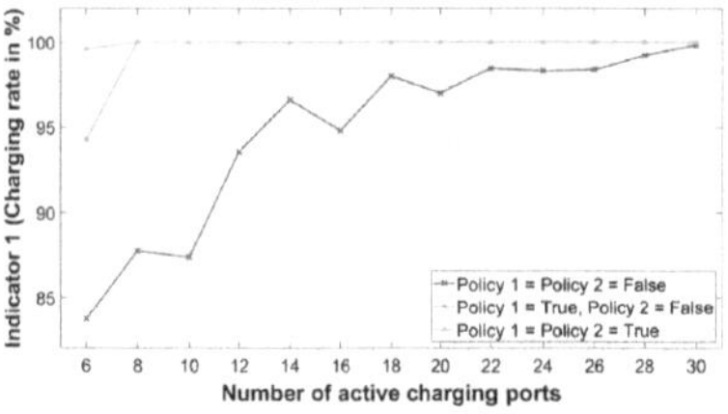

Fig. 8. 10 EVs < 30 Gasoline cars

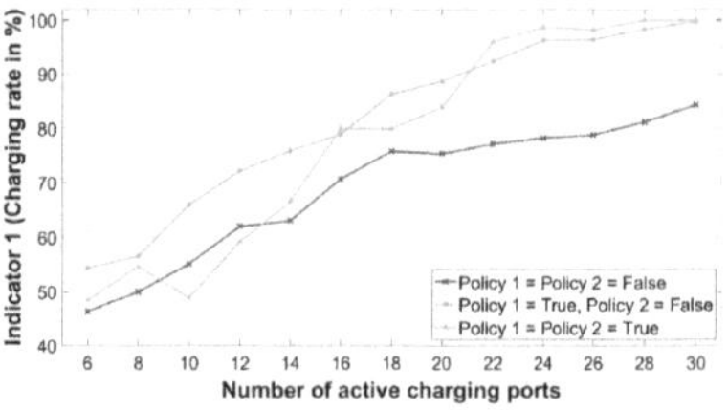

Fig. 9. 50 EVs > 30 Gasoline cars

Figure 8 and Fig. 9 indicate that banning gasoline cars from using active charging stations, enables a higher value for *Indicator 1* and therefore more EVs to be charged as needed. Introducing *Policy Level 2* does not significantly improve performance, as we expected by observing the Sobol analysis results in Fig. 4.

Moreover, Alternative (2) does not contribute to reducing the total electricity consumption, as illustrated in the plot below in Fig. 10. The peak consumption exceeds 24,000 kWh per month, representing more than 10% of the current monthly usage highlighting the risk of grid overload. Nonetheless, this simulation provides valuable insights for the operations team and VinUni leadership, serving as a reference in their decision-making process.

In addition to energy peaks, the profit VinFast derives from activating new charging ports experiences moderate fluctuations as we can see in Fig. 11, because more charging ports entail both higher monthly fees payable to VinUni and higher profit gained from EVs owners.

Looking at the simulation results in Fig. 10 and Fig. 11, we notice that both *Indicator 2* (monthly energy consumption) and *Indicator 3* (monthly profit) have a global maximum when the number of active charging ports at building C is 26. Although this value guarantees the maximum profit, the electricity grid overload may become a problem on the other hand. Another interesting suggestion could be to consider a different local optimum for *Indicator 3*, which is obtained when the active charging ports at building C are 18: this value ensures indeed a lower impact on the electricity grid, as shown in Fig. 10.

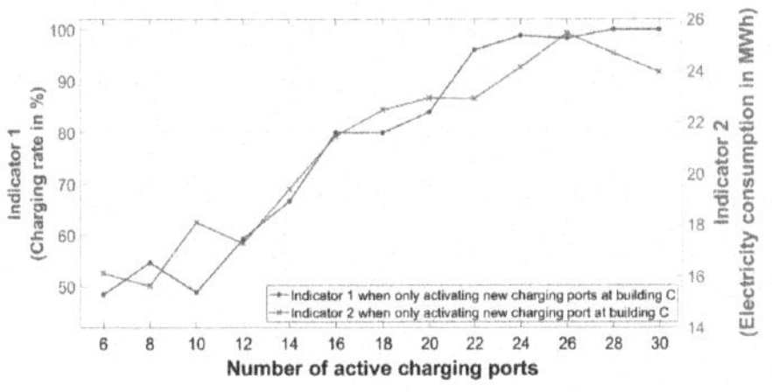

Fig. 10. Energy consumption

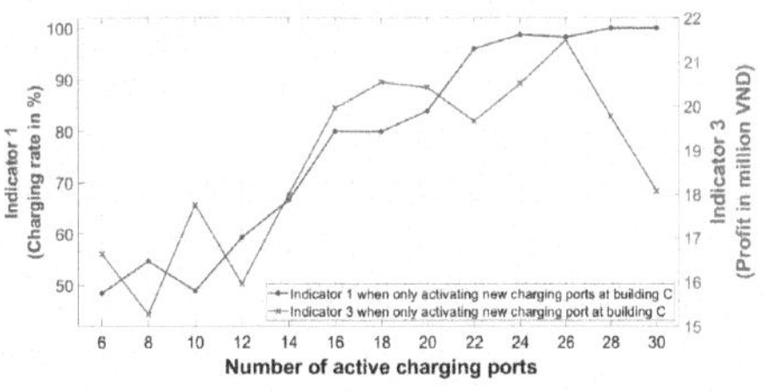

Fig. 11. Monthly profit

The results of the simulations and the data provided aim to be useful for the relevant departments in decision-making regarding the management of charging stations within VinUni. These insights can certainly be useful in the future when the number of EVs is likely to grow significantly.

5 Conclusions

In summary, the research has addressed the challenge of insufficient charging ports as the number of EVs rises in a university campus.

Our simulation enables policymakers to assess the impact of their policies on the rising number of EVs that can be charged and to forecast peak energy consumption for grid load management. Based on our analysis, it is strongly recommended that *Policy 1* - banning gasoline cars from parking at active charging stations - be implemented. This strategic move is poised to significantly enhance the availability of charged EVs when needed. Combining this policy with activating more charging ports would synergistically address the identified challenge. Implementing such policies holds the potential to amplify the effectiveness of activating additional charging ports.

Future research can expand by considering a network of charging stations, as our study focused only on those within the university campus. Enhancing model accuracy and runtime efficiency will also improve data computation and experiment execution. Incorporating renewable energy sources like solar and battery storage can help charging stations operate independently. However, a major challenge remains the lack of empirical data in the Vietnamese context, which hinders building a more accurate model.

Acknowledgments. This publication is based upon work supported by VinUniversity under Grant No. VUNI.2223.FT08

References

1. Ambrosino, L., Calafiore, G., Nguyen, K.M., Zorgati, R., Nguyen-Ngoc, D., El Ghaoui, L.: Optimizing electric vehicles charging through smart energy allocation and cost-saving. In: Book of Proceedings ESCC 2024 (2024). https://doi.org/10.48550/ARXIV.2409.08638
2. Bae, S., Kwasinski, A.: Spatial and temporal model of electric vehicle charging demand. IEEE Trans. Smart Grid **3**, 394–403 (2012). https://doi.org/10.1109/TSG.2011.2159278
3. Grimm, V., et al.: The ODD protocol for describing agent-based and other simulation models: a second update to improve clarity, replication, and structural realism. J. Artif. Soc. Soc. Simul. **23**(2) (2020). https://doi.org/10.18564/jasss.4259
4. IEA: Global EV outlook 2021 - analysis (2021). https://www.iea.org/reports/global-EV-outlook-2021
5. Jordán, J., Palanca, J., Martí, P., Julian, V.: Electric vehicle charging stations emplacement using genetic algorithms and agent-based simulation. Expert Syst. Appl. **197**, 116739 (2022). https://doi.org/10.1016/j.eswa.2022.116739
6. van der Kam, M., Peters, A., van Sark, W., Alkemade, F.: Agent-based modelling of charging behaviour of electric vehicle drivers. J. Artif. Soc. Soc. Simul. **22**(4), 7 (2019). https://doi.org/10.18564/jasss.4133
7. Mudiyanselage, M.W., et al.: A multiagent framework for electric vehicles charging power forecast and smart planning of urban parking lots. IEEE Trans. Transp. Electrification **10**(2), 2844–2857 (2024). https://doi.org/10.1109/TTE.2023.3289196
8. Nguyen, N.H., et al.: A method for assessing the feasibility of integrating planned unidirectional EV chargers into the distribution grid: a case study in Danang, Vietnam. Energies **16**(9) (2023). https://doi.org/10.3390/en16093741
9. Nossent, J., Elsen, P., Bauwens, W.: Sobol' sensitivity analysis of a complex environmental model. Environ. Model. Softw. **26**(12), 1515–1525 (2011). https://doi.org/10.1016/j.envsoft.2011.08.010
10. Shi, J., Zhang, W., Bao, Y., Gao, D.W., Wang, Z.: Load forecasting of electric vehicle charging stations: Attention based spatiotemporal multi-graph convolutional networks. IEEE Trans. Smart Grid **15**(3), 3016–3027 (2024). https://doi.org/10.1109/TSG.2023.3321116
11. Waraich, R.A., Galus, M.D., Dobler, C., Balmer, M., Andersson, G., Axhausen, K.W.: Plug-in hybrid electric vehicles and smart grids: investigations based on a microsimulation. Transp. Res. Part C: Emerg. Technol. **28**, 74–86 (2013). https://doi.org/10.1016/j.trc.2012.10.011, euro Transportation: selected paper from the EWGT Meeting, Padova, September 2009

12. Yi, Z., Chen, B., Liu, X.C., Wei, R., Chen, J., Chen, Z.: An agent-based modeling approach for public charging demand estimation and charging station location optimization at urban scale. Comput. Environ. Urban Syst. **101**, 101949 (2023). https://doi.org/10.1016/j.compenvurbsys.2023.101949

Calibrating Probabilistic Embeddings for Cross-Modal Retrieval

Fengchun Qiao(✉) and Xi Peng

Department of Computer and Information Sciences, University of Delaware, Newark, DE 19716, USA
{fengchun,xipeng}@udel.edu

Abstract. The core of cross-modal retrieval is to measure the content similarity between data of different modalities. The main challenge focuses on learning a shared representation space for multiple modalities where the similarity measurement can reflect the semantic closeness. The multiplicity of correspondences further escalates the challenge since all the possible matches should be ranked ahead of the negatives. Probabilistic embeddings are proposed to handle the multiplicity while suffering from similarity miscalibration. To address it, we propose to calibrate the similarity for probabilistic embeddings. The key idea is to estimate the density ratio between the distributions of the two modalities, and use it to calibrate the similarity measurement in the embedding space. To the best of our knowledge, we are the first to study the miscalibration in probabilistic embeddings. In addition, we further evaluate three pre-training tasks of language models, which is important for cross-modal but seldom investigated in previous studies. Extensive experiments as well as ablation studies on two benchmarks demonstrate its superior performance in tackling the multiplicity of cross-modal retrieval.

Keywords: Deep neural networks · Multimodal retrieval · Probabilistic models

1 Introduction

The two most prevailing modalities for displaying information in our daily lives are visual media and human language. It is critical to equip models with the capacity to comprehend and match such multimodal data. Cross-modal retrieval, a fundamental and essential problem in multimodal learning, has drawn intensive attention in recent years. Typically, cross-modal retrieval requires a shared representation space that allows computing a similarity measurement between the query and the retrieved data.

Building a shared representation space for multiple modalities is challenging due to the heterogeneity across different modalities. The multiplicity of correspondences further escalates the challenge: an image potentially matches with a number of different texts. Conversely, given a caption, there may be multiple manifestations of the caption in visual forms (Fig. 1(a)). The multiplicity

J. Kertesz et al. (Eds.): CSoNet 2024, LNCS 15417, pp. 174–187, 2025.
https://doi.org/10.1007/978-981-96-6389-7_15

poses new challenges for similarity measurement in cross modal retrieval since all the possible matches should be ranked ahead of the negatives. Most methods [27,32,34,47,49] ignore the multiplicity and use deterministic functions to map a sample as a single point in the embedding space (Fig. 1(a)). However, the single point representation can hardly handle the multiplicity. Recently, probabilistic embeddings [5,30,31] are proposed to map a sample as a Gaussian distribution in the embedding space, in order to cover a large area and increase the possibility to search for more possible matches.

The underlying assumption of probabilistic embeddings is that the two modalities are perfectly aligned and embeddings lie in a shared representation space. However, the assumption does not always hold in practice due to the modality heterogeneity [24,28,37]. As a result, the embedding spaces are partially rather than fully aligned (Fig. 1(b)). Besides, modality embeddings may easily fall out of the shared space when the variance is large and the overlap is small, yielding inaccurate similarity measurement between image-text pairs.

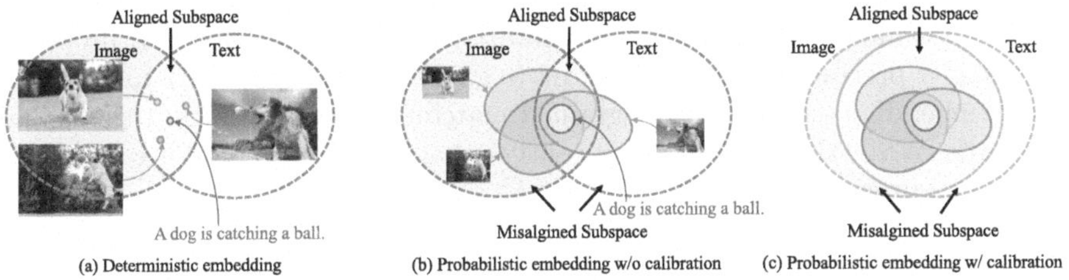

Fig. 1. (a) Deterministic embedding can hardly handle the multiplicity; b) Probabilistic embedding suffers from misaligned subspace; c) We propose a new method to enlarge the aligned subspace.

To narrow the aforementioned gap, we propose a novel calibration method for probabilistic embeddings in cross-modal retrieval. We propose to estimate the density ratio between the two distributions, and use it to calibrate the similarity measurement in the embedding space. The similarity calibration can effectively align the distributions between the two modalities and enlarge the shared representation space (Fig. 1(c)), facilitating more accurate one-to-many matching. Our method can be seamlessly integrated into current contrastive learning frameworks where matched pairs will be pulled closer and unmatched pairs will be pushed away in the embedding space. In addition to the similarity calibration, we further evaluate three pre-training tasks of language models, which plays the crucial role for cross-modal retrieval but seldom investigated in previous studies. To summarize, our contribution is multi-fold: 1) To the best of our knowledge, we are the first to study the miscalibration issue in probabilistic embeddings. 2) We propose to use density ratio between the two modalities to calibrate the similarity measurement between image-text pairs, enlarging the shared representation space and facilitating more accurate one-to-many matching. 3) Extensive experiments as well as ablation studies on two benchmarks demonstrate its superior performance in tackling the multiplicity for cross-modal retrieval.

2 Related Work

Cross-Modal Retrieval. Cross-modal retrieval for image and text modalities has been a prominent topic in multimodal learning research [10,18,47,48]. Most existing methods utilize one-to-one matching between image-text pairs within a shared embedding space. The prevalent approach involves maximizing the correlation between matched pairs within this embedding space. For example, [37] proposed canonical correlation analysis (CCA) to learn a shared subspace across the two modalities. More recently, deep neural networks have become popular for learning embedding functions in an end-to-end fashion. [1] introduced deep CCA (DCCA), while [49] extended this framework to high-dimensional image and text representations for cross-modal retrieval. Efforts have also been made to model the multiplicity of correspondences between modalities. [44] introduced Polysemous Visual-Semantic Embeddings (PVSE), which learn embedding functions by searching for multiple candidate representations for a given input. [17] proposed leveraging a pretrained object detector (e.g., Faster R-CNN [38]) to compute region embeddings, enabling fine-grained matching between image regions and text words. While this method significantly enhances performance, it comes with a high computational cost.

Probabilistic Embeddings. Probabilistic embeddings, as opposed to point embeddings, have been applied in various domains, such as image representation [2,19,29,42], multimodal learning [5,44], and human pose estimation [45]. [29] proposed hedged instance embedding (HIB) to capture uncertainty in the occluded N-digit MNIST dataset. In the context of cross-modal retrieval, [5] suggested learning probabilistic embeddings, representing each sample as a probabilistic distribution rather than a single vector. This approach inherently handles the multiplicity of correspondences between image and text modalities. However, probabilistic embeddings face challenges with similarity miscalibration and struggle to accurately capture one-to-many matching scenarios.

3 Method

We focus on cross-modal retrieval for vision and language data. Let $\mathcal{D} = (\mathcal{X}, \mathcal{Y})$ denote a collection of vision and language data, where $\mathcal{X}$ is a set of images and $\mathcal{Y}$ a set of captions. For a caption $\mathbf{y} \in \mathcal{Y}$ (respectively an image $\mathbf{x} \in \mathcal{X}$), there are multiple matching images $\{\mathbf{x}\}$ (respectively captions $\{\mathbf{y}\}$) due to the multiplicity. The goal is to achieve a shared subspace to measure the similarity between image-caption pairs. Typically, two mapping functions $f_\theta : \mathbf{x} \to \mathbf{u}$ and $g_\phi : \mathbf{y} \to \mathbf{v}$ will be learned where $\mathbf{u}$ and $\mathbf{v}$ are image and caption embeddings, respectively. Rather than point embeddings, $\mathbf{u}$ and $\mathbf{v}$ are probabilistic distributions to facilitate multiplicity. For each image-caption pair $(\mathbf{x_i}, \mathbf{y_j})$, we sample their representations as $\mathbf{u_i} \sim p_\theta(\mathbf{u_i} \mid \mathbf{x_i})$ and $\mathbf{v_j} \sim p_\phi(\mathbf{v_j} \mid \mathbf{y_j})$. The details of probabilistic embedding will be introduced in Sect. 3.2.

We define $p(m \mid \mathbf{x_i}, \mathbf{y_j})$ as the matching probability between $\mathbf{x_i}$ and $\mathbf{y_j}$. Taking image-to-text retrieval for example, let $(\mathbf{x_i}, \mathbf{y_j^+})$ be the positive pair and $(\mathbf{x_i}, \mathbf{y_j^-})$ be the negative pair. We expect $p(m \mid \mathbf{x_i}, \mathbf{y_j^+})$ should be larger than $p(m \mid \mathbf{x_i}, \mathbf{y_j^-})$:

$$\frac{p(m \mid \mathbf{u_i}, \mathbf{v_j^+})}{p(m \mid \mathbf{u_i}, \mathbf{v_j^-})} \geq \beta, \quad where \quad \beta > 1.$$

We apply negative logarithm to both sides:

$$(-\log p(m \mid \mathbf{u_i}, \mathbf{v_j^+})) - (-\log p(m \mid \mathbf{u_i}, \mathbf{v_j^-})) \leq -\log \beta.$$

To satisfy the above inequality, we organize model training in a triplet loss framework [41]. Given batch size N, we define the triplet loss $\mathcal{L}_\mathsf{t}$ for image-to-text retrieval as:

$$\mathcal{L}_\mathsf{t} = \sum_{i=1}^{N} \max(0, D(\mathbf{u_i}, \mathbf{v_j^+}) - D(\mathbf{u_i}, \mathbf{v_j^-}) + \alpha), \tag{1}$$

with distance kernel $D(\mathbf{u_i}, \mathbf{v_j}) = -\log p\,(m \mid \mathbf{u_i}, \mathbf{v_j})$ and margin $\alpha = \log \beta$. To form a triplet $(\mathbf{x_i}, \mathbf{y_j^+}, \mathbf{y_j^-})$, we perform online hard negative mining [43] to find $\mathbf{y_j^-}$ in a mini-batch. Similarly, the triplet loss $\mathcal{L}_\mathsf{i}$ for text-to-image retrieval as:

$$\mathcal{L}_\mathsf{i} = \sum_{j=1}^{N} \max(0, D(\mathbf{u_i^+}, \mathbf{v_j}) - D(\mathbf{u_i^-}, \mathbf{v_j}) + \alpha). \tag{2}$$

The overall loss function is: $\mathcal{L} = \mathcal{L}_\mathsf{t} + \mathcal{L}_\mathsf{i}$.

Following most existing works [7,12,33,37], we use cosine similarity to represent the matching probability:

$$p(m \mid \mathbf{u_i}, \mathbf{v_j}) = \mathbb{E}_{p(\mathbf{u_i})}\mathbb{E}_{p(\mathbf{v_j})}\mathbf{u_i}^T\mathbf{v_j}. \tag{3}$$

In Eq. 3, both $\mathbf{u_i}$ and $\mathbf{v_j}$ are normalized to lie on the unit hyper-sphere.

3.1 Similarity Calibration

We argue that the similarity measurement in Eq. 3 is questionable. The underlining assumption of $\mathbf{u_i}$ and $\mathbf{v_j}$ are well aligned in a shared subspace may not always hold true due to the modality heterogeneity as well as the discrepancy between f_θ and g_ϕ. To address this issue, we propose to calibrate $p(m \mid \mathbf{u_i}, \mathbf{v_j})$ toward more truthful similarity measurement:

$$p(m \mid \mathbf{u_i}, \mathbf{v_j}) = \mathbb{E}_{p(\mathbf{u_i})}\mathbb{E}_{p(\mathbf{v_j})}(\mathbf{u_i})^T(w \cdot \mathbf{v_j}), \tag{4}$$

where $w = \frac{p(\mathbf{u_i})}{p(\mathbf{v_j})}$. Let us consider three cases. (1) $w = 1$: The embeddings are well aligned in a share space which degrades to Eq. 3. (2) $w = C$: The misalignment of the embeddings is a constant across all the pairs. (3) $w = \frac{p(\mathbf{u_i})}{p(\mathbf{v_j})}$: The misalignment of the embeddings is a learnable variable where each image-text pair should have a unique w. Obviously, either (1) or (2) is a special (simplified) case of (3). After calibrating the similarity measurement, $\log p(m \mid \mathbf{u_i}, \mathbf{v_j})$ is equivalent to:

$$\begin{aligned} &\mathbb{E}_{p(\mathbf{u_i})}[\mathbb{E}_{p(\mathbf{v_j})} \log(\mathbf{u_i}^T \mathbf{v_j}) + \mathbb{E}_{p(\mathbf{v_j})} \log \frac{p(\mathbf{u_i})}{p(\mathbf{v_j})}] \\ &= \mathbb{E}_{p(\mathbf{u_i})}[\underbrace{\mathbb{E}_{p(\mathbf{v_j})} \log(\mathbf{u_i}^T \mathbf{v_j})}_{\textbf{Point matching}} - \underbrace{\mathrm{KL}(p(\mathbf{v_j})||p(\mathbf{u_i}))}_{\textbf{Distribution matching}}]. \end{aligned} \tag{5}$$

We highlight that Eq. 5 is the combination of *point matching* and *distribution matching*. The proposed calibration is capable of effectively aligning two embeddings and enlarging the aligned subspace (Fig. 1 (c)), facilitating accurate one-to-many matching.

3.2 Implementation

We introduce the implementation of mapping functions, probabilistic embeddings, and distribution matching.

Mapping Functions. We use ResNet-152 [9] to implement f_θ. The model is pre-trained on ImageNet [39]. We extract features after the average pooling layer and the features are transformed to D-dimensional embedding through a fully-connect layer. We use BERT [13] to implement g_ϕ. We leverage the final hidden state of the first token [CLS] as the features of the whole sequence and the features are transformed to D-dimensional embedding through a fully-connect layer.

Probabilistic Embeddings. We assume $\mathbf{u_i}$ and $\mathbf{v_j}$ follow multivariate Gaussian distribution in the embedding space: $p(\mathbf{u_i}) = \mathcal{N}(\mu_i, \mathbf{\Sigma_i})$, $p(\mathbf{v_j}) = \mathcal{N}(\mu_j, \mathbf{\Sigma_j})$. We apply image and text augmentation to estimate $(\mu_i, \mathbf{\Sigma_i})$ and $(\mu_j, \mathbf{\Sigma_j})$, respectively. For image augmentation, we assume access to a set Ψ, where each element is a specific image transformation. We can generate multiple augmentations by sampling from Ψ. For text augmentation, we use a fine-tuned T5 model [36] to get multiple paraphrased captions from the original caption. After estimating the distributions, we sample the embeddings from them: $\mathbf{u_i} \sim \mathcal{N}(\mu_i, \mathbf{\Sigma_i})$ and $\mathbf{v_j} \sim \mathcal{N}(\mu_j, \mathbf{\Sigma_j})$. Furthermore, we use the reparametrization trick [15] to enable efficient backpropagation.

Distribution Matching. KL divergence in Eq. 5 is asymmetric and well-known for the problem of vanishing gradient. To address it, we use Wasserstein distance [46] to minimize the discrepancy between $p(\mathbf{u_i})$ and $p(\mathbf{v_j})$, yielding more stable *distribution matching*. Concretely, we use 2-Wasserstein ($\mathcal{W}_2$) distance to align the distribution between $p(\mathbf{u_i})$ and $p(\mathbf{v_j})$. The $\mathcal{W}_2$ coupling distance between $p(\mathbf{u_i})$ and $p(\mathbf{v_j})$ on $\mathbb{R}^D$ is:

$$\mathcal{W}_2(p(\mathbf{u_i}); p(\mathbf{v_j})) := \inf \mathbb{E} \left(\|\mathbf{u_i} - \mathbf{v_j}\|_2^2 \right)^{1/2}, \tag{6}$$

where the infimum runs over all random vectors $(\mathbf{u_i}, \mathbf{v_j})$ of $\mathbb{R}^D \times \mathbb{R}^D$ with $\mathbf{u_i} \sim p(\mathbf{u_i})$ and $\mathbf{v_j} \sim p(\mathbf{v_j})$. Since we assume embeddings follow multivariate Gaussian distribution and the covariance matrix is a diagonal matrix, Eq. 6 is reduced to:

$$\mathcal{W}_2(p(\mathbf{u_i}); p(\mathbf{v_j}))^2 = \|\mu_\mathrm{i} - \mu_\mathrm{j}\|_2^2 + \left\| \mathbf{\Sigma_i^{1/2}} - \mathbf{\Sigma_j^{1/2}} \right\|_F^2,$$

where F is the Frobenius norm. We empirically demonstrate that 2-Wasserstein distance outperforms KL divergence by a large margin in Sect. 4.4.

Both f_θ and g_ϕ are fine-tuned on the target dataset in an end-to-end manner. We introduce the training details in Sect. 4.2.

4 Experiments

To evaluate the effectiveness of the proposed similarity calibration, we perform experiments in both image-to-text and text-to-image retrieval on two widely used datasets.

4.1 Datasets and Metrics

Table 1. Comparison (%) on Flickr30K [50]. Our method outperforms all baselines by a large margin in both *Image-to-Text* and *Text-to-Image* retrieval.

Method	Backbone	Image-to-Text			Text-to-Image		
		R@1	R@5	R@10	R@1	R@5	R@10
DAN [26]	VGG-19	41.4	73.5	82.5	31.8	61.7	72.5
RRF-Net [23]	ResNet-152	47.6	77.4	87.1	35.4	68.3	79.9
CMPM +CMPC [51]	ResNet-152	49.6	76.8	86.1	37.3	65.7	75.5
DAN [26]	ResNet-152	55.0	81.8	89.0	39.4	69.2	79.1
NAR [22]	ResNet-152	55.1	80.3	89.6	39.4	68.8	79.9
VSE++ [7]	ResNet-152	52.9	80.5	87.2	39.6	70.1	79.5
SCO [11]	ResNet-152	55.5	82.0	89.3	41.1	70.5	80.1
GXN [8]	ResNet-152	56.8	–	89.6	41.5	–	80.1
TIMAM [40]	ResNet-152	53.1	78.8	87.6	42.6	71.6	81.9
Ours	ResNet-152	**62.7**	**86.2**	**91.5**	**49.6**	**78.8**	**85.2**

Table 2. Comparison (%) on MS-COCO [20] 5K test set . Our approach achieves the best results in *Text-to-Image* retrieval on the 5K test set.

Method	Image-to-Text			Text-to-Image		
	R@1	R@5	R@10	R@1	R@5	R@10
VQA-A [21]	23.5	50.7	63.6	16.7	40.5	53.8
CMPM [51]	31.1	60.7	73.9	22.9	50.2	63.8
VSE++ [7]	41.3	71.1	81.2	30.3	59.4	72.4
SCO [11]	42.8	72.3	83.0	<u>33.1</u>	62.9	<u>75.5</u>
PVSE (K=1) [44]	41.7	73.0	83.0	30.6	61.4	73.6
PVSE [44]	**45.2**	<u>74.3</u>	<u>84.5</u>	32.4	<u>63.0</u>	75.0
PCME [5]	44.2	73.8	83.6	31.9	62.1	74.5
Ours	<u>44.8</u>	**75.1**	**84.8**	**33.8**	**64.8**	**76.4**

Datasets. We conducted experiments on the two widely-used benchmark datasets: Flickr30K [50] and MS-COCO [20], to evaluate our proposed model and compare with several state-of-the-art baselines. **Flickr30K**. This dataset consists of 31,783 images. Each image is described by 5 different sentences. Following the settings in previous work [4,16,35], this dataset is split into 29,783 training images, 1,000 validation images, and 1,000 testing images. **MS-COCO**. It is a large-scale dataset including 123,287 images, where each image is associated with 5 annotated sentences. Similarly, we followed the split of [4,16,35], *i.e.*, 113,287 images for training, 5,000 images for validation, and 5,000 images for testing. We report the results on the two evaluation settings: 1) MS-COCO 1K, the final result is calculated by averaging the results over 5-folds of 1K testing images; and 2) MS-COCO 5K, the evaluation result is directly calculated on the full 5K testing images.

Metrics. Recall@k (R@k). We report rank-1 (R@1), rank-5 (R@5), and rank-10 (R@10) results on both datasets. **Recall-Precision** (R-P). [25] proposed the Recall-Precision (R-P) metric as an alternative. For each query, we compute the ratio between matched items and top-r retrieved items, where r is the number of ground-truth matches. This precision metric has a promising property that a retrieval model achieves the highest R-P score if and only if it retrieves all the matched items before the negatives. Compared to Recall@k, R-P score can better evaluate the one-to-many matching for image-to-text retrieval. **Plausible Match Recall-Precision** (PMRP). [5] expands the existing ground truth matches to more plausible positive matches in a dataset through additional information (e.g. class labels for MS-COCO). In detail, a image-text pair $(\mathbf{x_i}, \mathbf{y_j})$ is viewed as positive if the binary label vectors for the two instances differ at most at ζ positions. In practice, they consider multiple criteria $\zeta \in \{0, 1, 2\}$ and average the results with those ζ values.

Table 3. Comparison (%) on MS-COCO [20] 1K test set.

Method	Image-to-Text			Text-to-Image		
	R@1	R@5	R@10	R@1	R@5	R@10
VQA-A [21]	50.5	80.1	89.7	37.0	70.9	82.9
CMPM [51]	56.1	86.3	92.9	44.6	78.8	89.0
VSE++ [7]	64.6	90.0	95.7	52.0	84.3	92.0
SCO [11]	**69.9**	92.9	97.5	56.7	87.5	94.8
PVSE (K=1) [44]	66.7	91.0	96.2	53.5	85.1	92.7
PVSE [44]	69.2	91.6	96.6	55.2	86.5	93.7
PCME [5]	68.8	91.6	96.7	54.6	86.3	93.8
Ours	69.7	**93.5**	97.8	**57.0**	**88.2**	**95.6**

4.2 Implementation Details

We use ResNet-152 [9] and BERT [6] as image and text encoder, respectively. We extract the 2048-dimensional feature after the average pooling layer. A fully-connect layer is then applied to transform the feature to the 512-dimensional embedding. The basic version of the pre-trained BERT [6] is utilized, equipped with 12 layers, 12 heads, 768 hidden units, and 110M parameters in total, to get the word embeddings with dimension of 768. We leverage the final hidden state of the first token [CLS] as the feature of the whole sequence and the feature is transformed to the 512-dimensional embedding through a fully-connect layer. We set the margin α in Eqs. 1 and 2 to 0.2 for all experiments. We use Adam optimizer [14] for model training with the mini-batch size of 64 and the epoches of 30. We set the initial learning rate as 0.0005 with decaying 10% of every 15 epochs.

4.3 Retrieval Comparison

Results on Flickr30K [50]**:** We compare our approach to previous state-of-the art methods. We report the results on the Flickr30K [50] in Table 1. Similar to the most methods, we use ResNet-152 [9] as the image encoder for fair comparison. Our method outperforms all methods by a large margin in both *Image-to-Text* and *Text-to-Image* retrieval. The superior performance demonstrates that the proposed similarity calibration can facilitate more accurate similarity measurement and correctly capture the multiplicity of correspondences.

Results on MS-COCO [20]**:** We compare our approach to previous state-of-the art methods. We report the results on 5k and 1k test sets in Tables 2 and 3. Our approach outperforms most of the baselines, and achieves the new state-of-the-art on the *Text-to-Image* on the 5K test set. We also compare our approach to other methods tailored for one-to-many matching: VSE++ [7], PVSE [44], and PCME [5]. Specially, PCME [5] is the first work that uses probabilistic

Table 4. Comparison (%) with methods tailored for one-to-many matching on MS-COCO [20]. Our approach achieves the new state-of-the-art on the both *Image-to-Text* and *Text-to-Image* tasks in terms of PMRP.

Method	1K Test Images				5K Test Images			
	Image-to-Text		Text-to-Image		Image-to-Text		Text-to-Image	
	PMRP	R@1	PMRP	R@1	PMRP	R@1	PMRP	R@1
VSE++ [7]	–	64.6	–	52.0	–	41.3	–	30.3
PVSE (K=1) [44]	40.3	66.7	41.8	53.5	29.3	41.7	30.1	30.6
PVSE (K=2) [44]	42.8	69.2	43.6	55.2	31.8	45.2	32.0	32.4
VSRN [17]	41.2	76.2	42.4	62.8	29.7	53.0	29.9	40.5
VSRN + AOQ [3]	44.7	**77.5**	45.6	**63.5**	33.0	**55.1**	33.5	**41.1**
PCME μ only [5]	45.0	68.0	45.9	54.6	34.0	43.5	34.3	31.7
PCME [5]	45.0	68.8	46.0	54.6	34.1	44.2	34.4	31.9
Ours	**45.2**	69.7	**46.3**	57.0	**34.6**	44.8	**35.2**	33.8

Table 5. Ablation study of similarity calibration on Flickr30K [50] and MS-COCO [20]. The proposed similarity calibration significantly improves both *Image-to-Text* and *Text-to-Image* retrieval.

Method	Flickr30K					MS-COCO				
	Image-to-Text			Text-to-Image		Image-to-Text			Text-to-Image	
	R@1	R@5	R-P	R@1	R@5	R@1	R@5	R-P	R@1	R@5
Ours	62.7	86.2	47.2	49.6	78.8	44.8	75.1	32.5	33.8	64.8
w/o Calibration	60.7	85.2	45.6	48.0	77.4	42.4	72.8	31.3	32.6	63.5
KL Divergence	61.0	85.4	46.5	47.8	77.0	43.5	73.7	31.9	33.2	64.2
JS Divergence	61.6	86.0	46.4	48.6	78.1	43.9	74.5	32.1	34.0	64.5

embeddings for cross-modal retrieval. In the 1K test set, our method outperforms all of these methods. In detail, our method outperforms PCME [5] by 0.95% and 2.4% in *Image-to-Text* and *Text-to-Image* retrieval, respectively. The results demonstrate that our method is capable of better capturing the one-to-many matching in both directions. We report the results with Plausible-Match R-Precision (PMRP) metrics (Sect. 4.1). Table 4 shows the results with state-of-the-art MS-COCO retrieval methods. As observed, in terms of PMRP, our approach outperforms previous SOTA PCME [5] in both 1K and 5K test images. It is worth noting that VSRN [17] uses Faster R-CNN [38]) to calculate region embeddings and build the fine-grained matching between regions and words, which accounts for the high performance in R@1.

4.4 Ablation Studies

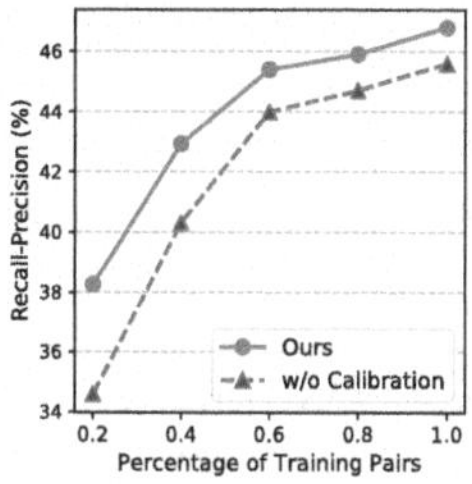

Fig. 2. Evaluation of similarity calibration on limited training data.

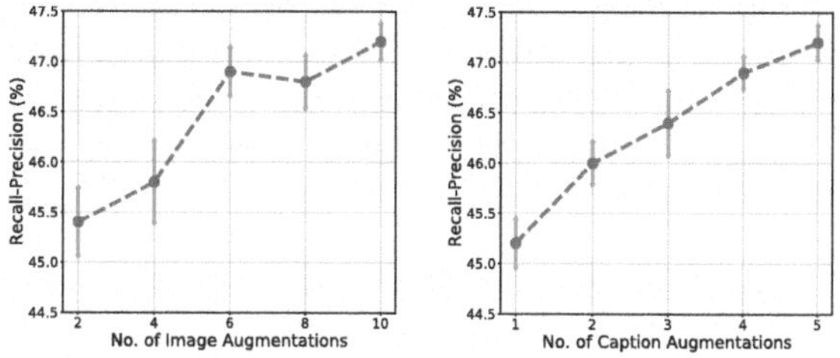

Fig. 3. Ablation study on the number of data augmentations. More augmentations contribute to higher R-P due to more accurate distribution estimation.

Validation of Similarity Calibration: The *similarity calibration* in Eq. 5 plays the key role in calibrating the similarity measurement and enlarging the shared representation space. We implement three variants for comparison: 1) Without Calibration: the model is only trained with *Point Matching* as shown in Eq. 5. 2) Kullback-Leibler (KL) divergence. 3) Jensen-Shannon (JS) divergence: $\mathrm{JSD}(p(\mathbf{u_i}), p(\mathbf{v_j})) = \frac{1}{2}[\mathrm{KL}(p(\mathbf{u_i}), q) + \mathrm{KL}(p(\mathbf{v_j}), q)]$, where $q = \frac{1}{2}[p(\mathbf{u_i}) + p(\mathbf{v_j})]$. Results on Flickr30K [50] and MS-COCO [20] are reported in Table 5. To further evaluate the effectiveness of the proposed similarity calibration, we conduct experiments with limited training data. Results of R-P on Flickr30K [50] are shown in Fig. 2. As observed, the improvements are more significant especially when the training data are extremely limited (38.3% v.s. 34.4% with 20% of training pairs). The Results demonstrate the effectiveness of the proposed similarity calibration for cross-modal retrieval.

Validation of Data Augmentation: We apply image and text augmentation to approximate the distributions of the two modalities. To better understand the effect of augmentation, we conduct experiments by varying the number of augmentations. In detail, we vary the number of image augmentations from 1 to 10 for each image, and vary the number of text augmentations from 1 to 5 for each caption. Note that, in both Flickr30K [50] and MS-COCO [20], we have 5 captions for each image. As a result, there will be 30 captions for each image if we create 5 augmentations for each caption. We report the results of Recall-Precision on different number of augmentations in Fig. 3. In both image and caption augmentations, more augmentations can consistently improve R-P due to more accurate distribution estimation.

5 Conclusion

In this paper, we introduced a novel calibration method for probabilistic embeddings in cross-modal retrieval. We estimate the density ratio between the distributions of the two modalities, and use it to calibrate the similarity measurement in the embedding space. Extensive experiments as well as ablation studies on two benchmarks demonstrate its superior performance in tackling the multiplicity of cross-modal retrieval.

Acknowledgments. This work is supported by the NSF CAREER Award No. 2340074, the NSF SAFE Award No. 2416937, the NSF III CORE Award No. 2412675, and the DoD DEPSCoR Award AFOSR FA9550-23-1-0494.

References

1. Andrew, G., Arora, R., Bilmes, J., Livescu, K.: Deep canonical correlation analysis. In: International Conference on Machine Learning, pp. 1247–1255. PMLR (2013)
2. Chang, J., Lan, Z., Cheng, C., Wei, Y.: Data uncertainty learning in face recognition. In: Proceedings of the IEEE/CVF Conference on Computer Vision and Pattern Recognition, pp. 5710–5719 (2020)
3. Chen, T., Deng, J., Luo, J.: Adaptive offline quintuplet loss for image-text matching. In: Vedaldi, A., Bischof, H., Brox, T., Frahm, J.-M. (eds.) ECCV 2020. LNCS, vol. 12358, pp. 549–565. Springer, Cham (2020). https://doi.org/10.1007/978-3-030-58601-0_33
4. Chen, T., Luo, J.: Expressing objects just like words: recurrent visual embedding for image-text matching. In: Proceedings of the AAAI Conference on Artificial Intelligence, vol. 34, pp. 10583–10590 (2020)
5. Chun, S., Oh, S.J., de Rezende, R.S., Kalantidis, Y., Larlus, D.: Probabilistic embeddings for cross-modal retrieval. In: Proceedings of the IEEE/CVF Conference on Computer Vision and Pattern Recognition (CVPR), pp. 8415–8424 (2021)
6. Devlin, J., Chang, M.W., Lee, K., Toutanova, K.: Bert: pre-training of deep bidirectional transformers for language understanding. In: NAACL-HLT (1) (2019)
7. Faghri, F., Fleet, D.J., Kiros, J.R., Fidler, S.: Vse++: improving visual-semantic embeddings with hard negatives. In: Proceedings of the British Machine Vision Conference (2016)
8. Gu, J., Cai, J., Joty, S.R., Niu, L., Wang, G.: Look, imagine and match: improving textual-visual cross-modal retrieval with generative models. In: Proceedings of the IEEE Conference on Computer Vision and Pattern Recognition, pp. 7181–7189 (2018)
9. He, K., Zhang, X., Ren, S., Sun, J.: Deep residual learning for image recognition. In: Proceedings of the IEEE/CVF Conference on Computer Vision and Pattern Recognition, pp. 770–778 (2016)
10. Hu, P., Zhen, L., Peng, D., Liu, P.: Scalable deep multimodal learning for cross-modal retrieval. In: Proceedings of the 42nd International ACM SIGIR Conference on Research and Development in Information Retrieval, pp. 635–644 (2019)
11. Huang, Y., Wu, Q., Song, C., Wang, L.: Learning semantic concepts and order for image and sentence matching. In: Proceedings of the IEEE Conference on Computer Vision and Pattern Recognition, pp. 6163–6171 (2018)

12. Huang, Z., et al.: Learning with noisy correspondence for cross-modal matching. Adv. Neural Inf. Process. Syst. **34** (2021)
13. Kenton, J.D.M.W.C., Toutanova, L.K.: Bert: pre-training of deep bidirectional transformers for language understanding. In: Proceedings of NAACL-HLT, pp. 4171–4186 (2019)
14. Kingma, D.P., Ba, J.: Adam: a method for stochastic optimization. arXiv:1412.6980 [cs.LG] (2014)
15. Kingma, D.P., Welling, M.: Auto-encoding variational bayes. In: International Conference on Learning Representations (2014)
16. Lee, K.H., Chen, X., Hua, G., Hu, H., He, X.: Stacked cross attention for image-text matching. In: Proceedings of the European Conference on Computer Vision (ECCV), pp. 201–216 (2018)
17. Li, K., Zhang, Y., Li, K., Li, Y., Fu, Y.: Visual semantic reasoning for image-text matching. In: Proceedings of the IEEE/CVF International Conference on Computer Vision, pp. 4654–4662 (2019)
18. Li, T., Ma, M., Peng, X.: Beyond accuracy: ensuring correct predictions with correct rationales. In: The Thirty-eighth Annual Conference on Neural Information Processing Systems (2024)
19. Li, T., Qiao, F., Ma, M., Peng, X.: Are data-driven explanations robust against out-of-distribution data? In: Proceedings of the IEEE/CVF Conference on Computer Vision and Pattern Recognition, pp. 3821–3831 (2023)
20. Lin, T.-Y., et al.: Microsoft COCO: common objects in context. In: Fleet, D., Pajdla, T., Schiele, B., Tuytelaars, T. (eds.) ECCV 2014. LNCS, vol. 8693, pp. 740–755. Springer, Cham (2014). https://doi.org/10.1007/978-3-319-10602-1_48
21. Lin, X., Parikh, D.: Leveraging visual question answering for image-caption ranking. In: Leibe, B., Matas, J., Sebe, N., Welling, M. (eds.) ECCV 2016. LNCS, vol. 9906, pp. 261–277. Springer, Cham (2016). https://doi.org/10.1007/978-3-319-46475-6_17
22. Liu, C., Mao, Z., Zang, W., Wang, B.: A neighbor-aware approach for image-text matching. In: ICASSP 2019-2019 IEEE International Conference on Acoustics, Speech and Signal Processing (ICASSP), pp. 3970–3974. IEEE (2019)
23. Liu, Y., Guo, Y., Bakker, E.M., Lew, M.S.: Learning a recurrent residual fusion network for multimodal matching. In: Proceedings of the IEEE International Conference on Computer Vision, pp. 4107–4116 (2017)
24. Ma, M., Ren, J., Zhao, L., Tulyakov, S., Wu, C., Peng, X.: SMIL: multimodal learning with severely missing modality. In: Association for the Advancement of Artificial Intelligence Conference on Artificial Intelligence (2021)
25. Musgrave, K., Belongie, S., Lim, S.-N.: A metric learning reality check. In: Vedaldi, A., Bischof, H., Brox, T., Frahm, J.-M. (eds.) ECCV 2020. LNCS, vol. 12370, pp. 681–699. Springer, Cham (2020). https://doi.org/10.1007/978-3-030-58595-2_41
26. Nam, H., Ha, J.W., Kim, J.: Dual attention networks for multimodal reasoning and matching. In: Proceedings of the IEEE Conference on Computer Vision and Pattern Recognition, pp. 299–307 (2017)
27. Nguyen, K.X., Qiao, F., Peng, X.: Adaptive cascading network for continual test-time adaptation. In: Proceedings of the 33rd ACM International Conference on Information and Knowledge Management (2024)
28. Nguyen, K.X., Qiao, F., Trembanis, A., Peng, X.: SeafloorAI: a large-scale vision-language dataset for seafloor geological survey. In: The Thirty-eight Conference on Neural Information Processing Systems Datasets and Benchmarks Track (2024)

29. Oh, S.J., Murphy, K.P., Pan, J., Roth, J., Schroff, F., Gallagher, A.C.: Modeling uncertainty with hedged instance embeddings. In: International Conference on Learning Representations (2018)
30. Peng, X., Qiao, F., Zhao, L.: Out-of-domain generalization from a single source: an uncertainty quantification approach. IEEE Trans. Pattern Anal. Mach. Intell. **46**(03), 1775–1787 (2024)
31. Qiao, F., Peng, X.: Uncertainty-guided model generalization to unseen domains. In: Proceedings of the IEEE/CVF Conference on Computer Vision and Pattern Recognition, pp. 6790–6800 (2021)
32. Qiao, F., Peng, X.: Topology-aware robust optimization for out-of-distribution generalization. In: The Eleventh International Conference on Learning Representations (2023)
33. Qiao, F., Peng, X.: Ensemble pruning for out-of-distribution generalization. In: Forty-First International Conference on Machine Learning (2024)
34. Qiao, F., Zhao, L., Peng, X.: Learning to learn single domain generalization. In: Proceedings of the IEEE/CVF Conference on Computer Vision and Pattern Recognition, pp. 12556–12565 (2020)
35. Qu, L., Liu, M., Cao, D., Nie, L., Tian, Q.: Context-aware multi-view summarization network for image-text matching. In: Proceedings of the 28th ACM International Conference on Multimedia, pp. 1047–1055 (2020)
36. Raffel, C., et al.: Exploring the limits of transfer learning with a unified text-to-text transformer. J. Mach. Learn. Res. **21**, 1–67 (2020)
37. Rasiwasia, N., et al.: A new approach to cross-modal multimedia retrieval. In: Proceedings of the 18th ACM International Conference on Multimedia, pp. 251–260 (2010)
38. Ren, S., He, K., Girshick, R., Sun, J.: Faster r-cnn: towards real-time object detection with region proposal networks. Adv. Neural. Inf. Process. Syst. **28**, 91–99 (2015)
39. Russakovsky, O., et al.: Imagenet large scale visual recognition challenge. Int. J. Comput. Vision (IJCV) **115**(3), 211–252 (2015)
40. Sarafianos, N., Xu, X., Kakadiaris, I.A.: Adversarial representation learning for text-to-image matching. In: Proceedings of the IEEE/CVF International Conference on Computer Vision, pp. 5814–5824 (2019)
41. Schultz, M., Joachims, T.: Learning a distance metric from relative comparisons. Adv. Neural. Inf. Process. Syst. **16**, 41–48 (2004)
42. Shi, Y., Jain, A.K.: Probabilistic face embeddings. In: Proceedings of the IEEE/CVF International Conference on Computer Vision, pp. 6902–6911 (2019)
43. Shrivastava, A., Gupta, A., Girshick, R.: Training region-based object detectors with online hard example mining. In: Proceedings of the IEEE Conference on Computer Vision and Pattern Recognition, pp. 761–769 (2016)
44. Song, Y., Soleymani, M.: Polysemous visual-semantic embedding for cross-modal retrieval. In: Proceedings of the IEEE/CVF Conference on Computer Vision and Pattern Recognition, pp. 1979–1988 (2019)
45. Sun, J.J., Zhao, J., Chen, L.-C., Schroff, F., Adam, H., Liu, T.: View-invariant probabilistic embedding for human pose. In: Vedaldi, A., Bischof, H., Brox, T., Frahm, J.-M. (eds.) ECCV 2020. LNCS, vol. 12350, pp. 53–70. Springer, Cham (2020). https://doi.org/10.1007/978-3-030-58558-7_4
46. Villani, C.: Topics in optimal transportation. No. 58. American Mathematical Soc. (2003)

47. Wang, Z., et al.: Camp: cross-modal adaptive message passing for text-image retrieval. In: Proceedings of the IEEE/CVF International Conference on Computer Vision, pp. 5764–5773 (2019)
48. Wei, X., Zhang, T., Li, Y., Zhang, Y., Wu, F.: Multi-modality cross attention network for image and sentence matching. In: Proceedings of the IEEE/CVF Conference on Computer Vision and Pattern Recognition, pp. 10941–10950 (2020)
49. Yan, F., Mikolajczyk, K.: Deep correlation for matching images and text. In: Proceedings of the IEEE Conference on Computer Vision and Pattern Recognition, pp. 3441–3450 (2015)
50. Young, P., Lai, A., Hodosh, M., Hockenmaier, J.: From image descriptions to visual denotations: new similarity metrics for semantic inference over event descriptions. Trans. Assoc. Comput. Linguist. **2**, 67–78 (2014)
51. Zhang, Y., Lu, H.: Deep cross-modal projection learning for image-text matching. In: Proceedings of the European Conference on Computer Vision (ECCV), pp. 686–701 (2018)

BCCNetAttention: Enhancing Breast Cancer Report Through Image Captioning with Convolution Neural Network and Transformers Architecture

Huong Hoang Luong[1,2], Nguyen Thai-Nghe[1], and Hai Thanh Nguyen[1(✉)]

[1] Can Tho University, Can Tho, Vietnam
ntnghe@cit.ctu.edu.vn, nthai.cit@ctu.edu.vn
[2] FPT University, Can Tho, Vietnam

Abstract. Artificial Intelligence (AI) is transforming the field of healthcare, which brings advancements to the diagnosis and treatment of various conditions, especially breast cancer. It is considered the most dangerous illness among women. Thus, AI technologies including machine learning, deep learning, and advanced data analytics offer promising solutions to this sickness. The primary goal of this study is to develop systems called BCCNetAttention (Breast Cancer Captioning with ResNet50 and Cross Attention) that can automatically interpret and describe the content of images in a way that is meaningful and coherent to humans. In more detail, this research employed the Convolutional Neural Network (CNN) model for feature extraction and the Transformer architecture with Future Masked Language Modeling (FMLM) to train the model in the HisBreast dataset. As a result, the proposed approach reached a surprise result based on two calculations with the highest scores from BLEU-1 to BLEU-4 and Rouge-L at 0.65, 0.69, 0.72, 0.73, and 0.71. The study also demonstrated the power of CNN and Transformer with Cross Attention architecture in breast cancer image captioning in the INBreast dataset, creating an effective pipeline in the breast cancer diagnosis process.

Keywords: Breast cancer · Captioning · Convolutional Neural Network · Transformer · Cross Attention · Future Masked Language Modeling

1 Introduction

Breast cancer remains one of the most prevalent and deadly types of cancer, affecting millions of women worldwide and surpassing lung, cervical, colon, and skin cancers in prevalence [1]. Following Female breast cancer incidence and mortality rates in the United States [2], white women reached the first position in incidence rates with 133.7 per 100,000. However, black women held the top mortality rate with 27.6 per 100,000. Continues Asian countries, a total of 29,729 new breast cancer cases were released in 2019 from the Korean Breast Cancer

J. Kertesz et al. (Eds.): CSoNet 2024, LNCS 15417, pp. 188–199, 2025.
https://doi.org/10.1007/978-981-96-6389-7_16

Society registry system and Korean Central Cancer Registry, which made it the most common illness in women of this nation [3]. An annual trend in Japanese Cancer Incidence and Mortality showed that breast cancer became a top type of cancer in females in 2016 [4]. Moreover, the Ho Chi Minh City Cancer Registry presented more than 14,222 new cases of breast cancer that had been reported between 1996 to 2015 [5].

Early and correct diagnosis is beneficial for effective treatment and better outcomes in breast cancer [6,7]. Traditional diagnostic approaches are useful, but they frequently rely on subjective interpretation resulting in variability in diagnoses. In recent years, artificial intelligence (AI) has emerged as a revolutionary tool in medicine that provides unprecedented accuracy and consistency in diagnostic procedures [8]. Furthermore, it has demonstrated amazing potential for analyzing complex medical data. In addition, image captioning [9] is one of the most used AI approaches besides classification [10] and segmentation [11]. Image captioning is the process of creating descriptive textual information from inputs to provide insight into medical pictures [9]. This capability is particularly useful in breast cancer diagnosis, where detailed image interpretation can aid in identifying critical features.

Central to this image analysis framework are the Convolutional Neural Network (CNN) model [12] and Transformer architecture [13]. Additionally, the Future Masked Language Modeling (FMLM) approach based on Bidirectional Encoder Representations from Transformers (BERT) [14] allows us to understand and generate contextual information from textual data. When combined with CNN, Transformers can significantly enhance the interpretative capabilities of diagnostic systems, providing richer and more accurate descriptions of medical images. In addition, Incorporating cross-attention mechanisms further amplifies the effectiveness of these models [15]. Cross-attention enables the model to focus on relevant parts of the image while generating captions, thereby improving the coherence and relevance of the descriptions. The main contributions to this study include:

- This study introduces a novel system called BCCNetAttention (Breast Cancer Captioning with ResNet50 and Cross Attention) designed to automatically interpret and describe the content of breast cancer images in a meaningful and coherent manner to aid in diagnosis and treatment.
- The research successfully integrates Convolutional Neural Networks (CNN) for feature extraction with Transformer architectures. Moreover, the study leveraged Future Masked Language Modeling (FMLM) based on Bidirectional Encoder Representations from Transformers (BERT) to enhance the capability to understand and generate contextual information from textual data.
- By combining cross-attention mechanisms, the system improves the relevance and coherence of the generated image captions that focus on important parts of the images thereby enhancing interpretative accuracy.
- The proposed approach demonstrates high performance on the HisBreast dataset, which achieved the top scores in BLEU-1 to BLEU-4 and Rouge-L

metrics (i.e., 0.65, 0.69, 0.72, 0.73, and 0.71 respectively). It also shows effectiveness on the INBreast dataset and demonstrates this is a robust pipeline for breast cancer diagnosis.

The research paper is divided into five main sections. It begins with an introduction in Sect. 1, followed by an in-depth review of the relevant literature in Sect. 2. Section 3 details the methodology, explaining the techniques used. Section 4 describes the experiments, their procedures, and evaluations. Finally, Sect. 5 summarizes the key findings and provides insights into limitations and future directions.

2 Related Works

Image captioning for medical images powerful aspect of deep learning. However, research papers that pay attention to this field are still extremely rare, especially in breast cancer captioning. According to Alexander Yalunin et al. [16], the experiment indicated that the EfficientNet model, Transformer architecture, and attention mechanism can be used for image captioning on the input mammograms and generate an attention map. Throughout various scenarios, the study presented that their MFEN2RUBERT model reached a surprise based on BLEU-1 BLEU-2 BLEU-3 BLEU-4, and Rouge-L at 0.662, 0.608, 0.567, 0.534, and 0.590, respectively. Besides, the paper has proven that BERT configurations were effective for report generation. However, the authors did not point out the state-of-the-art related works to compare with the research leading to a void hole for the research.

Jun Li et al. [17] proposed a novel pipeline for captioning breast, thyroid, and lung in Chinese. Their work has proven effective when the BLEU score from 1 to 4 reached 0.761, 0.710, 0.672, and 0.640. Moreover, Rouge-L also achieved a high score of 0.758. the paper pointed out several processes that help to extract potential prior knowledge, capture knowledge-related visual features, and generate a text sequence from visual features such as Knowledge Distiller (KD), Knowledge Matched Visual Extractor (KMVE), and Report Generator (RG). However, the study still has limits with words related to size, location, and number in the proposed reports.

In [18], the authors proposed an approach to generate medical reports for breast cancer images by combining the ResNet18 model and the Transformer architecture. The study conducted extensive experiments on two different datasets to evaluate the model's generalizability, using BLEU and Rouge-L as evaluation metrics. While the results were promising, there are still limitations, such as the need for improved data preprocessing and normalization.

In generating clinical reports and assisting radiologists in spotting breast cancer. Ankan Deria et al. [19] developed the InVERGe (Intelligent Visual Encoder for Bridging Modalities in Report Generation) model to generate reports based on images and explain the reasons behind the generated text using image-text alignment. The model indicated an acceptable score to demonstrate the effectiveness of their approach in BLEU-1 to 4 and Rouge-L at 0.453, 0.267, 0.185,

0.134, and 0.430 in the breast cancer dataset. Furthermore, the paper pointed out the CrossModal Query Fusion Layer (CMQFL) to identify the most suitable text-grounded image embedding, which promotes a more grounded vision and language representation. In opposite, the research not only paid attention breast dataset but also used the chest dataset which can lead to the dilution of the base information.

3 Methodology

3.1 Proposed Approach

The proposed BCCNetAttention (Breast Cancer Captioning with ResNet50 and Cross Attention) in Fig. 1 employs several novel techniques. First, it used CNN for feature extraction from breast cancer images. Specifically, the ResNet50 architecture is utilized due to its proven effectiveness in capturing deep features from medical images. ResNet50 enables the system to learn and extract intricate patterns and details from the images, which are crucial for accurate diagnosis and interpretation.

In addition, text generation in this study is enhanced by leveraging FMLM based on BERT. FMLM improves the system's ability to understand and generate contextual information from textual data. By masking future tokens during training, the model learns to predict the next word in a sequence, thereby capturing the dependencies and relationships between words in a bidirectional manner. Additionally, The system utilizes an encoder-decoder mechanism, where the encoder processes the input image features extracted by ResNet50 model and the decoder generates the corresponding textual descriptions.

The encoder takes the high-dimensional image features and transforms them into a series of lower-dimensional embeddings. These embeddings capture the essential information from the images, which is then passed to the decoder. The decoder is equipped with cross-attention mechanisms that generate the textual descriptions by attending to the relevant parts of the image embeddings. Cross-attention allows the decoder to focus on different regions of the image while generating each word in the caption, ensuring that the descriptions are aligned with the important features of the image.

By combining the strengths of CNNs for image feature extraction and Transformers for sequence-to-sequence learning, BCCNetAttention achieves high performance in generating meaningful and coherent captions for breast cancer images. The integration of ResNet50, FMLM, and cross-attention mechanisms results in a robust and effective pipeline, as evidenced by the top scores achieved on the HisBreast dataset in BLEU-1 to BLEU-4 and Rouge-L metrics, as well as on the INBreast dataset.

3.2 Dataset

This research employed two datasets for experiment scenarios. First, the HisBreast dataset [20] in Fig. 2A includes breast ultrasound pictures taken from Ca

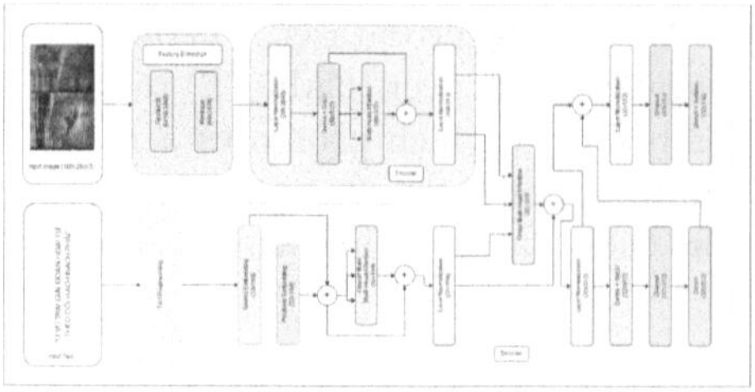

Fig. 1. The BCCNetAttention approach utilized the ability of the ResNet50 model, Transformer architecture, and Cross Attention algorithm.

Mau Province General Hospital in Vietnam. This dataset contains 972 samples that have a full description of breast tumor signs and characteristics, and diagnostic results from medical professionals. All material is offered in Vietnamese, making it accessible to local medical practitioners. In addition, The INbreast dataset [21] in Fig. 2B was gathered at Centro Hospitalar de S. João (CHSJ), Breast Centre in Porto including 410 full-field digital mammograms from 115 patients. This dataset is renowned for its excellent dependability and accuracy, which includes both impacted and post-mastectomy cases. Each DICOM-stored mammography includes manually labeled areas of interest (ROI) and medical reports translated from English to Vietnamese by professionals.

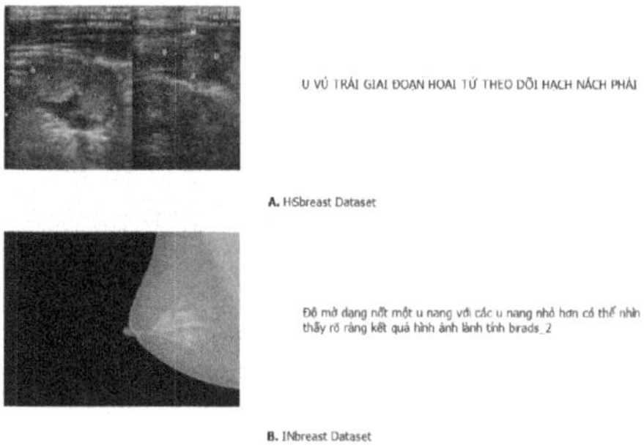

Fig. 2. The datasets with an example image and Vietnamese diagnosis

3.3 Text Re-processing

Effective text preprocessing is crucial for ensuring the quality and relevance of the data fed into the BCCNetAttention system. In Fig. 3, the preprocessing pipeline begins with the elimination of irrelevant diagnostic statements that do not contribute to the meaningful interpretation of breast cancer images. Next, special characters and HTML tags such as *
* and *& nbsp;* are removed to prevent any non-textual elements from interfering with the text analysis. Extra spaces are also eliminated to maintain consistency and readability. Additionally, numeric characters are carefully filtered. While most numeric characters are removed, specific numbers such as BIRAD scores or those followed by units are retained due to their diagnostic significance. Finally, the text is normalized to a consistent case format, converting all characters to either uppercase or normal case as needed. This normalization step ensures uniformity and helps in reducing variability caused by case differences, thus enhancing the ability to process and understand the text accurately.

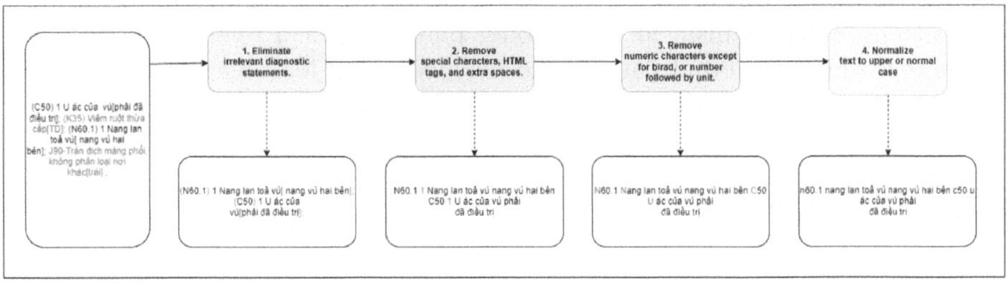

Fig. 3. The example of four main preprocess steps to enhance the ability to generate text, in which the red is the text that will be changed in the next step (Color figure online)

3.4 Convolution Neural Network with the ResNet50 Model

In the BCCNetAttention system, the ResNet50 model is responsible for the feature extraction process for breast cancer images. ResNet50 is a 50-layer deep residual network, which is designed to handle complex image recognition tasks by addressing the vanishing gradient problem that often hampers deep networks. By using ResNet50, the system can effectively dissect and understand the nuanced visual details within the images providing a rich set of features that serve as the foundation for generating coherent and contextually relevant image captions. In the BCCNetAttention system, the training and evaluation of models are conducted in an environment powered by Kaggle's NVIDIA TESLA P100 GPUs. Specifically, the dataset is divided into training, validation, and test sets in an 8-1-1 ratio. The training process spans 100 epochs, providing ample opportunities for the model to learn from the data. This training setup ensures that the models are well-equipped to handle the complexity and variability inherent in breast cancer image data.

3.5 Transformer Architecture with Encode and Decode

The proposed system employs a Transformer architecture that uses an encoder-decoder mechanism to generate descriptive captions for breast cancer images.

In Fig. 1, the encoder begins by processing embedded image features, first passing them through a Layer Normalization Layer to standardize the input and improve training stability. Besides, The decoder handles the embedded captions and starts with a Positional Embedding Layer, which combines input embeddings with positional encoding to retain the order of the words.

Future Masked Language Modeling (FMLM) based on Bidirectional Encoder Representations from Transformers (BERT) enhances the capability to generate contextual information from textual data. FMLM masks future tokens during training, allowing the model to predict the next word in a sequence while considering both past and future context. This bidirectional approach ensures that the generated captions are coherent and contextually accurate. Additionally, the cross-attention mechanism in the decoder plays a critical role by enabling the model to attend to relevant parts of the encoded image features while generating each word in the caption.

4 Experiments and Evaluation

4.1 Performance and Metrics

To optimize the efficiency and effectiveness of processing breast cancer images, we used a batch size of 16, and the image size was standardized to (224, 224). For optimization, we employed the AdamW optimizer with learning rate of 1e-4. This optimizer is a different version of the traditional Adam optimizer that includes weight decay. Because AdamW allows for faster convergence and improved generalization, it has been demonstrated to perform especially great in applications relating to CNN-Transformer hybrid architectures. To guarantee comprehensive learning and model adaption to the HisBreast and INBreast datasets, we fixed the number of epochs to 100.

In the evaluation, BLEU (Bilingual Evaluation Understudy) and Rouge-L metrics are crucial for assessing the quality of the generated image captions. Equation 1 measures the precision of n-grams in the generated text against reference texts calculating how many n-grams (i.e., n= 1,2,3,4) in the candidate caption appear in any of the reference captions. Mathematically, the BLEU score is computed as follows:

$$\text{BLEU} = BP \cdot \exp\left(\sum_{n=1}^{N} w_n \log p_n\right) \tag{1}$$

where BP is the brevity penalty to penalize short sentences, w_n is the weight for the n-gram, and p_n is the precision of n-grams in formular 1. BLEU-1 to BLEU-4 correspond to 1-gram to 4-gram precisions, indicating how closely the generated captions match the reference captions in terms of individual words up to sequences of four words.

Rouge-L measures recall, precision, and F1-score based on the longest common subsequence (LCS) between the candidate and reference texts in Eq. 2. The LCS captures the longest sequence of words that appears in both texts in the same order, emphasizing the preservation of sentence structure. The Rouge-L score is given by:

$$\text{Rouge-L} = \frac{(1+\beta^2) \cdot \text{Precision} \cdot \text{Recall}}{\text{Recall} + \beta^2 \cdot \text{Precision}} \tag{2}$$

where β is a balancing factor (usually set to 1, making the F1-score), Precision is the ratio of the length of the LCS to the length of the candidate caption, and Recall is the ratio of the length of the LCS to the length of the reference caption. These metrics collectively provide a comprehensive evaluation of the system's performance in generating accurate and contextually appropriate captions, with BLEU emphasizing precision and Rouge-L focusing on recall and structural similarity.

4.2 Scenario 1: Image Captioning with Convolution Neural Network and Transformer on the Description of HiSBreast Dataset

In the first scenario, Table 1 illustrates three experiments on different CNN models including VGG16, InceptionV3, and our proposed (i.e., ResNet50) with Transformer architecture. The results demonstrate the superiority of the proposed ResNet50 model. It achieves the highest scores across all metrics, with BLEU-1 at 0.532, BLEU-2 at 0.509, BLEU-3 at 0.523, BLEU-4 at 0.511, and Rouge-L at 0.545. In comparison, VGG16Transformer shows the lowest performance. The InceptionV3Transformer model performs better than the VGG16Transformer but still falls short of the proposed method. These results highlight the effectiveness of ResNet50 in extracting detailed features from breast cancer images, which significantly enhances the accuracy and coherence of the generated captions when combined with the Transformer architecture. Furthermore, Fig. 4 indicated the generated text matches almost correctly with preprocessed text. However, the proposed model seems unable to distinguish between left and right breast images.

Table 1. The results in the HiSBreast dataset for descriptions

Method	BLEU-1	BLEU-2	BLEU-3	BLEU-4	Rouge-L
VGG16Transformer	0.278	0.263	0.334	0.356	0.424
InceptionV3Transformer	0.393	0.365	0.416	0.426	0.507
Our	**0.532**	**0.509**	**0.523**	**0.511**	**0.545**

4.3 Scenario 2: Image Captioning with Convolution Neural Network and Transformer on the Diagnosis of HiSBreast Dataset

In Scenario 2, the experiment was conducted as in Scenario 1 with HiSBreast diagnosis, as shown in Table 2. The results indicate that the proposed ResNet50

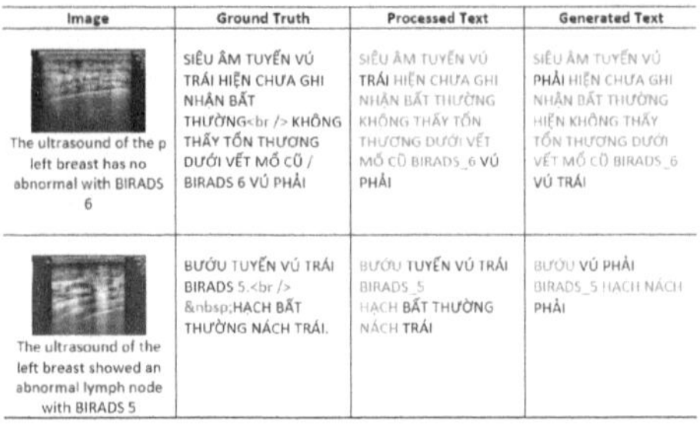

Fig. 4. The ground truth, processed text, and generated text in HiSBreast dataset descriptions, in which red color is removed, green color is a perfect match and orange is similar. (Color figure online)

model with Transformer architecture again outperforms the other models. Specifically, ResNet50 achieves BLEU-1, BLEU-2, BLEU-3, and BLEU-4 scores of 0.650, 0.692, 0.725, and 0.730, respectively, and a Rouge-L score of 0.713. These scores are significantly higher than those achieved by VGG16Transformer and InceptionV3Transformer. Figure 5 included in this scenario illustrates the ground truth, processed text, and generated text for diagnosis in the HiSBreast dataset. This visual representation emphasizes the high accuracy and contextual relevance of the captions generated by the proposed ResNet50 with Transformer architecture

Table 2. The results in the HiSBreast dataset for diagnosis

Method	BLEU-1	BLEU-2	BLEU-3	BLEU-4	Rouge-L
VGG16Transformer	0.490	0.545	0.589	0.598	0.584
InceptionV3Transformer	0.560	0.606	0.651	0.654	0.637
Our	**0.650**	**0.692**	**0.725**	**0.730**	**0.713**

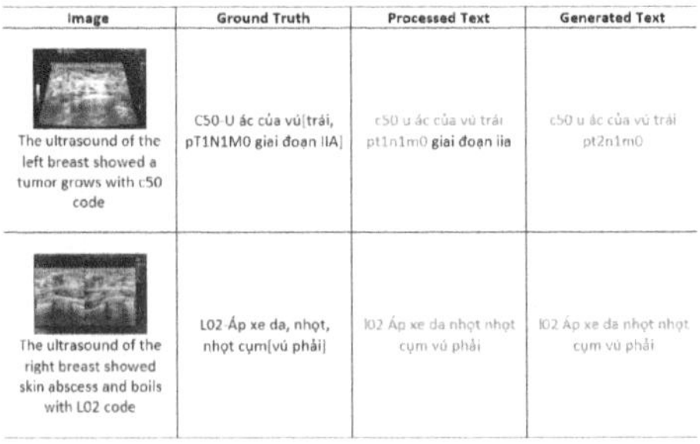

Fig. 5. The ground truth, processed text, and generated text in HiSBreast dataset diagnosis, in which red color is removed, green color is a perfect match (Color figure online)

4.4 Scenario 3: Image Captioning with Convolution Neural Network and Transformer on the Description of INBreast Dataset

Table 3. Image captioning with Convolution Neural Network and Transformer on the description of INBreast dataset

Method	BLEU-1	BLEU-2	BLEU-3	BLEU-4	Rouge-L
VGG16Transformer	0.304	0.259	0.282	0.275	0.423
InceptionV3Transformer	0.345	0.303	0.316	0.296	0.461
Our	**0.326**	**0.282**	**0.302**	**0.302**	**0.448**

In Scenario 3, the study extends to the INBreast dataset focusing on the report descriptions. In Table 3. Our proposed ResNet50 model, while slightly lower in BLEU scores compared to InceptionV3, achieves a higher Rouge-L score, with BLEU scores of 0.326, 0.282, 0.302, and 0.302, and a Rouge-L score of 0.448. In addition, Fig. 6 shows that our method needs to improve for long text captioning. However, the consistent performance across Different experiments demonstrates the robustness and adaptability of our proposed method in image captioning tasks.

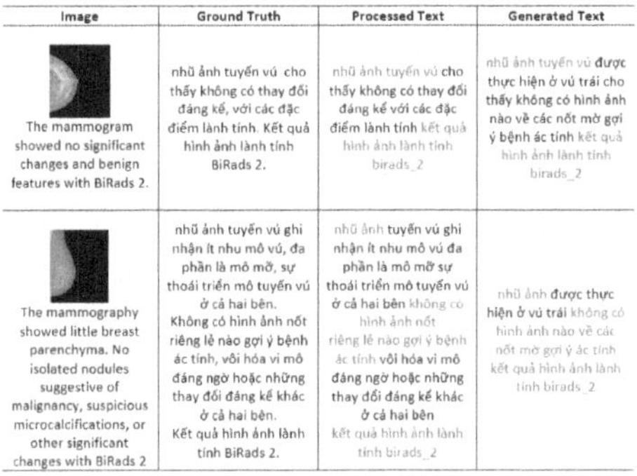

Fig. 6. The ground truth, processed text, and generated text in INBreast dataset description, in which red color is removed, green color is a perfect match and orange is similar. (Color figure online)

4.5 Comparison with State-of-the-Art Methods

The BCCNetAttention system demonstrates competitive performance compared to other state-of-the-art methods in image captioning on breast cancer datasets. As shown in Table 4, the proposed method shows robust performance, particularly in the higher-order n-gram precision metrics, underscoring its effectiveness in generating accurate and contextually relevant captions for breast cancer images.

Table 4. Comparison with other state-of-the-art methods in image captioning on breast dataset

Reference	Other Method	Year	Language	BLEU-1	BLEU-2	BLEU-3	BLEU-4	**Rouge-L**
Alexander Yalunin et al.	MFEN2RUBERT	2021	English	0.662	0.608	0.567	0.534	0.590
Jun Li et al.	CMFAvUG	2024	Chinese	0.761	0.710	0.672	0.640	0.758
Ankan Deria et al.	InVERGe	2024	English	0.453	0.267	0.185	0.640	0.430
Proposed			**Vietnamese**	**0.650**	**0.692**	**0.725**	**0.730**	**0.713**

5 Conclusion

In conclusion, BCCNetAttention can interpret and describe breast cancer images meaningfully and coherently to aid in diagnosis and treatment. Integrating CNNs for feature extraction with Transformer architectures, the system leverages ResNet50 to capture deep visual features and employs FMLM based on BERT to enhance textual understanding and generation. By incorporating cross-attention mechanisms, BCCNetAttention significantly improves the relevance and coherence of generated captions, focusing on critical image regions to enhance interpretative accuracy. The proposed approach demonstrates high performance on the HisBreast dataset, achieving top scores in BLEU-1 to BLEU-4 (i.e., 0.65, 0.69, 0.72, 0.73) and Rouge-L (i.e., 0.71). These results underscore the system's capability to generate accurate and contextually relevant captions, which makes it a valuable tool for improving breast cancer diagnosis and treatment through advanced AI-driven image captioning.

Acknowledgements. Luong Hoang Huong was funded by the Master, PhD Scholarship Programme of Vingroup Innovation Foundation (VINIF), code VINIF.2024.TS.067.

Data availability Statement. Availability of Data, Code, and Material

References

1. Chhikara, B.S., Parang, K., et al.: Global cancer statistics 2022: the trends projection analysis. Chem. Biol. Lett. **10**(1), 451–451 (2023)
2. Giaquinto, A.N., et al.: Breast cancer statistics, 2022. CA: Cancer J. Clin. **72**(6), 524–541 (2022)
3. Choi, J.E., et al.: Breast cancer statistics in Korea, 2019. J. Breast Cancer **26**(3), 207 (2023)
4. Katanoda, K., et al.: Updated trends in cancer in japan: incidence in 1985–2015 and mortality in 1958–2018-a sign of decrease in cancer incidence. J. Epidemiol. **31**(7), 426–450 (2021)
5. Pham, D.X., Ho, T., Bui, T.D., Ho-Pham, L.T., Nguyen, T.V.: Trends in breast cancer incidence in Ho Chi Minh city 1996–2015: a registry-based study. PLoS ONE **16**(2), e0246800 (2021)

6. Ginsburg, O., et al.: Breast cancer early detection: a phased approach to implementation. Cancer **126**, 2379–2393 (2020)
7. Bhushan, A., Gonsalves, A., Menon, J.U.: Current state of breast cancer diagnosis, treatment, and theranostics. Pharmaceutics **13**(5), 723 (2021)
8. Abbaoui, W., Retal, S., El Bhiri, B., Kharmoum, N., Ziti, S.: Towards revolutionizing precision healthcare: a systematic literature review of artificial intelligence methods in precision medicine. Inform. Med. Unlocked 101475 (2024)
9. Ghandi, T., Pourreza, H., Mahyar, H.: Deep learning approaches on image captioning: a review. ACM Comput. Surv. **56**(3), 1–39 (2023)
10. Chen, L., Li, S., Bai, Q., Yang, J., Jiang, S., Miao, Y.: Review of image classification algorithms based on convolutional neural networks. Remote Sensing **13**(22), 4712 (2021)
11. Cai, L., Gao, J., Zhao, D.: A review of the application of deep learning in medical image classification and segmentation. Annals Transl. Med. **8**(11) (2020)
12. Li, Z., Liu, F., Yang, W., Peng, S., Zhou, J.: A survey of convolutional neural networks: analysis, applications, and prospects. IEEE Trans. Neural Netw. Learn. Syst. **33**(12), 6999–7019 (2021)
13. Han, K., Xiao, A., Wu, E., Guo, J., Xu, C., Wang, Y.: Transformer in transformer. Adv. Neural. Inf. Process. Syst. **34**, 15908–15919 (2021)
14. Alaparthi, S., Mishra, M.: Bidirectional encoder representations from transformers (bert): a sentiment analysis odyssey. arXiv preprint arXiv:2007.01127 (2020)
15. Niu, Z., Zhong, G., Yu, H.: A review on the attention mechanism of deep learning. Neurocomputing **452**, 48–62 (2021)
16. Yalunin, A., Sokolova, E., Burenko, I., Ponomarchuk, A., Puchkova, O., Umerenkov, D.: Generating mammography reports from multi-view mammograms with bert. In: Findings of the Association for Computational Linguistics: EMNLP 2021, pp. 153–162 (2021)
17. Li, J., et al.: Ultrasound report generation with cross-modality feature alignment via unsupervised guidance. arXiv preprint arXiv:2406.00644 (2024)
18. Luong, H.H., Nguyen, H.T., Thai-Nghe, N.: Toward supporting breast cancer diagnosis based on captioning mammogram and ultrasound images. In: Thai-Nghe, N., Do, T.N., Benferhat, S. (eds.) Intelligent Systems and Data Science, pp. 71–85. Springer Nature Singapore, Singapore (2025)
19. Deria, A., Kumar, K., Chakraborty, S., Mahapatra, D., Roy, S.: Inverge: intelligent visual encoder for bridging modalities in report generation. In: Proceedings of the IEEE/CVF Conference on Computer Vision and Pattern Recognition, pp. 2028–2038 (2024)
20. Luong, H.H., Nguyen Thanh, H., Nguyen, T.N., Luong Thi Thu, H.: Hisbreast. Mendeley Data, V1, (2024)
21. Moreira, I.C., Amaral, I., Domingues, I., Cardoso, A., Cardoso, M.J., Cardoso, J.S.: Inbreast: toward a full-field digital mammographic database. Acad. Radiol. **19**(2), 236–248 (2012)

Visual Question Answering for Medical Data Using a Visio-Linguistic Model

Van Hieu Bui(✉), Quang Duc Tran, Kim Thanh Tran Thi, and Viet Tien Le

FPT University, Education Zone, Hoa Lac Hi-tech Park, Ha Noi, Vietnam
{hieubv10,ductqhe153732,thanhttkhe153476,tienlvhe151357}@fpt.edu.vn

Abstract. Medical Visual Question Answering (VQA) has become increasingly significant in aiding physicians with disease diagnosis and providing patients with detailed insights into their conditions. However, Medical VQA still lags behind general VQA due to challenges such as limited availability of accurate data and the complexity of medical terminology. Existing models frequently struggle with performance issues caused by the intricate nature of image and text encoders. Recent research has concentrated on improving fusion modules for integrating question and image features and employing pre-trained models with self-collected datasets, but often overlooks the value of question and image history. This paper proposes an approach that introduces an Associative Memory block to leverage historical questions and images, enhancing the vision-language context. Additionally, we incorporate a Prototype Learning block that utilizes hierarchical prototype learning on text and image embeddings through advanced Hopfield layers. Our approach focuses on identifying the most representative prototypes from text-image embeddings, enriched by associative memory, rather than learning direct text-image joint feature representations. This method facilitates a more nuanced representation of semantics for answering questions. Our proposed approach achieves the best performance on the VQA-RAD dataset, demonstrating a significant accuracy improvement of 0.45%.

Keywords: VQA · Medical Data · Visio-Linguistic Model

1 Introduction

Visual Question Answering (VQA) combines Computer Vision (CV) and Natural Language Processing (NLP) to provide answers to questions about images by analyzing their content [1]. Recently, Medical Visual Question Answering (Med-VQA) has emerged as a critical area of research, driven by its potential to enhance medical diagnostics and improve patient care.Med-VQA is a specialized task where a medical image is paired with a question, and the objective is to deliver an accurate response. This task requires the integration of computer vision, natural language processing, and medical expertise to support physicians, alleviate the burden on healthcare systems, and boost medical efficiency.

J. Kertesz et al. (Eds.): CSoNet 2024, LNCS 15417, pp. 200–211, 2025.
https://doi.org/10.1007/978-981-96-6389-7_17

Med-VQA systems can assist doctors in a manner akin to pathologists, analyzing body tissues to aid diagnoses [8]. They also function as knowledgeable assistants, offering additional perspectives to mitigate the risk of misdiagnoses and validate physicians' interpretations [15]. In automated health checks or online consultations, Med-VQA systems can provide reliable medical advice, counteracting the risks associated with misinformation from online sources.

Despite its promise, Med-VQA presents more complex technical challenges than general VQA. The development of large-scale medical VQA datasets is hindered by the high cost of expert annotations and the challenge of synthetically generating question-answer pairs from images. Additionally, Med-VQA models must handle fine-grained questions about microscopic lesions, often requiring advanced segmentation techniques and training on specialized medical knowledge rather than general language corpora.

Artificial intelligence has made strides in clinical decision support, particularly in automating medical image interpretation. Models such as PMC-VQA [20] and MUMC [7] have achieved state-of-the-art results by integrating medical visual content with text-based queries. Nonetheless, Med-VQA continues to face challenges, including diversity in questions, incorporation of supplementary medical information, interpretability, generalizability, and integration into medical workflows. A significant obstacle is the scarcity of large-scale labeled training data, which hinders Out-of-Distribution (OOD) generalization [21]. Recent studies suggest that models may rely excessively on question-answer distributions, potentially neglecting image content and exacerbating OOD generalization issues [21].

In response to these challenges, we propose a novel architectural model designed to address limitations in text recognition accuracy, speed, and resource utilization. Our approach introduces the Associative Memory Module (AMM), which utilizes a two-memory model-relational and item memories-that interact to refine their representations. Additionally, our model pioneers the use of Hopfield layers in Med-VQA, advancing the field of memorization and reasoning. We demonstrate the efficacy of our model with the best results on the VQA-RAD dataset, achieving significant improvements in accuracy, F1 score, and BLEU score. This research not only establishes new benchmarks but also makes substantial contributions to the broader field of medical artificial intelligence.

2 Related Work

Visual Question Answering (VQA) combines the fields of Computer Vision (CV) and Natural Language Processing (NLP) to enable systems to answer questions about images by analyzing visual content [1]. A standard VQA architecture includes four primary components: a visual encoder, a language encoder, a fusion algorithm, and an answering unit.

Visual Encoder: Visual encoders extract features from images using architectures such as VGGNet, ResNet, and more recent models like EfficientNet and Vision Transformer (ViT). These models are often initialized with pre-trained weights from datasets like ImageNet, although these weights may not fully capture medical image specifics. Researchers are exploring domain-specific pre-training to address this, as seen in work by Xiaoman Zhang et al. [20], who utilized pre-trained models on the PMC-VQA dataset. Given the limited size of medical VQA datasets (e.g., VQA-RAD [5], SLAKE-English [9]), methods like data augmentation and contrastive learning are being employed to improve model performance.

Language Encoder: On the language side, encoders such as LSTM, Bi-LSTM, GRU, and BERT are commonly used. BERT-based models, in particular, have shown superior performance due to advancements in contextual embeddings [3]. Despite progress, there is a need for further development in pre-training methods on larger and more diverse textual corpora, including models akin to GPT.

Fusion Algorithm: The fusion algorithm combines features from the visual and language encoders into unified representations. Techniques include attention mechanisms and pooling methods like concatenation, summation, and element-wise products. While pooling methods can combine features effectively, concatenation often results in average performance, and element-wise products can be computationally intensive [19].

Answering Components: The answering component produces the final output, typically using classification for discrete responses or text generation for more complex answers. Text generation in VQA is particularly challenging, as it requires maintaining contextual relevance and coherence throughout the response.

Prototype learning and memory networks significantly enhance Visual Question Answering (VQA) by improving data representation and contextual memory. Prototype learning focuses on selecting the most representative data points from a training set, using methods like K-Nearest Neighbors (KNN) for proximity-based selection and Learning Vector Quantization (LVQ) for manually chosen prototypes with fewer examples [13]. Recent methods use neural networks for autonomous prototype selection, including convolutional prototype learning, beneficial in tasks like semantic segmentation [2]. Our work applies a modern Hopfield network [12] for prototype learning, utilizing text-image embeddings to capture complex semantics and improve representation.

Memory networks provide a structured mechanism for storing and retrieving relevant information, essential in VQA for maintaining context over question sequences. Initially introduced by Weston et al. [16], memory networks have since incorporated neural sequence models and attention mechanisms [4], finding success in machine translation, image classification, and captioning tasks [17]. In Med-VQA, Pellegrini et al. [11] utilized hierarchical annotations to integrate context from prior interactions. Building on this, our approach uses an associative memory network with modern Hopfield layers [12] to advance memory retention and retrieval, enhancing learning and response accuracy.

3 Method

We present our model and training pipeline, illustrated in Fig. 1. The training process begins with encoding the input question and corresponding image. Visual features are extracted from the spatial layout of the final pooling layer of EfficientNet, while linguistic features are derived using RoBERTa [10]. These visual and linguistic features are then concatenated and passed into an associative memory module, which uses relational and item memories to store and compute relationships between the two feature types.

An encoder-decoder attention mechanism then identifies the most relevant regions and elements within the visual and linguistic features of the image and question. This mechanism assigns weights to each visual and linguistic feature vector, enhancing their representational power. The output from the associative memory module (AMM) is combined with the encoder-decoder attention output to further refine these visual-linguistic features.

Next, hierarchical prototype learning is performed on the enhanced features using prototype blocks, which incorporate modern Hopfield layers to capture complex semantic patterns. The final output from the prototype blocks is used to classify the answers.

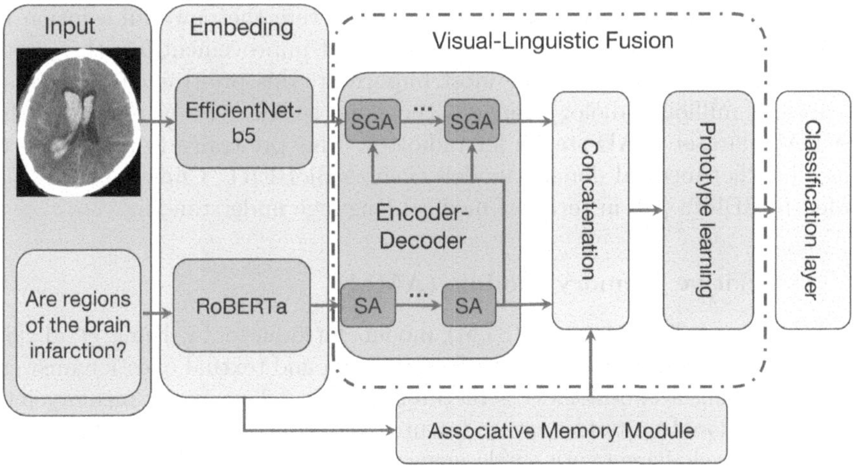

Fig. 1. Proposed Training Pipeline for Medical Visual Question Answering

3.1 Image Features Extraction

To extract features from images, we utilize the pre-trained EfficientNet [14]. The process begins with resizing the input images to a uniform size of 448 × 448 pixels, ensuring compatibility with EfficientNet's input requirements.

Once resized, the images are fed into the EfficientNet model. Specifically, we extract the outputs from the final convolutional layer of EfficientNet, denoted as Conv. These outputs are then processed through an additional convolutional layer, which transforms the feature maps into a feature space with a specified embedding size. The additional convolution serves two main purposes: it maps the feature maps to a desired embedding dimension tailored for subsequent processing and maintains flexibility with different hardware capacities and computational resources, as EfficientNet is designed to balance efficiency across various setups.

Following the additional convolution, we apply pooling layers with a pool size of 2 and a stride of 1. The final output of this process is a feature embedding matrix denoted as $I \in \mathcal{R}^{s \times d}$. Here, s represents the total number of spatial positions in the feature map, calculated as $H_{out} \times W_{out}$, where H_{out} and W_{out} are the height and width of the output feature map after pooling, and d denotes the embedding size.

3.2 Question Features Extraction

In order to extract contextual information from the questions, we decided to initialize the question encoder with pre-trained RoBERTa (RadBERT-RoBERTa-4 m) [18]. Initially, the Transformer model family has demonstrated its impressive performance although recurrent neural networks were the powerful solution in NLP for a long time. Transformer gives significant improvement in either accuracy or train costs. Next and the most important, this pre-trained model was built from 4 million radiology reports, the same as the type of images in the VQA-RAD dataset, RAD stands for radiology. This pre-trained model outperforms all earlier medical domain models such as BioBERT, Clinical-BERT and BioMed-RoBERTa [10] in terms of medical language understanding.

3.3 Associative Memory Module (AMM)

The SAM-Based Two-Memory (STM) model, introduced by Hung et al. [6], addresses memory limitations in Nth-farthest item and textual question answering by leveraging a two-memory structure. This model separates memory into item and relational units to capture features and structural relationships more effectively. The challenge with single-memory models is their difficulty in maintaining relational representations. To overcome this, the STM model incorporates distinct item and relational memories that interact to enhance each other's representations (see Fig. 2 for details).

In our approach, we adapt and extend this model by integrating the Self-attentive Associative Memory with outer product attention, as proposed by Hung et al. [6]. We modify the input to this model to better memorize both the items and the relationships between images and questions, thereby enriching the visual-linguistic features. This modification enhances the model's ability to capture and utilize complex semantic relationships between visual and textual data. The Associative Memory Module (AMM) dynamically updates its item

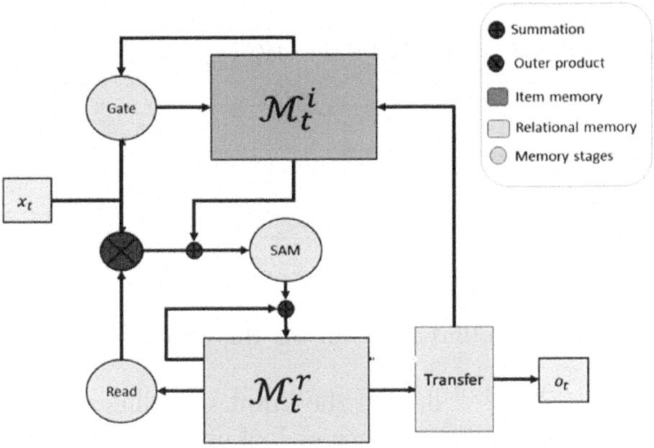

Fig. 2. Associative Memory Module [6]

memory $\mathcal{M}_{ti}$ using gating mechanisms at each timestep based on the input x_t. The outputs from both the relational memory and the item memory are added and passed as input to the Self-Attentive Memory (SAM). This process generates a novel relational representation, which is subsequently used to update the state of the relational memory $\mathcal{M}_t^r$. The relational memory transfers its insights to the item memory and contributes information to the final output value. Unlike conventional methods, which may struggle with memory reconstruction during the distillation process, our approach effectively captures bi-linear representations stored in the relational memory through high-dimensional transformations. This capability ensures that the output maintains a rich and meaningful representation, supporting both relational and item learning, even in vector form.

3.4 Prototype Learning Block

It is extremely challenging to directly learn authentic yet highly divergent semantic representations due to the significant modality gap between queries and medical images. To address this, we utilize the visual-linguistic feature space for prototype learning (see Fig. 3). Specifically, we incorporate the Hopfield layer and the self-attention layer within the prototype learning block. Each sub-layer employs a residual connection, followed by Normalization and Scale layers.

The original Hopfield layer, designed primarily for recognizing stored patterns or static queries, is further developed in the current Hopfield network [12]. Our goal is to enhance the network's ability to autonomously leverage clusters of high-level semantic concepts present in the data samples. This enhancement enables the network to systematically discover the most representative prototypes using the visual-linguistic features as input. These acquired prototypes can be viewed as code words representing more complex semantic concepts. The Hopfield layer utilized in this study is illustrated in Fig. 3.

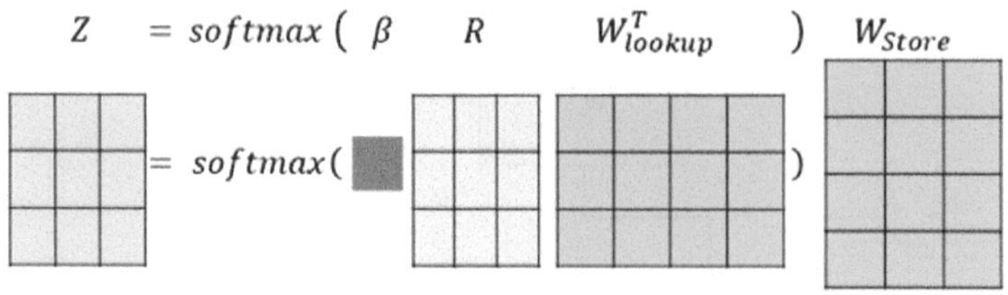

Fig. 3. The Illustration of the Hopfield layer. [12]

Formally, let $R \in \mathcal{R}^{(s+l)\times d}$ denote the input visuallinguistic feature R. The Prototype content and matrix prototype lookup matrix are then defined as W_{store} and $W_{lookup} \in \mathcal{R}^{n_{prot}\times d}$, where n_{prot} is the number of prototypes. The output $Z \in \mathcal{R}^{s\times d}$ can be formulated as:

$$Z = softmax(\beta R W^T_{lookup}) W_{store} \tag{1}$$

where $\beta = 1/\sqrt{d}$ is a scaling scalar. With Eq. 1, prototype learning can be achieved by the Hopfield layer from two perspectives:

1) Saving the stored patterns: Learning the most representative prototypes in W_{store}, where each row in W_{store} corresponds to a stored visual-linguistic prototype.
2) Using prototype learning: The learned prototypes from the lookup matrix W_{lookup} are used to represent the input visual-linguistic features X. Thus, the $softmax(\cdot)$ in the formula can be understood as the probability of each class (prototype) in the mapping.

3.5 Implementation

Dataset: The VQA-RAD dataset [11], released in 2018, focuses exclusively on radiology and is categorized into three main areas: abdomen, chest, and head. The dataset contains 315 radiology images, evenly distributed across these categories, and includes 3,515 question-answer pairs validated by clinicians. Each image may be associated with multiple questions, but for our implementation, we treat each question individually. Questions are classified into 11 categories, including color, abnormality, organ system, modality, attribute, counting, object/condition presence, positional reasoning, plane, size, and others. Approximately 58% of the answers are closed-ended, requiring brief responses, while the remaining answers are open-ended and can vary in length.

Code, Frameworks, and Environment: We extended the SAM model codebase [6], incorporating custom components for data processing, loading, training, testing, inference, and visualization. Our implementation uses Python and PyTorch, with tensor board for monitoring progress. We also utilize NumPy, Pandas, Matplotlib, and additional libraries like Einops, Pydash, torchinfo,

Shapely, Timm, Torch-Lightning, and Transformers. Implementation, debugging, and data analysis are conducted on Google Colab virtual machines (12.7 GB RAM, Intel Xeon CPU, GPU T4 with 15 GB VRAM), while training is performed on Vast.ai cloud platforms using RTX 3090 Ti GPUs (24 GB VRAM) and AMD Ryzen 9 5900X processors.

Hyperparameters: Table 1 presents a detailed breakdown of the hyperparameters used in our training process. Several adjustments were made compared to the original implementation to optimize performance. We set the input size of the image as 488×488 and the max padding size of the tokenizer for the question is 30. The Adam optimizer algorithm with a learning rate of 1e5 was our choice. We also incorporated the StepLR Scheduler during training to make the model learn better. as shown in Fig. 4.1. Then train the model batch size 16, and max num epochs 100. We must choose the hyper-parameter appropriate for each module because of the model trade-off between accuracy and resource. As shown in Table 2, a model is considered positive if it achieves highest performance with lowest resource so we use some combination of model hyper-parameters to evaluate before training.

Table 1. Table captions should be placed above the tables.

Learning rate	Epochs	Batch size	Prototypes	Memory slots
0.0001	100	16	500/1000/1500	1/6/12

4 Results

Our method outperforms the best approach, as shown in Table 2. Evaluations using the VQA-RAD dataset reveal that our model excels in both open-ended and overall performance metrics, achieving a 0.4% absolute improvement over Q2ATransformer, the leading method. Specifically, we see a 0.3% increase in open-ended scenarios and a 0.72% improvement in closed-ended scenarios. Compared to the best-performing models on closed-ended questions, our approach demonstrates a significant 11.19% absolute improvement on open-ended questions and a 4.43% overall gain. These results underscore the effectiveness of our approach, particularly in handling open-ended questions, validating our use of associative memory and prototype learning to enhance the network's memory and feature representation.

To identify the optimal generalization of our model, we first explored the effect of varying hidden sizes while keeping other parameters constant. Our experiments indicated that a hidden size of 1024 achieved better performance compared to smaller sizes, though it also increased the model size by 43 million parameters compared to a hidden size of 768, with only a marginal accuracy gain of 0.4%. Considering this trade-off between accuracy and resource utilization, we selected a hidden size of 768 for the final model to balance efficiency and competitive performance.

Table 2. Comparisons our method with the state-of-the-art methods on the VQA-RAD [11] test set.

Methods	Closed	Open	Overall
BAN-VQAMix [20]	74.0	53.8	65.9
CMSA-MTPT [32]	77.3	56.1	68.8
MMQ-BAN [5]	75.8	53.7	67.0
FITS [8]	82.0	68.2	76.5
hi-VQA [15]	-	-	76.3
Q2ATransformer [40]	81.2	79.19	80.48
Ours	81.98	79.39	80.93

The model's accuracy improved with larger hidden sizes and parameter counts. Specifically, a hidden size of 512 with 187.5 million parameters achieved 65.3% accuracy, while a hidden size of 768 with 213 million parameters yielded 73.8% accuracy. The highest accuracy of 74.2% was attained with a hidden size of 1024 and 255 million parameters, demonstrating that greater model capacity enhances performance.
Accuracy also varied with different maximum padding lengths. A padding length of 10 resulted in 62.4% accuracy, which improved to 73.8% with a padding length of 30. However, accuracy decreased to 68.1% with a padding length of 50, indicating that excessive padding may negatively impact performance.

4.1 The Impact of the Associative Memory Module

We adopt STM [6] as the AMM for our model, with the two memory modules serving as the relational and item memory. The AMM of our model uses a memory network strategy, directly capturing the bi-linear representations that are kept in the relational memory through high-dimensional transformations and enriching the visual- linguistic features. Our experiments on AMM are present on Table 3.

Table 3. Comparison of models with different hyper parameters of AMM

Model	Accuracy (%)	Time (s/epoch)
w/o AMM	62.4	61
nq = 1	68.8	65
nq = 6	75.2	96
nq = 12	79.7	119

As shown on Table 3, our model achieves groundbreaking accuracy with accuracy, but the training time is much higher without AMM. Furthermore, AMM helps models converge faster and learn better (See in Fig. 4a). Therefore, the memory module facilitates for the features fusion module learning a set of representative examples for each class. However, we also found that AMM consumes a lot of resources (See Fig. 4b). After all, AMM with nq = 12 We decided to trade-off resources for precision with one of the reasons presented in the next part. The usage is calculated on the entire model process with batch size 16 and similar to the above hyper-parameter.

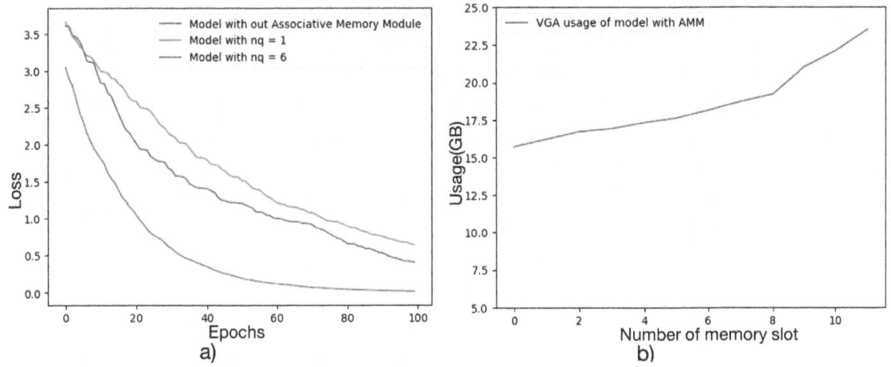

Fig. 4. GPU consumption of model on VQA-RAD [11]

4.2 The Impact of Prototype Learning

Prototype learning is a method that involves identifying a set of representative examples, or prototypes, for each class in a classification task. These prototypes encapsulate the essential features that distinguish one class from another. The Hopfield layer enhances this process by enabling hierarchical learning, allowing the model to capture both local and global semantic information from visual and textual embeddings. Table 4 shows the model accuracy for different numbers of prototypes and blocks used in prototype learning: The analysis of prototype learning configurations reveals that increasing the number of prototypes and blocks generally enhances model performance. With 500 prototypes, accuracy ranges from 79.96% to 80.47%, peaking at 80.47% with 10 blocks. For 1000

Table 4. The model accuracy (%) of each set number prototype and number of block prototype learning.

No of block	5	10	15
500	80.1	80.47	79.96
1000	80.24	80.93	80.24
1500	80.18	80.51	80.04

prototypes, the highest accuracy is 80.93% with 10 blocks, although it slightly decreases to 80.24% with 5 and 15 blocks. With 1500 prototypes, accuracy ranges from 80.04% to 80.51%, reaching its peak of 80.51% with 10 blocks. Overall, the optimal configuration is 1000 prototypes and 10 blocks, as this setup achieves the highest accuracy of 80.93%, with additional prototypes or blocks yielding only minimal improvements.

5 Conclusion

We introduced a novel architecture for medical Visual Question Answering (VQA) based on Associative Memory and Prototype Learning. Our model leverages Associative Memory to enhance visual features and Prototype Learning to represent different classes, addressing data limitations and improving model generalization. Benchmark experiments demonstrated that our architecture outperforms existing methods, excelling in visual and linguistic reasoning for medical questions. However, some limitations remain: the Associative Memory Module, while effective, consumes significant VRAM and may benefit from optimization or alternative core operators, and Prototype Learning did not perform as expected, indicating a need for improved architectural design. Future work will focus on refining these methods to further enhance model performance and contribute to advancements in VQA and multimodal systems.

References

1. Antol, S., et al.: Vqa: visual question answering. In: 2015 IEEE International Conference on Computer Vision (ICCV), pp. 2425–2433. IEEE Computer Society, Los Alamitos, CA, USA (2015)
2. Dong, N., Xing, E.: Few-shot semantic segmentation with prototype learning. arXiv preprint arXiv:1804.04754 (2018)
3. Khare, Y., Bagal, V., Mathew, M., Devi, A., Priyakumar, U.D., Jawahar, C.: Mmbert: multimodal bert pretraining for improved medical vqa. In: 2021 IEEE 18th International Symposium on Biomedical Imaging (ISBI), pp. 1033–1036 (2021). https://doi.org/10.1109/ISBI48211.2021.9434063
4. Kumar, A., et al.: Ask me anything: Dynamic memory networks for natural language processing. In: Proceedings of the International Conference on Machine Learning (2016)
5. Lau, J.J., Gayen, S., Abacha, A.B., Demner-Fushman, D.: A dataset of clinically generated visual questions and answers about radiology images. Sci. Data **5**, 1–10 (2018)
6. Le, H., Tran, T., Venkatesh, S.: Self-attentive associative memory. In: Proceedings of the International Conference on Machine Learning, pp. 5682–5691 (2020)
7. Li, P., Liu, G., He, J., Zhao, Z., Zhong, S.: Masked vision and language pretraining with unimodal and multimodal contrastive losses for medical visual question answering. In: Lecture Notes in Computer Science, pp. 374–383 (2023)
8. Lin, Z., et al.: Medical visual question answering: a survey. arXiv preprint arXiv:2111.10056 (2022)

9. Liu, B., Zhan, L.M., Xu, L., Ma, L., Yang, Y., Wu, X.M.: Slake: a semantically-labeled knowledge-enhanced dataset for medical visual question answering. In: 2021 IEEE 18th International Symposium on Biomedical Imaging (ISBI), pp. 1650–1654. IEEE (2021)
10. Liu, Y., et al.: Roberta: a robustly optimized BERT pretraining approach. arXiv preprint arXiv:1907.11692 (2019)
11. Pellegrini, C., Keicher, M., Özsoy, E., Navab, N.: Radrestruct: A novel vqa benchmark and method for structured radiology reporting. In: International Conference on Medical Image Computing and Computer-Assisted Intervention, pp. 409–419. Springer Nature Switzerland (October 2023)
12. Ramsauer, H., et al.: Hopfield networks is all you need. arXiv preprint arXiv:2008.02217 (2020)
13. Sato, A., Yamada, K.: Generalized learning vector quantization. In: Advances in Neural Information Processing Systems, vol. 8 (NeurIPS), pp. 423–429 (1996)
14. Tan, M., Le, Q.: Efficientnet: rethinking model scaling for convolutional neural networks. In: International Conference on Machine Learning, pp. 6105–6114. PMLR (2019)
15. Tschandl, P., et al.: Human-computer collaboration for skin cancer recognition. Nat. Med. **26**, 1229–1234 (2020)
16. Weston, J., Chopra, S., Bordes, A.: Memory networks. arXiv preprint arXiv:1410.3916 (2014)
17. Xu, K., et al.: Show, attend and tell: Neural image caption generation with visual attention. In: Proceedings of the International Conference on Machine Learning (2015)
18. Yan, A., et al.: Radbert: Adapting transformer-based language models to radiology. Radiology: Artif. Intell. **4**(4) (2022https://doi.org/10.1148/ryai.210258
19. Yu, Z., Yu, J., Xiang, C., Fan, J., Tao, D.: Beyond bilinear: generalized multimodal factorized high-order pooling for visual question answering. IEEE Trans. Neural Netw. Learn. Syst. **29**, 5947–5959 (2018). https://doi.org/10.1109/TNNLS.2018.2817340
20. Zhang, X., et al.: Pmc-vqa: Visual instruction tuning for medical visual question answering. arXiv preprint arXiv:2305.10415 (2023)
21. Zhang, Z., et al.: Challenges and solutions for out-of-distribution generalization in medical visual question answering. arXiv preprint (arXiv:2203.07564) (2022). https://arxiv.org/abs/2203.07564

Graph-Based Approaches for Image Space Exploration and Representative Set Selection

Alexander Veremyev[1], Alexander Semenov[2], Eduardo L. Pasiliao[3], and Vladimir Boginski[1](✉)

[1] University of Central Florida, Orlando, FL, USA
vladimir.boginski@ucf.edu
[2] University of Florida, Gainesville, FL, USA
[3] Air Force Research Laboratory, Eglin AFB, FL, USA

Abstract. We propose a new graph-based method for exploration and representative set selection in vector spaces for classification tasks, and demonstrate the results on a well-known MNIST dataset. Our method reveals significant variations in the similarity structure among vectors corresponding to different label classes. To better capture these differences, we construct similarity-based graphs (networks) with a balanced number of edges within each label class, rather than using a single similarity cutoff across all classes. This tailored approach provides deeper insights into class-specific similarities. We further analyze the resulting graphs by computing various global and local structural properties. Additionally, we introduce a representative set selection model based on independent and dominating sets. We validate the effectiveness of our approach by training a Convolutional Neural Network (CNN) on these representative sets and comparing performance against randomly selected sets of images of the same size.

Keywords: Image Classification · Graphs · Networks · Communities · Similarity Metrics · Representative Sets

1 Introduction

Understanding the data is one of the most important part in the machine learning process. It is necessary to explore and investigate what is going on in the dataset and how it relates to the considered problem (e.g., classification task) before applying the proper model. In machine learning models, vectors are used to represent the input (features) and the output data (labels). One of the most important aspect of data exploration and analysis is *similarity*, it is usually more revealing to look at relations among vectors in terms of similarity with each other rather than inspecting individual vector components (values at each dimension).

Graph/network-based representations provide intuitive and useful ways to uncover the complex structures of vector spaces based on their similarity with each other. Specifically, each vector (data point) in a dataset corresponds to a

J. Kertesz et al. (Eds.): CSoNet 2024, LNCS 15417, pp. 212–223, 2025.
https://doi.org/10.1007/978-981-96-6389-7_18

network node (vertex) and two nodes are connected by an edge if two corresponding vectors have high level of similarity (according to some similarity measure). Such representations of data are known as similarity-based networks [14]. They have been used to reveal specific patterns and organizing principles of vectors, representing data in various domains, e.g., semantic space [12], materials space [11], etc.

In this paper we explore the structure of image vector space using network analysis tools and concepts of a well-known MNIST dataset of 70K handwritten digits, which is considered to be the "Hello World" of machine learning, and one of the most studied dataset in Deep Learning. The training set of 60K images contains 10 approximately equal classes (digits) of images. We convert images into scaled vectors and use the cosine of an angle between vectors as a measure of their similarity.

The similarity-based network is constructed as follows, for a given cutoff level, there is an edge between two vectors if the similarity score (cosine) is higher than the given cutoff. Our first observation is that if we apply one similarity threshold to construct a similarity-based network, then the network will be highly imbalanced - the majority of edges (approx. 98%) will be between images of "1" whereas only about 2% of edges will be between images of other digits.

Since our goal is to analyze and compare structures of vector spaces of images in all label classes with each other, our first goal is to construct more balanced similarity-based networks in each class, e.g., the number of edges among images of the same class (digit) should be relatively similar in all classes. In order to achieve this, we computed and applied different similarity thresholds for each label class so that the network of images in each class has the same number of edges divided by its size, or, what is the same, same average degree. We constructed several such networks with various average degrees and investigate the most common structural properties. For example, we illustrate that the most *central* images in these networks usually represent the basic ways of how digits are written.

The constructed similarity-based networks of images can be viewed as the *backbones* of respective vector spaces, which incorporate the information about the corresponding classes of images. Based on this intuition, we demonstrate that network analysis provides an elegant and intuitive way for finding the representative set of data, i.e., the subset of data that captures the most information about the dataset. Specifically, we argue that the *maximum independent* and *minimum dominating* sets in the respective image networks are naturally the proper candidates for the representative sets. The maximum independent set in the similarity-based network of MNIST images in each class represents a subset of images such that no pair of images in it is similar to each other and any other image has at least one similar in this set. The minimum dominating set contains the minimum set of images such that any other image has at least one similar in this set.

Selecting a *representative set* of data [4,9] is an important problem in classification tasks, which is also known as instance or prototype selection problems [2,5]. To the best of our knowledge, there are no studies that propose representative set selection using maximum independent and minimum dominating sets in graph/network representations of the training dataset. To demonstrate the effectiveness of our representative set selection we use a Convolutional Neural Network (CNN) architecture, which shows very good performance on a MNIST dataset [1]. We compare the performance of CNN trained on the representative sets against the same CNN architecture trained on a randomly selected set of images from the training dataset of the same size. Our findings indicate that the identified representative sets achieve higher accuracy on the test set and contain more information about the dataset than random samples. Moreover, the performance of CNN trained on relatively large representative sets (about half of a training set) is usually even better than the one trained on all training set of data, which suggests that the identified representative sets do not have redundant samples (ensured by definition) that may negatively impact the training process.

The paper proceeds as follows. In Sect. 2 we provide more details on the MNIST dataset, analyze the similarity distributions among image vectors and discuss how to construct proper similarity-based networks. Section 3 investigates the basic structural characteristics of the constructed networks and provides intuitive interpretations of various interesting observations. Then, in Sect. 4 we discuss the basic requirements that a representative set of data should have and introduce the graph-theoretic concepts which naturally satisfy these requirements. Finally, Sect. 5 introduces the CNN architecture that we use, presents the results on performance of CNN trained on representative sets and randomly sampled data of the same size and discusses several insightful observations. Section 6 concludes the discussion.

2 MNIST Description and Similarity Network Construction

The MNIST database (Modified National Institute of Standards and Technology database) is a large database of handwritten digits that is commonly used for training various image processing systems. The MNIST database contains 60,000 training images and 10,000 testing images. Each MNIST data point is a gray scale image that is represented by 28×28 matrix with integer values from 0 to 255 (color intensity) accompanied by the corresponding label.

For the similarity network construction and analysis, we consider only training set of 60K images. We first convert matrices to 784 dimensional vectors (all matrix rows are consecutively stacked together) and then scaled all vectors to be between 0 and 1. To do that for each vector we first subtract the smallest value from all vector components and then divide all values by the highest value.

We compute cosine similarity between all pairs of vectors of 60K MNIST images in the training set. Figure 1 illustrates the histogram of the obtained similarity scores with 100 bins from 0 to 1. For example, the number of pairs of vectors with cosine similarity value in the interval (0.30, 0.31) is approximately 95M. Note that the total number of pairs of images is approximately 3.6B (60000×59999). We also plot similarity score histograms for the number of pairs belonging to the same classes (plot *in*) and the number of pairs of vectors from different classes (plot *out*). Since the area of our interest is high similarity score values, we also plot the right tails of histograms with similarity score greater than 0.7 to show more details (y axis is logarithmicaly scaled). Observe that even for high similarity scores, there are still pairs of images from different classes (representing different digits), but with high similarity scores.

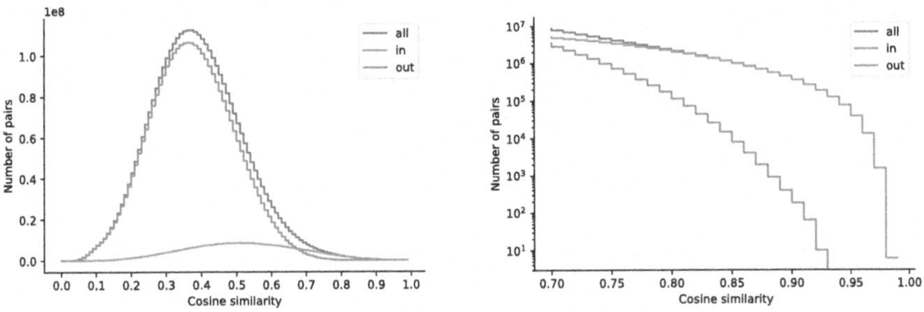

(a) (b)

Fig. 1. Cosine similarity score histogram of 60K images in the MNIST training set with 100 bins.

2.1 Selecting a Proper Similarity Score

To construct a threshold-based network in which there is an edge between two nodes if the cosine similarity between the corresponding vectors is above a certain threshold, we first need to find a reasonable similarity score cutoff. Since our goal is to try keep classes of vectors separate from each other and analyze network structure inside each class, we first find the highest similarity score between vectors in different classes.

The highest similarity score for pairs of vectors in different classes (digits) is 0.94 (Fig. 1b). Figure 2 shows 4 pairs of images with different digits with such similarity score. Hence, we first construct a network where there is an edge between two vectors if cosine similarity score between two vectors is greater than 0.94. In this network only edges between images in the same classes exist. Figure 3 depicts one of the connected component in the resulting network. Each node is drawn as the corresponding MNIST image.

(a) $cos(5,6) = 0.94$ (b) $cos(8,1) = 0.94$ (c) $cos(1,7) = 0.94$ (d) $cos(9,7) = 0.94$

Fig. 2. Pairs of images in different classes with highest cosine similarity.

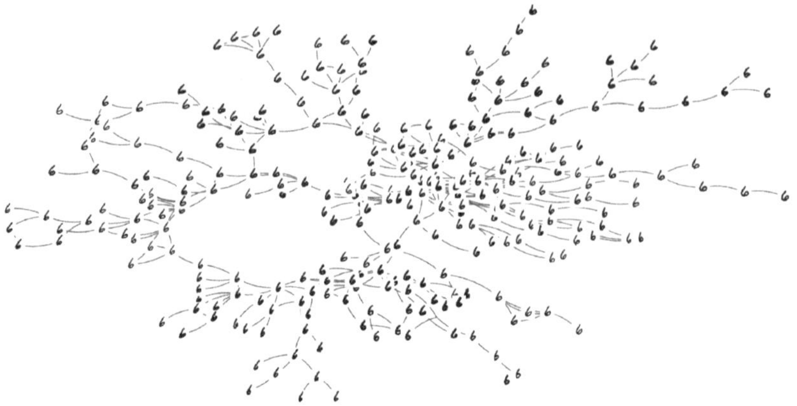

Fig. 3. One of the connected component of similarity-based network of MNIST images with 0.94 threshold with 280 nodes and 385 edges. All images are in the image class 6.

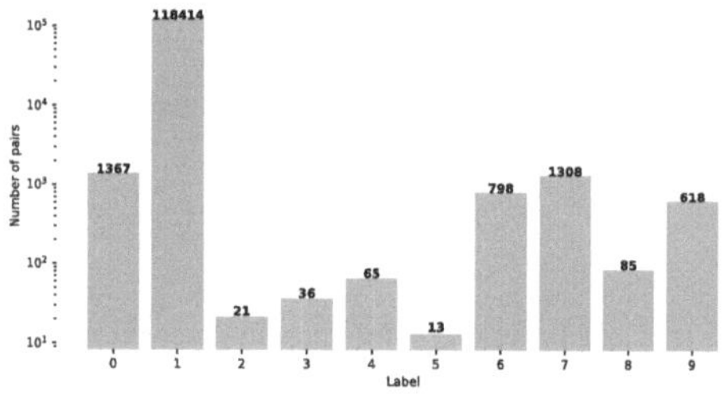

Fig. 4. Number of pairs of images with similarity score greater than 0.94 in each label class. Note that the vertical axis is scaled logarithmicaly. The number of edges in each class is highly imbalanced.

Figure 4 shows the number of edges inside each image class. We first note that the number of edges in the class of images of "1" is approximately 118K whereas only 13 edges are in the class of images of "5" (similarity score of the corresponding pairs is >0.94). Overall, we observe very high imbalances in the number edges inside each label class. Moreover, this pattern persists for other threshold levels as well.

Therefore, if one wants to construct a similarity-based network representing a backbone structure for each label class so that the resulting networks are somewhat balanced (have similar number of edge densities), and, at the same time, not too dense and not too sparse, then different similarity thresholds need to be used for different label classes.

Figure 5 plots the similarity cutoffs that should be used in order to have the similarity-based network in each label class to have certain (balanced) number of edges. We consider several possible cases: the number of edges equal to the number of images in each class (size), 3 times the size of the image class, 5, 10, 30 and 50 times the size of the image class. It is equivalent to require networks in

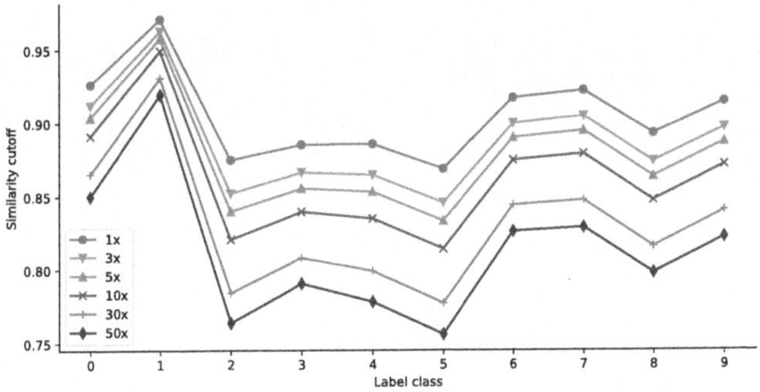

Fig. 5. Similarity cutoffs for each label class that should be used to make the similarity-based network to have the number of edges equal to the size (3x, 5x, 10x, 30x and 50x) of the image class (number of images)

each label class to have the same average node degree. The plot clearly illustrates the aforementioned observation about very high class structural imbalances, i.e., high difference in similarity score distributions among images in each label class. Overall, we can conclude that the images of "2" and "5" are most dissimilar to each other according to the cosine similarity score.

3 Basic Properties of MNIST Networks

In this section we illustrate the basic network properties when we construct MNIST networks for each label class with balanced number of edges, i.e., the number of edges divided by the number of images in a class (half of average node degree) is the same for all label classes.

Figure 6 shows the number of nodes in the largest connected components, the number of isolated nodes and other nodes in a couple of such networks. The main observation is that all networks are primarily composed by the set of isolated nodes and a connected component which spans almost all the remaining nodes. Moreover, the sizes of largest connected components are relatively similar across all label classes.

Figure 7 shows the distributions of degrees in the largest connected components of the same networks. For better visualization, we provide degree versus rank plots instead of commonly used degree versus frequency plots. We first sort all node degrees in non-increasing order, and then plot the node degree on the "y" axis versus its index on the "x" axis in this sequence. Observe that the degree sequences are very similar for networks in all label classes, despite the observed imbalances in similarity score distributions.

Our next goal is to use three popular network centrality metrics, *degree*, *betweenness* and *closeness* [3] to identify the most central images in each label class. The degree centrality counts the number of neighbors of each node, the betweenness centrality of a node considers how many shortest paths between

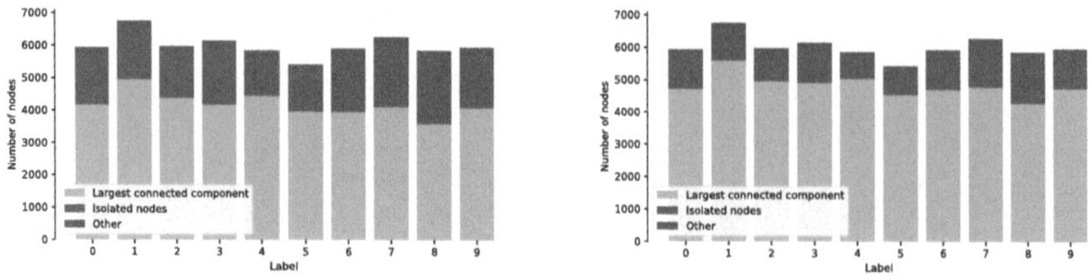

(a) 5x (b) 10x

Fig. 6. Largest connected components sizes and number of isolated nodes in MNIST networks for each label class with different number of edges: (a) 5 $\times$ size of the label class and (b) 10 $\times$ size of the label class

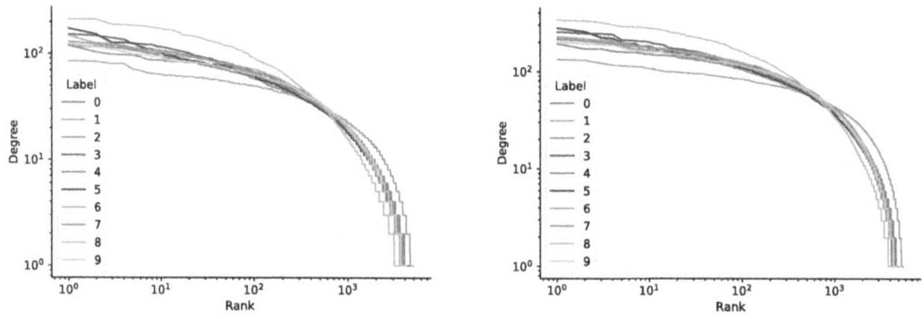

(a) 5x (b) 10x

Fig. 7. Distribution of degrees (degree of nodes plotted in the decreasing order) in largest connected components in MNIST networks for each label class with different number of edges: (a) 5 $\times$ size of the label class and (b) 10 $\times$ size of the label class

other network nodes traverse this node, and closeness centrality of a node considers the average distance from this node to other network nodes. All degree, betweenness and closeness centralities capture complementary aspects of node positions (locations) within a network [7]. Figure 8 shows 10 nodes (images) with highest degree, betweenness and closeness centralities in each label class. These images can be viewed as *the most central* in the corresponding image vector spaces, hence they capture the "basis" of handwritten digits, other variants are just deviations from this basis.

We have computed other characteristics of these networks to better understand their structural properties. Table 1 reports these characteristics of 2 MNIST networks constructed for "5x" and "10x" (the number of edges in each class is 5 or 10 times the label class size, respectively). The results are for the largest connected components (Largest CC) in these networks, which usually contain the majority of images (Fig. 6).

We observe that the maximum closeness centrality of a node (reported as the average distance from this node to other nodes) is substantially smaller than

(a) Degree (b) Betweenness (c) Closeness

Fig. 8. MNIST images with highest (a) degree, (a) betweenness and (b) closeness centralities in each label class in networks with "10x" number of edges, i.e., average node degree in each class is 20.

Table 1. Basic characteristics of MNIST networks for each label class. Two instances are considered: the number of edges is equal to 5 times the label class size and 10 times the label class size.

Label Class	0	1	2	3	4	5	6	7	8	9
Label Class size	5923	6742	5958	6131	5842	5421	5918	6265	5851	5949
Number of edges = 5 times the label class size										
Similarity Cutoff	0.903	0.958	0.840	0.855	0.853	0.833	0.890	0.894	0.864	0.887
Largest CC	4170	4948	4374	4169	4458	3974	3964	4110	3589	4090
Average Degree	14.2	13.6	13.6	14.6	13.1	13.6	14.9	15.2	16.3	14.5
Max Degree	119	85	118	151	119	172	147	129	210	123
Max Betweenness (%)	3.96	10.02	5.47	4.41	3.90	5.48	3.88	2.52	5.19	4.39
Max Closeness	3.56	6.40	3.35	3.18	3.70	3.47	3.51	3.71	3.01	3.63
Diameter	18	32	16	15	21	19	20	20	16	19
Average distance	5.45	9.11	5.06	4.78	5.68	5.36	5.39	5.71	4.69	5.51
Global Clustering	0.29	0.40	0.27	0.26	0.27	0.26	0.29	0.31	0.29	0.28
Average Local Clustering	0.33	0.42	0.30	0.30	0.31	0.31	0.32	0.33	0.31	0.32
Number of edges = 10 times the label class size										
Similarity Cutoff	0.891	0.949	0.821	0.840	0.835	0.814	0.875	0.879	0.847	0.871
Largest CC	4720	5588	4950	4895	5029	4524	4672	4753	4264	4711
Average Degree	25.1	24.1	24.0	25.0	23.2	23.9	25.3	26.3	27.4	25.2
Max Degree	214	133	218	255	192	279	228	218	337	201
Max Betweenness (%)	2.54	5.34	2.49	2.73	2.80	3.75	2.70	3.73	3.57	3.61
Max Closeness	3.08	5.35	2.91	2.84	3.28	3.03	3.17	3.32	2.67	3.25
Diameter	14	31	14	13	16	15	20	20	14	16
Average distance	4.68	7.53	4.34	4.26	4.86	4.62	4.82	5.04	4.15	4.80
Global Clustering	0.31	0.41	0.29	0.28	0.30	0.29	0.31	0.33	0.31	0.30
Average Local Clustering	0.38	0.45	0.35	0.34	0.35	0.35	0.35	0.36	0.35	0.37

the average distance within the corresponding connected component. It supports our idea that most images of the same digit have some short deviations from the "basis"

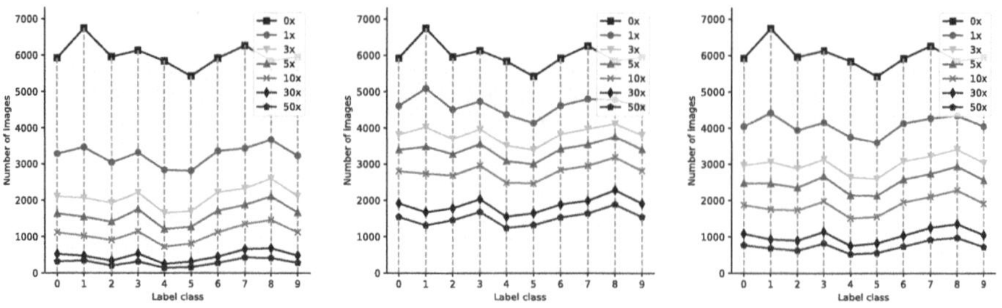

(a) Isolated nodes (b) Independent sets (c) Dominating sets

Fig. 9. Number of (a) isolated nodes, sizes of (b) maximum independent sets and (c) minimum dominating sets in similarity-based networks for each label class with 1x, 3x, 5x, 10x, 30x and 50x number of edges. The plot "0x" shows the total number of images in each label class.

Overall, we can conclude that the global network characteristics are somewhat similar to the ones calculated for other real-life networks [8] and indicate that these networks are also small-worlds [13] (that is, have high clustering coefficients, small diameters, and small average distances).

4 Selecting Representative Set of Images

In this section we consider some network concepts which might be appropriate for finding representative sets of data, based on the constructed similarity-based networks. A good representative set of images should capture the most information from the original dataset compared to other subsets of the same size. In a vector space terminology, it should be maximally diverse and have minimum redundant (very similar) vectors.

In the constructed similarity-based networks, the first sets of nodes, which, obviously, should be included in the representative sets are the *isolated* nodes, as the corresponding images have no other similar images in the same class according to the considered similarity threshold.

In addition, for any pair of similar images (connected by an edge) it would be reasonable to include only one of them into the representative set to avoid redundant information. Hence, to ensure that the elements of such a set are distributed across entire network, one may need to find the largest set with this property. In the context of graph theory and network analysis, this set is known to be the *maximum independent set*, i.e., the maximum set of nodes, such that no two nodes have an edge between them. The independent set is known to be *maximal* if it is not a subset of any other independent set. From the representative set perspective, maximal independent sets (of corresponding vectors) not only have minimum redundancy (there is no pair of similar vectors in this set), but also are guaranteed to span all possible area of the considered vector space, i.e., any other vector have at least one similar vector in this set (according to a desired similarity threshold). This can be easily showed by contradiction.

Another related concept arises from the following intuition: if a representative set captures the most information about the dataset, then any point in the dataset either belongs to the representative set or have at least one similar point in the representative set. In network analysis when edges represent similar objects this set is known as *dominating set*, i.e., a set of nodes, such that each node is either in this set, or has a neighbor belonging to this set. Since we are interested in finding as small representative set as possible with this property, then we need to find the minimum dominating set in the corresponding similarity-based networks.

Similarly to independent sets, a dominating set is known to be *minimal*, if any of its subset is not a dominating set. Simply speaking, removing any node from a dominating set will make it not dominating anymore. Hence, this set ensures that the corresponding representative set of vectors is not redundant.

Figure 9 plots the number of isolated nodes, maximum independent and minimum dominating sets identified in various MNIST networks. We observe that the number of nodes in independent and dominating sets are relatively similar for networks on all label classes with the same number of edges, which means that the corresponding representative sets are going to be balanced.

To find the maximum independent and minimum dominating sets we use their linear Integer Programming (IP) formulations (mathematical formulations omitted here due to space considerations) and Gurobi [6] solver to find solutions to these formulations.

5 CNN Performance Trained on Representative Sets

In this section, we illustrate the performance of a CNN trained on the considered representative sets (independent or dominating sets in MNIST networks obtained using models from the previous section) versus the one trained on the random sample of images of the same sizes. We use CNN since they are particularly useful for finding patterns in images to recognize objects.

Since there are many choices of CNN architectures, we tried to select the one that is quite simple and produce very high accuracy on a MNIST dataset. Ref. [1] provides a thorough analysis and discussion of such CNN architectures. Specifically, we use a CNN with two convolutional layers followed by fully connected layers. The first convolutional layer has 32 filters of size 3×3, and the second has 64 filters. Each convolution is followed by ReLU activation and 2×2 max pooling. The output is then passed through a fully connected layer of 128 units and an output layer with 10 units. The network achieves approximately 99% test accuracy after training.

The training process tries to find the weights of the connections in the CNN architecture in order to maximize the accuracy of the predictions on a training sample of images. Since the problem of finding a global maximum (highest possible accuracy score) is computationally challenging, the actual training process is stochastic and usually ends up finding a local maximum. Therefore, we perform 10 independent trainings for each case and report the average results

Table 2. CNN performance trained on representative sets (maximum independent and minimum dominating sets in a training set MNIST images) versus performance when trained on a random sample of images of the same size in each label class. Accuracy scores are given for test set (Test), all training set with 60K images (TrAll), and a subset of training images (TrSub) on which the CNN has been trained. Representative sets are obtained from networks constructed with various number of edges (1x, 3x, 5x, 10x, 30x and 50x) in each label class. The average values over 10 runs are reported in Accuracy and Time columns.

	Representative set						Random set			
			Accuracy				Accuracy			
Network	Size	Isol	Test	TrAll	TrSub	Time	Test	TrAll	TrSub	Time
	60000		0.9895	0.9958						
Independent set										
1x	46205	32372	0.9895	0.9952	0.9942	49.1	0.9887	0.9938	0.9955	48.9
3x	38100	20884	0.9907	0.9955	0.9940	40.1	0.9877	0.9919	0.9949	40.4
5x	33853	16128	0.9909	0.9955	0.9934	35.4	0.9887	0.9924	0.9959	35.6
10x	27886	10706	0.9898	0.9948	0.9921	29.2	0.9856	0.9895	0.9944	29.2
30x	18680	4664	0.9880	0.9923	0.9856	19.7	0.9845	0.9862	0.9940	19.9
50x	15155	2844	0.9890	0.9927	0.9863	15.9	0.9828	0.9842	0.9936	16.1
Dominating set										
1x	40689	32372	0.9900	0.9957	0.9948	42.7	0.9891	0.9934	0.9960	43.3
3x	29996	20884	0.9900	0.9945	0.9924	32.3	0.9875	0.9908	0.9954	31.7
5x	25027	16128	0.9882	0.9934	0.9911	26.7	0.9866	0.9890	0.9948	26.5
10x	18622	10706	0.9875	0.9922	0.9887	19.5	0.9845	0.9860	0.9939	19.8
30x	10319	4664	0.9866	0.9895	0.9837	10.9	0.9797	0.9793	0.9918	11.0
50x	7327	2844	0.9815	0.9825	0.9778	7.7	0.9756	0.9748	0.9912	7.7

which should better reflect the model performance. We use PyTorch [10] library for handling MNIST data extraction and manipulation, as well as the CNN architecture construction, training and performance measurement.

Table 2 reports the results on training time and accuracies of our CNN architecture trained on various representative and random subsets of a training set. For each case, we report the accuracy score on a test set (column Test), the accuracy score on all training set of 60K images (TrAll), as well as the accuracy score on a subset of a training set on which the CNN has been trained (TrSub).

There are some key observations from the results in the table that suggest that representative sets do capture information about the training dataset better than the random sample. Moreover, they also indicate that the representative sets tend to include more important (hardest to classify) cases from the training set and discard more common easy to classify images.

6 Concluding Remarks

In this study, we have shown the benefits of exploring the structure of image vector spaces using graph/network analysis tools and concepts. For illustrative purposes, we constructed and analyzed various similarity-based network using a training set of 60K images of a well-known MNIST dataset of handwritten digits. First, we showed that the similarity distributions among vectors vary significantly across different label classes, hence different similarity cutoff levels should be used for constructing more balanced networks for different label classes. We have also demonstrated that network representations provide an intuitive and easy to implement way for the representative set selection (i.e., maximum independent and minimum dominating sets), and validate it by comparing the CNN trained on such representative sets and randomly sampled set of images.

References

1. How to choose CNN Architecture for MNIST. https://www.kaggle.com/code/cdeotte/how-to-choose-cnn-architecture-mnist. Accessed3 Sept 2024
2. Blachnik, M., Kordos, M.: Comparison of instance selection and construction methods with various classifiers. Appl. Sci. **10**(11), 3933 (2020)
3. Boldi, P., Vigna, S.: Axioms for centrality. Internet Math. **10**(3–4), 222–262 (2014)
4. Borovicka, T., Jirina, M., Jr., Kordik, P., Jirina, M.: Selecting representative data sets. Advances Data Mining Knowl. Discov. Appl. **12**, 43–70 (2012)
5. Garcia, S., Derrac, J., Cano, J., Herrera, F.: Prototype selection for nearest neighbor classification: Taxonomy and empirical study. IEEE Trans. Pattern Anal. Mach. Intell. **34**(3), 417–435 (2012)
6. Gurobi Optimization, LLC. Gurobi Optimizer Reference Manual (2024)
7. Jackson, M.O., et al.: Social and economic networks, volume 3. Princeton university press Princeton (2008)
8. Newman, M.E.: The structure and function of complex networks. SIAM Rev. **45**(2), 167–256 (2003)
9. Pan, F., Wang, W., Tung, A.K., Yang, J.: Finding representative set from massive data. In: Fifth IEEE International Conference on Data Mining (ICDM'05), p. 8 IEEE (2005)
10. Paszke, A., et al. Pytorch: an imperative style, high-performance deep learning library. In: Advances in Neural Information Processing Systems, vol. 32 (2019)
11. Veremyev, A., et al.: Networks of materials: construction and structural analysis. AIChE J. **67**(3), e17051 (2021)
12. Veremyev, A., Semenov, A., Pasiliao, E.L., Boginski, V.: Graph-based exploration and clustering analysis of semantic spaces. Appl. Netw. Sci. **4**(1), 1–26 (2019). https://doi.org/10.1007/s41109-019-0228-y
13. Watts, D.J., Strogatz, S.H.: Collective dynamics of 'small-world' networks. nature **393**(6684), 440–442 (1998)
14. Zinoviev, D.: Complex network analysis in python: recognize-construct-visualize-analyze-interpret (2018)

Alzheimer's Disease Diagnosis with Enhanced Densely Connected Convolutional Networks

Hai Thanh Nguyen[1], Huong Hoang Luong[2](✉), Le Q. Hung[2], and Nam D. L. Tran[2]

[1] Can Tho University, Can Tho, Vietnam
[2] FPT University, Can Tho, Vietnam
huonghoangluong@gmail.com

Abstract. Alzheimer's disease (AD) affects million people worldwide, marked by progressive neurodegeneration leading to cognitive decline. Early detection is critical for effective treatment and disease management, yet it remains challenging due to the intricate nature of medical imaging. This study introduces an enhanced Densely Connected Convolutional Network (DenseNet-121) to detect stages of AD. Utilizing datasets associated with AD, the model was trained over 50 epochs with a batch size of 32, achieving an accuracy of 95%. These results highlight the model's potential for clinical integration, improving early diagnostic capabilities and advancing our understanding of AD progression.

Keywords: Alzheimer's disease · Deep learning · Disease diagnosis

1 Introduction

Alzheimer's disease (AD) is a progressive neurodegenerative disorder and the primary cause of dementia, significantly impairing memory, cognition, and executive functions. Over six million individuals in the United States are affected [1], with the World Health Organization identifying AD as the seventh leading cause of mortality globally. Despite its importance, early detection poses considerable challenges, particularly in distinguishing AD from other dementia subtypes during initial stages

Recent advancements and achievements in deep learning, particularly convolutional neural networks, have shown promise in detecting AD using ADNI-1 data. More specifically, High-resolution disease mapping and 3D-CNN architectures have been implemented to analyze specific brain regions. Notably, multimodal approaches like those of Lu [2] and Gupta [3] integrated ADNI-1 features to improve classification, achieving up to 96% accuracy. Ieracitano's [4] proposed EEG-based approach (89.8% accuracy) and Liu's [5] fine-tuned VGG-16 model (99.68%) for early-stage AD detection, underscoring the utility of CNNs in capturing spatial-temporal dependencies in brain imaging. However, these

J. Kertesz et al. (Eds.): CSoNet 2024, LNCS 15417, pp. 224–232, 2025.
https://doi.org/10.1007/978-981-96-6389-7_19

approaches face challenges in generalizing to broader datasets and achieving consistent results across complex AD stages. Korolev [6] demonstrates that comparable performance can be achieved by bypassing feature extraction steps and utilizing residual and plain 3D convolutional neural network architectures for Alzheimer's disease classification. Suriya Murugan (2021) [7] demonstrated the power of CNNs by generating high-resolution disease probability maps using local brain structures and a multi-layer perceptron.

Building the work in [8] deployed the classification with VGG-16, which achieved 98% accuracy, this study explores DenseNet-121's potential for improved accuracy and early-stage AD detection. Our key contributions include:

- A comparative analysis of DenseNet-121 versus some architectures for AD detection, focusing on early-stage diagnosis and differentiation from other dementia types.
- Implementation of data augmentation techniques (rotation, width/height shifts, shear, zoom, and horizontal flip) to improve the model robustness.

2 Proposed Methods

2.1 Dataset Collection

To evaluate the effectiveness of the proposed approach, this study utilizes two brain dataset including Alzheimer's Disease Neuro Imaging(ADNI) and ADNI-1 image . The first, ADNI-1 Dataset[1] (5,069 images), includes three categories: Non-demented (2,560 images, early/mild cognitive impairment), Very-mild-demented (1,792 images, intermediate stage), and Mild-demented (717 images, cognitive decline). The second, ADNI Dataset[2] (18,775 images), consists of five categories: Final AD (4,336 images, confirmed Alzheimer's), Final CN (3,780 images, cognitively normal), Final MCI (922 images, mild cognitive impairment), Final EMCI (240 images, early mild cognitive impairment), and Final LMCI (72 images, late-life mild cognitive impairment).

2.2 Data Preprocessing

Data preprocessing includes essential steps such as noise reduction, outlier removal, and data standardization, ensuring compatibility with machine learning algorithms. Images were resized to 100 × 100 pixels and normalized to a range of [0, 1] by dividing pixel values by 255, which enhances pattern recognition during training. These measures are critical for improving model performance and achieving robust results. The normalization of images can be performed using Eq. 1.

$$X_{norm} = \frac{X - X_{min}}{X_{max} - X_{min}}, \tag{1}$$

[1] https://www.kaggle.com/datasets/legendahmed/alzheimermridataset
[2] https://www.kaggle.com/datasets/melondoge/alzheimer5classmerged

where X_{min}, and X_{max} are the minimum and maximum pixel values. The images after that are appended to the images list, and the labels are appended to the lists. Then, the images in the images list are stacked into a single array, and the labels in the labels list are converted into a one-hot encoding. One-hot encoding is a valuable technique for assigning categories to a unique binary vector. It allows categorical data to be represented in a way compatible with machine learning algorithms. After resizing and normalizing, the images and labels are compiled into arrays, and labels are one-hot encoded for categorical representation. The dataset is then split into training, validation, and testing sets in a 60:20:20 ratio, ensuring balanced data distribution and preventing overfitting.

2.3 Data Augmentation

Data augmentation is well-known as a technique that allows us to greatly enhance the diversity and increase the training data size in the dataset, not by collecting new data but by creating new images from the existing images. These transformations enhance the dataset's variability, mitigating overfitting and enhancing generalization capability by minimizing biases from image similarity. For this study, we implemented specific augmentation parameters: a rotation range of 20°, width, and height shifts of 0.1, a shear range of 0.2, a zoom range of 0.2, and horizontal flips, with the fill mode set to "nearest." This approach preserved semantic content while increasing the robustness of the model against overfitting. Figure 1 illustrates the augmented images, showcasing transformations such as rotation, zoom, and flips.

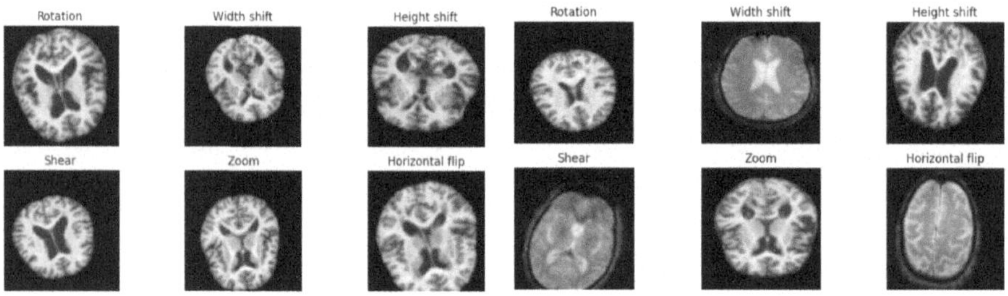

(a) ADNI-1 image dataset (b) ADNI dataset

Fig. 1. Some illustration of data augmentation

2.4 Deep Learning Architecture

This study leverages Dense Convolutional Network 121, namely DenseNet-121. It is a type of CNN model created by Gao Huang et al. in [9] in 2017. As in Fig. 2, we can see this model works by using all of the outputs from the L_1 layer to the ${L_{k-1}}^{th}$ layer as the input for the ${L_k}^{th}$ layer during the training process. Layers are connected directly with every other layer in the model. For the 'L' layers in the model, there are $L(L+1)/2$ connections. The feature maps of each layer of every previous layer are joined together and used as input data. So we can assume that at the model's L^{th} layer. Hyperparameters are critical to a model's training process, influencing how the model learns. In this study, we chose to train the model for 50 epochs with a batch size of 32 as optimal for our model. The learning rate, set to 0.0001, controls the magnitude of weight updates during training - a lower learning rate results in slower updates, promoting stability in the learning process. We conducted an exhaustive performance comparison between our proposed model and four other established architectures: DenseNet-121, VGG16, MobileNet, and ResNet50. We add two additional dense layers that come after the CNN layers but before the classification layer.

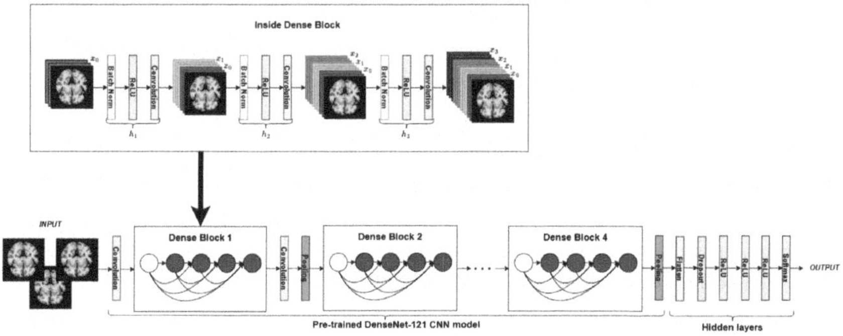

Fig. 2. The proposed architecture for Alzhimer's disease

3 Experimental Results

The performance of DenseNet-121 was evaluated through four primary classification scenarios:

- **Experiment 1: Classifying Non-demented and Mild-Demented**: The model demonstrated progressive accuracy improvements, achieving precise differentiation with added layers.

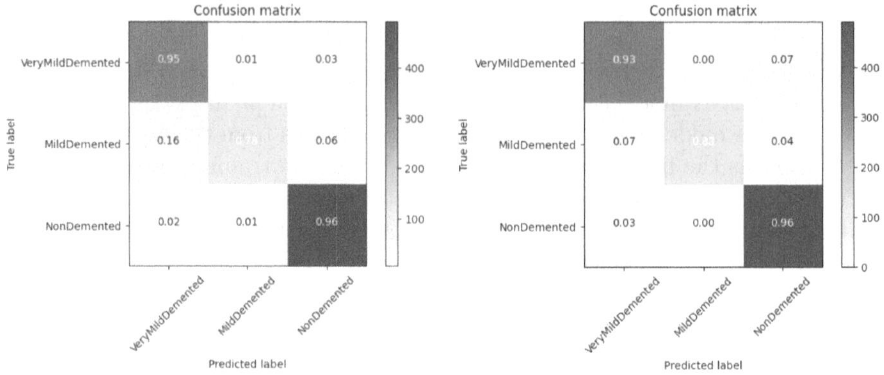

(a) Before data augmentation. (b) After data augmentation.

Fig. 3. The confusion matrices of Experiment 4: before and after adding three dense layers.

Table 1. The performance comparison of scenarios.

Scenario	train_acc	test_acc
Non-demented vs. Mild-demented	0.98	0.93
Non-demented vs. Mild-demented*	0.97	0.97
Non-demented vs. Very Mild-demented	0.93	0.88
Non-demented vs. Very Mild-demented*	0.98	0.94
Very Mild-demented vs. Mild-demented	0.97	0.89
Very Mild-demented vs. Mild-demented*	0.97	0.94
Non-demented, Very Mild-demented, and Mild-demented	0.99	0.91
Non-demented, Very Mild-demented, and Mild-demented*	0.99	0.95

(*The scenarios with three dense layers added.)

- **Experiment 2: Classifying Non-demented and Very Mild-Demented**: Accuracy increased significantly after architectural enhancements, with reduced misclassification rates.
- **Experiment 3: Classifying Very Mild-Demented and Mild-Demented**: Subtle distinctions between these stages were effectively captured, underscoring the model's sensitivity.
- **Experiment 4: Classifying Non-demented and Very Mild-Demented and Mild-Demented**: DenseNet-121 achieved 95% accuracy, outperforming other architectures such as VGG-16 (70%). This reinforces DenseNet-121 capability for handling more complex classification tasks in neurodegenerative

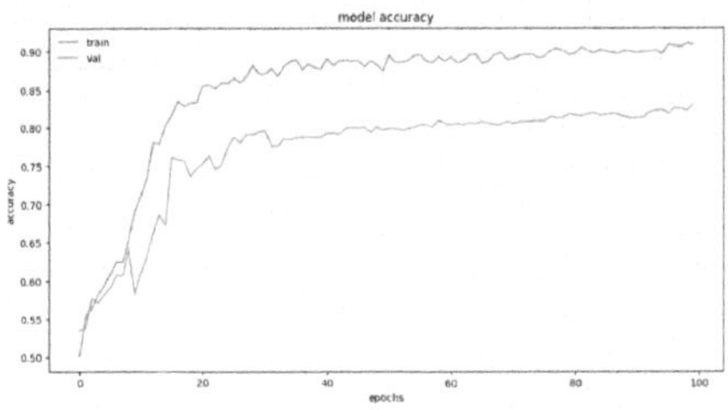

(a) The accuracy during the learning.

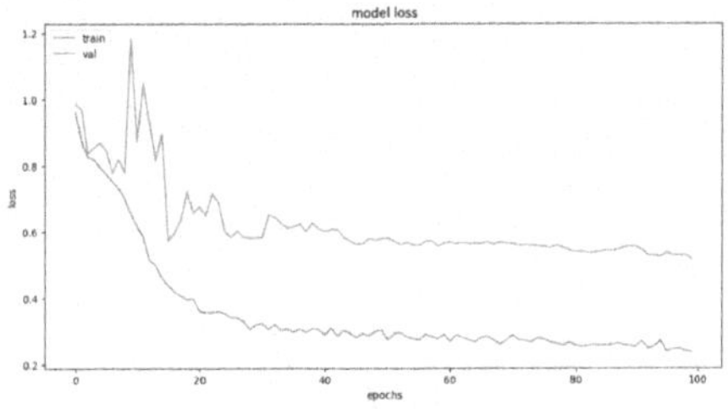

(b) The loss during the learning.

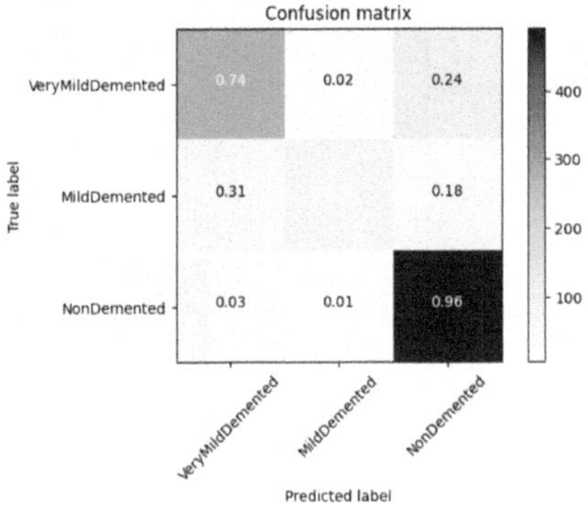

(c) The confusion matrix of the test set.

Fig. 4. The results of Experiment 4 with one dense layer added and without data augmentation.

diagnosis. The results of this scenario are visually represented in Fig. 3 displaying the confusion matrix. This matrix illustrates the model's classification performance, with diagonal elements showing correct classifications and off-diagonal elements indicating occasional misclassifications. All scenarios are shown in the Table 1.

We evaluated the architecture added more additional dense layers to optimize accuracy and complexity. Adding one dense layer improved accuracy from 80% to 85%, and three layers raised it to 95% (Fig. 4 and Fig. 5)) though some overfitting was observed. On the ADNI images dataset [15], DenseNet-121 outperformed VGG16, MobileNetV2, and ResNet50, achieving the highest accuracy (91%) and F1-score (0.91), highlighting its effectiveness in handling AD progression data in Table 2 and Table 3.

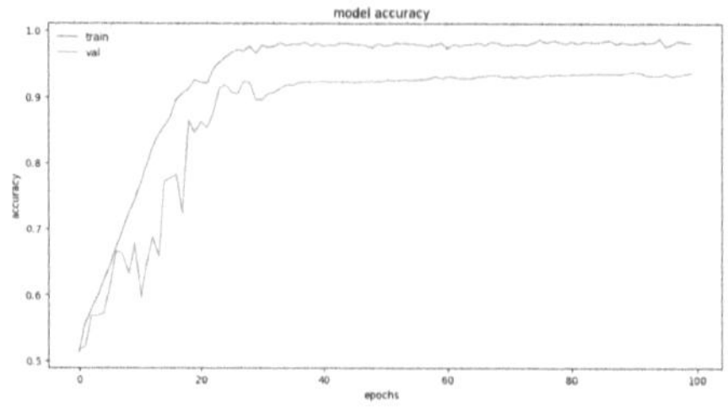

(a) The accuracy during the learning.

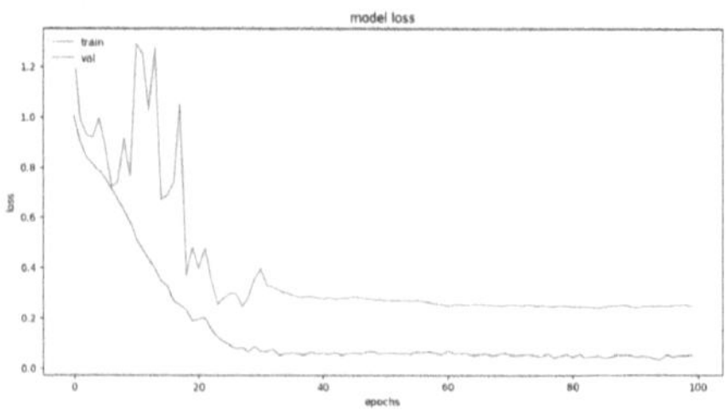

(b) The loss during the learning.

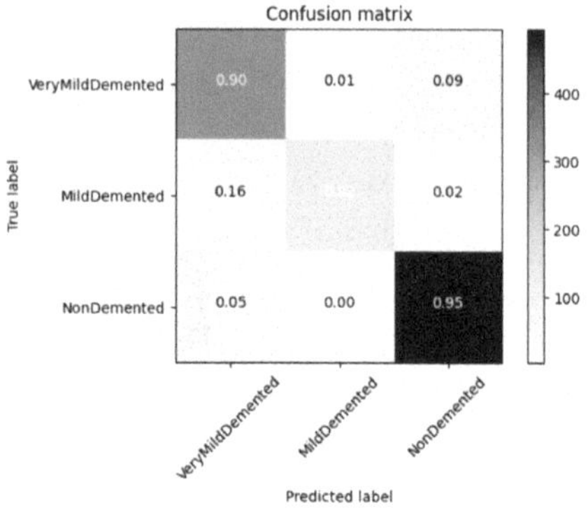

(c) The confusion matrix of the test set.

Fig. 5. The results of Experiment 4 with three dense layers added and with data augmentation

Table 2. The results on ADNI-1 and ADNI Datasets

Dataset	Architecture	train_acc	val_acc	train_loss	val_loss	test_acc	test_f1
ADNI-1	DenseNet-121	0.85	0.86	0.30	0.38	0.91	0.95
ADNI-1	MobileNetV2	0.64	0.56	0.73	1.00	0.61	0.57
ADNI-1	VGG 16	0.60	0.58	0.79	0.79	0.59	0.58
ADNI-1	Resnet50	0.70	0.73	0.67	0.63	0.68	0.68
ADNI	**DenseNet-121**	**0.91**	**0.86**	**0.24**	**0.48**	**0.91**	**0.91**
ADNI	VGG 16	0.90	0.85	0.25	0.49	0.90	0.90
ADNI	MobileNetV2	0.85	0.78	0.31	0.56	0.84	0.82
ADNI	Resnet50	0.92	0.86	0.23	0.34	0.88	0.88

Table 3. Performance comparison with previous studies.

References	DataSet	Architecture	Accuracy
Ref. [10]	ADNI-1	3D CNN	77% - 83%
Ref. [11]	Train: ADNI and Test: NRCD	CNNs	90%
Ref. [12]	ADNI	Multimodal stacked DPN	55%
Ref. [13]	ADNI	Multimodal structural	89%
Ref. [14]	ADNI	CNN	91%
Ref. [8]	Custom Dataset	Multimodal input	98%
Ours	**ADNI-1 and ADNI**	**Multimodal input**	**95% and 85%**

4 Conclusion

The DenseNet-121 architecture exhibited strong potential in detecting and classifying AD stages, with high accuracy across multiple cognitive impairment levels. This highlights its viability for integration into clinical workflows to enhance early diagnosis and disease management. Future research should prioritize extending the model to larger, more diverse datasets and exploring real-time implementation to improve accessibility and facilitate timely medical interventions.

References

1. Association, A.: Alzheimer's Dementia **19**(4), 1598–1695 (2023). DOI: https://doi.org/10.1002/alz.13016
2. Lu, D., Initiative, A., Popuri, K., Ding, G.W., Balachandar, R., Beg, M.F.: Multimodal and multiscale deep neural networks for the early diagnosis of alzheimer's disease using structural mr and fdg-pet images. Sci. Rep. **8**, 1–13 (2018)
3. Gupta, Y., Lee, K.H., Choi, K.Y., Lee, J.J., Kim, B.C., Kwon, G.R.: Early diagnosis of alzheimer's disease using combined features from voxel-based morphometry and cortical, subcortical, and hippocampus regions of mri t1 brain images. PLoS ONE **14**, e0222446 (2019)
4. Ieracitano, C., Mammone, N., Bramanti, A., Hussain, A., Morabito, F.C.: A convolutional neural network approach for classification of dementia stages based on 2d-spectral representation of eeg recordings. Neurocomputing **323**, 96–107 (2019)
5. Liu, M., Shalaginov, M.Y., Liao, R., Zeng, T.H.: A deep convolutional neural network for early diagnosis of alzheimer's disease. In: 2022 IEEE-EMBS Conference on Biomedical Engineering and Sciences (IECBES), pp. 58–61 (2022)
6. Korolev, S., Safiullin, A., Belyaev, M., Dodonova, Y.: Residual and plain convolutional neural networks for 3d brain mri classification. In: 2017 IEEE 14th International Symposium on Biomedical Imaging (ISBI 2017), pp. 835–838 (2017)
7. Murugan, S., et al.: Demnet: a deep learning model for early diagnosis of alzheimer diseases and dementia from mr images. IEEE Access. **9**, 90319–90329 (2021)

8. Luong, H.H., Vo, P.T., Phan, H.C., Tran, N.L.D., Le, H.Q., Nguyen, H.T.: Fine-tuning vgg16 for alzheimer's disease diagnosis. In: Conference on Complex, Intelligent, and Software Intensive Systems, pp. 68–79. Springer, Heidelberg (2023). https://doi.org/10.1007/978-3-031-35734-3_8
9. Huang, G., Liu, Z., Van Der Maaten, L., Weinberger, K.Q.: Densely connected convolutional networks. In: Proceedings of the IEEE Conference on Computer Vision and Pattern Recognition, pp. 4700–4708 (2017)
10. Rieke, J., Eitel, F., Weygandt, M., Haynes, J.-D., Ritter, K.: Visualizing convolutional networks for MRI-based diagnosis of alzheimer's disease. In: Stoyanov, D., et al. (eds.) MLCN/DLF/IMIMIC -2018. LNCS, vol. 11038, pp. 24–31. Springer, Cham (2018). https://doi.org/10.1007/978-3-030-02628-8_3
11. Ahmed, S., et al.: Ensembles of patch-based classifiers for diagnosis of alzheimer diseases. IEEE Access **7**, 73373–73383 (2019)
12. Shi, J.X., Zheng, Y.L., Zhang, Q., Ying, S.: Multimodal neuroimaging feature learning with multimodal stacked deep polynomial networks for diagnosis of alzheimer's disease. IEEE J. Biomed. Health Inf. **22**, 173–183 (2018)
13. Cui, R., Liu, M., Li, G.: Longitudinal analysis for alzheimer's disease diagnosis using rnn. In: 2018 IEEE 15th International Symposium on Biomedical Imaging (ISBI 2018), pp. 1398–1401 (2018)
14. Ullanat, V., Balamurali, V., Rao, A.: A novel residual 3-d convolutional network for alzheimer's disease diagnosis based on raw mri scans. In: 2020 IEEE-EMBS Conference on Biomedical Engineering and Sciences (IECBES), pp. 82–87 (2021)
15. Petersen, R.C., et al.: Alzheimer's disease neuroimaging initiative (adni): clinical characterization. Neurology **74**(3), 201–209 (2010). https://doi.org/10.1212/WNL.0b013e3181cb3e25

Energy-Based Learning for Robust Fake News Detection: A Graph Neural Network Approach with Trainable Cost Function

Mao Nguyen[1,2], Dang Le[1,2], Tan Huynh[1,2], Minh Phan[1,2], Thien Pham[1,2], and Tho Quan[1,2(✉)]

[1] Faculty of Computer Science and Engineering, Ho Chi Minh City University of Technology (HCMUT), Ho Chi Minh City, Vietnam
{nxmao.sdh232,dang.le246,tan.huynhxinchao,minh.phanpvd, pcthien.sdh20,qttho}@hcmut.edu.vn
[2] Vietnam National University Ho Chi Minh City, Ho Chi Minh City, Vietnam

Abstract. Nowadays, the widespread and harmful fake news has generally become a significant consideration. Fake news has the ability to evolve and create huge difficulties for human detection. Therefore, machine learning-based approaches to differentiate fake and real news have emerged as a predominant strategy. Historically, many previous content-based deep learning methods struggle with new types of fake news due to their reliance on static learned patterns. As a result, recent approaches have shifted to using *Graph Neural Network* (GNN) to include a more comprehensive context and prior knowledge. In this paper, we introduce a novel and robust framework that combines GNN and energy-based learning. Specifically, by leveraging the energy score in updating the trainable cost function, our method maximizes the energy gap between real and fake news, significantly enhancing detection performance. The experimental results demonstrate our promising output compared to that of state-of-the-art methods.

Keywords: Evidence-based fake news detection · Graph neural network · Energy-based model

1 Introduction

The proliferation of the Internet and social media has increased the spread of fake news, leading to misleading reviews, fake accounts, and harmful websites. To address this urgent challenge, researchers are actively developing machine learning models to detect false information in the early stage, primarily through content-based and evidence-based approaches. Content-based models mainly focus on linguistic patterns and fraud detection within text, such as analyzing writing styles and the relationships among readers and spreaders [1,2]. However, they often lack the contextual understanding needed to detect new types of fake news. To resolve the problem, evidence-based models use external resources

J. Kertesz et al. (Eds.): CSoNet 2024, LNCS 15417, pp. 233–241, 2025.
https://doi.org/10.1007/978-981-96-6389-7_20

to verify claims by comparing semantic structures [3–7]. One recent evidence-based method [8] has introduced a graph-based technique to model the relationships between words in claims and evidence sentences as graphs. By using a graph structure, this technique does an outstanding job of capturing far-reaching information. However, the metrics used in above methods are mostly well-known scores, such as softmax-based scores, which are biased and unreliable for anomaly detection. In contrast, the energy score is superior in *Out Of Distribution* (OOD) detection, as it can be derived from a purely discriminative model without explicitly relying on a density estimator [9,10]. In this study, we apply a GNN method for fake news detection, building word-level networks as part of an evidence-based approach and combining energy-based loss with cross-entropy loss to fine-tune the model, aiming for enhanced performance.

Our contributions can be outlined as follows: (1) We address the fake news detection problem from two perspectives: first, as a standard supervised classification task, and second, by treating fake news as an OOD sample and framing its detection as an OOD detection problem. (2) By integrating the graph learning structure with an energy-bounded learning objective, we train a model that effectively learns an embedding space to distinguish fake and real news. (3) Experiments on two datasets illustrate the comparable results with other baselines. This study introduces a promising direction for future research, suggesting the integration of an energy-based loss function with traditional objectives for enhanced fake news detection.

2 Related Work

2.1 Fake News Detection

Fake news detection is a *Natural Language Processing* (NLP) task that focus on identifying and classifying false news [11,12]. Approaches in this field are commonly divided into content-based and evidence-based methods. Content-based methods solely rely on neural networks to extract features such as semantic meaning, sentiments, and writing styles of news for verification [13]. In addition, some researchers also use information in social media such as user profiles [14], and comments [15] for news checking. Evidence-based methods, on the other hand, collect evidences from reliable sources on the internet, emphasizing semantic relationships between claims and evidences. DeClarE [3] was the first system to apply evidences in fake news detection by using BiLSTMs and attention mechanisms to evaluate the relevance of words within evidences to a claim. The following works further refine these methods by integrating attention models to capture semantic embeddings at different levels. For instance, HAN [4] computes coherence and entailment at the sentence level between claims and their supporting evidence, while EHIAN [5] employs self-attention mechanisms to capture interactions at both the word and sentence levels. Recent works improve this by combining hierarchical interactions to strengthen claim verification: MAC [6], CICD [7]. Besides, GET [8] further contributes by leveraging graph structures and neighborhood aggregation to integrate long-distance relevant information.

2.2 Energy-Based Out-of-Distribution Detection

Recent works [16,17] have established a connection between neural classifiers and *Energy-based Models* (EBMs). A classifier $f_y(x) : \mathbb{R}^D \to \mathbb{R}^K$ maps an input instance to a K-dimensional logits vector, which the EBMs then uses to define an energy function based on the predicted logits. Given an input x, the energy score is calculated using an energy function $E(x)$ [9]:

$$E(x) = -\log \sum_{j=1}^{K} e^{f_j(x)}. \tag{1}$$

where $f_j(x)$ denotes the jth entry of the logits vector.

The energy score calculated via $E(x)$ serves as an effective indicator for OOD detection due to its property that in-distribution data generally have lower energy scores compared to OOD data [9]. Additionally, energy score can be used as a regularization loss when OOD training data is available [9]:

$$\mathcal{L}_{energy} = (max(0, E(x_{in}) - m_{in}))^2 + (max(0, m_{out} - E(x_{out}))^2 \tag{2}$$

where m_{in} and m_{out} are threshold parameters.

3 Method

In this section, we propose our model for fake news detection task leveraging the power of graph structure and energy-based models. Our model consisted of four major components, which are illustrated in Fig. 1. The main input of the problem is denoted as tuples $(c, s, \mathcal{E}, p)$ where c denotes the claim to be verified, $s \in \mathbb{R}^{1\times H}$ represents its speaker, and $\mathcal{E} = \{e_1, e_2, ..., e_{n_e}\}$ is a collection of n_e related evidence and their publishers $p \in \mathbb{R}^{n_e \times H}$. The goal of this work is to classify each tuple $(c, s, \mathcal{E}, p)$ as either fake or real news.

3.1 Graph Construction

We represent each unique word in a document as a node in the graph, merging all instances of the same word into a single node to capture long-distance relationships. Each node is embedded using the 300-dimensional pre-trained GloVe model [18]. The graph's structure, described by an adjacency matrix, captures node connections via a sliding window method [19], where each center word is connected to other words in its window context; connected nodes are marked as 1 in the matrix, unconnected as 0. To ensure numerical stability [20], we also normalize the adjacency matrix as: $L = D^{\frac{-1}{2}}(A + I)D^{\frac{-1}{2}}$, where D is the diagonal degree matrix (i.e., $D_{ii} = \sum_j A_{ij}$), I represents the identity matrix.

We represent the normalized adjacency matrices and node embedding matrices for claim c and evidence e as $L^c \in \mathbb{R}^{N_c * N_c}$, $L^e \in \mathbb{R}^{N_e * N_e}$, $H^c \in \mathbb{R}^{N_c * d}$, $H^e \in \mathbb{R}^{N_e * d}$ respectively. N_c and N_e are the number of nodes in graph c and evidence graph e, while d is the node embedding dimension.

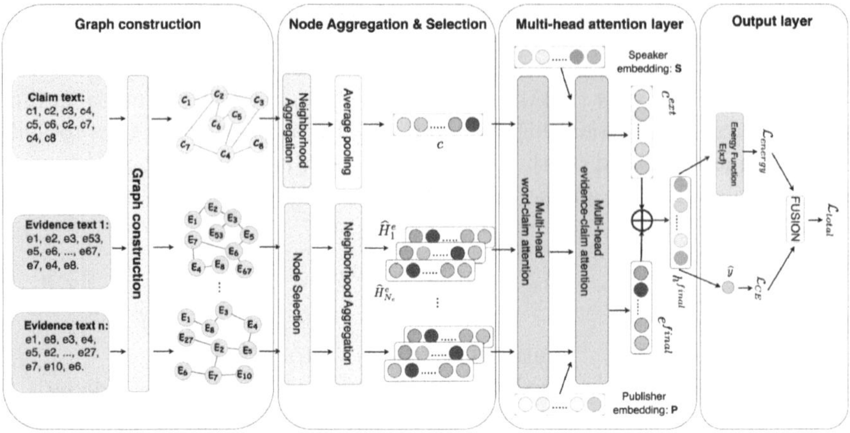

Fig. 1. The architecture of our proposed model. It consists of: (1) Graph construction, (2) Neighborhood Aggregation & Selection, (3) Multi-head attention layer, (4) Output layer.

3.2 Node Aggregation and Selection

After obtaining a normalized adjacency matrix L^c for a claim c, we leverage its node features and topological structure using GNN to capture intra-document word interactions. As previous work [8], we employ *Gated Graph Neural Network* (GGNN) [21] on both claim and evidence graphs allowing nodes to integrate information from their adjacent neighbors. This helps maintain the balance between self-features and neighboring information. The formulas for new embedding of ith node in a graph L^c are expressed as: $\widehat{H}_i^c = GGNN(L^c, H^c)$.

Similarly, we apply $GGNN$ on each evidence e to get the representation $\widehat{H}_i^e$ for each word in e. After applying $GGNN$, evidence e is modeled as a matrix $\widehat{H}^e = [\widehat{H}_1^e \oplus \widehat{H}_2^e \oplus ... \oplus \widehat{H}_{N_e}^e] \in \mathbb{R}^{N_e \times d}$ where $\oplus$ is the stacking operation.

Note that for each claim, we applied an averaging pooling layer to get the final representation $c \in \mathbb{R}^d$.

Evidence often contains irrelevant information that can mislead predictions. Following [8], we use $GGNN$ to compute attention scores based on self and topological features. By selecting the *top-k* nodes with the highest scores, we filter out irrelevant information, enhancing robustness to graph size. The refined evidence graph is denoted as L_{out}^e.

3.3 Multi-head Attention Layer

We need to integrate the normalized Laplacian matrix L_{out} and new node embeddings $\widehat{H}$ to generate the final embedding. Inspired by earlier research [6], we employ word-to-claim and evidence-to-claim multi-head attention mechanisms which measure the influence of each word and each evidence on the claim, respectively.

Word-to-Claim Multi-head Attention. After applying neighborhood aggregation and node selection, we obtained a new embedding matrix for each evidence as $\widehat{H}^e \in \mathbb{R}^{N_e \times d}$. As suggested by previous work [6], we use a multi-head attention mechanism to assess the relevance of each word in the evidence to the claim, capturing varying semantic weights:

$$A^{'} = Softmax_{col}(tanh([\widehat{H}^e||C].W_1).W_2) \in \mathbb{R}^{N_e \times head_1} \tag{3}$$

where C is created by stacking N_e vector c, $W_1 \in \mathbb{R}^{2d \times a'}$, $W_2 \in \mathbb{R}^{a' \times head_1}$, $head_1$ is the number of attention heads. Intuitively, A' denotes $head_1$ separate attention weights assigned to the N_e words of the evidence e. The $Softmax_{col}$ function normalizes each column of matrix A' by the softmax operation. The new representation for evidence e is formulated as:

$$e_{n_e} = Flatten(A^{'}.\widehat{H}^e) \tag{4}$$

where the function $Flatten(.)$ flattens result matrix $A^{'}.\widehat{H}^e$ into a vector $e \in \mathbb{R}^{head_1.d}$. For brevity, two Eq. 3 and Eq. 4 is represent as: $MATT(\widehat{H}^e, c)$

Evidence-to-Claim Multi-head Attention. Previous research [6] has shown that the credibility of a claim is influenced by the speaker who made the claim and the reputation of the evidence publisher. Following Vo and Lee [6] the extended representation of claim and evidence are: $c^{ext} = [c||s]$, $e_i^{ext} = [e_i||p_i]$ respectively. After extending the representation of speakers and publishers, we use the same attention mechanism as word-to-claim multi-head attention to capture the interaction between a claim and its supporting evidence. The new embedding of relevant evidence of a claim is generated as:

$$E^{ext} = [{e_1}^{ext} \oplus {e_2}^{ext} \oplus ... \oplus {e_{n_e}}^{ext}] \in \mathbb{R}^{n_e \times (head_1.d+H)} \tag{5}$$

$$e^{final} = MATT(E^{ext}, c^{ext}) \in \mathbb{R}^{head_2.(head_1.d+H)} \tag{6}$$

Finally, we get the final representation of a claim and their embedding in one vector h^{final} by concatenating two vectors c^{ext} and e^{final} as:

$$h^{final} = [c^{ext}||e^{final}] \in \mathbb{R}^{(d+H)+head_2.(head_1.d+H)} \tag{7}$$

3.4 Output Layer and Energy-Based Loss Function

In this final layer, we input the final representation h^{final} of a claim and its evidence into a *Multilayer Perceptron* (MLP) to output the logits value.

$$f_y(h^{final}) = MLP(h^{final}) \tag{8}$$

These logits are used to derive a categorical distribution using the softmax function:

$$\widehat{y} = \frac{e^{f_y(h^{final})}}{\sum_{j=1}^{K} e^{f_j(h^{final})}} \tag{9}$$

We train our model to minimize the standard cross-entropy loss, which can be expressed as:

$$\mathcal{L}_{CE} = -ylog(\widehat{y}) + (1-y)log(1-\widehat{y}) \tag{10}$$

Although training with cross-entropy loss does distinguish the energy values between fake and real news, the energy gap might not always be optimal for differentiation. Therefore, we propose an energy-bounded loss function, where the model will create an energy gap by pulling down the energy score of the real documents and pulling up the energy score of the fake ones. The energy regularization loss $\mathcal{L}_{energy}$ [9] is defined as:

$$\mathcal{L}_{energy} = (max(0, E(h^{final}_{real}) - m_{real}))^2 + (max(0, m_{fake} - E(h^{final}_{fake}))^2 \tag{11}$$

$$E(x) = -log(\sum_{j=1}^{K} e^{f_j(h^{final})}) \tag{12}$$

Finally, the training objective is a combination of the standard cross-entropy loss and an energy regularization loss:

$$\mathcal{L}_{total} = (1-\alpha).\mathcal{L}_{CE} + \alpha.\mathcal{L}_{energy} \tag{13}$$

where α is a hyperparameter that controls the importance of the regularization loss term.

4 Experiments

4.1 Datasets and Baselines

We used two public datasets, Politifacts and Snopes, are provided and preprocessed in previous work [4], to validate our model. These datasets offers comprehensive collections of fact-checked claims and supporting evidence.

We collect some other baseline performance from the content-based approach and evidence-based approach. By comparing them and our baseline, we can provide more evidence for the potential of applying Energy-based scores in the field of fake news detection. Details about collected baselines are listed as follows:

- **Content-based baselines**:
  - LSTM [22] utilizes the hidden layers of LSTM to represent each word and applies average pooling to obtain the final representation of the claim.
  - TextCNN [23] utilizes a 1-d convolution neural network to model claim text.
  - BERT [24] utilizes a pre-trained BERT classifier to generate a claim representation by feeding the [CLS] token into a trainable linear layer.
- **Evidence-based baselines**:
  - NSMN [25] assess the conflict or support between each evidence-claim pair by assigning a score, then calculates the average score across all evidence.

- DeClarE [3] consists of a BiLSTMs layer to collect contexts for each claim, and an attentive layer to aggregate all the information, producing the final representation for these claims.
- HAN [4] utilizes a Coherence-based Evidence attention mechanism, which captures crucial evidence for each claim.
- EHIAN [5] employs a self-attention mechanism to identify important evidence components, and then integrates article source features to enhance the semantic understanding of the evidence.
- MAC [6] employs a Hierarchical Multihead Attentive framework to capture both word-level and sentence-level semantics.
- CICD [7] designs a new loss function that emphasizes both word-level and sentence-level semantics to enhance interpretability in claim verification.
- GET [8] applies a graph structure on both claims and evidence to integrate far-reaching information and uses an attention mechanism to model claim-evidence interactions.

4.2 Implementation Details

Following previous works [6], we randomly selected 10% inputs in each dataset to create a validation set. For the remaining 90% inputs, we conducted a 5-fold cross-validation experiment to assess the performance of our model. We used 4-folds for training and 1-fold for validation. We implemented our method and the baselines in Pytorch and ran experiments on NVIDIA RTX 4060. Adam optimizer was utilized with 0.0001 learning rate and weight decay $\lambda = 0.001$. The maximum length of words in each claim and evidence are 30 and 100, respectively. Each words embedding size is 300, it is 128 for sentences embedding. The loss weight hyperparameter α is chosen from $\{0.05, 0.1, 0.15, 0.2, 0.25, 0.3\}$. The proportion of the selected node (top_k) is set to 0.6.

4.3 Results

Table 1 presents a comparison of our model's performance with ten other methods, measured by Precision, Recall, and F1 scores, using results from GET [8]. Our model generally surpasses previous methods and is competitive with state-of-the-art models. It achieves the highest F1-Macro and F1-Micro scores of 0.804 and 0.846 on the Snopes dataset and 0.692 and 0.697 on the Politifacts dataset.

These results demonstrate the proposition that energy-based learning can enhance GNN-based fake news detection. Specifically, our model outperforms pattern-based methods such as LSTM, TextCNN, and BERT, which rely solely on text patterns and lack semantic information. While performance fluctuates across datasets, our model achieves higher Precision and F1 scores on the Snopes dataset when Fake News is the positive class, though the GET model slightly surpasses it in Recall. For True News as the positive class, our model's Precision and Recall declined, with GET and CICD models taking the lead. In the Politifacts dataset, where data distribution is more complex, our models faced some challenges; however, it generally maintained the highest scores across metrics, with GET slightly surpassing it in F1 for Fake News as the positive class.

Table 1. Overall comparisons among different models on two datasets

Dataset	Snopes									Politifacts								
Methods	F1-Macro	F1-Micro	True News as Positive			Fake News as Positive				F1-Macro	F1-Micro	True News as Positive			Fake News as Positive		
			F1	Precision	Recall	F1	Precision	Recall			F1	Precision	Recall	F1	Precision	Recall
LSTM	0.621	0.719	0.430	0.484	0.397	0.812	0.791	0.837	0.606	0.609	0.618	0.632	0.613	0.593	0.590	0.604
TextCNN	0.631	0.720	0.450	0.482	0.430	0.812	0.799	0.826	0.604	0.607	0.615	0.630	0.610	0.592	0.591	0.604
BERT	0.621	0.716	0.431	0.477	0.407	0.810	0.793	0.830	0.597	0.598	0.608	0.619	0.599	0.586	0.577	0.597
NSMN	0.680	0.761	0.520	0.576	0.482	0.841	0.820	0.864	0.602	0.604	0.611	0.631	0.600	0.593	0.582	0.610
DeClarE	0.725	0.786	0.594	0.610	0.579	0.857	0.852	0.863	0.653	0.652	0.675	0.667	0.683	0.631	0.637	0.625
HAN	0.752	0.802	0.636	0.625	0.647	0.868	0.876	0.861	0.661	0.660	0.679	0.676	0.682	0.643	0.650	0.637
EHIAN	0.784	0.828	0.684	0.617	0.768	0.885	0.882	0.890	0.676	0.679	0.689	0.686	0.693	0.655	0.675	**0.636**
MAC	0.786	0.833	0.687	0.700	0.686	0.886	0.886	0.887	0.672	0.673	0.718	0.675	0.735	0.643	0.676	0.617
CICD	0.789	0.837	0.691	0.632	**0.775**	0.893	0.890	0.895	0.682	0.685	0.702	**0.689**	0.714	0.657	0.691	0.629
GET	0.800	0.846	0.705	**0.721**	0.694	0.895	0.890	**0.902**	0.691	0.694	0.723	0.687	0.764	**0.660**	0.708	0.629
Our Model	**0.804**	**0.846**	**0.714**	0.712	0.717	**0.895**	**0.896**	0.894	**0.692**	**0.697**	**0.731**	0.683	**0.788**	0.653	**0.722**	0.600

5 Conclusion

In this work, we propose a method that integrates GNN with energy-based learning for fake news detection. By leveraging graph structures, relevant information is captured through the aggregation of data among nodes. Additionally, by treating the fake news problem as an OOD detection task, we employ an energy loss function to establish a clear energy gap. This approach assigns lower energy levels to real news and higher levels to fake news, improving the distinction between the two. We conducted experiments to demonstrate the success of our proposed method with different approaches. The combination of graph structure with energy-based learning is essential for this success.

However, the limited amount of real news makes it challenging to develop a robust distribution. In future work, we plan to augment the dataset of real articles to increase in-distribution data and achieve a more reliable distribution. Additionally, we will also investigate various graph structures to further improve the performance of our model.

Acknowledgement. This research is funded by Murata Science Foundation under grant number 24VH09. We acknowledge Ho Chi Minh City University of Technology (HCMUT), VNU-HCM for supporting this study.

References

1. Ajao, O., Bhowmik, D., Zargari, S.: Sentiment aware fake news detection on online social networks. In: ICASSP 2019 - 2019, pp. 2507–2511 (2019)
2. Zhou, X., Zafarani, R.: Network-based fake news detection: a pattern-driven approach. ACM SIGKDD Explor. Newsl., 48–60 (2019)
3. Popat, K., Mukherjee, S., Yates, A., Weikum, G.: DeClarE: debunking fake news and false claims using evidence-aware deep learning. In: EMNLP, pp. 22–32 (2018)
4. Ma, J., Gao, W., Joty, S., Wong, K.F.: Sentence-level evidence embedding for claim verification with hierarchical attention networks. In: Proceedings of the 57th Annual Meeting of the Association for Computational Linguistics (2019)

5. Wu, L., Rao, Y., Yang, X., Wang, W., Nazir, A.: Evidence-aware hierarchical interactive attention networks for explainable claim verification. In: Proceedings of the 29th IJCAI, pp. 1388–1394 (2021)
6. Vo, N., Lee, K.: Hierarchical multi-head attentive network for evidence-aware fake news detection. In: EACL (2021)
7. Wu, L., Rao, Y., Lan, Y., Sun, L., Qi, Z.: Unified dual-view cognitive model for interpretable claim verification. arXiv preprint arXiv:2105.09567 (2021)
8. Xu, W., Wu, J., Liu, Q., Wu, S., Wang, L.: Evidence-aware fake news detection with graph neural networks (2022). https://arxiv.org/abs/2201.06885
9. Liu, Y., Sadegh, M., Liu, B., He, X.: Energy-based out-of-distribution detection. Proceedings of the 37th ICML, pp. 1234–1243 (2020)
10. Wu, Q., Chen, Y., Yang, C., Yan, J.: Energy-based out-of-distribution detection for graph neural networks. In: The 11th ICLR (2023)
11. Shu, K., Sliva, A., Wang, S., Tang, J., Liu, H.: Fake news detection on social media: a data mining perspective. SIGKDD Explor. Newsl., 22–36 (2017)
12. Zhou, X., Zafarani, R.: A survey of fake news: fundamental theories, detection methods, and opportunities. ACM Comput. Surv. (CSUR) **53**(5), 1–40 (2020)
13. Przybyła, P.: Capturing the style of fake news. In: AAAI Conference on Artificial Intelligence (2020)
14. Kumar, S., Carley, K.M.: Tree lstms with convolution units to predict stance and rumor veracity in social media conversations. In: Proceedings of the 57th Annual Meeting of the Association for Computational Linguistics, pp. 5047–5058 (2019)
15. Bovet, A., Makse, H.A.: Influence of fake news in twitter during the 2016 us presidential election. Nat. Commun. **10**(1), 7 (2019)
16. Xie, X., Raigorodskii, A., Jiang, X.: Energy-based models for deep learning. In: Advances in Neural Information Processing Systems (NeurIPS) (2016)
17. Grathwohl, P., Goldstein, T., Chen, R.T.Q., Bettencourt, J., Duvenaud, D.: Flow matching for generative modeling. In: Proceedings of the 37th ICML (2020)
18. Pennington, J., Socher, R., Manning, C.D.: Glove: global vectors for word representation. In: Proceedings of the EMNLP, pp. 1532–1543 (2014)
19. Yu, X., Xu, W., Cui, Z., Wu, S., Wang, L.: Graph-based hierarchical relevance matching signals for ad-hoc retrieval. In: WWW 2021, pp. 778–787 (2021)
20. Berg, R.v.d., Kipf, T.N., Welling, M.: Graph convolutional matrix completion. arXiv preprint arXiv:1706.02263 (2017)
21. Li, Y., Tarlow, D., Brockschmidt, M., Zemel, R.: Gated graph sequence neural networks. arXiv preprint arXiv:1511.05493 (2015)
22. Hochreiter, S., Schmidhuber, J.: Long short-term memory. Neural Comput. **9**, 1735–1780 (1997). https://doi.org/10.1162/neco.1997.9.8.1735
23. Wang, W.Y.: "liar, liar pants on fire": a new benchmark dataset for fake news detection (2017). https://arxiv.org/abs/1705.00648
24. Devlin, J., Chang, M.W., Lee, K., Toutanova, K.: Bert: pre-training of deep bidirectional transformers for language understanding. In: NAACL (2019)
25. Nie, Y., Chen, H., Bansal, M.: Combining fact extraction and verification with neural semantic matching networks. AAAI Press (2019)

The Multifaceted Role of Trust and Reputation in the Digital Age: A Comprehensive Review

Thi Kim Anh Vo(✉)

Ton Duc Thang University, 19 Nguyen Huu Tho Street, Tan Phong Ward, District 7, Ho Chi Minh City, Vietnam
vothikimanh@tdtu.edu.vn

Abstract. This study delves into the intricate dynamics of trust and reputation within the digital landscape, with a particular focus on social media networks. It explores the multifaceted ways in which these constructs influence and are influenced by a range of factors, including social media marketing strategies, information quality, user engagement, and corporate social responsibility. By synthesizing insights from recent research, this paper elucidates the pivotal role of trust in shaping online interactions, fostering brand loyalty, driving consumer purchase decisions, and facilitating political engagement. Furthermore, it underscores the critical importance of reputation management for both individuals and organizations navigating the complexities of the digital age. Ultimately, this study offers a comprehensive understanding of the interplay between trust and reputation in the digital realm, providing valuable insights for researchers, practitioners, and policymakers alike.

Keywords: Trust · Reputation · Social Media

1 Introduction

In the ever-evolving digital landscape, the concepts of trust and reputation have become intertwined, shaping the very fabric of online interactions. Trust, the willingness to rely on others despite inherent risks, and reputation, the collective perception of an entity's trustworthiness, are the bedrock upon which digital relationships are built [4, 11, 16]. Social media platforms, with their expansive reach and interactive nature, have emerged as vibrant arenas where trust and reputation are both cultivated and contested.

The significance of trust in the digital age cannot be overstated. It serves as the lubricant that facilitates cooperation, collaboration, and exchange in the online world. Whether it's engaging in e-commerce transactions, sharing personal information, or participating in online communities, trust is the essential ingredient that enables individuals and organizations to navigate the complexities of the digital realm. Reputation, in turn, acts as a powerful beacon, signaling trustworthiness and influencing how others perceive and interact with individuals and organizations in the digital space [5, 12, 17].

Social media platforms have not only amplified the importance of reputation but have also democratized its formation. The visibility and reach of these platforms allow

J. Kertesz et al. (Eds.): CSoNet 2024, LNCS 15417, pp. 242–249, 2025.
https://doi.org/10.1007/978-981-96-6389-7_21

information, both positive and negative, to be disseminated rapidly, shaping public perceptions and influencing trust at an unprecedented scale [3, 9]. In this environment, individuals and organizations must proactively manage their online reputations to foster trust and credibility among their audiences.

This article embarks on a journey to explore the multifaceted roles of trust and reputation in the digital age, with a particular emphasis on the dynamic world of social media. It delves into the intricate dance between these two concepts, examining how they influence and are influenced by a myriad of factors, including social media marketing activities, information quality, user engagement, and corporate social responsibility. By synthesizing insights from a rich tapestry of recent research studies, this article aims to provide a comprehensive understanding of the dynamics of trust and reputation in the digital landscape. It seeks to illuminate the pathways through which trust is built and maintained, and how reputation serves as both a shield and a sword in the digital arena. Ultimately, this article offers valuable insights for researchers, practitioners, and policymakers alike, empowering them to navigate the complexities of the digital world with confidence and integrity.

2 Positioning Within the Existing Literature

In the realm of social media, the dynamics of reputation and trust are both intricate and impactful. While prior research has illuminated various facets of these concepts, a comprehensive understanding of their interplay, particularly within the context of social media marketing, remains elusive [11, 15]. This study is driven by the imperative to bridge this gap, delving into the multifaceted ways in which reputation and trust intertwine to shape online behaviors and relationships.

Building upon the foundation laid by previous scholars, we aim to extend their work by examining the specific mechanisms through which social media marketing activities influence brand trust, brand equity, and brand loyalty. The existing literature suggests that social media marketing activities can significantly impact brand trust and loyalty [9, 13]. We will further explore the mediating role of trust in these relationships, shedding light on the underlying processes that drive consumer perceptions and behaviors, aligning with previous research that highlights the importance of trust as a mediator in the relationship between social media marketing and brand outcomes [1, 2, 17]. Furthermore, we will investigate the potential moderating effects of factors such as consumer engagement and perceived authenticity, recognizing that these elements can significantly impact the effectiveness of social media marketing efforts, as evidenced by prior studies [5, 6].

By integrating insights from diverse research streams and employing rigorous methodological approaches, this study aspires to contribute to the growing body of knowledge on reputation and trust in the digital age. We anticipate that our findings will not only enhance theoretical understanding but also offer practical implications for marketers and communicators navigating the complexities of the social media landscape (Fig. 1).

The above figure illustrates the relationship between prior research and the current study in the context of reputation and trust in social media. It highlights that while prior research has explored various aspects of these concepts, there is a limited understanding of their interplay, particularly concerning social media marketing's impact on

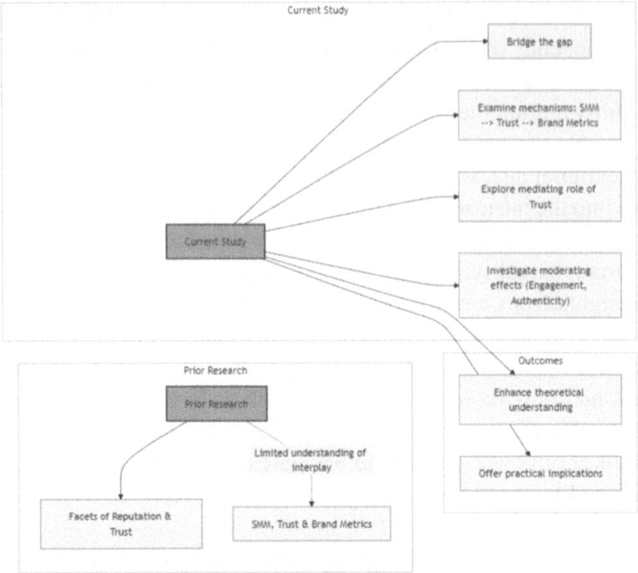

Fig. 1. Bridging the Gap: The Current Study's Role in Understanding Reputation and Trust in Social Media Marketing

brand metrics. The current study aims to address this gap by examining the mechanisms through which social media marketing influences brand trust, brand equity, and brand loyalty, with a focus on the mediating role of trust and the moderating effects of consumer engagement and perceived authenticity. The study's anticipated outcomes include enhancing theoretical understanding and offering practical implications for marketers and communicators.

3 Methodology

To unravel the complexities of trust and reputation in the digital age, this study adopts a systematic literature review methodology (Fig. 2). This approach ensures a rigorous and comprehensive examination of the existing research landscape, enabling us to identify key themes, patterns, and insights related to the interplay of trust and reputation in various digital contexts.

The review process will involve a systematic search of relevant academic databases, utilizing a combination of keywords and search terms related to trust, reputation, social media, digital marketing, and online behavior. The search will be limited to peer-reviewed articles published in reputable journals within the last five years to ensure the inclusion of the most recent and relevant research.

The selected articles will undergo a thorough screening process based on predefined inclusion and exclusion criteria. The criteria will focus on the relevance of the articles to the research topic, the rigor of their methodological approaches, and the clarity of their findings. The selected articles will then be subjected to a detailed analysis, extracting key information related to the research questions, theoretical frameworks, methodological approaches, findings, and implications.

The extracted data will be synthesized and organized thematically to identify patterns, trends, and gaps in the existing literature. This synthesis will facilitate a comprehensive understanding of the current state of knowledge on trust and reputation in the digital age, paving the way for the development of new insights and actionable recommendations.

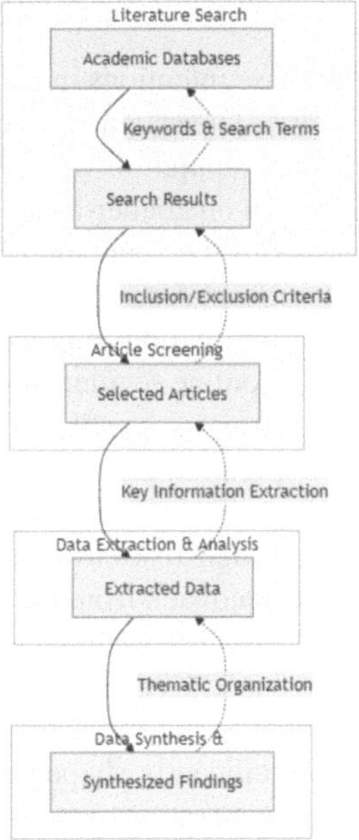

Fig. 2. Systematic Literature Review Process

4 Results and Discussion

The review underscores the symbiotic relationship between trust and reputation in the digital landscape. They are not isolated entities but rather intertwined forces that mutually reinforce each other. A positive reputation begets trust, and trust, in turn, strengthens and solidifies reputation. This dynamic is particularly pronounced in the realm of social media, where brands strategically leverage marketing activities to cultivate trust and loyalty [9].

Social media marketing activities, when thoughtfully designed and executed, can significantly impact brand trust and loyalty. Tactics such as personalization, entertainment, and promotions resonate with consumers, fostering a sense of connection and positive association with the brand [9]. However, the efficacy of these activities hinges on the perceived quality of information shared. Accuracy, reliability, and relevance are paramount in shaping a brand's reputation and nurturing trust among its audience [3,

10]. User engagement, encompassing active participation and interaction, further contributes to this virtuous cycle, as it signals a brand's responsiveness and commitment to its community [17, 19].

In the context of e-commerce, trust emerges as a pivotal mediator, influencing consumer purchase intentions. It acts as a bridge between social media marketing efforts and brand loyalty, as well as between brand equity and the ultimate decision to buy [1, 2]. Moreover, the reputation of the e-retailer, coupled with assurances of privacy and security, significantly impacts consumer trust, ultimately shaping their online shopping behavior [8, 14].

The formation of customer purchase intentions in online shopping has garnered significant attention recently. This study [7] investigates whether gender plays a role in how individuals utilize trust and perceived reputation when forming purchase intentions in online retail. Based on existing research on gender-based differences in online shopping behavior, it is proposed that females prioritize reputation while males prioritize perceived trust when developing purchase intentions. A sample of 727 respondents in Sweden was used to test these propositions, and the findings supported the proposed associations. The implications of these findings for online retailers are subsequently explored.

Beyond the commercial sphere, trust is equally vital in online communities and social networks, where it fosters cooperation and collaboration. The history of positive interactions between individuals, known as dyadic embeddedness, is a powerful predictor of trust, even in uncertain and high-risk environments like cryptomarkets [24]. Reputation systems, which aggregate feedback from multiple sources, also contribute to trust development, although their effectiveness can be undermined by malicious actors and biased information [4, 18].

The political arena is not immune to the influence of trust. Trust in social media platforms and political actors can significantly shape political involvement and participation, particularly among younger generations who are digital natives [10, 17]. The quality of information shared and the perceived reputation of social media platforms are critical factors in fostering trust, which in turn influences political engagement and activism [10].

Trust and reputation are crucial in all forms of communication, including human-to-human, human-machine, and machine-to-machine interactions. While cloud computing and the Internet of Things (IoT) offer numerous benefits, they also introduce security and privacy concerns. The growing number of devices connected to the IoT necessitates addressing issues like user trustworthiness and the identification of malicious actors. Fog computing, or edge computing, enhances cloud-based IoT by delivering cloud services closer to the network's edge, which can help mitigate security, privacy, and trust challenges. To address these challenges, a context-aware trust evaluation model is proposed to assess user trustworthiness in a Fog-based IoT environment. This model employs a context-aware multi-source trust and reputation-based evaluation system for effective user trustworthiness assessment. Additionally, context-aware feedback and a feedback crawler system are utilized to ensure unbiased, effective, and reliable trust evaluations. A monitor mode is also introduced to track the behavior and trustworthiness of potentially malicious or untrustworthy users. The model's adaptability is enhanced through the use of tunable factors that can be adjusted according to the system's specific requirements.

Simulations and results demonstrate the effectiveness and reliability of this approach in evaluating user trustworthiness (Fig. 3).

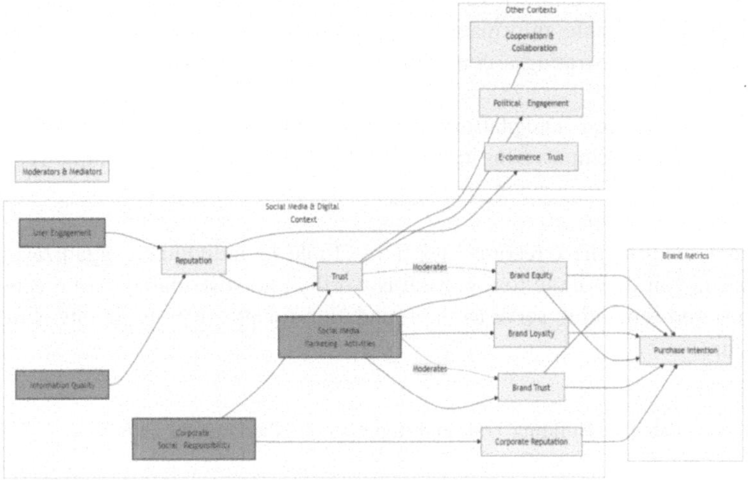

Fig. 3. Trust and Reputation: The Cornerstones of the Digital Ecosystem

The figure visually articulates the complex interplay of trust and reputation within the digital landscape and their far-reaching implications. At its core, the diagram highlights the bidirectional relationship between trust and reputation, suggesting they mutually reinforce each other. It underscores the influence of social media marketing activities, information quality, and user engagement on shaping reputation. Furthermore, it illustrates how trust serves as a linchpin, not only moderating the impact of social media marketing on brand metrics like brand equity and brand loyalty but also playing a pivotal role in fostering cooperation and collaboration, political engagement, and e-commerce trust. The figure also emphasizes the significance of corporate social responsibility in cultivating both trust and corporate reputation. Overall, this visual representation offers a holistic perspective on the multifaceted dynamics of trust and reputation in today's digital age.

5 Conclusion and Recommendations

In summation, this comprehensive review underscores the intricate and dynamic relationship between trust and reputation in the digital age, particularly within the context of social media. The findings highlight the multifaceted ways in which these two constructs intertwine and influence various online behaviors and outcomes. Social media marketing, information quality, user engagement, and corporate social responsibility emerge as critical factors in shaping reputation and fostering trust. Trust, in turn, acts as a powerful mediator, impacting brand loyalty, purchase intention, and political engagement.

To thrive in the digital world, individuals should cultivate a positive online reputation by managing their presence and ensuring their actions align with their values. Authentic engagement and sharing accurate information are crucial for building trust.

Organizations should prioritize trust-building in their social media strategies. This involves sharing reliable information, encouraging user engagement to build relationships, and demonstrating a commitment to social responsibility to enhance their reputation.

Finally, policymakers and platform developers must actively promote trust and combat misinformation. Empowering users with tools to manage their online reputations and fostering transparency among platforms and political actors are vital for facilitating meaningful engagement.

By implementing these recommendations (Table 1), individuals, organizations, and policymakers can contribute to a more trustworthy and sustainable digital ecosystem, where trust and reputation serve as the foundation for positive online interactions and relationships.

Table 1. Building Trust and Reputation in the Digital Landscape

Stakeholder	Recommendations
Individuals	1. Manage your online presence 2. Engage authentically online 3. Share accurate information
Organizations	1. Prioritize trust in social media marketing 2. Share reliable information 3. Foster user engagement 4. Demonstrate social responsibility
Policymakers & Platform Developers	1. Combat misinformation 2. Empower users 3. Encourage transparency

Future research should delve deeper into the nuanced dynamics of trust and reputation in the digital age, exploring the impact of emerging technologies, platforms, and cultural factors. By continuing to unravel the complexities of these constructs, we can gain a more profound understanding of their role in shaping online interactions and relationships, ultimately contributing to a more informed and empowered digital society.

References

1. Haudi, H., et al.: The effect of social media marketing on brand trust, brand equity, and brand loyalty. Int. J. Data Netw. Sci. **6**(1), 1–15 (2022)
2. Seo, E., et al.: The effect of social media usage characteristics on e-WOM, trust, and brand equity: focusing on users of airline social media. Sustainability **12**(4), 1691 (2020)
3. Park, S., et al.: Global mistrust in news: the impact of social media on trust. Int. J. Media Manag. **22**(1), 1–14 (2020)

4. Ramya, G., et al.: A review on various applications of reputation-based trust management. Int. J. Interact. Mob. Technol. (iJIM) **15**(10), 87–102 (2021)
5. Ryu, E., Han, E.: Social media influencer's reputation: developing and validating a multidimensional scale. Sustainability **13**(2), 631 (2021)
6. Fatmawati, I., Fauzan, N.: Building customer trust through corporate social responsibility: the effects of corporate reputation and word of mouth. J. Asian Finance Econ. Bus. **8**(3), 793–805 (2021)
7. Oghazi, P., et al.: From mars to venus: alteration of trust and reputation in online shopping. J. Innov. Knowl. **6**(1), 1–10 (2020)
8. Varma, M., et al.: Impact of social media, security risks, and reputation of e-retailer on consumer buying intentions through trust in online buying: a structural equation modeling approach. J. Crit. Rev. **7**(1), 1–10 (2020)
9. Althuwaini, S.: The effect of social media activities on brand loyalty for banks: the role of brand trust. Adm. Sci. **12**(4), 148 (2022)
10. Hamid, R., et al.: The role of social media in the political involvement of millennials. Span. J. Mark. ESIC **26**(1), 1–10 (2022)
11. Baber, P., Baber, R.: Influence of social media marketing efforts, e-reputation, and destination image on intention to visit among tourists: application of SOR model. J. Hosp. Tour. Insights **6**(1), 1–10 (2022)
12. Stravinskiene, J., et al.: Impact of corporate reputation dimensions on consumer trust. Eng. Econ. **32**(2), 177–192 (2021)
13. Salhab, H., et al.: The impact of social media marketing on purchase intention: the mediating role of brand trust and image. Int. J. Data Netw. Sci. **7**(3), 591–600 (2023)
14. Yan, X., et al.: Relationship between corporate social responsibility, organizational trust, and corporate reputation for sustainable performance. Sustainability **14**(14), 8737 (2022)
15. Dvorský, J., et al.: The impact of corporate reputation and social media engagement on the sustainability of SMEs: perceptions of top managers and the owners. Equilibrium **18**(3), 779–811 (2023)
16. Kumari, K., et al.: Role of corporate social responsibility in corporate reputation via organizational trust and commitment. J. Adm. **3**(2), 42–63 (2021)
17. Karunasingha, A., Abeysekera, N.: The mediating effect of trust on consumer behavior in social media marketing environments. South Asian J. Mark. (2022)
18. Geraldine, L., et al.: The effect of social media marketing on brand image, brand trust, and purchase intention of Somethinc skincare products in Surabaya. J. Entrep. Bus. **3**(2), 1 (2022)
19. Hatamleh, I.H., et al.: Trust in social media enhancing social relationships. Soc. Sci. **12**(7), 1–22 (2023)

Energy-Driven Riemannian Block-Matching

Dung Ngoc Le Ha[1,2] and Hiep Xuan Huynh[1(✉)]

[1] Can Tho University, Can Tho City, Viet Nam
hxhiep@ctu.edu.vn
[2] Can Tho University of Technology, Can Tho City, Viet Nam

Abstract. This study introduces BM-RED, a Block-Matching method combining Energy Distance with the Riemannian metric. By mapping optical flow vectors onto a unit sphere in Riemannian space, it captures nonlinear motion characteristics. Evaluated on the Sintel dataset, BM-RED excels in subtle movements (e.g., facial expressions) and complex motion (e.g., tree and background scenes), improving stability and sensitivity. Results show that Riemannian Energy Distance (RED) provides a robust geometric representation, achieving accurate estimates in challenging scenarios like occlusion and non-uniform motion.

Keywords: Motion estimation · Optical flow · Energy distance · Riemannian distance · Computer vision

1 Introduction

Motion Estimation [3] plays a crucial role in the field of computer vision and video processing, with the aim of determining object movements between consecutive frames in a video sequence. This field has wide-ranging applications, from video compression and behavior recognition to robotic control and virtual reality systems [2]. Energy Distance [4] enhances Block-Matching for motion estimation by measuring differences between probability distributions of pixel values, unlike traditional methods like SAD or SSD [8] that focus on pixel intensity. This approach captures complex changes, including geometric deformations and subtle shape alterations.

By integrating Energy Distance with Riemannian geometry [5], Block-Matching effectively handles curved or non-linear spaces, enabling accurate tracking of motion involving translation, rotation, and deformation [6]. This is particularly useful for complex motions like human body movement or elastic material deformat.

This article is organized into seven sections: Sect. 1 provides an overview of motion estimation and the problem at hand; Sect. 2 Briefly discusses motion estimation using Block-Matching. Section 3 details the steps for computing motion vectors between two consecutive frames using BM-RED. Section 4 presents models for motion estimation with BM-RED. Section 5 describes evaluation methods

J. Kertesz et al. (Eds.): CSoNet 2024, LNCS 15417, pp. 250–257, 2025.
https://doi.org/10.1007/978-981-96-6389-7_22

for BM-RED estimation. Section 6 shows experimental results across three different scenarios of the Sintel dataset. The final part concludes with the results of the proposed methods.

2 BM-RED: Enhanced Block-Matching with Riemannian Energy Distance

The Block-Matching method, widely used in motion estimation [7], divides frames into blocks and searches for their positions in the next frame, minimizing differences using metrics like SAD or SSD. While effective for basic motion, it struggles with complex scenarios. Recent advancements, such as diamond and adaptive rood search patterns [9,10], have improved efficiency and accuracy. Additionally, machine learning, particularly deep learning [11], has further enhanced performance. Traditional metrics like SAD or SSD fail to handle complex variations like deformations and rotations, prompting the development of more sophisticated similarity measures.

As in traditional approaches, optical flow estimation in Riemannian space remains an optimization problem. However, the Riemannian manifold's metric tensor modifies distance measurements between pixels in curved space, influencing the solution methodology. The objective is to minimize the Riemannian distance between consecutive frames by finding the optimal displacement vector field $v(x, y)$.

3 The Main Computational Steps of BM-RED

The proposed BM-RED method uses two consecutive images as input. Each block is mapped to the Riemannian space M through the function φ, The RED between corresponding points on M and calculated based on these Riemannian distances, The block with the smallest RED to B_i is selected as the matching block.

3.1 Riemannian Space

An image block B of size mxn is represented as a set of points on M 1,

$$B = \{p_{ij} \in M \mid 1 \leq i \leq m, 1 \leq j \leq n\} \tag{1}$$

Assume that each pixel in an image block is represented as a point on the Riemannian manifold M with a metric tensor g. Riemannian distance between two points p and q on a Riemannian manifold M is given by (2)

$$d_M(p, q) = \inf_{\gamma \in \Gamma_{p,q}} \int_0^1 \left\| \frac{d\gamma(t)}{dt} \right\|_{g(\gamma(t))} dt \tag{2}$$

where γ is a curve L connecting p and q, and $\frac{d\gamma(t)}{dt}$ is the tangent vector to $\gamma(t)$ at $\gamma(t)$. The norm $\|\cdot\|_{g(\gamma(t))}$ is calculated with respect to the metric tensor g at each point along the curve. In geometry, the metric tensor is a tool used to measure distances and angles in a space. Using the unit sphere as the metric tensor in Riemannian geometry enables more accurate modeling and computation on curved surfaces, which Euclidean geometry cannot handle effectively. For the unit sphere S^2 in $\mathbb{R}^3$ the metric tensor g in spherical coordinates (θ, φ) is given by (3).

$$g = [1 \quad 0][0 \quad sin^2\theta] \tag{3}$$

where $(\theta \in [0, \pi])$ is the latitude (polar angle) and $(\varphi \in [0, 2\pi])$is the longitude (azimuthal angle). The Riemannian distance on the unit sphere S^2 can be calculated using the metric tensor in spherical coordinates. For two points on the unit sphere, the Riemannian distance is the length of the shortest path (geodesic) between these two points $p = (\theta_1, \varphi_1)$ v $q = (\theta_2, \varphi_2)$ given by equation (4)

$$d(p, q) = \arccos(\sin\theta_1 \sin\theta_2 \cos(\varphi_1 - \varphi_2) + \cos\theta_1 \cos\theta_2) \tag{4}$$

3.2 Riemannian Energy Distance

Let $X = \{x_1, ..., x_n\}$ and $Y = \{y_1, ..., y_m\}$ be two sets of points on unit sphere, Energy Distance $D(X, Y)$ can be computed using the following equation (5).

$$D(X, Y) = 2E[d(X, Y)] - E[d(X, X')] - E[d(Y, Y')] \tag{5}$$

Combining the above factors, the *Riemannian Energy Distance* equation for the unit sphere metric tensor can be rewritten as (6), $(\theta_{x_i}, \varphi_{x_i})$ is the spherical coordinates of the point x_i in the set X.

$$\begin{aligned} D_{Riemannian}(X, Y) = 2E[d_{Riemannian}(X, Y)] - E[d_{Riemannian}(X, X')] \\ -E[d_{Riemannian}(Y, Y')] \end{aligned} \tag{6}$$

Where

$E[d_{Riemannian}(X, Y)] = \frac{2}{nm}\sum_{i=1}^{n}\sum_{j=1}^{m} \arccos(\sin\theta_{x_i} \sin\theta_{y_j} \cos(\varphi_{x_i} - \varphi_{y_j}) + \cos\theta_{x_i} \cos\theta_{y_j})$

$E[d_{Riemannian}(X, X')] = \frac{1}{n^2}\sum_{i=1}^{n}\sum_{j=1}^{n} \arccos(\sin\theta_{x_i} \sin\theta_{x_j} \cos(\varphi_{x_i} - \varphi_{x_j}) + \cos\theta_{x_i} \cos\theta_{x_j})$

$E[d_{Riemannian}(Y, Y')] = \frac{1}{m^2}\sum_{i=1}^{m}\sum_{j=1}^{m} \arccos(\sin\theta_{y_i} \sin\theta_{y_j} \cos(\varphi_{y_i} - \varphi_{y_j}) + \cos\theta_{y_i} \cos\theta_{y_j})$

3.3 The Block-Matching process using RED

Given I_1 and I_2 as two frames in the video. Each frame is divided into blocks B_i of size kxk For each block B_i in I_1, we find the block B_{j*} in I_2 such that:

$$B_j^* = \arg\min_j D_{Riemannian}(B_i, B_j) \tag{7}$$

where $D_{Riemannian}(B_i, B_j)$ is the Energy Distance between the two blocks, computed using the Riemannian distance as defined above.

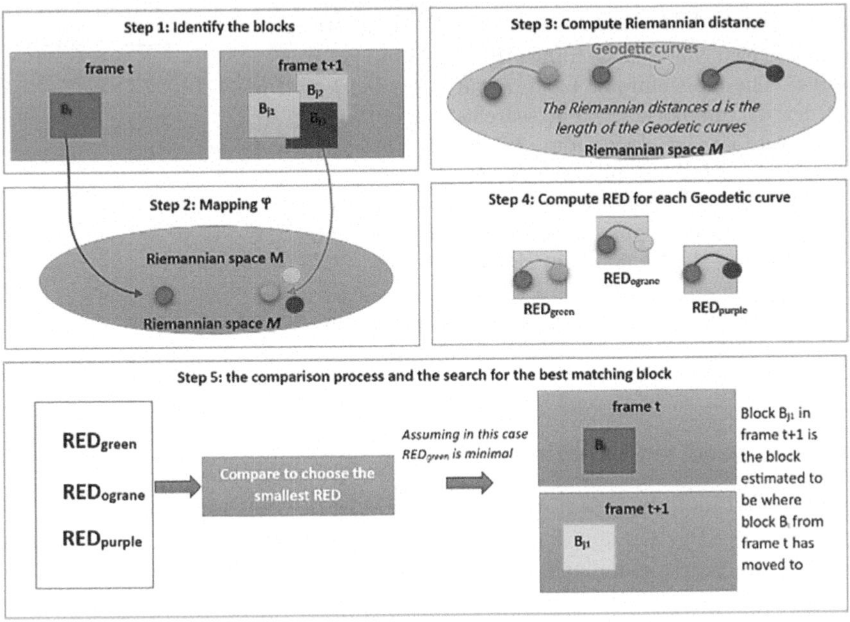

Fig. 1. Diagram representing the motion vector estimation process with BM-RED.

4 Motion Estimation with BM-RED Algorithm

Figure 1 illustrates the BM-RED in which Block-Matching process using energy distance with Riemannian to estimate motion. *Video frames*: Two frames are displayed at the top of the image, representing two consecutive frames in the video frame t, frame $t+1$; *Blocks* in frame t, we have block B_i that needs to be matched. In frame $t+1$, there are three candidate blocks B_{j1}, B_{j2}, and B_{j3}; *RED*: symbolizing the Riemannian manifold M. φ *mapping*: The blocks from the pixel space are mapped into the Riemannian space via the function φ. *Geodesic curve*: A dashed curve represents the geodesic path between two points on the manifold. The Riemannian distance is calculated along this curve. *Matching process*: Arrows from block B_i in frame t to the candidate blocks in frame $t+1$ represent the comparison process and the search for the best matching block.

5 Experiment

5.1 Experimental Datatsets

The dataset is derived from the animated short film 'Sintel' by the Blender Foundation, featuring high-quality graphics and offering complex scenarios involving motion, lighting, and image detail. Sintel also known as the MPI Sintel Flow Dataset developed by Butler et al. [1].

Algorithm 1. BM-RED for complex motion estimation

Require: Two consecutive frames I_1 v I_2 in video
Ensure: The most suitable block B_j^* in I_2 for block B_i from I_1

"Identify the block B_i to be searched for in frame I_1 "
"Identify the set of candidate blocks $\{B_j\}$ from frame I_2"
for every candidate blocks B_j in $\{B_j\}$ **do**
    Map B_i and B_j into the Riemannian space M:
    Compute the Riemannian distance $d\_R(\varphi(B_i), \varphi(B_j))$ over M:
    Compute the Riemannian Energy Distance $D\_R(B_i, B_j)$:
end for
Select the best matching block $B_j^* = armin_j D\_R(B_i, B_j)$
return B_j^*

5.2 Tool used for Experiment

The proposed models were tested on the *EDR* tool. This tool was developed by our team using Python and deployed on a Google Colab T4 GPU. It includes the following functions: calculating the Riemannian Energy Distance between two blocks, estimating motion vectors with BM-RED, and visualizing the results with video.

5.3 Evaluation Metrics

The Angular error (AE) is used to measure the angular deviation between the direction of the estimated and actual velocity vectors [12]. Let (u_{es}, v_{es}) is estimated motion vector and ground truth: (u_{gt}, v_{gt})

$$AE = \arccos\left(\frac{u_{\text{es}} \cdot u_{\text{gt}} + v_{\text{es}} \cdot v_{\text{gt}} + 1}{\sqrt{(u_{\text{es}}^2 + v_{\text{es}}^2 + 1)(u_{\text{gt}}^2 + v_{\text{gt}}^2 + 1)}}\right) \tag{8}$$

The formula using 3D vectors (u,v,1) adds 1 to both the numerator and denominator to avoid issues when one of the velocity vectors is zero. The reference range is in degrees $(0 - 180^o)$, where a value closer to 0 indicates the smallest angular difference.

5.4 Scenario 1: Estimation with Complex Motion

We performed facial motion recognition on a dataset focused on scenes with extensive facial movements. The subset of data was taken from *ambush*5, *ambush*6, and *bandage*1.

- EPE values are reported as mean ± standard deviation.
- Lower values indicate better performance.
- Best results for each sequence are highlighted in bold

Table 1. Performance Comparison of BM-RED for Complex Motion Estimation.

Consecutive frames	AE ambush_5	AE ambush_6	AE bandage_1
Frame 1–2	4.4781	28.5790	2.1122
Frame 2–3	4.2601	33.1153	3.8720
Frame 3–4	3.5006	35.46102	5.4845
Frame 4–5	2.8761	31.3495	3.0507
Frame 5–6	2.5943	29.1995	1.7865
Frame 6–7	2.4103	16.6774	1.4640
Frame 7–8	2.04285	13.4896	1.7081
Frame 8–9	2.8802	15.5788	1.7368
Frame 9–10	2.9477	22.00611	1.8459
Frame 10–11	3.9308	31.0620	2.1083
Mean AE	**3.192 ± 0.170**	**25.652 ± 1.330**	**2.517 ± 0.139**
Best Result	**2.043 (Frame 7–8)**	**13.490 (Frame 7–8)**	**1.464 (Frame 6–7)**

The results highlight BM-RED's strong performance on complex motion. For ambush5, it maintained a stable mean AE of 3.192 0.170 pixels, significantly outperforming traditional methods with AE values above 5.0. In the challenging ambush6 sequence, with rapid movements, the mean AE reached 25.652 1.330 but showed consistent improvement, achieving its best performance in frames 7-8 (AE: 13.490 0.785). In bandage1, BM-RED excelled, achieving its best performance with a mean AE of 2.517 0.139, effectively capturing subtle expressions and gradual movements

The visual results show that for local motions, BM-RED provides good results compared to the ground truth (*ambush_5* and *bandage_1*); however, when dealing with more complex and abundant motions, the performance decreases (*ambush_6*).

5.5 Scenario 2: Estimation with Minimal Motion

In this section, we experiment with the proposed method to estimate motion for objects with nonlinear motion, specifically the movement of trees and plants in the wind. The subset of data was taken from *bamboo_1*, *bamboo_2*, *bandage_2*. Table 2 summarizes the errors between the estimated vectors and the ground truth.

Figure 3 shows the discrepancy in estimating motion vectors for consecutive frames with minimal motion, where the error rate compared to the ground truth is negligible.

Table 2. Performance Comparison of BM-RED for Minimal Motion Estimation

Consecutive frames	AE bamboo_1	AE bamboo_2	AE bandage_2
Frame 1–2	0.7683	0.5775	0.9312
Frame 2–3	0.8057	0.7244	1.1037
Frame 3–4	0.7768	0.7529	1.4528
Frame 4–5	0.7732	0.8636	1.7316
Frame 5–6	0.7459	0.6101	2.0305
Frame 6–7	0.8071	0.5146	2.2042
Frame 7–8	0.8465	0.5871	2.2836
Frame 8–9	0.8285	0.7997	2.3024
Frame 9–10	2.9477	0.7815	2.3537
Frame 10–11	0.8726	0.9524	2.5090
Mean AE	**1.017 0.054**	**0.716 0.039**	**1.890 0.097**
Best Result	**0.746 (Frame 5–6)**	**0.515 (Frame 6-7)**	**0.931 (Frame 1-2)**

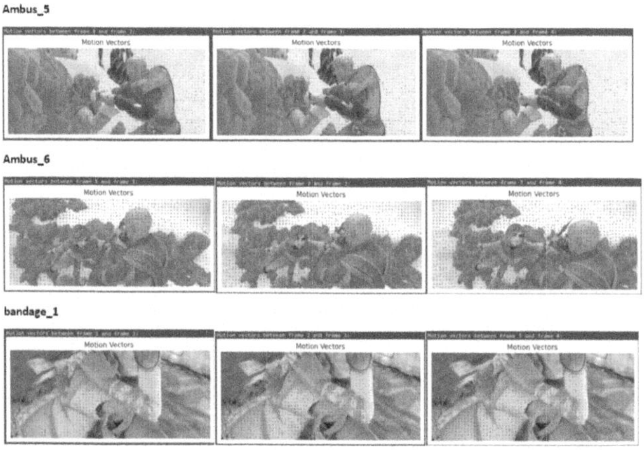

Fig. 2. Visualization of motion vectors with complex motion

6 Conclusion

This article proposes enhancing motion estimation in Block-Matching by using Energy Distance Riemannian as the cost function. The method employs Riemannian metrics for block distance measurement and integrates similarity matrices from ranking values and contextual attributes. Experiments on two real-world datasets demonstrate significant improvements, addressing sparse data issues and boosting performance.

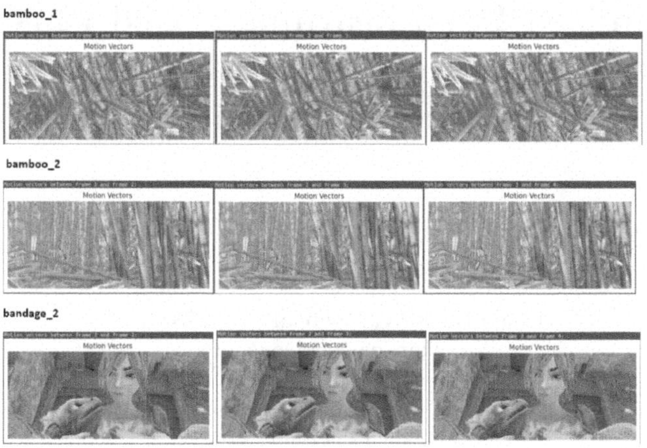

Fig. 3. Visualization of motion vectors with minimal motion

References

1. Butler, D.J., Wulff, J., Stanley, G.B., Black, M.J.: A naturalistic open source movie for optical flow evaluation. In: Fitzgibbon, A., Lazebnik, S., Perona, P., Sato, Y., Schmid, C. (eds.) ECCV 2012. LNCS, vol. 7577, pp. 611–625. Springer, Heidelberg (2012). https://doi.org/10.1007/978-3-642-33783-3_44
2. Wang, Z., Chen, J., Hoi, S.: Deep learning for image super-resolution: a survey. IEEE Trans. Pattern Anal. Mach. Intell. **43**(10), 3365–3387 (2020)
3. Cuevas, E., Zaldivar, D., Pérez-Cisneros, M.: A novel multi-threshold segmentation approach based on differential evolution optimization. Expert Syst. Appl. **37**(7), 5265–5271 (2010)
4. Székely, G.J., Rizzo, M.L.: Energy statistics: a class of statistics based on distances. J. Stat. Plan. Inference **143**(8), 1249–1272 (2013)
5. Pennec, X., Fillard, P., Ayache, N.: A Riemannian framework for tensor computing. Int. J. Comput. Vision **66**, 41–66 (2006)
6. Srivastava, A., Klassen, E.P.: Functional and Shape Data Analysis, 1st edn. Springer, Berlin (2016)
7. Barjatya, A.: Block matching algorithms for motion estimation. IEEE Trans. Evol. Comput. **8**(3), 225–239 (2004)
8. Bhattacharjee, K., Kumar, S., Pandey, H.M., Pant, M., Windridge, D., Chaudhary, A.: An improved block matching algorithm for motion estimation in video sequences and application in robotics. Comput. Electr. Eng. **68**, 92–106 (2018)
9. Zhu, S., Ma, K.-K.: A new diamond search algorithm for fast block-matching motion estimation. IEEE Trans. Image Process. **9**(2), 287–290 (2000)
10. Nie, Y., Ma, K.-K.: Adaptive rood pattern search for fast block-matching motion estimation. IEEE Trans. Image Process. **11**(12), 1442–1449 (2002)
11. Ren, S., He, K., Girshick, R., Sun, J.: Faster R-CNN: towards real-time object detection with region proposal networks. IEEE Trans. Pattern Anal. Mach. Intell. **39**(6), 1137–1149 (2016)
12. Baker, S., Scharstein, D., Lewis, J.P., Roth, S., Black, M.J., Szeliski, R.: A database and evaluation methodology for optical flow. Int. J. Comput. Vision **92**, 1–31 (2011)

Optimized Deep Learning Based Phishing Email Detection Using BERT and Hill Climbing Algorithm

Akshat Gaurav[1], Brij B. Gupta[2(✉)], Arcangelo Castiglione[3], Shavi Bansal[4], and Kwok Tai Chui[5]

[1] Ronin Institute, Montclair, NJ 07043, USA
akshat.gaurav@ieee.org
[2] Department of Computer Science and Information Engineering, Asia University, Taichung City, Taiwan
gupta.brij@gmail.com
[3] University of Salerno, Fisciano, Salerno, Italy
arcastiglione@unisa.it
[4] Insights2Techinfo, Jaipur, India
shavi@insights2techinfo.com
[5] Department of Electronic Engineering and Computer Science, Hong Kong Metropolitan University, SAR, Hong Kong, China
jktchui@hkmu.edu.hk

Abstract. Prevention of cybersecurity risks in contemporary communication systems depends on phishing email detection. This work presents an optimal deep learning method using the Hill Climbing (HC) algorithm for hyperparameter optimization and BERT for feature extraction to improve phishing detection. Using a Kaggle dataset, the model was trained with balanced precision, recall, and F1-scores for phishing and safe emails with a 95% accuracy. In terms of decreased loss and improved generalization, a comparative study encompassing GRU, LSTM, RNN, Logistic Regression, and SVM showed the suggested method's excellence. The results highlight how well feature extraction combined with optimization methods could help to identify phishing emails in practical environments.

Keywords: Phishing Detection · BERT · Hill Climbing Algorithm

1 Introduction

For people and businesses, the rising danger of phishing emails on today's digital terrain causes great anxiety. Usually including false emails meant to fool recipients into revealing sensitive information, phishing assaults have gotten ever more complex and common. With estimates of 96% of cyberattacks being phishing attacks and daily more than 3.4 billion phishing emails end by the attackers [10,11]. This concerning number emphasizes how urgently this widespread problem has to be addressed.

J. Kertesz et al. (Eds.): CSoNet 2024, LNCS 15417, pp. 258–269, 2025.
https://doi.org/10.1007/978-981-96-6389-7_23

Phishing efforts have very large financial consequences. Successful phishing efforts may cause millions of dollars in damages for companies; this is shown by well-publicized incidents involving big companies [5,7]. Moreover, the effects go beyond only instant money loss; phishing attempts could cause long-term harm to reputation and client confidence loss [13]. The expenses related to remedial actions and the use of security protocols to stop next attacks aggravate the economic load [15].

Different detection and prevention techniques have been suggested to help against the growing flood of phishing attacks. Natural language processing and artificial intelligence, among other machine learning methods, have shown potential in raising phishing detection system accuracy [1,3,12].

1.1 Contribution

The main contributions of this work are the inclusion of the Hill Climbing technique for hyperparameter optimization in phishing email detection and BERT for feature extraction. Comparatively to conventional models, this combo greatly increases generalization and model correctness. Moreover, the suggested approach presents a strong way to improve email communication systems' cybersecurity.

1.2 Organization

The rest of the paper is organized as follows: Sect. 2 presents the related work. The details of the proposed approach are presented in Sect. 3. Section 4 presented the results. Finally, Sect. 5 concludes the paper.

2 Related Work

As sophisticated attacks have grown in recent years, phishing and spam email detection have attracted more and more interest from experts. Phishing emails have becoming increasingly difficult to spot with the rise of generative artificial intelligence because AI-generated emails show different trends than conventional phishing efforts. Creating a corpus of such emails and using many machine learning methods for detection allows Eze, Chibuike Samuel, and Lior Shamir (2024) [8] to present a fresh strategy to identify AI-generated phishing emails. Their efforts draw attention to the differences between phishing emails produced by artificial intelligence and conventional ones, therefore stressing the requirement of many detection techniques to counter AI-based assaults. To maintain resilience in future detections, their method does, however, depend on training on both AI-generated and human-generated emails.

Taghandiki, Kazem (2023) [16] on spam detection using conventional machine learning techniques, on contrast, Their work shows a 96% accuracy rate using MLP for spam identification using the spaCy natural language processing toolkit and Naive Bayes (NB), Decision Tree (C4.5), and Multilayer Perceptron (MLP).

Although their method is confined to a Gmail dataset and does not handle sophisticated or AI-generated phishing emails, allowing opportunity for development in addressing more difficult assaults even if it is successful.

Mishra, A., & Gupta, B. B. (2018) [14] introduces a phishing detection system, CUMP, that leverages URI and CSS matching to effectively identify phishing websites, including zero-day attacks. This method capitalizes on the observation that phishers replicate URI patterns and CSS styles to mimic legitimate sites, achieving high true positive and true negative rates.

Expanding on the usage of sophisticated models, Uddin, Mohammad Amaz, and Iqbal H. Sarker (2024) [18] provide a refined, fine-tuned DistilBERT model for phishing email detection. Using Explainable-AI (XAI) methods like LIME and Transformer Interpret to improve transparency in phishing detection, their work tackles preprocessing and class imbalance. Though the results are encouraging, their method calls for large computing resources and validation across many datasets, which might be a constraint for more general uses.

Vajrobol et al. (2024) [19] enhances phishing detection by applying mutual information and logistic regression to analyze URLs, achieving an impressive accuracy of 99.97%. The research identifies key features that are particularly informative in distinguishing phishing URLs, offering valuable insights for cybersecurity professionals to strengthen defenses.

Regarding optimization, Thomas, Merly, and B. Meshram (2024) [17] provide a fresh strategy using the Aquila Optimization (AO) algorithm to fine-tune the hyperparameters of a Stacked Auto Encoder (SAE) for email categorization. In terms of accuracy, their model beats Logistic Regression (LR) and LSTM-based GRU models; yet, depending on certain features and hyperparameters can restrict its performance on bigger or more complicated datasets.

Gupta, B. B., & Jain, A. K. (2020). [9] introduces a language-independent, search engine-based phishing detection method that effectively identifies phishing sites across multiple languages. By integrating five heuristics, the method enhances detection accuracy, addressing gaps where legitimate sites may not yet be indexed by search engines, achieving a high true positive rate of 98.15% and a low false positive rate of 0.05%.

Bagui, Sikha, et al. (2021) [4] combine deep learning (DL) and machine learning (ML) models by means of deep semantic analysis for phishing email identification. According to their research, CNN with word embedding beats all other models in accuracy-96.34%. Deep learning techniques, however, need more computing time than conventional ML models, which might be troublesome for real-time detection in settings with constrained processing capacity.

Almomani et al. [2] enhances phishing detection by utilizing 10 carefully selected semantic features related to URL, domain, HTML, JavaScript, and abnormal characteristics, making the classification process more robust. A comparative analysis of 16 machine learning models demonstrated that GradientBoostingClassifier and RandomForestClassifier achieved the highest accuracy (around 97%) in detecting phishing sites.

These research highlight the need of using cutting-edge methods like deep learning, artificial intelligence-driven models, and optimization algorithms for phishing and spam detection taken as whole. Still, the trade-off between accuracy and processing efficiency is a difficult one, particularly given real-time applications and the emergence of phishing emails produced by artificial intelligence.

3 Proposed Model

In this section, we describe the complete procedure of the proposed approach, including data collection, feature extraction using BERT, hyperparameter optimization using the Hill-Climbing algorithm, and finally, training the deep learning model. The process is represented mathematically as follows:

3.1 Data Collection

Let the dataset D consist of N email samples, where each sample $x_i \in D$ is labeled as either phishing or safe:

$$D = \{(x_1, y_1), (x_2, y_2), \dots, (x_N, y_N)\}, \quad y_i \in \{0, 1\} \tag{1}$$

where $y_i = 1$ represents a phishing email and $y_i = 0$ represents a safe email.

3.2 Feature Extraction Using BERT

BERT is used to convert each email x_i into a feature vector $f_i \in \mathbb{R}^d$, where d is the dimension of the feature space:

$$f_i = \text{BERT}(x_i), \quad f_i \in \mathbb{R}^d \tag{2}$$

Thus, the feature set for the entire dataset becomes:

$$F = \{f_1, f_2, \dots, f_N\}, \quad F \in \mathbb{R}^{N \times d} \tag{3}$$

3.3 Hyperparameter Optimization Using Hill Climbing Algorithm

Let θ represent the set of hyperparameters for the deep learning model, including learning rate, number of layers, and number of units per layer. The Hill Climbing algorithm iteratively searches for the optimal hyperparameter set θ^* that minimizes the objective function $\mathcal{L}(\theta)$, where $\mathcal{L}(\theta)$ is the loss function of the model:

$$\theta^* = \arg\min_{\theta} \mathcal{L}(\theta) \tag{4}$$

At each iteration t, the algorithm evaluates a new candidate θ_t, compares it to the current best solution, and updates accordingly:

$$\theta_{t+1} = \begin{cases} \theta_t & \text{if } \mathcal{L}(\theta_t) \leq \mathcal{L}(\theta_{t+1}) \\ \theta_{t+1} & \text{otherwise} \end{cases} \tag{5}$$

3.4 Training the Deep Learning Model

After determining the optimal hyperparameters θ^*, the deep learning model M is trained using the extracted features F and corresponding labels Y:

$$M(F, \theta^*) = \hat{Y}, \quad \hat{Y} = \{\hat{y}_1, \hat{y}_2, \ldots, \hat{y}_N\} \tag{6}$$

The model minimizes the loss function $\mathcal{L}(\theta^*)$ over the training data to improve prediction accuracy:

$$\mathcal{L}(\theta^*) = -\sum_{i=1}^{N} [y_i \log(\hat{y}_i) + (1 - y_i) \log(1 - \hat{y}_i)] \tag{7}$$

where $\hat{y}_i$ is the predicted probability of the i-th email being phishing.

3.5 Final Model Prediction

After training, the model M is used to classify new emails based on their BERT-extracted features:

$$\hat{y}_{\text{new}} = M(\text{BERT}(x_{\text{new}}), \theta^*) \tag{8}$$

where $\hat{y}_{\text{new}}$ represents the predicted label (phishing or safe) for a new email x_{new}.

4 Results and Discussion

4.1 Dataset Representation

This work evaluated our proposed deep learning model for phishing email detection using a publicly accessible Kaggle dataset [6]. The dataset comprises two classes- "Safe Email" and "Phishing Email". Figures 1 show the class distribution. The dataset reveals a modest class imbalance, as shown by around 10,000 safe emails and 6,000 phishing emails. This mismatch may compromise the model's capacity to identify phishing emails, the minority class correctly. While other techniques-such as data re-sampling or cost-sensitive learning-can be used to solve this imbalance, in this work, we concentrate on increasing the performance of the deep learning model via feature extraction using BERT and hyperparameter adjustment using the Hill Climbing Algorithm.

4.2 Performance of Hill Climbing (HC) Algorithm

Following BERT model feature extraction, we optimized the hyperparameters of the deep learning model using the Hill Climbing (HC) technique. The following figures show the HC algorithm's performance across the optimization phase.

With a runtime varying between 46 and 52 s, Fig. 2 shows the algorithm's running throughout 100 iterations. Although the Hill Climbing method investigates many hyperparameter combinations, the very constant computing time

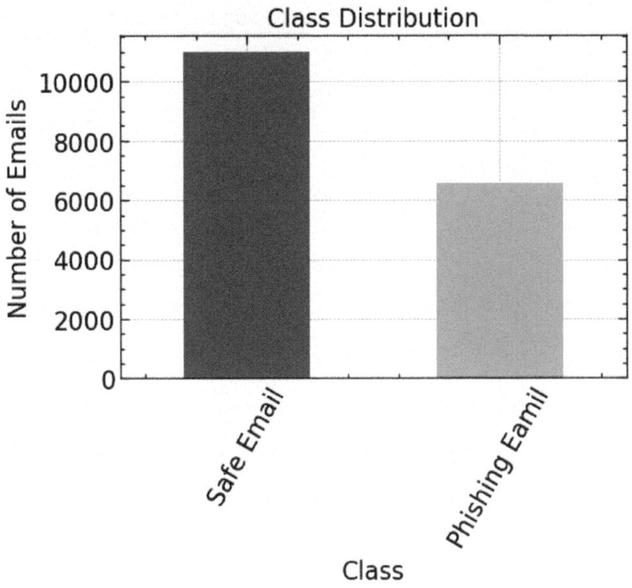

Fig. 1. Class Distribution

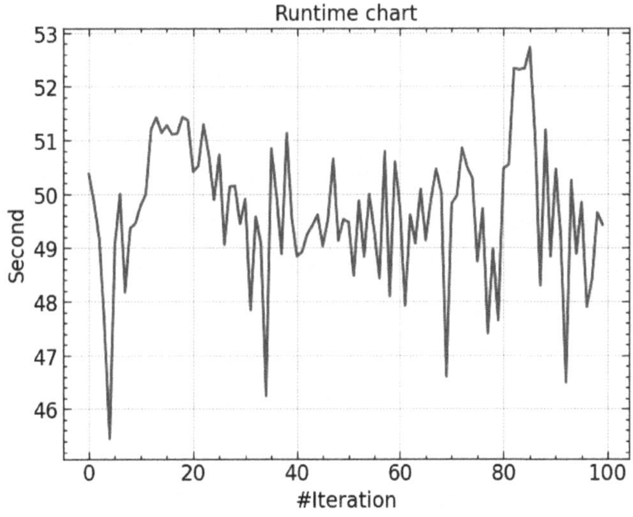

Fig. 2. Runtime of HC

indicates that it maintains constant processing efficiency throughout the optimization process.

Figure 4, the Global Objective Chart, shows how the objective function value falls over repetitions. The constant decrease in the objective value shows that

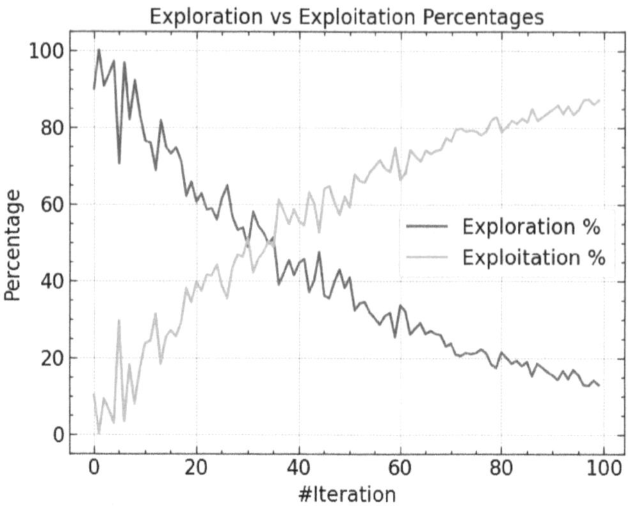

Fig. 3. Exploration against Exploitation of HC

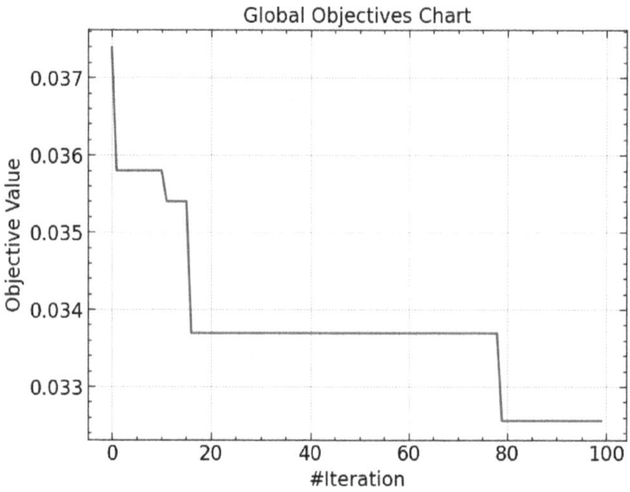

Fig. 4. Global Objective of HC

the HC method efficiently maximizes the model by gradually reducing the objective function. After around 80 iterations, the objective value converges around 0.033, indicating that the method finds an optimum solution within a reasonable amount of iterations, avoiding over-exploration or too high computing cost.

We find the equilibrium between exploration and exploitation throughout the optimization process in Fig. 3. As shown by a larger proportion of exploration, the method first focuses more on discovery. But as the iterations go on, the

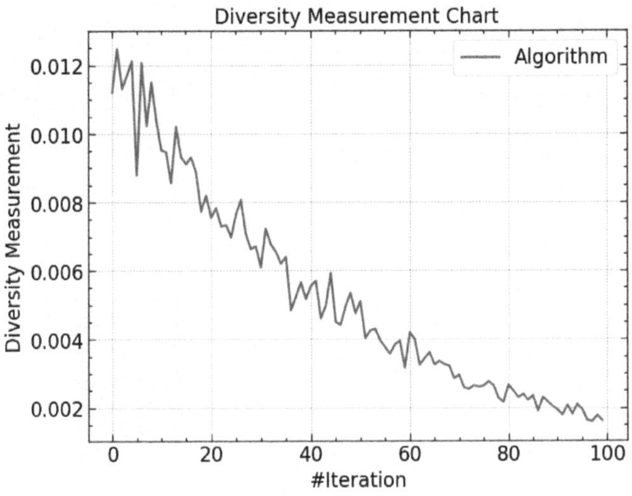

Fig. 5. Diversity of HC

method progressively moves toward exploitation, stressing the improvement of the answer in a more confined search area. This change from exploration to exploitation is a desired characteristic that guarantees early coverage of a large search space before concentrating on fine-tuning the performance of the model.

At last, the Diversity Measurement Chart (Fig. 5) shows how the search space closes with time. As the HC method converges toward an ideal set of hyperparameters, the variety of the solutions reduces. As the algorithm narrows down on the optimal answer, this decrease in variety is predicted as it reduces variation and focuses on small changes instead of broad investigation.

4.3 Performs of Deep Learning Model

Following the Hill Climbing algorithm's optimum hyperparameter acquisition, we trained the deep learning model for five consecutive evaluations. Together with macro and weighted averages, Fig. 6 shows the classification report, including accuracy, recall, F1-score, and support for every class.

Strong performance in phishing email detection helped the model reach an overall accuracy of 95%. The accuracy, recall, and F1-score for the "Safe Email" class (0.0) were 0.92, 0.96, and 0.94, respectively, meaning the model efficiently detects safe emails with the lowest false positives. The accuracy, recall, and F1-score for the "Phishing Email" class (1.0) were 0.97, 0.95, and 0.96, thereby stressing the model's capacity to precisely identify phishing emails while preserving a low false negative rate.

Consistent at 0.95, the macro average and weighted average for accuracy, recall, and F1-score help to further validate the model's balanced performance across both classes. This categorization report shows how well the improved deep learning model manages phishing and safe emails.

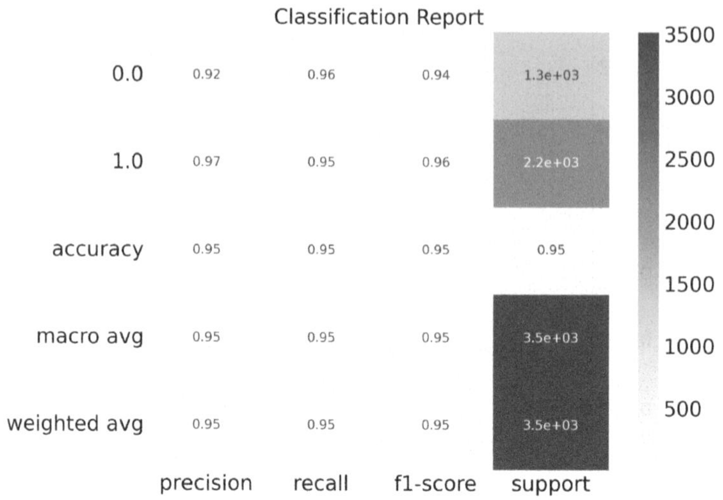

Fig. 6. Classification Report

Apart from the classification report, we assessed the model's performance using a confusion matrix-as shown in Fig. 7. The confusion matrix thoroughly analyzes the model's forecasts for the "Safe Email" and "Phishing Email" classes.

Out of 1,295 genuine safe emails, the model properly categorized 1,239 as safe and 56 as phishing emails, according to the matrix. Analogous to 2,213 phishing emails, the algorithm correctly categorized 2,103 as phishing and 110 misclassified safe emails.

With quite a few misclassifications, these findings show that the model is rather good in identifying phishing emails. Crucially, in reducing the hazards connected with phishing attempts, the number of false negatives-110 phishing emails expected as safe-is low relative to the overall amount of phishing emails. Furthermore, the limited number of false positives (56 safe emails expected as phishing) shows how strong the model is in preserving a low false positive rate, guaranteeing little disturbance in legitimate email processing.

The confusion matrix highlights the great accuracy of the enhanced deep learning model in separating safe and phishing emails, therefore supporting the results of the classification report.

4.4 Comparative Analysis

We performed a comparison study against many conventional models, including GRU, LSTM, RNN, Logistic Regression, a Simple Neural Network, and SVM, thereby validating the performance of our optimal deep learning model. Figures 8 show for every model the loss comparison throughout five epochs.

Our suggested model (blue line) routinely beats the other models in terms of reducing loss, converging to the lowest loss value at the conclusion of the

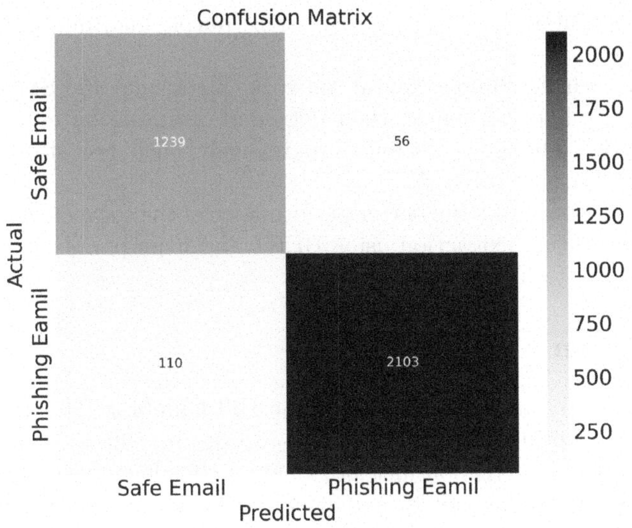

Fig. 7. Confusion Matrix

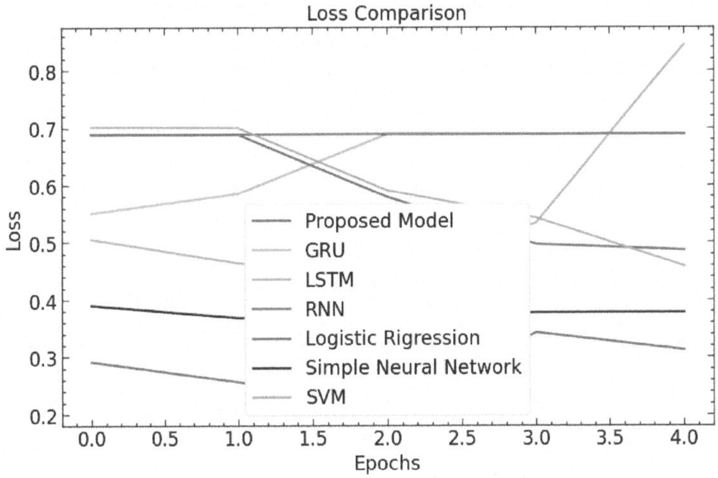

Fig. 8. Comparative Analysis. (Color figure online)

training period, as the figure shows. Our model's loss shows effective learning and optimization as it constantly falls throughout epochs.

Models such as LSTM (orange line) and GRU (green line) first perform well, then show spikes in loss beyond the second epoch, suggesting possible overfitting or data generalizing problems. Redline RNN shows little capacity to learn from the dataset in this situation as it maintains a high and flat loss curve. Though it begins with a larger loss, logistic regression (purple line) improves somewhat with time.

Although both the Simple Neural Network (black line) and SVM (gray line) exhibit comparable performance, their degree of optimization falls short of our suggested model. Though it declines progressively, their loss stays larger than our ideal deep learning method.

This comparison shows the better performance of the suggested model, which gains from the feature extraction using BERT and hyperparameter tuning with the Hill Climbing technique.

5 Conclusion

Using BERT for feature extraction and the Hill Climbing (HC) algorithm for hyperparameter optimization, this work proposes an efficient deep learning-based phishing email detection method. Using a Kaggle dataset, the model was trained with great accuracy of 95%. It performed efficiently regarding precision, recall, and F1 scores across safe and phishing emails. Comparative investigation using conventional models like GRU, LSTM, RNN, Logistic Regression, and SVM showed even more the superiority of the proposed model, which displayed reduced loss and greater generalization. The results verify that phishing email detection is much improved by combining BERT with hyperparameter tuning utilizing HC. This method may be practically used to raise cybersecurity standards.

Acknowledgment. This research work is supported by National Science and Technology Council (NSTC), Taiwan Grant No. NSTC112-2221-E-468-008-MY3.

References

1. Alakbarov, R.: An optimization model for task scheduling in mobile cloud computing. Int. J. Cloud Appl. Comput. (IJCAC) **12**(1), 1–17 (2022)
2. Almomani, A., et al.: Phishing website detection with semantic features based on machine learning classifiers: a comparative study. Int. J. Semant. Web Inf. Syst. (IJSWIS) **18**(1), 1–24 (2022)
3. Andriu, A.: Adaptive phishing detection: harnessing the power of artificial intelligence for enhanced email security. Roman. Cyber Secur. J. **5**, 3–9 (2023). https://doi.org/10.54851/v5i1y202301
4. Bagui, S., Nandi, D., Bagui, S., White, R.J.: Machine learning and deep learning for phishing email classification using one-hot encoding. J. Comput. Sci. (2021)
5. Bhardwaj, A., Kaushik, K.: Predictive analytics-based cybersecurity framework for cloud infrastructure. Int. J. Cloud Appl. Comput. (IJCAC) **12**(1), 1–20 (2022)
6. Chakraborty, S.: Phishing email detection (2023). https://doi.org/10.34740/KAGGLE/DSV/6090437. https://www.kaggle.com/dsv/6090437
7. Cooper, M., Levy, Y., Dringus, L.: Subject matter experts' feedback on a prototype development of an audio, visual, and haptic phishing email alert system. Online J. Appl. Knowl. Manag. **8**, 107–121 (2020). https://doi.org/10.36965/ojakm.2020.8(2)107-121

8. Eze, C.S., Shamir, L.: Analysis and prevention of ai-based phishing email attacks. Electronics (2024). https://doi.org/10.3390/ELECTRONICS13101839
9. Gupta, B.B., Jain, A.K.: Phishing attack detection using a search engine and heuristics-based technique. J. Inf. Technol. Res. (JITR) **13**(2), 94–109 (2020)
10. Jain, A.K., Gupta, B.B.: Phishing detection: analysis of visual similarity based approaches. Secur. Commun. Netw. **2017**(1), 5421046 (2017)
11. Lappas, D., Karampelas, P.: Designing an email attack by analysing the victim's profile. an alternative anti-phishing training method. In: European Conference on Cyber Warfare and Security, vol. 22, pp. 257–266 (2023). https://doi.org/10.34190/eccws.22.1.1178
12. Li, S., Qin, D., Wu, X., Li, J., Li, B., Han, W.: False alert detection based on deep learning and machine learning. Int. J. Semant. Web Inf. Syst. (IJSWIS) **18**(1), 1–21 (2022)
13. M., S., Pais, A.: Classification of phishing email using word embedding and machine learning techniques. J. Cyber Secur. Mobil. (2022). https://doi.org/10.13052/jcsm2245-1439.1131
14. Mishra, A., Gupta, B.B.: Intelligent phishing detection system using similarity matching algorithms. Int. J. Inf. Commun. Technol. **12**(1–2), 51–73 (2018)
15. Salloum, S., Gaber, T., Vadera, S., Shaalan, K.: A systematic literature review on phishing email detection using natural language processing techniques. IEEE Access **10**, 65703–65727 (2022). https://doi.org/10.1109/access.2022.3183083
16. Taghandiki, K.: Building an effective email spam classification model with spacy (2023)
17. Thomas, M., Meshram, B.B.: Optimizing hyperparameters for enhanced email classification and forensic analysis with stacked autoencoders. Int. J. Netw. Secur. Appl. (2024). https://doi.org/10.5121/IJNSA.2024.16102
18. Uddin, M.A., Sarker, I.H.: An explainable transformer-based model for phishing email detection: a large language model approach (2024). https://doi.org/10.48550/ARXIV.2402.13871
19. Vajrobol, V., Gupta, B.B., Gaurav, A.: Mutual information based logistic regression for phishing url detection. Cyber Secur. Appl. **2**, 100044 (2024)

Intestate Inheritance Allocation Algorithm According to Thai Law Using Bottom-up Pruning Approach

Sorawit Chokphantavee, Sirawit Chokphantavee, and Somrudee Deepaisarn(✉)

Sirindhorn International Institute of Technology, Thammasat University, Bangkok 12120, Pathum Thani, Thailand
somrudee@siit.tu.ac.th

Abstract. The field of legal assistance systems has gained significant attention for its benefits, such as increased efficiency in legal case processing, reduced workload of legal practitioners, and improved accessibility. While there are several developments in this domain, only a handful of inventions address the inheritance calculation, and to the best of our knowledge, none directly handle the intestate inheritance allocation per the Thai Civil and Commercial Code. Therefore, we developed a novel algorithm to automate such a process utilizing the rule-based algorithm and tree-based algorithm, which include the recursive non-binary tree construction, bottom-up pruning, and result allocation. This algorithm can correctly allocate inheritance for all test cases, indicating its potential for adoption in practical applications in the future.

Keywords: Thai Law · Inheritance Allocation · Civil and Commercial Code · Algorithm · Family Tree

1 Introduction

In today's technological-driven era, it is indisputable that the integration of cutting-edge tools and algorithms has become part of our lives. This also holds for the legal domain. Legal practitioners vastly benefit from these technological breakthroughs, allowing them to retrieve legal documents and information quickly and accurately using various techniques and deep learning models [7,9,12]. Another significant focus within this domain, which has currently received massive attention from scholars, is to automate the legal text classification [1,3,5,8] and court judgment prediction tasks [6,11].

Nevertheless, shifting our focus toward a more specific legal task, such as intestate inheritance allocation and management, there are very few tools and algorithms to support legal experts in such tasks, especially in Thai law. Most existing literature and online applications [4] that aim to address this intestate inheritance allocation task are mainly created for Islamic law. In [13], they proposed a system to calculate the inheritance distribution for each heir in the family

J. Kertesz et al. (Eds.): CSoNet 2024, LNCS 15417, pp. 270–279, 2025.
https://doi.org/10.1007/978-981-96-6389-7_24

as per Islamic law by adopting the concept of ontology for the Arabic language. As a result, this system was named "AraFamOnto". Another notable work by Bin Awae and Limsiroratana [2] proposed a web-based application for intestate inheritance management designed explicitly for Islamic law used in Thailand. As opposed to any other existing inheritance allocation system, this system has one distinctive feature: the ability to fairly distribute indivisible property, namely land, houses, or jewelry, by utilizing the Knapsack algorithm in combination with the modified Bin packing algorithm. Although this system is applicable in some areas of Thailand where Islamic law is widely used, it does not account for the broader Thai population. The majority of Thai citizens rely on inheritance laws stipulated in the Thai Civil and Commercial Code (CCC), which use a completely different rule compared to Islamic law. This signified the importance of developing a specialized tool or algorithm tailored to streamline intestate inheritance calculations under the Thai CCC. Especially, those that can handle the special case as per the right of representation, a legal principle that theoretically allows rights in the de cujus' estate to be passed down through generations indefinitely until it reaches the first living and eligible heir of the stirpes.

In this work, we developed an algorithm that can perform the intestate inheritance allocation that can also handle the sophisticated scenarios concerning the rights of representation by leveraging the rule-based algorithm extracted from the legal provision related to inheritance together with the tree-based data structure, and our proposed bottom-up pruning algorithm.

2 Methodology

Our algorithm receives the family tree, which can be represented as a list of nodes and their connecting edges, as input and returns the allocation ratio of intestate property for each eligible heir and excludes the others. Each node corresponds to an individual in the family tree and retains specific properties, namely their familial role relative to the inheritor (de cujus), their status (whether deceased or alive), and the inheritance allocation ratio to be assigned, which is essential for further calculation of our algorithm. Then, initially, our algorithm will utilize the rule-based method, which relies upon the logical and legal principle extracted from the relevant legal provision related to inheritance. This step alone is sufficient for dealing with simple cases where the representative heir is not presented. However, if there is a representative heir as per the right of representation under the Thai Civil and Commercial Code (CCC), the follow-up step for the tree-based processing with bottom-up pruning and result allocation will be triggered (tree-based algorithm). Figure 1 illustrates the algorithm used for different parts of the family tree.

2.1 Intestate Inheritance Rule Extraction from Law Code

To develop this algorithm, we first need to fathom the legal provisions governing the intestate inheritance allocation under the Thai CCC. This will be

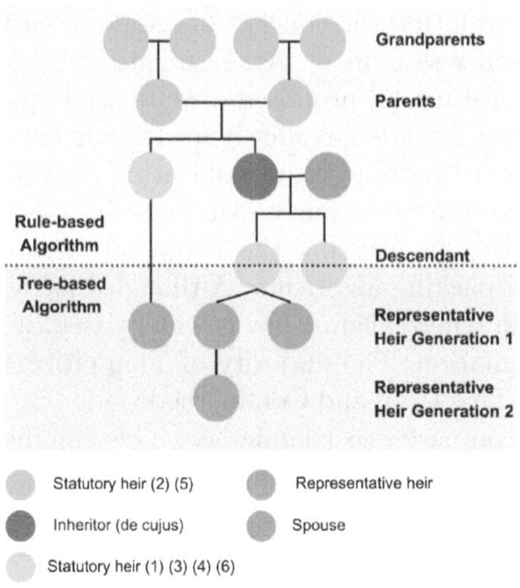

Fig. 1. An illustration of an example of a family tree and the corresponding algorithm used to process each part of the tree. The rule-based algorithm handles all the inheritance allocation of statutory heirs according to Section 1629 and spouses, while the tree-based algorithm manages representative heirs across multiple generations according to Section 1639. Each color denotes different types of heirs and the de cujus.

useful for the core logic extraction from the law and provide a clear guideline for implementing such an algorithm. The predominant legal section for inheritance allocation in intestate cases is Section 1629 under the Thai CCC, which details the order in which the estate of the de cujus must be distributed among statutory heirs when no will has been established. The statutory heir, according to this section, consists of 6 classes ordered as follows: descendants (children of the de cujus regardless of legitimacy), parents (mother and legitimate father of the de cujus), brothers and sisters of full blood, brothers and sisters of half blood, grandparents, uncles, and aunts.

Then, Section 1630 states that the heir of a lower degree, as defined in Section 1629, has no right to inherit the estate of the de cujus if an heir of a higher degree is surviving or being represented. This principle is commonly known as the "nearer exclude the remote" rule [10]. However, this rule does not apply between the first and second levels heir. Therefore, if both descendants and parents of the de cujus are present, the parent of the de cujus will be treated as if they were descendants and entitled to the same proportion of inheritance. Section 1633 states that the inheritance should be distributed equally among heirs in the same class.

Another crucial section is Section 1635 regarding the legitimate spouse's share in de cujus estate. This section states that the surviving legitimate spouse of the deceased is entitled to a predetermined fraction of the inheritance based on the degree of the remaining statutory heir. If the heir, according to Section 1629 (1), survives or has a representative, the lawful spouse of the de cujus shall entitled to an equal share of that of a descendant. However, suppose the de cujus has no heir according to Section 1629 (1) or such an heir deceased before the de cujus and having no representative, but there is an heir according to Section 1629 (2) or (3). In that case, the legitimate spouse is entitled to one-half of the inheritor's estate. Then, if the de cujus solely has heirs according toSection 1629 (4), (5), or (6), the spouse shall receive two-thirds of the inheritance. Lastly, if there is no heir as per Section 1629, the surviving spouse shall grant the estate of the de cujus in its entirety.

Next, understanding Section 1639 is vital for handling the scenarios in which there is a representative heir. This section allows the direct descendant of heirs, according to Section 1629 (1), (3), (4), or (6), to represent such heir for the sake of inheritance in the case where such heir is deceased or is excluded before the death of the inheritor. Lastly, Section 1753 of the CCC details the edge case where the deceased individual does not have any eligible heir according to the law, and no final will has been established, such individual's estate shall be devolved on the state in its entirety.

With all the legal sections and the logic mentioned above (except Section 1639), the rule-based algorithm can be programmatically implemented. First, the algorithm will identify and record the number of living heirs of the highest degree. Nonetheless, if there exist heirs according to both Section 1629 (1) and (2), this algorithm will count all heirs from both classes. Then, the system will allocate a portion of the inheritor's estate to the lawful spouse using the above-mentioned criteria. Subsequently, the remaining inheritance will be distributed to the eligible heir equally by utilizing the remaining inheritance fraction as a dividend and the number previously obtained as a divisor. After that, the entitlement portion of the inheritance will be allocated to each node accordingly. An example of the rule-based allocation process is depicted in Fig. 2.

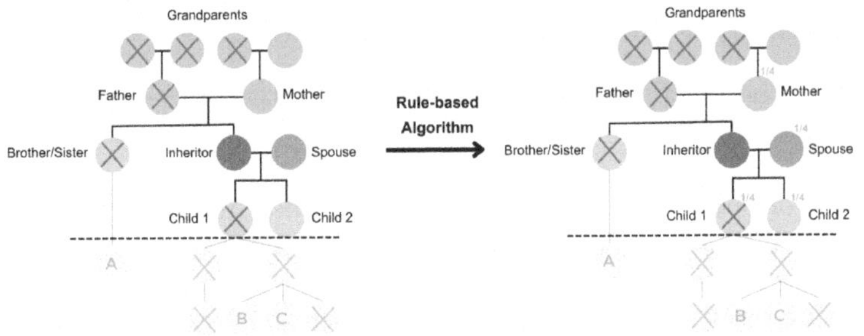

Fig. 2. The diagram demonstrates the calculation using the rule-based algorithm on an example case. According to Section 1630, the surviving parent and surviving child are entitled to an equal share of the estate. Additionally, the surviving legitimate spouse is entitled to the same share as a child, as stated in Section 1635 (1). Although Child 1 is already deceased, it has representative heirs who are alive. Therefore, the system allocates the same equal share to such node, which will be used for further processing using the tree-based algorithm.

2.2 Recursive Tree Construction

The rule-based algorithm described in the previous section allows us to compute the allocation ratio for all six classes of the statutory heir and spouse. However, it cannot deal with the rights of representation. Therefore, a particular algorithm designed to handle such cases is necessary. Among numerous existing algorithms and data structures, we reckon that the tree data structure seems to be the most suitable. The chief rationale behind using the tree-based structure to cope with the rights of representation case is that, as described in Sect. 2.1, the right to inherit of heirs according to Section 1639 can be bequeathed to the direct descendant of such heirs over and over until it reaches the first surviving heir of the stirpes.

Moreover, it is possible that at each generation the stirpes may also split into multiple sub-stirpes. As a result, we decided to use a non-binary tree data structure with recursive construction. The non-binary tree allows each branch to split into multiple sub-branches, and tree construction using recursion allows for more dynamic tree formation without the need for a predetermined structure of the final tree.

The recursive tree construction algorithm works as follows. First, the algorithm determines the root node of the tree, which is the heir node as per Section 1629 (1), (3), (4), or (6), which has some living representative heir. Then the algorithm identifies whether the root has any child nodes. If no child nodes exist, the algorithm immediately terminates by returning the root node. Otherwise, all the child nodes will be added to the children's list of the root. Subsequently, the algorithm will recursively call itself on each child node, ensuring that all the nodes that correspond to the representative heir in the following generations are linked to the root node forming a complete non-binary tree as required for the following step.

2.3 Bottom-Up Pruning and Inheritance Allocation

Nevertheless, the inheritance allocation process for the representative heirs cannot yet be done directly on the constructed tree since one limitation still remains and will lead to incorrect allocation results. Such a limitation is the existence of a branch or sub-branch of the representative heir wherein every individual in such branch is already deceased or so-called "the deceased branch". Without the further processing step to eliminate such a branch before we calculate the allocation result, leading to nodes within such a deceased branch incorrectly receive the fraction of the inheritance. To address this problem, we developed a "Bottom-up pruning" algorithm to remove the deceased branch. The idea underlying this algorithm is to step back and prune the irrelevant node along the deceased branch recursively until it finally arrives at its root node or all irrelevant nodes are pruned out. To clarify, this recursive algorithm will be called by all dead leaf nodes. Then it will begin by first checking whether such a node is a root or not, if it is a root such a node will be returned and the recursion will be terminated, otherwise, the algorithm will step back to the parent of this node.

After that, it checks whether there is any alive leaf node of the node that calls the algorithm (not parent node) or not, if there exists none of the alive leaves of such node then we will remove such node from the list of children node of its parent, effectively pruning it from the tree. Lastly, the algorithm will be called on the parent to continue this process up the tree until it reaches the root node or all necessary pruning has been completed.

After obtaining these pruned trees, the final step is to perform the inheritance allocation for the representative heirs by propagating the inheritance from its root nodes down each pruned tree recursively. Technically, each root node (the heir node with representative according to Section 1639) will call the recursive function for inheritance allocation propagation. This function will first inspect the root node for its children, in cases where no child node is present the recursion is terminated, returning the node calling this function. Conversely, if some child nodes do exist, the algorithm will count the number of all child nodes, then divide the allocation ratio of the calling node by such number, essentially splitting the allocation ratio equally among representative heirs of the same level, before assigning this new value to all child nodes. After that, these child nodes will in turn call the allocation propagation function to continue the recursion until all the representative heirs receive their inheritance ratio. Lastly, the algorithm will return the allocation result of all alive nodes that receive the fraction of inheritance. Figure 3 displays the bottom-up pruning and allocation step, which is the subsequent step of the rule-based algorithm shown in Fig. 2.

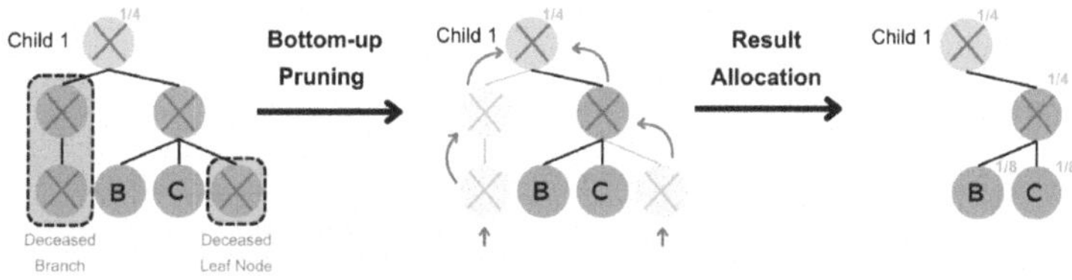

Fig. 3. The illustration of the tree-based algorithm process including the bottom-up pruning algorithm and result allocation. The process begins at the deceased leaf node and steps back to its parent until it reaches the root node and pruning out the deceased node along the way. Finally, the allocation result then propagates down the pruned tree from the root node.

2.4 Evaluation of the Algorithm

To evaluate the proposed algorithm, we created a total of 30 different test cases, which can be categorized into three difficulty levels, easy (Test Case 1–10), moderate (Test Case 11–20), and challenging (Test Case 21–30). The easy test case is created to mainly evaluate the rule-based algorithm part, specifically, the case in which the family tree consists of the heirs according to Sections 1629 (1) and (2) only. The test cases of moderate difficulty also used to validate the rule-based algorithm, include all six classes of statutory heirs as per Section 1629 in the family tree. Lastly, challenging test cases are created to ensure that the tree-based algorithm, which was developed to handle the right of representation as stipulated in Section 1639, can perform the calculation and allocation accurately. The calculation result produced by the algorithm for each test case then underwent the validation step performed by human evaluators.

3 Results and Discussion

In this work, we developed an algorithm to calculate the intestate inheritance distribution according to the CCC. The algorithm takes the family tree represented as lists of nodes and edges as input and performs the calculation accordingly, resulting in a list of the proportion of the inheritor's estate entitled to each eligible heir per the law. The algorithm works by first utilizing the rule-based algorithm to allocate the results among the six classes of statutory heirs (Section 1629), as the example shown in Fig. 2. After that, if the statutory heir who deceased before the de cujus but is eligible for inheritance has the representative according to Section 1639, the algorithm will further use the tree-based algorithm to process such cases. The tree-based algorithm mainly consists of three phases, namely recursive tree-construction, described in Sect. 2.2, and the bottom-up pruning algorithm and result allocation step, as explained in Sect. 2.3 and Fig. 3. Finally, the algorithm returns the final allocation result of each eligible heir as depicted in Fig. 4.

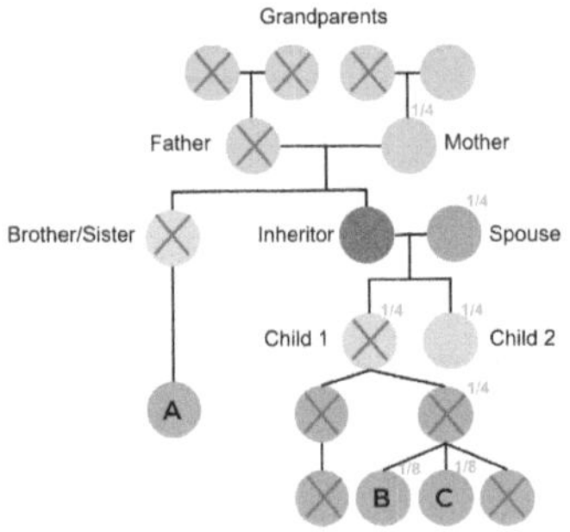

Allocation Result	
Mother	1/4
Spouse	1/4
Child 2	1/4
Representative B	1/8
Represenative C	1/8

Fig. 4. The final allocation result of an example family tree. The allocation result table in this figure shows the fraction of estate entitled to each heir. Note that the fraction assigned to the deceased node in the family tree is only done to propagate the result to the surviving descendants of the stirpes. Hence, this value is advertently excluded from the final allocation result table.

Then, the proposed algorithm was evaluated against a total of 30 test cases with three difficulty levels to ensure its validity. Table 1 comprised of four columns including `Test Case` column indexing the test case we used to evaluate our algorithm, `Heir List` determine all heirs presented in a given test case, and `Allocation Result` list the fraction of inheritance received by each heir ordered in respect of the heir list. As demonstrated in Table 1, our proposed algorithm can correctly calculate every single test case. This potentially results from the carefully craft rule-based algorithm extracted from legal understanding and logic along with the tree-based algorithm to operate recursively which allows it to handle the complicated inheritance allocation according to the right of representation. This algorithm can operate flawlessly in an intestate inheritance allocation case but it does not account for a testate case where the inheritor has established the final will. Note that the latter is out of the scope of this proposed algorithm.

Table 1. Test cases for validating the performance of the proposed intestate inheritance calculation algorithm. This proposed algorithm can correctly calculate the result for all test cases (*).

Test Case	Heirs List	Allocation Result* (All are correct.)
1	F, M	1, 0
2	$F, M, C1, C2$	1/4, 1/4, 1/4, 1/4
3	$F, M, SP, C1$	0, 0, 1/2, 1/2
4	$F, M, SP, C1$	0, 0, 0, 1
5	$F, M, SP, C1$	Devolve on the state
6	$F, M, SP, C1$	1/4, 1/4, 1/2, 0
7	$F, M, SP, C1, C2, C3$	1/5, 1/5, 1/5, 1/5, 1/5, 0
8	$F, M, SP, C1, C2, C3$	1/3, 0, 1/3, 0, 0, 1/3
9	$F, M, SP, C1, C2, C3$	1/6, 1/6, 1/6, 1/6, 1/6, 1/6
10	$F, M, SP, C1, C2, C3, C4$	0, 1/3, 0, 0, 1/3, 0, 1/3
11	$F, M, SP, SB1, SB2$	0, 0, 1/2, 1/4, 1/4
12	$F, M, SP, SB1, SB2$	0, 0, 1/2, 0, 1/2
13	$G1, G2, G3, G4, F, M, SP$	1/6, 0, 0, 1/6, 0, 0, 2/3
14	$F, M, SP, HS1, HS2, C1$	0, 0, 2/3, 0, 1/3, 0
15	$G1, G2, G3, G4, F, M, UA1, SP, C1$	0, 0, 0, 0, 1/4, 1/4, 0, 1/4, 1/4
16	$G1, G2, G3, G4, F, M, UA1, UA2, SP$	0, 0, 0, 0, 0, 0, 1/3, 0, 2/3
17	$F, M, SP, SB1, SB2, HS1, C1, C2, C3$	0, 0, 0, 1/2, 1/2, 0, 0, 0, 0
18	$G1, G2, G3, G4, F, M, SP, SB1, C1, C2, C3$	0, 0, 0, 0, 1/3, 0, 1/3, 0, 0, 1/3, 0
19	$G1, G2, G3, G4, F, M, SP, SB1, C1, C2, C3$	Devolve on the state
20	$G1, G2, G3, G4, F, M, UA1, UA2, SP, C1, C2$	0, 0, 0, 0, 0, 0, 0, 0, 1/3, 1/3, 1/3
21	$F, M, SP, C1, C2, R1_{C2}, R2_{C2}, R3_{R1}$	0, 1/3, 1/3, 1/3, 0, 0, 0, 0
22	$F, M, SP, C1, C2, R1_{C1}, R2_{C1}, R3_{C1}, R4_{R2}, R5_{R2}$	1/5, 1/5, 1/5, 0, 1/5, 1/15, 0, 1/15, 1/30, 1/30
23	$F, M, SB1, C1, C2, C3, C4, C5, R1_{C1}, R2_{C2}, R3_{C2}, R4_{C3}, R5_{C4}, R6_{R5}, R7_{C5}$	1/7, 1/7, 0, 0, 0, 0, 0, 0, 1/7, 1/14, 1/14, 1/7, 0, 1/7, 1/7

(continued)

Table 1. (*continued*)

Test Case	Heirs List	Allocation Result* (All are correct.)
24	$F, M, SP, SB1, SB2, C1, C2, R1_{SB1}, R2_{SB1}, R3_{SB2}, R4_{SB2}$	0, 0, 1/2, 0, 0, 0, 0, 1/4, 0, 1/8, 1/8
25	$F, M, SP, SB1, SB2, HS1, HS2, HS3, C1, R1_{SB1}, R2_{SB2}, R3_{HS1}, R4_{HS1}$	0, 0, 2/3, 0, 0, 0, 1/9, 1/9, 0, 0, 0, 1/18, 1/18
26	$G1, G2, G3, G4, F, M, UA1, UA2, SP, R1_{UA1}, R2_{UA1}, R3_{R1}$	0, 0, 0, 0, 0, 0, 0, 1/6, 2/3, 0, 0, 1/6
27	$G1, G2, G3, G4, F, M, UA1, SP, C1, C2, C3, R1_{C1}, R2_{C1}, R3_{R1}, R4_{R1}, R5_{UA1}$	0, 0, 0, 0, 0, 0, 0, 1/3, 0, 0, 1/3, 0, 1/6, 1/12, 1/12, 0
28	$F, M, SP, SB1, C1, C2, C3, R1_{C1}, R2_{C1}, R3_{R2}, R4_{SB1}$	1/3, 1/3, 0, 0, 0, 0, 0, 1/3, 0, 0, 0
29	$G1, G2, G3, G4, F, M, SP, SB1, C1, C2, R1_{C1}, R2_{C1}, R3_{R1}, R4_{R2}, R5_{R2}, R6_{R2}, R7_{SB1}$	0, 0, 0, 0, 0, 1/4, 1/4, 0, 0, 1/4, 0, 0, 0, 1/8, 1/8, 0, 0
30	$F, M, SP, SB1, C1, C2, C3, R1_{C1}, R2_{C1}, R3_{R2}, R4_{SB1}$	Devolve on the state

Remarks I: F = legitimate father, M = mother, SP = legitimate spouse, Ci = the ith child, SBi = the ith sibling, HSi = the ith half-sibling, $G1$ = Paternal grandfather, $G2$ = Paternal grandmother, $G3$ = Maternal grandfather, $G4$ = Maternal grandmother, UAi = the ith uncles or aunts, Ri_x = the representative heir of heir x with running number i. Where i is a positive integer.
Remarks II: The child or descendant of the de cujus may refer to a legitimate child, an illegitimate child who gets registered as a lawful child by the de cujus (father), or a legally adopted child according to Section 1627 of the CCC.
Remarks III: Any heir marked in red implies that such heir is deceased (died) or being excluded before the death of the de cujus.

4 Conclusion and Future Work

This work proposed an algorithm to automate intestate inheritance allocation according to the CCC by combining the rule-based logic from the law code with a recursive tree construction and bottom-up pruning algorithms to handle the complex case of rights of representation. The evaluation of the proposed algorithm against multiple test cases shows that the algorithm accurately distributes inheritance according to the intestate inheritance rule. This algorithm can potentially lead to more efficient processing of legal cases related to intestate inheritance and reduces the workload for legal professionals. Future directions include integrating this algorithm into a legal assistance application with a chat-like interface for interacting with the user and developing a web application to visualize the family tree and calculate the allocation result. This would ultimately result in a tool that allows individuals, with or without knowledge of the underlying legal provision, to calculate inheritance conveniently and accurately.

Acknowledgments. The first author (So.C.) acknowledges the ETS Scholarship awarded by Sirindhorn International Institute of Technology, Thammasat University.

Disclosure of Interests. The authors have no competing interests to declare that are relevant to the content of this article.

References

1. Aguiar, A., Silveira, R., Pinheiro, V., Furtado, V., Neto, J.A.: Text classification in legal documents extracted from lawsuits in Brazilian courts. In: Britto, A., Valdivia Delgado, K. (eds.) BRACIS 2021. LNCS (LNAI), vol. 13074, pp. 586–600. Springer, Cham (2021). https://doi.org/10.1007/978-3-030-91699-2_40
2. Bin Awae, I., Limsiroratana, S.: Inheritance management method for set of indivisible item based on islamic law. In: Proceedings of the 2017 International Conference on Data Mining, Communications and Information Technology, pp. 1–6 (2017)
3. Chalkidis, I., Fergadiotis, M., Malakasiotis, P., Aletras, N., Androutsopoulos, I.: LEGAL-BERT: the muppets straight out of law school. In: Cohn, T., He, Y., Liu, Y. (eds.) Findings of the Association for Computational Linguistics: EMNLP 2020, pp. 2898–2904. Association for Computational Linguistics, Online (2020). https://doi.org/10.18653/v1/2020.findings-emnlp.261. https://aclanthology.org/2020.findings-emnlp.261
4. Cheema, S.: Distribution of inheritance under islamic law: an appraisal of online inheritance calculators. J. Islamic Thought Civilizat. **11**(1), 112–131 (2021)
5. Chen, H., Wu, L., Chen, J., Lu, W., Ding, J.: A comparative study of automated legal text classification using random forests and deep learning. Inf. Process. Manag. **59**(2), 102798 (2022)
6. Kowsrihawat, K., Vateekul, P., Boonkwan, P.: Predicting judicial decisions of criminal cases from thai supreme court using bi-directional gru with attention mechanism. In: 2018 5th Asian Conference on Defense Technology (ACDT), pp. 50–55. IEEE (2018)
7. Nguyen, H.T., Phi, M.K., Ngo, X.B., Tran, V., Nguyen, L.M., Tu, M.P.: Attentive deep neural networks for legal document retrieval. Artif. Intell. Law **32**(1), 57–86 (2024)
8. Shaheen, Z., Wohlgenannt, G., Filtz, E.: Large scale legal text classification using transformer models. arXiv preprint arXiv:2010.12871 (2020)
9. Socatiyanurak, V., et al.: Law-u: legal guidance through artificial intelligence chatbot for sexual violence victims and survivors. IEEE Access **9**, 131440–131461 (2021). https://doi.org/10.1109/ACCESS.2021.3113172
10. Soonthornpan, P.: Problems concerning the representation of the heir for the purpose of receiving inheritance. KASEM BUNDIT J. **17**(2), 1–15 (2016). https://so04.tcithaijo.org/index.php/jkbu/article/view/72242
11. Strickson, B., De La Iglesia, B.: Legal judgement prediction for UK courts. In: Proceedings of the 3rd International Conference on Information Science and Systems, pp. 204–209 (2020)
12. Sugathadasa, K., et al.: Legal document retrieval using document vector embeddings and deep learning. In: Arai, K., Kapoor, S., Bhatia, R. (eds.) SAI 2018. AISC, vol. 857, pp. 160–175. Springer, Cham (2019). https://doi.org/10.1007/978-3-030-01177-2_12
13. Zouaoui, S., Rezeg, K.: Islamic inheritance calculation system based on Arabic ontology (arafamonto). J. King Saud Univ.-Comput. Inf. Sci. **33**(1), 68–76 (2021)

Numerical Modelling of River Flood: A Case Study in the Nhat Le River Basin, Vietnam

Nguyen Van Luc[1], Dinh Nhat Quang[1], Nguyen Trung Viet[1], Huynh Quang Nghi[2], and Nguyen Ngoc Doanh[2(✉)]

[1] Thuyloi University, 175 Tay Son, Dong Da, Hanoi, Vietnam
[2] COSMOS Lab, Center For Environmental Intelligence and College of Engineering and Computer Science, VinUniversity, Da Ton, Gia Lam, Hanoi, Vietnam
doanh.nn@vinuni.edu.vn

Abstract. This paper discusses the creation and use of the numerical model for flood assessment in the Nhat Le river basin, Vietnam. In particular, the hydrodynamic model based on Mike Flood has been calibrated and validated with the observed water levels at gauging stations, flood marks, and flood extent derived from Sentinel 1 satellite imagery in the historical flood events of October 2010 and October 2020. The well-validated model was adopted to determine the flood damage risk for the structures and relevant elements located in the basin. The developed mathematical model allows one to assess the flood risk in the Nhat Le river basin, as well as the implementing and planning for individual recovery measures and general shelter. It can also be used to help make decisions like any combination of land use, land-cover types, socio-economic activities, building patterns, and flood control strategies.

Keywords: Numerical modelling · flood inundation modelling · river flooding · flood risk · flood control strategies · decision-support system

1 Introduction

Flooding is the phenomenon of river water rising over a certain period and then receding. Among various types of natural disasters, floods are always regarded as one of the most common and severe, causing significant consequences throughout human history. Most countries around the world regularly suffer from the impacts of flooding disasters. According to calculations by the Swiss Re Institute, floods caused over USD 82 billion in global economic losses in 2021, accounting for nearly one-third of total natural disaster-related losses. In Europe alone, floods caused USD 43 billion in damage and resulted in 240 deaths; in Henan Province, China, the economic loss was USD 17.5 billion, with 320 fatalities, and more than a million people displaced. These figures are based on insurance claims, so the actual figures are likely much higher.

Vietnam is one of the countries heavily affected by flooding. The mortality rate among populations directly exposed to storms and floods is 0.3% [1]. According to statistics from the Department of Dyke Management and Disaster Prevention, Typhoon

J. Kertesz et al. (Eds.): CSoNet 2024, LNCS 15417, pp. 280–291, 2025.
https://doi.org/10.1007/978-981-96-6389-7_25

Yagi (September 2024) alone resulted in 292 deaths, 37 missing persons, and economic losses exceeding USD 2 billion. Every year, the East Sea experiences between 6 and 10 typhoons. Quang Binh province, located in central Vietnam, has a narrow and steep terrain, sloping from west to east. Rivers and streams are short and steep, causing floods to rise rapidly and flow at high speeds. This characteristic makes floods a highly destructive natural disaster for the province. Between 2007 and 2011, Quang Binh experienced 16 floods, causing 93 deaths and 354 injuries [1]. According to the report of Quang Binh province, in 2022, floods submerged 914 houses, caused 8,300 m of irrigation canals and 2,400 m of dikes to erode or be washed away, damaged two reservoirs, and flooded 9,380 ha of rice fields, 557 ha of crops, and 917 ha of aquaculture. Additionally, roads and coastal areas suffered severe erosion, with total damages estimated at VND 286.7 billion.

With the concern of various countries and socio-economic organizations, numerous projects aimed at enhancing disaster response capabilities have been implemented, especially in developing countries [2]. Of these, flood early warning systems are a top priority [3]. The development of warning systems and the dissemination of information about flood situations play a crucial role in flood prevention and control. The prompt, continuous, and timely delivery of information enables authorities at all levels, sectors, and residents to be proactive in flood response. The sooner this information reaches users, the more effective the preventive and responsive measures. Timely and appropriate flood prevention measures can minimize damage caused by floods and also save costs in organizing preventive actions.

Many scientists have made efforts to research solutions for predicting and controlling flood situations to minimize their harmful effects [3]. Calculating design floods, flood management, and flood forecasting are essential scientific tasks and are integral to the design, evaluation, and operation of reservoirs [4]. A flood event can be described by a multivariable function, including peak flow, total flood volume, and flood duration [5]. While bridge, culvert, or channel design often focuses on determining the peak flow corresponding to a specific frequency, it is crucial to consider the entire flood event when designing dams and reservoirs.

The pressing issue is how to model flood events, providing a basis for flood forecasting and warning, helping residents and authorities proactively and flexibly respond. The most common method of flood simulation today is the use of physically-based models [6], which simulate and predict flood-related information (such as peak flow, flood depth, inundation extent, and flood duration) using hydrological and hydraulic models. With detailed input data and extended computation periods, physical-based models offer highly accurate results. However, this approach is mainly used for validating results, training datasets, or studying and assessing the causes and mechanisms of past floods, providing valuable knowledge to improve flood risk management methods. Popular models include Delft3D, MIKE, SOBEK-1D, and HEC-RAS [7–10].

This paper aims at developing the numerical model for flood inundation in Nhat Le river basin in Vietnam as well as assess the effects of the historical flood event in 2020.

This study endeavors to construct a numerical model capable of accurately simulating flood inundation within the Nhat Le river basin in Vietnam. By leveraging advanced modeling techniques, the research seeks to comprehend the complex hydrodynamics governing flood events in this region. Furthermore, the developed model will be applied to retrospectively analyze the historical flood of 2020, aiming to gain valuable insights into the extent of inundation, peak water levels, and potential impacts on local communities. This analysis will provide a foundation for informed decision-making regarding flood risk management and mitigation strategies in the Nhat Le river basin.

The paper is organized as follows: Sect. 2 is about study area and data collection; Sect. 3 presents numerical modelling for flood inundation including model setup, model calibration and validation, and results discussion; Sect. 4 is dedicated to conclusion.

2 Study Area and Data Collection

2.1 Study Area

The Nhat Le River Basin, located in Quang Binh province, Vietnam, is a crucial hydrological system susceptible to frequent flooding events (see Fig. 1a). The basin's topography, characterized by mountainous terrain and narrow valleys, combined with heavy monsoon rainfall, creates favorable conditions for floods (see Fig. 1c). The region's geological structure, consisting of limestone formations with limited infiltration capacity, further exacerbates the flooding risk. Additionally, deforestation and land degradation within the basin have contributed to increased erosion and sedimentation, clogging river channels and reducing their capacity to handle floodwaters. These factors, coupled with climate change-induced shifts in rainfall patterns, have made the Nhat Le River Basin particularly vulnerable to flooding, posing significant threats to local communities and infrastructure.

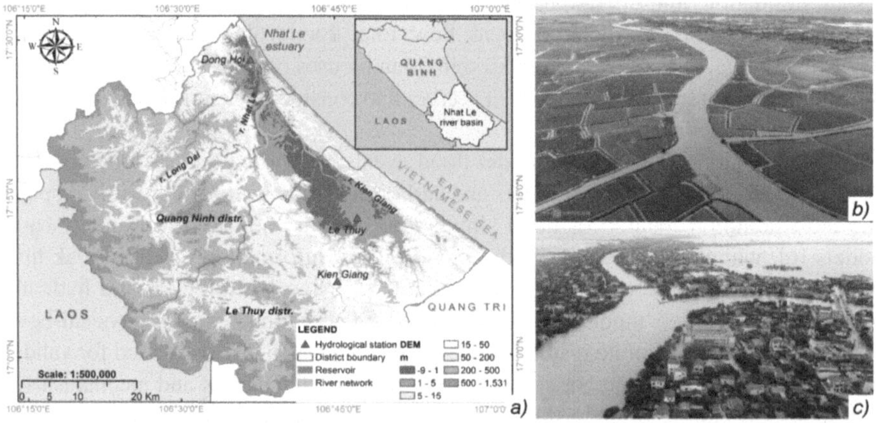

Fig. 1. (a) Nhat Le river basin; (b) Kien Giang river; and (c) Flooding in Kien Giang river

The Nhat Le River system comprises three primary tributaries: Kien Giang, Long Dai, and Le Thuy. These rivers originate in the mountainous regions of central Quang Binh, converging to form the Nhat Le River, which flows eastward through the province before emptying into the East Vietnamese Sea. The interplay between these tributaries contributes to the unique hydrological dynamics of the Nhat Le River system, which plays a crucial role in supporting local livelihoods and ecosystems.

The October 2020 floods in Quang Binh province, particularly affecting the Nhat Le River basin, were a historic event. A series of tropical storms and depressions, combined with heavy rainfall, led to unprecedented water levels and widespread flooding. The Nhat Le River basin, already prone to flooding due to its geographical characteristics, experienced severe inundation, causing significant damage to infrastructure, agriculture, and residential areas. The floodwaters overwhelmed levees, inundated villages, and disrupted transportation networks. The event highlighted the vulnerability of the region to extreme weather events and underscored the need for improved flood management strategies and infrastructure to mitigate future impacts.

2.2 Data Collection

To develop accurate and reliable flood inundation model for Nhat Le river basin, a diverse range of data was collected as follows:

i) **Topographic data** such as digital elevation models (DEMs); topographic maps on a scale of 1:2,000 (for Dong Hoi city) and 1:10,000 (for Le Thuy and Quang Ninh districts) collected from the Department of Surveying, Mapping, and Geographic Information of Vietnam; cross-sectional data for 11 rivers from several research projects and studies undertaken within the study region (see Table 1). These data provide detailed information on land surface elevations and watercourse networks.

Table 1. Collected cross-sectional data of the Nhat Le river system.

No.	River	Length (km)	Number of sections	Surveyed year
1	Kien Giang	50.3	66	2019, 2021,2022
2	Long Dai	34.9	48	2019, 2021
3	Nhat Le	16.9	30	2019, 2021
4	Le Ky	17.4	32	2019, 2021
5	Hoi Dai	7.0	12	2019
6	Sao Vang	6.8	9	2019
7	Phu Vinh	12.4	27	2021
8	Cam Ly	10.7	11	2021
9	Phu Hoa	11.0	09	2022
10	An Ma	6.7	07	2021
11	Thanh Son	14.0	13	2021

ii) **Hydrological data**, encompassing precipitation records, river flow measurements, and water level gauges, are crucial for understanding the dynamics of water movement. Within this research, hydrological data at three stations: Kien Giang, Le Thuy, and Dong Hoi were collected and used for calibrating and validating the numerical model.

iii) **Flood marks and flood extent**: In order to calibrate and validate the hydrodynamic and inundation model for the Nhat Le River basin, data on flood marks observed during the catastrophic flood events of October 2010 and October 2020 had been gathered (see Fig. 2a). In addition, surface water on October 18th, 2020 was extracted from Sentinel-1 radar images by utilizing remote sensing and Google Earth Engine [11] in order to validate the simulated inundation area (see Fig. 2b). These data were crucial for model domain selection and validation of flood simulation results.

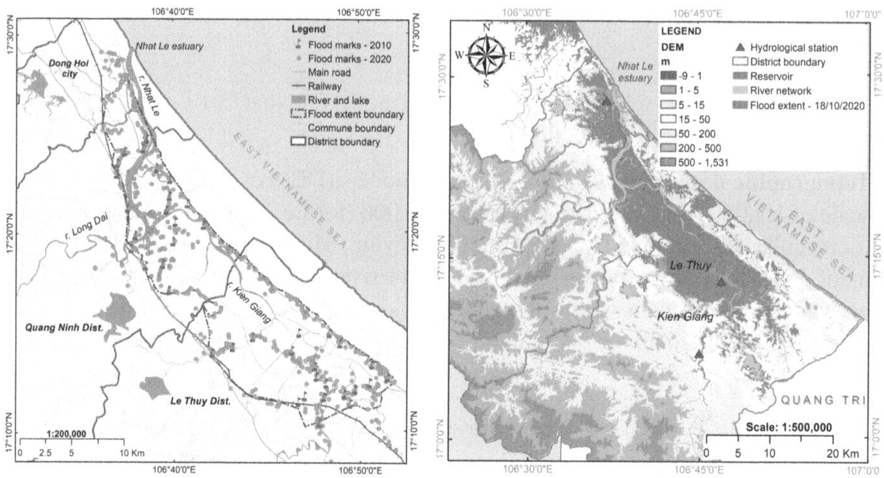

Fig. 2. (a) Flood marks in 2010 and 2020; b) Flood extent on the 18th of October 2020, derived from Sentinel 1 image

3 Numerical Modelling for Flood Inundation

Numerical models are widely employed to simulate flood inundation, providing valuable insights into flood extent, depth, and velocity. These models typically involve several key steps as presented in Fig. 3.

Model Selection: Appropriate numerical models are chosen based on factors such as the scale of the study area, complexity of the terrain, and desired level of detail. The MIKE software suite, developed by the Danish Hydraulic Institute, serves as the foundation for the modeling tools employed to simulate flooding in the Nhat Le River basin. This selection is driven by its comprehensive capabilities and robust numerical methods. MIKE's ability to integrate hydrodynamic and hydrological processes allows for a holistic understanding of flood dynamics. Its advanced numerical methods enable high-resolution simulations, capturing intricate details of flood extent, depth, and velocity.

Additionally, MIKE's user-friendly interface, extensive database, and global applications make it a versatile and reliable tool for flood modeling in various geographic and climatic settings.

Data Acquisition: Essential data for model calibration and validation were gathered, including topographic data, hydrological data, historical flood marks and flood extent as presented in SubSect. 2.2.

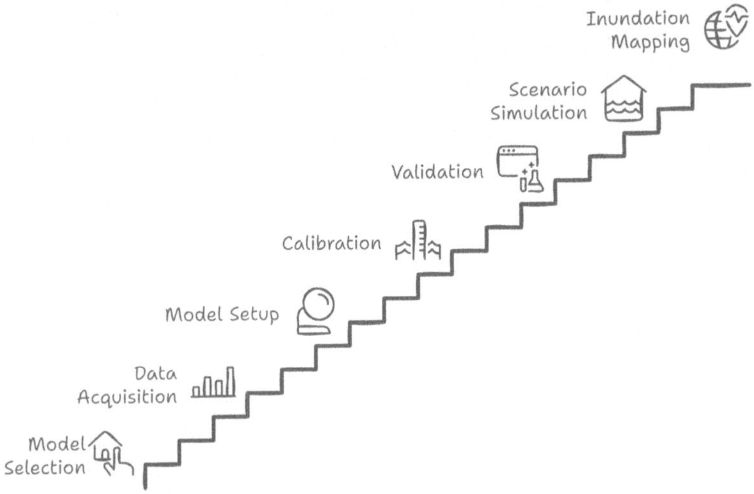

Fig. 3. Flowchart for Flood Inundation modelling

3.1 Model Setup for Nhat Le River Basin

Model Domain: A 2D flood model was developed to simulate overland flow in the Nhat Le River basin, with its domain defined based on historical flood marks and flood extent derived from Sentinel-1 during the historical flood events in October 2020. The domain encompasses the entire area of interest, including the river basin, floodplain, and potential areas of flooding (see Fig. 4).

Mesh Generation: Mesh generation is a critical step in flood inundation modeling, as it discretizes the continuous space into a finite number of elements. Balancing computational cost with desired accuracy, the finite element mesh discretizes the study area into 63,362 nodes and over 104,077 elements (see Fig. 4a). The element size in plain areas, residential areas, and areas near structures (e.g., transportation systems, irrigation canals, dikes, etc.) is set to 50–100 m, 30–40 m, and 5–10 m, respectively. In addition, to account for the influence of topographic variations, a high-density transportation network was integrated into the 2D flood inundation model. The model specifically considers the impact of major transportation routes like National Highway (NH) 1, NH 1A, and the Ho Chi Minh Highway, etc., which play a crucial role in surface runoff and were thus incorporated into the model.

2D Terrain Digitalization: Figure 4b presents the terrain generated for the 2D model based on the terrain data described in SubSect. 2.2 and interpolated using the aforementioned grid system. The computed terrain is highly detailed, including the elevated contours of hills and coastal dunes, as well as the flood-prone areas in the centers of Le Thuy, Quang Ninh districts, and Dong Hoi city.

Coupling of 1D and 2D Models in Mike Flood: enhances flood inundation modeling by capturing both river behavior and floodplain dynamics. It is worth noting that the 1D model (Mike 11) for Nhat Le river system was inherited from the Project "*Research on Digital Transformation in the Flood Warning Methods for the Community: An Experimental Flood Warning System for Nhat Le river basin, Quang Binh Province*" funded by Ministry of Agricultural and Rural Development and was well validated using river water level data from gauging sites during the historical flood events in 2010 and 2020. The 2D model (Mike 21) operates in two dimensions, allowing for spatially distributed simulations across the floodplain. Mike 21 uses lateral links to connect with Mike 11, forming the Mike Flood model setup as shown in Fig. 4b.

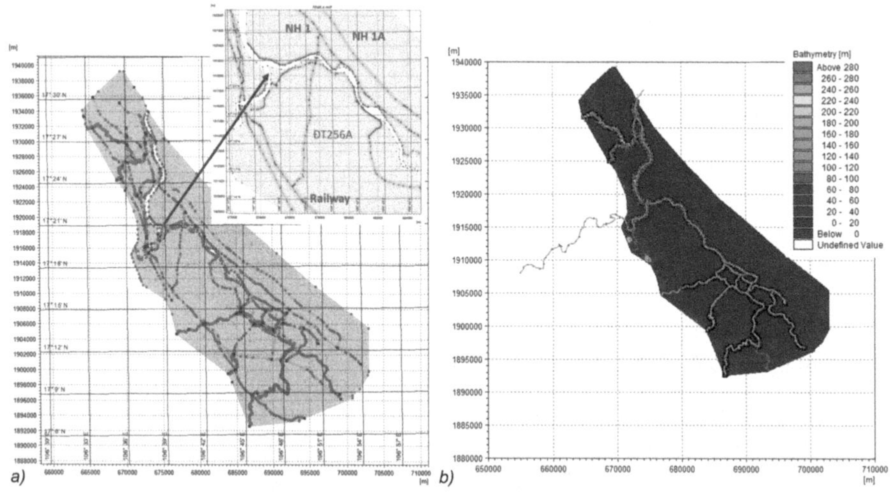

Fig. 4. (a) 2D model domain and mesh; and (b) coupling of 1D and 2D models in Mike Flood

3.2 Model Calibration and Validation

Calibration and validation are critical steps in the development and application of flood inundation models. Calibration involves adjusting model parameters to ensure that the model accurately reproduces historical flood events. Within this research, the model's performance was evaluated against the October 2010 flood using the observed water levels at gauging stations and 25 flood marks recorded in the study area in 2010. Figure 5 indicated a good fit between the simulated and observed hydrographs: i) the peak water level error was minimal at 0.09 m; and ii) the Nash-Sutcliffe efficiency was a satisfactory 0.811.

Figure 6 shows a comparison between the simulated maximum inundation depths and the observed flood elevations in 2010. The model's performance is validated by the close agreement between the simulated and measured data. While there are some minor discrepancies in water levels, the overall accuracy of the model is high, with less than a 20% difference. Figure 7 presents the modeling results of flood inundation in the Nhat Le river basin, overlaid with the locations of flood marks from 2010. This indicates that the calibrated 2D model is reliable for further applications.

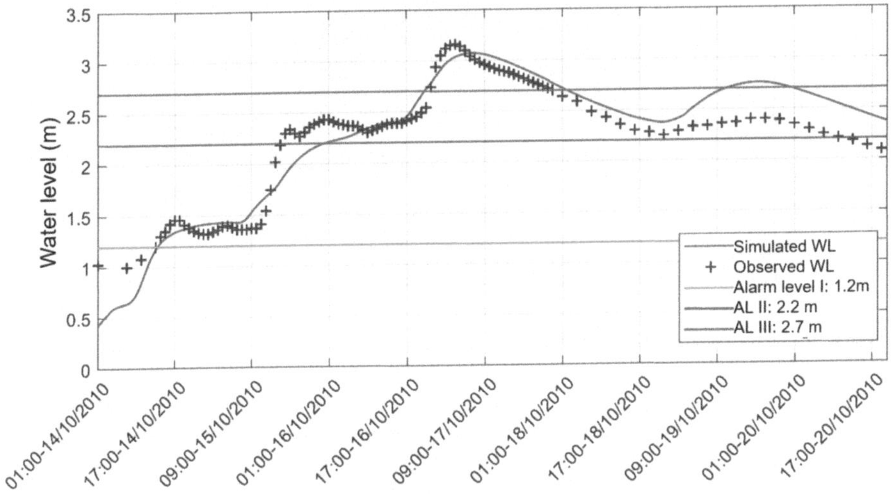

Fig. 5. Comparison of simulated and observed water level hydrographs at Le Thuy station during the October 2010 flood

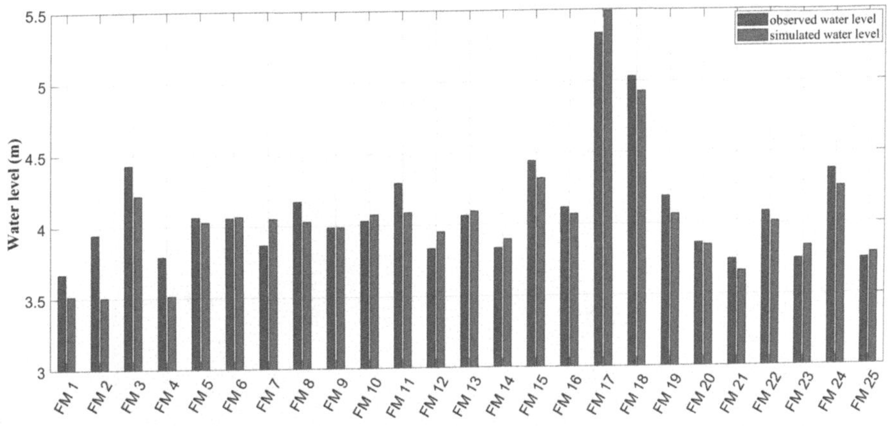

Fig. 6. Comparison of water surface elevation and extracted data at flood mark locations from the 2010 flood simulation results

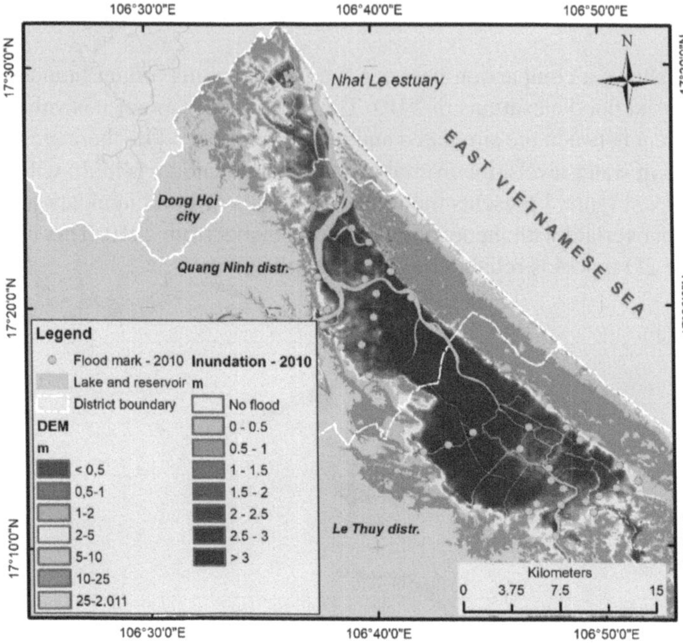

Fig. 7. Flood marks and simulated flood inundation during the flood events in October 2010

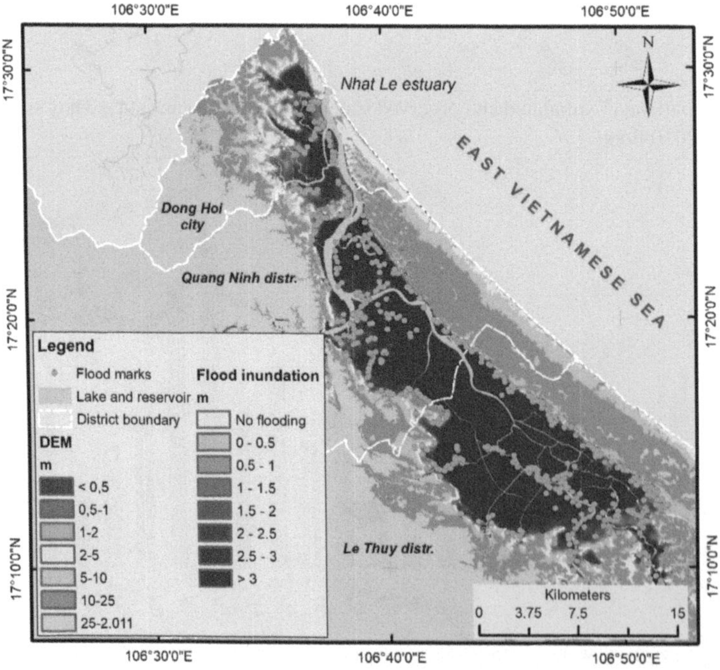

Fig. 8. Flood marks and simulated flood inundation during the flood events in October 2020

Further validation was conducted using the October 2020 flood event. Figure 8 displays the simulated flood inundation, while Fig. 2b presents the interpreted flood inundation from radar imagery on October 18, 2020. A comparison of the two reveals a high degree of agreement. The main discrepancies occur in the coastal dune areas, which are sparsely populated and thus have minimal impact on the overall assessment. These discrepancies are considered negligible given the model's limitations. Table 2 quantifies the discrepancy between the simulated and radar-derived inundated areas on October 18, 2020. The results show a close match, with the radar image analysis indicating a total inundated area of 22,602 ha, which is only 114 ha or 0.51% greater than the simulated area. These findings highlight the accuracy of the numerical model in predicting flood extent.

Table 2. Comparison of flooded areas between simulation results and satellite image analysis.

District/City	Flooded area (ha)		Difference	Difference
	Satellite	Simulation	(ha)	(%)
Le Thuy	12,423.32	12,006.59	416.73	1.85%
Quang Ninh	7,880.72	7,798.32	82.40	0.37%
Dong Hoi	2,298.16	2,683.23	(385.07)	1.71%
Total	**22,602.20**	**22,488.13**		**3.93%**

The calibrated 2D flood model, which was calibrated using 2010 inundation depth data and validated against 2020 observations, has proven to be accurate and reliable. This model can be confidently used for subsequent research.

3.3 Inundated Area and Affected Building

Figure 8 presents the simulated flood inundation of the Nhat Le river basin corresponding to the flood event from October 14–24, 2022. The inundated areas are primarily concentrated in low-lying areas (elevation 2–5 m) between the mountainous region and the dune areas (elevation 5–30 m). The bar chart in Fig. 9a showing the inundated area in hectares (ha) for Le Thuy and Quang Ninh districts and Dong Hoi city under different categories of flood depth. Some key observations are: i) Le Thuy has the largest inundated area, followed by Quang Ninh and Dong Hoi. Most of the inundated area in Le Thuy and Quang Ninh districts is due to flooding depths between 1–2 m and 2–3 m; ii) Dong Hoi city has a significant portion of its inundated area due to flooding depths greater than 3 m; iii) Le Thuy has a small area inundated by flooding depths less than 1 m. Quang Ninh and Dong Hoi have a similar amount of area inundated by flooding depths less than 1 m and between 2–3 m. Overall, the simulation results indicate that Le Thuy district was the most severely affected by flooding, with a significant portion of its area inundated to various depths.

The bar chart in Fig. 9b showing the number of affected buildings Le Thuy and Quang Ninh districts and Dong Hoi city under different categories of flood depth. It is clearly show that: i) Le Thuy district has the highest number of affected buildings, followed by Quang Ninh district and Dong Hoi city. Most affected buildings in Le Thuy and Quang Ninh experienced flooding depths between 1–2 m; ii) Dong Hoi has a significant number of buildings affected by flooding depths greater than 3 m; and iii) Le Thuy has a small number of buildings affected by flooding depths less than 1 m. Quang Ninh and Dong Hoi have a similar number of buildings affected by flooding depths less than 1 m and between 2–3 m. Overall, the chart indicates that Le Thuy was the most severely affected by flooding, with a significant number of buildings experiencing moderate to severe flooding.

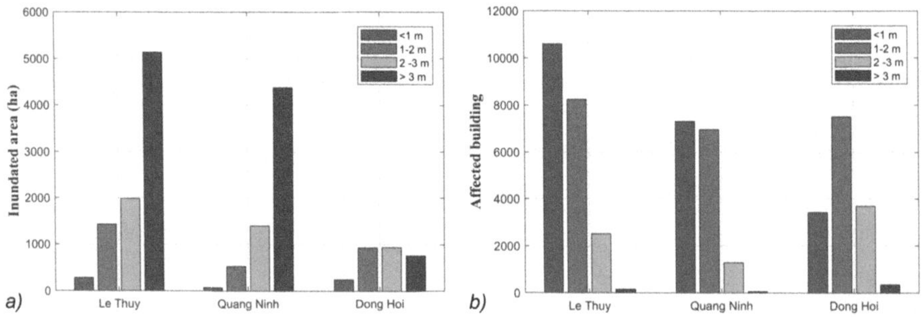

Fig. 9. (a) Inundated area; and (b) Number of affected buildings during the historical flood event in October 2020

4 Conclusions

This research has successfully developed a numerical model for flood inundation in the Nhat Le river basin, Vietnam by utilizing the MIKE software package. The model incorporates a comprehensive representation of the basin's topography and hydrological processes, enabling accurate simulations of flood extent and depth.

The model's calibration and validation against historical flood events in 2010 and 2020 demonstrated its reliability and accuracy in predicting flood inundation patterns. The findings from the model can be used to inform flood risk assessment, disaster management planning, and decision-making for infrastructure development in the Nhat Le river basin.

Acknowledgments. This research was supported by the Ministerial-level Research Project, entitled '*Research on Digital Transformation in the Flood Warning Methods for the Community: An Experimental Flood Warning System for Nhat Le river basin, Quang Binh Province*', and the research project entitled "*Coupling Mathematical Modelling and Computer Modelling Approaches to Support Flood Inundation Prediction: A Case Study of Dong Hoi City, Quang Binh Province, Vietnam*" under the program Mathematics for Humanity, International Centre for Mathematical Sciences (ICMS), Edinburgh, UK. The authors also would like to thank The Vietnamese Climate Science and Environmental Modelling Network (VCSEMN), Vietnam Institute for Advanced Study in Mathematics for providing them a great opportunity to collaborate in this project.

Disclosure of Interests. The authors declare no conflict of interest.

References

1. Bon, T.V., Ngoc, V.V., Han, P.T., Quynh, V.P.: Some research findings on human risk due to flooding in the Kien Giang and Long Dai river basins, Quang Binh province. J. Water Resour. Sci. Technol. **28** (2015)
2. Kumbier, K., Carvalho, R.C., Vafeidis, A.T., Woodroffe, C.D.: Investigating compound flooding in an estuary using hydrodynamic modelling: a case study from the Shoalhaven River, Australia. Nat. Hazards Earth Syst. Sci. **18**(2), 463–477 (2018). https://doi.org/10.5194/nhess-18-463-2018
3. Merkuryeva, G., Merkuryev, Y., Sokolov, B., Potryasaev, S., Zelentsov, V., Lektauers, A.: Advanced river flood monitoring, modelling and forecasting. J. Comput. Sci. **10** (2014). https://doi.org/10.1016/j.jocs.2014.10.004
4. Jain, S.K., Singh, V.P.: Reservoir sizing. In: Jain, S.K., Singh, V.P. (eds.) Developments in Water Science, Volume 51: Water Resources Systems Planning and Management, vol. 51, pp. 555–612. Elsevier (2003) https://doi.org/10.1016/S0167-5648(03)80064-3
5. Wang, H., et al.: Multivariable flood risk and its dynamics considering project reasonable service life in a changing environment. J. Hydrol. **590**, 125524 (2020). https://doi.org/10.1016/j.jhydrol.2020.125524
6. Micovic, Z., Schaefer, M.G., Barker, B.L.: Sensitivity and uncertainty analyses for stochastic flood hazard simulation. In: Petropoulos, G.P., Srivastava, P.K. (eds.) Sensitivity Analysis in Earth Observation Modelling, pp. 213–234. Elsevier (2017). https://doi.org/10.1016/B978-0-12-803011-0.00011-2
7. Suman, A., Akther, F.: River flood modelling using SOBEK: a case study from Ciliwung catchment, Indonesia. Int. J. Eng. Res. **3**, 662–668 (2014). https://doi.org/10.17950/ijer/v3s11/1108
8. Hoang Thai, B., Ngoc Anh, T., Dang Dinh, K.: Simulation of flood inundation using MIKE FLOOD model in Nhat Le river system - Quang Binh province. VNU J. Sci. **26**, 285–294 (2010)
9. Ghosh, M., Mohanty, M.P., Kishore, P., Karmakar, S.: Performance evaluation of potential inland flood management options through a three-way linked hydrodynamic modelling framework for a coastal urban watershed. Hydrol. Res. **52**(1), 61–77 (2020). https://doi.org/10.2166/nh.2020.123
10. Yalcin, E.: Two-dimensional hydrodynamic modelling for urban flood risk assessment using unmanned aerial vehicle imagery: a case study of Kirsehir, Turkey. J. Flood Risk Manag. **12**(S1), e12499 (2019). https://doi.org/10.1111/jfr3.12499
11. Minh, V.A., Quang, D.N., Tinh, N.X., Ribbe, L.: Spatio-temporal dynamics monitoring of surface water bodies in Nhat Le River Basin, Vietnam, by Google Earth Engine. J. Water Clim. Change **15**(3), 1262–1281 (2024). https://doi.org/10.2166/wcc.2024.574

Thai Legal Fact Classification of Property-Related Offences Using Finetuned BERT Modelling

Sirawit Chokphantavee, Sorawit Chokphantavee, and Somrudee Deepaisarn(✉)

Sirindhorn International Institute of Technology, Thammasat University, Bangkok 12120, Pathum Thani, Thailand
somrudee@siit.tu.ac.th

Abstract. Legal natural language processing has recently received a surge in interest from experts due to its potential application in various domains. One of the most popular tasks in this area is legal case categorization and judgment prediction, which can be seen as a classification problem. Previous attempts at the classification task mostly employ traditional methods, such as the static embedding method in combination with machine learning or deep learning models. Even though such approaches can achieve a notable performance, they have yet to reach state-of-the-art performance. With the significant leap in text and natural language processing, namely the advent of transformer-based models, along with their consistent improvement, we see the opportunity to adopt this development to the legal classification task. Our proposed modeling pipeline, the WangchanBERTa-SFT-sc, can outperform the baseline model using the fastText embedding method and conventional machine learning models on the binary classification of whether or not the case is related to property offence, reaching exceptional test accuracy and F1-score of 94.5%. This finding highlights the capability and importance of contextual comprehension in dealing with the text classification task in a specific and highly sophisticated environment, particularly the legal domain.

Keywords: Thai Law · Text Classification · Natural Language Processing (NLP) · Bidirectional Encoder Representations from Transformers (BERT) · Property-Related Offences

1 Introduction

Law is, undoubtedly, one of the most crucial foundations that play a significant role in upholding order and peace for any human society. Despite its importance, for a long time, those who could fully capitalize, understand, categorize, or interpret such rules were limited to solely lawyers and legal professionals. Due to the rapid population growth and, consequently, the number of cases,

J. Kertesz et al. (Eds.): CSoNet 2024, LNCS 15417, pp. 292–301, 2025.
https://doi.org/10.1007/978-981-96-6389-7_26

many legal practitioners are experiencing a substantial increase in workload. In response to this pressing issue, more researchers and computer scientists aim to address such a problem and support lawyers using advanced methods in natural language processing and artificial intelligence.

This domain, the legal natural language processing, covers a broad spectrum of tasks from information extraction [7,18], summarization [8], and document retrieval [4,15,16], to the classification of legal cases. Among these tasks, one of the approaches that attract considerable attention from scholars is the automatic legal text classification due to its potential value in alleviating the labor-intensive process of categorizing vast amounts of textual documents. Besides such capability, this task can also serve as a vital constituent for developing a more advanced intelligent legal system. One notable work by Chen H. et al. [3] implements the domain concept extraction methods to acquire the features, perform PCA for feature extraction, and then utilize the random forest model for classification. Such a method achieves 84.49% accuracy in the multiclass classification of 30,000 US case documents into 50 categories. Another work by Aletras et al. [1] developed a machine learning system for predicting the violation of human rights from the case of the European Court of Human Rights (ECHR) utilizing n-gram and topic clustering to construct features and SVM as a classifier obtaining an average accuracy of 79%. For the context of Thai legal text analysis, [9] introduces a novel method for judicial decision prediction for Thai criminal cases with the adoption of a Bi-directional Gated Recurrent Unit (Bi-GRU) model in cooperation with an attention mechanism. Such an approach consumes both the factual case description and the pertinent legal provision text as input, with the attention mechanism to evaluate their relevancy, making a prediction regarding the judicial outcomes (guilty or not), attaining an average macro F1-score of 63.35% and 66.67% for average micro F1-score.

In this work, we develop a pipeline for classifying whether the case is associated with the offence against property or not, given the textual input of scenario description in the Thai language solely. We experimented with the combination of fastText word embedding and various traditional machine learning models, as well as the transformer-based WangchanBERTa model [11] for text classification on a partition of the Thai Supreme Court Cases (TSCC) dataset [9]. This development for accurate classification holds great benefits as it can alleviate the workload of legal practitioners by offering more efficient case management, which in turn leads to a swifter legal decision-making process, especially for the domain of property-related offences. Since property offences are among the most prevalent criminal offences in Thailand, and contain a broad range of provisions, making the discernment of such a category is particularly valuable. Moreover, this work can also be adapted to the classification of other legal aspects or even used as the foundation for further development of a more advanced intelligent legal system.

2 Methodology

2.1 Thai Supreme Court Cases Dataset (TSCC)

In this study, we conducted the experiment on the TSCC Judgement dataset primarily developed in [9]. This dataset consists of approximately 1,000 records of Supreme Court decisions for criminal cases spanning over three major categories, namely offences against life and body, offences against property, and offences against fame. Since our main task is to determine whether the given scenario or fact is related to an offence against property or not, we have to process the dataset further as follows. First, we extract all the property-related cases, which comprise 408 records, from the TSCC Judgement dataset, then randomly sample the other categories to match the same number of records, ensuring the balanced data record between the two classes. As a result, we end up with a dataset of 816 data records. Then, as we are interested in the facts about the scenario only, we need to exclude the judicial discretion enclosed in `<discr>` tag. This can be done by substituting the following Regular Expression (RegEx) `<discr>[^<]*</discr>` with an empty string. Lastly, we modified the label by annotating all the records related to offences against property with 1 and other offences with 0. Lastly, we split the dataset into training and test sets in an 80:20 manner using a stratified splitting scheme. The statistics of each split are detailed in Table 1.

Table 1. Class-wise Distribution of Training and Test Sets for Property-Related and Other Offences.

Dataset Split	Property-related (label=1)	Others (label=0)	Number of support (%)
Training set	326	326	652 ($\sim$ 80%)
Test set	82	82	164 ($\sim$ 20%)
Total	408	408	816 (100%)

2.2 FastText Embedding with Different Machine Learning Classifiers

In this study, we first experimented with combinations of the static embedding method, the fastText [2], and several traditional machine learning models, namely k-Nearest Neighbor (KNN), Support Vector Machine (SVM), Random Forest Classifier (RFC), and Multi-layer perceptron (MLP), for classifying property-related offences. This fastText embedding model was implemented in Python programming language by leveraging the gensim library [13]. We particularly selected the fastText model pre-trained on the Thai Wikipedia corpus, which has a total vocabulary size of around 107,000 tokens. With this embedding model, each token in the given sequence was transformed into a vector with a dimension of 300. Subsequently, we then computed the approximate embedding vector for the entire sequence using the averaging scheme as illustrated in Equation (1). Once the embedding of each input sequence is derived, it is then used to train each machine learning classifier implemented using sci-kit learn library [12], and the models built can be evaluated against the test dataset.

$$\mathbf{v}_s = \frac{1}{N} \sum_{i=1}^{N} \mathbf{v}_i \tag{1}$$

where $\mathbf{v}_s$ indicates the vector representation of the given sequence, N represents number of tokens in the sequence, and $\mathbf{v}_i$ describes the fastText embeddings of the ith token in the sequence.

To ensure the robustness, performance, and generalization of our model, we performed the hyperparameter tuning by adopting the grid search 5-fold cross-validation strategy on the training dataset, adapting the different variables for each machine learning model as follows.

k-nearest neighbors (KNN)

- `n_neighbors`: 3, 5, 7, and 9
- `weights`: uniform and distance
- `p`: 1 (Manhattan distance) and 2 (Euclidean distance)

Random forest classifier (RFC)

- `n_estimators`: 50, 100, and 200
- `max_depth`: None, 10, 20, and 30
- `min_samples_split`: 2, 5, and 10

Multi-layer perception (MLP)

- `hidden_layer_sizes`: (50,), (100,), and (100, 50)
- `activation`: relu, tanh, and logistic
- `solver`: adam and sgd
- `alpha`: 0.0001, 0.001, and 0.01

Support vector machine classifier (SVM)

- `C`: 0.1, 1, and 10
- `kernel`: linear, rbf, and poly
- `gamma`: scale and auto

Using the average accuracy of the 5-fold cross-validation as the criterion, we then selected the hyperparameters in such a way that maximizes such average accuracy. As a result, we obtain the parameters as such the `n_estimators` of 5, `p` of 2, and uniform weighting strategy for KNN. For RFC, the suitable according to the same grid search cross-validation scheme is as follows: `max_depth` of 10, with `min_samples_split` of 2, and 50 estimators. The optimal MLP architecture is one hidden layer of 50 neurons, with tanh activation function, L2 regularization parameter `alpha` of 0.01, and Adam optimizer. Lastly, for the SVM model, the optimal hyperparameter is C of 10, with linear kernel and scale kernel coefficient. After that, we constructed these models with the corresponding optimal hyperparameters, then trained these models on the whole training set and performed the final evaluation on the test set.

2.3 Transformer-Based Classification Model

Another approach that we experimented with is the contextualized embedding and classification using a transformer-based model, Bidirectional Encoder Representations from Transformers (BERT) [5]. For this study, we utilized the BERT model for the Thai language, developed in [11], the WangChanBERTa model. This model is a RoBERTa [10] variant of the BERT model pre-trained on 78.5 GB of Thai corpora. We employed the transformers library [17] to perform supervised finetuning on the WangChanBERTa model for binary text classification with an objective to predict whether the input case description is related to property or not. Note that for this task, we utilized only the embedding of the `[CLS]` token as a vector representation of the input sequence having a dimension of 768.

Similar to the procedure mentioned in Sect. 2.2, we also performed the hyperparameter tuning using grid search 5-fold cross-validation to find the optimal parameter for the model. The hyperparameters varied in our experiments are the following:

- `learning_rate`: 1e–5, 3e–5, and 5e–5
- `num_train_epochs`: 5 and 10

By evaluating the average accuracy over 5-fold, we obtained the optimal hyperparameters for training the WangchanBERTa model on this binary text classification task: The optimal learning rate is 5e-05 with 5 training epochs. Finally, we similarly created the model with such hyperparameters, trained it on the whole training data, and evaluated the result on the test data.

3 Results and Discussion

In this study, we performed the binary classification on the fact description of legal cases in order to distinguish the property-related scenarios according to the Criminal Code of Thailand from the cases under other categories. The classification performance of various pipelines evaluated on the test set is demonstrated in Table 2. The pipelines considered include the combination of fastText embedding together with traditional machine learning techniques, namely KNN, RFC, MLP, and SVM, as well as the BERT-based deep learning approach, the supervised finetuned WangchanBERTa. The metrics for evaluation measure are precision, recall, F1-score, and accuracy.

Table 2. Binary classification performance for distinguishing the offences against the property from other criminal offences evaluated on the test dataset.

Pipeline	Precision	Recall	F1-score	Accuracy
fastText + KNN	0.800	0.829	0.814	0.811
fastText + RFC	0.857	0.878	0.867	0.866
fastText + MLP	0.854	0.927	0.889	0.884
fastText + SVM	0.843	0.915	0.877	0.872
WangchanBERTa-SFT-sc	**0.951**	**0.939**	**0.945**	**0.945**

Remarks: Our proposed pipeline is in bold.

Among these pipelines, the approach that exerts the highest performance as per our experiment setup is the supervised finetuned WangchanBERTa for the binary classification task of whether or not the context concerns offences related to property, achieving the outstanding result of 94.5% accuracy and F1-measure, with an even higher precision sitting at 95.1% and slightly lower recall of around 93.9% on the test dataset. Such an exceptional figure of precision, recall, F1 score, and accuracy reflects the capability of the model to capture the contextual relationship between words as well as its ability to discern the subtle differences in word usage more effectively than the static word embedding such as fastText in conglomeration with traditional machine learning models. As evidenced by Fig 1, the finetuned transformer-based model can correctly associate phrases and terms related to property such as "taking away", "stealing", and "money deposit" with the predicted label of being the property-related case. This also holds true when considering the scenario of other criminal cases, such as offences against life and body. As can be seen from the figure, the model can effectively attribute the negative contribution of words like "kill" and "deceased" toward the predicted outcome of the case being offences against property.

The confusion matrix in Fig 2 further confirms the effectiveness of our proposed WangchanBERta-SFT-sc model in classifying property-related cases against other criminal cases, having solely 4 false-positive predictions and 5 false-negative predictions. Upon a deeper analysis of the incorrectly predicted cases, we found that the majority of false-positive predictions have a similar disposition being in other categories but having an association with property offences. For instance, in the case of the defendant giving false testimony to officials against the plaintiff, accusing the plaintiff of theft while in reality, the plaintiff is innocent. Other examples are mostly in similar themes where the actual case is within defamation but contains the accusation of some party of fraud or theft. This close resemblance between keywords and the surrounding context of such examples will likely be the major culprit engendering such faulty positive predictions. For the false-negative prediction cases, there are some ambiguities in a similar manner to the previously discussed false-positive cases. To illustrate, one scenario describes the case where the defendant stole the firearm from the plaintiff and used it to shoot another person. Though such a case includes a lot

An example of property-related case

พฤติการณ์ของจำเลยที่ลักและเอาไปเสียซึ่งสมุดบัญชีเงินฝากของผู้เสียหายแล้วปลอมใบถอนเงินของธนาคารโจทก์ร่วมเอาไปแสดงต่อพนักงานของโจทก์ร่วมเพื่อขอเบิกถอนเงิน

(The defendant's behavior was to steal and take away the money deposit book of the victim and then forge a bank withdrawal slip from the co-plaintiff, the bank, and show it to the employees of the co-plaintiff to request a withdrawal of money.)

An example of other criminal case

จำเลยได้รับค่าจ้าง 100,000 บาท จากผู้อื่นให้ฆ่าผู้ตาย

(The defendant was paid 100,000 baht by another person to kill the deceased.)

Fig. 1. The examples illustrate the contribution of each word toward the final prediction of being the case under offences against property or not using the Shapely value implemented using the SHAP library [14]. The red color indicates the positive contribution of such a word toward the final result being property-related offences, while blue represents the negative contribution, with the color intensity reflecting how strongly each word contributes to the final prediction. The English translation of each example sentence is shown in the parentheses below the original sentence written in Thai. (Color figure online)

of the description of offences against the life and body of another person, the first and crucial part for which the plaintiff files the case is the act of theft. This contradiction may possibly make the model focus on the incorrect part of the message that the description aims to convey, leading to faulty yet reasonable predictions. These misclassifications, in turn, emphasize the complexity of the legal case text descriptions and highlight the sophisticated nature of the legal case classification task.

Although pipelines with fastText embedding and traditional machine learning cannot perform well on par with the WangchanBERTa-SFT-sc method, they still offer competitive performance, especially those based on the MLP and SVM having 88.4% and 87.2% accuracy, respectively, with corresponding F1 scores of 88.9% and 87.7%. Such a result proved the integration between fastText embedding with these 2 machine learning models to be quite effective in coping with this binary classification task. Moreover, though slightly lower than that of the BERT-based model, the relatively high recall, 92.7% for MLP and 91.5% for SVM, also indicates the strength of these two models in identifying the property-related case. Following closely behind is the fastText + RFC model with a slightly different statistic, it can be seen that for this model, the recall is a lot worse compared to MLP and SVM but this comes with a slightly superior precision. The worst method among all the tested models is the KNN + fastText with around 81% accuracy. The plausible reason for this is due to the nature of the KNN as an instance-based learning method in conglomeration with the possible curse of

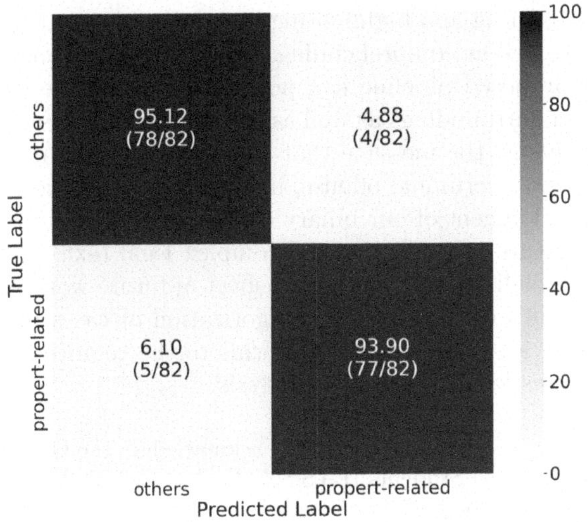

Fig. 2. Confusion matrix demonstrates the binary classification result for property-related legal cases analysis evaluated on the test dataset using the supervised finetuned WangchanBERTa model (WangchanBERTa-SFT-sc). Each cell of the confusion matrix displays the percentage of predicted labels per true label, with the instance count in the parentheses.

dimensionality that may be presented from the high dimensional word embedding. To illustrate, the KNN models, which use distance calculation as a main criterion, without the training phase to extract the pattern or abstraction from the data, make the performance of such model depend heavily on the suitability and quality of the word embedding. This, together with the fact that word embedding vector usually resides in high dimensions, which, according to [6], leads to the distance calculations becoming less meaningful. Therefore, these premises explain the lower performance of the KNN model.

4 Conclusion and Future Work

This study addresses the legal case classification problem of distinguishing the offence against the property from other criminal offences from the given case description or fact. Our highest performance model, the WangchanBERTa-SFT-sc (transformer-based model), achieves outstanding accuracy and F1-score, reaching 94.5% for both metrics. The proposed transformer-based model outperforms all the baseline methods using the combination of the static embedding model, the fastText, and traditional machine learning models such as KNN, RFC, SVM, and MLP. The results signify that for the task of binary text classification in such a specific domain as the legal domain, contextual understanding is crucial for achieving high performance, as demonstrated by the superior performance of the WangchanBERTa-SFT-sc model. Since it is a transformer-based model, it specializes in capturing and highlighting important keywords using the attention mechanism as well as comprehending the surrounding context of the word. As a result, our proposed pipeline can potentially detect the subtle change in keywords and their surroundings as well as the change in sentence structure that may completely change the message that it conveys or even make it fall under different categories of a criminal offense, making it possess such a performance. The successful development of our binary classification model for legal text lays a foundation for future research in more complex legal text classification tasks as well as other specialized domains. One aspect of future work we would like to explore more in-depth details for the categorization of cases into specific legal provisions, utilizing a technique that conforms to the cognitive process of legal professionals, such as legal component analysis.

Acknowledgments. The first author (Si.C.) acknowledges the Graduate Scholarship Program for Excellent Thai Students (ETS Scholarship) awarded by Sirindhorn International Institute of Technology, Thammasat University.

Disclosure of Interests. The authors have no competing interests to declare that are relevant to the content of this article.

References

1. Aletras, N., Tsarapatsanis, D., Preoţiuc-Pietro, D., Lampos, V.: Predicting judicial decisions of the European court of human rights: a natural language processing perspective. PeerJ Comput. Sci. **2**, e93 (2016)
2. Bojanowski, P., Grave, E., Joulin, A., Mikolov, T.: Enriching word vectors with subword information. Trans. Assoc. Comput. Linguist. **5**, 135–146 (2017)
3. Chen, H., Wu, L., Chen, J., Lu, W., Ding, J.: A comparative study of automated legal text classification using random forests and deep learning. Inf. Process. Manag. **59**(2), 102798 (2022)
4. Chusri, T., Arsaibun, S., Chokesuwattanaskul, P., Chuangsuwanich, E., Rutherford, A.T.: Few-shot law retrieval system for supreme court cases. In: 2023 20th International Joint Conference on Computer Science and Software Engineering (JCSSE), pp. 84–89. IEEE (2023)
5. Devlin, J.: Bert: transformers for language understanding. arXiv preprint arXiv:1810.04805 (2018)
6. Domingos, P.: A few useful things to know about machine learning. Commun. ACM **55**(10), 78–87 (2012)
7. García-Constantino, M., et al.: Cliel: context-based information extraction from commercial law documents. In: Proceedings of the 16th Edition of the International Conference on Artificial Intelligence and Law, pp. 79–87 (2017)
8. Kanapala, A., Pal, S., Pamula, R.: Text summarization from legal documents: a survey. Artif. Intell. Rev. **51**, 371–402 (2019)
9. Kowsrihawat, K., Vateekul, P., Boonkwan, P.: Predicting judicial decisions of criminal cases from Thai supreme court using bi-directional gru with attention mechanism. In: 2018 5th Asian Conference on Defense Technology (ACDT), pp. 50–55. IEEE (2018)

10. Liu, Y., et al.: Roberta: a robustly optimized BERT pretraining approach. CoRR arxiv:1907.11692 (2019)
11. Lowphansirikul, L., Polpanumas, C., Jantrakulchai, N., Nutanong, S.: Wangchanberta: pretraining transformer-based thai language models. arXiv preprint arXiv:2101.09635 (2021)
12. Pedregosa, F., et al.: Scikit-learn: machine learning in python. J. Mach. Learn. Res. **12**, 2825–2830 (2011)
13. Řehůřek, R., Sojka, P.: Software framework for topic modelling with large corpora. In: Proceedings of the LREC 2010 Workshop on New Challenges for NLP Frameworks, pp. 45–50. ELRA, Valletta (2010). http://is.muni.cz/publication/884893/en
14. Scott, M., Su-In, L., et al.: A unified approach to interpreting model predictions. Adv. Neural. Inf. Process. Syst. **30**, 4765–4774 (2017)
15. Socatiyanurak, V., et al.: Law-u: legal guidance through artificial intelligence chatbot for sexual violence victims and survivors. IEEE Access **9**, 131440–131461 (2021)
16. Sugathadasa, K., et al.: Legal document retrieval using document vector embeddings and deep learning. In: Arai, K., Kapoor, S., Bhatia, R. (eds.) SAI 2018. AISC, vol. 857, pp. 160–175. Springer, Cham (2019). https://doi.org/10.1007/978-3-030-01177-2_12
17. Wolf, T., et al.: Transformers: state-of-the-art natural language processing. In: Proceedings of the 2020 Conference on Empirical Methods in Natural Language Processing: System Demonstrations, pp. 38–45. Association for Computational Linguistics, Online (2020). https://www.aclweb.org/anthology/2020.emnlp-demos.6
18. Zadgaonkar, A.V., Agrawal, A.J.: An overview of information extraction techniques for legal document analysis and processing. Int. J. Electr. Comput. Eng. (2088-8708) **11**(6) (2021)

Agent-Based Modeling Approach in Single Fish Population Management

Tran Thi Quynh Anh[1], Tri Nguyen-Huu[2,3], and Doanh Nguyen-Ngoc[1(✉)]

[1] COSMOS Lab, CEI, VinUniversity, Hanoi, Vietnam
{23anh.ttq,doanh.nn}@vinuni.edu.vn
[2] ACROSS Lab, Thuyloi University, Hanoi, Vietnam
[3] COSMOS Lab, UMMISCO, IRD, Bondy, France
tri.nguyen-huu@ird.fr

Abstract. Maximum Sustainable Yield (MSY) and Maximum Economic Yield (MEY) are key concepts in population and resource management, critical for optimizing exploitation and ensuring long-term sustainability. MSY represents the largest possible yield that maintains the resources' ability to regenerate, while MEY maximizes the economic benefits. Traditional models, such as Schaefer's logistic growth, provide valuable insights but often oversimplify ecological dynamics, social influences, and spatial factors. In contrast, Agent-Based Modeling (ABM) offers a dynamic and flexible approach by simulating complex interactions between agents and their environment and incorporating stochastic events, thus better capturing real-world complexities. This paper explores the potential of ABM to enhance the understanding of MSY and MEY in fisheries management, using the case of anchovy fisheries in the Gulf of Thailand as a study. Results from simulations demonstrate ABM's effectiveness in analyzing both biological and economic outcomes, revealing differences between traditional and ABM-derived estimates of MSY and MEY. While still in the early stages of application, ABM shows promising results for fisheries management, making it valuable for both scientists and stakeholders. The research may also open various developing and applicating opportunities in similar fields. However, it also suffers from some notable drawbacks in the development stage such as intensive requirements of time and resources, thorough consideration of the model's realism trade-off, and lack of initial input.

1 Introduction

MSY and MEY are crucial in population and sustainable science. Determining MSY and MEY is crucial for optimizing resource exploitation, conserving the population, and maintaining a balanced ecosystem while maximizing revenue. Assuming the population follows the logistic growth model, MSY represents the largest yield that allows the resource to regenerate by harvesting the surplus amount, maintaining the population at the highest growth rate. When the population size is smaller than the point of highest growth rate, the surplus is small

J. Kertesz et al. (Eds.): CSoNet 2024, LNCS 15417, pp. 302–316, 2025.
https://doi.org/10.1007/978-981-96-6389-7_27

and not economically beneficial. Conversely, a larger population limits regeneration factors, reducing the surplus to zero (Bousquet et al. 2008). On the other hand, MEY relates to the effort required to achieve the most economic benefits, balancing total revenue and total cost. The level of effort at MEY is generally lower than at MSY, as increasing the effort level beyond MSY reduces the surplus.

In fisheries management research, various modeling and simulation methods have been used to improve accessibility and comprehension for stakeholders without technical specialties. Most notable are mathematical models, such as Schaefer's logistic growth model, which play a vital role in analyzing and conceptualizing these terms. While these models excel in delivering precise and clear functional relationships, they often neglect dynamic spatial and temporal factors, variability in environment and ecology, social and economic influence, and individual differences. This shortcoming necessitates a new modeling approach, ABM, that better captures the complex interactions of these elements over space and time.

An agent-based model is a computational model that simulates the impacts of autonomous agents' behaviors and interactions on a complex system in various fields, including social sciences, economic trends, and environmental sciences. ABM explores how the agents' behaviors and interactions with other agents and the environment can lead to complex and often unexpected phenomena at higher levels. Consequently, the method has good use in studying: interactions among multiple management institutions, incorporation of cognitive and behavioral sciences in fisheries science and practices, and social consequences of management institutions. For stated reasons, ABM is an ideal - flexible and descriptive - approach for demonstrating changes in fisheries behaviors and exploring new hypotheses or consequences that real-life experiments are not feasible. Moreover, it provides a clear visualization of interactions among multiple individuals, the ability to incorporate cognitive and behavioral into the field, and a straightforward picture of social influences and consequences on the system (Seijo et al. 1998). There are several growing applications of ABM in fishery management, one noteworthy example is FishMORPH - An agent-based model to predict salmonid growth and distribution responses under natural and low flows (Phang et al. 2016). Although the applications of ABM in fishery management are limited, they are steadily increasing. It is worth noting that there is currently no documented use of the ABM approach to determine MSY and MEY in fishery management. As a result, this paper aims to introduce the applications of ABM in establishing the concepts of MSY and MEY in fishery management.

This paper is formatted as follows: Sect. 2 will discuss modeling in ODD structure, Sect. 3 presents the results and discussions, and Sect. 4 concludes the findings.

2 Overview

2.1 Case Study

The model represents anchovy (Stolephorus commersonnii) fishery in the Gulf of Thailand. This species is distributed near the eastern coast of Africa, from the Gulf of Aden to Zanzibar, northern Madagascar, eastward to Hong Kong, and Papua New Guinea. They form schools at depths between 0 and 50 m and rely on surface plankton, particularly copepods and prawn larvae. This schooling behavior helps them reduce predation and increase feeding efficiency. Spawning occurs throughout the year, with peaks in August, October, and January (Hata et al. 2021). It plays a crucial role in various aspects such as ecology, culinary arts, nutrition, and particularly in many of Vietnam's industries. In Vietnam, they are a key ingredient in iconic products like fish sauce, contributing to economic growth and providing livelihoods for coastal communities. Excessive fishing has resulted in a 50% decline in stocks from 2011–2012 to 2020, and the situation is worsening. The Ministry of Agriculture and Rural Development has emphasized the need for sustainable anchovy management to preserve traditional fish sauce production and ensure the sustainable exploitation of anchovy resources. Due to the recent fishing restrictions, the fishery is now only operational during March and April.

This model is operated on the GAMA platform since GAMA supports various types of files such as CVS files, GIS files, and even 3D files, allows a wide range of application domains, including urban mobility, climate change adaptation, epidemiology, and disaster evacuation strategy design, integrates with other software and languages like R and Python, is designed for both computer scientists and non-computer scientists, GAMA offers an intuitive interface for creating and running simulations and provides powerful visualization capabilities, interactive features, and connection to other databases and external tools (Taillandier et al. 2019).

2.2 Purpose and Patterns

The model illustrates interactions between anchovy distribution, fishing fleets, and food availability within an archipelago environment. It aims to reveal dynamics related to fish and human activities and environmental elements, such as islands and food distribution. We outline a general pattern of fish population behavior in response to fishing and food availability.

2.3 Entities, State Variables, and Scales

The following entities are included in the model: agents including fish groups and fishing boats, grid cells representing a virtual sea area, and the observer or global environment defining islands' shapes and food amount (Table 1 and Fig. 1).

In the model, the fish group is depicted by black circles, with larger circles indicating larger groups. The big red squares represent fishing boats that pursue

Table 1. State variables

Entity	Variable name	Variable type and unit	Meaning
Fish group	num_group	Integer, dynamic, groups	The initial number of fish groups
	biomass	Float number, dynamic, biomass unit	The biomass of each fish group
Boat	num_boat	Integer, static, boats	The number of boats
	catch_rate	Float number, static	The proportion of fish to be caught by the boat (range: 0.1–1)
	c	Float number, static, biomass unit	The cost of each boat, assumed to be the same for all boats
Food	K	Integer, static, food unit	The environment's maximum food amount
	num_food	Integer, dynamic, agent	The initial number of food agents
	growth_rate	Float number, static	The rate at which food regenerates
	amount	Float number, food unit	Total food amount of a food agent
Environment	island_shapes	List of shapes, static	List of geometries representing the islands' shapes
	list_areas	List of integers, static	List of areas around islands where food is located
Cell	food_amount	Float number, static, biomass unit	The amount of food inside a cell

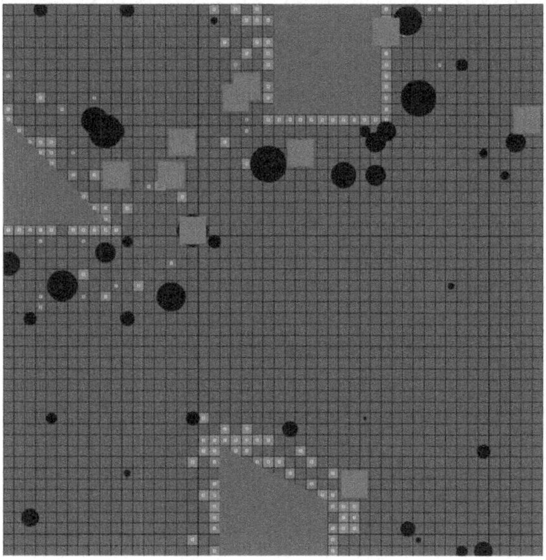

Fig. 1. Model interface

and capture fish. Meanwhile, the large brown blocks symbolize islands, and food is indicated by a heat map that ranges from blue, signifying scarce food, to red, denoting abundant food.

The model's spatial extent is a square of 50×50 square cells, each cell is 10 km long, hence the total area is $250000\,\text{km}^2$. The resolution is relatively acceptable in examining the behavior of fish and ships inside a closed sea surrounded by islands but not optimal. The model runs at a 1-month time step, assuming that the anchovy swims an average of 30 km and the ship sails an average of 50 km in a straight line. The model runs for 300 months, which is equivalent to 25 years.

2.4 Process Overview and Scheduling

The model is developed to cover interactions between anchovy schools, fishing boats, and food development. There are seven processes: one related to food spawning (updating the amount of food in the environment), four related to anchovy (biomass reducing, feeding, migrating, and reproducing), two related to boats (fishing and sailing).

1. Food distribution update: At the start of each cycle, the distribution of food sources along the coast is refreshed. This means that the availability and location of food for the fish are adjusted, setting the stage for the upcoming interactions.
2. Fish group behaviors
   (a) Biomass reduction: The anchovy schools experience a reduction in their biomass. This loss occurs due to natural factors like aging and metabolic activities, which reduce the overall size of the fish population.
   (b) Feeding: Fish groups begin to feed on the food sources in their immediate surroundings, gaining biomass proportion to food amount and current biomass.
   (c) Migration: When there is no nearby food source, the fish will target and migrate towards the closest available location. This migration ensures that fish schools can sustain themselves by constantly seeking out new food resources.
   (d) Interaction: During the feeding and migration processes, fish groups have a probability of colliding and merging.
   (e) Reproduction: Once a year, when the biomass of a fish school reaches a certain threshold, the school will reproduce. This event adds new generations, ensuring the continuity of the species.
   (f) Die: The process involves evaluating the biomass to determine if it falls below a specific threshold. If it does, then the fish group dies.
3. Fishing boat behaviors:
   (a) Expense update: The expense increases by total cost of the fishing fleet.
   (b) Catching fish: Simultaneously with the fish feeding and migrating, fishing boats catch nearby fish schools. The fishing activity competes directly with the fish schools' natural behaviors toward gaining biomass and reproducing, leaves impacts the overall fish population.
   (c) Sailing: When there is no fish in the neighborhood area, the boat chases the nearest fish group or moves toward a food source, as fish gather around the area. This behavior maximizes the yield.

3 Design Concepts

3.1 Basic Principles

This study examines a conservation issue in fishery management using Schaefer's model. Schaefer's model is a fundamental concept in population dynamics, specifically used to describe the growth of biological populations under harvesting. It integrates the logistic growth model with a harvesting term, representing the population's response to natural growth and exploitation. The model is widely used in fisheries management to determine maximum sustainable yield (MSY) and maximum economic yield (MEY) (Seijo et al. 1998), the largest amount of harvesting to ensure sustainability and to achieve the highest profit respectively. Moreover, an agent-based approach is utilized to validate the MSY and MEY in a simulated environment and gain insights from the oscillation nature of fish and food relations.

3.2 Emergence

The key results of the model are Schaefer's patterns in fishery and how closely they align with the model's. Specifically, the outcomes are shaped by the interplay between the fishing boats' catch rates and the growth and reproduction of fish schools. The growth and reproduction rate of anchovies are heavily influenced by population density. The rates decrease as the population reaches carrying capacity, or the minimum biomass needed for reproduction. Additionally, the interaction between food availability and anchovy schools relies on their quantity and growth rate. Similar to the previous point, the anchovy population experiences faster growth as food quantity approaches carrying capacity and slower growth as it decreases toward zero.

3.3 Adaptation

The main adaptive behavior of this model is repositioning. It is modeled as direct objective-seeking, to find out locations with food for anchovy schools and fish biomass for the fishing fleets. The agents relocate only when their current location lacks food or fish. The fish schools select their next location based on the closest distance, while the boats rely on intuition to identify locations with the highest probability of finding fish.

3.4 Objectives

The objective for relocation of fish and boat agents is measured by the quantity of food amount and anchovy biomass in the neighborhoods. This allows them to maximize their chance of survivability and profit. The neighborhoods are covered in different eye-sight distances of two agent types.

3.5 Learning

The model only includes simple learning for the boats to choose the nearest location with a high concentration of food to maximize the likelihood of catching, as fish tend to gather around those.

3.6 Prediction

The model is predicted to generate higher revenue around a value of fishing effort, or the MEY value, and the fish population is extinct after a long time if the fishing effort is higher than a fishing effort value, or MSY.

3.7 Sensing

Anchovy groups and fishing boats are assumed to be able to perfectly sense the current availability of all agents in cells within a specified radius of their current cell. This radius is constant over time and space but different between types of agents.

3.8 Interaction

The agents interact directly through changes in state variables such as biomass, food amount, and catch. They also interact indirectly, for example, through competition for food sources. This model depicts two types of interactions. The first type involves interactions between fish and food, or between boats and fish. The second type involves interactions among different groups of fish. In this system, anchovy and food, as well as fishing fleets and anchovy groups, act as predators and prey, with one type of agent consuming the other. Notably, the number of boats remains independent of both fish population and food quantity. The second type of interaction occurs among fish groups; if the group number does not exceed the maximum biomass, groups are likely to merge when they encounter one another.

3.9 Stochasticity

The usage of randomness is integrated into the processes of initialization, fish migration, reproduction, and food respawning. Initially, the locations of food sources and the biomass of fish groups are randomly distributed. When migrating, if no food source is visible, the fish agent selects a random cell in its neighborhood as a new destination. The reproduction and respawning processes occur randomly, with a probability of 1 in 12, and are subject to a threshold because, in reality, the spawning season of anchovies and the availability of food in the sea can vary due to seasonal and geographical factors.

3.10 Collectives

The fish group agent is structured as a single entity that disregards individual behavior, as anchovies typically swim in schools and rarely separate.

3.11 Observations

The results are graphed on a line chart. The revenue generated by fishing boats follows Schaefer's model. Variables recorded at the end of the simulation to determine MSY and MEY consist of the total fish population, total amount of food, carrying capacity, fishing effort which is calculated by multiplying the number of boats with catch efficiency, and yield. For the assessment of fish density, each island's food allocation range, the average biomass of fish in the food range, and the average food quantity are documented.

4 Details

4.1 Initialization

Upon initialization, there are 10000 food units and 500 independent fish groups. The grid is partitioned into 8 neighborhoods, with each cell able to accommodate multiple agents. All fish groups are given random biomass ranges from 15 kg to 20 kg. The islands are established using a set of (x, y) coordinates to define the area they cover, and the information about the areas is then used to specify the range of food distribution. Afterward, the initial number of boats and their catch rate are chosen depending on specific cases.

4.2 Input

The model does not use input data to represent time-varying processes, such as environmental processes.

4.3 Submodels

Fish density: To gain insights into the relations between food distribution areas and fish density, we conducted a simulation in which the initial number of boats was set to 0. The islands' areas were kept constant with different values to examine whether a larger food distribution area would lead to a greater fish density. Our findings confirmed this hypothesis. However, further evidence or test cases are needed to substantiate this result.

5 Simulation and Discussion

5.1 Results

To obtain Schaefer's MSY and MEY values and the model's MSY and MEY for the fixed condition (K = 10000 food unit, num_group = 500 agents, num_food

= 500 agents, time = 300 months), various simulations are run with different num_boat from 1 to 20 and catch_rate from 0.1 to 1 to assess the variations in yield, profit, and num_fish. From the model, 1520 different scenarios were simulated and recorded as follows (Fig. 2).

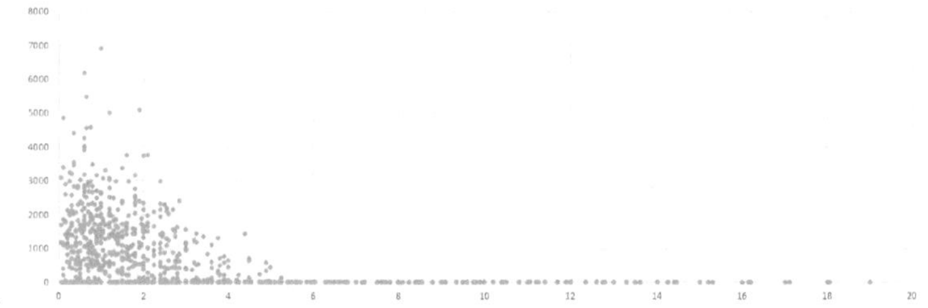

Fig. 2. Fishing Effort vs Remaining Anchovy Population chart.

This chart illustrates the relationship between fishing effort on the x-axis (in effort unit) and the remaining fish population on the y-axis (in biomass unit) at the end of the simulation. As a general trend, the data points are concentrated towards the left side of the graph, suggesting that high fishing efforts correspond to lower remaining populations. For fishing effort levels above 5, the population mostly approaches 0, which implies the maximum effort to achieve sustainability or E_MSY of this model is approximately 5. Below the MSY point, the population varies from 0 to almost 7000 biomass units, indicating that stochastic events can lead to the depletion of the population (Fig. 3).

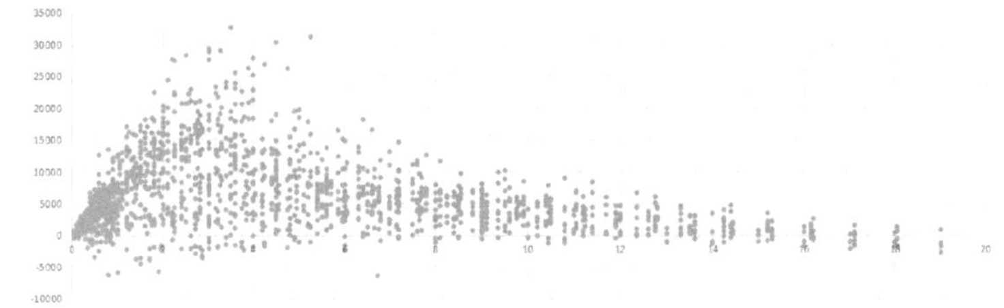

Fig. 3. Fishing Effort vs Profit chart.

The x-axis denotes the fishing effort in effort units and the y-axis represents the profit generated in fish biomass units, ranging from negative values (losses) to significant positive values. As per the model, the profit initially increases until it reaches around 3 effort units, after which it becomes more concentrated around small values, indicating that further efforts result in limited or negative gains. This trend suggests diminishing returns, where increased fishing effort may not necessarily lead to higher profits and could result in losses. From the definition, E_MEY is determined by calculating the average fishing effort of the top 25% highest profit data points, which is found to be 3.195 units.

For further clarification, some charts compare the remaining fish population and profit over time if we fix catch_rate at 0.3 and run simulations for the number of boats equal 5, 10, and 20 accordingly (Fig. 4).

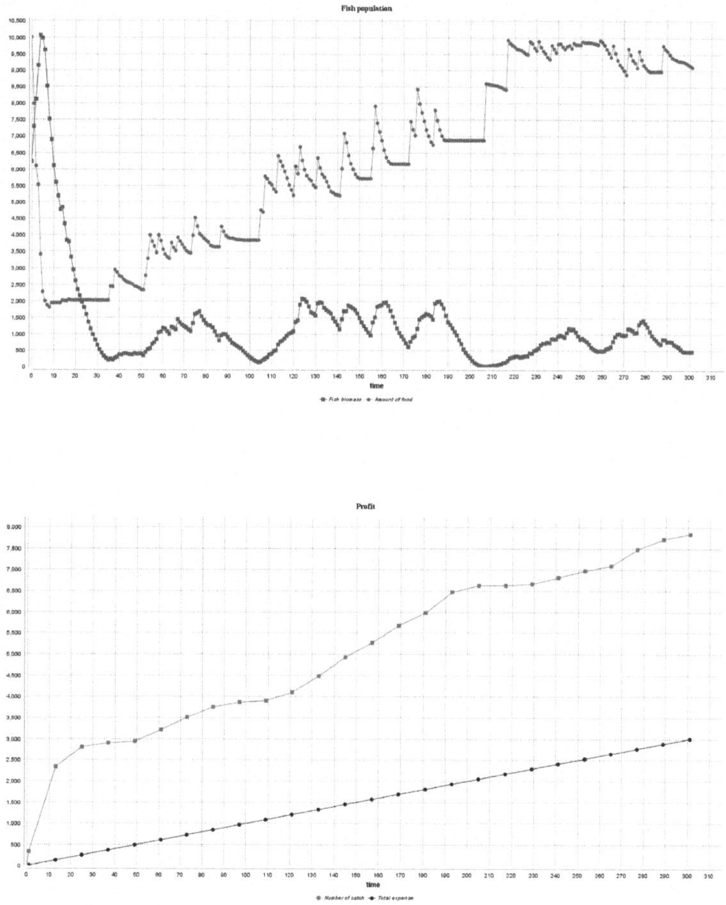

Fig. 4. Number of boats equals 5, effort equals 1.5, which is below MEY and MSY.

The fish population fluctuates significantly because the effort is small and does not affect strongly the fish stock. As a result, the total yield is quite low, 8 000 biomass units (Fig. 5).

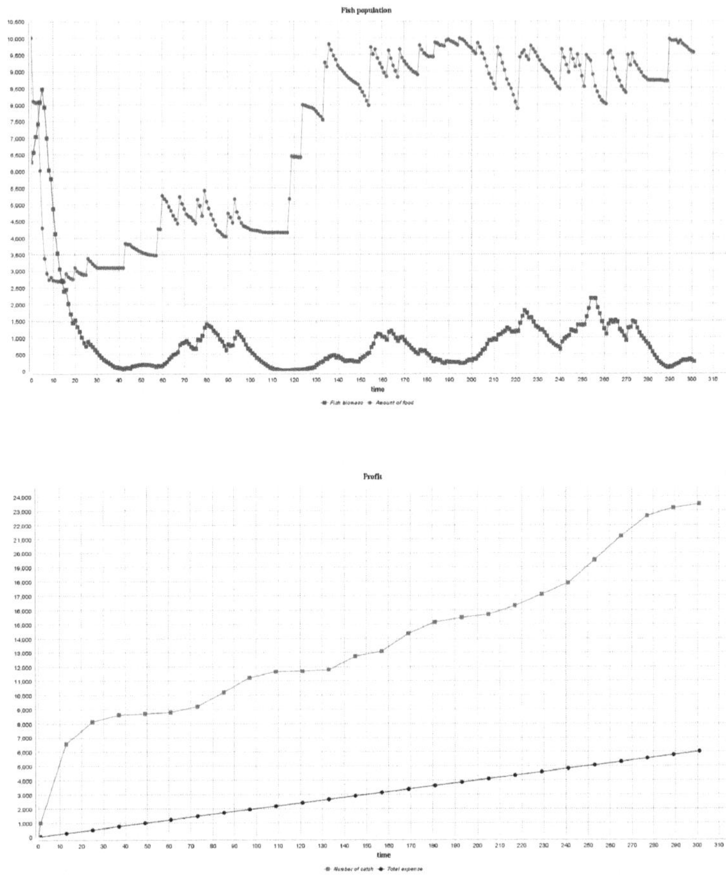

Fig. 5. Number of boats equals 10, effort equals 3, which is about MEY effort.

The fish population fluctuates less remarkably compared to the previous result. As can be seen at the start and in the middle of the simulation, the peak and the foot are not too far from each other. The yield, consequently, is higher than and approximate three times as the previous ones (Fig. 6).

The fish population does not fluctuate and drops dramatically to depletion in 120 months. Therefore, the yield can not be increased and stops at 11 000 biomass units. Furthermore, the fishing cost will gradually surpass the yield and the model returns a negative gain.

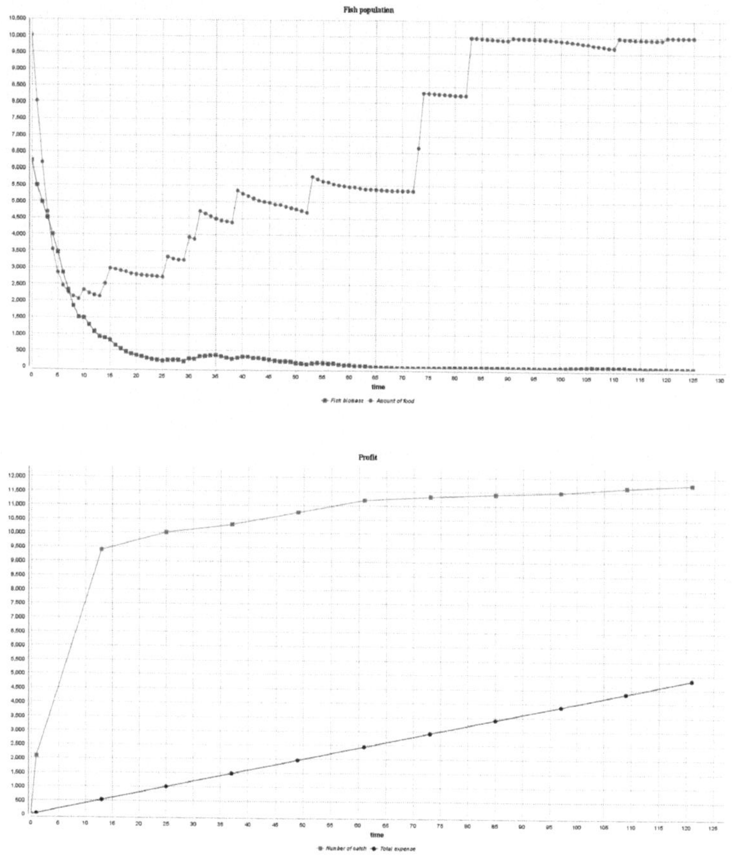

Fig. 6. Number of boats equals 20, effort equals 6, which is beyond MSY.

6 Comparisons

The general concept of MSY and MEY is developed based on data analysis, biological assessments, and dynamics models. Although this approach provides a direct sustainability goal, a clear guideline, and a flexible framework, it has difficulties estimating due to data limitations, environmental variations, and ecological complexities. Another important factor that this concept ignores is social and economic influences (Haddon 2011, Hilborn et al. 1992). The ABM approach to MSY and MEY heritages from the general MSY and MEY concept thus extends the existing strengths such as expansion to the scope of purpose and flexibility to incorporate in various conditions. On top of that, it exhibits several strengths in data collection. These include efficient data collection, reduced time and costs, and flexibility for testing various scenarios. Moreover, this approach possesses adaptability to environmental complexities, and the ability to integrate economic and social factors.

According to Seijo, Schaefer's model freezes the catch rate coefficient and calculates the fishing effort in terms of the number of boats. The yield $Y(E)$ is expressed as:

$$Y(E) = qEK(1 - qEr)$$

This parabolic function represents yield $Y(E)$ according to fishing effort E and reaches its peak at $E = \frac{r}{2q}$, with q being each boat's catch rate, K being the environment's carrying capacity, and r being the fish population growth rate.

Applying Schaefer's equation, the ABM model's fishing effort, calculated by multiplying the boat quantity and the catch rate, at maximum sustainable yield (MSY) is half the growth rate. In this simulation, with the fish doubling their biomass monthly, the annual growth rate is 12. Therefore, the fishing effort at MSY is 6 effort units.

To obtain the fishing effort at maximum economic yield (MEY), Schaefer's model uses:

$$E_{\text{MEY}} = E_{\text{MSY}} \times \frac{\text{catch rate} \times \text{carrying capacity} - \text{total expense}}{\text{catch rate} \times \text{carrying capacity}}$$

According to Seijo et al. (1998), this value is approximately 2/3. As a result, MEY is achieved at 4 effort units (Table 2).

Table 2. Comparison of MSY and MEY values between Schaefer's model and the ABM model

	Schaefer's model	ABM model
MSY (effort units)	6	5
MEY (effort units)	4	3.195

The ABM model's results are approximately 20% off compared to Schaefer's model.

Schaefer's MSY and MEY derive from the Gordon-Schaefer logistic growth model, a mathematical model that illustrates how the fish population grows more gradually as it nears the carrying capacity or depletion point and accelerates when it reaches approximately half the carrying capacity. Therefore, this approach is simpler to calculate than the general concept and has higher possibilities to predict future growth (Hilborn et al. 1992). Furthermore, it is a crucial concept that sets the foundation for fishery management, aiding scientists and policy-makers in sustainability actions (Caddy et al. 1995). However, Schaefer's concepts suffer criticisms for oversimplifying environmental variability and population dynamics including static carrying capacity, constant recruitment rate, and overlooking individual characteristics (Haddon et al. 2011, Hilborn et al. 1992). This approach also has a significant limitation in that it may not be accessible to non-academic audiences, including policy-makers and, notably, many individuals in the fishing industry. The ABM model for MSY and MEY exhibits stochasticity and emphasizes individual characteristics. Therefore, it can simulate complex conditions involving multiple species, predict future trends across various aspects, and identify emergent points or patterns related to specific conditions. Notably, the ABM approach is known for visual representations, facilitating a clearer understanding and interpretation of complex systems. This visual emphasis not only enhances the model's accessibility but also makes it more comprehensive to diverse audiences, including stakeholders who may not have expertise.

7 Conclusion

This study highlights the strengths and limitations of both traditional and agent-based approaches to determining MSY and MEY in fisheries management. While Schaefer's logistic growth model provides a straightforward, mathematically rigorous framework for resource optimization, it often overlooks key ecological, social, and economic complexities. The ABM method addresses these shortcomings by simulating interactions between agents, environment, and economic factors, offering a more flexible and descriptive analysis. It also expands the model's scope of purpose, some examples include observing the dynamics between fish schools and the environment, predicting the effectiveness of fishing policies, and developing a sufficient fishing strategy. In the case of anchovy fisheries in the Gulf of Thailand, ABM results aligned reasonably well with traditional MSY and MEY estimates, though differences in effort levels indicate that ABM may better capture the nuances of real-world scenarios. ABM's ability to incorporate behavioral and environmental variables, alongside its visual outputs, makes it a powerful tool for stakeholders and policymakers aiming for sustainable resource management. Although the application of ABM in fisheries management is still limited, this study underscores its potential to refine and expand upon traditional models, offering a more holistic approach to resource exploitation and conservation.

Nonetheless, the ABM approach also possesses some difficulties such as requiring significant time and resource investment and challenges in achieving accurate replication. In addition, The agent-based model's scope significantly influences the necessary resources and time, which can vary from cost-effective and instantaneous to expensive and enduring. Furthermore, the model's realism is often compromised due to uncertainty propagation, limitations in incorporating numerous parameters and functions, and over-fitting. To address these drawbacks, it's recommended to carefully develop a minimally but adequately realistic scope, including essential parameters, complexity levels, and the combination of different approaches. Moreover, this research project on the anchovy (Stolephorus commersonnii) in the Gulf of Thailand lacks initial input data, potentially limiting its ability to achieve the necessary level of realism as the model does not account for the impact of a multi-species ecosystem on the concepts of MSY and MEY. Therefore, a future approach should consider integrating multi-species in fishery management. An interesting exploration for further advancement regarding how this model could be applied to fields beyond fisheries management, such as wildlife population conservation, deforestation rate optimization, and the husbandry industry.

Acknowledgements. This publication is based upon work supported by VinUniversity under project VUNIĊEI.FS_0001 Digital Twin Platform to Empower Communities towards an Eco-friendly and Heathy Future

References

Bousquet, N., Duchesne, T., Rivest, L.: Redefining the maximum sustainable yield for the Schaefer population model including multiplicative environmental noise. J. Theor. Biol. **254**(1), 65–75 (2008). https://doi.org/10.1016/j.jtbi.2008.04.025

Caddy, J.F., Mahon, R.: Reference points for fisheries management. In: FAO Fisheries Technical Paper No. 347 (1995)

Haddon M.: Modelling and quantitative methods in fisheries (2011)

Hata, H., Lavoué, S., Motomura, H.: Taxonomic status of nominal species of the anchovy genus *Stolephorus* previously regarded as synonyms of *Stolephorus commersonnii* Lacepède 1803 and *Stolephorus indicus* (van Hasselt 1823), and descriptions of three new species (Clupeiformes: Engraulidae). Ichthyol. Res. (2021)

Hilborn, R., Walters, C.J.: Quantitative fisheries stock assessment: choice, dynamics and uncertainty (1992)

Phang, S.C., et al.: FishMORPH - an agent-based model to predict salmonid growth and distribution responses under natural and low flows. Sci. Rep. **6**(1), 1–13 (2016). https://doi.org/10.1038/srep29414

Seijo, J.C., Defeo, O., Salas, S.: Fisheries bioeconomics: theory, modelling and management. In: FAO Fisheries Technical Paper No. 368 (1998)

Taillandier, P., et al.: Building, composing and experimenting complex spatial models with the GAMA platform. GeoInformatica **23**(2), 299–322 (2019). https://doi.org/10.1007/s10707-018-00339-6

Townsend, C.R., Begon, M., Harper, J.L.: Essentials of Ecology. Wiley-Blackwell, Hoboken (2008)

Visual-Based Navigation of Educational Mobile Robot Using Transfer Learning with Teachable Machine

Nutchanon Yongsatianchot, Pradya Prempraneerach(✉), Pakorn Uttayopas, Yutana Chongjarearn, Akkharawoot Takhom, Pattiya Thongkruer, and Kanchana Silawarawet

Faculty of Engineering, Thammasat School of Engineering, Thammasat University, Pathumthani, Thailand
ppradya@engr.tu.ac.th

Abstract. To encourage students' interest in modern technologies-specifically Artificial Intelligent (AI) and robotic/automation-a training program, using a mobile robot platform with visual feedback has been developed for high-school or undergraduate students. This educational mobile robot allows students to gain various skills and concepts, including micro-controller and AI programming, visual feedback from camera, and data communication via WiFi. In this study, we use a two wheeled differential-drive mobile robot controlled by an LN298 motor driver. This robot is also equipped with an ultrasonic sensor for object detection and an ESP32-CAM for visual feedback. Thus, this setup helps students to learn about mechanical construction, electronics, and Arduino programing. Using the web-based Teachable Machine, students can explore concepts of deep learning and learn how to train/create AI models, allowing for sign images to be visual-based navigation for this robot. Lastly, sign images captured by the ESP32-CAM can be classified in real-time by the deep-learning model on a web client, which can be accessed on a smartphone, through two-way communication using a WebSocket program.

Keywords: Visual Navigation · Mobile Robot · Transfer Learning · Teachable Machine · Websockets

1 Introduction

Robots are becoming an increasingly important part of our daily activities, such as household chores [1, 2] and human-robot interaction in industrial settings [3]. Additionally, they also have been deployed in industrial workspace with more efficient and safer functions [4] and gradually equipped with autonomous function/operation [5]. Mobile robots, one of the significant robotic fields, were initially used for transporting tools/products in factories along predefined paths. Several types of locomotion, such as wheels, legs, propeller, etc., have been employed with mobile robots. Currently, the mobile robot, equipped with localization and positioning systems, can perform several complex tasks in both industrial/home applications.

J. Kertesz et al. (Eds.): CSoNet 2024, LNCS 15417, pp. 317–327, 2025.
https://doi.org/10.1007/978-981-96-6389-7_28

Recently, autonomous mobile robots have gained attentions from various fields, such as manufacturing, healthcare, and agriculture, due to advancements in robotic technologies [6, 7]. The mobile robots are required to locate themselves, plan paths between positions, and navigate through environments. Vision is an important feedback mechanism used to provide robots with awareness of their surroundings for navigation. Techniques such as Simultaneous Localization and Mapping (SLAM), enable robots to create a map of their environment while simultaneously tracking their location within it [8, 9]. These capabilities can be improved by integrating artificial intelligence into the system, allowing robots to better understand the world around them and plan their paths in real time [10–13]. In particular, deep learning techniques such as Convolutional Neural Networks (CNNs) are utilized to provide vision feedback for object detection and identification, facilitating decision-making in autonomous mobile robots [14, 15].

To introduce students to robotics technology, a simple two-wheeled differential-drive mobile robot is used as an educational platform for hands-on learning and training. Sensors and a camera are integrated into the robot to help students develop skills in microcontroller programming. Furthermore, machine vision using deep learning algorithms is implemented for object detection, classification, and autonomous navigation, providing students with an introduction to artificial intelligence (AI). This paper proposes a visual navigation concept for the educational mobile robot. This paper is organized as follows: Sect. 2 presents a kinematics and component/structure of this mobile-robot. The virtual-based navigation using deep learning from Teachable Machine as well as websocket programming are described in Sect. 3. Operation of this robot used the ESP32-CAM and ultrasonic sensor, as well as training outcomes are explained/discussed in Sect. 4. Lastly, Sect. 5 concludes learning results using this mobile robot platform.

2 Mobile Robot Kinematics and Structure

A mobile robot with left and right differential-drive wheels and additional front and rear caster wheels was chosen as an educational platform due to its stability, simple mechanics, and low cost. Using an ESP-32 CAM microcontroller as the main controller further simplifies the robot's structure and construction, as well as a further integration of the deep learning model in the visual navigation system.

2.1 Kinematics of Educational Mobile Robot

The mobile robot used two independent fixed standard wheels as drive wheels mounted on each side of the robot's circular chassis. To ensure stability, two caster wheels, used as passive wheels, were mounted at the front and rear of the robot's chassis. The robot's velocities can be calculated based on the robot heading angle θ and the velocities of its drive wheels, designated as ϕ_R for the right wheel and ϕ_L for the left wheel. Thus, its kinematics can be expressed as:

$$\xi_I = \begin{bmatrix} \cos\theta & 0 \\ \sin\theta & 0 \\ 0 & 1 \end{bmatrix} \begin{bmatrix} v \\ \omega \end{bmatrix} \tag{1}$$

where $\xi_I = [\dot{x}, \dot{y}, \dot{\theta}]^T$ is a vector representing the robot's velocities relative to the global frame. This vector consists of the robot's linear velocities in the horizontal ($\dot{x}$), and vertical ($\dot{y}$), directions, as well as its angular velocity $\dot{\theta}$. Meanwhile, its velocities relative to its own frame are given by $v = \frac{r}{2}(\phi_R + \phi_L)$ f for linear velocity, and $\omega = \frac{r}{L}(\phi_R - \phi_L)$ for angular velocity where r is the wheel radius and L is the distance between the two wheels (Fig. 1).

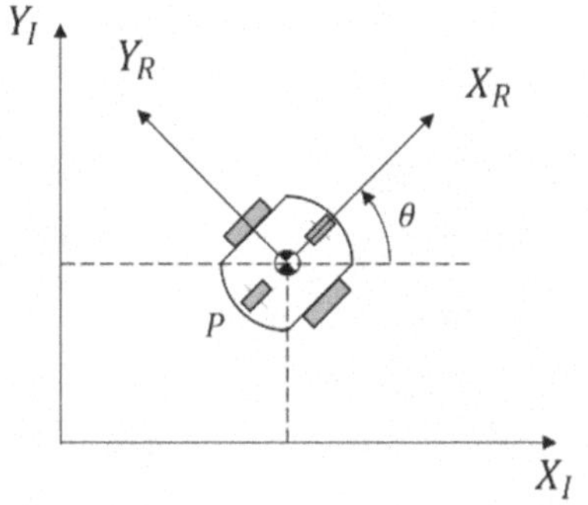

Fig. 1. Global coordinate (X_I, Y_I) and local coordinate (X_R, Y_R) systems of this mobile robot for kinematic analysis.

2.2 Components of Educational Mobile Robot

The mobile robot comprises three main components: 1) an ESP32-CAM with OV2640 camera, 2) an IOE-SR05 ultrasonic sensor module, and 3) the circular chassis with two differential-drive wheels and two caster wheels, as shown in Fig. 2. The ESP32-CAM is a compact and versatile development board that combines the ESP32 microcontroller with a camera module. Developed by Espressif Systems, this board features built-in Wi-Fi and Bluetooth capabilities, making it ideal for Internet of Things (IoT) projects and remote monitoring applications. The ESP32-CAM includes an OV2640 camera capable of capturing 2-megapixel images, along with a microSD card slot for local storage. Its small form factor, low power consumption, and affordable price have made it suitable for classroom settings and for small robotic applications. Moreover, the LN298 motor-drive module is used as a main driver of two gearhead DC motors and as a 5-VDC voltage supply for ESP32-CAM. A main power source of this mobile robot is supplied by two 3.7-V lithium polymer batteries.

Our chosen ultrasonic sensor is the IOE-SR05 ultrasonic ranging sensor Module, a compact sensor with a printed circuit board measuring 2.2 × 3.6 cm, suitable for our small robot. The model features five pins: a wide voltage input (supporting 3 V–5.5 V), a serial output, an enable pin, and two ground connections. The module automatically transmits eight 40 kHz square waves every 18 ms and detects whether there is a signal return. When a signal is received, the module processes it internally and outputs distance information through the TXD pin. The model outputs 4 bytes at a time in the following order: 1) Head: A start byte with a value of 0xFF for validation, 2) H_DATA: the upper 8 bits of the distance data, 3) L_DATA: the lower 8 bits of the distance data, and 4) SUM: a validation byte equal to the lower 8 bits of the sum of Head, H_DATA, and L_DATA. Using this data, we can calculate the distance as H_DATA * 256 + L_DATA. When the range is exceeded, the sensor automatically returns the data FF AA AA 53. A wiring diagram of the ESP32-CAM with the IOE-SR05 ultrasonic sensor and the LN298 motor drivers is shown in Fig. 3.

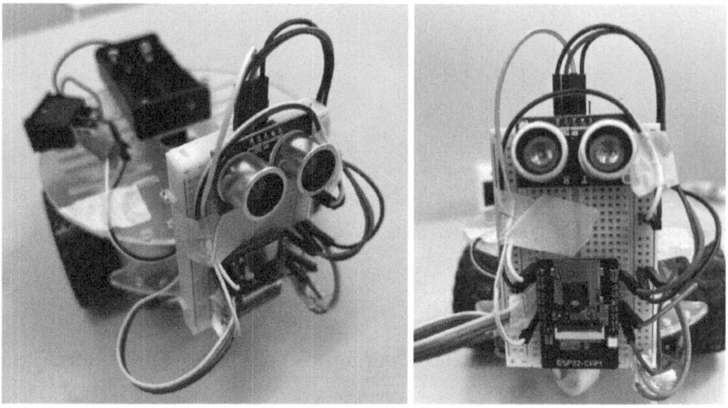

Fig. 2. The educational mobile robot after fully assembly, used in this training.

Pins on LN298 & IOE-SR05 boards	Pins on the ESP32 Cam board
IN1 – LN298	GPIO 14
IN2 – LN298	GPIO 15
IN3 – LN298	GPIO 13
IN4 – LN298	GPIO 12
ENA – LN298	GPIO3 (UOR)
ENB – LN298	GPIO1 (UOT)
TrigPin – SR05	GPIO 16
EchoPin – SR05	GPIO 2
5V	5V
GND	GND

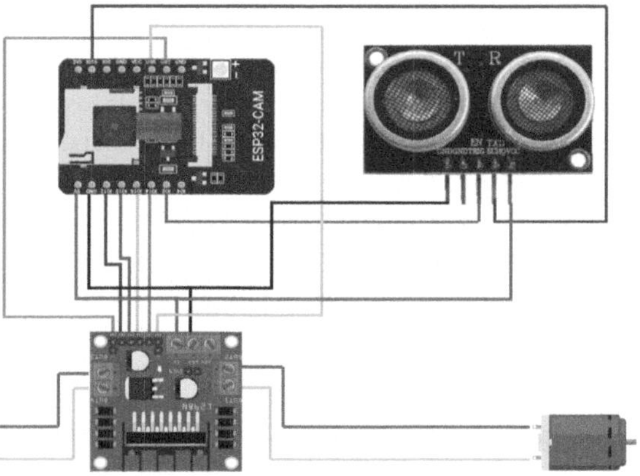

Fig. 3. The wiring diagram of this educational mobile robot. The ESP32-CAM microcontroller and the IOE-SR05 ultrasonic module are correspondingly at the top center and the top right of the diagram. The LN298 motor-drive module locates at the bottom center of the diagram, which connects to two motors. Table on the left shows how to connect ESP32-CAM with the ultrasonic and motor modules. GPIO (General-Purpose Input/Output) can be used for ESP32 input and output connections with external hardwares.

3 Visual-Based Navigation Using Deep Learning

To enable the robot to be autonomous, a transfer learning technique is applied. The robot will learn to recognize signs presented in front of it through a ESP32-CAM and react with predefined commands. As the core component of the robot's navigation, the visual processing system interfaces with the trained deep learning model from Teachable Machine, a web-based machine learning model, through the WebSocket communication protocol, which will be detailed in the subsequent section.

3.1 MobileNets Transfer Learning by Teachable Machine

Teachable Machine, developed by Google (https://teachablemachine.withgoogle.com), is a web-based tool for easily and quickly creating deep learning models without prior programming and deep learning knowledge. Therefore, it is suitable for high-school students to get hands-on experience with the deep learning. Teachable Machine can train three different types of the deep-learning models to classify images, audio, and body positions or poses. In this project, we focused on the image model of Teachable Machine for instructing students.

Teachable Machine uses TensorFlow.js, a library for the deep learning in Javascript, to train and to test the models directly on the web browser. The image model is based on MobileNets, which are small, low-latency, low-power models. The MobileNet is designed to be used under resource-constraint use cases, such as web and mobile applications [16]. The MobileNet is a portable Convolutional Neural Networks (CNN) architecture, based on a depthwise separable convolution, which factorized a standard convolution into a depthwise convolution and a 1 x 1 convolution. The MobileNet is pretrained on the ImageNet dataset [17] and can be effectively fine-tuned for new image classes using a small dataset, making it one of the popular Transfer Learning (TL) technique.

There are three main steps for using Teachable Machine:

1. First, students collect and group image datasets into several specified categories that we want the TL model to learn/train.
2. Then, students train the TL model by Teachable Machine on web browser. Students can instantly test the trained model using a real-time image from their webcams or using new uploaded images to verify its ability to correctly classify new datasets. Figure 4 displays the interface of Teachable Machine.
3. Finally, students can easily export their TL models for their projects by inserting them into the website with a simple code snippet. The model can then be downloaded to a local host or an online host from Teachable Machine-provided servers. For this training program, the TL models are hosted online by Teachable Machine, where the model interaction can be accessed through a URL.

We provide students with 50 sign images per class for three different classes (left, right, and stop), as illustrated in Fig. 5. Students are encouraged to examine an effect of the number of trained images on the learning accuracy by adding their own images into their trained dataset. In addition, a simple webpage, developed by Javascript, is given to student so that they can paste the URL of their Teachable Machine model to run and to interact with the ESP32 microcontroller.

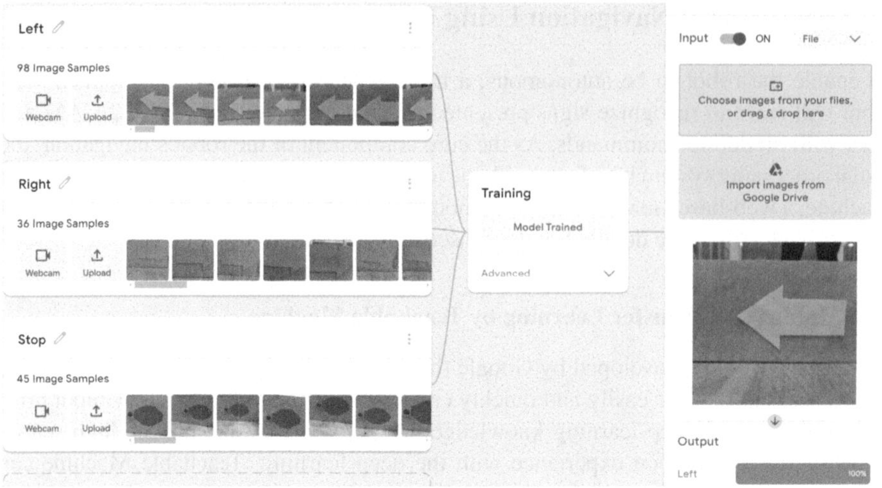

Fig. 4. Teachable Machine Interface: The left-hand column is where students can create classes and insert trained image samples. In this case, there are 3 classes: left, right, and stop signs. The middle column is the training control panel. The right column is where students can test their model and see the output or prediction in real time.

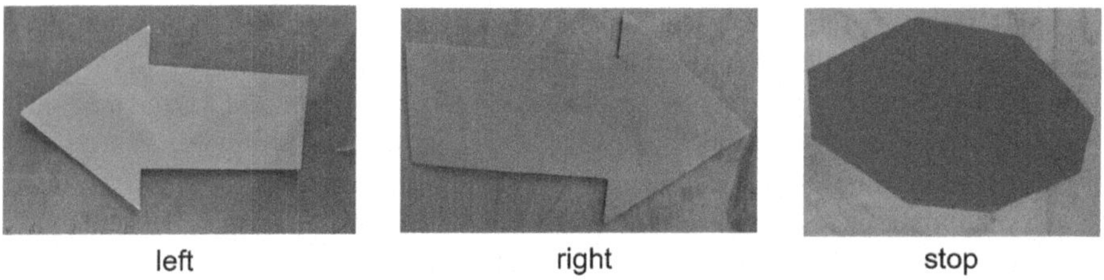

Fig. 5. Examples of signage images of three different classes (1. Left, 2. Right, 3. Stop).

3.2 Websockets: ESP-32 and Teachable Machine Communication

Furthermore, we implement a real-time communication system using WebSocket protocol, enabling bidirectional data exchange between the ESP32-CAM microcontroller and a web client. Unlike the traditional HTTP request-response cycles, WebSocket allows continuous, full-duplex communication over a single TCP connection, significantly improving efficiency and reducing latency.

According to our setup, the ESP32-CAM serves as a WebSocket server on port 81. Upon receiving a "capture" command, it transmits captured image frames to connected clients. On the client side, JavaScript code manages the WebSocket connection, handling connection events and processing incoming messages. When the client receives image data, it displays the image and predict image class using the Teachable Machine model. Then, a real-time image, refreshed every second, along with the predicted class probabilities are shown to students on the developed webpage, and the highest probability class is sent back to the ESP32-CAM as a single class number. Students can access this developed webpage on their smartphones, which are connected to the same Wi-Fi network as the ESP32 WebSocket.

This process creates a feedback loop where the system can capture images, transmit, analyze images, and provide robot's responds in near real-time. This approach demonstrates how WebSocket can be effectively used in IoT and deep learning applications to create a responsive system with a minimal delay between data transmission and robot's processing.

4 Operation and Training of Educational Mobile Robot

In this section, we first discuss the operation of the mobile robot. Then, we explain what and how we teach students using this robot. Finally, we present and discuss the results of our training program.

Figure 6 illustrates an overall logical operation of this mobile robot. First, the ultrasonic module calculates the distance between the robot and the wall/obstacle. When the robot moves close to the wall, its movement stops. Afterward, the ESP32-CAM is activated to capture the sign image on the wall. This image is then transmitted to the Teachable Machine model, hosted on the developed website. The TL model processes the image and sends its prediction result back to the ESP32 microcontroller, which subsequently issues a command for the robot to turn left, or turn right, or remain stationary (stop).

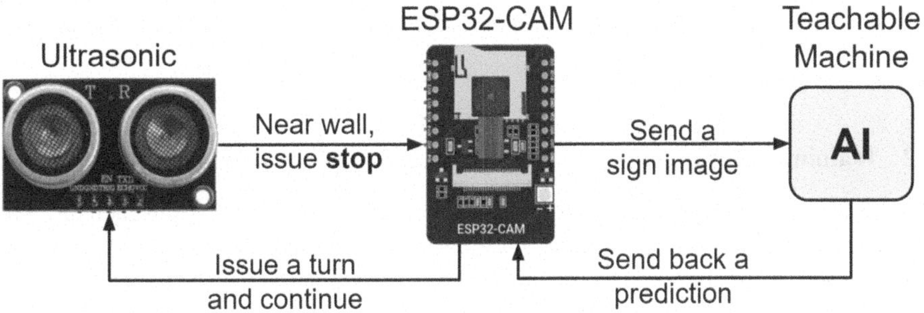

Fig. 6. The overall control logic of this educational mobile robot.

4.1 ESP32-CAM and Arduino Programing

To program the ESP32-CAM, we employed the Arduino Integrated Development Environment (IDE), leveraging its user-friendly interface and C/C++-based language to ease students into programming. The Arduino IDE serves as an effective educational tool, allowing students to write, compile, and upload code to their mobile robot projects with minimal setup complexity. This approach enables students to focus on core programming concepts and the robot control logic. By integrating the ESP32-CAM with Arduino in our mobile robot projects, students can gain hands-on experience in several areas, such as motor control, sensor integration, wireless communication, and basic computer vision. Particularly, a logical operation of the ultrasonic sensor is explained in Fig. 7. This practical application of technologies not only reinforces programming skills but also introduces students to the interdisciplinary nature of robotics, combining elements of computer science, electrical engineering, and mechanical design.

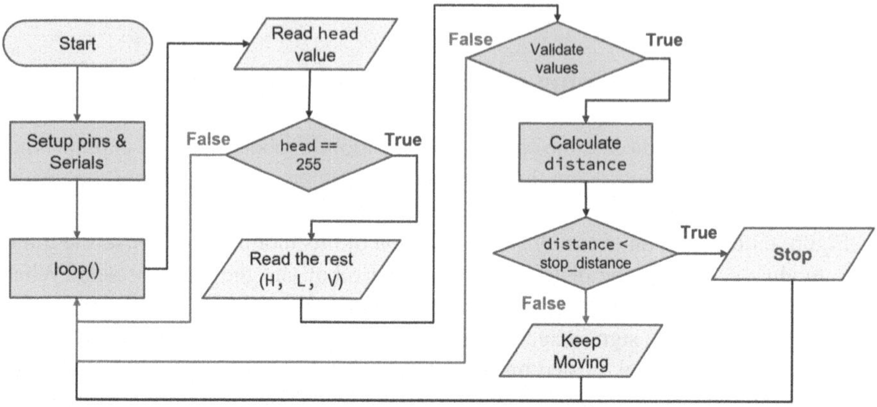

Fig. 7. A flowchart of the ultrasonic sensor's operation, which is used to teach students, help stopping robot motion after computing distance between the robot and surrounding obstacles. The key part is the validation of the ultrasonic data which include checking the head data and the validation value. Another important part is the logic for stopping the robot. If the distance from the ultrasonic is lower than the user-defined threshold (stop_distance), then the robot stops.

4.2 Training Program of Visual-Based Navigation of This Mobile Robot

The training program spans a two-day period, running from 9 am to 4 pm each day. On the first day, students learn Arduino IDE, basic programming in Arduino, basic deep learning within Teachable Machine, and WiFi communication using WebSockets. The second day begins with assembling the mobile robot and programming its motor control during the morning session. In the afternoon session, students connect the ESP32-CAM and ultrasonic sensor to the mobile robot, which unites the ultrasonic sensor, visual feedback using the ESP32-CAM, trained TL model, and motor controls all together, as shown in Fig. 6. Lastly, at the end of the second day, all students get a chance to compete using their mobile robot to navigate in a small maze box according to left/right arrows and stop signs, pre-installed on the maze wall, illustrated in Fig. 8. Students could run their trained TL model on their smartphone after signage image was transmitted from the ESP32-CAM to the smartphone in real time.

A total of 77 Thai students participated in the TSE training program between April 30th and May 1st, 2024. Following the training, we analyzed feedbacks from 20 students across three different aspects: 1) program satisfaction, 2) instructor performance, and 3) meeting expectations. As shown in Fig. 9, the training program received a high average satisfaction score of 4.5 out of 5.0, and students reported that the knowledge

Fig. 8. Student competition is held on the last day of training to test out their mobile robot using the visual-based navigation according to sign images on the maze wall.

and experience gained from the TSE training program exceeded their expectations with an average score of 4.7 out of 5.0.

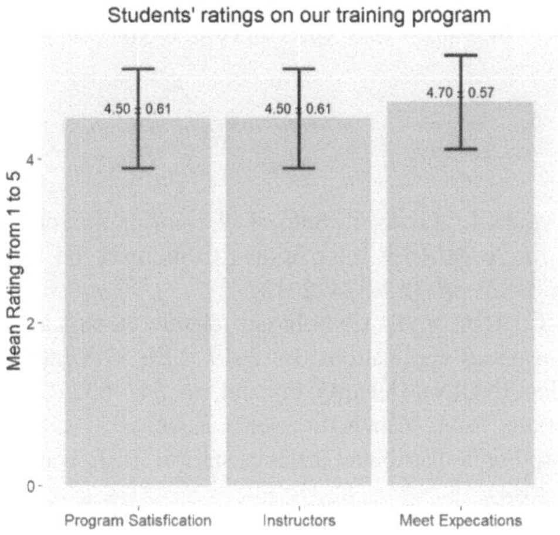

Fig. 9. Feedback from 20 students, whom attended the TSE training program on April 30th and May 1st, 2024, from three different aspects. Error bars show one standard deviation from their mean values.

5 Conclusion/Future Works

The educational mobile-robot platform with visual feedback for navigation serves as an effective teaching tool for high-school and undergraduate students across various disciplines, including mechanical engineering, electrical engineering, and computer science. This training program enables students to develop multiple skills and understand key concepts: microcontroller and AI programming, camera-based visual feedback, and WiFi data communication. The simple mobile robot, comprising two differential-drive wheels and two caster wheels, utilizes two DC motors with an LN298 motor driver. It controls its motion through Arduino programming using the ultrasonic sensor for forward obstacle detection and an ESP32-CAM for visual feedback. Furthermore, students learn how to train the deep learning model with sign images on Teachable Machine website by Google Creative Lab. Integration of real-time images from the ESP32-CAM with deep learning model can be accomplished by WebSocket program for two-way communication between the ESP32-CAM microcontroller and a web client on a smartphone.

To maintain student engagement throughout the training program, continuous evaluations of each topic are conducted during the two-day period, culminating in a mobile-robot competition that integrates all acquired knowledges and skills on the final day. After the two-day training at Thammasat School of Engineering, students provided high rating feedback in terms of learning satisfaction, instructor knowledge, meeting expectation from this training experience.

Acknowledgments. Authors would like to thank the Faculty of Engineering, Thammasat School of Engineering, Thammasat University for financial support of this educational training program.

Disclosure of Interests. All authors have no competing interests to declare that are relevant to the content of this article.

References

1. Pantofaru, C., Takayama, L., Foote, T., Soto, B.: Exploring the role of robots in home organization. In: 2012 7th ACM/IEEE International Conference on Human-Robot Interaction (HRI), Boston, MA, USA, pp. 327–334 (2012)
2. Luo, R.C., Lin, H.-C., Hsu, Y.-T.: CNN based reliable classification of household chores objects for service robotics applications. In: 2019 IEEE 17th International Conference on Industrial Informatics (INDIN), Helsinki, Finland, pp. 547–552 (2019)
3. Avanzini, G.B., Ceriani, N.M., Zanchettin, A.M., Rocco, P., Bascetta, L.: Safety control of industrial robots based on a distributed distance sensor. IEEE Trans. Control Syst. Technol. **22**(6), 2127–2140 (2014)
4. Chu, T.S., Culaba, A.B., Jose, J.A.C.: Robotics in the fifth industrial revolution. In: 2022 IEEE 14th International Conference on Humanoid, Nanotechnology, Information Technology, Communication and Control, Environment, and Management (HNICEM), Boracay Island, Philippines (2022)
5. Garcia, L., Jimenez, M.A., De Santos, P.G., Armada, M.: The evolution of robotics research. IEEE Robot. Autom. Mag. **14**(1), 90–103 (2007)
6. Bonin-Font, F., Ortiz, A., Oliver, G.: Visual navigation for mobile robots: a survey. J. Intell. Robot. Syst. **53**, 263–296 (2008)

7. Yasuda, Y.D.V., Martins, L.E.G., Cappabianco, F.A.M.: Autonomous visual navigation for mobile robots: a systematic literature review. ACM Comput. Surv. **53**(1) (2020)
8. Sasiadek, J.Z., Monjazeb, A., Necsulescu, D.: Navigation of an autonomous mobile robot using EKF-SLAM and FastSLAM. In: 2008 16th Mediterranean conference on Control and automation, pp. 517–522 (2008)
9. Panigrahi, P.K., Bisoy, S.K.: Localization strategies for autonomous mobile robots. A review. J. King Saud Univ. Comput. Inf. Sci. **34**(8), (2022)
10. Casarrubias-Vargas, H., Petrilli-Barceló, A., Bayro-Corrochano, E.: EKF-SLAM and machine learning techniques for visual robot navigation. In: 2010 20th International Conference on Pattern Recognition, Istanbul (2010)
11. Zhang, Y., Feng, W., Yang, Z., Zhou, Z., Zhu, Z., Wang, W.: Visual navigation of mobile robots in complex environments based on distributed deep reinforcement learning. In: 2022 6th Asian Conference on Artificial Intelligence Technology (ACAIT), Changzhou, China (2022)
12. Pengyu, Y., Jing, X., Huan, Z., Ding, L.: Experimental research on deep reinforcement learning in autonomous navigation of mobile robot. In: 14th IEEE Conference on Industrial Electronics, and Applications (ICIEA). Waseda University, Tokyo, Japan (2019)
13. Hikaru, S., Tadahi, H., Satoru, K.: A study on vision-based mobile robot learning by deep Q-network. In: Proceedings of the SICE Annual Conference of the Society of Instrument and Control Engineering of Japan (SICE). Kanazawa University, Kanazawa, Japan (2017)
14. Foroughi, F., Chen, Z., Wang, J.: A CNN-based system for mobile robot navigation in indoor environments via visual localization with a small dataset. World Electr. Veh. J. **12**(3), 134 (2021)
15. Gao, H., Cheng, B., Wang, J., Li, K., Zhao, J., Li, D.: Object classification using CNN-based fusion of vision and LIDAR in autonomous vehicle environment. IEEE Trans. Ind. Inf. **14**(9), 4224–4231 (2018)
16. Howard, A.G., et al.: MobileNets: efficient convolutional neural networks for mobile vision applications. arXiv:1704.04861 (2017)
17. ImageNet Large Scale Visual Recognition Challenge 2015 (ILSVRC2015). https://image-net.org/challenges/LSVRC/2015/

NFTs in Knowledge Management: Utilizing Blockchain Applications for Data Sharing

Phat T. Tran-Truong[1,2](✉), P. H. T. Trung[3], N. T. K. Ngan[4], T. B. Nam[3], T. D. Khoa[3], H. G. Khiem[3], T. Q. Bao[3], D. M. Hieu[3], and N. T. Anh[3]

[1] Department of Software Engineering, Faculty of Computer Science and Engineering, Ho Chi Minh City University of Technology (HCMUT), 268 Ly Thuong Kiet Street, District 10, Ho Chi Minh City, Vietnam
phatttt@hcmut.edu.vn

[2] Vietnam National University Ho Chi Minh City, Linh Trung Ward, Thu Duc District, Ho Chi Minh City, Vietnam

[3] FPT University, Can Tho city, Vietnam

[4] FPT Polytechnic, Can Tho city, Vietnam

Abstract. The intersection of blockchain technology and knowledge management is changing the way academic content is stored, accessed, and disseminated. This paper explores the potential of NFTs and decentralized architectures to enhance the efficiency and security of knowledge management systems, particularly in academic settings. Traditional knowledge management models, which are reliant on physical and digital repositories, face limitations in accessibility, copyright protection, and data integrity. Blockchain technology offers a secure and transparent method for knowledge transfer and access control, while decentralized approaches such as cloud computing provide scalability and flexibility. Our proposed framework integrates blockchain and NFTs to address these challenges, offering a method for secure and efficient knowledge dissemination. We evaluate the practicality of this framework by implementing smart contracts on four EVM-compatible platforms: Binance Smart Chain, Polygon, Fantom, and Celo. The evaluation assesses the performance, scalability and cost effectiveness of the system.

Keywords: Knowledge Management · Blockchain · Smart Contracts · Non-Fungible Tokens (NFTs) · Data Sharing

1 Introduction

The intersection of blockchain technology with knowledge management is driving a transformation in the way academic content is stored, accessed, and disseminated [4,5]. With the advent of digital technologies like Non-Fungible Tokens (NFTs) and decentralized architectures, there is an emerging need to re-evaluate traditional knowledge management systems. In our paper, we explore the potential of these technologies to enhance the efficiency and security of knowledge

J. Kertesz et al. (Eds.): CSoNet 2024, LNCS 15417, pp. 328–335, 2025.
https://doi.org/10.1007/978-981-96-6389-7_29

management, particularly in academic settings. The classical architecture of academic knowledge management, predominantly reliant on physical and digital repositories managed by librarians, has been the cornerstone of scholarly communication. This model, characterized by its structured interaction between human agents and information repositories, has facilitated a continuous cycle of learning and contribution among scholars [8,9]. However, with the progression of digital technology, this traditional system reveals its limitations, particularly in terms of accessibility, copyright protection, and data integrity.

Traditional academic knowledge management systems (as illustrated in Fig. 1), centered around physical and digital repositories, have facilitated scholarly communication for centuries. However, these systems often struggle with scalability, accessibility, and data integrity. As libraries grow, managing vast physical collections and ensuring timely access to information becomes increasingly difficult. In addition, manual processes involved in cataloging, maintenance, and copyright management are time-consuming and error-prone. The limitations of traditional library systems are further exacerbated by the challenges of maintaining accurate and up-to-date information. Physical resources, such as books and journals, are inherently static and can quickly become outdated. This can hinder research and learning, particularly in rapidly evolving fields. Moreover, the reliance on centralized repositories makes these systems vulnerable to security breaches and data loss.

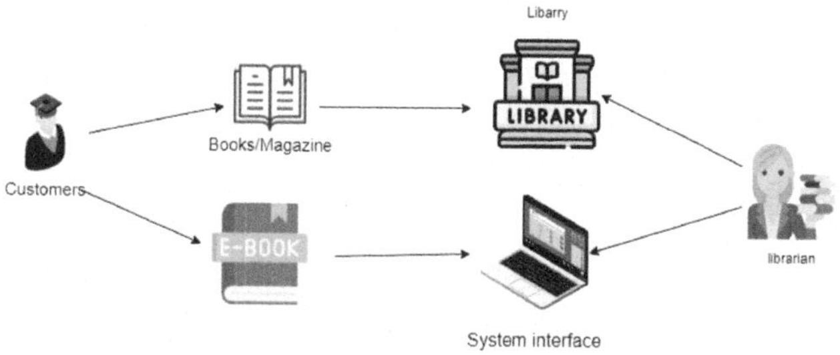

Fig. 1. Traditional Knowledge Management System Model (e.g., Libraries)

Our approach addresses these challenges by proposing an architectural framework that integrates blockchain and NFTs into the knowledge management system. This architecture aims to overcome the limitations of traditional systems, particularly in terms of data security, copyright protection, and accessibility. By leveraging the immutable and transparent nature of blockchain, coupled with the unique identification features of NFTs, our system introduces a novel method of managing and disseminating knowledge [7]. To evaluate the practicality of our proposed system, we have implemented smart contracts on four notable Ethereum Virtual Machine (EVM)-compatible platforms: Binance Smart Chain, Polygon, Fantom, and Celo. This diverse set of platforms offers a comprehensive landscape for testing various aspects of our system, from transaction creation to

NFT management. The evaluation aims to evaluate the performance, scalability, and cost effectiveness of the system in a real world setting.

2 Related Work

2.1 Blockchain-Enabled Knowledge Management System

Recent explorations into blockchain technology in the realm of knowledge management reveal its potential to enhance these traditional systems. Studies by Pfeiffer et al. [9] and Nyame et al. [8] have highlighted the use of blockchain for secure and transparent knowledge transfer and access control. Further, the works of Bartling and Fecher [1], and Qin et al. [10] illustrate the broader applications of blockchain in knowledge creation and organizational management. These studies lay the groundwork for understanding blockchain's role in a more decentralized and secure approach to knowledge management.

2.2 Cloud-Based Knowledge Management System

In parallel, the integration of the decentralize approaches (e.g., cloud computing) in knowledge management systems has been gaining traction. The adaptability of independence cloud-based services to modern technological advancements has been noted by Depeige and Boulanger [2], and Khoshnevis and Khanlari [3]. Their research underscores the scalability and flexibility offered by cloud services in managing knowledge. However, challenges in data security and system integrity persist, highlighting the need for a more robust solution [6].

3 Approach

Figure 2 shows a blockchain-based approach to knowledge management that incorporates e-books and distributed ledger technology. The workflow begins with the conversion of physical books or magazines into electronic documents, represented by the e-book icon in the diagram. This digitization step is crucial for making knowledge resources more easily distributable and accessible in modern information systems. Once converted to an e-book format, the digital content is then saved into a centralized system, likely a database or content management platform. The system interface serves as the core of this knowledge management approach, facilitating several key functions. It acts as the central hub for storing and organizing the digitized content, as well as providing a user interface for customers to access and study the materials.

An important aspect of this workflow is the integration of distributed ledger technology. This technology, often associated with blockchain systems, enhances the security and traceability of the knowledge management process. The diagram shows bidirectional data synchronization between the system interface and the distributed ledger, ensuring that information remains consistent and up-to-date across the network. The workflow also incorporates smart contracts

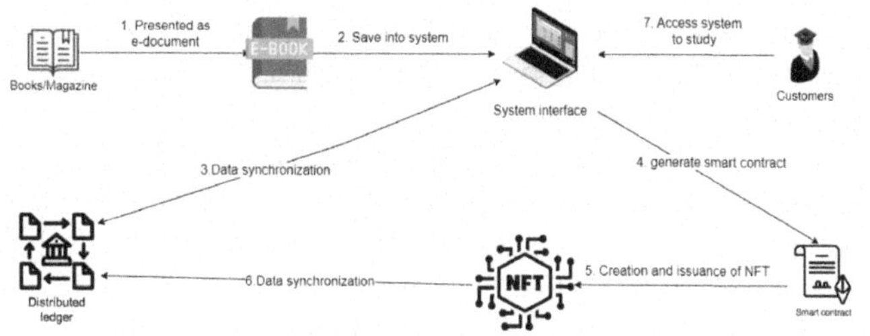

Fig. 2. Knowledge Management System Workflow Using Blockchain Technology

and NFTs as part of the knowledge management process. The system generates smart contracts, which are self-executing contracts with the terms of the agreement directly written into code. These smart contracts likely govern access rights, usage terms, or other conditions related to the digital content. Following the creation of smart contracts, the system issues NFTs, which are unique digital assets that can represent ownership or specific rights to the e-book content. The inclusion of NFTs suggests an attempt to establish clear provenance and potentially enable new models of content licensing or ownership in the digital realm. Both the smart contracts and NFTs are integrated into the distributed ledger, maintaining a secure and transparent record of these digital assets and their associated rights.

4 Evaluation

4.1 Transaction Fee Analysis

The analysis of transaction fees across different blockchain platforms provides crucial insights into the cost implications of deploying blockchain-based knowledge management systems (i.e., Table 1).

Table 1. Transaction fee

	Contract Creation	Create NFT	Transfer NFT
BNB Smart Chain	0.027311 BNB ($16.04)	0.00109162 BNB ($0.64)	0.00056991 BNB ($0.33)
Fantom	0.0095767 FTM ($0.001)	0.000405167 FTM ($0.000)	0.0002380105 FTM ($0.000)
Polygon	c 0.0068405000328344 MATIC($0.000)	0.000289405001273382 MATIC($0.000)	0.000170007500748033 MATIC($0.000)
Celo	0.00709722 CELO ($0.004)	0.0002840812 CELO ($0.000)	0.0001554878 CELO ($0.000)

On the BNB Smart Chain, the transaction fee for contract creation is 0.027311 BNB, which translates to approximately $16.04. This relatively high fee reflects the computational resources required to deploy smart contracts on this platform. For creating an NFT, the fee is substantially lower at 0.00109162 BNB ($0.64), while transferring an NFT incurs a fee of 0.00056991 BNB ($0.33).

These fees indicate that while the initial deployment of contracts is expensive, the costs associated with ongoing operations, such as NFT creation and transfer, are more manageable.

When it comes to Fantom, it presents a stark contrast in terms of transaction fees. The cost for contract creation is 0.0095767 FTM, approximately $0.001, which is significantly lower compared to BNB Smart Chain. Similarly, creating an NFT costs 0.000405167 FTM, effectively negligible in USD, and transferring an NFT costs 0.0002380105 FTM. The minimal fees on Fantom suggest that it is a highly cost-effective platform for both deploying and managing blockchain-based applications, making it an attractive option for projects with budget constraints.

For the cases of Polygon, it also demonstrates low transaction fees. The fee for contract creation is 0.0068405000328344 MATIC, which is negligible in USD terms. The costs for creating and transferring NFTs are 0.000289405001273382 MATIC and 0.000170007- 500748033 MATIC, respectively, both effectively zero in USD. This low-cost structure is advantageous for users who need to execute numerous transactions, as it minimizes the financial burden associated with blockchain operations.

Finally, Celo's transaction fees are similarly low, with the cost for contract creation being 0.00709722 CELO, roughly $0.004. The fees for creating and transferring NFTs are 0.0002840812 CELO and 0.0001554878 CELO, respectively, both amounting to negligible USD values. Celo's fee structure indicates that it, like Fantom and Polygon, offers a cost-effective environment for deploying and managing blockchain applications.

4.2 Burn Fee

The analysis of burn fees described in Table 2 offers insight into the cost implications associated with the destruction of tokens during various operations. Burn fees are crucial because they reflect the economic cost of reducing the circulating supply of tokens, which can impact both the cost structure of blockchain applications and the overall tokenomics of the platform.

Table 2. Burn fee

	Contracts Creation	Create NFT	Transfer NFT
BNB Smart Chain	0.0027311 BNB ($1.6)	0.00109162 BNB ($0.064)	0.{4}56991 BNB ($0.03)
Fantom	do not mention	do not mention	do not mention
Polygon	0.{10}0328344 MATIC ($0.00)	0.{10}01273382 MATIC($0.00	0.{12}0748033 MATIC($0.00)
Celo	do not mention	do not mention	do not mention

For the BNB Smart Chain (i.e., about 10% of the corresponding functions), the burn fee for contract creation is 0.0027311 BNB, which is approximately $1.60. This fee indicates the cost incurred when deploying a smart contract and removing a portion of the tokens from circulation. The burn fee for creating an NFT on this platform is 0.00109162 BNB, translating to $0.064. This cost, though relatively small, adds up with frequent transactions, impacting the overall cost of NFT operations. Additionally, the burn fee for transferring an NFT is 0.00056991 BNB, which amounts to about $0.03. These fees demonstrate that while the burn fees for individual transactions are modest, they still represent a significant consideration in the ongoing operational costs. On the Polygon network, the burn fees are recorded as effectively zero in USD terms, though the nominal values in MATIC are provided. For contract creation, the burn fee is listed as 0.0000328344 MATIC, which translates to a negligible amount in USD. Similarly, the burn fees for creating and transferring NFTs are 0.00001273382 MATIC and 0.00000748033 MATIC, respectively, both amounting to zero in USD. The minimal burn fees on Polygon indicate that it is highly cost-efficient, especially for applications requiring numerous transactions and operations.

In contrast, the Fantom and Celo platforms do not mention burn fees in the provided data, implying either the absence of such fees or their negligible impact on the overall cost structure. This lack of burn fees can be a significant advantage for these platforms, making them more cost-effective for users who engage in frequent transactions and deployments. The absence of burn fee data for Fantom and Celo, coupled with the negligible fees on Polygon, suggests that these platforms might be more financially viable for projects sensitive to cost fluctuations and tokenomics. This advantage is particularly relevant for applications that necessitate frequent transactions and smart contract deployments, where cumulative costs can significantly impact the project's sustainability and financial planning.

4.3 Gas Limit Analysis

Table 3 shows the gas limits, which determines the maximum amount of computational work that can be executed in a single transaction, thereby influencing the complexity and size of operations that can be performed.

Table 3. Gas limit

	Contract Creation	Create NFT	Transfer NFT
BNB Smart Chain	2,731,100	109,162	71,991
Fantom	2,736,200	115,762	72,803
Polygon	2,736,476	115,762	72,803
Celo	3,548,610	142,040	85,673

On the BNB Smart Chain, the gas limit for contract creation is set at 2,731,100 units. This substantial limit allows for the execution of complex smart contracts, which is essential for deploying sophisticated blockchain applications. For creating an NFT, the gas limit is significantly lower at 109,162 units, reflecting the relatively simpler computational requirements of this operation. Similarly, the gas limit for transferring an NFT is 71,991 units, which is sufficient for the straightforward task of moving digital assets between addresses.

Fantom's gas limits are slightly higher than those of the BNB Smart Chain for all operations. The gas limit for contract creation on Fantom is 2,736,200 units, marginally exceeding the BNB Smart Chain's limit. This small difference suggests that Fantom allows for a slightly higher degree of complexity in smart contract execution. The gas limit for creating an NFT on Fantom is 115,762 units, and for transferring an NFT, it is 72,803 units. These higher limits indicate that Fantom provides slightly more computational resources for these operations, potentially enhancing their efficiency and performance.

Polygon's gas limits closely mirror those of Fantom, with a gas limit of 2,736,476 units for contract creation. The slight increase over Fantom's limit suggests a similar capacity for handling complex smart contracts. The gas limits for creating and transferring NFTs on Polygon are 115,762 units and 72,803 units, respectively, identical to those on Fantom. This consistency highlights Polygon's comparable ability to handle NFT-related operations with sufficient computational resources. Celo stands out with the highest gas limits among the evaluated platforms. The gas limit for contract creation on Celo is 3,548,610 units, significantly higher than those on BNB Smart Chain, Fantom, and Polygon. This higher limit indicates that Celo can support more complex smart contracts and potentially larger-scale applications. The gas limit for creating an NFT on Celo is 142,040 units, and for transferring an NFT, it is 85,673 units. These increased limits suggest that Celo provides more computational resources for these operations, which could translate into better performance and efficiency, particularly for applications requiring extensive data processing and transaction handling.

The gas limit analysis reveals that while all evaluated platforms offer substantial computational resources for various blockchain operations, there are notable differences. BNB Smart Chain provides adequate limits for most applications but is slightly lower than Fantom and Polygon, which offer similar and slightly higher limits for contract creation and NFT operations. Celo, with its significantly higher gas limits, stands out as the platform that can support the most complex and resource-intensive applications. These findings help in selecting the appropriate platform based on the computational requirements of blockchain-based knowledge management systems.

5 Conclusion

In conclusion, this paper has examined the potential of integrating blockchain technology and NFTs into knowledge management systems to enhance security, accessibility, and efficiency. Traditional models of knowledge management, while foundational, have shown limitations in the face of advancing digital technologies. The immutable and transparent nature of blockchain, combined with the unique identification features of NFTs, offers a robust solution to these challenges. Our proposed framework addresses issues related to data security, copyright protection, and accessibility by leveraging these technologies. The implementation of smart contracts on Binance Smart Chain, Polygon, Fantom, and Celo demonstrates the feasibility of this approach across different platforms. The evaluation results indicate that our system is not only scalable and cost-effective but also capable of maintaining high performance in real-world settings. These findings suggest that adopting blockchain and NFT technologies in knowledge management systems can significantly improve the way academic content is managed and shared.

Acknowledgement. We acknowledge the support of time and facilities from Ho Chi Minh City University of Technology (HCMUT), VNU-HCM for this study.

References

1. Bartling, S.: Blockchain for science and knowledge creation. In: Haring, R. (ed.) Gesundheit digital, pp. 159–180. Springer, Heidelberg (2019). https://doi.org/10.1007/978-3-662-57611-3_10
2. Depeige, A., Doyencourt, D.: Actionable knowledge as a service (akaas): leveraging big data analytics in cloud computing environments. J. Big Data **2**(1), 1–16 (2015)
3. Khoshnevis, S., Rabeifar, F.: Toward knowledge management as a service in cloud-based environments. Int. J. Mechatron. Electr. Comput. Technol. **2**(4), 88–110 (2012)
4. Le, H.T., et al.: Introducing multi shippers mechanism for decentralized cash on delivery system. Int. J. Adv. Comput. Sci. Appl. **10**(6) (2019)
5. Le, N., et al.: Assuring non-fraudulent transactions in cash on delivery by introducing double smart contracts. Int. J. Adv. Comput. Sci. Appl. **10**(5), 677–684 (2019)
6. Liu, Z.Q., Dorozhkin, E., Davydova, N., Sadovnikova, N.: Effectiveness of the partial implementation of a cloud-based knowledge management system. Int. J. Emerg. Technol. Learn. (iJET) **15**(13), 155–171 (2020)
7. Mittal, U., Gedeon, T., Caldwell, S.: Managing knowledge provenance using blockchain. In: 2018 9th IEEE International Conference on Cognitive Infocommunications (CogInfoCom), pp. 000241–000246. IEEE (2018)
8. Nyame, G., Qin, Z., Obour Agyekum, K.O.B., Sifah, E.B.: An ecdsa approach to access control in knowledge management systems using blockchain. Information **11**(2), 111 (2020)
9. Pfeiffer, A., Bezzina, S., Wernbacher, T., Vella, V., Dingli, A., Serada, A.: The use of blockchain-supported reward systems for knowledge transfer between generations. In: Academic Conferences International Limited (2020)
10. Qin, R., Yuan, Y., Wang, F.Y.: Blockchain-based knowledge automation for cpss-oriented parallel management. IEEE Trans. Comput. Soc. Syst. **7**(5), 1180–1188 (2020)

Blockchain-Driven Pediatric Vaccine Management: Utilizing RSA-Encrypted NFTs, and IPFS for Secure Solutions

Phat T. Tran-Truong[1,2](✉), H. V. Khanh[3], M. N. Triet[3], K. L. Bang[3], M. D. Hieu[3], N. N. Hung[3], and K. T. N. Ngan[4]

[1] Department of Software Engineering, Faculty of Computer Science and Engineering, Ho Chi Minh City University of Technology (HCMUT), 268 Ly Thuong Kiet Street, District 10, Ho Chi Minh City, Vietnam
phatttt@hcmut.edu.vn

[2] Vietnam National University Ho Chi Minh City, Linh Trung Ward, Thu Duc District, Ho Chi Minh City, Vietnam

[3] FPT University, Can Tho city, Vietnam

[4] FPT Polytechnic, Can Tho city, Vietnam

Abstract. Effective vaccination is crucial for public health, however, traditional paper-based systems are prone to errors and inefficiencies. This paper proposes a blockchain-based solution, leveraging smart contracts to automate data management processes, RSA-encrypted NFTs to provide tamper-proof digital certification of vaccination events and InterPlanetary File System (IPFS) for decentralized data storage. By doing this, our approach not only ensures the immutability and accessibility of vaccination records, but also enhance the security, transparency, and efficiency of pediatric vaccine management as a whole. Our system is then evaluated in term of performance efficiency and transaction fees across multiple EVM-supported blockchain platforms, including Binance Smart Chain, Polygon, Fantom, and Celo to highlight practical implementation insights for transparent and trustworthy blockchain-driven vaccine management system.

Keywords: Pediatric Vaccine · Blockchain · Smart Contracts · Non-Fungible Tokens (NFTs) · Decentralized Storage

1 Introduction

Vaccination stands as a cornerstone of public health, critical in safeguarding populations against a spectrum of diseases. With the global transition towards digitalization, there is a pressing need to reevaluate and refine the mechanisms underpinning vaccination record-keeping and management. Recent studies [5,7] have explored various dimensions of this domain, ranging from simultaneous vaccination administration, the promise of blockchain-based solutions, the intricacies of decentralized systems, to the quality and accessibility of vaccination information online. Global challenges, such as the COVID-19 pandemic, underscore the imperative of efficient and transparent vaccine management.

J. Kertesz et al. (Eds.): CSoNet 2024, LNCS 15417, pp. 336–343, 2025.
https://doi.org/10.1007/978-981-96-6389-7_30

On the flip side, the traditional vaccine management model has been instrumental in ensuring that children receive timely and safe vaccinations. This model, as shown in Fig. 1, is based on a collaborative effort between parents or guardians, healthcare providers, and vaccination centers. In which key components/actors are: Parents/Guardians Make informed decisions about your child's health, including vaccination schedules; Vaccine Logbook: A paper-based record of vaccinations administered; Vaccination Center: The facility where vaccines are administered; and the vaccine Certificate: Official documentation of completed vaccinations.

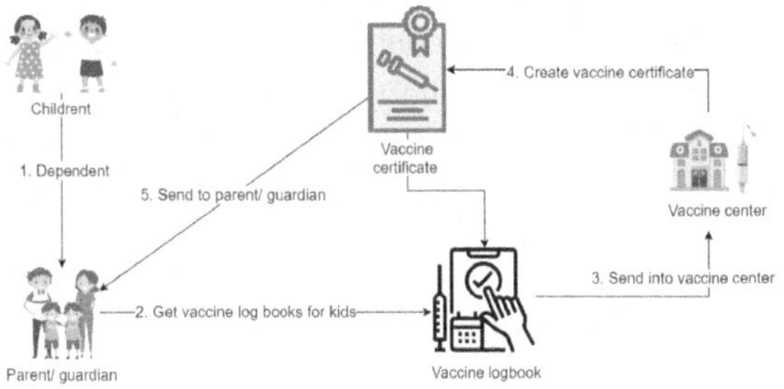

Fig. 1. Traditional vaccine management process for children

In this paper, we propose a comprehensive approach to pediatric vaccine management, aimed at providing a secure and efficient system for vaccine records using blockchain technology, RSA-encrypted NFTs, and smart contracts. Our contributions include introducing a blockchain-centric framework that enhances the security and integrity of vaccine records while ensuring accessibility to authorized parties. We utilize RSA-encrypted NFTs to digitally certify each vaccination event, making the records tamper-proof and transparent. Smart contracts are leveraged to automate and streamline the vaccine management process, reducing the likelihood of human errors and improving overall efficiency. The system is designed for cross-platform compatibility, with implementations across multiple EVM-supported blockchain platforms, including Binance Smart Chain, Polygon, Fantom, and Celo, ensuring flexibility and scalability. Additionally, by integrating the IPFS, we ensure durable and decentralized storage of vaccination data, enhancing accessibility and security.

2 Related Work

The management and record-keeping of vaccinations are pivotal in public health. Numerous strategies have been explored to optimize these processes, including simultaneous vaccine administration, as proposed by Zhao et al. [9], to boost coverage rates. Blockchain technology has emerged as a promising solution for managing vaccination records. Alnssayan et al. [1] highlighted its potential to address data integrity concerns inherent in traditional systems. Halim et al. [3] introduced a decentralized system for Malaysia, leveraging IPFS and blockchain to enhance data integrity and accessibility. Beyond technological advancements, the cold chain remains a critical factor in vaccine efficacy. Feyisa et al. [2] emphasized the importance of maintaining cold chain integrity, particularly in regions like Ethiopia. Digital platforms have also been explored to promote vaccination and educate the public. Kolff et al. [4] investigated the role of digital platforms in influencing public health initiatives. However, Modanloo et al. [6] highlighted a gap in high-quality online resources for parents, particularly those offering pain management advice during vaccinations. Our proposed blockchain-based healthcare system aims to address these challenges and opportunities by leveraging blockchain technology and smart contracts to enhance healthcare operations while prioritizing data security, transparency, and patient empowerment.

3 Approach

3.1 Phase One: Blockchain-Based Approach for Vaccine Management in Children

Building on the model discussed in our previous article [8], we aim to enhance the system for securing children's vaccination data by integrating RSA-encrypted NFTs. Our proposed approach utilizes advanced technologies such as Smart Contracts, RSA-encrypted NFTs, IPFS, and Blockchain. Figure 2 shows the architecture of this approach again, introducing several components to address the limitations of the traditional model. These components include a User Interface for easy navigation and data entry, a Personal Identification Code for secure identification, Smart Contracts to automate and validate vaccination procedures, NFTs for digitizing and verifying individual vaccination records, IPFS for decentralized and durable data storage, and a Distributed Ledger to maintain a transparent and immutable record of all transactions and interactions. Our blockchain-based approach offers a secure and transparent solution to address these challenges by a six-step process:

Step 1: Child's Dependence on Parents or Guardians. Children rely on their parents or guardians for their well-being, including healthcare decisions. This makes parental involvement crucial in ensuring timely and appropriate vaccinations.

Step 2: Initialization Through Personal Identification. Parents or guardians create a digital vaccine record for their child by providing personal information, health history, and previous vaccination details.

Step 3: Creation of RSA-Encrypted NFT Smart Contract. The child's vaccination information is encrypted and securely stored as an NFT on the blockchain, guaranteeing data integrity and immutability.

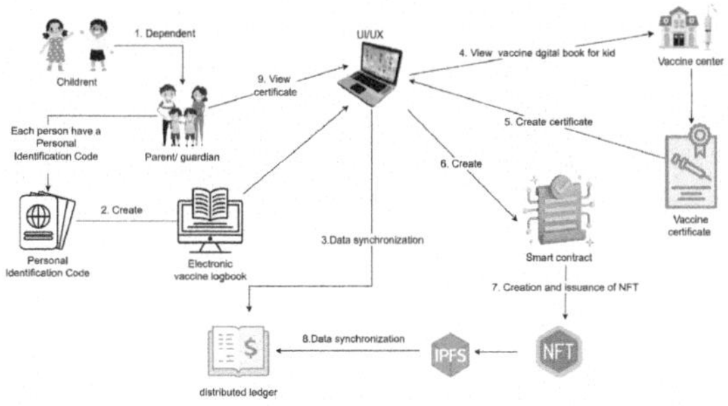

Fig. 2. Blockchain-Based Approach for Vaccine Management in Children

Step 4: Verification at the Vaccination Center. Healthcare professionals at the vaccination center access the child's secure digital record on the blockchain. This allows them to verify the child's vaccination history, determine necessary vaccinations, and review any relevant health information.

Step 5: Vaccination and Certificate Issuance. Subsequent to vaccination, the vaccination center updates the child's digital record and issues a secure digital vaccination certificate, which is immutably recorded on the blockchain.

Step 6: Continuous Monitoring by Parents or Guardians. Parents or guardians can log in to the system to monitor their child's vaccination records, update health information, and ensure timely vaccinations.

3.2 Phase Two: Integration of RSA-Encrypted NFTs and Smart Contracts for Vaccine Management in Children

The diagram (Fig. 3) outlines a methodical approach to managing children's vaccination records using RSA-encrypted NFTs to ensure secure and private access. In our system, guardians, such as parents or legal custodians, and the vaccination center are the primary users who interact with the vaccination records through distinct public keys within the blockchain framework. At the outset, each guardian is assigned a unique public key (referred to as public key A in the diagram), which is essential for accessing their child's vaccination records. The NFTs, which represent the vaccination records, are encrypted using RSA encryption, a widely recognized method for securing sensitive data. The encrypted NFT is linked to the guardian's public key, ensuring that only they can access and manage their child's vaccination data.

In parallel, vaccination centers are allocated a separate public key (public key B). When a doctor needs to access a child's vaccination records, the NFT is decrypted using the corresponding private key that matches public key B. This decryption process allows for secure and controlled viewing of vaccination records

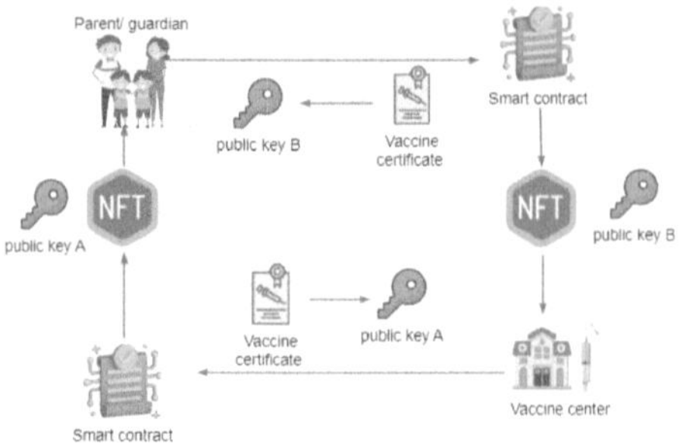

Fig. 3. Schematic representation of a Vaccine Management in Children model using RSA-encrypted NFTs

by healthcare professionals. RSA encryption ensures that the data is transmitted and viewed without the risk of unauthorized access or exposure. Smart contracts within the blockchain manage the permissions and actions associated with these NFTs. They execute predefined rules that govern who can access the vaccination records, under what conditions, and what actions can be taken. For example, a smart contract may be programmed to grant access to a new doctor when a child visits a new vaccination center or to update the vaccination records upon receiving new information.

4 Evaluation

4.1 Efficiency

To assess the efficiency of using RSA-encrypted NFTs to secure and manage children's vaccination records, we conducted a performance evaluation on two types of data: image files (e.g., vaccination certificates) and text records (e.g., vaccination schedules). The evaluation of time efficiency in the RSA key generation, encryption, and decryption processes for images within the vaccine management system for children is summarized in Table 1. The time taken for generating the RSA key ranged from 30,108 microseconds to 301,008 microseconds, with an average of approximately 146,687 microseconds, indicating a significant computational requirement for this initial step. The encryption of the image was quicker, with times ranging from 8,111 microseconds to 11,635 microseconds, averaging around 9,744 microseconds, which supports the need for efficient documentation processes. In contrast, the decryption of the image was the most time-consuming, ranging from 255,306 microseconds to 269,676 microseconds, with an average of 262,883 microseconds. This extended time for decryption underscores the computational demands of the RSA algorithm, balancing the need for data security with processing efficiency.

Similarly, the evaluation of time efficiency in the RSA key generation, encryption, and decryption processes for text within the vaccine management system for children is summarized in Table 2. The time taken for generating the RSA

Table 1. Evaluation of Time Efficiency in RSA Key Generation, Encryption, and Decryption for Image in Microseconds

RSA (image)	1	2	3	4	5	6	7	8	9	10
Generating key	75356	95235	38750	78216	98703	95067	54002	301008	75905	98625
Encrypting image	10678	9685	8111	9330	9393	10638	11635	10350	10979	10646
Decrypting image	262878	265051	269676	255449	258359	265588	255306	258615	259331	260586

key ranged from 24,110 microseconds to 168,443 microseconds, with an average of approximately 78,356 microseconds, reflecting the computational demand of this initial step. The encryption of text data was consistently rapid, showing a time of 0 microseconds across all trials, indicating negligible time required for this process. Decryption times varied, ranging from 501 microseconds to 1,508 microseconds, with an average of 1,011 microseconds. This demonstrates the efficiency of handling routine data entries within the system while ensuring secure and quick access to vaccination records.

Table 2. Evaluation of Time Efficiency in RSA Key Generation, Encryption, and Decryption for Text in Microseconds

RSA (text)	1	2	3	4	5	6	7	8	9	10
Generating key	109072	161201	58533	54586	24110	94431	168443	31826	46018	82341
Encrypting text	0	0	0	0	0	0	0	0	0	0
Decrypting text	594	1413	1160	1274	501	1084	1378	1508	502	998

The RSA encryption mechanism exhibits relatively consistent performance across different data types. Nonetheless, the key generation and, particularly, the decryption processes are computationally demanding. This inherent trade-off between security and efficiency must be carefully considered when deploying RSA encryption in pediatric vaccine management systems. The findings presented in Tables 1 and 2 underscore the need for a robust yet efficient encryption solution to effectively manage vaccination records.

4.2 Testing on EVM-Supported Platforms

Transaction Fee Analysis: To conduct our analysis, we examine four Ethereum Virtual Machine (EVM)-compatible blockchain platforms and compares transaction fees, detailed in Table 3: Binance Smart Chain (BNB), Fantom (FTM), Polygon (MATIC), and Celo (CELO) for a framework enhancing vaccine management in children using RSA-encrypted NFTs and smart contracts. The table also shows the token market values for these platforms as of January 27, 2024, at 7:00:00 AM UTC, highlighting the economic context for adopting these blockchain technologies in the vaccine management system.

Table 3. Transaction fee

	Transaction Creation	Create NFT	Transfer NFT
BNB	0.0273134 BNB ($16.47)	0.00109162 BNB ($0.66)	0.00057003 BNB ($0.34)
Fantom	0.00957754 FTM ($0.00)	0.000405167 FTM ($0.00)	0.0002380105 FTM ($0.00)
Polygon	0.006840710032835408 MATIC ($0.01)	0.000289405001852192 MATIC ($0.00)	0.000170007501088048 MATIC ($0.00)
Celo	0.007097844 CELO ($0.005)	0.0002840812 CELO ($0.000)	0.0001554878 CELO ($0.000)

Firstly, on BNB, transaction fees are 0.0273134 BNB ($16.47), minting an NFT costs 0.00109162 BNB ($0.66), and transferring an NFT costs 0.00057003 BNB ($0.34). These fees position Binance Smart Chain as an efficient platform, albeit potentially costlier than alternatives. Secondly, Fantom presents a cost-effective alternative, with the price for executing a new transaction set at 0.00957754 FTM, a nominal amount in dollar terms. Fees for NFT creation and transfer on Fantom's network are recorded at 0.000405167 FTM and 0.0002380105 FTM, respectively, both translating to minimal dollar values. This suggests that Fantom offers a more affordable solution for managing transactions, particularly for activities involving NFTs. Thirdly, the Polygon network lists the fee for starting a transaction at 0.006840710032835408 MATIC, or just $0.01. Creating an NFT on Polygon is extremely cost-effective at 0.000289405001852192 MATIC, and transferring an NFT costs 0.000170007501088048 MATIC. Both expenses are negligible, indicating a minimal financial impact for operations on this platform. Finally, Celo's network charges 0.007097844 CELO for initiating a transaction, which equates to about $0.005. The fees for NFT creation and transfer are 0.0002840812 CELO and 0.0001554878 CELO, respectively, both amounting to less than a cent. These figures position Celo as an economically viable choice for transaction management within the system.

The comparative analysis of transaction costs presented in the table is crucial for stakeholders contemplating the integration of blockchain technology into vaccine management. These costs have a direct bearing on the financial feasibility of blockchain solutions and should be carefully assessed in the context of the specific operational requirements of the vaccine management system.

5 Conclusion

In conclusion, this paper proposes a comprehensive blockchain-enabled framework for pediatric vaccine management, incorporating RSA-encrypted NFTs and smart contracts. The proposed system addresses critical challenges in current vaccination record-keeping processes, enhancing data security, transparency, and operational efficiency. Our cross-platform implementation demonstrates the system's versatility and scalability. Future research will explore further refinements and evaluate the long-term economic implications of widespread adoption.

Acknowledgement. We acknowledge the support of time and facilities from Ho Chi Minh City University of Technology (HCMUT), VNU-HCM for this study.

References

1. Alnssayan, A.A., Hassan, M.M., Alsuhibany, S.A.: Vacchain: a blockchain-based emr system to manage child vaccination records. Comput. Syst. Sci. Eng. **40**(3) (2022)
2. Feyisa, D.: Cold chain maintenance and vaccine stock management practices at public health centers providing child immunization services in jimma zone, oromia regional state, ethiopia: multi-centered, mixed method approach. Pediatric health, medicine and therapeutics, pp. 359–372 (2021)
3. Halim, F.H., Rashid, N.A.M., Johari, N.F.M., Rahman, M.A.H.A.: Decentralized children's immunization record management system for private healthcare in malaysia using ipfs and blockchain. JOIV: Inter. J. Inform. Visualiz. **6**(4), 890–896 (2022)
4. Kolff, C.A., Scott, V.P., Stockwell, M.S.: The use of technology to promote vaccination: a social ecological model based framework. Human Vaccines Immunotherapeutics **14**(7), 1636–1646 (2018)
5. Le, H.T., et al.: Patient-chain: patient-centered healthcare system a blockchain-based technology in dealing with emergencies. In: Shen, H., et al. (eds.) PDCAT 2021. LNCS, vol. 13148, pp. 576–583. Springer, Cham (2022). https://doi.org/10.1007/978-3-030-96772-7_54
6. Modanloo, S., Stacey, D., Dunn, S., Choueiry, J., Harrison, D.: Parent resources for early childhood vaccination: an online environmental scan. Vaccine **37**(51), 7493–7500 (2019)
7. Son, H.X., et al.: Toward a blockchain-based technology in dealing with emergencies in patient-centered healthcare systems. In: Bouzefrane, S., Laurent, M., Boumerdassi, S., Renault, E. (eds.) MSPN 2020. LNCS, vol. 12605, pp. 44–56. Springer, Cham (2021). https://doi.org/10.1007/978-3-030-67550-9_4
8. Trong, N., et al.: Blockchain-enhanced pediatric vaccine management: A novel approach integrating nfts, ipfs, and smart contracts. In: International Conference on Services Computing, pp. 63–78. Springer (2023). https://doi.org/10.1007/978-3-031-51674-0_5
9. Zhao, Z., Smith, P.J., Hill, H.A.: Evaluation of potentially achievable vaccination coverage with simultaneous administration of vaccines among children in the united states. Vaccine **34**(27), 3030–3036 (2016)

Classify Bone Fractures in X-ray Images

Tu N. Hoa[1,2], An N. Ho[1,2], Vi T. N. Ly[1,2], Son T. Huynh[1,2], and Binh T. Nguyen[1,2(✉)]

[1] AISIA Research Lab, University of Science, Ho Chi Minh City, Vietnam
ngtbinh@hcmus.edu.vn
[2] Vietnam National University, Ho Chi Minh City, Vietnam

Abstract. Bone fractures are prevalent injuries that necessitate prompt and precise diagnosis to ensure effective treatment. Traditionally, fractures are diagnosed using data from X-rays, magnetic resonance imaging (MRI), or computed tomography (CT) scans. This study aims to assist physicians by employing artificial intelligence to classify X-ray images as fractured or non-fractured. To achieve this, we evaluated the performance of 20 models. The models tested include AlexNet, ResNet, DenseNet, VGG, MobileNet, EfficientNet, RegNet, and RepVGG. DenseNet, MobileNet, and EfficientNet performed best, achieving a test F1-Score of 0.79.

Keywords: Biomedical image classification · Bone fractures · Deep learning · CNN · X-ray

1 Introduction

In recent years, Deep Learning (DL) has been famous for its revolution in various fields, ranging from healthcare to autonomous driving. In the beginning, its "deep" structure takes inspiration from the human brain structure; by stacking many neurons into layers (from three to several hundred or even thousands), DL models can be trained to process particular data and generate a suitable output in a short time. These networks can automatically extract useful features from data and also capture the underlying relationships between them despite their complex architectures. Up to this point, it is undeniable that DL has become the center stage in terms of technological advancements and real-world downstream applications. Fig 1 illustrates a brain neuron (**A**) and an ANN structure (**B**). They both process multiple input signals, and the output is passed on to other states after being processed. Each cell body processes the inputs in very distinct ways. The ANN consists of interconnected artificial neurons, where each neuron functions as a simple classifier model that generates a decision signal based on the weighted sum of evidence [9].

One of the most outstanding characteristics of DL models is that they are trained rather than manually programmed. They require less fine-tuning and expert oversight, which helps DL surpass many conventional methods in various tasks. For example, the famous dataset, the MNIST database, comprises

J. Kertesz et al. (Eds.): CSoNet 2024, LNCS 15417, pp. 344–356, 2025.
https://doi.org/10.1007/978-981-96-6389-7_31

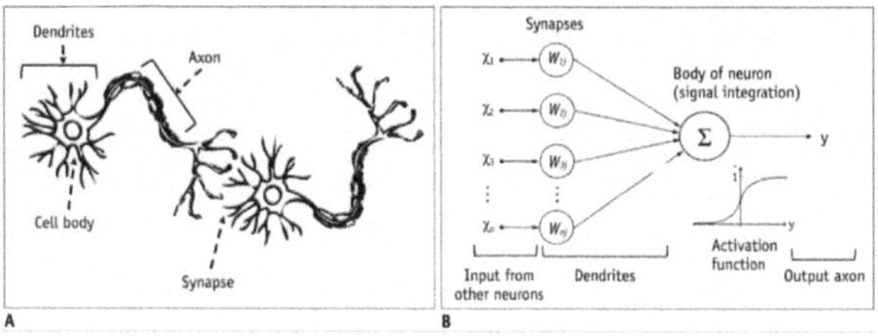

Fig. 1. Conceptual analogy between real neurons (A) and artificial neurons (B) [9]

handwritten digits and includes 60,000 training examples and 10,000 test examples. Many methods have been established for solving this problem, but in the end, deep learning emerged as the top choice due to its fast and highly accurate results.

On the other hand, a fracture is a partial or complete break in the bone[1]. The causes for the disease might be varied, such as physical trauma, overuse, and health conditions that weaken bone strength, for example, osteoporosis, which is the leading cause of bone fractures. More importantly, old age can be a severe risk for a fracture since human bones will typically weaken with age, along with having varied conditions that decrease bone quality over time.[2]. To be more specific, osteoporosis is a condition affecting the skeletal system. It is characterized by low bone mass and deterioration of bone tissue, which leads to weaker and more porous bones, increasing the risk of fractures. It is known as a common cause of broken bones in the elderly, with approximately 6.8 million cases coming to medical attention each year in the United States. Fractures comprise 16% of all musculoskeletal injuries in the U.S. annually, with approximately 6.3 million occurring each year[3].

Furthermore, the symptoms of a fracture are diverse due to many factors, namely its location, the patient's age, previous health status, the wound's severity, and so on. While bone fractures might typically heal well after being appropriately treated, complications can occur under some circumstances. For example, the bone may heal in the wrong position or shift during the recovery process. In children, bone fractures can adversely impact bone growth, potentially leading to deformities.

The most common and valuable method for detecting a fracture is through X-rays, which produce clear images of the bone. These can also show the type of fracture the patient experiencing and precisely pinpoint its location in the body. The most common method for evaluating a fracture is through X-rays, which produce clear images of the bone. They can also reveal the fracture type and precisely pinpoint its location within the bone. Nowadays, radiologists around the globe face a growing volume of complex imaging tests, making it more difficult for

[1] https://www.hopkinsmedicine.org/health/conditions-and-diseases/fractures.
[2] https://www.medicalnewstoday.com/articles/173312#types.
[3] https://u.osu.edu/productdesigngroup3/sample-page/.

them to complete readings on time and produce accurate reports [9]. However, deep learning technology offers potential solutions by quantitatively analyzing suspicious lesions and facilitating faster report generation through automatic reporting and voice recognition. These advancements could enhance diagnostic accuracy and streamline the clinical workflow. Despite the deep learning model's great influences on musculoskeletal radiology diagnosis, such as detecting fractures in areas like the proximal humerus, hand, and ankle on X-rays, AI algorithms, up to now, have neither been widely used in clinical nor being accepted by the FDA (Food and Drug Administration). According to the ACRDSI's AI Center in 2023, only 22 algorithms have received approval to date [10].

Because of the limited number of approved methods currently used in clinical settings, additional research and examination are necessary to develop more effective diagnostic methods for bone fractures in the future. In light of this, this research's key contributions encompass an extensive survey and experimental analysis utilizing state-of-the-art (SOTA) CNN models for classification purposes. We identified the optimal model for accurately distinguishing between fractured and non-fractured X-ray images. These results aim to support non-specialists in triage, particularly in emergency departments where bone fractures are frequently encountered.

With the results presented in this paper, we aim to expedite the selection of appropriate state-of-the-art models for related topics and generate outstanding outcomes that will ultimately improve patient care.

2 Related Works

Convolutional neural networks (CNNs) have different applications in automated fracture detection and classification. Asma Alzaid et al. [2] systematically investigated various CNN architectures, including ResNet, DenseNet, VGG, and Inception, to classify peri-prosthetic femur fractures (PFFs). They studied a computer-aided diagnosis (CAD) tool for detecting and classifying PFFs.

Fatih et al. [16] investigated the classification problem of shoulder fractures using deep learning ensemble models, focusing on the MURA dataset, which consists of musculoskeletal radiographs. This research evaluated the effectiveness of 26 pre-trained deep learning models, including ResNet, ResNeXt, DenseNet, VGG, Inception, and MobileNet, alongside their Spinal Fully Connected (Spinal FC) variations. To further enhance the accuracy of fracture classification, the researchers proposed two ensemble learning models, EL1 and EL2, which leveraged the strengths of the highest-performing pre-trained models. The results demonstrated that the EL2 model achieved superior test accuracy and Cohen's kappa values, while the EL1 model recorded the highest area under the receiver operating characteristic curve (AUC). Specifically, the EL2 model reached approximately 84.7% test accuracy, a Cohen's kappa value of 0.694, and an AUC of 0.886. These findings underscore the utility of ensemble learning techniques in improving diagnostic performance. Furthermore, this study emphasized the critical role of transfer learning in the medical image classification process.

Using pre-trained models and ensemble learning approaches contributed to more robust and accurate predictions.

The significance of these results shows the relevant potential to support clinical decision-making, offering radiologists a powerful tool for identifying shoulder fractures with greater precision. Integrating multiple deep learning models improved the overall diagnostic accuracy and showcased the viability of leveraging ensemble learning methods to address the inherent variability in medical imaging data. This combination of models is particularly beneficial in real-world clinical scenarios, where diverse patient cases require nuanced and reliable diagnostic solutions.

3 Methodology

3.1 Problem Formulation

Fracture detection and classification from X-ray images are essential in assisting physicians in diagnosing and treating injuries accurately and efficiently. The main objective of this study is to explore deep learning-based methods for binary classification of X-ray images into two groups: fractured and non-fractured.

However, this process faces many challenges due to the sophistication and diversity of fracture types, uneven image quality, and differences in bone structure in different age groups. In particular, cases of patients who have undergone treatment for fractures can also be accurate. As medical data are rare and limited, we decided to use the FracAtals dataset [1], including various types of bone fractures. Also, this dataset has been well-labeled and can be used for different models. The total number of X-ray images used is 4083, with 717 fractured images and 3366 non-fractured pictures. Besides, we mainly focus on images of the hand, shoulder, hip, and leg.

3.2 Deep Learning Approaches

Various deep-learning-based methods have been developed and employed to classify X-ray images of the bone in PNG format. These methods include different convolutional neural network (CNN) architectures with unique structures and layers. Specifically, models such as AlexNet [8], ResNet (18, 34, 50, 101, 152) [4,5], DenseNet (169, 201) [7], VGG (16, 19) [13], MobileNet (V2, V3) [6,12], EfficientNet (b0, b1, b7, v2) [14,15], RegNet [11], and RepVGG [3] have been utilized due to their strong performance in image classification tasks. These publicly available CNN-based models have been optimized for feature extraction and image analysis.

AlexNet. AlexNet has five convolutional layers, with three fully connected layers. The first convolutional layer uses 96 filters of size 11×11 with a stride of 4, followed by a ReLU activation and a 3×3 max pooling layer with a stride of 2. The second convolutional layer employs 256 filters of size 5×5 with a stride of

1, followed by a ReLU activation and a 3×3 max pooling layer with a stride of 2. The third and fourth convolutional layers utilize 384 filters of size 3×3 with a stride of 1, each followed by a ReLU activation. The fifth convolutional layer uses 256 filters of size 3×3 with a stride of 1, followed by a ReLU activation and a 3×3 max pooling layer with a stride of 2. The convolutional layers' output is flattened and passed through two fully connected layers.

ResNet. In a convolutional neural network, ResNet, each layer incorporates residual connections that allow gradients to flow more easily through the network during training. The ResNet architecture is characterized by its use of residual blocks, where each block contains two or more convolutional layers with skip connections that bypass one or more layers. In this study, we use the robust architectures of ResNet18, ResNet34, ResNet50, ResNet101, and ResNet152.

DenseNet. DenseNet has different layers, each receiving input from all preceding layers, enhancing feature reuse and gradient flow. DenseNet169 has 169 layers organized into dense blocks, with each block concatenating the outputs of previous layers before applying convolution. Transition layers use 1×1 convolution and 2×2 average pooling to reduce feature maps and downsample. DenseNet201 extends this to 201 layers, adding more dense blocks and transition layers, maintaining a growth rate of 32 feature maps per layer to capture more intricate patterns.

MobileNet. MobileNet is a lightweight and efficient convolutional neural network designed for mobile and embedded applications. MobileNetV2 introduces inverted residual blocks with depthwise separable convolutions and linear bottleneck layers, using 3×3 depthwise convolutions and ReLU6 activations to reduce computational cost while maintaining accuracy. MobileNetV3 builds on this with Squeezeand-Excitation (SE) blocks for better channel-wise attention and the Hard Swish (H-Swish) activation for improved performance. Both versions aim to optimize efficiency and accuracy for mobile devices.

RegNet. RegNet emphasizes a flexible, efficient design with a novel scaling approach. RegNet-Y_16GF uses a regularized, modular design for performance and efficiency. It consists of stages with increasing feature dimensions, using depthwise separable convolutions and linear bottleneck layers. The key feature is its balanced parameterization strategy for efficient scalability and robust performance.

EfficientNet. EfficientNet achieves a balance between accuracy and efficiency through a compound scaling method. EfficientNet-B0 uses depthwise separable convolutions, squeeze-and-excitation layers, and Swish activations. EfficientNet-B1 and EfficientNet-B7 increase depth, width, and resolution for higher accuracy. EfficientNet-V2-S incorporates efficient training and Hard Swish activations for improved performance.

RepVGG. RepVGG integrates ResNet and VGG to optimize performance. RepVGG_A00 combines 3×3 convolutional layers with residual connections, enhancing gradient flow and training efficiency. The architecture includes convolutional blocks with residual connections, periodic 2×2 max pooling for downsampling, and global average pooling for feature aggregation before classification, avoiding fully connected layers.

3.3 Evaluation Metrics

Precision and Recall. For imbalanced datasets, where the number of data points in different classes varies significantly, *Precision* and *Recall* become crucial metrics.

Precision (Positive Predictive Value - PPV) is defined as the ratio of correctly predicted positive cases. The formula for Precision is:

$$PPV = \frac{TP}{TP + FP}$$

This metric calculates the ratio of true positive points (TP) among the points classified as positive (TP + FP). A high precision value indicates a high level of accuracy in predicting positive points.

On the other hand, **Recall (True Positive Rate - TPR)**, also known as Sensitivity, measures the ratio of true positive cases. The formula for Recall is:

$$TPR = \frac{TP}{TP + FN}$$

Recall is the ratio of true positive points (TP) among the points that are actually positive (TP + FN). A high recall value suggests high sensitivity, which translates into a low rate of missed actual positive points. Thus, while high precision corresponds to fewer false positives (low FP), high recall corresponds to fewer missed positives (low FN).

F1 Score. The F1 score computes the average of precision and recall, where the relative contribution of both of these metrics is equal to the F1 score. The formula for Recall is:

$$F1 = \frac{2 \times \text{Precision} \times \text{Recall}}{\text{Precision} + \text{Recall}}$$

This score ranges between 0 and 1, with a higher F1 score indicating better classification performance. When both Precision and Recall are equal to 1, the F1 score equals 1. Conversely, when both Precision and Recall are low, the F1 score approaches 0.

4 Experiments

Based on the goal of examining the performance of different SOTA CNN models on diagnosing bone fracture, we choose the FracAtlas dataset [1], which contains thousands of X-ray images and published by the authors in [1]. This dataset was collected from three hospitals in Bangladesh from 2021 to 2022 and annotated by experts in radiology and orthopedists with years of experience to adapt to the demand for advanced machine-learning algorithms in computer-aided diagnosis. The FracAtlas has 4083 scans (the hand, leg, hip, and shoulder regions) that are converted to JPG format. The ages of all subjects in the dataset range from 8 months to 78 years. About 62% of the subjects are male and 38% female. Additionally, due to the privacy of patients, all sensitive information presented in the scans was replaced with an arbitrary image name. After being annotated, the images were cross-checked again to solve all conflicts and then manually annotated with the help of makesense.ai (https://github.com/SkalskiP/make-sense). Afterward, the masks were validated by the medical officer. The FracAtlas is chosen because of the following reasons:

(i) Compared to other existing musculoskeletal datasets, the FracAtlas includes fracture X-ray scans from diverse regions of the body, which helps models extract more comprehensive features.
(ii) Each fracture instance has been carefully labeled with its own mask or bounding box, which will improve the precision of computer vision tasks such as classification, localization, and segmentation.
(iii) The wide age range of patients in the dataset is also an advantage. It allows models to extract value information for distinguishing between fractures and non-fractures due to the unique bone structures at specific ages.
(iv) Since this dataset is publicly available, it will be a significant advantage for others interested in the same field.

Analysis of Distribution. The whole FracAtlas has 4083 X-ray images and 4497 locales, which contain 396 different aspect scans of the same region within the same image. There are 717 images for the abnormal set distributed unevenly across the abovementioned regions. Aside from the known ones such as 'Hand,' 'Shoulder,' 'Hip,' and 'Leg,' Table 1 also shows the number of Orthopedic Fixation Devices (Hardware) and images with a multi-view of the same part.

Table 1. The distribution of different locales

Region of Interest	Fractured	Non-Fractured
Hand	437	1101
Shoulder	63	286
Hip	63	275
Leg	263	2009
Hardware	97	2
Multi-view	80	316

As illustrated in Table 1, the distribution of fractured and non-fractured images varies significantly across different regions of interest. To further visualize these distributions and highlight any patterns in the data, Fig. 2 presents a graphical representation of the image counts for each locality.

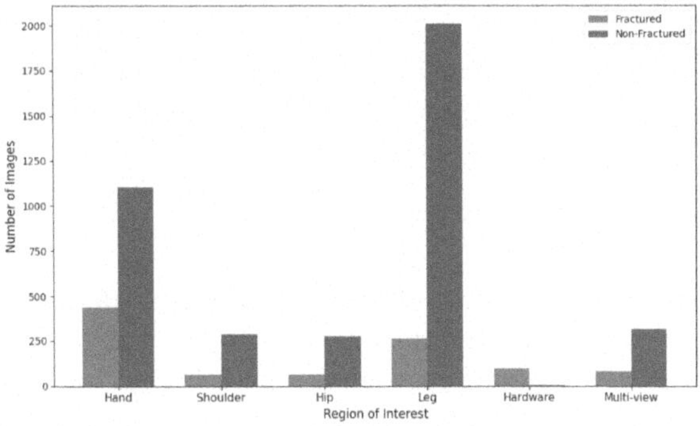

Fig. 2. The distribution of images of different localities

Dataset Partitioning. For this study, due to the imbalance between the amount of Fractured and Non-fractured scans, we chose to split the FracAtlas dataset with 80% of the images allocated to the training set and the remaining 20% to the testing set, as shown in Table 2 below.

Table 2. Dataset partitioning

Set	Fractured	Non-fractured
Training set	571	2695
Testing set	146	671

4.1 Experimental Settings

The experiments detailed in this paper were conducted on COLAB, utilizing an NVIDIA Tesla T4 GPU equipped with 15 GB of VRAM and 12 GB of RAM. The packages used included torch-vision, seaborn, scikit-learn, matplotlib, and torch. The program codes, written using the PyTorch deep learning library, are publicly available in one GitHub repository[4]. The proposed models were trained

[4] https://github.com/ddearie/CODE-CLASSFICATION-IMAGE/tree/master.

and evaluated on the FracAtlas dataset. We adopted a transfer learning strategy to leverage prior knowledge and accelerate the training process. Pre-trained weights from various classification models on the ImageNet dataset were utilized as the starting point for our models. The classification procedures employed a learning rate of 0.0001, an epoch count of 20, the Adam optimizer, and the cross-entropy loss function across multiple models, including AlexNet, ResNet (18, 34, 50, 152), DenseNet (169, 201), VGG (16, 19), MobileNet (v2, v3), EfficientNet (b0, b1, b7, v2), RegNet, and RepVGG (A0). The initial learning rate was adaptive, decreasing tenfold every ten epochs to enhance the network's learning performance.

4.2 Experimental Results

Data Augmentation. As shown above, the FracAtlas dataset shows a significant imbalance between the Fractured and Non-Fractured classes, which can adversely impact model evaluation results, especially in classification tasks. To address this, we used data augmentation to increase the number of Fractured class images in the FracAtlas dataset. This process involved creating new images by rotating the originals up to 10 °C to the right or left.

Data Processing. One critical step in the data processing was ensuring that the initial images, which had varying resolutions and three channels, were resized to a uniform size of $320 \times 320 \times 3$ pixels. This resolution was chosen as it is the most compatible for studies on similar datasets. Apply preprocessing steps to remove noise and avoid negatively impacting the model's classification process, helping the model achieve more accurate predictions:

(i) **Region detection**: After converting the images to grayscale, apply a dual threshold using the Otsu thresholding method to create a binary grayscale image, where the threshold is determined to minimize the variance within each class (background and foreground).
(ii) **Edge detection**: Apply edge detection to the processed grayscale image to determine boundaries and crop the original image based on the calculated boundary values, improving image quality and size-related information.
(iii) **CLAHE transformation (Contrast Limited Adaptive Histogram Equalization)**: Divide the input image into several regions, each containing a separate histogram that is adjusted based on a user-defined clipping limit. The output is a contrast-enhanced image.
(iv) **Normalization and Standardization**: Finally, normalize the image values to a uniform range, where the mean is 0 and the standard deviation is 1.

Classification Results. To accurately and comprehensively evaluate the results of classification problems, it is essential to obtain precision, recall, and F1 scores for each class from every classification model. Precision indicates the

Table 3. Comparison of experimental results in bone fracture classification on the FracAtlas dataset.

Model	Class	Acc	Precision	Recall	F1 Score
AlexNet	Fractured	0.90	0.74	0.64	0.69
	Non Fractured		0.93	0.95	0.94
VGG 16	Fractured	0.92	0.81	0.74	0.78
	Non Fractured		0.95	0.96	0.95
VGG 19	Fractured	0.91	0.78	0.66	0.71
	Non Fractured		0.93	0.96	0.94
ResNet 18	Fractured	0.90	0.76	0.65	0.70
	Non Fractured		0.93	0.96	0.94
ResNet 34	Fractured	0.92	0.83	0.71	0.76
	Non Fractured		0.94	0.97	0.95
ResNet 50	Fractured	0.91	0.82	0.65	0.72
	Non Fractured		0.93	0.97	0.95
ResNet 101	Fractured	0.91	0.85	0.61	0.71
	Non Fractured		0.92	0.98	0.95
ResNet 152	Fractured	0.90	0.81	0.66	0.73
	Non Fractured		0.93	0.97	0.95
DenseNet 169	Fractured	0.93	0.87	0.72	0.79
	Non Fractured		0.94	0.98	0.96
DenseNet 201	Fractured	0.92	0.86	0.68	0.76
	Non Fractured		0.93	0.98	0.96
MobileNet V2	Fractured	0.93	0.82	0.75	0.79
	Non Fractured		0.95	0.97	0.96
MobileNet V3	Fractured	0.91	0.84	0.62	0.71
	Non Fractured		0.92	0.97	0.95
EfficientNet B0	Fractured	0.92	0.81	0.75	0.78
	Non Fractured		0.95	0.96	0.95
EfficientNet B1	Fractured	0.93	0.82	0.76	0.79
	Non Fractured		0.95	0.96	0.96
EfficientNet B7	Fractured	0.93	0.86	0.72	0.78
	Non Fractured		0.94	0.97	0.96
EfficientNet V2	Fractured	0.90	0.76	0.67	0.71
	Non Fractured		0.93	0.96	0.94
RegNet Y 16GF	Fractured	0.90	0.88	0.53	0.66
	Non Fractured		0.91	0.98	0.94
RepVGG A0	Fractured	0.90	0.76	0.65	0.70
	Non Fractured		0.93	0.96	0.94

proportion of predicted positive values that are correct. Recall, also known as the true positive rate, measures the proportion of actual positives that are correctly identified. It is worth noting that the F1-score is the harmonic mean of precision and recall. It provides a balanced and fair measure of both, ensuring a comprehensive evaluation of our results.

Analysis of Models Based on Precision, Recall, and F1 Scores: From the provided classification report, we can analyze which model has the highest and lowest Precision, Recall, and F1 Score for the "Fractured" class and the "Non Fractured" class.

The highest and lowest scores for the 'Fractured' class: (1)**Precision (Highest)**: RegNet Y 16GF with 0.88; (b) **Recall (Highest)**: EfficientNet B1 with 0.76; (c) **F1 Score (Highest)**: DenseNet 169, EfficientNet B1, and MobileNet V2 all with 0.79; (d) **Precision (Lowest)**: RegNet Y 16GF with 0.53; (e) **Recall (Lowest)**: AlexNet with 0.64; (f) **F1 Score (Lowest)**: RegNet Y 16GF with 0.66.

Performance of Selected Models: DenseNet 169 achieves high scores in Precision (0.87), Recall (0.72), and F1 Score (0.79); MobileNet V2 achieves high scores in Precision (0.82), Recall (0.75), and F1 Score (0.79); and EfficientNet B1 achieves high scores in Precision (0.82), Recall (0.76), and F1 Score (0.79) for the "Fractured" class. These performances indicate balanced and robust models for accurately identifying fractures.

RegNet Y 16GF: RegNet Y 16GF has the lowest Recall (0.53) and F1 Score (0.66) for the "Fractured" class, despite having the highest Precision (0.88). The high Precision but low Recall indicates that while RegNet Y 16GF is very accurate when it predicts a fracture, it misses many actual fracture cases.

Overall, DenseNet 169, MobileNet V2, and EfficientNet B1 exhibit strong performance with balanced high Precision, Recall, and F1 Scores, making them reliable for fracture classification tasks. In contrast, RegNet Y 16GF, while achieving high Precision, suffers from low Recall and F1 Score, making it less suitable for scenarios where missing fractures could be critical. This analysis underscores the crucial role of balancing Precision and Recall to ensure comprehensive and accurate fracture detection.

5 Conclusion and Future Works

This study aimed to explore and identify the most optimal model for classifying bone X-ray images as either normal or abnormal (fractured). To achieve this goal, the initial objective was to classify fracture images using 18 different classification models. Among these, DenseNet169, EfficientNet b1, MobileNetV2, and VGG16 demonstrated the best performance compared to the others. Overall, these models provide valuable reference results that can assist doctors in diagnosing bone fractures through X-ray images. With the support of these classification models, determining whether an X-ray image indicates a bone fracture becomes more efficient and reliable.

Future research on fracture classification tasks using the FracAtlas dataset can be extended through several approaches. One potential avenue is to enhance the quality of training image datasets, which could improve model performance. Additionally, implementing novel methods and incorporating emerging models could further advance the accuracy and robustness of fracture detection and classification. These developments will contribute to more effective and precise diagnostic tools for medical professionals.

Acknowledgment. Son T Huynh was funded by the PhD Scholarship Programme of Vingroup Innovation Foundation (VINIF), code VINIF.2024.TS.006.

References

1. Abedeen, I., Rahman, M.A., Prottyasha, F.Z., Ahmed, T., Chowdhury, T.M., Shatabda, S.: FracAtlas: a dataset for fracture classification, localization and segmentation of musculoskeletal radiographs. Sci. Data **10**(1) (2023). https://doi.org/10.1038/s41597-023-02432-4
2. Alzaid, A., Wignall, A., Dogramadzi, S., Pandit, H., Xie, S.Q.: Automatic detection and classification of peri-prosthetic femur fracture. Int. J. Comput. Assist. Radiol. Surg. **17**(4), 649–660 (2022). https://doi.org/10.1007/s11548-021-02552-5
3. Ding, X., Zhang, X., Ma, N., Han, J., Ding, G., Sun, J.: Repvgg: making vgg-style convnets great again. In: 2021 IEEE/CVF Conference on Computer Vision and Pattern Recognition (CVPR), pp. 13728–13737 (2021).https://doi.org/10.1109/CVPR46437.2021.01352
4. He, K., Zhang, X., Ren, S., Sun, J.: Deep residual learning for image recognition. In: Proceedings of the IEEE Conference on Computer Vision and Pattern Recognition (CVPR), pp. 770–778 (2016a)
5. He, K., Zhang, X., Ren, S., Sun, J.: Identity mappings in deep residual networks. In: Leibe, B., Matas, J., Sebe, N., Welling, M. (eds.) ECCV 2016. LNCS, vol. 9908, pp. 630–645. Springer, Cham (2016). https://doi.org/10.1007/978-3-319-46493-0_38
6. Howard, A., et al.: Searching for mobilenetv3. In: Proceedings of the IEEE International Conference on Computer Vision (ICCV), pp. 1314–1324 (2019)
7. Huang, G., Liu, Z., Maaten, L., Weinberger, K.: Densely connected convolutional networks. In: Proceedings of the IEEE Conference on Computer Vision and Pattern Recognition (CVPR), pp. 4700–4708 (2017)
8. Krizhevsky, A., Sutskever, I., Hinton, G.: Imagenet classification with deep convolutional neural networks. In: Advances in Neural Information Processing Systems (NIPS) (2016)
9. Lee, J.G., et al.: Deep learning in medical imaging: general overview. Korean J. Radiol. **18**(4), 570–584 (2017)
10. Mello-Thoms, C., Mello, C.A.: Clinical applications of artificial intelligence in radiology. Br. J. Radiol. **96**(1150), 20221031 (2023)
11. Radosavovic, I., Kosaraju, R., Girshick, R., He, K., Dollár, P.: Designing network design spaces. In: Proceedings of the IEEE Conference on Computer Vision and Pattern Recognition (CVPR), pp. 10428–10436 (2020)
12. Sandler, M., Howard, A., Zhu, M., Zhmoginov, A., Chen, L.C.: Mobilenetv2: inverted residuals and linear bottlenecks. In: Proceedings of the IEEE Conference on Computer Vision and Pattern Recognition (CVPR), pp. 4510–4520 (2018)

13. Simonyan, K., Zisserman, A.: Very deep convolutional networks for large-scale image recognition. arXiv preprint arXiv:1409.1556 (2014)
14. Tan, M., Le, Q.: Efficientnet: rethinking model scaling for convolutional neural networks. In: Proceedings of the 36th International Conference on Machine Learning (ICML), pp. 6105–6114 (2019)
15. Tan, M., Pang, R., Le, Q.: Efficientnetv2: smaller models and faster training. In: Proceedings of the 39th International Conference on Machine Learning (ICML) (2021)
16. Uysal, F., Hardalaç, F., Peker, O., Tolunay, T., Tokgöz, N.: Classification of shoulder x-ray images with deep learning ensemble models. MDPI (2021). https://doi.org/10.3390/app11062723

Classifying Historical Cuisines Using Word Embeddings and Machine Learning Models: A Comparative Study

Y. Ece Demiral and Ali M. M. Alsahag(✉)

University of Amsterdam, Amsterdam, The Netherlands
ece.demiral@student.uva.nl, a.m.m.alsahag@uva.nl

Abstract. Historical menus serve as valuable archival records that reflect culinary practices, consumption patterns, and environmental changes. However, limited research has explored their potential in understanding shifts in culinary trends. This study addresses this gap by investigating the effectiveness of word embeddings and optimization techniques in classifying cuisine patterns using historical menu data. By comparing traditional, ensemble, and deep learning models, the paper focuses on using word embeddings for multi-class classification. TF-IDF embeddings consistently provided superior performance, especially in traditional models like Support Vector Machines and ensemble methods such as Random Forest, achieving the highest accuracy, 0.9059, and F_1-score, 0.9011, when combined with Word2Vec. Findings indicate that selection of mere embedding does not effect the model's performance for this classification task, hybrid embeddings with hyperparameter optimization improve classification performance. Future research should investigate transformer-based models to better capture ingredient and cuisine nuances.

Keywords: historical menus · word embedding · hyperparameter optimization · supervised learning

1 Introduction

Restaurant menus reflect culinary preferences and food consumption patterns, providing insight into ingredient availability and evolving cultural values shaped by economic and political trends. According to Bourdieu, these patterns also reveal societal stratification through food choices, reflecting acquired capital and aesthetic trends [7,10]. Analyzing these trends offers insights into culinary practices, such as cuisine dominance across regions [23].

Prior research has explored the relationship between environmental changes and cuisine evolution but has only focused on cuisine classification based on ingredients [31]. As ingredient diversity per menu declines, understanding these patterns becomes crucial for predicting cuisine types and their cultural implications. Recent advances in machine learning allows for efficient analysis of such

J. Kertesz et al. (Eds.): CSoNet 2024, LNCS 15417, pp. 357–364, 2025.
https://doi.org/10.1007/978-981-96-6389-7_32

patterns through multi-class classification tasks. Although traditional models using TF-IDF have been common approach, research on word embeddings' effect and the application of deep learning architectures for cuisine prediction remain underexplored. This study fills this gap by employing machine learning on multicultural recipe data from RecipeNLG[1] and Yummly's "What's Cooking" dataset to predict cuisines from ingredient lists. By utilizing hyperparameter optimization and comparing the effect of word embedding selection this research aims to improve model performance in multi-class cuisine prediction tasks. This study addresses the question: To what extent do hyperparameter optimization and word embedding selection improve multi-class classification models for cuisine prediction?

2 Related Work

Cuisine classification using machine learning is an evolving area intersecting data science and gastronomy. While traditional qualitative approaches required significant manual effort from domain experts, advancements in machine learning enabled more automated analysis of culinary data, revealing consumption patterns and connections between ingredients, cuisines, and gastronomic practices [12]. This section reviews recent work on cuisine prediction focusing on multi-class classification, model selection, hyperparameter optimization, and word embeddings.

As a machine learning technology, Natural Language Processing (NLP) is increasingly applied to various domains, including to food-related tasks such as sentiment analysis on restaurant reviews and food detection [1]. Early works in cuisine classification, such as Kalajdziski et al., employed Naïve Bayes, Neural Networks, and Support Vector Machines (SVM) with TF-IDF vectorization to compare predictive accuracy [20], while recent studies extended this by treating recipes as text classification problems, experimenting with traditional models and Transformer-based models [29]. Despite advancements in large language models and transformers for understanding text, research focused specifically on menus remains limited, restricting their availability as a benchmark for this study [22].

Model selection is important for balancing complexity and accuracy in cuisine prediction. Ensemble learning methods like Random Forests and boosting algorithms, including AdaBoost and XGBoost, offer superior generalization and bias-variance trade-offs compared to traditional models [17]. Random Forests, though effective, are prone to overfitting noisy data, while boosting algorithms like Gradient Boosting Machine (GBM) and XGBoost reduce bias through iterative learning and excel in scalability and handling large datasets efficiently [16,32]. These models are particularly relevant for cuisine prediction, where the complexity of the data can vary significantly between recipes and ingredient lists.

In contrast to these, deep learning architectures such as Convolutional Neural Networks (CNN), Recurrent Neural Networks (RNN), and Long-Short Term

[1] https://recipenlg.cs.put.poznan.pl/.

Memory (LSTM) networks are well-suited for handling sequential data like recipes [4]. RNNs and LSTMs excel at capturing dependencies between ingredients, enhancing classification accuracy compared to simpler models like TF-IDF-encoded classifiers. While Transformer-based models like BERT perform well in NLP tasks, LSTMs can surpass BERT on smaller, specialized datasets like the recipe ingredients analyzed in this study, which employs CNN, RNN, and LSTM architectures [13].

Hyperparameter optimization is crucial for maximizing model performance to enhance accuracy, reduce training time, and improve generalizability [6]. Making the selecting of these values a vital part of analysis. Manual searches often limit scalability, while advanced techniques like Bayesian optimization, gradient-based methods, and frameworks like Optuna address these challenges effectively [2]. However, grid search can outperform Bayesian methods on a smaller dataset with a fixed grid space such as in this study [3].

Word embeddings are integral to text-based classifiers. Frequency-based embeddings like TF-IDF and Count Vectorization are widely used in cuisine classification due to their simplicity [29], while Word2Vec, Glove, and FastText provide richer semantic understanding [25]. Despite their advantages, embedding ensemble methods remain underexplored for recipe-specific contexts [8].

The reviewed literature highlights the need for further exploration of model optimization techniques and the impact of word embeddings on cuisine classification. Although several models have been applied successfully, more research is needed to determine the optimal combination of hyperparameters, vectorization techniques, and model architectures for accurate and efficient cuisine prediction. This study aims to address these gaps by comparing various classification models and embeddings, focusing on improving accuracy while mitigating issues such as overfitting, precision-recall trade-offs, and computational inefficiency.

3 Methodology

This chapter outlines the methodology for tracking changes in food consumption patterns using restaurant menus. Given the range of influences on dining habits, including historical, social, and ethical factors, a systematic analysis is crucial. This study explores these dynamics by comparing various models and feature engineering methods. The experimental pipeline consists of three steps: data handling and preprocessing, classification, and evaluation.

3.1 Data Handling and Preprocessing

The datasets are preprocessed by data cleaning, feature encoding, and text processing. For culinary datasets text processing and dimensionality reduction were applied to improve the datasets' suitability for classifiers. Datasets used in this study include The New York Public Library's "What's on the Menu?" initiative, Yummly's "What is Cooking" dataset, and the RecipeNLG dataset. By exploring classifiers both with the historical menus and cuisine-recipe dataset of Yummly, this study aims to provide a comparative case study approach.

The "What's on the Menu?" includes up to 45,000 menus, with a wide range of dishes from 1840 s to the 2000 s This study focuses on Waldorf Astoria Hotel menus to address potential biases form overrepresented menus and provides a balanced historical perspective. The dataset of Yummly provides information on twenty cuisines, and is employed to compare the performance of classifiers with literature. Lastly, RecipeNLG dataset includes over two million recipes with ingredient lists and cooking instructions. This dataset helps to match dishes from historical menus to modern ingredients and cuisines. Exact matching with ingredient lists is used to enhance reliability.

3.2 Experimental Construction and Evaluation

Model selection was deliberately designed, building upon existing research on cuisine prediction models [20] in an attempt to understand the impact of word-embeddings on model performance by extending the prior research on cuisine prediction. For a narrowed the scope, this study employed the following traditional models: Multinomial Naïve Bayes (MNB), Logistic Regression (LR), K-Nearest Neighbouring (KNN), Decision Tree (DT), and Support Vector Machine algorithms (SVM); ensemble learning models bagging with Random Forest and boosting with XGBoost (XGB) and AdaBoost (AB). The application of deep learning included neural network models: Convolutional, Recurrent, and its successor Long-Short Term Memory. For computational efficiency, a predetermined tuning approach was used for neural networks [27]. Literature suggests that large batch sizes lack a regularizing effect, while smaller batches introduce noise, which aids the process but increases computational cost. Their experiments identified 64 as the optimal batch size, balancing accuracy, training time, and overfitting prevention [26]. Furthermore, each model were trained with ten epochs, an Adaptive Moment Estimation optimizer and Mean Squared Error for the loss function of the LSTM model [24].

There are several points to underline for this paper's model selections. While Logistic Regression is an inherently binary classification algorithm, alternative applications for multi-class classification are available [28]. Another inherently binary model SVM can be applied for this task by alternating between kernels. For this study, Grid Search included linear, polynomial, and radial basis function (RBF) kernels. Gradient descent adaptation rule calculation was employed, which was irrespective of the initial hyperparameter value of regularization, and used 0.1 as kernel parameter.

Evaluation metrics included accuracy, precision, recall, and F_1-scores, with the confusion matrix used for detailed performance analysis. Stratified sampling was employed to manage class distributions. Macro-averaged precision and recall were used to assess model performance. Statistical significance was tested using paired t-test, and significance threshold was set as 0.05. While there are emerging recommendations favoring stricter thresholds to control the false discovery rate, this study opts for ensuring transparency through reporting exact p-values rather than merely indicating significance [11].

4 Results and Discussion

This section discusses the results in relation to research questions, ethics, limitations, and future work. The findings confirm previous studies on cuisine prediction and provide insights into the impact of word embeddings on hyperparameter-optimized models. Earlier studies mainly used TF-IDF vectorization. The SVM achieved the highest accuracy of 0.873 with an F_1-score of 0.8479, while the RF reached an accuracy of 0.8621 and an F_1-score of 0.8476. However, RF with W2V embedding showed improved performance, with 0.9059 accuracy and a 0.8972 F_1-score. The count vectorizer, performing 8.669% worse than W2V, outperformed it in the SVM and AB models. Including TF-IDF and other context-free vectorizers in the analysis of cuisine and menu datasets ensured a controlled comparison, balancing internal and external validity [30]. TF-IDF consistently outperformed other embeddings in accuracy and balanced the recall-precision trade-off across various models. Traditional models like LR, MNB, KNN, and ensemble methods such as XGB and RF performed better with TF-IDF and CountVectorizer. Using TF-IDF alone, the SVM achieved an accuracy of 0.7536, slightly lower than the 0.79 reported by Jayaraman et al. [18]. However, combining Word2Vec and TF-IDF led to a significant accuracy increase to 0.903, with an F_1-score of 0.9011 and a p-value of 0.008, supporting the effectiveness of hybrid vectorization techniques, consistent with Kilimci et al.'s findings on text classification [21].

Traditional models showed a 15.14% improvement in accuracy with TF-IDF compared to CV, with Word2Vec performing less effectively due to its continuous-valued vectors not aligning with traditional models like LLR and MNB [19]. DT achieved an accuracy of 0.6239 with TF-IDF, while RF reached 0.7522. These results are consistent with Alshanketi's findings for RF with TF-IDF resulting in an accuracy of 0.76, surpassing those reported by Sharma et al. for DTs reported as 0.5037 [5]. Combined with TF-IDF, Random Forests achieved a macro-averaged accuracy of 0.8032. Bearing in mind, its previous achievements, we can denote TF-IDF's efficiency in handling textualized ingredients. RRNs and CNNs achieved accuracies of 0.6872 and 0.7657, respectively, using TF-IDF. Training Word2Vec on recipe texts outperformed the previous research baseline by 21.75%, resulting in a statistically significant improvement with a p-value of 0.0005 compared to p-value of significance 0.05. Nevertheless, Keras embedding surpassed this without a statistically significant difference (p-value = 0.96¿ 0.05, z-score = 0.048). Building upon the hypothesis on whether ensemble embeddings can outperform non-hybrid approaches concerning the accuracy, the inclusion of TF-IDF in Keras further improved the performance to 0.7718.

The applied methods successfully extracted temporal trends and cuisines from historical menus. Cuisine prediction accuracies varied significantly between

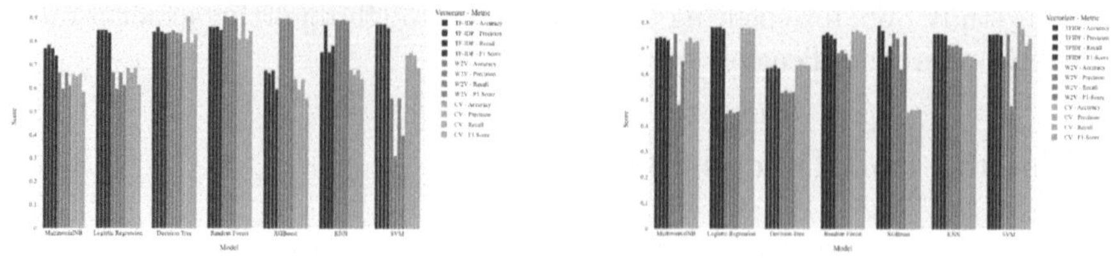

(a) Comparison of traditional and ensemble models with different word embedding combinations using the menu dataset.

(b) Comparison of traditional and ensemble models with different word embedding combinations using the cuisine dataset.

Fig. 1. Comparison of different datasets applications

models ($p = 0.013$), though vectorizer performance was consistent. This variance is likely explained by the class imbalance in historical menu cuisine labels. A closer examination of cuisine distributions over time, indicates that some cuisine categories were not well-represented in certain decades.

To adapt the models, ingredients were matched with labeled cuisine classes using a rule-based approach with single-character-change logic, offering higher efficiency than probabilistic matching for large datasets. One ethical concern is the assumption that recipes remain constant over time, potentially leading to biased results and impacting external validity [15]. A diverse, multilingual dataset was used to mitigate this effect [9]. Another concern is the focus on hotel menus, which may reflect wealthier individuals' dining habits, introducing temporal bias; however, these menus provide valuable insights into both touristic and local dining experiences, useful for studying broader culinary trends [7]. Lastly, reproducibility is limited for algorithms sensitive to random initialization and data conditions. Future studies should maintain consistent preprocessing for replication [14]. Despite these challenges, the study offers a thorough analysis of model performance across datasets and techniques.

5 Conclusion

This study explored the use of advanced machine-learning techniques, including ensemble word embeddings for predicting cuisines to analyse food consumption patterns. While previous research focused on nutritional aspects and traditional methods, this study addressed the application of modern techniques to historical menu data to predict the cuisine of a dish to seek cuisine dominance trends. The results indicated that word embedding choices did not significantly impact average model performance for multi-class classification, with a p-value of 0.186, well above the 0.05 significance threshold. Among the embeddings, TF-IDF consistently performed well, while Word2Vec showed high variability, particularly affecting traditional models like LR and MNB. The combination of Word2Vec with RF achieved the highest accuracy, 0.7644 for the cuisine dataset and 0.9059 for the menu dataset. In conclusion, incorporating word embeddings did not achieve generalizable improvements for multi-class classification. However, their combination managed to outperform deep learning models. Future research should consider advanced embeddings such as BERT or GPT, further explore the effectiveness of hybrid approaches, and expand to more diverse historical menus. Additionally, investigating hierarchical methods could deepen the understanding of food classification.

Acknowledgements. I would like to express my sincere gratitude to my supervisor, Marieke van Erp, for her invaluable support and guidance during this research project and my internship at KNAW Humanities Cluster. I am also deeply grateful to the University of Amsterdam for the Excellence and Merit Scholarship that made this study possible. For additional information or access to the appendix, readers are encouraged to contact the authors.

References

1. Adak, A., Pradhan, B., Shukla, N.: Sentiment analysis of customer reviews of food delivery services using deep learning and explainable artificial intelligence: systematic review. Foods **11**(10) (2022)
2. Akiba, T., Sano, S., Yamamoto, S., Koyama, M., Harada, K.: Optuna. In: Proceedings of International Conference on Knowledge Discovery & Data Mining, pp. 2623–2631. ACM (2019)
3. Alibrahim, H., Ludwig, S.A.: Hyperparameter optimization: Comparing genetic algorithm against grid search and bayesian optimization. In: 2021 IEEE Congress on Evolutionary Computation (CEC), pp. 1551–1559 (2021)
4. Alom, M.Z., et al.: A state-of-the-art survey on deep learning theory and architectures. Electronics (2019)
5. Alshanketi, F.: Machine learning model for predicting the cuisine category from a dish ingredients. In: 2023 International Conference on Smart Computing and Application (ICSCA), pp. 1–6 (2023)
6. Andonie, R.: Hyperparameter optimization in learning systems. J. Membrane Comput., 1–13 (2019). https://doi.org/10.1007/s41965-019-00023-0
7. Bourdieu, P.: Distinction. Routledge, London, England (2024)
8. Catellier, R., Vaiter, S., Garreau, D.: On the robustness of text vectorizers (2023)
9. Chen, F., Wang, L., Hong, J., Jiang, J., Zhou, L.: Unmasking bias in artificial intelligence. J. Am. Med. Inform. Assoc. **31**(5), 1172–1183 (2024)
10. Costa, C., Murphy, M.: Bourdieu and the application of habitus across the social sciences. In: Bourdieu, Habitus and Social Research. Palgrave Macmillan, London (2015)
11. Di Leo, G., Sardanelli, F.: Statistical significance. European Radiol. Expe. **4**(1), 18 (2020)
12. van Erp, M., et al.: Using natural language processing and artificial intelligence to explore the nutrition and sustainability of recipes and food. Front. Artifi. Intell. **3** (2021)
13. Ezen-Can, A.: A comparison of lstm and bert for small corpus. ArXiv abs/arXiv:2009.05451 (2020)

14. Fan, C., Chen, M., Wang, X., Wang, J., Huang, B.: A review on data preprocessing techniques toward efficient and reliable knowledge discovery from building operational data. Front. Energy Res. **9**, 652801 (2021). https://doi.org/10.3389/fenrg.2021.652801
15. Ferrara, E.: Fairness and bias in artificial intelligence. Sci **6**(1), 3 (2023)
16. Florek, P., Zagdański, A.: Benchmarking state-of-the-art gradient boosting algorithms for classification (2023)
17. Ganaie, M., Hu, M., Malik, A., Tanveer, M., Suganthan, P.: Ensemble deep learning: a review. Eng. Appli. Artifi. Intel. **115** (2022)
18. Jayaraman, S., Choudhury, T., Kumar, P.: Analysis of classification models based on cuisine prediction using machine learning. In: 2017 International Conference On Smart Technologies For Smart Nation (SmartTechCon), pp. 1485–1490 (2017)
19. Johnson, S.J., Murty, M.R., Navakanth, I.: A detailed review on word embedding techniques with emphasis on word2vec. Multimedia Tools Appli. **83**, 37979–38007 (2024)
20. Kalajdziski, S., Radevski, G., Ivanoska, I., Trivodaliev, K., Stojkoska, B.R.: Cuisine classification using recipe's ingredients. In: 2018 MIPRO, pp. 1074–1079 (2018)
21. Kilimci, Z.H., Akyokuş, S.: Deep learning- and word embedding-based heterogeneous classifier ensembles for text classification. Complex **2018**, 7130146:1–7130146:10 (2018)
22. Kumar, P.: Large language models (llms): survey, technical frameworks, and future challenges. Artif. Intell. Rev. **57**, 260 (2024)
23. Li, H., Hou, J., Chen, Y., Liu, K.: À la Carte: turning historical menu into menu network. In: Doucet, A., Isaac, A., Golub, K., Aalberg, T., Jatowt, A. (eds.) TPDL 2019. LNCS, vol. 11799, pp. 370–374. Springer, Cham (2019). https://doi.org/10.1007/978-3-030-30760-8_36
24. Lipton, Z.C., Kale, D.C., Elkan, C.P., Wetzel, R.C.: Learning to diagnose with LSTM recurrent neural networks. CoRR abs/ arXiv: 1511.03677 (2015)
25. Morales-Garzón, A., Gómez-Romero, J., Martín-Bautista, M.J.: A word embedding-based method for unsupervised adaptation of cooking recipes. IEEE Access **9**, 27389–27404 (2021)
26. Radiuk, P.: Impact of training set batch size on the performance of convolutional neural networks for diverse datasets. Inform. Technol. Manag. Sci. **20**, 20–24 (2017)
27. Roy, S., Mehera, R., Pal, R., et al.: Hyperparameter optimization for deep neural network models: a comprehensive study on methods and techniques. Innovations Syst. Softw. Eng. (2023)
28. Shah, B., Bhavsar, H., Bhavsar, H.: Overview of deep learning in food image classification for dietary assessment system. Intell. Syst. Technol. Appli. (2021)
29. Sharma, T., Upadhyay, U., Bagler, G.: Classification of cuisines from sequentially structured recipes. In: 2020 IEEE, pp. 105–108 (2020)
30. Trafimow, D.: A new way to think about internal and external validity. Perspect. Psychol. Sci. **18**(5), 1028–1046 (2023)
31. Trostler, N., Gvion, L.: Trends in restaurant menus. Nutr. Today **42**(6), 255–262 (2007)
32. Zhao, C., Peng, R., Wu, D.: Bagging and boosting fine-tuning for ensemble learning. IEEE Trans. Artifi. Intell. **5**(4), 1728–1742 (2024)

Tracing Farmers' Protests Online in Europe 2024

Andrzej Jarynowski[1,2](✉), Alexander Semenov[3], Daniel Platek[4], and Vitaly Belik[1]

[1] System Modeling Group, Institute of Veterinary Epidemiology and Biostatistics, Freie Universität Berlin, Berlin, DE, Germany
[2] Polish Hygienic Society, Wrocław, PL, Poland
ajarynowski@gmail.com
[3] University of Florida, Gainesville, FL, USA
[4] Institute of Political Studies of the Polish Academy of Sciences, Warsaw, PL, Poland

Abstract. To the best of our knowledge, this is the first pan-European study on farmers' protests on the Internet in 2024. This research systematically compares digital traces from January to July 2024 in online media coverage of protests across three languages: Polish, German, and Flemish. The findings reveal significant differences in media coverage and sentiment across the three regions. Polish protests received the most attention per capita and elicited the strongest negative emotions. The study also shows that traditional media dominate Polish discourse, whereas social media play a more prominent role in German and Flemish discussions. Furthermore, the study highlights that topics, such as animal welfare and food security, are underrepresented in traditional media. It also underscores how the 2024 protests differ from earlier ones due to public support related to the costs of eco-transformation and the involvement of far-right political groups in the protest discourse.

Keywords: Social Media Analysis · Veterinary Anthropology · Natural Language Processing

1 Introduction

The European Union's Green Deal aims to make agriculture more sustainable, with a particular focus on livestock production [1]. This initiative has led to the formation of alliances opposing these changes, including livestock farmers, far-right groups, agricultural parties, and religious organizations [3,14]. Conversely, environmental activists and animal rights groups advocate for these measures, highlighting their environmental and animal welfare benefits [6,15].

Traditional and social media not only reflect reality [4,7] but also shape it. This paper examines the online representation of farmers' protests in Poland, Germany, and the Flemish-speaking regions.

J. Kertesz et al. (Eds.): CSoNet 2024, LNCS 15417, pp. 365–372, 2025.
https://doi.org/10.1007/978-981-96-6389-7_33

2 Related Work

Pre-existing social conflicting matter of the animal production conditions has been manifesting in reconfiguration of social relations by strengthening the tendency issuing farm animal protection in the general population (mostly urban) and '"hijacking" profitability and cultural values of farmers [11]. Dietary or consumption changes, government decisions, animal welfare, and health issues causing protest movements have been actively discussed on social media [8]. There are many studies, mainly from Indian Subcontinent about digital reflection on farmers protests (we are using this knowledge as a reference), however European perspective from 2024 is still missing upon submission of this paper [8,12].

3 Data Processing and Methods

We collected internet data using Brand24 from January 1 to July 31, 2024, focusing on online representations of farmers' protests across different countries and languages. The data sources included X (former Twitter), Facebook, Instagram, TikTok, Telegram, forums, YouTube, and news outlets. Protest-specific hashtags trended across various countries, helping to unify and amplify farmer voices and been used for anti protesters. The keywords "farmers' protest" in the respective languages are shown below. We used these keywords, including their variations and declensions (for Polish), to ensure comprehensive coverage.

- **Protest Rolników**: Mentions with keywords such as *protest*, *protesty*, *strajk rolników*, *rolnicze* in Polish.
- **Bauernproteste**: Mentions with #Bauernproteste in German-speaking regions.
- **Boerenprotest**: Mentions with #boerenprotest in Flemish-speaking regions.

Table 1. Comparison of Online Mentions and Reach Across Languages.

	Protest Rolników	Bauernproteste	Boerenprotest
Total mentions	38,807	32,140	5,938
Mentions per million users	862.38	321.40	237.52
Social media mentions	17,526 (45.2%)	20,194 (62.8%)	4,500 (75.8%)
Non-social media mentions	21,281 (54.8%)	11,946 (37.2%)	1,438 (24.2%)
Positive mentions	1,055 (3%)	2,285 (8%)	670 (12%)
Negative mentions	12,682 (33%)	4,221 (14%)	924 (16%)
Social media reach	193,553,475 (49%)	317,294,530 (57.9%)	36,735,197 (59.2%)
Non-social media reach	202,523,172 (51.1%)	30,451,764 (42.1%)	25,351,015 (40.8%)

Social media may reflect and strengthen offline relations of activation possibility, as powerful actors from both protesting and anti protesting site should posses

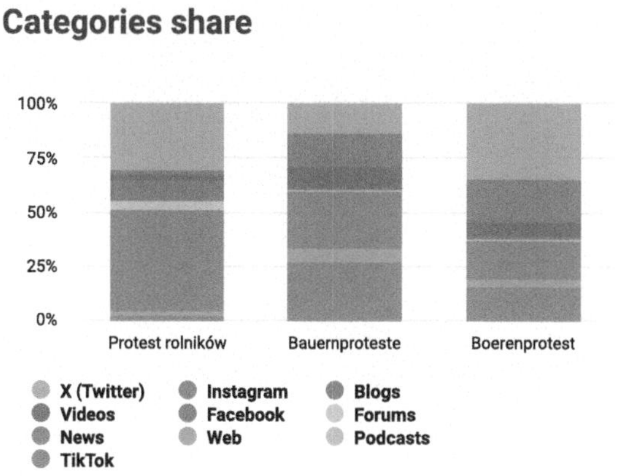

Fig. 1. Distribution of Media Types Discussing Protests.

marketing potential to engage in social media [11]. Protests in Poland garnered significantly more attention per capita than those in other regions (Table 1). The reach data shows how many people were exposed to protest-related content, with Germany having the highest reach, especially in social media.

Natural Language Processing (NLP) techniques were employed to extract keywords, topics, and sentiment analysis from the collected data. It is done by leveraging deep learning and pre-trained language models to determine whether social media mentions are positive, negative, or neutral. Mentions refer to the number of posts, comments, articles, and materials from traditional and social media. Reach estimates the number of people exposed to the content. In NLP, positive sentiment indicates favorable emotions, while negative sentiment reflects unfavorable ones.

For *Protest Rolników*, a bubble graph representing the frequency of keywords was produced. We counted all appearances of variations of keywords describing Breeders, Food (a) and non-food (b) animal products, and Other topics such as epizootics.

Moreover, for Polish protests the topic modeling was done (transformer-based with contextual embeddings to cluster texts into coherent topics).

4 Results

4.1 Comparison of Protests

All protests analyzed constitute counter-protests, often accompanied by the phenomenon of hashtag hijacking.

The farmer protests were most intense in Polish media, approximately three times more mentions per capita than in other languages (Table 1). This reflects the significance of agriculture in Poland's economy and the tensions over imports of Ukrainian products.

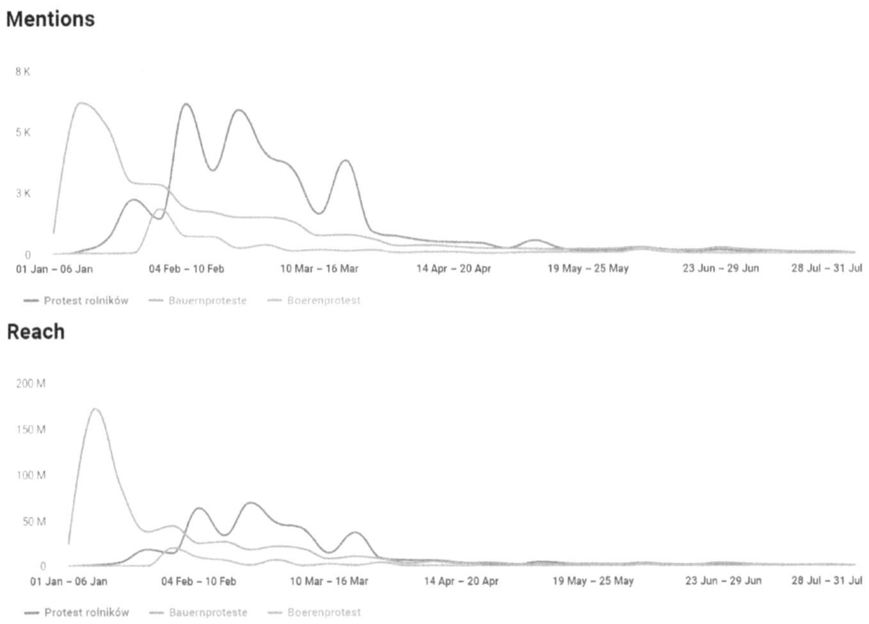

Fig. 2. Time Evolution of Mentions and Reach.

The Fig. 1 illustrates the distribution of media types (social vs. traditional) used to discuss the protests across the three languages. It is clear that traditional media dominates in Polish, whereas social media is more prevalent in German and Flemish discussions.

Each language community exhibits different media preferences for discussing protests. In Polish social media dominates, whereas TikTok and Instagram are less popular. These patterns result from both regional media preferences and differences in protest agendas, composition of disputants (fraction of pro and anti protesters) and forms across countries.

4.2 Time Evolution of Protest Intensity

The plots (Fig. 2) indicate that reach declines faster than mentions, particularly in Germany, suggesting that while the volume of discussions remains, the audience size shrinks over time.

The sequence of on-the-ground protests began in Germany, followed by the Benelux countries, and finally in Poland. The protests in Poland lasted the longest (at least until the onset of the first necessary spring fieldwork), and the duration of the wave was also the broadest in Poland.

The reach declines faster than mentions, most noticeably in Germany.

In Poland the protests reached their peak in terms of the number of mentions and reach of media mentions on February 9th due to the mass nature of the

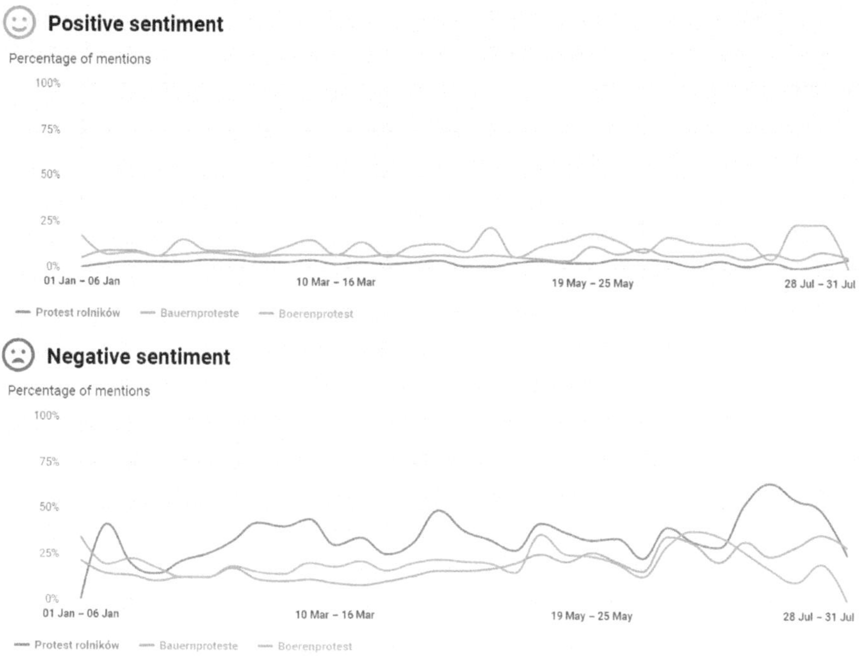

Fig. 3. Sentiment Analysis Over Time.

protests, which noticeably affected the daily lives of most country residents, often through local media. On February 27th, video materials allegedly showing blocked ambulances dominated Polish-language content on X, reaching beyond the usual protest opposition groups.

Bauernproteste (German protests) were primarily against the planned agricultural cuts by the German government, including the removal of tax advantages for agricultural diesel, however in the course preparation in early 2024 of the range of postulates were extended. German tractors clog Berlin as farmer protests peak on January 15th.

Nitrogen emissions and animal welfare topics, which triggered farmers' protests in the Benelux (Boerenprotest) in recent years [5,9], continue to be a source of unrest in 2024. On January 30 and February 1, Benelux farmers attempted to dispose of manure in front of the European Parliament and the EU Commission, prompting a response from the police, including the use of force.

4.3 Time Evolution of Emotional Load

In Polish media, the share of negative emotions increases after the EU elections in June, while it decreases in other languages (Fig. 3). The protests on March 6th reached a level of emotional engagement on social media comparable to the events of February 9th and 20th. In Germany, the share of negative emotions grows over time, whereas the Benelux region shows the highest share of positive emotions.

4.4 Deep Discourse Analysis in Polish Protests

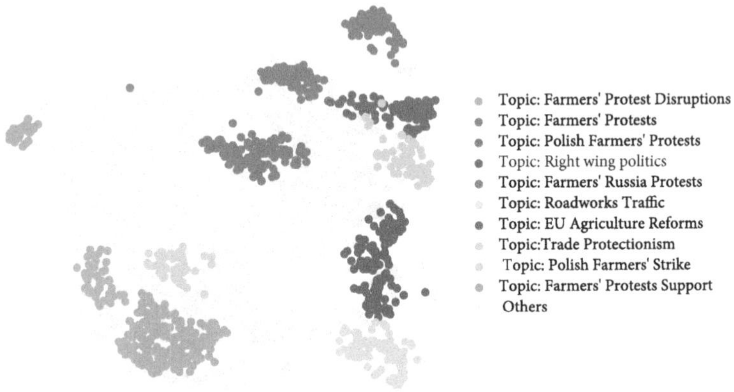

Fig. 4. Topic modeling 15-29.03.2024 for Poland

Depending on the medium, 5–20% of mentions contain animal-related content. The majority of the discourse focuses on eggs and poultry (Fig. 5) due to the possible ban on cage farming and imports from Ukraine.

5 Discussion

Empirical analysis of traditional media in Polish, Flemish, and German from 2024 shows an under representation of serious topics such as animal welfare and food security threats. Instead, media focus primarily on economic issues (e.g., subsidies) and logistics (e.g., road blockades). High-reach media used critical or omitting framing of protests as general in Poland (with low coverage by traditional media) and of specific topics in all countries. Conflicts between interest groups may be manipulated by foreign intelligence services which, was postulated by dis/mis-information checkers. In Poland (Fig. 4) as well in other analyzed countries far right political sector were involved in protests discourse [10]. Short-form video content on platforms like TikTok, Instagram, Facebook, and YouTube gained traction, showcasing protest actions and farmer perspectives while also serving as a means to spread misinformation against protesters (e.g., allegations regarding ambulance rerouting on February 27th). However restrictions on domestic animal production in Benelux and Poland are a more significant issue than current imports of Ukrainian plant products.

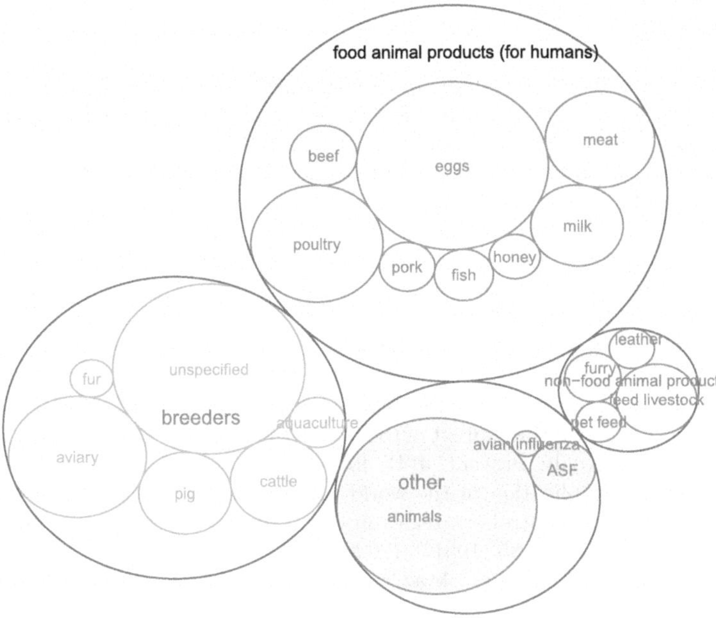

Fig. 5. Keywords Related to Animal Discourse 15.01–13.02 in Poland

6 Conclusion

We confirm fashion like phenomena (Fig. 2, mainly reach component) of the protest perception, as the public interest peak not in the culmination of physical protest, but in the start of series of the protest [13]. There is an observed 'cancel culture' towards farmer postulates (low penetration in traditional media) concerning animal production in the mainstream media [12]. Europeanized farmers have been confirmed to have limited representation [2] in the mainstream media (mostly opposite side have access to it). We show, that analyzing only one medium (as usually done in scientific literature) may give very biased picture of the events (Fig. 1) and only inter-medium triangulation can explain the phenomenon. Media coverage of protests is limited, with farmers underrepresented in mainstream outlets. Some social media, especially TikTok, is used to promote protests (mainly in Flemish and German speaking Internet).

Acknowledgments. The first author has participated as an observer in protests in all three settings. He engaged in discussions with protesters, counter-protesters, and local residents affected by the protests for better understand of the situation.

References

1. Barreiro Hurle, J., et al.: Modelling environmental and climate ambition in the agricultural sector with the capri model. Technical report, Joint Research Centre (Seville site) (2021). http://dx.doi.org/10.2760/98160
2. Chabanet, D.: Protest in the EU: A Path toward Democracy?, pp. 95–112. Palgrave Macmillan UK, London (2011)
3. Dobbins, C.E., Masambuka-Kanchewa, F., Lamm, A.J.: A systematic literature review of the intersection between social media and cultural identity: Implications for agricultural and environmental communication. J. Appli. Commun. **105**(2), COV–COV (2021)
4. Eysenbach, G.: How to fight an infodemic: the four pillars of infodemic management. J. Med. Internet Res. **22**(6), e21820 (2020)
5. Jarynowski, A.: Agroterrorism involving biological agents and related threats in Poland and Europe in the context of the Covid-19 pandemic and the war in ukraine. Terrorism Stud. Analy. Prevent. **4**(4), 405–444 (2023)
6. Jori, F., et al.: Application of the world café method to discuss the efficiency of African swine fever control strategies in european wild boar (sus scrofa) populations. Prev. Vet. Med. **185**, 105178 (2020)
7. Łódzki, B., et al.: Medialny obraz rzeczywistości. Studia Socialia Cracoviensia **91**(16), 121–136 (2017)
8. Neogi, A.S., Garg, K.A., Mishra, R.K., Dwivedi, Y.K.: Sentiment analysis and classification of Indian farmers' protest using twitter data. Inter. J. Inform. Manag. Data Insights **1**(2), 100019 (2021)
9. Noya, S.: The relationship between the Dutch farmers protest on October 1st 2019 and the social media attention that the protest received. PhD thesis (2021)
10. Pospieszna, P., Płatek, D., Piotrowski, G., Monkos, A.: Pillarized networks in a polarized civil society: a structure of far-right networks in poland. Nationalities Papers, pp. 1–16 (2023). https://doi.org/10.1017/nps.2023.47
11. Rodak, O.: Hashtag hijacking and crowdsourcing transparency: social media affordances and the governance of farm animal protection. Agric. Hum. Values **37**(2), 281–294 (2020)
12. Sandhu, A., Waraich, G.S.: The protest: A battle of media narratives. In: The Indian Farmers' Protest of 2020–2021, pp. 187–202. Routledge India
13. Sushko, I., Gardini, L., Matsuyama, K.: Dynamics of a generalized fashion cycle model. Chaos, Solitons Fractals **126**, 135–147 (2019)
14. van der Ploeg, J.D.: Farmers' upheaval, climate crisis and populism. J. Peasant Stud. **47**(3), 589–605 (2020)
15. Vicente, J., et al.: Science-based wildlife disease response. Science **364**(6444), 943–944 (2019)

Gradient Upsampling for Enhanced Image Resolution and Classification

Alexander Semenov[1(✉)], Chaity Banerjee Mukherjee[2], Vladimir Boginski[3], Eduardo L. Pasiliao[4], and Tathagata Mukherjee[2]

[1] University of Florida, Gainesville, FL, USA
asemenov@ufl.edu
[2] University of Alabama in Huntsville, Huntsville, AL, USA
[3] University of Central Florida, Orlando, FL, USA
[4] Air Force Research Laboratory, Eglin AFB, FL, USA

Abstract. We propose a novel method for image *gradient upsampling* that leverages adaptive convolution with learnable kernels to add weighted permutations of the input image pixels back to the image in a constrained manner in order to enhance the image gradient resolution. The proposed approach dynamically adjusts pixel values based on local patterns of pixels in the input image that define the gradients in the image. Traditional upsampling techniques, such as unpooling and nearest-neighbor interpolation rely on predefined rules and often result in blurred or jagged edges due to their inability to adapt to image content. Moreover, these and other image upsampling techniques like those based on deep learning, focus on enhancing the spatial information in the input with the goal of enhancing the human visual perceptual experience. However, the goal of our approach is to enhance the gradient information in the image in order to help gradient based learners learn better latent space features for inference tasks. Our approach uses trainable convolutional kernels that learn to extract and amplify intricate gradient based features during training by subdividing the input images into overlapping patches and applying element-wise transformations. We show the efficacy of the proposed method by enhancing the gradient information in images of the FashionMNIST dataset.

Keywords: Gradient Enhancement · Gradient Upsampling · Upsampling · Pixel Permutation · Neural networks

1 Introduction

Image upscaling is a fundamental task in image processing, aimed at increasing the spatial resolution of an image while preserving or enhancing its visual quality [13,14,18,25]. This process typically involves expanding the dimensions of an image by interpolating additional pixels, which can be achieved through various computational techniques, and is used in such applications as superresolution [8]. These methods aim to create new pixels using the existing information contained in the image which leads to better spatial resolution and enhanced visual quality. Thus the goal of such methods is to enhance the quality of the image such that

J. Kertesz et al. (Eds.): CSoNet 2024, LNCS 15417, pp. 373–382, 2025.
https://doi.org/10.1007/978-981-96-6389-7_34

the new enhanced image is perceived to be of higher quality by the human visual system. Though such enhancements can lead to better interpretation of images by human beings, they may have detrimental effect on the quality of inference achieved through Artificial Intelligence (AI), especially the ones using deep neural networks which are known to be sensitive to small changes in their input [24]. Succinctly, though these methods enhance the image quality, they may not improve the quality of inference using deep feature learning techniques.

Deep neural networks learn features from images for target tasks using gradient information present in the training images. During testing, inference is done by using the gradient information present in the test images to map the image to an appropriate section of the latent space which can then be used for the final inference. Since the way deep neural networks perceive images is different from that of the human visual system, in order to enhance the learning ability of neural networks, gradient augmentation methods hold more promise as opposed to up-sampling techniques. It must be noted that gradient augmentation techniques will not improve the visual quality of the image but will help the neural network better learn information from the input image due to the enhanced gradient related information. In this work we propose a novel method for image gradient enhancement, called *gradient upsampling* using an adaptive convolutional strategy with learnable kernels. The proposed approach enhances the "image gradient resolution" by dynamically adjusting pixel values based on local gradient patterns. Traditional upscaling methods, such as unpooling [29] and nearest-neighbor or edge-directed interpolation [15], often rely on predefined rules to fill in missing pixels, which can result in blurred or jagged edges. Unpooling layers, for instance, reverse pooling operations in CNNs but do not inherently enhance image detail or gradient information, as they primarily insert zeros or average values into expanded regions, smoothing out gradients in the process.

In contrast, gradient upsampling utilizes a convolutional kernel that learns to upscale the gradient information in images by extracting and amplifying intricate gradient features during training. By subdividing the input image into overlapping patches and applying element-wise transformations, our approach adapts to the image content, preserving crucial details like edges and textures while enhancing the gradients with the goal of helping the neural network learn effective representations of the image. This adaptive mechanism allows our proposed method to outperform conventional upscaling techniques for the task of representation learning by producing gradient enhanced high-resolution images. We define a *high-resolution gradient enhanced image* as one where the image gradient information is enhanced through the addition of pixels to the input image. Note that though the resulting image has more pixels, the enhancement is in the gradient information only and may or may not lead to the creation of visually appealing images. This makes our method suitable for applications that require automated inference with low resolution noisy input images, like in the field of medical image processing. By enhancing the gradients of the noisy input images, we allow the underlying deep representation learning algorithm to better learn the image content and map the same to the latent space for further inference. In order to test our gradient upsampling technique, we use the proposed approach on images from the FashionMNIST dataset.

The rest of the paper is organized as follows: in Sect. 2 we discuss previous work related to upsampling and convolution based image enhancement techniques, in Sect. 3 we describe the proposed gradient upsampling technique and finally in Sect. 4 we describe the experiments and results. Finally, we conclude in Sect. 5.

2 Related Work and Contributions

Recent work in image upsampling has focused on leveraging advanced machine learning techniques, particularly deep learning models, to achieve high-quality outputs. Here we provide a list of methods used for the task of image upsampling, though we must point out again that these methods have the goal if enhancing the visual quality of the images in a way that affects the human perceptual system. They do not focus on the task of gradient information enhancement for augmenting deep feature learning tasks. Deep convolutional neural networks (CNNs) have become the dominant method for image upsampling in recent years, offering significant improvements over traditional interpolation techniques. One way to upscale image resolution is through a 2D transposed convolution (also known as a fractionally-strided convolution or deconvolution), as proposed in [28]. A version of deconvolution is presented in [20], where it is used for image segmentation. An application of deconvolution layers is super-resolution, which focuses on reconstructing high-resolution images from low-resolution inputs [9,17]. Another variant, known as the pixel deconvolution network, is presented in [7]. The "checkerboard" pattern issue and methods to prevent it are discussed in [1]. Traditional image upscaling methods are based on filtering approaches, such as those proposed in [6] and [18]. Additionally, random forests have been employed for image super-resolution [22]. Super-Resolution CNNs (SRCNN) introduced the concept of using CNNs to learn the mapping between low and high-resolution images [5]. SRCNN features three convolutional layers: (1) a 9×9 layer for patch extraction, generating 64 feature maps; (2) a 1×1 layer for non-linear mapping, reducing them to 32; and (3) a 5×5 layer for reconstruction, producing the high-resolution output. Trained end-to-end on the Y channel in YCrCb space, SRCNN outperforms traditional methods like bicubic interpolation and sparse coding. Generative Adversarial Networks (GANs) have shown remarkable results in image upsampling: (1) SRGAN (Super-Resolution GAN) [13] uses a perceptual loss function to generate photo-realistic high-resolution images. EnhanceNet [21] combines adversarial training with texture matching loss for improved texture synthesis. There are methods based on the idea of *progressive growing of GANs* which gradually increases the resolution of generated images during training, allowing for the creation of high-resolution images. Specialized network architectures for image upsampling have been studied and implemented. For example ESRGAN (Enhanced SRGAN) [26] improves upon SRGAN with a Residual-in-Residual Dense Block (RRDB) design. RealSR [2] uses a deep recursive residual network to achieve state-of-the-art results. LIIF (Learning Continuous Image Representation) [3] proposes approach to represent images as continuous functions, allowing for arbitrary upsampling ratios. Incorporating attention mechanisms into upsampling networks has yielded promising results: (1) SAN [4] uses second-order channel attention to capture feature correlations, and (2) HAN [19] employs layer attention for feature adaptation. of different levels. Applications of upsampling include: (1) Face Super-Resolution [11] enhances low-resolution facial images; (2) Medical Imaging employs tailored methods for upsampling scans, with [16] offering further references; (3) Satellite Imagery: Models designed to enhance the resolution of aerial and satellite photographs have been considered for traditional and small SAT data [12]. Research is also being conducted on making upsampling more computationally efficient; ESPCN (Efficient Sub-Pixel CNN) [23] performs most computations in the low-resolution space, reducing computational complexity while IMDN (Information Multi-Distillation Network) [10] is designed for efficient super-resolution on mobile devices.

While the proposed method shares some conceptual similarities with transposed convolution, such as increasing the spatial dimensions of the input, it is a fundamentally different technique. In standard transposed convolution, the output is constructed through overlapping applications of the kernel, where contributions from multiple positions in the input are summed to produce each element in the output. This involves a specific pattern of weight sharing and addition due to strides and padding, leading to overlapping regions in the output that are summed together. In contrast, the method described here performs element-wise multiplication of extracted submatrices with the kernel and then concatenates the results without any overlapping or summation. Each element in the output is influenced by a single position in the input, and there is no accumulation of values from multiple input positions. Therefore, although both methods aim to upsample the input, the underlying operations and mathematical foundations are different resulting in different outcomes; the first one leads to enhancement of spatial image resolution and information whereas the latter leads to enhancement of the gradient information through a locally constrained permutation achieved through learning convolution filters and concatenating the filter responses.

3 Method Description and Implementation

The proposed method was implemented in the `UpConv2d` class using PyTorch and differs from the classic image scaling techniques such as nearest-neighbor interpolation, bilinear interpolation, bicubic interpolation and other deep learning based techniques discussed in Sect. 2. Traditional upsampling algorithms typically use some type of interpolation to estimate pixel values at new coordinate locations in the image based on the values at neighboring pixels. For instance, bilinear interpolation computes the output pixel value as a weighted average of the four nearest input pixels, resulting in smoother images but potentially blurring sharp edges, hence diluting the gradient information in the image.

In contrast, our method operates by extracting overlapping submatrices from the input tensor and performing element-wise multiplication with a trainable kernel K. This is followed by rearranging the results to get a constrained permutation to form the upsampled output. Mathematically, each output region is computed as:

$$R_{i,j} = A_{i,j} \odot K,$$

where $A_{i,j}$ are the extracted submatrices and $\odot$ denotes element-wise multiplication. The output is then reconstructed by assembling these $R_{i,j}$ matrices without overlap, leading to an increased spatial dimension.

Unlike interpolation-based methods (deep learning or otherwise) that rely on fixed mathematical formulas or function estimation techniques to estimate pixel values, our approach allows the model to learn how to upsample the gradient information in the input data effectively through training. This learned gradient upsampling can capture complex patterns and features in the data through gradient enhancement, resulting in better performance of deep feature learning algorithms for specific tasks. This is due to the possibility of learning better gradient based features which can be used for inference, unlike the classical methods that enhance spatial image information at the cost of potentially diluting the gradient information.

3.1 Method Formulation

The `UpConv2d` function performs an operation that upsamples the gradient of an input square matrix A of size $M \times M$ using a kernel matrix K of size $K \times K$. The output is a larger matrix B obtained through the following process: we extract all possible $K \times K$ submatrices from A by sliding the kernel over A with a stride of 1. The number of positions where the kernel fits is given by:

$$P = M - K + 1$$

Thus, we obtain $P \times P$ submatrices $A_{i,j}$, where $i, j = 1, 2, \ldots, P$. For each extracted submatrix $A_{i,j}$, we perform an element-wise multiplication with the learned kernel K:

$$R_{i,j} = A_{i,j} \odot K$$

where $\odot$ denotes element-wise multiplication. Note that each $R_{i,j}$ is a $K \times K$ matrix. The resulting matrices $R_{i,j}$ are arranged in a grid to form the output matrix B. Specifically, they are concatenated without overlap, resulting in B having dimensions:

$$\text{Size of } B = (P \times K) \times (P \times K)$$

Substituting P, we get:

$$\text{Size of } B = ((M - K + 1) \times K) \times ((M - K + 1) \times K)$$

The method is illustrated in Fig. 1. In the PyTorch implementation of the `UpConv2d` class, the upsampling operation is realized by unfolding the input tensor to extract all possible submatrices $A_{i,j}$ of size $K \times K$, as described in the previous formulas. Specifically, the `unfold` function is used to generate these submatrices along the height and width dimensions. Each submatrix is then element-wise multiplied with the weight matrix K, corresponding to the operation $R_{i,j} = A_{i,j} \odot K$. The resulting tensors $R_{i,j}$ are then rearranged and reshaped to form the output tensor B, with dimensions given by $((M - K + 1) \times K) \times ((M - K + 1) \times K)$, matching the output size derived earlier.

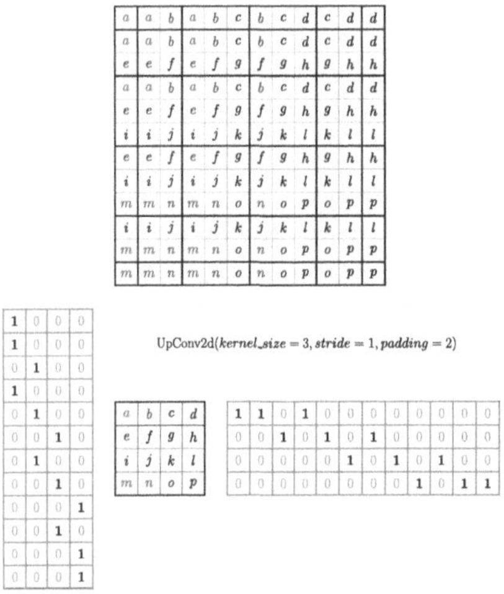

(a) UpConv2d illustration

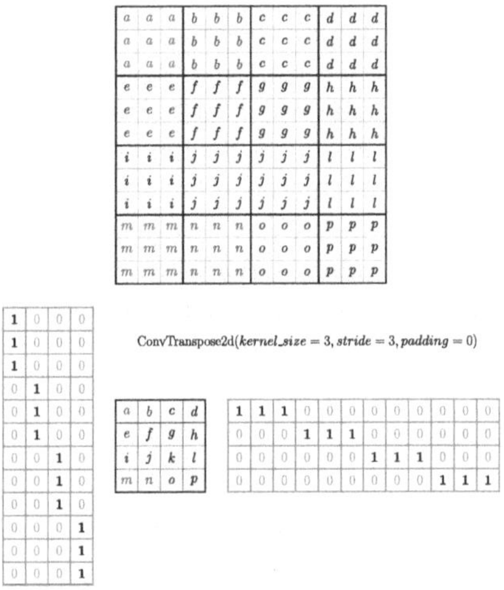

(b) ConvTranspose2d illustration

Fig. 1. Comparison of UpConv2d and ConvTranspose2d illustrations.

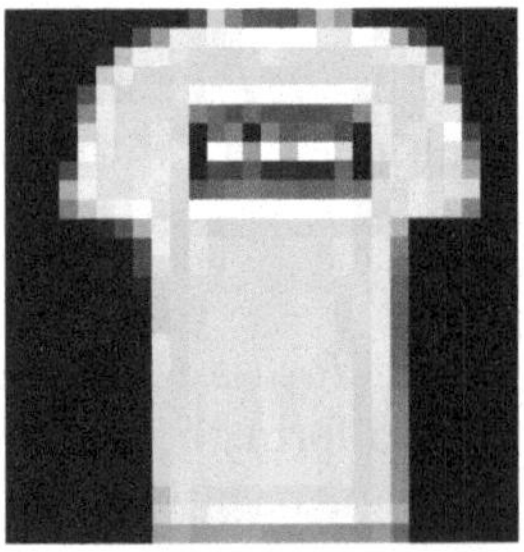

(a) Original Image 1

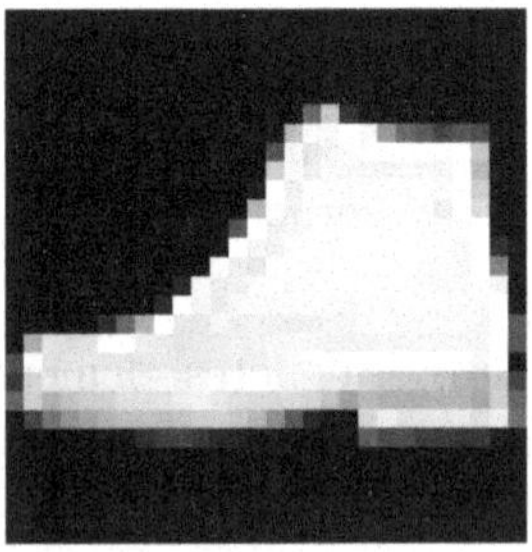

(b) Original Image 2

Fig. 2. Two original images

(a) Upsampled with 3x3 matrix of ones

(b) Upsampled with 3x3 matrix

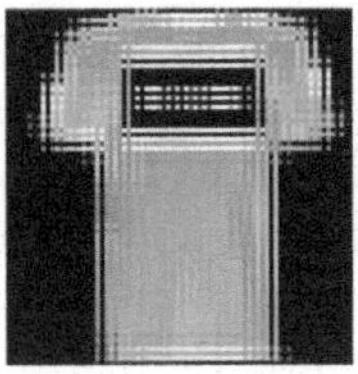

(c) ReLU of upsampled image with 3x3 matrix of ones

(d) ReLU of upsampled image with 3x3 matrix

(e) ReLU of negative upsampled image with 3x3 matrix of ones

(f) ReLU of negative upsampled image with 3x3 matrix

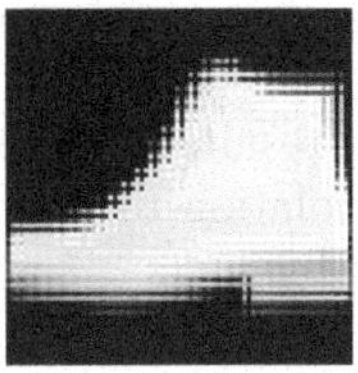

(g) Upsampled with 3x3 matrix of ones (alt)

(h) Upsampled with 3x3 matrix (alt)

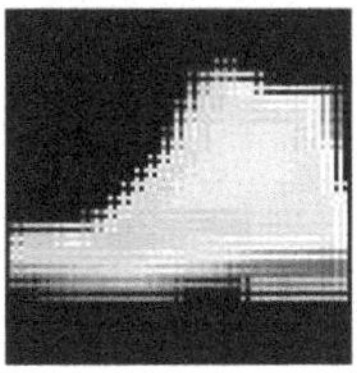

(i) ReLU of upsampled image with 3x3 matrix of ones (alt)

(j) ReLU of upsampled image with 3x3 matrix (alt)

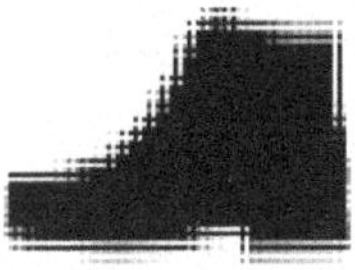

(k) ReLU of negative upsampled image with 3x3 matrix of ones (alt)

(l) ReLU of negative upsampled image with 3x3 matrix (alt)

Fig. 3. Comparison of upsampling and ReLU transformations from two of images.

4 Experiments

We employed a convolutional neural network (CNN) architecture comprising two convolutional layers and two fully connected layers. The first convolutional layer applies 8 filters of size 3×3 with stride $s = 1$ and padding $p = 1$ to the input, followed by a ReLU activation function and a max pooling layer with kernel size 2×2 and stride $s = 2$. The second convolutional layer also applies 8 filters of size 3×3 with stride $s = 1$ and padding $p = 1$, followed by another ReLU activation and a max pooling layer of the same configuration. We used FashionMNIST for evaluation [27]. We have upscaled the images using nearest neighbor method, and compared it with UpConv upscaling. Examples of upsampled images (see Fig. 2) and their transformations are shown in Fig. 3.

The output from the convolutional layers is flattened into a vector of size $8 \times 21 \times 21$ and passed through a fully connected layer with 32 neurons, followed by a ReLU activation function and a dropout layer with a dropout rate of 0.5 to prevent overfitting. Finally, the network outputs predictions through a second fully connected layer with 10 neurons, corresponding to the target classes.

The plots in Fig. 4a and 4b depict the comparison of our method, UpConv2D, against the nearest-neighbor interpolation method in terms of training loss and testing accuracy over several epochs. In the loss plot, UpConv2D shows a consistently lower training loss compared to nearest-neighbor interpolation. The accuracy plot demonstrates that UpConv2D achieves higher testing accuracy across all epochs. These results show that UpConv2D outperforms the traditional nearest-neighbor interpolation in both minimizing training error and enhancing model accuracy (see Table 1).

Table 1. Comparison of testing accuracy between our method (UpConv2D) and nearest-neighbor interpolation.

Method	Testing Accuracy (%)
Nearest-neighbor interpolation	88.49
UpConv2D (our approach)	**89.72**

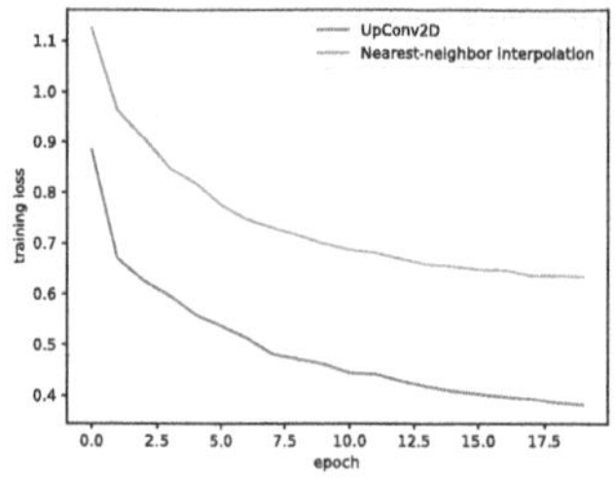

(a) Loss

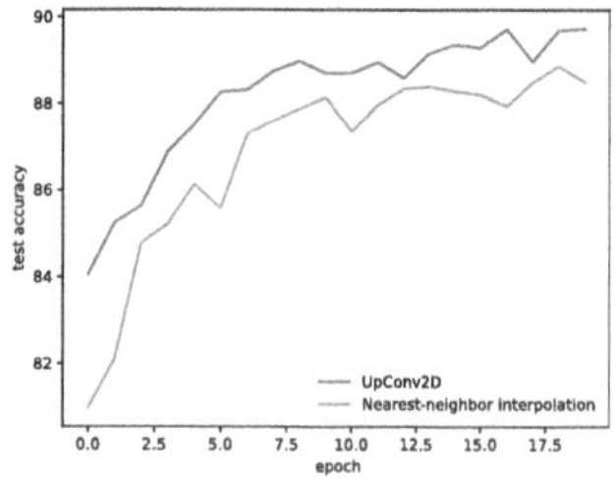

(b) Testing accuracy

Fig. 4. Neural Network performance: (a) Loss; (b) Testing accuracy.

5 Concluding Remarks

In this paper, we proposed a new technique for enhancing image resolution via gradient upsampling. The results obtained on the well-known Fashion MNIST dataset suggest that our approach can potentially be useful for transforming and enhancing the images in the considered dataset, as well as for improving the accuracy of image classification on the test dataset. These preliminary results suggest that the proposed approach is promising and needs to be studied in the future research from the perspectives of both further enhancements of the models and testing the respective models on a variety of image datasets.

References

1. Aitken, A., Ledig, C., Theis, L., Caballero, J., Wang, Z., Shi, W.: Checkerboard artifact free sub-pixel convolution: A note on sub-pixel convolution, resize convolution and convolution resize. arXiv preprint arXiv:1707.02937 (2017)
2. Cai, J., Zeng, H., Yong, H., Cao, Z., Zhang, L.: Toward real-world single image super-resolution: A new benchmark and a new model. In: Proceedings of the IEEE/CVF International Conference on Computer Vision, pp. 3086–3095 (2019)
3. Chen, Y., Liu, S., Wang, X.: Learning continuous image representation with local implicit image function. In: Proceedings of the IEEE/CVF Conference on Computer Vision and pattern recognition, pp. 8628–8638 (2021)
4. Dai, T., Cai, J., Zhang, Y., Xia, S.-T., Zhang, L.: Second-order attention network for single image super-resolution. In: Proceedings of the IEEE/CVF Conference on Computer Vision and Pattern Recognition, pp.11065–11074 (2019)
5. Dong, C., Loy, C.C., He, K., Tang, X.: Image super-resolution using deep convolutional networks. IEEE Trans. Pattern Anal. Mach. Intell. **38**(2), 295–307 (2015)
6. Duchon, C.E.: Lanczos filtering in one and two dimensions. J. Appl. Meteorol. Climatol. **18**(8), 1016–1022 (1979)
7. Gao, H., Yuan, H., Wang, Z., Ji, S.: Pixel transposed convolutional networks. IEEE Trans. Pattern Anal. Mach. Intell. **42**(5), 1218–1227 (2019)
8. Giachetti, A., Asuni, N.: Real-time artifact-free image upscaling. IEEE Trans. Image Process. **20**(10), 2760–2768 (2011)
9. Guo, M., et al.: Rapid image deconvolution and multiview fusion for optical microscopy. Nat. Biotechnol. **38**(11), 1337–1346 (2020)
10. Hui, Z., Gao, X., Yang, Y., Wang, X.: Lightweight image super-resolution with information multi-distillation network. In: Proceedings of the 27th ACM International Conference on Multimedia, pp. 2024–2032 (2019)
11. Jiang, J., Wang, C., Liu, X., Ma, J.: Deep learning-based face super-resolution: a survey. ACM Comput. Surv. (CSUR) **55**(1), 1–36 (2021)
12. Karwowska, K., Wierzbicki, D.: Using super-resolution algorithms for small satellite imagery: a systematic review. IEEE J. Selected Topics Appli. Earth Observat. Remote Sensing **15**, 3292–3312 (2022)
13. Ledig, C., et al.: Photo-realistic single image super-resolution using a generative adversarial network. In: Proceedings of the IEEE Conference on Computer Vision and Pattern Recognition (CVPR) (July 2017)
14. Lehmann, T.M., Gonner, C., Spitzer, K.: Survey: interpolation methods in medical image processing. IEEE Trans. Med. Imaging **18**(11), 1049–1075 (1999)
15. Li, X., Orchard, M.T.: New edge-directed interpolation. IEEE Trans. Image Process. **10**(10), 1521–1527 (2001)
16. Li, Y., Sixou, B., Peyrin, F.: A review of the deep learning methods for medical images super resolution problems. Irbm **42**(2), 120–133 (2021)
17. Liu, H., et al.: Arbitrary-scale super-resolution via deep learning: a comprehensive survey. Inform. Fusion **102**, 102015 (2024)
18. Mitchell, D.P., Netravali, A.N.: Reconstruction filters in computer-graphics. ACM Siggraph Comput. Graph. **22**(4), 221–228 (1988)
19. Niu, B., et al.: Single image super-resolution via a holistic attention network. In: Vedaldi, A., Bischof, H., Brox, T., Frahm, J.-M. (eds.) ECCV 2020. LNCS, vol. 12357, pp. 191–207. Springer, Cham (2020). https://doi.org/10.1007/978-3-030-58610-2_12

20. Noh, H., Hong, S., Han, B.: Learning deconvolution network for semantic segmentation. In: Proceedings of the IEEE International Conference on Computer Vision, pp. 1520–1528 (2015)
21. Sajjadi, M.S., Schölkopf, B., Hirsch, M.: Enhancenet: Single image super-resolution through automated texture synthesis. arXiv preprint, arXiv:1612.07919 (2016)
22. Schulter, S., Leistner, C., Bischof, H.: Fast and accurate image upscaling with super-resolution forests. In: Proceedings of the IEEE Conference on Computer Vision and Pattern Recognition (CVPR) (June 2015)
23. Shi, W., et al.: Real-time single image and video super-resolution using an efficient sub-pixel convolutional neural network. In: Proceedings of the IEEE Conference on Computer Vision and Pattern Recognition, pp. 1874–1883 (2016)
24. Su, J., Vargas, D.V., Sakurai, K.: One pixel attack for fooling deep neural networks. IEEE Trans. Evol. Comput. **23**(5), 828–841 (2019)
25. Wang, Q., Yuan, Y.: Learning to resize image. Neurocomputing **131**, 357–367 (2014)
26. Wang, X., et al.: ESRGAN: enhanced super-resolution generative adversarial networks. In: Leal-Taixé, L., Roth, S. (eds.) ECCV 2018. LNCS, vol. 11133, pp. 63–79. Springer, Cham (2019). https://doi.org/10.1007/978-3-030-11021-5_5
27. Xiao, H., Rasul, K., Vollgraf, R.: Fashion-mnist: a novel image dataset for benchmarking machine learning algorithms (2017)
28. Zeiler, M.D., Krishnan, D., Taylor, G.W., Fergus, R.: Deconvolutional networks. In: 2010 IEEE Computer Society Conference on Computer Vision and Pattern Recognition, pp. 2528–2535 (2010)
29. Zeiler, M.D., Taylor, G.W., Fergus, R.: Adaptive deconvolutional networks for mid and high level feature learning. In: 2011 International Conference on Computer Vision, pp. 2018–2025. IEEE (2011)

Advanced Heuristic Solution for the Hospital-Resident Matching with Ties Problem

Uyen T. Nguyen[1(✉)] and Sang X. Tran[2]

[1] Institute of Engineering and Technology, Vinh University, Nghean, Vietnam
uyennt@vinhuni.edu.vn
[2] Cyber School, Vinh University, Nghean, Vietnam
sangtx@vinhuni.edu.vn

Abstract. The Hospitals/Residents with Ties problem (HRT) can yield stable matchings of varying sizes. A well-known NP-hard task is to find a stable matching of maximal size in any HRT situation, known as MAX-HRT. In this study, we report a heuristic search strategy designed specifically to tackle MAX-HRT. First, we randomly assign residents to hospitals. Next, we solve one undominated blocking pair at a time until we find the best solution, iteratively improving this assignment. We conduct a series of experiments to assess the performance of our algorithm against adaptive search techniques and hospital-proposing methods. Results indicate that our strategy provides improved efficiency in terms of both execution time and solution quality, especially when working with large-scale MAX-HRT instances.

Keywords: Hospitals/Residents with Ties problem · MAX-HRT · Undominated Blocking Pairs · Weakly Stable Matching

1 Introduction

The Hospitals/Residents with Ties (HRT) problem [7,8] is one of many-to-one stable matching problems, which is extended from the well-known one-to-one Stable Marriage (SM) problem [3]. The HRT problem has recently received lots of attention from researchers because of its important role in many applications, such as the National Resident Matching Program (NRMP) in the US [19], the Evolution of the Labor Market for Medical Interns and Residents [19], the Scottish Pre-registration house officer Allocations (SPA) matching scheme [6], or the Canadian Resident Matching Service (CaRMS) in Canada, the problem of assigning users to servers in a large distributed Internet service [12].

An instance I of HRT comprises a set n of residents and a set m of hospitals. Each resident and hospital rank a subset of the hospitals and residents, respectively, in order of preference consisting of ties. Moreover, each hospital has a limited number of assigned residents, called the hospital's capacity. When ties are allowed in the residents' and hospitals' preference lists, three criteria

J. Kertesz et al. (Eds.): CSoNet 2024, LNCS 15417, pp. 383–394, 2025.
https://doi.org/10.1007/978-981-96-6389-7_35

of stable matchings are given, consisting of *weak stability*, *strong stability*, and *super-stability* [8]. Weak stability allows a matching where no resident-hospital pair mutually prefers each other over their current assignments, even when preferences are tied. This criterion is relatively flexible, as it only prevents mutually preferred switches without imposing further constraints. Strong stability imposes stricter conditions by requiring that no resident-hospital pair, even with slight mutual preference, prefers each other over their current assignments, thus eliminating any desire for a swap. Super-stability is the most stringent of all, ensuring that no resident or hospital could ever prefer an alternative pairing under any circumstance, thereby completely removing the possibility of unsatisfied pairings [8,21].ou Among these criteria, the problem of finding weakly stable matchings has been an active field of research for several years since its practical applications. Irving et al. [21] showed that weakly stable matchings of an arbitrary instance of HRT always exist and have different sizes, so it is natural to find those of maximum size such that there is the maximum number of residents assigned to hospitals. Such a problem has been known as MAX-HRT and shown to be NP-hard [14] and therefore, finding an efficient algorithm to deal with MAX-HRT is a challenge for researchers.

Our Contributions: In this paper, we propose a heuristic search algorithm to solve MAX-HRT. Our motivation is derived from the two following problems: (*i*) reducing the average execution time for MAX-HRT of large sizes. To do this, our idea is only to consider a resident which can yield a blocking pair and finds an undominated blocking pair from the resident's point of view instead of all residents at each iteration, as shown in [17] and [20]; and (*ii*) maximizing the number of residents assigned to hospitals. Here, we propose a strategy to improve the stable matching size by promoting under-subscribed hospitals in the same ties and unassigned residents without restarting from a random matching. Our experimental results show that our algorithm outperforms AS-HRT [17] and Hospital-proposing [10] algorithms, which are efficient for MAX-HRT in recent years, in terms of execution time and solution quality for MAX-HRT of large sizes.

Organization: The rest of the paper is structured as follows. Section 2 provides the literature review on HRT problem. Section 3 presents notations and proprieties of studied problem. Section 4 introduces the proposed algorithm and theoretical analysis. Experimental computation is provided in Sect. 5. Finally, we conclude this work in Sect. 6.

2 Related Work

An instance I of HRT comprises a set n of residents and a set m of hospitals. Each resident and hospital rank a subset of the hospitals and residents, respectively, in order of preference consisting of ties. Moreover, each hospital has a limited number of assigned residents, called the hospital's capacity. When ties are allowed in the residents' and hospitals' preference lists, three criteria of stable matchings are given, consisting of *weak stability*, *strong stability*, and *super-stability* [8]. Among these criteria, the problem of finding weakly stable matchings has been an active field of research for several years since its practical applications. Irving et al. [21] showed that weakly stable matchings of an arbitrary instance of HRT always exist and have different sizes, so it is natural to find those of maximum size such that there is the maximum number of residents assigned to hospitals. Such a problem has been known as MAX-HRT and shown to be NP-hard [14] and therefore, finding an efficient algorithm to deal with MAX-HRT is a challenge for researchers.

In recent years, almost all the algorithms that have been proposed to solve MAX-HRT are approximate since MAX-HRT is NP-hard. Manlove et al. [14] proved that the maximum size of stable matchings is at most twice the minimum size of stable matchings for any instance of HRT. Irving and Manlove [7] proposed two heuristic algorithms for the restricted version of MAX-HRT in which ties are allowed to appear in only hospitals' lists. Kira'ly [10] proposed two 3/2−linear time approximation algorithms for MAX-HRT, one is applied for the case when ties are allowed to appear only on the hospitals' lists, and the other is applied for the general case where ties are allowed to appear on both residents' and hospitals' lists. Kwanashie et al. [11] presented an integer programming (IP) model to solve MAX-HRT. Given an instance of HRT, they first remove all the acceptable pairs in the residents' and hospitals' lists that cannot appear in any stable matching by using *hospitals-offer* and *residents-apply* algorithms [7], and thus reducing the number of the variables in their IP model. Munera et al. [17] proposed an algorithm, namely AS-HRT, to solve MAX-HRT. They convert an instance of HRT into an instance of SMTI (Stable Marriage problem with Ties and Incomplete lists) [9,14] and apply their previous adaptive search algorithm [18] for the SMTI instance to find a solution of MAX-HRT. Recently, Viet et al. [20] proposed a heuristic algorithm based on the min-conflict algorithm [16] to deal with MAX-HRT. This algorithm achieved better solution quality and execution time in comparison to other previous research works. However, it still exposed a weakness in execution time for MAX-HRT of large sizes.

3 Preliminaries

This section reminds the HRT problem and definitions related to this paper [8, 13]. The Hospitals/Residents with Ties (HRT) [13,15] is an extension of the stable marriage incomplete with ties (SMTI) [3] problem. The HRT problem is a wellknown matching problem and recently, it has been attracting much attention from the research community due to its important role in a wide range of applications such as the National Resident Matching Program (NRMP) in the US [19], the Evolution of the Labor Market for Medical Interns and Residents [19], the Scottish Pre-registration house officer Allocations (SPA) matching scheme [6], the Canadian Resident Matching Service (CaRMS) in Canada, and even issues like assigning users to servers in large distributed Internet services [12].

An HRT instance of size $n \times m$ of HRT includes a set of n residents, denoted by $\mathcal{R} = \{r_1, r_2, \cdots, r_n\}$, and a set of m hospitals, denoted by $\mathcal{H} = \{h_1, h_2, \cdots, h_m\}$, in which each $r_i \in \mathcal{R}$ ranks a subset of $\mathcal{H}$ in its preference list and each $h_j \in \mathcal{H}$ ranks a subset of $\mathcal{R}$ in its preference list. Moreover, each h_j has a *capacity* $c_j \in \mathbb{Z}^+$ to allow the maximum number of residents that can be assigned to it. We denote the rank of h_j in r_i's preference list by $R_{r_i}(h_j)$ and the rank of r_i in h_j 's preference list by and $R_{h_j}(r_i)$.

We denote a set of *acceptable* pairs by $\mathcal{A} = \{(r_i, h_j) \in \mathcal{R} \times \mathcal{H}\}$, where r_i and h_j appear in the preference list of each other. Thus, if (r_i, w_j) is an acceptable pair, then $R_{r_i}(h_j) > 0$ and $R_{h_j}(r_i) > 0$. If a resident r_i strictly prefers a hospital h_j to a hospital h_k, then we denote by $R_{r_i}(h_j) < R_{r_i}(h_k)$. If a resident r_i prefers a hospital h_j and a hospital h_k, then we denote by $R_{r_i}(h_j) = R_{r_i}(h_k)$.

An matching $\mathcal{M}$ of an HRT instance is a set of acceptable pairs $\mathcal{M} = \{(r_i, h_j), (r_i, \emptyset); |\mathcal{M}(s_i)| \leq 1$ for all $s_i \in \mathcal{R}$, $|\mathcal{M}(p_j)| \leq c_j\}$ for all $p_j \in \mathcal{P}$ meaning that each s_i belongs to at most one pair. If $(r_i, h_j) \in \mathcal{M}$, we say that r_i is assigned to h_j, denoted by $\mathcal{M}(r_i) = \{h_j\}$, and h_j is assigned to the set of residents r_i, denoted by $\mathcal{M}(h_j) = \{r_i\}$. If r_i is unassigned in $\mathcal{M}$, we denote by $\mathcal{M}(r_i) = \emptyset$. We say that a hospital $h_j \in \mathcal{H}$ is *under-subscribed* if $|\mathcal{M}(h_j)| < c_j$, *full* if $|\mathcal{M}(h_j)| = c_j$, or *over-subscribed* if $|\mathcal{M}(h_j)| > c_j$. A pair $(r_i, h_j) \in \mathcal{R} \times \mathcal{H}$ is a *blocking pair* for a matching $\mathcal{M}$ in I if:

1. $(r_i, h_j) \in \mathcal{A}$.
2. $\mathcal{M}(r_i) = \emptyset$ or $R_{r_i}(h_j) < R_{r_i}(\mathcal{M}(r_i))$.
3. $|\mathcal{M}(h_j)| < c_j$ or $R_{h_j}(r_i) < R_{h_j}(\mathcal{M}(h_j))$.

Given two blocking pairs $(r_i, h_j) \in \mathcal{R} \times \mathcal{H}$ and $(r_i, h_k) \in \mathcal{R} \times \mathcal{H}$, we say that (r_i, h_j) *dominates* (r_i, h_k) from the resident's point of view if $R_{r_i}(h_j) < R_{r_i}(h_k)$. A blocking pair $(r_i, h_j) \in \mathcal{R} \times \mathcal{H}$ is called an *undominated blocking pair*, if there exists no blocking pair that dominates it from the resident's. A matching $\mathcal{M}$ is called *weakly stable* if it admits no blocking pairs, otherwise, it is called *unstable*. *size*$(\mathcal{M})$ is the matching size of $\mathcal{M}$, i.e. the number of acceptable pairs assigned in a stable matching $\mathcal{M}$. If *size*$(\mathcal{M}) = n$, then $\mathcal{M}$ is called *perfect*, otherwise, $\mathcal{M}$ is called *non-perfect*. Irving et al. [8] showed that weakly stable matchings of an HRT instance have different sizes. In order for every person paired, we need to find a matching that is not only weakly stable but also of maximum size. This problem is known as MAX-HRT [13] and NP-hard [9] and therefore, finding an efficient algorithm to solve the problem of large sizes is a challenge for researchers (Table 1).

4 Proposed Algorithm

This section, we propose a heuristic search algorithm to solve MAX-HRT, so called HS-HRT. Our idea for HS-HRT to solve MAX-HRT is to improve the stability of an unstable matching by eliminating some blocking pairs through iterations. To do this efficiently, we remove an *undominated blocking pair* (UBP) instead of blocking pairs for an unstable matching at a time. It should be noted

Table 1. An HRT instance

Resident' preferences	Hospital' preferences	Capacity
r_1: h_1 h_3	h_1: r_3 (r_2 r_5) (r_1 r_7 r_8)	$c_1 = 2$
r_2: (h_1 h_4)	h_2: r_3 r_8 (r_5 r_6) r_7 r_4	$c_2 = 2$
r_3: h_1 h_2	h_3: (r_1 r_4 r_6) r_5	$c_3 = 2$
r_4: (h_2 h_3 h_4)	h_4: r_2 r_6 r_4	$c_4 = 2$
r_5: (h_1 h_2) h_3		
r_6: h_4 h_2 h_3		
r_7: h_1 h_2		
r_8: (h_1 h_2)		

that the concept of UBP was given in [4], and then it was applied to solve the SMTI problem [5,18].

Our HS-HRT to solve MAX-HRT is given in Algorithm 1. At the beginning, the algorithm creates a random matching $\mathcal{M}$ consisting of acceptable pairs $(r_i, h_j) \in \mathcal{A}$ and unassigned residents, assigns $\mathcal{M}$ to the best matching $\mathcal{M}_{best}$ and sets each resident $r_i \in \mathcal{R}$ to be active. Besides, the algorithm initializes a variable, denoted by $z(r_i)$, to count the number of hospitals assigned to each resident $r_i \in \mathcal{R}$ to zero, a variable, denoted by $z(h_j)$, to count the number of residents assigned to each resident $h_i \in \mathcal{H}$ to zero, and saves the original rank of every $r_i \in \mathcal{R}$, denoted by $R^{\dagger}_{r_i}(h_j)$. It should be noted that both $z(r_i)$ and $z(h_j)$ are used only in Algorithm 2, while $R^{\dagger}_{r_i}(h_j)$ is used for recovering the h_j's rank in r_i's rank list since while finding an UBP for r_i, the h_j's rank will be deleted in r_i's rank list. At each iteration, if there exists an active resident r_i, the algorithm finds a hospital h_k and a waiting list $W(r_i)$. HS-HRT finds an undominated blocking pair UBP, (r_i, h_k) and a set of hospitals $h_t \in \mathcal{H}$, $W(r_i)$ that $R_{r_i}(h_t) < R_{r_i}(\mathcal{M}(r_i))$ or $R_{r_i}(h_t) = R_{r_i}(h_k)$. If there exists no such a hospital h_k, meaning that r_i does not yield any blocking pair for $\mathcal{M}$ and so r_i is set to become inactive. Otherwise, the algorithm finds $h_j = \mathcal{M}(r_i)$, removes the UBP (r_i, h_k) for $\mathcal{M}$ by assigning h_k to r_i in $\mathcal{M}$, and sets r_i to become inactive. Then, the algorithm recovers the h_j's rank in every resident r_l that $W(r_l) = h_j$ and sets r_l to become reactive so that r_l can find a hospital for it in the next iterations. After that, the algorithm checks if $|\mathcal{M}(h_k)| > c_k$, then it removes the pair (r_w, h_k) such that $|\mathcal{M}(h_k)| = c_k$, where r_w is the worst resident assigned to h_j, and sets r_w to become reactive. It should be noted that when the algorithm finds the next active resident of the last active resident r_i, it backs to find an active resident from r_1. If there exists no active resident, meaning that the algorithm reaches a stable matching $\mathcal{M}$, then the algorithm checks if $|\mathcal{M}_{best}| < |\mathcal{M}|$, it assigns $\mathcal{M}$ to $\mathcal{M}_{best}$. If $|\mathcal{M}_{best}| = n$, meaning that all residents are assigned to hospitals, the algorithm returns a perfect matching $\mathcal{M}_{best}$. Otherwise, it means that the algorithm finds a non-perfect matching and we consider this is the case of getting stuck at a local minimum. Therefore, the algorithm calls the function given in Algorithm 2 to overcome the local minimum and continues the next iteration. The algorithm terminates when it finds a perfect matching or reaches a given maximum number of iterations. In the latter case, the algorithm returns a stable matching of maximum size found so far.

Algorithm 1: HS-HRT Algorithm

Input: An instance I, maximum iter max_iter
Output: A stable matching $\mathcal{M}$
`// Phase 1: Pre-processing`
$\mathcal{M} :=$ a random matching
$\mathcal{M}_{best} := \mathcal{M}$
$a(r_i) := 1, \forall r_i \in \mathcal{R}$
$z(r_i) := 0, \forall r_i \in \mathcal{R}$
$z(h_j) := 0, \forall h_j \in \mathcal{H}$
$R^{\dagger}_{r_i}(h_j) := R_{r_i}(h_j)$
$iter := 0$
$r_i := \emptyset$
`// Phase 2: Main HS`
while $iter \leq max\_iter$ **do**
  $iter := iter + 1$
  if *there exists no active resident* **then**
    $\mathcal{M}_{best} := \mathcal{M}$
    if $(|\mathcal{M}_{best}| = n)$ **then** break;
  $\mathcal{M}' :=$ `Improve(`$\mathcal{M}$`)`
  if $\mathcal{M}' = \mathcal{M}$ **then** break;
  $\mathcal{M} := \mathcal{M}'$
  $r_i :=$ the next active resident of r_i;
  $[h_k, W(r_i)] :=$ `UBP(`$r_i, \mathcal{M}$`)`;
  if $h_k \neq \varnothing$ **then**
    $\mathcal{M} := \mathcal{M} \setminus \{(r_i, h_j)\} \cup \{(r_i, h_k)\}$
    $a(r_i) := 0$
    for *each* $r_l | W(r_l) = h_j$ **do**
      $R_{r_l}(h_j) := R^{\dagger}_{r_l}(h_j)$
      $a(r_l) := 1$
    if $|\mathcal{M}(h_k)| > c_k$ **then**
      $r_w := h_k$'s worst non-empty resident;
      $\mathcal{M} := \mathcal{M} \setminus \{(r_w, h_k)\}$;
      $a(r_w) := 1$;
  else
    $a(r_i) := 0$;
return $\mathcal{M}_{best}$.

Algorithm 2: Improve of stable matching

Input: a stable matching $\mathcal{M}$
Output: a new matching $\mathcal{M}$

function Improve($\mathcal{M}$)
  for *each unassigned* $r_u \in \mathcal{R}$ **do**
    find $(r_i, h_k) \in \mathcal{M}$ that $R_{h_k}(r_i) = R_{h_j}(r_u)$ and $z(r_u) \geq z(r_i)$;
    $\mathcal{M} := \mathcal{M} \setminus \{(r_i, h_k)\} \cup \{(r_u, h_k)\}$;
    $z(r_u) := z(r_u) + 1$;
    $a(r_u) := 0$;
    $a(r_i) := 1$;
    $R_{r_u}(h_k) := R^{\dagger}_{r_u}(h_k)$;
  end
  for *each under-subscribed* $h_t \in \mathcal{H}$ **do**
    find $(r_i, h_k) \in \mathcal{M}$ that $R^{\dagger}_{r_i}(h_k) = R^{\dagger}_{r_i}(h_t)$ and $z(h_t) \geq z(h_k)$;
    $\mathcal{M} := \mathcal{M} \setminus \{(r_i, h_k)\} \cup \{(r_i, h_t)\}$;
    $z(h_t) := z(h_t) + 1$;
    $R_{r_i}(h_t) := R^{\dagger}_{r_i}(h_t)$;
    for *each* r_w *such that* $W(r_w) = h_k$ **do**
      $R_{r_w}(h_k) := R^{\dagger}_{r_w}(h_k)$;
      $a(r_w) := 1$;
    end
  end
  return $\mathcal{M}$;
end function

5 Experimental Evaluation

This section describes experiments to compare the average execution time and solution quality found by our HS-HRT with those found by the AS-HRT algorithm [17]. We generated HRT instances by letting $p_1 \in [0.1, 0.8]$ and $p_2 \in [0.0, 1.0]$ with step of 0.1. We implemented all these algorithms in Matlab 2019a software and ran them on a computer with Core i7-8550U CPU 1.8 GHz and 16 GB RAM in Windows 10.

Experiment 1. In this experiment, we randomly generated 100 HRT instances for each combination of parameters n, m, p_1, and p_2, where $n = 200$, $m = 20$, $p_1 = 0.1, 0.2, \cdots, 0.8$, and $p_2 = 0.0, 0.1, \cdots, 1.0$ (the total of instances was 8800). This means that each resident ranks about from 4 to 18 hospitals and each hospital ranks about 40 to 180 residents when p_1 decreases from 0.8 to 0.1, respectively. For each generated instance, we set $c_j = n/m = 10$ for all $h_j \in \mathcal{H}$ $(j = 1, 2, \cdots, m)$. By this setting, the total of capacities of hospitals is equal to n, i.e. $\sum_{j=1}^{m} c_j = n$, and this allows every resident can assign to hospitals in its preference list. Obviously, if $\sum_{j=1}^{m} c_j < n$, then there exists at least one resident unassigned to hospitals, meaning that we cannot find any perfect matching for HRT instances. However, if $\sum_{j=1}^{m} c_j > n$, then we can find easierly perfect matchings for HRT instances. In addition, we set the maximum number of iterations in both HS-HRT and AS-HRT to 5000.

Figure 1(a) shows the percentage of perfect matchings found by HS-HRT and AS-HRT when p_1 varies from 0.6 to 0.8 with step 0.1 and p_2 varies from 0.0 to 1.0 with step 0.1. It should be noted that when p_1 varies from 0.1 to 0.5 with step 0.1, both HS-HRT and AS-HRT result in 100% of perfect matchings and therefore, we do not show the results for these values of p_1. We see that when p_1 increases from 0.6 to 0.8, the percentage of perfect matchings found by both HS-HRT and AS-HRT decreases since the number of hospitals ranked in each resident decreases and vice versa, making the number of acceptable pairs in generated instances decreases. When $p_2 = 0$, meaning that the residents' and hospitals' preference lists do not contain ties, HS-HRT and AS-HRT find the same percentage of perfect matchings since all stable matchings have the same size [7]. When p_2 varies from 0.1 to 1.0, HS-HRT finds a much higher percentage of perfect matchings than those of AS-HRT. Figure 1(b) shows the average number of unassigned residents in stable matchings. Again, when $p_2 = 0$, HS-HRT and AS-HRT find the same number of unassigned residents in stable matchings since all stable matchings have the same size. When p_2 varies from 0.1 to 1.0, HS-HRT finds a much smaller number of unassigned residents than those of AS-HRT in non-perfect matchings. This means that HS-HRT finds better maximum stable matchings than those of AS-HRT in this experiment.

Figure 1(c) shows the average execution time of HS-HRT and AS-HRT. When p_1 increases from 0.6 to 0.8, the average execution time of HS-HRT and AS-HRT increases slightly. When p_2 increases from 0.0 to 0.9, the average execution time of HS-HRT and AS-HRT decreases slightly. When $p_2 = 1.0$, the average execution time of HS-HRT is almost the same as that when $p_2 = 0.9$, while the average execution time of AS-HRT decreases significantly. We can see that the average execution time of HS-HRT increases from about $10^{-2.5}$ seconds to $10^{-2.1}$ seconds, while that of AS-HRT increases from about $10^{-1.4}$ seconds to $10^{0.9}$ seconds for every value of p_1 and p_2. This means that HS-HRT runs about 12 to 1000 times faster than AS-HRT. Figure 1(d) shows the average number of iterations used by HS-HRT and AS-HRT. When p_2 varies from 0.1 to 1.0, the average number of iterations of HS-HRT is only slightly changed, while that of AS-HRT decreases significantly for p_2 from 0.9 to 1.0. We see that HS-HRT uses a much smaller number of iterations than those of HS-HRT to find stable matchings. This explains that HS-HRT runs much faster than AS-HRT as shown in Fig. 1(a).

Experiment 2. In this experiment, we randomly generated 100 HRT instances for each combination of values n, m, p_1, and p_2 given in *Experiment 1*, but we set the capacity c_j of hospital h_j in each generated instance to a random integer number in $[0.1q, 0.4q]$, where q is the total number of residents ranked by hospital

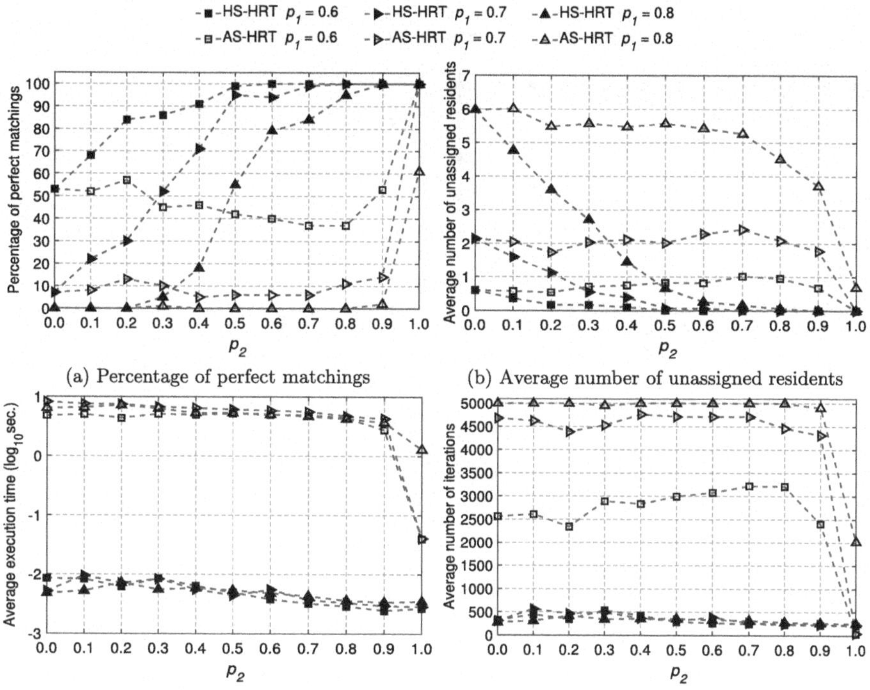

(a) Percentage of perfect matchings (b) Average number of unassigned residents

(c) Average execution time (d) Average number of iterations

Fig. 1. HS-HRT vs. AS-HRT for $n = 200$, $m = 20$ and $c_j = n/m$ $(j = 1, 2, \cdots, m)$

h_j for all $h_j \in \mathcal{H}$ $(j = 1, 2, \cdots, m)$. This can be understood that a hospital h_j ranks q residents but chooses from 10% to 40% residents in its rank list. Figure 2 shows the results of this experiment. We see that when $p_1 = 0.6$ or $p_1 = 0.7$, both HS-HRT and AS-HRT find much easily stable matchings than those when $c_j = n/m$ and therefore, they use less time and number of iterations to find stable matchings. Again, we see that HS-HRT not only finds a higher percentage of perfect matchings than those of AS-HRT, but also finds a smaller number of unassigned residents than those of AS-HRT in stable matchings. Besides, HS-HRT runs much faster and uses much fewer iterations than AS-HRT.

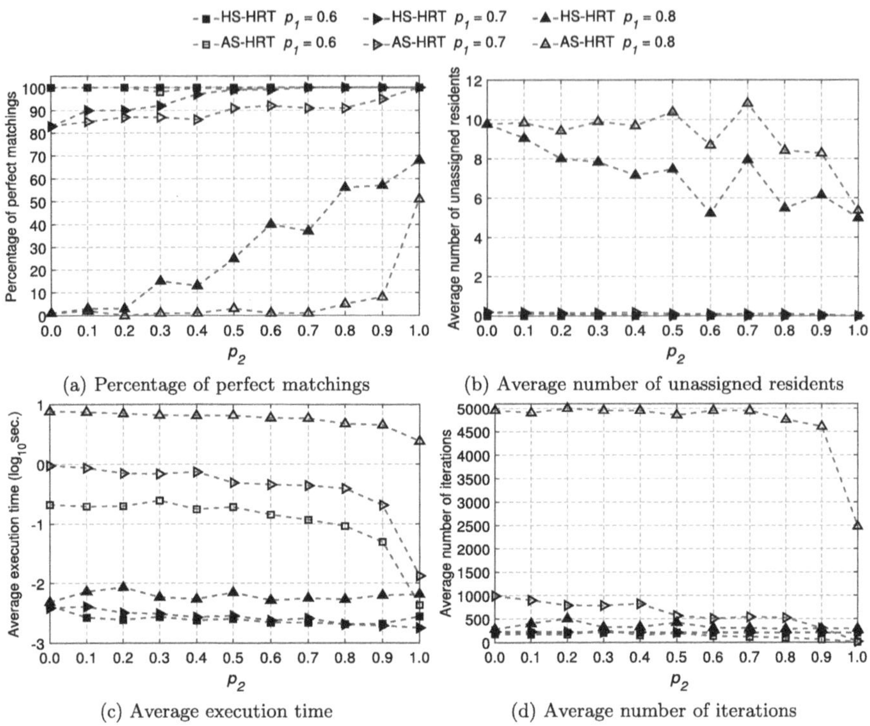

Fig. 2. HS-HRT vs. AS-HRT for $n = 200$, $m = 20$ and $c_j = [0.1q, 0.4q]$ ($j = 1, 2, \cdots, m$)

6 Conclusion

This paper introduces a heuristic algorithm named HS-HRT designed to tackle the MAX-HRT problem. The algorithm begins by generating a random matching and iteratively refines it to find a maximum stable matching. In each iteration, it identifies and removes undominated blocking pairs associated with active residents, progressively improving the stability of an initially unstable matching. If the algorithm encounters a non-perfect matching, it repairs the acceptable pairs within the matching and continues the process until it either finds a perfect matching or reaches the maximum number of iterations. If the latter occurs, the algorithm returns the largest stable matching discovered up to that point. Experimental results demonstrate that HS-HRT not only achieves a significantly higher percentage of perfect matchings but also outperforms the AS-HRT and HP-HRT algorithms in terms of speed when addressing the MAX-HRT problem. Future work will focus on adapting the proposed algorithm to other variants of the SMTI problem, such as HRC [15], SPA-ST [1] or SR [2].

References

1. Abraham, D.J., Irving, R.W., Manlove, D.F.: The student-project allocation problem. In: Proceedings of the 14th International Symposium, pp. 474–484. Kyoto, Japan (2003)
2. Cseha, A., Irving, R.W., Manlove, D.F.: The stable roommates problem with short lists. Theory Comput. Syst. **63**(1), 128–149 (2019)
3. Gale, D., Shapley, L.S.: College admissions and the stability of marriage. Am. Math. Mon. **9**(1), 9–15 (1962)
4. Gelain, M., Pini, M.S., Rossi, F., Venable, K.B., Walsh, T.: Local search for stable marriage problems with ties and incomplete lists. In: Proceedings of 11th Pacific Rim International Conference on Artificial Intelligence, pp. 64–75. Daegu, Korea (2010)
5. Gelain, M., Pini, M.S., Rossi, F., Venable, K.B., Walsh, T.: Local search approaches in stable matching problems. Algorithms **6**(4), 591–617 (2013)
6. Irving, R.W.: Matching medical students to pairs of hospitals: a new variation on a well-known theme. In: Bilardi, G., Italiano, G.F., Pietracaprina, A., Pucci, G. (eds.) ESA 1998. LNCS, vol. 1461, pp. 381–392. Springer, Heidelberg (1998). https://doi.org/10.1007/3-540-68530-8_32
7. Irving, R.W., Manlove, D.F.: Finding large stable matchings. J. Exp. Algorithmics **14**(2), 1.2–1.2:30 (2009)
8. Irving, R.W., Manlove, D.F., Scott, S.: The hospitals/residents problem with ties. In: Proceedings of the 7th Scandinavian Workshop on Algorithm Theory, pp. 259–271. Bergen, Norway (2000)
9. Iwama, K., Miyazaki, S., Morita, Y., Manlove, D.: Stable marriage with incomplete lists and ties. In: Proceedings of International Colloquium on Automata, Languages, and Programming, pp. 443–452. Prague, Czech Republic (1999)
10. Király, Z.: Linear time local approximation algorithm for maximum stable marriage. Algorithms **6**(1), 471–484 (2013)
11. Kwanashie, A., Manlove, D.F.: An integer programming approach to the hospitals/residents problem with ties. In: Proceedings of the International Conference on Operations Research, pp. 263–269. Erasmus University Rotterdam (2013)
12. Maggs, B.M., Sitaraman, R.K.: Algorithmic nuggets in content delivery. ACM SIGCOMM Comput. Commun. Rev. **45**(3), 52–66 (2015)
13. Manlove, D.F.: The hospitals/residents problem. In: Kao, M.Y. (ed.) Encyclopedia of Algorithms. Springer, Boston, MA (2008)
14. Manlove, D.F., Irving, R.W., Iwama, K., Miyazaki, S., Morita, Y.: Hard variants of stable marriage. Theoret. Comput. Sci. **276**(1–2), 261–279 (2002)
15. Manlove, D.F., McBride, I., Trimble, J.: "Almost-stable" matchings in the hospitals/residents problem with couples. Constraints **22**(1), 50–72 (2017)
16. Minton, S., D.Johnston, M., B.Philips, A., Laird, P.: Minimizing conflicts: a heuristic repair method for constraint satisfaction and scheduling problems. Artif. Intell. **58**(1–3), 161–205 (1992)
17. Munera, D., Diaz, D., Abreu, S., Rossi, F., Saraswat, V., Codognet, P.: A local search algorithm for SMTI and its extension to HRT problems. In: Proceedings of the 3rd International Workshop on Matching Under Preferences, pp. 66–77. Glasgow, United Kingdom (2015)
18. Munera, D., Diaz, D., Abreu, S., Rossi, F., Saraswat, V., Codognet, P.: Solving hard stable matching problems via local search and cooperative parallelization. In: Proceedings of the Twenty-Ninth AAAI Conference on Artificial Intelligence, pp. 1212–1218. Austin, Texas (2015)

19. Roth, A.E.: The evolution of the labor market for medical interns and residents: a case study in game theory. J. Polit. Econ. **92**(6), 991–1016 (1984)
20. Uyen, N.T., Giang, N.L., Thang, N.T., Viet, H.H.: A min-conflicts algorithm for maximum stable matchings of the hospitals/residents problem with ties. In: Proceedings of 2020 RIVF International Conference on Computing and Communication Technologies, pp. 1–6. Ho Chi Minh City, Vietnam (2020)
21. W.Irving, R., F.Manlove, D., Scott, S.: The stable marriage problem with master preference lists. Discrete Appl. Math. **156**(15), 2959–2977 (2008)

Comparison on Basic Image Augmentation Techniques for Skin Disease Image Classification Model Development

Nawarerk Chalarak(✉)

Thammasat University, Bangkok 12121, Pathum Thani, Thailand
nawarerk@tu.ac.th

Abstract. This study investigates the impact of different image augmentation techniques on the performance of an EfficientNet model for skin disease classification. Three augmentation methods, including random rotation, random zoom, and random flip, were applied to generate distinct training datasets, which were then evaluated against a control dataset without augmentation. The results revealed that the random flip technique achieved the highest performance, with an accuracy of 84% and an F1-score of 80.47%, along with superior sensitivity (80.57%) and specificity (95.85%). Random zoom also enhanced model accuracy and robustness, while random rotation showed limited improvement, particularly in sensitivity. This study provides insights into the effectiveness of different image augmentation techniques in enhancing the performance and generalizability of AI models for skin disease classification. The findings emphasize the importance of augmentation in improving model generalizability and performance in clinical applications.

Keywords: Image Augmentation · Image Classification · Skin Disease Image

1 Introduction

1.1 Skin Disease

Skin diseases affect millions of individuals worldwide, exerting significant impact on both physical health and quality of life [1, 2]. Conditions such as eczema, psoriasis, acne, and various forms of skin cancer can lead to discomfort, disfigurement, and severe psychological distress [1]. The burden of skin diseases is not only borne by the individuals affected but also by healthcare systems, which must allocate considerable resources to diagnose and manage these conditions [2]. The global prevalence of skin diseases underscores the importance of accurate and timely diagnosis to facilitate effective treatment and minimize complications. However, diagnosing skin diseases remains a complex and time-consuming process that requires significant expertise, particularly given the subtle variations that can differentiate one condition from another.

The traditional diagnostic method for skin diseases typically involves a patient consultation, clinical examination, and potentially a biopsy for histopathological analysis

J. Kertesz et al. (Eds.): CSoNet 2024, LNCS 15417, pp. 395–402, 2025.
https://doi.org/10.1007/978-981-96-6389-7_36

[3]. This multi-step approach, while thorough, is inherently time-intensive and can lead to delays in treatment, especially in regions where dermatological specialists are scarce. In such contexts, the waiting period for an accurate diagnosis can exacerbate patient anxiety and lead to disease progression.

1.2 AI-Supported Diagnostic Process

Given these challenges, there is a pressing need for innovative solutions that can streamline the diagnostic process. Artificial intelligence (AI) has emerged as a promising tool to augment medical decision-making across various specialties, including dermatology [4, 5]. Specifically, image classification models have shown great potential in assisting with the initial assessment of skin diseases [6, 7]. These models are designed to analyze clinical images of skin lesions and classify them into predefined categories, thus providing preliminary diagnostic support that can guide further medical evaluation [8]. By leveraging AI, healthcare providers can potentially reduce diagnostic turnaround times, improve accessibility to expert-level diagnostic support, and alleviate the burden on dermatologists [9].

However, the development of robust AI classification models is not without its challenges. One of the primary requirements for training effective image classification models is a substantial dataset of labeled images. In the field of dermatology, acquiring such datasets poses significant difficulties. High-quality clinical images must be carefully labeled by experts to ensure accurate ground truth data for model training. This labeling process is labor-intensive and requires significant domain expertise, which further limits the availability of large-scale datasets. Moreover, skin disease datasets must capture sufficient variability in terms of skin types, lesion characteristics, and image acquisition conditions to enable the model to generalize effectively across diverse patient populations.

1.3 Skin Disease Image Augmentation

To mitigate the challenge of limited labeled data, researchers have increasingly turned to image augmentation techniques. Image augmentation refers to the process of artificially expanding a dataset by creating modified versions of images through various transformations [10]. These transformations can include basic operations such as rotation, scaling, and flipping, as well as more advanced methods that alter color properties or simulate natural variations in the appearance of skin lesions. Augmentation helps simulate a wide range of possible real-world scenarios that the model might encounter, making it better equipped to handle variability in clinical practice.

The importance of image augmentation is underscored by the unique characteristics of skin disease images [3]. Unlike generic images used for tasks such as object detection or scene classification, skin disease images often exhibit subtle distinctions between different conditions [11, 12]. These differences may manifest in texture, color distribution, shape, and border irregularities. Effective augmentation strategies must therefore preserve the clinically relevant features of lesions while introducing variability that prevents overfitting and enhances model performance. The choice of augmentation techniques must be carefully considered to maintain the integrity of the data and ensure that the resulting augmented images still reflect realistic clinical scenarios.

Despite the promise of augmentation, the selection and implementation of appropriate techniques require careful consideration and empirical validation. The efficacy of different augmentation strategies may vary depending on the specific characteristics of the dataset and the AI model architecture. Therefore, ongoing research is essential to identify the most effective augmentation approaches for skin disease classification and to establish best practices for their application. This research will contribute to a deeper understanding of how augmentation impacts model training in the context of medical imaging. Through a experimental analysis, we aim to provide insights that can guide future research and practical implementation in the field of dermatological AI.

This research contributes to the field of medical image analysis by systematically evaluating the impact of different image augmentation techniques on the performance of an EfficientNet model for skin disease classification. By comparing metrics such as accuracy, sensitivity, specificity, and F1-score, the study identifies the most effective augmentation strategies, particularly highlighting the superior performance of random flip augmentation. Furthermore, the findings emphasize the importance of augmentation in improving model generalizability and robustness, especially in scenarios with limited labeled datasets. This work provides practical insights for optimizing AI-based diagnostic tools and lays the foundation for future research exploring advanced augmentation methods and larger, diverse datasets.

2 Methodology

This section outlines the methodological framework designed to investigate the impact of different image augmentation techniques on the performance of an AI model for skin disease image classification. The objective is to evaluate how specific augmentations influence the accuracy and robustness of the model's predictions, using EfficientNet-B4 as the underlying architecture. The experimental design includes three augmentation strategies applied individually to generate distinct training and testing datasets, followed by model training and performance comparison.

All experiments in this study were conducted on a MacBook Pro equipped with a 2.3 GHz Quad-Core Intel Core i7 processor, Intel Iris Plus Graphics 1536 MB, and 32 GB of 3733 MHz LPDDR4X memory. This machine provided computational power for training the EfficientNet models and performing image augmentation tasks.

2.1 Data Collection and Preprocessing

The dataset used for this study comprises clinical images of various skin diseases sourced from publicly available and verified databases, ensuring a representative sample of common conditions and skin types. The skin disease images used in this study were sourced from Dermnet, a publicly available dataset containing over 23,000 images of skin diseases classified into 23 categories [13]. For this research, images of five common skin diseases in Thailand were selected from the dataset to ensure relevance and applicability. Prior to augmentation, the images are resized to a consistent dimension of 64×64 pixels to align with the input requirements of the EfficientNet model.

2.2 Image Augmentation Techniques

Three augmentation techniques were selected to generate separate datasets:

Random Rotation. This technique applies a random rotation to each image within a predefined range of −0.4 * pi to 0.4 * pi (using keras RandomRotation()), simulating different perspectives of skin lesions that might be encountered in clinical scenarios.

Random Zoom. Random zooming is used to augment images by varying the scale, manipulating the image size for a maximum of 20% increase or decrease. This method mimics slight variations in distance and image focus during image capture.

Random Flip. Horizontal and vertical flips are applied randomly to create flipped versions of the images, introducing variability in orientation without altering diagnostic features.

Each augmentation technique was applied to the original dataset to generate three augmented datasets, including random rotation, random zoom, and random flip. A fourth dataset is the original non-augmented dataset.

2.3 Model Architecture and Training Procedure

EfficientNet, a high-performance convolutional neural network known for its ability to balance computational efficiency and accuracy, was chosen for this study. EfficientNet, introduced in 2019, is a convolutional neural network (CNN) model designed for image classification tasks. Developed by Tan, et al. [14], the EfficientNet family consists of models ranging from EfficientNet-B0 to EfficientNet-B7, with increasing levels of complexity and performance as the model number rises. These models are designed to improve accuracy when more computational resources are available.

The key innovation of EfficientNet lies in its compound scaling method, which uniformly scales the network's depth, width, and resolution using a highly effective compound coefficient. This approach ensures that the network achieves better efficiency and accuracy compared to traditional scaling techniques. The EfficientNet architectures were developed using a multi-objective neural architecture search, which optimizes both accuracy and computational efficiency, making these models particularly suitable for resource-constrained environments and applications requiring high performance.

The EfficientNet-B4 variant was utilized due to its well-established performance on medical imaging tasks [14, 15]. The final classification layer was modified to output predictions relevant to the skin disease categories under study, including Acne-cystic, Eczema-chronic, Lentigo-adults, Psoriasis-chronic-plaque, and Hives-urticaria-acute.

Each augmented dataset was split into training (80%) and testing (20%) subsets. The model was trained separately on each dataset for 20 epochs with a batch size of 32, using the Adam optimizer. Data augmentation was performed in real-time during training, ensuring that each epoch presented a unique view of the dataset.

2.4 Evaluation Metrics

The performance of the models in this study was evaluated using accuracy, sensitivity, specificity, and F1-score, as described in Tanantong, et al. [16] and Srijiranon, et al.

[17]. Accuracy measures the proportion of correct predictions out of the total predictions and is calculated by testing each model using the test dataset. Sensitivity evaluates the model's ability to correctly identify positive cases, while specificity measures its ability to correctly predict negative cases. Both sensitivity and specificity were computed as the average values across the five selected skin disease classes.

The F1-score, also referenced in Tanantong, et al. [16], is a harmonic mean of precision and recall, providing a balanced measure of the model's performance, especially for imbalanced datasets. In this study, the F1-score was determined using predictions on images of varying sizes in the test dataset, offering additional insights into the robustness of the model under different conditions.

3 Results

3.1 Results Comparison

The trained models were evaluated on their respective test sets, and the results were documented for comparison. Table 1 presents the performance metrics for each dataset.

Table 1. Accuracy and F1-Score for each augmentation technique.

Augmentation Technique	Accuracy	F1-Score	Sensitivity	Specificity
Random rotation	79%	73.66%	72.23%	94.45%
Random zoom	83%	80.04%	78.15%	95.71%
Random flip	84%	80.47%	80.57%	95.85%
No augmentation	83%	79.97%	78.44%	95.66%

3.2 Results Analysis

The results of the study indicate distinct impacts of different image augmentation techniques on the performance of an EfficientNet model trained for skin disease classification. The performance metrics considered include accuracy, F1-score, sensitivity, and specificity. Each metric provides unique insights into the strengths and weaknesses of the model under different augmentation conditions.

Random Rotation. The model trained on the dataset augmented with random rotation achieved an accuracy of 79% and an F1-score of 73.66%. These results indicate that while the model performed reasonably well in classifying skin disease images, its precision and balance between precision and recall, as represented by the F1-score, were relatively lower compared to other augmentation techniques. The sensitivity, which measures the model's ability to correctly identify positive cases, was 72.23%, suggesting moderate effectiveness in capturing true positives. However, the specificity, at 94.45%, was notably high, demonstrating that the model was proficient in correctly identifying negative cases.

This disparity between sensitivity and specificity implies that the model may have a tendency to under-detect true positive cases while being stringent in identifying non-cases.

Random Zoom. The dataset with random zoom augmentation yielded an accuracy of 83% and an F1-score of 80.04%. This method performed better than random rotation, as indicated by both higher accuracy and F1-score. The sensitivity was 78.15%, indicating an improvement in identifying true positive cases compared to the model trained with random rotation. The specificity was also higher at 95.71%, reinforcing the model's capability to accurately detect negative cases. The balanced improvement in both sensitivity and specificity suggests that random zoom augmentation helped the model achieve a more robust performance by introducing scaled variations that simulate realistic clinical scenarios.

Random Flip. The model trained with random flip augmentation demonstrated the highest performance across the metrics with an accuracy of 84% and an F1-score of 80.47%. The sensitivity was 80.57%, reflecting the model's superior ability to identify true positive cases, and the specificity was 95.85%, which was the highest among all the tested augmentation techniques. The use of random flips allowed the model to learn from images presented in different orientations, contributing to a better balance in correctly predicting both positive and negative cases. This suggests that flipping images horizontally and vertically can effectively simulate variations encountered in clinical settings without altering key diagnostic features, leading to improved overall model performance.

No Augmentation. The model trained on the original, non-augmented dataset achieved an accuracy of 83% and an F1-score of 79.97%, comparable to the performance of the model trained with random zoom. The sensitivity was 78.44%, and the specificity was 95.66%. These results show that, while the baseline model performed relatively well, it did not achieve the highest metrics across the board. This finding emphasizes the potential benefits of using augmentation techniques to enhance the training dataset and improve model generalizability.

3.3 Summary of Results

Overall, the application of image augmentation techniques demonstrated clear benefits for model performance. The model trained with random flip augmentation showed the highest accuracy (84%) and F1-score (80.47%), as well as the best sensitivity (80.57%) and specificity (95.85%), indicating that this technique provided the most comprehensive enhancement to the dataset. Random zoom also improved model performance compared to the non-augmented control, while random rotation yielded lower sensitivity and F1-score, suggesting limited efficacy for this specific task. These findings underscore the importance of selecting appropriate augmentation techniques to optimize the development of AI models for skin disease classification.

4 Conclusion

This study evaluated the effects of three image augmentation techniques, including random rotation, random zoom, and random flip, on the performance of an EfficientNet-B4 model for skin disease classification. The results demonstrated that applying image augmentation significantly impacts model performance, with variations in the outcomes depending on the technique used. Among the augmentation methods tested, random flip proved to be the most effective, yielding the highest accuracy (84%) and F1-score (80.47%). This approach also showed superior sensitivity (80.57%) and specificity (95.85%), highlighting its ability to enhance model generalizability by introducing diverse orientations that mimic real-world scenarios. Random zoom augmentation also improved the model's metrics over the non-augmented baseline, indicating its utility in simulating variable image scales. In contrast, random rotation, while increasing specificity to a high level (94.45%), resulted in lower sensitivity (72.23%) and F1-score (73.66%), suggesting limited efficacy for optimizing model robustness in identifying true positives.

The findings underscore the importance of incorporating effective augmentation strategies in training pipelines to improve the performance of AI models used for medical image classification. Image augmentation enhances the diversity of training data and helps prevent overfitting, ultimately leading to models that are better equipped to handle variability in clinical practice.

Future research could expand on this work by exploring more complex augmentation techniques, such as generative models like GANs for synthetic data creation [18, 19], or self-supervised learning approaches to further augment training datasets. Additionally, studying the impact of combined or sequential application of different augmentations could yield insights into optimizing data diversity. It would also be beneficial to assess the effectiveness of these augmentation techniques on larger, multi-institutional datasets to validate their generalizability across different patient populations and imaging conditions.

Acknowledgement. The authors gratefully acknowledge the financial support provided by Faculty of Science and Technology, Thammasat University, Contact No. SciGR 26/2567. This work was supported by Thammasat University Research Unit in Data Innovation and Artificial Intelligence.

Disclosure of Interests. The author has no competing interests to declare that are relevant to the content of this article.

References

1. Basra, M.K.A., Shahrukh, M.: Burden of skin diseases. Expert Rev. Pharmacoecon. Outcomes Res. **9**(3), 271–283 (2009)
2. Jafferany, M., Pastolero, P.: Psychiatric and psychological impact of chronic skin disease. Prim. Care Companion CNS Disord. **20**(2), 27157 (2018)
3. Zhu, C.-Y., et al.: A deep learning based framework for diagnosing multiple skin diseases in a clinical environment. Front. Med. **8**, 626369 (2021)

4. Naylor, C.D.: On the prospects for a (deep) learning health care system. JAMA **320**(11), 1099–1100 (2018)
5. Panesar, A.: Machine Learning and AI for Healthcare. Springer, Coventry (2019)
6. Nafi'iyah, N., Yuniarti, A.: A convolutional neural network for skin cancer classification. Int. J. Inform. Commun. Technol. **11**(1), 76–84 (2022)
7. Anand, V., et al.: An automated deep learning models for classification of skin disease using dermoscopy images: a comprehensive study. Multimedia Tools Appl. **81**(26), 37379–37401 (2022)
8. Shaheen, M.Y.: Applications of artificial intelligence (AI) in healthcare: a review. ScienceOpen Preprints (2021)
9. Abunadi, I., Senan, E.M.: Deep learning and machine learning techniques of diagnosis dermoscopy images for early detection of skin diseases. Electronics **10**(24), 3158 (2021)
10. Shorten, C., Khoshgoftaar, T.M.: A survey on image data augmentation for deep learning. J. Big Data **6**(1), 60 (2019)
11. Goceri, E.: Diagnosis of skin diseases in the era of deep learning and mobile technology. Comput. Biol. Med. **134**, 104458 (2021)
12. Zhang, B., et al.: Opportunities and challenges: classification of skin disease based on deep learning. Chin. J. Mech. Eng. **34**(1), 112 (2021)
13. Saifan, R., Jubair, F.: Six skin diseases classification using deep convolutional neural network. Int. J. Electr. Comput. Eng. (2088–8708) **12**(3) (2022)
14. Tan, M., Le, Q.: EfficientNet: rethinking model scaling for convolutional neural networks. In: International Conference on Machine Learning. PMLR (2019)
15. Rattanawin, P., Pakinsee, T., Songmuang, P.A.: GoogLeNet performance approach for COVID-19 detection using chest X-ray images. In: 2023 15th International Conference on Knowledge and Smart Technology (KST). IEEE (2023)
16. Tanantong, T., Nantajeewarawat, E., Thiemjarus, S.: False alarm reduction in BSN-based cardiac monitoring using signal quality and activity type information. Sensors **15**(2), 3952–3974 (2015)
17. Srijiranon, K., Lertratanakham, Y., Tanantong, T.: A hybrid framework using PCA, EMD and LSTM methods for stock market price prediction with sentiment analysis. Appl. Sci. **12**(21), 10823 (2022)
18. Zhao, C., et al.: Dermoscopy image classification based on StyleGAN and DenseNet201. IEEE Access **9**, 8659–8679 (2021)
19. Chungnoy, K., Tanantong, T., Songmuang, P.: Bee-inspired knowledge transfer: synthesizing data for enhanced deep learning explainability. Indones. J. Electr. Eng. Comput. Sci. **36**(2), 1052–1069 (2024)

Tourist Behavior-Based Buddhist Tourism Recommendation Using Image Classification

Surachart Buachum[1], Kritanat Chungnoy[1,2], and Phattaramon Klaasa[1(✉)]

[1] Faculty of Management Science, Chandrakasem Rajabhat University, Bangkok, Thailand
phattaramon.k@chandra.ac.th

[2] Faculty of Science and Technology, Thammasat Universit, Bangkok, Thailand

Abstract. This research presents a Buddhist tourism recommendation system aimed at enhancing personalized travel experiences through image classification and tourist behavior analysis. Focusing on Buddhist landmarks in Thailand, the system uses Convolutional Neural Networks (CNNs) to classify and categorize key features of Buddhist sites, such as architectural styles and religious symbols. Recommendations are generated based on tourist preferences, gathered from sources such as social media and surveys, which reveal patterns in spiritual, historical, and cultural interests. The system architecture includes a Data Collection Layer for gathering images and user interactions, a Data Preprocessing Layer for cleaning and augmenting the data, and a Classification Layer for feature extraction. The AI Engine Layer employs hybrid filtering methods, combining collaborative and content-based filtering to provide context-aware recommendations. A Personalization Module in the Application Layer customizes the user interface to enhance engagement. The system aims to distribute tourist traffic more evenly, promote lesser-known sites, and support cultural preservation by offering tailored experiences. The dataset for image classification consists of 1,000 images of Buddhist Phra That, categorized into 11 classes, sourced from travel blogs and social media. The dataset was split into 80% for training and 20% for testing. The results show that the model performs well overall, with a high F1-score of 0.91, demonstrating its effectiveness in classifying images and delivering relevant recommendations.

Keywords: Tourist Behavior · Buddhist Tourism · Image Classification

1 Introduction

Buddhist tourism holds significant value across Asia, particularly in nations where Buddhism is a major religion, such as Thailand, Sri Lanka, Japan, and Myanmar. Buddhist landmarks like temples, stupas, and ancient architecture attract both domestic and international tourists, serving not only as leisure destinations but as pathways for visitors to connect deeply with Buddhist history, culture, art, and teachings, fostering a unique spiritual and cultural experience. In the digital age, technology significantly enhances Buddhist tourism experiences. Travelers increasingly rely on digital tools for trip planning, accessing destination information, and making decisions based on personal interests. Advanced technologies like Artificial Intelligence (AI), Machine Learning, and

J. Kertesz et al. (Eds.): CSoNet 2024, LNCS 15417, pp. 403–410, 2025.
https://doi.org/10.1007/978-981-96-6389-7_37

Image Classification can analyze tourist behaviors and preferences, enabling personalized and engaging destination recommendations. This research aims to develop a Buddhist tourism recommendation system that uses Image Classification to analyze images of Buddhist sites of interest to travelers and suggest similar destinations based on art, culture, and religious context. AI-driven systems not only make travel experiences more meaningful and personalized but also support the preservation of cultural and religious heritage by promoting lesser-known sites, helping to distribute tourism more evenly and reduce overcrowding at popular locations. Focusing on Thailand's Buddhist heritage, particularly its revered pilgrimage sites known as "Phra Borommathat" or "Phra That" which hold cultural, historical, and spiritual significance, this study uses image data from widely shared online sources to build a prototype recommendation system for tourism destinations. Table 1 presents a list of notable Phra That sites across Thailand that are central to this study's focus.

Table 1. Number of Phra Borommathat and Phra That in Thailand.

Regions in Thailand	Number of Places
North of Thailand	390
Northeast of Thailand	173
Central-East-West of Thailand	81
South of Thailand	36
Total	**680**

2 Literature Review

2.1 Buddhist Tourism and Recommender Systems

Buddhist tourism, a specialized segment within the broader tourism industry, has garnered increasing interest from scholars and practitioners due to its potential to blend spiritual, cultural, and historical experiences. Destinations in Southeast Asia, such as Thailand, Sri Lanka, and Myanmar, play a pivotal role as pilgrimage hubs, featuring Buddhist landmarks like temples and stupas. These sites offer visitors not only leisure opportunities but also avenues for spiritual enrichment, cultural exchange, and historical learning [2]. With advancements in digital technology, recommender systems have become integral in enhancing tourist experiences by personalizing destination suggestions. For Buddhist tourism, these systems employ data-driven approaches to align recommendations with tourists' specific interests, such as historical significance, cultural heritage, or spiritual pursuits [3, 5]. By guiding users toward lesser-known yet meaningful sites, recommender systems contribute to a richer and more diversified exploration of Buddhist culture.

2.2 Image Classification in Tourism

Image classification has emerged as a transformative tool in the tourism industry, enabling automated identification and categorization of destination features. Powered by deep learning techniques like Convolutional Neural Networks (CNNs), image classification facilitates the recognition of visual elements such as landmark architecture, natural surroundings, and ambiance [1]. In the context of Buddhist tourism, where visual and symbolic elements such as pagodas, stupas, and statues play a central role, image classification enhances the ability to link visually similar sites. By analyzing these attributes, personalized destination recommendations can be tailored to tourists' preferences, further promoting lesser-known landmarks and providing a unique cultural experience [6].

2.3 Behavior Analysis in Tourism Recommendation

Understanding tourist behavior is essential for developing effective recommendation systems. Behavioral data, sourced from surveys, social media, travel apps, and reviews, offers insights into tourist preferences and motivations [7]. Patterns such as preferred activities, destination types, and influencing factors can be leveraged to create tailored suggestions. For example, tourists seeking spiritual fulfillment may be drawn to meditation retreats or iconic Buddhist temples, while history enthusiasts might prefer ancient architectural sites. In Buddhist tourism, behavior analysis enables the system to recommend destinations aligned with specific religious, cultural, or historical interests, ensuring a personalized and meaningful experience for users.

3 Methodology

3.1 Data Collection

The dataset for this research comprises 1,000 images of Thai Buddhist pagodas, categorized into 10 distinct classes based on prominent landmarks, along with one additional class for miscellaneous locations. These images were sourced from reliable online platforms, such as travel blogs and social media, ensuring diverse and representative data for the study. The images were resized to 128×128 pixels to standardize input dimensions for the CNN model. To improve training efficiency, pixel values were normalized to a range of [0, 1]. The dataset distribution is summarized in Table 2.

3.2 Image Classification Model Development

This study utilizes a Convolutional Neural Network (CNN) for robust image data analysis and classification. The model was designed and fine-tuned to capture the unique characteristics of Thai pagodas, such as architectural styles and symbolic elements.

- Model Selection: A CNN architecture was chosen for its proven capability to extract spatial features and classify visual data effectively.

Table 2. Dataset of PhraThat images

No.	Class Name	Location (Province)	Number of Images
1	Chaiya	Surat Thani	100
2	Chedi Nakhon Si Thammarat	Nakhon Si Thammarat	100
3	Chae Haeng	Nan	100
4	Doi Suthep	Chiang Mai	100
5	Doi Tung	Chiang Rai	100
6	Hariphunchai	Lamphun	100
7	Lampang Luang	Lampang	100
8	Phanom	Nakhon Phanom	100
9	Sri Chom Thong	Chiang Mai	100
10	Sri Song Rak	Loei	100
	Total		**1,000**

- Data Preparation: The dataset was divided into training, validation, and testing subsets, with 80% allocated for training and 20% for testing. Augmentation techniques, including rotation, flipping, and brightness adjustments, were applied to enhance the dataset and mitigate overfitting.
- Model Architecture: The CNN consists of the following layers:
  - Convolutional Layer: A layer with 128 filters and a kernel size of 3 × 3, using ReLU activation for feature extraction.
  - Pooling Layers: Two Max Pooling layers (pool size: 2 × 2) to reduce spatial dimensions while retaining critical features.
  - Dense Layers: Two dense layers capture complex patterns, and a final dense layer with a soft-max activation function outputs probabilities for 10 classes.
  - Flatten Layer: This layer flattens intermediate outputs into a vector for dense layer processing.
- Model Training: Training was conducted on a GPU-enabled setup to handle computational demands. Key hyperparameters included:
  - Learning Rate: 0.0001 (Adam optimizer).
  - Batch Size: 128 samples.
  - Epochs: 100 iterations for model convergence.
  - Loss Function: Categorical Cross-entropy, suitable for one-hot encoded multi-class classification.
- Performance Evaluation: Metrics such as precision, recall, accuracy, and F1-score were calculated. A confusion matrix (Table 3) was utilized to assess the model's predictive performance and identify areas for improvement.

Table 3. Confusion matrix

	Predicted Positive	Predicted Negative
Actual Positive	True Positive (TP)	False Negative (FN)
Actual Negative	False Positive (FP)	True Negative (TN)

This matrix helps in calculating various performance metrics, such as Precision, Recall, Accuracy, and F1-score as equations:

$$Precision = TP / (TP + FP) \quad (1)$$

$$Recall = TP / (TP + FN) \quad (2)$$

$$F1 - score = 2 \times (Precision + Recall) / (Precision \times Recall) \quad (3)$$

The model achieved an overall F1-score of 0.91, with high precision and recall across most classes. For instance, "Chaiya" and "Chedi Nakhon Si Thammarat" achieved perfect scores, while "Doi Tung" showed room for improvement.

3.3 Tourist Behavior Analysis

Understanding tourists' behaviors and interests is essential for tailoring the recommendation system appropriately. The tourist behavior analysis will be conducted using the following methods:

- Survey Data Collection: A survey will be conducted among tourists who have visited Buddhist landmarks to gather data on their preferences, such as types of pagodas they favor and the factors influencing their choice (e.g., spiritual significance, historical value, or visual appeal).
- Data from Digital Platforms: Data from social media, travel apps, and review websites will be analyzed to identify patterns in tourist behaviors, such as visit frequency, location preferences, and types of content shared or liked (e.g., images of pagodas).
- Behavior Classification: Tourists will be grouped according to their interests, such as "spiritual seekers," "history enthusiasts," or "cultural lovers," to recommend pagodas that match each group's preferences.
- Statistical Analysis: The collected data will be analyzed statistically to determine correlations between tourists' behaviors and the types of pagodas they prefer, which will help refine the recommendation system.

3.4 Recommendation System Design

The recommendation system will be developed using a hybrid approach, combining both image classification and behavior analysis to recommend appropriate tourist destinations (see Fig. 1).

- Integration of Image Classification and Behavior Analysis: The image classification model will be a key component of the recommendation system, suggesting similar places based on the visual characteristics of pagodas. Meanwhile, tourists' behavioral data will help personalize the recommendations, such as suggesting spiritually significant pagodas for spiritual seekers.
- Recommendation Algorithm: The system will use content-based recommendation algorithms based on interactions with the locations (e.g., likes or visits) and collaborative filtering based on the preferences of other tourists with similar interests.
- Personalized Recommendations: The system will combine image and behavioral data to recommend pagodas that match the individual tourist's interests, providing comprehensive information such as historical and cultural details, as well as activities available at the location.

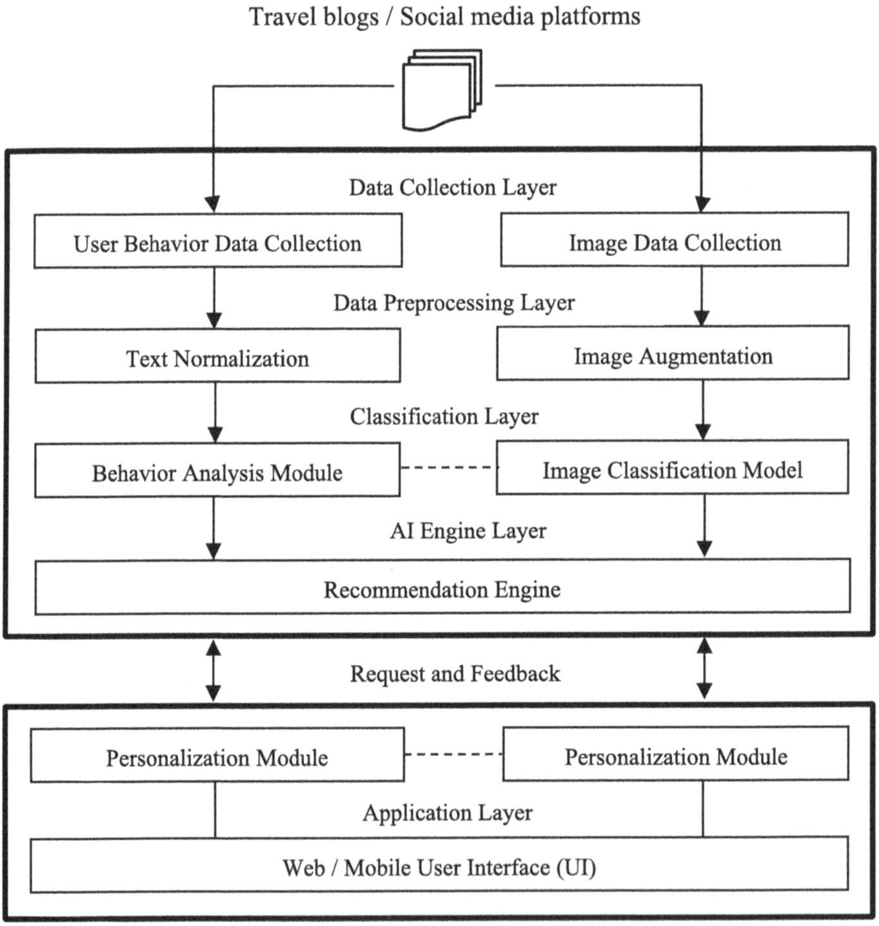

Fig. 1. System Architecture

Table 4. Precision, Recall, and F1-scores

Class Name	Precision	Recall	F1-Score
Chedi Nakhon Si Thammarat	1.00	1.00	1.00
Chae Haeng	1.00	1.00	1.00
Chaiya	1.00	1.00	1.00
Doi Suthep	0.67	0.67	0.67
Doi Tung	1.00	0.50	0.67
Hariphunchai	1.00	1.00	1.00
Lampang Luang	1.00	1.00	1.00
Phanom	0.67	1.00	0.80
Sri Chom Thong	1.00	0.67	0.80
Sri Song Rak	1.00	1.00	1.00
Overall	**0.94**	**0.89**	**0.91**

Table 4 shows that the model performs well overall, with high precision (0.94), recall (0.89), and F1-score (0.91). Most classes, such as "Chedi Nakhon Si Thammarat" and "Hariphunchai," exhibit perfect precision, recall, and F1-scores, indicating strong predictive accuracy. However, some classes, like "Doi Tung" and "Phanom," have slightly lower recall or F1-scores, suggesting room for improvement in identifying these instances. Overall, the model demonstrates effective performance across all classes.

4 Conclusion

The Buddhist tourism recommendation system combines CNN-based image classification with behavior analysis to offer a personalized experience for tourists exploring Buddhist heritage. Its architecture, including data collection, preprocessing, and transfer learning, ensures accurate recommendations by identifying key features of Buddhist sites. The AI Engine's hybrid filtering aligns suggestions with users' preferences, while the Application Layer provides an adaptive interface for better engagement. This system enhances user experience, promotes sustainable tourism by recommending lesser-known sites, and eases congestion, helping preserve heritage. Future work will focus on expanding multilingual support and integrating diverse data sources to provide deeper cultural insights and more personalized recommendations for a global audience.

References

1. Jin, X., Liu, S., Zhang, J.: Tourism image classification based on deep learning: a review and future directions. J. Tour. Res. **15**(2), 95–110 (2020)
2. Nguyen, T.H.: Buddhist tourism in Southeast Asia: a study of tourism flows and economic impacts. Tour. Econ. **22**(3), 521–536 (2016)

3. Ricci, F., Rokach, L., Shapira, B: Recommender systems Handbook. Springer, New York (2015)
4. Wang, S., Li, J., Zhang, Z.: Behavioral analysis of tourism choices using big data. Tour. Manag. Perspect. **30**, 10–20 (2019)
5. Xu, X., Wu, H., Liu, Y.: The role of recommender systems in promoting Buddhist tourism. Tour. Manag. **76**, 104052 (2021)
6. Zhou, Y., Chen, L., Liu, W.: Leveraging image classification for personalized tourism recommendations. J. Comput. Sci. Technol. **15**(1), 58–73 (2022)
7. Zhang, J., Wang, Y., Li, Z.: Tourist behavior and preferences analysis for personalized recommendations. Tour. Manag. **65**, 32–42 (2018)

AI Implementations on Circular Economy: A Systematic Literature Review

Pattarapol Tongyodkaew(✉) and Pokpong Songmuang

Thammasat University, Klong Luang 12120, Pathum Thani, Thailand
Pattarapol.ton@dome.tu.ac.th

Abstract. The transition from a linear to a circular economy (CE) emphasizes sustainable production and consumption by promoting resource efficiency, reuse, and recycling. This systematic literature review explores how artificial intelligence (AI) technologies, particularly machine learning (ML), can enhance various stages of CE, including raw material extraction, product design, manufacturing, distribution, and waste management. A total of 14 peer-reviewed studies published between 2020 and 2024 were analyzed, identifying key applications and trends in AI-driven CE practices. Findings highlight that AI optimizes processes such as sustainable concrete design, CO2 tracking across supply chains, smart water distribution networks, and automated waste sorting. Although AI presents significant opportunities to increase resource efficiency and reduce waste, challenges remain, such as high computational requirements and the need for quality data. This review underscores the potential of AI as a critical enabler of circular strategies, while also pointing to the importance of further research to address current limitations.

Keywords: Circular Economy · Artificial Intelligent · Machine Learning · Systematic literature review

1 Introduction

Circular Economy (CE) is one of the models of production and consumption believed to help extends the life cycle of products. In a circular economy, products and the materials are highly valued. This fact contrasts with the traditional, linear economic model based on a 'take-make-consume-throw away' pattern [1]. At the end of a product's life, the materials used to make it are kept in the economy and reused wherever possible, meaning that switching to CE from linear economy is the way forward [1]. This research proposes that AI could be integrated into every step of CE, from production, purchasing, consumption, collection and processing waste. In this study, we adopt the definition and the composition of the circular economy as provided by the European Parliament (see Fig. 1), which describes it as "a model of production and consumption, which involves sharing, leasing, reusing, repairing, refurbishing and recycling existing materials and products as long as possible. In this way, the life cycle of products is extended [1]."

Over the years, AI has continuously developed, and humans have been trying to integrate it into almost every aspect of our lives, aiding us regardless of what we want to

J. Kertesz et al. (Eds.): CSoNet 2024, LNCS 15417, pp. 411–419, 2025.
https://doi.org/10.1007/978-981-96-6389-7_38

Fig. 1. The circular economy model composition we adopted from European Parliament

achieve with more precision and efficiency. Sustainability is one aspect that is beneficial not only to humans but to the world. Tools like Machine Learning are sure to help us do what humans can't efficiently. This systematic literature review will show trends of how AI, specifically Machine Learning, can be fused into steps of the circular economy to enhance resource efficiency, reduce waste, and promote sustainable practices. This review aims to identify key areas where AI technologies can optimize circular economy processes by examining current research and case studies.

2 Research Methodology

We adopted certain elements of the systematic literature review (SLR) methodology to examine published articles on the implementation of AI in the circular economy (CE) from January 2020 to May 2024. This time frame extends beyond the conclusion of Federica et al.'s (2021) systematic literature review in July 2020 [2], allowing us to capture the evolution of AI and technology in this domain. Our approach is instrumental in identifying gaps and unexplored areas within the research field. Precisely, we followed key aspects of the SLR methodology outlined by Federica et al. (2021) while making necessary adaptations to suit our research objectives. Our literature search was conducted using the SCOPUS database, selected for its extensive collection of peer-reviewed articles.

In the search and retrieval of articles in the field of AI and CE in the SCOPUS database, the queries are: TITLE-ABS-KEY ("Circular Economy" OR "Circular Manufacturing") AND ("Artificial Intelligence") AND ("Machine Learning") Since Circular Manufacturing is also a keyword in interests we also use it. The search ranges from 2020 to 2024. Document types are limited to Articles in English. After that, we conduct the selection process to find the eligible articles. The search process showed 38 articles, of which only 26 were seen fit to the content we are looking to review after the first selection process from their titles and abstracts from these three factors that we would see as non-eligible for this review. First are papers that are not focused on CE, second are those that are a review itself, and last are those that are not focused on CE and ML but used ML to conduct their study. Then, in the second selection from each entire text reading, we discarded 13 papers. Seven of which are exploring and evaluating existing research, three of which we cannot perform an integral reading of the paper, and Three are discarded because they are not focused on CE and ML but used ML to conduct their study. Which results in 13 Final samples of papers (see Fig. 2).

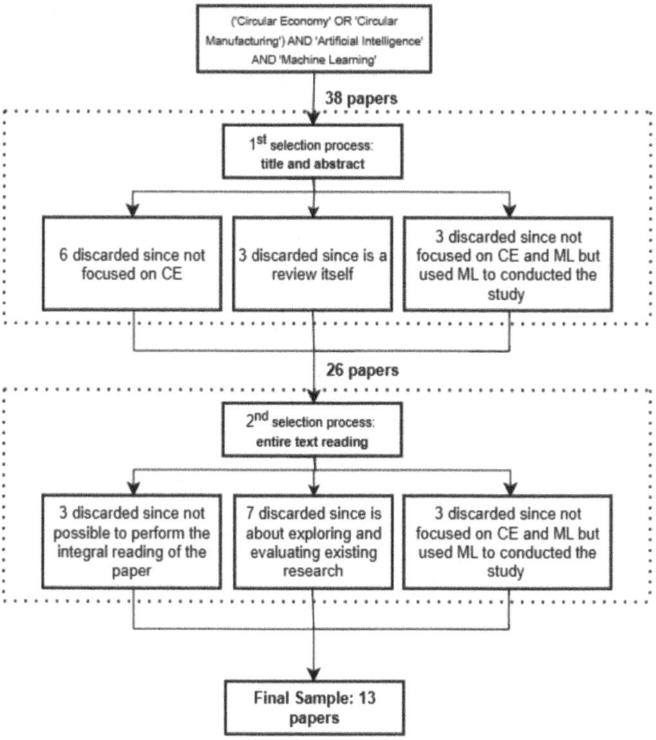

Fig. 2. Selection process of eligible papers for the review

3 AI in Raw Material

From one paper on ML being implemented in the raw materials side of CE strategies. The study for *Unleashing the Alternative Food Potential of Microalgae*, conducted by Mohamed et al. (2023) [3], ML, Artificial Neural Networks (ANN) to be exact, has been very helpful in integrating and analyzing vast amounts of omics data, improving growth rate through identifying genetic modifications, assisting in optimizing cultivation conditions to maximize biomass production and protein content, and toxicity prediction, ensuring the safety of the produced microalgae-based proteins.

4 AI in Sustainable Design

A circular economy will require designing products so they can be easily recycled or disassembled (for repair, reuse, or resource recovery). This means designing consumer products with fewer raw materials or capital equipment designed for serviceability, modularity, and refurbishment.

We have found three papers about ML being implemented on sustainable design. First, Ulucan, Gunduzalp, Yildirim, Alatas, and Alyamac (2024) present a new meta-heuristic approach for predicting sustainable concrete compressive strength [4]. A Feed Forward Neural Network (FFNN), a ML model, was used to predict the final-age compressive strength of sustainable concrete produced from post-earthquake construction and demolition wastes. This was with the purpose of reducing environmental degradation and conserving rapidly decreasing natural resources (Ulucan et al. 2024, introduction section). In the second paper Panagoulias, Sarmas, Marinakis, Virvou, Tsihrintzis, and Doukas (2023) proposes an Intelligent decision support for energy management with tailored explainability of artificial intelligence analytics [5]. Machine Learning is also used for making an interactable system that can aid humans in making decisions tailored to their professions [6]. A personalized explainable artificial intelligence in the intelligent decision support system that helps stakeholders make informed decisions about energy management and efficiency in buildings by combining AI and optimization algorithms (Panagoulias et al. 2023, introduction section). Said study has implemented a stacked ensemble model, including a Support Vector Classifier, Gaussian Naive Bayes, Random Forest (RF), K-Nearest Neighbors Classifier, Extreme Gradient Boosting (XGBoost), and Logistic Regression as a Meta-model. And the third paper, for architects, there is research to develop a working ML model, with Neural networks, Deep Neural Networks, and Convolutional Neural Networks (CNN), that could aid architects in the early design phases of developing environmentally conscious design models or a regenerative architectural design.

5 AI in Production

In production, the first paper used machine learning to design a circularity accounting network for the impact of product's CO2 emissions and sequestration along global supply chains using ANN [7]. In this system, For Object Estimators, neural networks are trained to recognize objects, encode their features, and uses Chain predictor models to predict CO2 consumption values for objects based on their features and positions in the production-consumption process. These include image detector models such as ImageNet, single-shot detector models, and autoencoder-based image detectors. This means improving coordination between different stages of the production supply chain, ensuring materials and components are used efficiently. And easier control over carbon emissions in the supply chain overall. In the second paper, several ML models has been used to optimize Hydrogen production processes [8]. Such as K-nearest neighbor (KNN) and RF Support Vector Machine (SVM), Gradient boosting machine, Decision Tree, Permutation variable index and Boruta. Their results indicate that KNN and RF models proves to be the most efficient in predicting green H2 production in this study's cases. Which would help in cost savings and an improvement in efficiency during Hydrogen production.

6 AI in Distribution

On the topic of distribution we have found an application of machine learning with optimization practices for smartening water distribution networks (WDN). In this study, ANN has been implemented to evaluate an energy based performance of the WDN, optimize the energy recovery capacity and predict the Micro-Hydropower's behavior used in the WDN [9]. With ANN implementation, a sensor to smarten the network and energy harvesting process has been created. The results shown ANN performed by selecting the best validation performance in the first epoch. This concludes that the WDN model could successfully optimize the energy recovery potential with consideration of improving the hydraulic parameters of WDN by the combination of Taguchi and Response Surface Methodology methods with the prediction ability enhanced by ANN.

7 AI in Waste Management

We have found six papers of AI being implemented in waste management. First paper, A study focusing on recycling construction and demolition waste (CDW). They have used machine learning with U-Net architecture, widely used for image segmentation, to develop a deep learning-based segmentation model for the instance segmentation of overlapping particles in 3D laser triangulation images of CDW [10]. The model aims to aid the particle size distribution monitoring in recycling, which would lead to more efficient use of resources and a reduction in waste [10]. Second paper, For effective recycling various ML models, such as ANNs, random forest, polynomial regression, are used to predict the behavior of sensor-based sorting units based on information on the input material flow. Which demonstrates the potential of data-driven process models thus paving the way towards improved design and operation of sorting plants and a more circular future [11]. Third paper, In a more grand scheme, ML is used to identify key attributes, such as local governance, employment, and technological research, that influence sustainable waste management. This helps in providing actionable insights for policymakers to improve waste management systems [12]. Rough Set-based Machine Learning has been used to generate interpretable if-then rules that link cities and countries key attributes to waste management performance. Fourth paper, A study on creation of

CNN architecture developed by ML and used for waste image classification which would come to perform better than the baseline classifier [13]. The model comes in two sizes, big and small, the small model being more suitable for embedded application on low-cost devices with limited specifications, the big model being more generalizable but with poorer performance [13]. The classification consists of five convolutional 2D layers of various neuron sizes [13]. This means that this could aid in an Automatic waste sorting. The ML models used in this study are SVM, decision trees, KNN. Fifth paper, this study proposes AI based automated solution for sorting COVID related medical waste streams, which was an emerging COVID problem, from other waste types and, at the same time, ensures data-driven decisions for recycling in the context of CE [14]. The waste type classification is done based on image-texture dependent features using models such as KNN, SVM, ANN [14]. Their method also involves a feature-fusion-based approach for obtaining the necessary features for waste classification. Sixth paper, the study focuses on predicting municipal solid waste generation (MSWG) using data-driven models, while addressing the challenges of non-linear and non-stationary nature of waste data [15]. MSWG is influenced by dynamic factors like temperature, population, income, etc. Used ML techniques are such as Gene Expression Programming (GEP) and Online Sequential Extreme Learning Machine. The authors also utilize the Intrinsic Time-Scale Decomposition method as a pre-processing technique to improve the accuracy of the prediction models.

8 Discussion

This review examined 14 studies that demonstrate how AI, especially ML, enhances various stages of the CE, including raw materials, design, production, distribution, and waste management. Waste management emerged as a key area, where AI-driven models facilitate in various management. The applications highlight AI's ability to improve resource efficiency, reduce environmental impact, and support sustainable decision-making across sectors. The findings reveal that AI and ML is an effective enabler of CE principles across multiple areas. In raw materials, AI supports sustainable practices by optimizing production and reducing environmental impact, as seen in microalgae cultivation. In design, ML models assist in predicting material behavior, creating sustainable architectures, and improving energy management. AI also enhances production by monitoring emissions and recognizing objects and their features and optimizing processes like hydrogen production. Additionally, it ensures efficient water distribution and improves waste management through automated sorting, recycling, and predictive waste generation models. These findings suggest that AI can bridge gaps in CE by making processes more intelligent, adaptable, and resource-efficient. Still, there are Several limitations in the findings of this study, such as many of the found AI applications are still in the experimental or theoretical phase, High computational requirements and the reliance on extensive, high-quality datasets limit AI's feasibility in industries with constrained technological and data resources, limiting their direct impact in real-world industrial settings. Additionally, because some AI models require high computational power, contrasting and raising concerns about the energy efficiency of AI technologies themselves, potentially contradicting sustainability goals of CE. The scalability of AI-driven solutions in CE shows both promise and barriers. Positive indicators are modular

AI applications like decision support systems and predictive analytics, which can be easier to adapt across industries. While for example, automated waste sorting systems using CNNs have proven adaptable for different waste streams. The limitations highlight the need for further designing, development and testing of AI and ML applications to ensure the broad yet sustainable adoption. To conclude, a summary of AI benefits are reported in Table 1.

Table 1. AI benefits in CE in different strategies

CE Strategy	AI Benefits
Raw Material	Uses ANN models to analyze omics data, identify genetic modifications, and optimize microalgae cultivation conditions, improving biomass yield and protein content [3]
Sustainable Design	Predicts the compressive strength of concrete made from post-earthquake demolition waste, helping conserve resources and reduce environmental degradation through FFNN models [4] Assists energy management and optimization in smart buildings using a stacked ensemble model combining AI algorithms like SVM, Random Forest, and XGBoost [5] Supports architects in creating sustainable, regenerative designs with early-phase planning tools using CNN, DNN, and other neural networks [6]
Production	Uses ANN to monitor CO2 emissions across supply chains by recognizing objects and predicting their carbon consumption, enabling precise tracking and reduction of environmental impact [7] Optimizes green hydrogen production by employing KNN and Random Forest models, identifying cost-effective production parameters and improving process efficiency [8]
Distribution	Uses ANN to enhance water distribution networks by optimizing energy recovery potential through smart sensors, improving hydraulic performance and micro-hydropower capacity [9]
Waste Management	Implements U-Net deep learning models for accurate particle size distribution in 3D images of construction and demolition waste, enhancing recycling efficiency [10] Predicts the behavior of sensor-based sorting units for different waste flows using ML models, improving the design and operation of sorting plants [11] Identifies key governance, employment, and research factors that influence sustainable waste management, providing actionable insights to policymakers through Rough Set-based models [12] Automates waste classification using CNN models designed for embedded systems, enabling cost effective and accurate sorting across various waste types [13] Sorts COVID-related medical waste with KNN, SVM, and ANN models, using a feature-fusion approach to ensure effective recycling and safe waste management [14] Forecasts municipal waste generation using GEP and extreme learning machines, accounting for dynamic factors like temperature, income, and population changes to improve waste management strategies [15]

9 Conclusion

This systematic literature review has highlighted the potential of AI, particularly Machine Learning, to enhance and optimize various aspects of the circular economy. AI's capabilities are demonstrated across multiple processes throughout CE, including raw material, sustainable design, production, distribution, and waste management. Through predictive analytics, automation, and data-driven insights, AI can streamline processes, improve resource efficiency, reduce waste, and promote sustainable practices. These advancements align closely with the core principles of CE, which emphasize resource conservation, material reuse, and waste reduction.

One of the key findings is that AI provides actionable solutions to specific challenges, such as forecasting material performance, enhancing hydrogen production efficiency, and developing automated waste-sorting mechanisms. Furthermore, AI-powered decision-making systems help stakeholders make more informed choices such like energy management, sustainable architecture, and municipal waste planning. These applications not only improve the efficiency but also create opportunities for innovation, cost savings, and environmental benefits. However, the study also underscores the need for further exploration, particularly in scaling AI applications from theoretical models to real-world deployments. The integration of AI into CE offers significant environmental and economic benefits, contributing to global sustainability efforts by facilitating the transition from a linear to a circular economy. Yet, the deployment of AI technologies is not without challenges. Limitations such as access to high-quality data, the complexity of AI models, and concerns about the energy consumption required for machine learning models must be addressed to ensure sustainable adoption. While AI presents a transformation of an opportunity to enhance CE practices, the successful implementation of these technologies requires great collaborative efforts between researchers, industry stakeholders, and policymakers. Future research should focus on expanding the scope of AI applications across industries, conducting large-scale projects, implementing and adapting what we have already found in other part of the processes, and developing sustainable AI systems. Through these efforts, AI can unlock new pathways for circular practices, helping societies achieve both economic growth and environmental sustainability.

Acknowledgments. This study is not funded.

Disclosure of Interests. The authors declare that they have no known competing financial interests or personal relationships that could have appeared to influence the work reported in this paper.

References

1. European Parliament. https://www.europarl.europa.eu/topics/en/article/20151201STO05603/circular-economy-definition-importance-and-benefits. Accessed 2 Nov 2024
2. Acerbi, F., Forterre, D.A., Taisch, M.: Role of artificial intelligence in circular manufacturing: a systematic literature review. IFAC-PapersOnLine **54**(1), 367–372 (2021)
3. Helmy, M., Elhalis, H., Liu, Y., Chow, Y., Selvarajoo, K.: Perspective: multiomics and machine learning help unleash the alternative food potential of microalgae. Adv. Nutr. **14**(1), 1–11 (2023)
4. Ulucan, M., Gunduzalp, E., Yildirim, G., Alatas, B., Alyamac, K.E.: Optimizing sustainable concrete compressive strength prediction: a new particle swarm optimization-based metaheuristic approach to neural network modeling for circular economy and disaster resilience. Struct. Concr. (2024)
5. Panagoulias, D.P., Sarmas, E., Marinakis, V., Virvou, M., Tsihrintzis, G.A., Doukas, H.: Intelligent decision support for energy management: a methodology for tailored explainability of artificial intelligence analytics. Electronics **12**(21), 4430 (2023)
6. Płoszaj-Mazurek, M., Ryńska, E., Grochulska-Salak, M.: Methods to optimize carbon footprint of buildings in regenerative architectural design with the use of machine learning, convolutional neural network, and parametric design. Energies **13**(20), 5289 (2020)

7. Jesse, F.F., Antonini, C., Luque-Vilchez, M.: A circularity accounting network: CO2 measurement along supply chains using machine learning: Una red de contabilidad de la circularidad: Medición del CO2 a lo largo de las cadenas de suministro mediante aprendizaje automático. Revista de Contabilidad **26**(Spec.), 21–33 (2023)
8. Kabir, M.M., et al.: Machine learning-based prediction and optimization of green hydrogen production technologies from water industries for a circular economy. Desalination **567**(116992), 116992 (2023)
9. Nakhaei, M., Akrami, M., Gheibi, M., Daniel Urbina Coronado, P., Hajiaghaei-Keshteli, M., Mahlknecht, J.: A novel framework for technical performance evaluation of water distribution networks based on the water-energy nexus concept. Energy Convers. Manag. **273**(116422), 116422 (2022)
10. Wu, X., Kroell, N., Greiff, K.: Deep learning-based instance segmentation on 3D laser triangulation data for inline monitoring of particle size distributions in construction and demolition waste recycling. Resour. Conserv. Recycl. **205**(107541), 107541 (2024)
11. Kroell, N., et al.: Towards digital twins of waste sorting plants: developing data-driven process models of industrial-scale sensor-based sorting units by combining machine learning with near-infrared-based process monitoring. Resour. Conserv. Recycl. **200**(107257), 107257 (2024)
12. Gue, I.H.V., Lopez, N.S.A., Chiu, A.S.F., Ubando, A.T., Tan, R.R.: Predicting waste management system performance from city and country attributes. J. Clean. Prod. **366**(132951), 132951 (2022)
13. Nnamoko, N., Barrowclough, J., Procter, J.: Solid waste image classification using deep convolutional neural network. Infrastructures **7**(4), 47 (2022)
14. Kumar, N.M., et al.: Artificial intelligence-based solution for sorting COVID related medical waste streams and supporting data-driven decisions for smart circular economy practice. Process Saf. Environ. Prot. Trans. Inst. Chem. Eng. Part B **152**, 482–494 (2021)
15. Fan, L., Abbasi, M., Salehi, K., Band, S.S., Chau, K.-W., Mosavi, A.: Introducing an evolutionary-decomposition model for prediction of municipal solid waste flow: application of intrinsic time-scale decomposition algorithm. Eng. Appl. Comput. Fluid Mech. **15**(1), 1159–1175 (2021)

AquaSense: Smart System for Water Quality Monitoring and Reporting Using Empathy

Wiwit Suksangaram[1] and Mahasak Ketcham[2(✉)]

[1] Phetchaburi Rajabhat University, Phetchaburi 76000, Thailand
[2] King Mongkut's University of Technology North Bangkok, Bangkok 10800, Thailand
mahasak.k@it.kmutnb.ac.th

Abstract. This research focuses on the development of a water quality monitoring and improvement system tailored to the needs of Koi fish farmers, utilizing the Design Thinking (DT) approach. By leveraging both qualitative and quantitative research methods, the study identifies critical requirements and pain points in Koi fish farming and proposes a technological solution that integrates real-time data monitoring, automated water quality adjustment, and behavior analysis through a mobile application. This study aims to evaluate the performance of a water quality monitoring application, utilizing a Line chatbot as the primary communication tool for users. The application's efficiency was assessed by three experts, with results indicating an excellent performance level, achieving 83.33% efficiency. In addition, user testing among the general public revealed a high level of satisfaction with the system, with an overall satisfaction score of 4.37 and a standard deviation (S.D.) of 0.75, classified as very good. The findings suggest that this application holds significant potential for real-world implementation. Recommendations for future development include enhancing the application by integrating modern design principles and staying abreast of emerging technologies. These improvements will ensure that the system remains efficient and responsive to user needs in the long term.

Keywords: Water Quality Monitoring · Application Efficiency · User Satisfaction · Expert Evaluation · Emerging Technologies · Real-World Implementation

1 Introduction

The practice of Koi fish farming originated in Japan as a result of advancements in aquaculture aimed at producing high-quality Koi with desirable aesthetic characteristics. Initially, the cultivation of Koi gained prominence during the late 19th and early 20th centuries, when breeders focused on developing fish with elongated, graceful tails and refined body shapes, making them suitable for ornamental purposes and international competitions. Despite its popularity, Koi farming presents several challenges, particularly in maintaining optimal water quality, which is critical for the health and development of the fish. Poor water conditions, such as the presence of pathogens or

J. Kertesz et al. (Eds.): CSoNet 2024, LNCS 15417, pp. 420–432, 2025.
https://doi.org/10.1007/978-981-96-6389-7_39

contaminants, can severely affect the growth and wellbeing of Koi, leading to increased mortality rates or compromised health. Effective temperature regulation is another essential aspect of Koi farming, as Koi are highly sensitive to fluctuations in water temperature. Inadequate temperature control can hinder growth and contribute to the onset of diseases, such as bacterial infections. Moreover, ensuring appropriate oxygen levels in the water is vital, as oxygen is necessary for the fish's physiological functions and overall growth. Insufficient oxygen supply can result in respiratory issues and diminished health outcomes in Koi. Additionally, the use of chemical treatments to control diseases in aquaculture poses risks, as chemical residues may accumulate in the water, negatively impacting both the fish and the environment. Consequently, the judicious and regulated application of chemical substances is necessary to mitigate these risks. Koi farming requires specialized techniques that differentiate it from other forms of aquaculture due to the emphasis on producing aesthetically appealing fish with high-quality traits. This necessitates careful management of feeding practices, stringent control of water quality, and constant health monitoring. However, many breeders face challenges in dedicating sufficient time and resources to the systematic management of their Koi ponds. The increasing popularity of Koi farming extends beyond Japan, with global interest growing, particularly within artistic and competitive arenas. As a result, Koi breeding has evolved into a significant profession, offering substantial economic opportunities. In parallel, the field has attracted academic attention from researchers and students in aquaculture and environmental sciences, particularly those interested in controlled-environment fish farming. This academic focus seeks to advance scientific understanding and develop improved technologies to enhance the efficiency and sustainability of Koi farming. Given these challenges, there is a growing recognition of the need for technological solutions to assist Koi breeders in monitoring and maintaining optimal water quality. Proposed innovations include the development of automated water quality improvement systems and real-time reporting tools accessible via mobile applications. These advancements aim to alleviate the burden of manual monitoring, providing breeders with more efficient and effective means of ensuring the health and longevity of their Koi populations.

Design Thinking (DT) is a widely recognized and applied process in organizations, aimed at problem-solving and fostering innovation. Its creative and intuitive nature distinguishes DT from purely analytical approaches [1–16]. A key advantage of DT lies in its ability to generate product or service innovations by placing a strong emphasis on understanding users' needs at a deep level. This process also facilitates better decision-making by mitigating cognitive biases, promotes learning, and drives organizational culture towards innovation. Although design research has its roots in the 1960s, applying design principles within a business context remains relatively new. Earlier studies primarily focused on identifying the characteristics of DT and its relevance to business and management. In recent years, research has expanded to examine the applications, conditions, and impacts of DT, with an increasing use of quantitative methods to assess DT's effects. Given DT's growing popularity in practice, this research seeks to apply DT principles to the design of a Smart System for Water Quality Monitoring and Reporting, leveraging its problem-solving framework to create innovative and user-centered solutions. This application of DT offers the potential to significantly enhance the effectiveness and efficiency of water quality monitoring through the integration of intuitive design and cutting-edge technology.

2 Related Work

2.1 Theories of Satisfaction

Shelly [17] studied the concept of satisfaction and concluded that it is characterized by two types of human feelings: positive and negative emotions. Positive emotions are those that, once experienced, create a feedback loop that enhances feelings of happiness or further positive emotions. This suggests that happiness is a complex emotion with a significant impact on individuals, surpassing other positive feelings. Negative and positive emotions, along with happiness, are intricately interconnected, forming a complex emotional system. This system of emotions is referred to as the Satisfaction System, in which satisfaction arises when the balance of positive emotions outweighs negative emotions.

2.2 Human-Centered Design (HCD)

Human-Centered Design (HCD) [18] is an approach to problem-solving that focuses on creating solutions specifically for "end users" or those who will directly benefit from the solution. A key phase in HCD is empathy, often described as "putting oneself in another's shoes" to truly understand the user's problems from their perspective. This empathy phase involves gaining deep insights into how users feel or think when confronted with certain situations or challenges, simulating the experience as if one were facing the same issues. Once empathy is established, the next phase involves ideation generating as many potential solutions as possible. This stage emphasizes the idea that there is rarely just one way to solve a problem. Multiple ideas are brainstormed, and then the most viable ones are taken forward for further development into prototypes. Prototyping makes abstract ideas tangible, enabling clearer visualization of potential solutions. For instance, in the case of a physical device, paper models or 3D-printed mock-ups can be created. For software solutions, this might involve writing code or designing mockup interfaces. These prototypes are then tested with the end users, who provide feedback on the solutions. Throughout this process, the designer shares their thought process with users to ensure that the final solution accurately addresses the users' needs.

3 Methodology

3.1 Understanding the Target Group (Empathy)

A deep understanding of the target group's issues is a crucial step in identifying their core needs. This study employs both quantitative and qualitative research tools to gather comprehensive insights. The quantitative approach involves the use of an online questionnaire administered through Microsoft Forms, while the qualitative method includes in-depth interviews to provide richer, more nuanced data. Target Group The target group for this study consists of individuals directly involved in Koi fish farming, a group with specialized knowledge and experience in this field. Data collection from this group will be conducted through in-depth interviews and online surveys. This dual approach aims to capture both the explicit needs and the underlying challenges faced by Koi fish farmers, facilitating a thorough understanding of the complexities involved in their practices.

3.2 Data Collection Method

The data collection process involved carefully selecting questions to gather information from the target group, focusing on understanding the needs of Koi fish farmers. In depth interviews were employed, using open ended questions to explore various dimensions such as the participants' experiences, behaviors, and emotions. The questions were designed based on a thorough review of relevant literature and previous research to ensure their appropriateness for the target group. The selected open-ended interview questions are detailed in Table 1. This approach aimed to capture a comprehensive understanding of the challenges and needs faced by Koi fish farmers.

Table 1. In-depth Interview Questions.

No.	Questions
1	What challenges do Koi fish farmers face?
2	How interested are you in using technology to help solve these challenges?
3	What conveniences or facilities do Koi fish farmers require?
4	How do you assess the water quality for fish farming?

3.3 Empathy Map for Koi Fish Farmers

Goals

- Ensure that Koi fish are healthy, well-developed, and thriving.
- Achieve high market value for the Koi fish.
- Maintain a quality rearing environment (water, temperature, air, sunlight) that matches standards in Japan.

Think & Feel

- High maintenance costs are a concern.
- Busy schedule leads to limited time for proper care and observation.

Hear

- Koi fish farming is a popular and expansive market.
- Koi fish are imported from Japan, often through auctions, with prices ranging from hundreds of thousands to millions.
- Some breeders outsource the care of their Koi fish to Japan before bringing them back for competitions in Thailand.
- Experiences of winning awards in Koi fish competitions.
- There are established standards of beauty for Koi fish.
- Breeders often maintain multiple tanks for different purposes, such as personal enjoyment, sales, or competitions.

See

- Breeders are communicative, friendly, and provide straightforward information.
- Many are still developing their expertise in Koi fish farming.
- They are willing to invest in things that bring them happiness, including their passion for Koi fish.
- Breeders often exhibit an affinity for brand-name goods and show an interest in IoT technology.

Say & Do

- Express dissatisfaction with the difference in the quality of water and air compared to Japan.
- Have limited time to observe the rearing environment, fish behavior, and water quality.
- Lack of oxygen-level monitoring equipment.
- Use surveillance cameras but acknowledge it is not the same as personal observation.
- Small fish size may be attributed to factors such as diet, breed, tank size, water quality, or disease.
- Power outages result in fish deaths due to low oxygen levels.
- No historical data on fish or water conditions is collected.
- Daily feeding and monitoring are necessary, and new fish require quarantine.

Pain Points

- Water pollution.
- Water quality in Thailand differs from Japan.
- High temperatures in Thailand (ideal temperature for Koi is between 24–25 °C).
- Fish diseases.
- Low oxygen levels during power outages lead to fish deaths.
- Limited time for monitoring fish behavior, water quality, and environmental factors.

- Lack of tools and technology to assist in these tasks.

Gains

- Need tools and technology to help monitor and improve water quality.
- Desire for technology that can assist in monitoring Koi fish behavior.

3.4 Defining the Problem (Define)

Persona: The persona created to represent the target group is a university professor who is also a Koi fish farmer. This individual seeks a water quality monitoring and improvement system, coupled with technology for monitoring the behavior of Koi fish.
Interests, Goals, Pain Points, and Motivations:
Name: Mr. Mau Lor-Ruay (pseudonym)

- **Gender:** Male
- **Age:** 40–50 years
- **Occupation:** University professor and researcher
- **Hobbies/Interests:** Gardening, car modification, shooting, amulet collection
- **Marital Status:** Married (no children)
- **Interest:** Water quality monitoring systems, automated water quality adjustment systems, and alert technology for Koi ponds.
- **Goals:**
  - Ensure water temperature control
  - Monitor pH levels and adjust water quality automatically
  - Implement a system to monitor Koi fish behavior with data reporting and mobile alerts.
- **Pain Points:**
  - Limited time to monitor the pond environment
  - Lack of tools to measure pH and oxygen levels
  - Surveillance cameras do not provide sufficient information about water quality and fish behavior
  - No historical data collection
- **Motivations:**
  - Advanced water quality improvement technologies
  - Tools to monitor Koi fish behavior in real-time
  - Easy-to-use systems with low maintenance costs

Challenges

- Thailand's hot climate (ideal temperature for Koi is 24–25 °C)
- Desire for water quality comparable to Japan
- Frequent power outages affecting oxygen levels in ponds
- High susceptibility of Koi to disease
- High cost of Koi fish

Needs & Expectations

- Easy-to-use, cost-effective solutions
- Technologies that address current problems
- Modern, automated systems that require minimal effort

Technology & Communication Tools

- Water temperature measurement devices
- pH and oxygen level monitoring systems
- Automatic water quality adjustment systems
- Fish behavior monitoring technology
- **Tools used:**
- Line Application, smartphones, computers, notebooks
- **Content Type:**
- Digital display showing real-time water quality data (temperature, pH, oxygen levels)
- Clear, easy-to-read reports with simple visuals

Brands & Influences
Not brand loyal, prefers technology that fits their needs (Tables 2 and 3).

Table 2. Customer Journey Map: Water Quality Monitoring & Reporting System

Phase	Activities	Touch Points	Problems	Opportunities
Interest	Searching for water quality monitoring systems with alert features for Koi ponds	Websites, Koi breeder forums, equipment stores	Scattered information, lack of reliable user reviews	Develop an app for real-time monitoring, provide comprehensive user reviews
Information Search	Gathering data from websites, inquiring with fellow Koi breeders	Social media, YouTube reviews	Websites not updated, difficult to find accurate reviews	Regularly update websites, feature customer testimonials

(*continued*)

Table 2. (*continued*)

Phase	Activities	Touch Points	Problems	Opportunities
Comparison	Comparing prices and features across models and stores	Online forums, equipment stores	High prices, no flexible payment options	Offer installment payment options
Purchase Decision	Finalizing purchase and making payment	Online payments, equipment stores	High cost, complex installation	Provide easy installation guides, offer product demonstrations
Usage	Learning to operate the system and monitoring tools	Pond environment, online guides	Time-consuming setup, unfamiliar with the equipment	Simplify the user manual, create instructional videos
Customer Service	Contacting support for advice or repairs	Call centers, online help	Difficulty reaching customer support, no replacement equipment	Improve support channels, offer backup equipment during repairs
Repeat Purchase	Recommending the system to fellow Koi breeders	Social media, personal recommendations	Lack of post-purchase support	Provide special offers or discounts for repeat customers

Table 3. Customer Journey Map: Reporting System via Application

Phase	Touch Points	Problems	Opportunities
Needs	Monitoring environment but lacking tools for pH, oxygen level, and fish behavior	Unable to track environmental conditions consistently	Develop a system to measure water quality in real-time through mobile apps
Data Selection	Water temperature and pH monitoring systems	Surveillance cameras cannot detect water quality or fish behavior	Integrate real-time data into the app, viewable daily or weekly
Report Generation	Real-time processing with mobile alerts	No historical data collection	Enable historical data storage for trend analysis
Notifications	Customizable alerts through mobile apps	Lack of real-time notifications for critical changes in water quality	Provide notification options via Line or other mobile apps

3.5 Solution Design

Utilizing the Design Thinking approach, the research team developed a conceptual framework for a Smart Water Quality Monitoring and Improvement System. This system is designed to address the specific needs and challenges identified through user research. The proposed solution includes the following components. The following solutions were proposed to address the needs of Koi fish farmers.

- **Water Quality Monitoring System**: Includes sensors for temperature, pH, and oxygen levels, with real-time data accessible via mobile applications. The system is powered by electricity or solar energy.
- **Fish Behavior Monitoring**: Uses underwater cameras and sonar technology to track fish activity, with AI-based behavior analysis.
- **Automated Water Adjustment**: Automatically adjusts water conditions based on collected data to maintain optimal water quality for Koi fish.
- **User-Friendly Interface**: A digital dashboard displaying all relevant data, including temperature, pH, oxygen levels, and behavior patterns. Customizable alerts can be sent to the user's smartphone.
- **Historical Data Access**: Allows users to view past water quality data and fish behavior trends, providing insights for better decision-making.

These solutions aim to offer ease of use, low cost, and reliable technology, tailored specifically to the needs of Koi fish farmers.

3.6 Hardware Design

The design and development of a system for monitoring server room temperature and humidity using IoT involves several key hardware components. These include a computer for program development, a server, and a microcontroller (MCU). The chosen MCU for this project is the ESP8266, which is highly suitable for IoT applications. Additionally, a DHT sensor is used to measure temperature and humidity levels, and various electronic accessories are incorporated to support the functionality of the system. Together, these components form the hardware foundation for real time environmental monitoring within the server room.

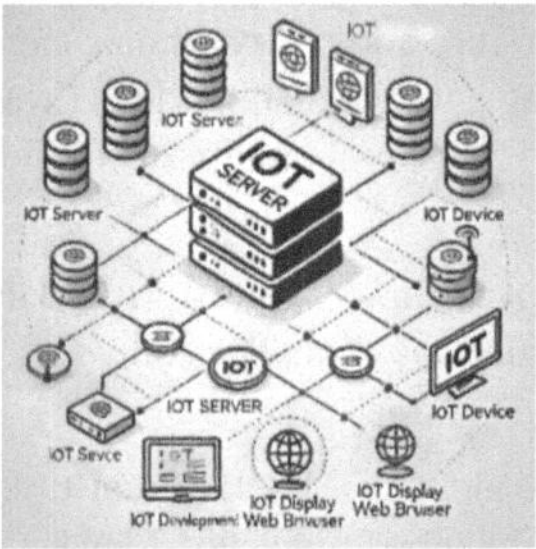

Fig. 1. Logical Diagram Overview of IoT system.

This Fig. 1 represents an IoT (Internet of Things) network that connects various devices and systems through an IoT server or IoT private cloud. Here's a breakdown of the components. IoT Server: At the center of the network, the IoT server serves as the main hub for managing data and communications between devices. It receives data from multiple IoT devices, processes it, and coordinates responses. IoT Devices: These are the various endpoints that collect data or perform tasks. In the context of a server room, these could include sensors for temperature, humidity, or other environmental factors. Each

IoT device communicates with the server through a wireless network. IoT Development and Management: This represents the systems or tools used for developing, managing, and maintaining the IoT ecosystem. It could involve programming interfaces or dashboards for system management. IoT Display (Web Browser): The display system, likely accessed via a web browser, allows users to view real-time data and manage the IoT network. This interface presents visualizations of the data collected by the IoT devices and offers insights for decision-making. Connectivity: All components are interconnected through wireless signals (Wi-Fi), enabling real-time communication between devices, the server, and the management systems.

4 Results

Phase	Interest	Search	Comparison	Purchase Decision	Usage	Customer Service	Repurchase
Activities	Purchase water quality testing equipment and water quality improvement systems with warning systems for use with koi ponds.	-Search for information on the Web -Ask for information from fish farmers - Walk around electrical appliance stores	-Start comparing the prices and features of each model and each store.	Make payment	Study the tools and learn how to use them, which may include reading manuals and watching demonstration videos.	Call to inquire about information or ask for advice in case of sending for repair.	Introduce friends to the Koi fish breeding group
Touch Point		-Web/Social -Fish farming group page -Electrical appliance store	-Watch reviews, features on Youtube. -Ask from real users	Payment by card	Homemade kraft pond	-Call for information -View information via Web	Web
Problem	There is no time to observe the environment in which fish are kept.	- Information is scattered - Website is not updated	- Hard to find reviews from real users - Durability of the device - Accuracy of water temperature measurement	-Price is quite high -No payment terms	-Take time to study the manual -A place suitable for the equipment	- Difficult to call the call center No repairs during delivery - Spare equipment waiting to be used	
Opportunity	There is an application that connects to your mobile phone, allowing you to view the water temperature at all times.	Update the website all the time Develop a modern website that is easy on the eyes	-Collect lots of buyer review images for advertising -Choose tools designed for specific usage environments and maintenance [illegible]	-Add multiple payment channels -Can pay for products in installments	-Staff provides basic equipment installation advice -Recommend products that are appropriate for the size of the aquarium	- Add a channel to contact customers.	-Promotion -Special discount for old customers

Fig. 2. Customer Journey Chart Overview of Demand for Thermometers Water Quality Monitoring Equipment

This Fig. 2 presents the customer journey map is a vital tool that enables businesses to gain insight into the various stages customers go through when interacting with products or services. By analyzing these stages, companies can identify pain points and opportunities for improving customer experience. This paper presents the results of a customer journey analysis focused on a water quality monitoring system for koi fish farming. The journey map is structured around seven key phases: interest, information search, comparison, decision-making, use, customer service, and after-sales service. Each phase highlights the challenges customers face and the opportunities for businesses to enhance service offerings. The journey begins with customers expressing interest in purchasing water quality monitoring equipment and an alert system for koi fish farming. The main issue encountered at this stage is the lack of time or knowledge about where to start in maintaining water quality for the fish. This presents an opportunity for businesses to develop digital platforms, such as mobile applications, that provide step-by-step guidance, saving customers time and effort in finding the necessary information. Once customers have decided to pursue a purchase, they begin searching for information from various sources, such as websites, social media, and electronic equipment stores. A common problem in this phase is the scattered and often outdated nature of the information found across different platforms. The opportunity here lies in maintaining up-to-date, comprehensive online resources, ensuring that customers can easily access relevant, accurate information to make informed decisions. Comparison Phase,

During the comparison phase, customers typically rely on product reviews and user feedback, often from platforms like YouTube or direct inquiries with experienced users. The challenge at this stage is the conflicting nature of user reviews, which can lead to confusion. Businesses can address this issue by consolidating customer feedback and presenting structured, objective reviews that clearly outline the strengths and weaknesses of each product. Decision-Making Phase, At this point, customers proceed to purchase, often using credit cards or online payment systems. The primary obstacle encountered is the high cost of equipment, coupled with a lack of flexible payment options such as installment plans. This issue presents an opportunity for businesses to introduce flexible payment methods, such as installment options or promotional discounts, to ease the financial burden on customers and make the products more accessible. Use Phase, Following the purchase, customers engage in setting up and using the equipment. However, they frequently encounter difficulties with complex user manuals, which complicates the installation and operation process. An opportunity exists to simplify these manuals or provide interactive video tutorials that offer clear, step-by-step guidance, making it easier for customers to utilize the equipment effectively. Customer Service Phase, in cases where customers require assistance, they typically reach out to customer service via phone or online platforms. The main challenge here is the difficulty in obtaining specialized support for the equipment. Businesses can enhance the customer experience by expanding the range of available customer service channels and improving the responsiveness and accessibility of support, especially for technical issues. After-Sales Service Phase, in the final phase, customers may purchase additional products or seek further guidance on product usage. A common issue is the complexity of returning items or claiming warranties. To address this, businesses can streamline the return process and offer loyalty programs or special promotions for repeat customers, encouraging long-term engagement and satisfaction. This analysis of the customer journey highlights critical insights into the overall customer experience, identifying key pain points and opportunities for improvement across all stages of the buying process. By addressing these issues, businesses can enhance service delivery, improve customer satisfaction, and develop strategies that better align with customer needs and expectations. These findings provide a framework for businesses to implement targeted improvements that foster stronger customer relationships and increase sales potential (Fig. 3).

Fig. 3. Prototype

5 Conclusion

Evaluation of System Efficiency by Expert Group. The evaluation of system efficiency conducted by an expert group reveals that the system demonstrates a high level of satisfaction in several key areas. The assessment was based on the following criteria. User Requirement Fulfillment received an average score of 4.33 (S.D. = 0.57), which is classified as good. This score reflects the system's capability to adequately meet the basic needs and requirements of its users. User Interaction with the System scored an average of 4.66 (S.D. = 0.57), categorized as very good. This indicates that the system facilitates efficient and effective communication and interaction with users. System Accuracy also received an average score of 4.66 (S.D. = 0.57), classified as very good, demonstrating the system's reliability and accuracy in performing its designated functions. System Efficiency achieved an average score of 4.66 (S.D. = 0.57), also classified as very good, highlighting the system's high performance in supporting users' operations. The overall average score across all categories is 4.57 (S.D. = 0.57), which is classified as very good. This result reflects the system's overall efficiency and its ability to satisfactorily meet the needs of its users. Based on these evaluation results, it can be concluded that the developed system demonstrates high efficiency, particularly in areas such as user interaction, system accuracy, and operational effectiveness. These factors contribute to the system's reliability and suitability for implementation in contexts where it is required to support user needs efficiently. The positive assessment by the expert group indicates that the system is well positioned for deployment in practical applications. Based on the test results and performance evaluation of the water quality monitoring application by three experts, the findings indicate that the application achieved an excellent efficiency rating of 83.33%. Additionally, the user testing by general users revealed a high level of satisfaction with the Line chatbot system, with an overall satisfaction score of 4.37 (S.D. = 0.75), classified as very good. The application demonstrates significant potential for real-world implementation, based on the data collected and the insights gained. Future iterations should focus on enhancing the application by incorporating modern design principles and keeping pace with emerging technologies. These improvements will ensure that the system remains up-to-date and relevant for future developments in the field of water quality monitoring.

References

1. Brown, T.: Design thinking. Harv. Bus. Rev. **86**(6), 84–92 (2008)
2. Mansoori, Y., Lackeus, M.: Comparing effectuation to discovery-driven planning, prescriptive entrepreneurship, business planning, lean startup, and design thinking. Small Bus. Econ. **54**(3), 791–818 (2020). https://doi.org/10.1007/s11187-019-00153-w
3. Nakata, C.: Design thinking for innovation: considering distinctions, fit, and use in firms. Bus. Horiz. **63**(6), 763–772 (2020). https://doi.org/10.1016/j.bushor.2020.07.008
4. Liedtka, J.: Perspective: linking design thinking with innovation outcomes through cognitive bias reduction. J. Prod. Innov. Manag. **32**(6), 925–938 (2015). https://doi.org/10.1111/jpim.12163
5. Beckman, S.L., Barry, M.: Innovation as a learning process: embedding design thinking. Calif. Manag. Rev. **50**(1), 25–56 (2007). https://doi.org/10.2307/41166415
6. Elsbach, K.D., Stigliani, I.: Design thinking and organizational culture: a review and framework for future research. J. Manag. **44**(6), 2274–2306 (2018). https://doi.org/10.1177/0149206317744252
7. Kolko, J.: Design thinking comes of age. Harv. Bus. Rev. **93**(9), 66–71 (2015)
8. Appleyard, M.M., Enders, A.H., Velazquez, H.: Regaining R&D leadership: the role of design thinking and creative forbearance. Calif. Manag. Rev. **62**(2), 12–29 (2020). https://doi.org/10.1177/0008125619897395
9. Suci, A., Maryanti, S., Hardi, H., Sudiar, N.: Embedding design thinking paradigm in a university's business assistance to small business. Syst. Pract. Act. Res. (2021). https://doi.org/10.1007/s11213-021-09565-w
10. Thompson, L., Schonthal, D.: The social psychology of design thinking. Calif. Manag. Rev. **62**(2), 84–99 (2020). https://doi.org/10.1177/0008125619897636
11. Tiberius, V., Schwarzer, H., Roig-Dobon, S.: Radical innovations: between established knowledge and future research opportunities. J. Innov. Knowl. **6**(3), 145–153 (2021). https://doi.org/10.1016/j.jik.2020.09.001
12. Tranfield, D., Denyer, D., Smart, P.: Towards a methodology for developing evidenceinformed management knowledge by means of systematic review. Br. J. Manag. **14**, 207–222 (2003). https://doi.org/10.1111/1467-8551.00375
13. Vetterli, C., Uebernickel, F., Brenner, W., Petrie, C., Stermann, D.: How deutsche bank's IT division used design thinking to achieve customer proximity. MIS Q. Exec. **15**(1), 37–53 (2016)
14. Welsh, M.A., Dehler, G.E.: Combining critical reflection and design thinking to develop integrative learners. J. Manag. Educ. **37**(6), 771–802 (2013). https://doi.org/10.1177/1052562912470107
15. Wrigley, C., Mosely, G., Tomitsch, M.: Design thinking education: a comparison of massive open online courses. She Ji **4**(3), 275–292 (2018). https://doi.org/10.1016/j.sheji.2018.06.002
16. Wrigley, C., Nusem, E., Straker, K.: Implementing design thinking: understanding organizational conditions. Calif. Manag. Rev. **62**(2), 125–143 (2020). https://doi.org/10.1177/0008125619897606
17. Shelly, D.F.: Tackling family member compensation. Am. Print. **215**, p2 (1995)
18. Kluge, A., Termer, A.: Human-centered design (HCD) of a fault-finding application for mobile devices and its impact on the reduction of time in fault diagnosis in the manufacturing industry. Appl. Ergon. **59**(Part A), 170–181 (2017). ISSN 0003-6870. https://doi.org/10.1016/j.apergo.2016.08.030.LNCS

Machine Learning on Metabolomic Profiles from Fecal to Identify Plant-Based Food Intake

Natnicha Charoenwong[1,3], Krerkpon Rattanapoom[1,3], Umaporn Uawisetwathana[2,3], Awanwee Petchkongkaew[1,3,4], Kritanat Chungnoy[5], Surasit Uypatchawong[6(✉)], and Pokpong Songmuang[1]

[1] Faculty of Science and Technology, Thammasat University, Bangkok, Thailand
[2] National Center for Genetic Engineering and Biotechnology (BIOTEC), National Science and Technology Development Agency (NSTDA), Khlong Nueng, Thailand
[3] International Joint Research Center on Food Security (IJC-FOODSEC), Bangkok, Thailand
[4] Institute for Global Food Security, Queen University Belfast, Belfast, UK
[5] Faculty of Management Science, Chandrakasem Rajabhat University, Bangkok, Thailand
[6] Faculty of Science and Technology, Sakon Nakhon Rajabhat University (SNRU), Sakon Nakhon, Thailand
surasit@snru.ac.th

Abstract. Plant-based diets have gained significant attention due to their health benefits and environmental sustainability. Infants are unable to communicate their dietary intake. Fecal metabolites provide an alternative approach to accurately assess consumed foods. This study applied machine learning (ML) techniques-including Random Forest (RF), Support Vector Machine (SVM), Gradient Boosting (GB), and Extreme Gradient Boosting (XGB)-to analyze fecal metabolomic profiles associated with plant-based diets. A total of 159 metabolite features were selected based on the coefficient of variation (CV) criterion for analysis using ML models to predict food intake. For each single food, the dataset was divided into six categories, each corresponding to a specific plant-based food: Almond, Avocado, Barley, Broccoli, Oats, and Walnut. In the "multi-food" approach, samples from all six plant-based foods were combined into a single dataset for prediction. Our results showed that the GB model achieved the highest average accuracy when predicting each of the six datasets separately across all plant-based foods (single food). However, when combining all six datasets into one (multi-food) for prediction, the SVM model provided the best predictive performance. Future research should explore the application of deep learning techniques to gain deeper insights into the data and enhance model performance.

Keywords: Machine learning · Fecal metabolites · Food intake · Infants · Plant-based food

1 Introduction

Infants' dietary challenges because they cannot express what they eat. Infants rely entirely on their caregivers to monitor their food intake, but parents might

J. Kertesz et al. (Eds.): CSoNet 2024, LNCS 15417, pp. 433–445, 2025.
https://doi.org/10.1007/978-981-96-6389-7_40

miss important details [1]. According to research, accurate assessment of infant diets is essential for their growth and development, but traditional methods like asking parents are not always reliable [24].

One of the main problems is that infants cannot describe any discomfort or abnormal reactions to food, making it harder to detect issues like allergies, intolerances, or nutritional deficiencies. Detecting what babies eat becomes even more important in clinical settings. Researchers are now exploring advanced methods, such as analyzing fecal samples to track what infants consume and how their bodies are processing the nutrients. This approach could provide more accurate information about infant diets [18,25].

There is growing interest in plant-based diets because of their health benefits and positive impact on the environment. Researchers have started using a scientific method called metabolomics, which studies small molecules in the body, known as metabolites. By studying feces, scientists can learn a lot about how the gut processes food and what someone has eaten [20] [16].

In recent years, ML has become an important tool for analyzing metabolomics data, and helps scientists analyze large and complex data sets to find patterns. Four main ML methods-RF, SVM, GB, and XGB-have been successful in identifying important metabolites related to diet in many research [14,17,19,33].

2 Literature Review

2.1 Infants and Case Studies of Dietary Challenges

Infants are unable to describe what they have eaten, especially those under the age of two, rely on non-verbal cues such as crying, changes in behavior, or physical symptoms to signal discomfort or abnormal responses to food [18].

In some cases, infants show signs of abnormal food reactions through symptoms such as vomiting, diarrhea, skin rashes, or excessive crying after eating certain foods. Identifying these allergies are crucial, but it can be difficult when infants can not directly express their pain or discomfort [16].

Healthcare professionals use various methods to assess infant feeding problems, such as growth tracking, allergy testing, or the analysis of stool samples. For instance, fecal analysis can provide insights into the infant's digestion and how their body is processing nutrients [11,16].

2.2 Fecal Metabolome

Metabolomics is the large-scale study of metabolites, which are the end products of metabolism. These metabolites can be analyzed in different biological samples such as blood, urine, or feces, and they provide insight into the body's functions and responses to various factors like diet and disease [32].

Fecal metabolomics provide an objective method for measuring what a person has consumed. Studies have shown that specific metabolites in feces are linked to the consumption of plant-based foods such as fruits, vegetables, and grains [5].

2.3 Machine Learning Model Classification

ML has become an essential tool for analyzing large datasets and predictions. In classification, ML models are trained to recognize patterns in data and then categorize new data based on those patterns. Some of the most widely used ML models for classification are RF, SVM, GB, and XGB [4,14,17].

RF model is a type of ensemble learning method, which means it combines multiple decision trees to make predictions. Each tree in the forest is built using a random subset of the data, and the final prediction is made based on the majority vote of the trees [6].

SVM works by finding a hyperplane that best separates the data into different categories. It is particularly effective when dealing with high-dimensional data, such as datasets with many features [13].

GB is more advanced method that builds decision trees sequentially, with each tree correcting the errors of the previous ones. This method tends to work well with small to medium-sized datasets. The key strength of GB is that it focuses on minimizing the errors in each step [21].

XGB is an improved version of GB. It was developed to be faster and more efficient, especially when working with large datasets. XGB uses additional techniques to prevent overfitting and optimize the speed of training [7].

In conclusion, RF, SVM, GB, and XGB are four of the most commonly used ML models for classification tasks. Each model offers distinct advantages depending on the dataset and the problem at hand [15,23,29].

3 Methodology

3.1 Fecal Metabolomics

The publicly available data about fecal metabolome from plant-based food intake were collected from research articles [2,12,22,26,27,30,31], with ethical approval for human. The researchers conducted the experiment on a single plant-based food, dividing healthy participants into two groups. Group 1 consumed a regular diet, while group 2 consumed a regular diet supplemented with one type of plant-based food at each meal. Fecal samples were collected and analyzed for metabolites using untargeted metabolomics with a GC-MS instrument.

3.2 Data Preprocessing

The preprocessing steps applied to the raw fecal metabolite data were designed to ensure the dataset's quality for machine learning analysis. Initially, six experimental datasets were sourced from publicly available research articles, comprising 309 metabolite features. To address missing values within the dataset [10], a random imputation method was employed, where missing entries were filled with a value randomly selected between 0 and one-half of the minimum value observed for that metabolite each respective metabolite [26]. This study employed the CV criterion for feature selection. The CV was calculated for each metabolite feature to assess variability across the dataset. Metabolite features with CV of less than 100 in at least 60% of the samples were retained for further analysis, reducing the number of metabolite features to 153 [28].

3.3 Machine Learning Model

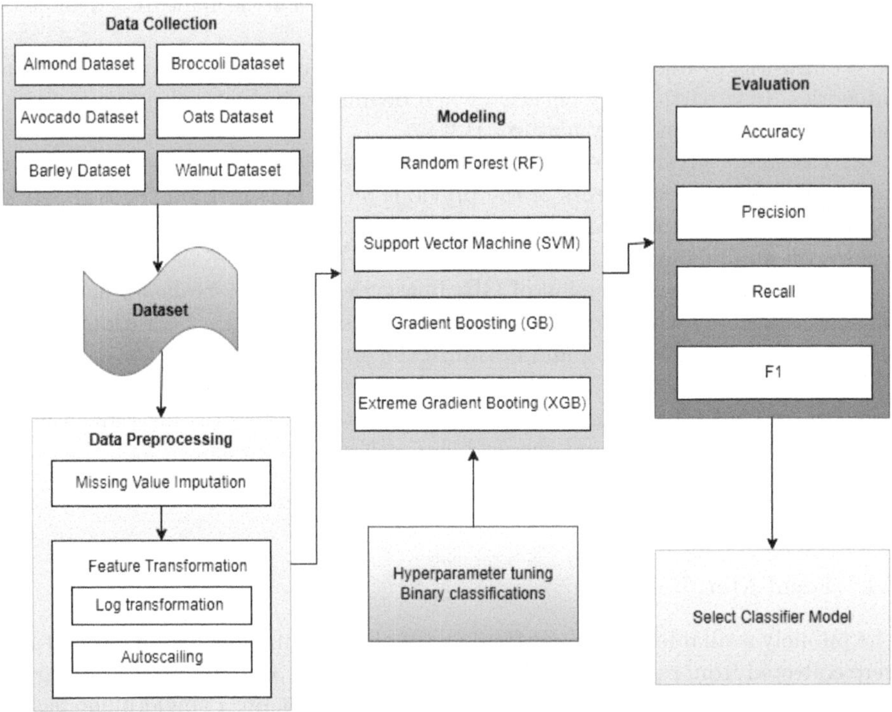

Fig. 1. Data analysis workflow

This workflow diagram represents the process of building a classifier model with several stages, from data collection to model evaluation and selection (Fig. 1). Different datasets related to various types of plant-based food-Almond(n=15), Avocado(n=20), Barley(n=15), Broccoli(n=15), Oats(n=15), and Walnut(n=18) -were collected. These datasets contain information on fecal metabolite profiles associated with each food type (single food) [8], the model can learn patterns that indicate the consumption of each type. On the other hand, the collected data from each food type is combined into a single dataset (multi-food) for processing (n=98). Feature transformation, which includes log transformation and autoscaling to normalize the data and ensure comparability across features. After feature transformation, hyperparameter tuning and binary classifications are conducted using four different ML models: RF, SVM, GB, and XGB [3]. Data was split using 70:30 ratio, where 70% was allocated to the training set and 30% to the testing set. This ratio was chosen as the limited size of the dataset. Therefore, this split ratio is deemed appropriate for training and evaluating the classification of ML models. Multiple ML algorithms are applied to classify dietary intake based on metabolite profiles. Using a train-test split ratio of 70:30, the models were trained on 70% of the data and then used to classify the remaining 30% of the samples. The best-performing classifier model is selected based on performance: accuracy, precision, recall, and F1 score [9].

4 Results

4.1 Single-Food Machine Learning Classification Models

Table 1 presents the performance of four different ML classification models-RF, SVM, GB, and XGB-for classifying six types of plant-based foods (Almond, Avocado, Barley, Broccoli, Oats, and Walnut) based on fecal metabolite data. The metrics shown for each model are precision, recall, F1-score, and accuracy for each plant-based food. RF achieves perfect accuracy with almond and walnut(1.00). For avocado, barley, broccoli, and oats, RF shows moderate performance with accuracy scores of 0.69, 0.60, 0.70, and 0.60, respectively. SVM shows high accuracy for avocado (0.88) and walnut (0.91). For almond, broccoli, barley and oats, SVM has moderate performance with accuracy scores of 0.60, 0.70, 0.70, and 0.50, respectively. GB demonstrates perfect scores for almond and walnut with accuracy of 1.00, showing its strength in these food classes. GB has moderate performance for avocado (0.81 accuracy), broccoli (0.60 accuracy), barley (0.90 accuracy), and oats (0.70 accuracy). XGB shows perfect accuracy for almond and walnut, with accuracy of 1.00. For broccoli, barley and oats, XGB shows moderate performance with accuracy scores of 0.60, 0.70, and 0.50, respectively. However, avocado showing the lowest accuracy (0.56).

Table 2 outlines the optimization parameters used for four ML models to enhance their performance in predicting individual plant-based foods and a combined multi-food dataset. The numbers 1 to 7 in the "Optimized" columns correspond to the specific datasets: 1 for almond, 2 for avocado, 3 for barley, 4 for broccoli, 5 for oats, 6 for walnut, and 7 for a dataset comprising all six plant-based foods combined (multi-food). The optimal model performance on optimization parameter settings for each ML model was adapted from the methodology [3]. Each model has undergone a hyperparameter optimization process tailored to each dataset, leading to the selection of the most suitable parameters for the specific food or multi-food classification.

Table 1. Single-food machine learning classification.

Model	Plant-based food	Class	precision	recall	f1-score	accuracy
Random Forest (RF)	Almond	Almond	1.00	1.00	1.00	1.00
		No Almond	1.00	1.00	1.00	
	Avocado	Avocado	0.64	1.00	0.78	0.69
		No Avocado	1.00	0.29	0.44	
	Barley	Barley	0.57	0.80	0.67	0.60
		No Barley	0.67	0.40	0.50	
	Broccoli	Broccoli	0.67	0.80	0.73	0.70
		No Broccoli	0.75	0.60	0.67	
	Oats	Oats	0.67	0.40	0.50	0.60
		No Oats	0.57	0.80	0.67	
	Walnut	Walnut	1.00	1.00	1.00	1.00
		No Walnut	1.00	1.00	1.00	
Support Vector Machine (SVM)	Almond	Almond	0.67	0.40	0.50	0.60
		No Almond	0.57	0.80	0.67	
	Avocado	Avocado	0.82	1.00	0.90	0.88
		No Avocado	1.00	0.71	0.83	
	Barley	Barley	1.00	0.40	0.57	0.70
		No Barley	0.63	1.00	0.77	
	Broccoli	Broccoli	0.50	1.00	0.67	0.70
		No Broccoli	0.00	0.00	0.00	
	Oats	Oats	0.50	0.60	0.55	0.50
		No Oats	0.50	0.40	0.44	
	Walnut	Walnut	0.83	1.00	0.91	0.91
		No Walnut	1.00	0.83	0.91	
Gradient Boosting (GB)	Almond	Almond	1.00	1.00	1.00	1.00
		No Almond	1.00	1.00	1.00	
	Avocado	Avocado	0.75	1.00	0.86	0.81
		No Avocado	1.00	0.57	0.73	
	Barley	Barley	0.83	1.00	0.91	0.90
		No Barley	1.00	0.80	0.89	
	Broccoli	Broccoli	0.60	0.60	0.60	0.60
		No Broccoli	0.60	0.60	0.60	
	Oats	Oats	1.00	0.40	0.57	0.70
		No Oats	0.63	1.00	0.77	
	Walnut	Walnut	1.00	1.00	1.00	1.00
		No Walnut	1.00	1.00	1.00	
Extreme Gradient Boosting (XGB)	Almond	Almond	1.00	1.00	1.00	1.00
		No Almond	1.00	1.00	1.00	
	Avocado	Avocado	0.56	1.00	0.72	0.56
		No Avocado	0.00	0.00	0.00	
	Barley	Barley	0.67	0.80	0.73	0.70
		No Barley	0.75	0.60	0.67	
	Broccoli	Broccoli	0.67	0.40	0.50	0.60
		No Broccoli	0.57	0.80	0.67	
	Oats	Oats	0.50	0.40	0.44	0.50
		No Oats	0.50	0.60	0.55	
	Walnut	Walnut	1.00	1.00	1.00	1.00
		No Walnut	1.00	1.00	1.00	

In the RF model, the n_estimators parameter, which controls the number of trees in the forest, has been optimized across various values, with barley (3), broccoli (4), and multi-food (7) performing best at 100 trees, while almond (1) achieved optimal performance at 200 trees. The max_depth parameter, which limits tree depth, was typically set to 10 or 30 depending on the dataset, controlling model complexity and aiding in avoiding overfitting.

The max_features parameter, specifying the number of features considered at each split, was often optimized to 'sqrt,' although 'log2' was selected for broccoli. Parameters like min_samples_split and min_samples_leaf, which prevent overfitting by specifying minimum samples required to split a node or form a leaf, vary across datasets; for instance, broccoli (4) had min_samples_split set at 8, while almond (1) was set at 2.

Table 2. Optimization parameters for machine learning models

Technique	Parameter	Search Space	Optimized						
			1	2	3	4	5	6	7
RF	*n_estimators*	[50,100, 150,200]	200	50	100	100	50	50	100
	max_depth	[10,20,30]	30	10	10	30	30	10	10
	max_features	['auto', 'sqrt', 'og2']	sqrt	sqrt	sqrt	Log2	sqrt	sqrt	sqrt
	min_samples _split	[2,4,6,8]	2	6	6	8	4	8	8
	min_samples _leaf	[1,2,3,4,5]	5	4	4	3	5	1	2
SVM	*C*	[0.1, 1, 10, 100]	100	1	1	0.1	1	10	100
	gamma	[1, 0.1, 0.01, 0.001]	0.1	1	0.1	0.001	0.01	0.01	0.001
	kernel	['rbf', 'poly', 'sigmoid']	sigmoid	sigmoid	rbf	sigmoid	rbf	sigmoid	sigmoid
GB	*subsample*	[0.55,0.65, 0.7,0.75,1.0]	0.75	0.55	1.00	1.00	0.65	0.55	0.55
	n_estimators	[20,50, 100,150]	150	100	50	100	50	100	50
	learning_rate	[0.05, 0.075,0.1]	0.075	0.05	0.05	0.05	0.05	0.05	0.05
	max_depth	[5, 10, 20]	5	20	20	5	10	10	20
XGB	*subsample*	[0.55,0.65, 0.7,0.75,1.0]	1.00	0.75	0.55	0.75	0.55	0.55	0.70
	min_child _weight	[1,2,3,4,5]	1	1	1	1	1	1	1
	n_estimators	[20,50, 100,150]	20	20	50	100	150	20	50
	learning_rate	[0.1,0.2,0.3, 0.4,0.5]	0.1	0.3	0.3	0.3	0.5	0.2	0.1
	max_depth	[5,10,20]	5	20	5	5	5	5	5

For the SVM model, the regularization parameter C and gamma were optimized to control margin and decision boundary flexibility. For most datasets, C was set at 0.1 to 100. The gamma parameter, which influences the reach of each support vector, was typically set to 0.1 or 0.01 for most foods. The choice of kernel-a function that defines the transformation of data into higher dimensions-varied as well, with sigmoid used for most foods, while the rbf (radial basis function) kernel was selected for barley and oats.

In the GB model, the subsample parameter, which controls the fraction of data used for each boosting iteration, was optimized across different levels. Barley (3) and broccoli (4) showed optimal performance at a higher subsample rate of 1.0. The n_estimators parameter, representing the number of boosting rounds, was generally higher for single-food datasets (such as 150 for almond), while multi-food (7) achieved better results with fewer estimators (50). The learning_rate, which shrinks each tree's contribution, was often set at 0.05 or 0.075 for single-foods. The max_depth parameter, controlling tree complexity, was set to values (5, 10, or 20) across all foods.

For the XGB model, the subsample was optimized to values ranging from 0.55 to 1.0, with almond (1) performing best at full subsample (1.0), while multi-food (7) achieved optimal results at 0.7. The min_child_weight, which adds regularization by requiring a minimum sum of weights in child nodes, was generally set to 1 across all foods. The n_estimators and learning_rate were optimized with food using fewer estimators and a lower learning rate to prevent overfitting, whereas oats used higher values to enhance their predictive performance. Finally, the max_depth parameter was generally set low at 5 for all foods except for avocado (2).

4.2 Multi-food Machine Learning Classification Models

Table 3 represents the performance of four different ML classification models-RF, SVM, GB, and XGB-for multi-food classification, where samples from all plant-based foods (Almond, Avocado, Barley, Broccoli, Oats, and Walnut) were combined into a single dataset. The table shows precision, recall, F1-score, and accuracy for each food type across the different models. RF achieves an overall accuracy of 0.77. RF has lower precision, recall, and F1-score for barley (F1-score of 0.50) and oats (F1-score of 0.20). SVM achieves the highest overall accuracy of 0.86, making it the best performance in the multi-food classification. SVM shows perfect scores (1.00) across all metrics for almond, avocado, broccoli, and walnut. This shows that SVM can accurately classify these foods in the multi-food dataset. GB achieves an overall accuracy of 0.83, slightly lower than SVM but still competitive. GB also performs well for almond, avocado, broccoli, and walnut, achieving F1-scores of 1.00 for these classes, except for almond (0.91) and avocado (0.94). GB has difficulty classifying barley (F1-score of 0.62) and oats (F1-score of 0.29). XGB has the lowest overall accuracy of 0.74 among the four models, making it the least effective for multi-food classification. XGB achieves high F1-scores for almond (0.89), broccoli (1.00), and walnut (0.92), showing it can classify these foods reasonably well. XGB has lower performance for barley (F1-score of 0.36) and oats (F1-score of 0.22).

5 Discussion

5.1 Machine Learning Classification Models for Single-Food

Best model for single-food prediction is GB (Table 1). It achieves the best average accuracy across the six individual food datasets, making it the most reliable model for single-food classification. All models show variation in performance across different foods. Almond and walnut consistently yield high scores, while broccoli and avocado tend to have lower scores, indicating these foods may be harder to classify accurately.

Table 3. Multi-food machine learning classification.

Model	Plant-based food	Precision	Recall	F1-score	Accuracy
Random Forest (RF)	Almond	1.00	1.00	1.00	0.77
	Avocado	1.00	0.89	0.94	
	Barley	0.43	0.60	0.50	
	Broccoli	1.00	1.00	1.00	
	Oats	0.20	0.20	0.20	
	Walnut	1.00	0.83	0.91	
Support Vector Machine (SVM)	Almond	1.00	1.00	1.00	0.86
	Avocado	1.00	1.00	1.00	
	Barley	0.50	1.00	0.67	
	Broccoli	1.00	1.00	1.00	
	Oats	0.00	0.00	0.00	
	Walnut	1.00	1.00	1.00	
Gradient Boosting (GB)	Almond	0.83	1.00	0.91	0.83
	Avocado	1.00	0.89	0.94	
	Barley	0.50	0.80	0.62	
	Broccoli	1.00	1.00	1.00	
	Oats	0.50	0.20	0.29	
	Walnut	1.00	1.00	1.00	
Extreme Gradient Boosting (XGB)	Almond	1.00	0.80	0.89	0.74
	Avocado	0.89	0.89	0.89	
	Barley	0.33	0.40	0.36	
	Broccoli	1.00	1.00	1.00	
	Oats	0.25	0.20	0.22	
	Walnut	0.86	1.00	0.92	

GB generally outperforms the other models for single-food classification, while SVM has been noted to perform best when all six foods are combined in a multi-food dataset. The low classification performance was observed in the case of oat samples. This is likely due to the similarity in the fecal metabolite profiles between group 1 (those consuming a regular diet) and group 2 (those consuming a regular diet supplemented with oats). The number and quantity of features in the metabolite profiles of these two groups were closely comparable, making it challenging for the ML models to accurately distinguish between them. Consequently, this led to reduced accuracy in the classification results.

Table 2 demonstrates that optimal model performance in classifying different plant-based foods depends heavily on fine-tuned parameter settings for each ML model. RF, SVM, GB, and XGB models each required unique parameter adjustments tailored to specific datasets-ranging from individual foods and a combined multi-food dataset. The parameter settings were applied to the fecal metabolite profiles, and the optimized parameter settings most suitable for the data and the ML models were identified. By utilizing these optimized settings, the models achieved the highest possible accuracy. This customized tuning reflects the diverse nature of the data for each food type, as different foods exhibit varying metabolite features, requiring specific configurations to achieve the best predictive accuracy.

5.2 Machine Learning Classification Models for Multi-food

SVM is the best Model for Multi-Food Classification. SVM achieves the highest overall accuracy (0.86), making it the most reliable model for classifying multiple plant-based foods in a single dataset. All models show consistent difficulty in classifying Oats and Barley, suggesting that the features of these foods might be less distinct in the metabolite data, leading to lower classification performance. While SVM performs the best overall, GB and RF are also effective, with RF showing particularly strong classification for certain foods like broccoli and almond. Other models may be useful depending on specific food categories. However, Oats and Barley remain challenging to classify accurately across all models.

6 Conclusion

ML models were evaluated for classifying plant-based foods based on fecal metabolite data. GB is recommended for single-food classification, while SVM is preferred for multi-food classification. However, further work is needed to improve classification accuracy for Oats and Barley, as these foods remain challenging across all models, and could investigate use of deep learning methods to obtain more detailed insights from the data and improve model accuracy.

Acknowledgments. We would like to extend their sincere gratitude to Shinn et al.(2022) for making the data publicly available, which was essential for the completion of this study. Special thanks are also due to faculty of computer sciences, Thammasat University and International Joint Research Center On Food Security (IJC-FOODSEC) which contributed to the success of this work, for their support, including providing the necessary equipment, funding, and research facilities that made this work possible.

Disclosure of Interests. The authors have no competing interests to declare that are relevant to the content of this article.

References

1. Almeida, C.C., Mendonça Pereira, B.F., Leandro, K.C., Costa, M.P., Spisso, B.F., Conte-Junior, C.A.: Bioactive compounds in infant formula and their effects on infant nutrition and health: a systematic literature review. Int. J. Food Sci. **2021**(1), 8850080 (2021)
2. Baer, D.J., Gebauer, S.K., Novotny, J.A.: Walnuts consumed by healthy adults provide less available energy than predicted by the atwater factors. J. Nutr. **146**(1), 9–13 (2016)
3. Bifarin, O.O.: Interpretable machine learning with tree-based shapley additive explanations: application to metabolomics datasets for binary classification. PLoS ONE **18**(5), e0284315 (2023)
4. Bishop, C.M., Nasrabadi, N.M.: Pattern recognition and machine learning, vol. 4. Springer (2006)
5. Braundmeier-Fleming, A., et al.: Stool-based biomarkers of interstitial cystitis/bladder pain syndrome. Sci. Rep. **6**(1), 26083 (2016)
6. Breiman, L.: Random forests. Mach. Learn. **45**, 5–32 (2001)
7. Chen, T., Guestrin, C.: Xgboost: a scalable tree boosting system. In: Proceedings of the 22nd ACM SIGKDD International Conference on Knowledge Discovery and Data Mining, pp. 785–794 (2016)
8. Chungnoy, K., Songmuang, P.: Missing values imputation framework for mixed datasets. In: 2023 IEEE International Conference on Cybernetics and Innovations (ICCI), pp. 1–5. IEEE (2023)
9. Chungnoy, K., Tanantong, T., Songmuang, P.: Bee-inspired knowledge transfer: synthesizing data for enhanced deep learning explainability. Indonesian J. Electr. Eng. Comput. Sci. **36**(2), 1052–1069 (2024)
10. Chungnoy, K., Tanantong, T., Songmuang, P.: Missing value imputation on gene expression data using bee-based algorithm to improve classification performance. PLoS ONE **19**(8), e0305492 (2024)
11. De Filippis, F., et al.: High-level adherence to a mediterranean diet beneficially impacts the gut microbiota and associated metabolome. Gut **65**(11), 1812–1821 (2016)

12. Edwards, C.G., et al.: Effects of 12-week avocado consumption on cognitive function among adults with overweight and obesity. Int. J. Psychophysiol. **148**, 13–24 (2020)
13. Evgeniou, T., Pontil, M.: Support vector machines: Theory and applications. In: Advanced Course on Artificial Intelligence, pp. 249–257. Springer (1999)
14. Galal, A., Talal, M., Moustafa, A.: Applications of machine learning in metabolomics: disease modeling and classification. Front. Genet. **13**, 1017340 (2022)
15. Ghosh, T., Sazonov, E.: A comparative study of deep learning algorithms for detecting food intake. In: 2022 44th Annual International Conference of the IEEE Engineering in Medicine & Biology Society (EMBC), pp. 2993–2996. IEEE (2022)
16. Holmes, E., Wilson, I.D., Nicholson, J.K.: Metabolic phenotyping in health and disease. Cell **134**(5), 714–717 (2008)
17. Johnson, C.H., Ivanisevic, J., Siuzdak, G.: Metabolomics: beyond biomarkers and towards mechanisms. Nat. Rev. Mol. Cell Biol. **17**(7), 451–459 (2016)
18. JoMay, C., Danny, A., et al.: Fecal metabolomics of healthy breast-fed versus formula-fed infants before and during in vitro batch culture fermentation (2014)
19. Lhasiw, N., Tanantong, T., Sanglerdsinlapachai, N.: Thai conversational chatbot classification using bilstm and data augmentation. In: International Conference on Data Science and Artificial Intelligence, pp. 127–141. Springer (2023). https://doi.org/10.1007/978-981-99-7969-1_10
20. McEvoy, C.T., Temple, N., Woodside, J.V.: Vegetarian diets, low-meat diets and health: a review. Public Health Nutr. **15**(12), 2287–2294 (2012)
21. Natekin, A., Knoll, A.: Gradient boosting machines, a tutorial. Front. Neurorobot. **7**, 21 (2013)
22. Novotny, J.A., Gebauer, S.K., Baer, D.J.: Discrepancy between the atwater factor predicted and empirically measured energy values of almonds in human diets. Am. J. Clin. Nutr. **96**(2), 296–301 (2012)
23. Oliveira Chaves, L., et al.: Applicability of machine learning techniques in food intake assessment: a systematic review. Crit. Rev. Food Sci. Nutr. **63**(7), 902–919 (2023)
24. Robinson, S., Fall, C.: Infant nutrition and later health: a review of current evidence. Nutrients **4**(8), 859–874 (2012)
25. Rodriguez-Herrera, A., et al.: Early-life fecal microbiome and metabolome dynamics in response to an intervention with infant formula containing specific prebiotics and postbiotics. Am. J. Physiol.-Gastrointestinal Liver Physiol. **322**(6), G571–G582 (2022)
26. Shinn, L.M., et al.: Fecal metabolites as biomarkers for predicting food intake by healthy adults. J. Nutr. **152**(12), 2956–2965 (2022)
27. Shinn, L.M., et al.: Fecal metagenomics to identify biomarkers of food intake in healthy adults: findings from randomized, controlled, nutrition trials. J. Nutr. **154**(1), 271–283 (2024)
28. Songmuang, P., Ueno, M.: Bees algorithm for construction of multiple test forms in e-testing. IEEE Trans. Learn. Technol. **4**(3), 209–221 (2010)

29. Tanantong, T., Parnkow, M.: A survey of automatic text classification based on thai social media data (2022)
30. Thompson, S.V., et al.: Avocado consumption alters gastrointestinal bacteria abundance and microbial metabolite concentrations among adults with overweight or obesity: a randomized controlled trial. J. Nutr. **151**(4), 753–762 (2021)
31. Thompson, S.V., Swanson, K.S., Novotny, J.A., Baer, D.J., Holscher, H.D.: Gastrointestinal microbial changes following whole grain barley and oat consumption in healthy men and women. FASEB J. **30**, 1–406 (2016)
32. Tilman, D., Clark, M.: Global diets link environmental sustainability and human health. Nature **515**(7528), 518–522 (2014)
33. Uypatchawong, S., Chanamarn, N.: Enhancing surface water quality prediction efficiency in northeastern Thailand using machine learning. Indonesian J. Electr. Eng. Comput. Sci. **36**(2), 1189–1198 (2024)

Dynamic Threshold for Image Retrieval

Varintorn Sithisint[1], Awirut Phuseansaart[1], Jittapat Chanyarungroj[1], Thittaporn Ganokratanaa[1], and Mahasak Ketcham[2(✉)]

[1] King Mongkut's University of Technology Thonburi, Bangkok 10140, Thailand
thittaporn.gan@kmutt.ac.th

[2] King Mongkut's University of Technology North Bangkok, Bangkok 10800, Thailand
maoquee@hotmail.com

Abstract. Content-based image retrieval (CBIR) with a static threshold often encounters limitations due to the varying characteristics of queries in different image galleries. In this paper, we propose an approach to address this challenge by introducing dynamic threshold determination for image retrieval. Our method dynamically adjusts the threshold for each gallery based on the distribution of galleries close to that gallery in feature space. By tailoring the threshold to the specific characteristics of each gallery, our approach aims to enhance retrieval accuracy and relevance. We evaluate our method using the ROxford dataset and compare it with the best static threshold. Our approach yields significant enhancements in macro F1 scores across diverse dataset complexities. In the ROxford (medium) scenario, we observed an 12.4% improvement over the static threshold baseline, while in the ROxford (hard) setting, we achieved a 6.41% enhancement. The LogoSearch dataset achieved a 2.72% enhancement.

Keywords: Image retrieval · Computer Vision · Artificial intelligence

1 Introduction

Content-based image retrieval (CBIR) [1–3] plays a crucial role in numerous applications, ranging from image search engines to e-commerce and medical imaging. The ability to retrieve relevant images based on their visual content is essential for tasks requiring efficient access to large image databases. Traditional CBIR systems typically rely on static thresholds to determine image similarity, which can pose significant challenges in adapting to the diverse characteristics of query images and image galleries. such as changes in pose or scale for objects in the same category, may confuse systems relying on static thresholds.

The limitations of static thresholding methods have motivated the exploration of alternative approaches to enhance CBIR performance. In this paper, we propose a novel approach to address these challenges by introducing dynamic

T. Ganokratanaa—Lecturer at King Mongkut's University of Technology Thonburi.

J. Kertesz et al. (Eds.): CSoNet 2024, LNCS 15417, pp. 446–454, 2025.
https://doi.org/10.1007/978-981-96-6389-7_41

threshold determination for image retrieval. Unlike static thresholds, which apply a uniform threshold for all queries, our method dynamically adjusts the threshold for each gallery based on the distribution of queries that are close to that particular gallery in feature space.

The key motivation behind our approach is to improve retrieval accuracy and relevance by tailoring the threshold to the specific characteristics of each gallery and its proximal queries. By considering the distribution of galleries within each gallery, our method aims to better capture the nuances of image similarity, leading to more accurate retrieval results.

To evaluate the effectiveness of our proposed approach, we conducted experiments using the Oxford5k dataset [4] and LogoSearch dataset, a widely used benchmark dataset for CBIR research. We compare the performance of our method with that of the best static thresholding approach, focusing on metrics such as macro F1 scores to assess retrieval accuracy.

2 Related Works

Image retrieval is the task of retrieving visually similar images from a database based on a query image. It has been an active area of research with various approaches proposed to improve retrieval performance. Lin Song *et al.* [5] propose a privacy-preserving threshold-based image retrieval scheme using the convolutional neural network (CNN) model and a secure k-nearest neighbor (kNN) algorithm. The threshold is determined by the user during the query process. Sunitha *et al.* [6] introduces an efficient Content-Based Satellite Image Retrieval (CBSIR) system for large datasets, employing a Threshold-centered Checking (TC) method. The system aims to bridge the "semantic gap" between low-level image features and high-level user concepts, enhancing retrieval accuracy. They utilize predefined, static thresholds to evaluate the relevance of retrieved images. And local feature descriptors (e.g., SIFT [7], SURF [8]) have been widely used for feature extraction. Similarity measures like Euclidean distance or cosine similarity are then employed to rank images based on their similarity to the query.

CLIP model [9] leverages a transformer architecture trained on a large-scale dataset of image-text pairs, enabling it to learn rich semantic representations of both images and corresponding textual descriptions. This capability empowers CBIR systems to perform image retrieval based on semantic similarity, facilitating more meaningful and contextually relevant search results.

FAISS [10], which stands for "Facebook AI Similarity Search," is a library developed by Facebook AI Research for efficient similarity search and clustering of high-dimensional vectors. It is designed to handle large-scale datasets and provides fast, memory-efficient algorithms for nearest neighbor search, similarity search, and clustering tasks. In the context of our research paper, we utilize FAISS to compute distances between feature vectors encoded by the CLIP model. By leveraging FAISS for similarity search in the latent space generated by CLIP, we can efficiently identify images that are most like a given query image, facilitating content-based image retrieval with improved speed and scalability.

Static thresholding methods rely on predetermined threshold values to classify gallery images, irrespective of the variability in query characteristics across different image datasets. This inflexible approach often leads to suboptimal retrieval performance, particularly when faced with diverse query scenarios and image galleries with varying content distributions.

Adaptive thresholding [11] is a powerful technique in image processing, particularly for binarization and segmentation. Unlike conventional thresholding, which applies a static, global threshold across an image, adaptive thresholding dynamically adjusts the threshold value for different regions based on local characteristics such as contrast, texture, and illumination. This adaptability is crucial for handling images with non-uniform lighting or complex patterns, allowing for more accurate segmentation and feature extraction.

However, in the domain of image retrieval, static thresholding methods are often employed, which fail to account for the varying characteristics of query and gallery images. This limitation can result in suboptimal retrieval performance, especially in diverse datasets. To address this, the paper proposes a novel approach that adjusts the threshold for each gallery dynamically, based on the distribution of queries that are proximal to the gallery in the feature space.

3 Methods

3.1 Feature Extraction and Encoding

We employ a CLIP encoder to extract features from both query and gallery images as illustrated in Fig. 1, mapping them into a latent space of size 1024. These encoded representations serve as the basis for subsequent distance calculations.

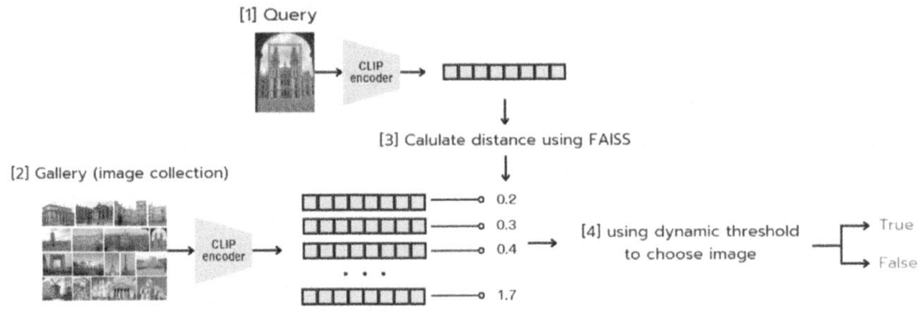

Fig. 1. Our Image Retrieval Framework

3.2 Distance Calculation

Once we obtain the latent space representations of both query and gallery images, we employ the FAISS library to compute the distances between these latent vectors. A smaller distance indicates a higher degree of similarity between the images in the feature space. Therefore, by measuring distances using FAISS, we can effectively quantify the similarity between query and gallery images, facilitating accurate content-based image retrieval.

3.3 Static Threshold Comparison

Traditionally, image retrieval systems have relied on static thresholds to classify gallery images, determining whether they match a given query or not. However, the efficacy of this method is hindered by the diverse characteristics of queries across different image galleries, leading to suboptimal performance. we employ a grid search technique within the static threshold framework to determine the most suitable threshold for each training dataset. This allows us to compare the performance of static thresholds against our dynamic thresholding method effectively.

3.4 Dynamic Threshold Determination

To address the limitations of static thresholds, our approach introduces dynamic threshold determination for image retrieval. This entails adjusting the threshold for each gallery dynamically, based on the distribution of queries that closely align with that specific gallery in feature space.

3.4.1 Calculation of Mean Distance

Initially, as illustrated in Fig. 2, for each gallery image, we compute the mean distance to its top n most similar images within the same gallery. This process is repeated for varying values of n, such as 10, 30, and 50. Subsequently, we calculate the global mean (M), representing the average distance in mean distance of each gallery ($\overline{x}$).

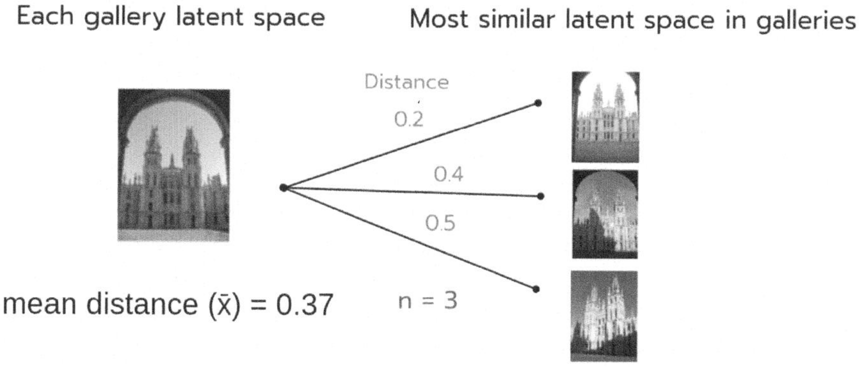

Fig. 2. Calculation of Mean Distance

3.4.2 Dynamic Threshold Computation

The dynamic threshold (Dt) for each gallery is then determined as the difference between the mean distance of the gallery ($\overline{x}$) and the global mean (M). This calculation effectively captures the distribution of distances within each gallery.

$$D_t = \overline{x} - M \tag{1}$$

where:

- D_t is the dynamic threshold specific to each gallery.
- $\overline{x}$ is the mean distance of each gallery.
- M is the global mean.

3.4.3 Dynamic Threshold Computation

Finally, we adjust the threshold for each gallery using the formula:

$$t_{\text{new}} = t_{\text{static}} + D_t w \tag{2}$$

where:

- t_{new} is the new threshold.
- t_{static} is the static threshold.
- D_t is the dynamic threshold specific to the gallery.
- w is a weight parameter.

In determining the optimal value for the weight parameter (w), we conduct a grid search across the dataset used in our experiments. This exhaustive search method allows us to systematically explore various combinations of w values and evaluate their performance in the context of our retrieval task.

By iteratively updating the thresholds based on the distribution of distances within each gallery, our approach aims to enhance the accuracy and relevance of content-based image retrieval, guided by the optimal weight parameter determined through grid search.

4 Experiments

We evaluate the efficacy of our proposed method using the ROxford and LogoSearch datasets, comparing its performance against the conventional static threshold approach. The experiments focus on macro F1 scores, a widely-used metric that balances precision and recall in multi-class classification tasks, demonstrating the potential of our dynamic thresholding method to enhance content-based image retrieval (CBIR) performance.

Initially, we establish a baseline using the CLIP encoder and FAISS as our base model. We evaluate both the best static threshold and our dynamic threshold method. To determine the optimal static threshold, we perform a grid search across the datasets. Subsequently, we incorporate this optimal static threshold

(T_{static}) into our dynamic threshold formula, conducting another grid search to identify the optimal weight (w) and dynamic threshold (D_t). This iterative refinement ensures the parameters chosen yield the most effective retrieval outcomes.

4.1 Dynamic Threshold vs. Static Threshold

Our experiments reveal that incorporating a weight into the dynamic threshold formula results in a range of weights that outperform the static threshold in terms of macro F1 scores. For example, as shown in Fig. 3a, in the ROxford (MEDIUM) and ROxford (HARD) dataset, macro F1 scores improve significantly as the weight is optimized.

On the ROxford dataset:

- In the **medium** setting, the dynamic thresholding method elevates the macro F1 score from 0.302 to 0.3394, representing an 12.4% improvement over the static threshold baseline.
- In the **hard** setting, it boosts the macro F1 score from 0.2620 to 0.2788, indicating a 6.4% improvement.

These results highlight the dynamic thresholding method's capacity to adapt to varying dataset complexities and deliver enhanced performance compared to static thresholding.

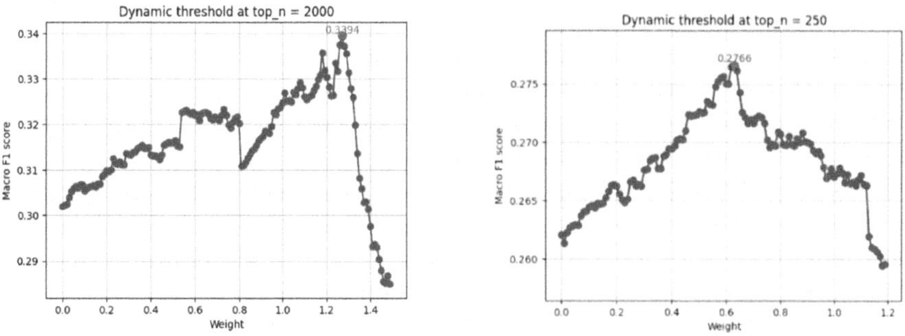

(a) Macro F1 scores for ROxford (MEDIUM). The optimal performance ($w = 1.27$) achieves a macro F1 score of 0.3394.

(b) Macro F1 scores for ROxford (HARD). The optimal performance ($w = 0.62$) achieves a macro F1 score of 0.2766.

Fig. 3. Varying weight in Dynamic Threshold effect macro F1 scores for ROxford (HARD) and ROxford (MEDIUM)

4.2 Experimental Results

To validate the effectiveness of our proposed dynamic thresholding method, we conducted extensive experiments on two datasets: ROxford [4] and LogoSearch. These datasets are widely recognized in content-based image retrieval (CBIR) research due to their varying levels of complexity and real-world applicability.

The **ROxford** dataset [4] consists of images depicting urban landmarks and is divided into three levels of difficulty: easy, medium, and hard. We focused on the medium and hard difficulty levels, where the distinction between relevant and irrelevant images is less obvious, providing a rigorous test for our dynamic thresholding approach.

The **LogoSearch** dataset is a private dataset used in one of the competitions in *Super AI Engineer Season 3*. It presents an image search challenge where the goal is to retrieve images similar to a query image while minimizing the retrieval of irrelevant images. This dataset adds diversity to our evaluation and demonstrates the applicability of our method to different types of image retrieval tasks.

In these experiments, we compared the performance of our dynamic thresholding method against a static threshold baseline using the macro F1 score as the primary evaluation metric. The macro F1 score measures the balance between precision and recall across multiple classes, making it well-suited for assessing retrieval performance in diverse datasets.

Table 1 summarizes the results across the datasets. Our dynamic thresholding method consistently outperformed the static threshold baseline:

- **ROxford (MEDIUM):** The static threshold achieved a macro F1 score of 0.302. By incorporating our dynamic thresholding method, the score improved to 0.3394, representing a 12.4% enhancement. This improvement highlights the ability of our method to adapt to the feature distribution of each query, leading to more accurate retrieval results.
- **ROxford (HARD):** In this more challenging scenario, the static threshold resulted in a macro F1 score of 0.2620. Our dynamic thresholding approach elevated the score to 0.2788, corresponding to a 6.4% improvement. This demonstrates the robustness of our method in handling complex retrieval tasks where distinguishing relevant images is more difficult.
- **LogoSearch:** The static threshold achieved an impressive macro F1 score of 0.9488 on this dataset. However, our dynamic thresholding method further improved the score to 0.9746, corresponding to a 2.72% increase. Despite the already high baseline performance, our method was able to enhance retrieval accuracy, demonstrating its effectiveness even on datasets with high initial performance.

Table 1. Comparison of results on the ROxford and LogoSearch datasets.

Dataset	Macro F1 Score		Parameters
	Static Threshold	Dynamic Threshold	
ROxford (MEDIUM)	0.302	**0.3394 (12.4% ↑)**	top_n=1000, w=0.93
ROxford (HARD)	0.2620	**0.2788 (6.4% ↑)**	top_n=250, w=0.63
LogoSearch	0.9488	**0.9746 (2.72% ↑)**	top_n=1000, w=1.53

5 Conclusions

In this study, we addressed the limitations of content-based image retrieval (CBIR) systems utilizing static thresholds by proposing a dynamic threshold determination approach. Our method dynamically adjusts the threshold for each gallery based on the distribution of galleries in feature space, thereby tailoring retrieval parameters to the specific characteristics of each image collection. Through experimentation on the ROxford dataset, we compared the performance of our dynamic thresholding approach with the best static threshold, utilizing metrics such as macro F1 score to evaluate CBIR performance.

The results of our evaluation demonstrate the efficacy of the proposed dynamic thresholding method in enhancing CBIR performance. Specifically, our approach yielded significant improvements in macro F1 scores across diverse dataset complexities. In the ROxford (medium) scenario, we observed an 12.4% enhancement over the static threshold baseline, while in the ROxford (hard) setting, we achieved a 6.41% improvement. The LogoSearch dataset achieved a 2.72% enhancement.

These findings highlight the potential of dynamic threshold determination for addressing the challenges associated with static thresholding in CBIR systems. This dynamic threshold can be applied not only to the CLIP model but also to many other models that transform images into latent space or spatial space.

Acknowledgements. This work is supported by the Department of Mathematics, King Mongkut's University of Technology Thonburi

References

1. Kaushik, M., Sharma, R., Vidhyarthi, A.: Analysis of spatial features in cbir system. Inter. J. Comput. Appli. **54**(17), 11–15 (2012)
2. Smeulders, A., Worring, M., Santini, S., Gupta, A., Jain, R.: Content-based image retrieval at the end of the early years. IEEE Trans. Pattern Anal. Mach. Intell. **22**(12), 1349–1380 (2000)
3. Jain, S., Zaveri, T., Prajapati, K., Patel, S.: Deep learning feature map for content-based image retrieval system for remote sensing application. Inter. J. Image Mining **2**(1), 1 (2016)

4. Radenovic, F., Iscen, A., Tolias, G., Avrithis, Y., Chum, O.: Revisiting oxford and paris: large-scale image retrieval benchmarking. In: Proceedings of the IEEE Conference on Computer Vision and Pattern Recognition (CVPR) (2018)
5. Song, L., Miao, Y., Weng, J., Choo, K.-K.R., Liu, X., Deng, R.H.: Privacy-preserving threshold-based image retrieval in cloud-assisted internet of things. IEEE Internet Things J. **9**, 13598–13611 (2022)
6. Thenmozhi, S., Thamarai Selvi, S.: An efficient content-based satellite image retrieval system for big data utilizing threshold-based checking method. Earth Sci. Inform. **14**, 1847–1859 (2021)
7. Lowe, D.G.: Distinctive image features from scale-invariant keypoints. Int. J. Comput. Vision **50**(2), 91–110 (2004)
8. Bay, H., Tuytelaars, T., Van Gool, L.: SURF: speeded up robust features. In: Leonardis, A., Bischof, H., Pinz, A. (eds.) ECCV 2006. LNCS, vol. 3951, pp. 404–417. Springer, Heidelberg (2006). https://doi.org/10.1007/11744023_32
9. A. Radford, et al.: Learning transferable visual models from natural language supervision, arXiv preprint, arXiv: 2103.00020 (2021)
10. Johnson, J., Douze, M., Jégou, H.: Billion-scale similarity search with gpus. IEEE Trans. Big Data **7**(3), 535–547 (2019)
11. Roy, P., Dutta, S., Dey, N., Dey, G., Chakraborty, S., Ray, R.: Adaptive thresholding: a comparative study. In: 2014 International Conference on Control, Instrumentation, Communication and Computational Technologies (ICCICCT), pp. 1182–1186 (2014)

Evaluating Salary Prediction Models for Graduates Using Dimensionality Reduction and Machine Learning Techniques

Surasit Uypatchawong, Kritanat Chungnoy, and Pokpong Songmuang(✉)

Faculty of Science and Technology, Thammasat University, Bangkok, Thailand
surasit.uyp@dome.tu.ac.th, kittanutc@gmail.com

Abstract. This research investigates the effectiveness of predicting future salaries for graduates using academic performance data from Sakon Nakhon Rajabhat University. The study applies five machine learning models-Decision Tree Regression, Random Forest Regression, Support Vector Regression (SVR), K-Nearest Regression, and Gradient Boosting Regression-on datasets both with and without dimensionality reduction. Principal Component Analysis (PCA) and Feature Selection were used as dimensionality reduction methods to streamline the dataset. However, the results indicate that dimensionality reduction did not improve prediction accuracy; in fact, the original dataset without dimensionality reduction yielded the lowest Root Mean Square Error (RMSE) across all models, with GBR achieving the best result at 1856.59. This finding suggests that dimensionality reduction may lead to a loss of crucial information, especially in datasets containing diverse academic records and course enrollment requirements. Consequently, future research should explore grouping similar data to increase predictive accuracy and applying multi-prediction models to each group. This approach may help retain important features and improve the effectiveness of salary predictions for graduate students.

Keywords: Salary Prediction · Dimensionality Reduction · Machine Learning

1 Introduction

Predicting the salary of graduates has become an important and widely discussed topic in recent years, especially in societies where rapid changes in the economy and labor markets are occurring. Predicting post-graduation income can provide valuable information to educational institutions, students, and related organizations. For instance, educational institutions can use this information to improve their courses and teaching methods to increase employment opportunities and develop skills that meet labor market needs. Additionally, students can use this

J. Kertesz et al. (Eds.): CSoNet 2024, LNCS 15417, pp. 455–465, 2025.
https://doi.org/10.1007/978-981-96-6389-7_42

information to plan their careers and make informed decisions about further studies. This research focuses on predicting the salary of graduates from Sakon Nakhon Rajabhat University, a university that plays a vital role in the local community.

Many studies have shown that using Machine Learning techniques to predict employee salaries can yield effective results. For example, Das et al. [3] applied Linear Regression and Polynomial Regression techniques to predict employee salaries, and their data showed that Polynomial Regression was particularly effective at capturing nonlinear relationships in the data, leading to more accurate predictions. Similarly, Ayua et al. [1] used Polynomial Regression to develop a salary prediction system for employees, incorporating exchange rate data as a significant variable in the predictions, which improved the model's performance for nonlinear data.

Matbouli and Alghamdi [8] presented a framework for salary prediction across different occupational groups using various types of Machine Learning models, including Gaussian Process Regression and Artificial Neural Networks, to estimate annual salaries based on economic activities and major job roles. Their findings showed that the Gaussian Process Regression model reduced errors by over 80% compared to Multiple Linear Regression.

This study uses data from Sakon Nakhon Rajabhat University over the period 2018–2022, with a total of 11,305 records and 4,074 attributes, covering various factors that influence salary, such as academic performance, personal characteristics, and economic factors. The research employs five Machine Learning techniques: Decision Tree Regression, Random Forest Regression, Support Vector Regression, K-Neighbors Regression, and Gradient Boosting Regression. The goal is to identify the most effective method for predicting salary, providing insights that reflect the earning potential of graduates.

The structure of this paper is divided into four main sections: The Literature Review, which discusses related works on using Machine Learning to predict graduates' income and evaluates the effectiveness of each selected method; the Proposed Method section, which describes the steps of applying each of the five techniques to predict and analyze data to choose the most suitable method; the Result section, which presents experimental findings and compares the performance of each method; and finally, the Conclusion, which summarizes the research findings, key insights, and future directions.

2 Literature Review

Salary prediction has gained considerable attention in recent years due to its impact on employee motivation, job satisfaction, and career planning. Research in this area has integrated various machine learning (ML) and statistical techniques to predict salaries across industries and occupations. Studies have examined personality traits [5], emotional intelligence (EI) [6], and machine learning models as key factors influencing salary prediction.

Personality traits have long been linked to career outcomes, with traits from the Big Five model, such as Extraversion and Conscientiousness, often correlating positively with higher salaries [2,13]. Emotional intelligence plays an essential role by enhancing the predictive power of personality traits. De Haro, Castejon, and Gilar's study in 2020 demonstrated that dimensions of EI, particularly clarity and repair, partially mediate the effect of traits like Neuroticism and Extraversion on early-career salary, suggesting that EI may be a valuable addition to personality-based salary models [4].

In addition to individual factors, organizational characteristics and economic activities significantly influence salary outcomes. Matbouli and Alghamdi (2022) proposed a predictive framework that incorporates economic activities and organization size as variables. Using supervised ML models like Bayesian Gaussian Process Regression (GPR) [10,11] and artificial neural networks (ANN) [9,12,14], their model accurately predicted salaries across various sectors in Saudi Arabia. This framework shows that ANN and GPR models provide significant accuracy improvements over traditional multiple linear regression (MLR) by considering organizational characteristics such as industry type [8].

Machine learning techniques have proven highly effective in salary prediction, often surpassing traditional statistical methods. Recent studies have compared models like linear regression, random forest, and neural networks to determine their effectiveness. Kablaoui and Salman (2022) applied these models to a large dataset, revealing that neural networks outperform both linear regression and random forest in prediction accuracy, though linear regression was faster in training time. This finding suggests that choosing a model for salary prediction may involve balancing accuracy and computational efficiency depending on the data and use case [7].

Another model for salary prediction, developed by Ayua, Malgwi, and Afrifa (2023), focuses on non-academic staff in Nigerian universities, integrating the exchange rate (XR) as an economic indicator. Using a polynomial regression (PR) model, they achieved a 97.2% accuracy rate, showing how XR fluctuations affect salary predictions. This approach demonstrates PR's ability to handle non-linear relationships and highlights the importance of external economic factors in salary prediction models [1]. Additionally, Das et al. (2021) explored using linear and polynomial regression to model past salary data and predict future salary growth. Polynomial regression, in particular, offers a valuable tool for modeling nonlinear salary trends over time [3].

Across the literature, advanced ML techniques frequently demonstrate improved accuracy in salary prediction. While multiple regression models are commonly used, more sophisticated techniques like random forests, support vector machines (SVM) [14], and neural networks can capture complex, nonlinear relationships in large datasets. Studies comparing multiple models have found that models such as SVM often achieve higher accuracy than traditional regression techniques, especially in diverse datasets. Despite this, simpler linear models remain useful as a baseline for model comparisons, as seen in Matbouli and

Alghamdi's research, where linear regression served as a benchmark for evaluating improvements offered by more complex models [7,8].

In conclusion, an integrated approach combining personality traits, EI, economic factors, and machine learning models creates a robust framework for salary prediction. By accounting for both intrinsic (e.g., personality, EI) and extrinsic (e.g., economic conditions, organizational characteristics) factors, predictive models can provide valuable insights for employers and employees alike. Future research may continue to refine these models by incorporating additional factors, further enhancing the accuracy and applicability of salary prediction.

3 Proposed Method

This study presents a machine learning pipeline for predicting salaries using educational and employment data of students. The process begins by merging these two data sources to form a complete dataset, which then undergoes several preprocessing steps, including the removal of outliers, handling of missing values, dimensionality reduction through Principal Component Analysis (PCA), and feature selection to retain relevant predictors. An exploratory data analysis (EDA) is performed to gain insights into the data, involving statistical analysis and visualization to understand underlying patterns. The modeling phase tests several regression algorithms-Decision Tree Regression, Random Forest Regression, Support Vector Regression, K-Nearest Neighbors Regression, and Gradient Boosting Regression-to identify the most effective model for salary prediction. Finally, model performance is evaluated using Mean Square Error (MSE) and Root Mean Square Error (RMSE) to measure accuracy, providing a comprehensive approach to understanding the relationship between educational and employment factors and their impact on salary predictions (see Fig. 1).

3.1 Dataset

The dataset used in this research comes from two main sources: the educational dataset and the student employment status dataset. The educational dataset includes information on students' academic performance in each registered course, along with the grades received. This dataset contains 12 attributes and a total of 547,279 instances. The student employment status dataset, on the other hand, is compiled by the university one year after students graduate. It includes details on the occupation and salary of each graduate at that time, with 41 attributes and a total of 11,305 instances. All data were collected from Sakon Nakhon Rajabhat University from 2018 to 2022, covering both academic information and post-graduation employment status.

For this experiment, it was necessary to transform the educational dataset and merge it with the student employment status dataset to make it suitable for analysis. We combined the two datasets and conducted data transformation and data preprocessing to obtain a more complete dataset that clearly reflects factors influencing graduate income. A sample of the dataset is shown in Fig. 2, and the

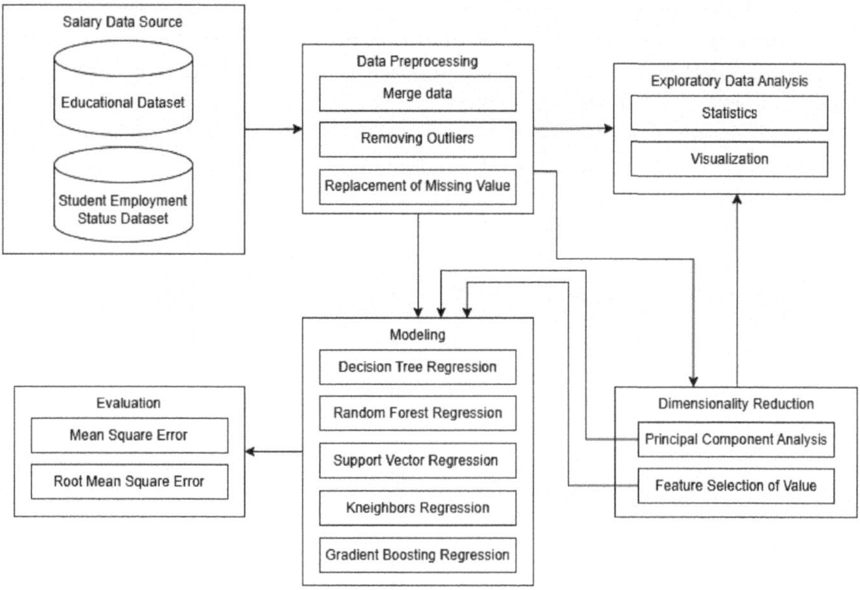

Fig. 1. Working diagram of the proposed method

steps of merging and preparing the data are further explained in Sect. 3.2, Data Preprocessing.

	OLDID	PROG	LEV_NAME	COURSE_ID	NAME_T	SECTION	GNAME	TERM	DESCRIP	STD_TYPE_NAME	GPA	CREDIT
0	521192251	วิทยาศาสตร์	ค.บ. 5 ปี	01550101	ภาษาอังกฤษเพื่อการสื่อสาร	M	C	1/52	ฝึกทักษะเพื่อพัฒนาการฟังและการพูดภาษาอังกฤษที่...	ป.ตรี ภาคปกติ	2.43	3
1	521192251	วิทยาศาสตร์	ค.บ. 5 ปี	04000102	คอมพิวเตอร์สารสนเทศขั้นพื้นฐาน	M	C+	1/52	ความรู้เบื้องต้นเกี่ยวกับคอมพิวเตอร์และเทคโนโลย...	ป.ตรี ภาคปกติ	2.43	3
2	521192251	วิทยาศาสตร์	ค.บ. 5 ปี	24011101	ฟิสิกส์ทั่วไป 1	B	F	1/52	การวัดและความแม่นยำในการวัด ปริมาณสเกลาร์และเ...	ป.ตรี ภาคปกติ	2.43	3
3	521192251	วิทยาศาสตร์	ค.บ. 5 ปี	24011301	ปฏิบัติการฟิสิกส์ทั่วไป 1	B	D+	1/52	ปฏิบัติการเกี่ยวกับเทคนิคเบื้องต้นและหลักปฏิบั...	ป.ตรี ภาคปกติ	2.43	1
4	521192251	วิทยาศาสตร์	ค.บ. 5 ปี	24021101	เคมีทั่วไป 1	B	C	1/52	หลักการพื้นฐานทางเคมี ทฤษฎีพื้นฐานทางเคมี หลั...	ป.ตรี ภาคปกติ	2.43	3
5	521192251	วิทยาศาสตร์	ค.บ. 5 ปี	24021301	ปฏิบัติการเคมีทั่วไป 1	B	C	1/52	ปฏิบัติการเกี่ยวกับเทคนิคเบื้องต้นและหลักปฏิบั...	ป.ตรี ภาคปกติ	2.43	1
6	521192251	วิทยาศาสตร์	ค.บ. 5 ปี	24031101	ชีววิทยาทั่วไป 1	B	D+	1/52	การกำเนิดชีวิต วิวัฒนาการโดยการคัดเลือกจากธรร...	ป.ตรี ภาคปกติ	2.43	3
7	521192251	วิทยาศาสตร์	ค.บ. 5 ปี	24031301	ปฏิบัติการชีววิทยาทั่วไป 1	B	B	1/52	ปฏิบัติการเรื่องการใช้กล้องจุลทรรศน์ คุณสมบั...	ป.ตรี ภาคปกติ	2.43	1
8	521192251	วิทยาศาสตร์	ค.บ. 5 ปี	01500102	จริยธรรมเพื่อการดำเนินชีวิต	E	B	1/53	วิเคราะห์ความหมายของจริยธรรมในทัศนะของปรัชญาและ...	ป.ตรี ภาคปกติ	2.43	3
9	521192251	วิทยาศาสตร์	ค.บ. 5 ปี	21002201	คณิตศาสตร์และคอมพิวเตอร์สำหรับครูวิทยาศาสตร์	B	A	1/53	อนุกรมไม่รู้จบ เวคเตอร์และการวิเคราะห์เวคเตอร...	ป.ตรี ภาคปกติ	2.43	3

Fig. 2. Dataset of Educational Data

3.2 Data Preprocessing

The data preprocessing process in this research begins with Merging Datasets by combining academic performance data from the educational dataset with student salary information from the student employment status dataset. After merging, we obtained a total of 11,305 rows and 4,074 attributes, encompassing both academic and employment status information after graduation.

Following the merging process, we conducted an outlier detection to ensure that the data used for analysis is of high quality and reliability. The results of the outlier detection are shown in Fig. 3, with the salary data range for further analysis set between 9,750–15,000 baht.

Next, since some parts of the educational dataset contain missing values, particularly grades for courses that students were not required to register for based on their curriculum, we addressed this issue by replacing missing values with zero(0) to enhance data completeness.

The outcome of this preprocessing process is the Final dataset, which is complete and ready for further predictive analysis.

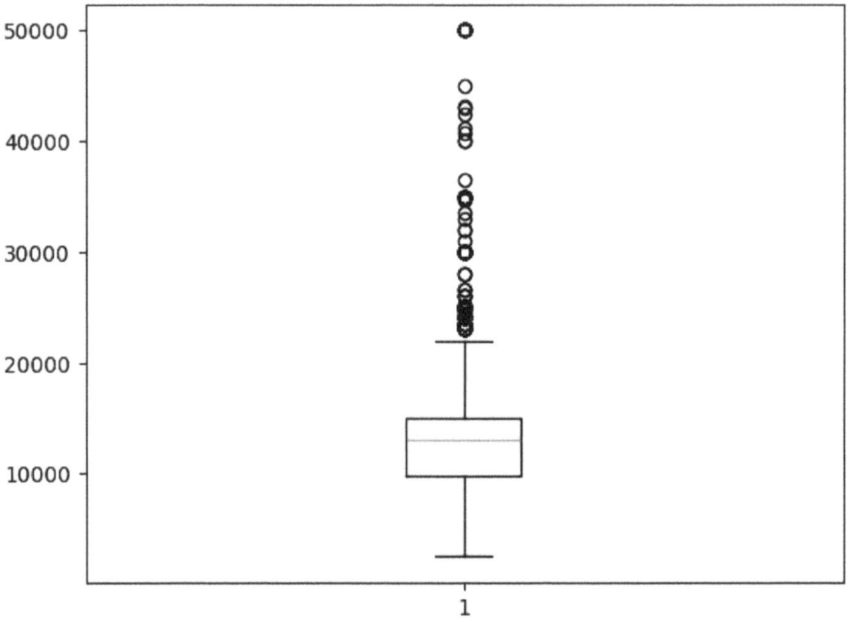

Fig. 3. The results of the outlier detection

3.3 Experiment Setting

This research focuses on studying the effectiveness of salary prediction. In the experiment, Principal Component Analysis and Gini impurity methods were applied to reduce the size of the features. The researcher hypothesizes that reducing the size of the data with missing values replaced in a way that may not align with real-world semantics could lead to improved prediction accuracy. In this study, missing data was replaced with a value of zero in the attributes representing grades for each course. Semantically, a zero might suggest a grade of F, but in reality, the missing data occurred because certain courses were not required in the students' curriculum. This may result in salary predictions that deviate from reality. It is expected that data dimensionality reduction will enhance the prediction performance.

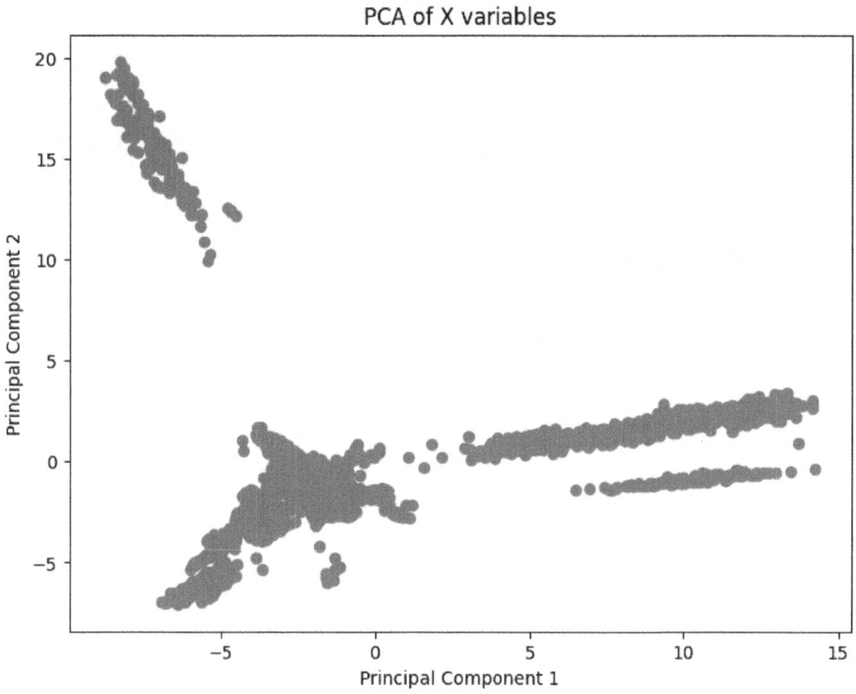

Fig. 4. The results of Principal Component Analysis

Two methods were chosen to compare performance and validate the hypothesis. The first method is PCA, which reduces the data's dimensionality. The results of PCA are shown in Fig. 4, and the dataset processed through PCA is referred to as the Final dataset with PCA (FDPCA). The second method is Gini impurity, used to select only the most relevant features for prediction. A sample result of the Gini impurity process is displayed in Fig. 5, with 100 features selected for the experiment. This dataset is called the Final dataset with Gini Impurity (FDGI).

We will test the prediction performance of the dimensionality-reduced datasets by using all three datasets-FD, FDPCA, and FDGI-in prediction with five Machine Learning techniques: Decision Tree Regression, Random Forest Regression, Support Vector Regression, K-Neighbors Regression, and Gradient Boosting Regression. This will allow for a comparison of each method's effectiveness in producing accurate predictions.

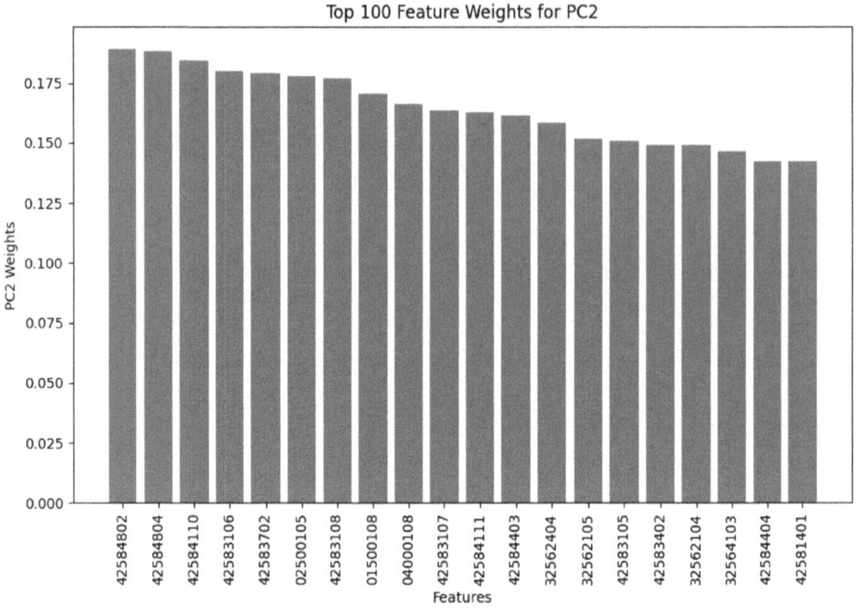

Fig. 5. A sample result of the Gini impurity

3.4 Evaluation

This experiment compares the performance of salary prediction across datasets processed with different dimensionality reduction methods. The evaluation metrics used are Mean Square Error (MSE) and Root Mean Square Error (RMSE) from experiments conducted with five Machine Learning techniques. The MSE is calculated using the following equation:

$$\text{MSE} = \frac{1}{n}\sum_{i=1}^{n}(y_i - \hat{y}_i)^2 \tag{1}$$

where y_i represents the actual value, $\widehat{y}_i$ is the predicted value, and n is the number of observations.

The Root Mean Square Error (RMSE) is derived from the MSE, as shown in the following equation:

$$\text{RMSE} = \sqrt{\frac{1}{n}\sum_{i=1}^{n}(y_i - \hat{y}_i)^2} \tag{2}$$

By comparing the MSE and RMSE values for each dataset, we can determine the effectiveness of each dimensionality reduction method in enhancing prediction accuracy.

4 Result

This section explains the experimental results of building a model to predict students' future salaries using both dimensionality-reduced datasets and datasets without dimensionality reduction. Five models were used: Decision Tree Regression, Random Forest Regression, Support Vector Regression (SVR), K-Nearest Regression, and Gradient Boosting Regression. The results indicate that reducing the dimensionality of the data did not enhance prediction performance. As shown by the RMSE values in Table 1, the lowest RMSE in all predictive models was achieved using the Final Dataset without dimensionality reduction, with GBR having the lowest RMSE of 1856.59. From this experiment, it can be concluded that dimensionality reduction may not decrease prediction error and could potentially increase it. This is likely because the dataset contains students from various fields of study, or the same field but in different programs, resulting in differences in course enrollment. When dimensionality reduction is applied, some grade data for certain students may be removed, leading to the loss of important information for building an accurate predictive model.

It is important to highlight the meanings of MSE (Mean Squared Error) and RMSE (Root Mean Squared Error) in the context of this research. MSE represents the average of the squared differences between the predicted and actual values, providing an overall measure of prediction error. However, since MSE is in squared units, it can be difficult to interpret directly in terms of the original data. RMSE, derived as the square root of MSE, converts this error back to the original unit of measurement (in this case, salary), making it easier to understand and compare the magnitude of prediction errors across different models. A lower RMSE indicates a more accurate predictive model. Therefore, in this study, RMSE serves as a critical metric for evaluating model performance, with the GBR model achieving the most accurate predictions by minimizing this error.

Table 1. Performance of the used machine learning models to predict salary.

Model	FD		FDPCA		FDGI	
	mse	rmse	mse	rmse	mse	rmse
DTR	6145324.00	2478.98	7427802.68	2725.40	6213292.28	2492.65
RFR	3523321.73	1877.05	4318779.67	2078.17	3689484.26	1920.80
SVR	3551158.64	1884.45	3632607.93	1905.94	3937638.29	1984.35
kNR	3601262.52	1897.70	4247528.48	2060.95	3808716.23	1951.59
GBR	3446909.47	**1856.59**	3722223.88	1929.31	3666174.34	1914.73

5 Conclusion

This research studied the prediction of future salaries for students using both dimensionality-reduced datasets and datasets without dimensionality reduction, applying five machine learning techniques: Decision Tree Regression, Random Forest Regression, Support Vector Regression (SVR), K-Nearest Regression, and Gradient Boosting Regression. The results indicated that dimensionality reduction did not improve prediction performance. On the contrary, the dataset without dimensionality reduction (Final Dataset) produced the lowest RMSE across all predictive models, with GBR achieving the lowest RMSE of 1856.59. This outcome suggests that dimensionality reduction may lead to the loss of important information, given that the dataset contains students from various fields of study and programs with different course enrollments. As a result, some grade data that could be essential for prediction may be excluded. Therefore, this research concludes that dimensionality reduction may not be advantageous for complex datasets requiring comprehensive information to build accurate predictive models.

To address this limitation, future research could explore segmenting student data into groups before constructing predictive models. This approach may enhance prediction accuracy by focusing on the unique characteristics of each group. However, a drawback of segmentation is that it reduces the data size from the original sample, which may impact the effectiveness of the predictive models. As a solution, researchers could refine the preprocessing steps by grouping similar data and applying a multi-prediction model approach to predict each data group individually. This strategy has the potential to improve both the accuracy and effectiveness of predictions, especially in datasets with diverse student characteristics.

Furthermore, future work could incorporate advanced feature selection techniques such as Gini Impurity or similar methods. These techniques can be employed to identify and rank the most relevant features incrementally, cutting off at the optimal number of features that best fit the dataset. This stepwise selection approach could reduce noise and redundancy in the data, ultimately enhancing the performance of the predictive models. Combining effective feature selection with segmentation and tailored multi-model predictions may yield a robust framework for addressing the challenges of diverse and complex datasets.

References

1. Ayua, S.I., Malgwi, Y.M., Afrifa, J.: Salary prediction model for non-academic staff using polynomial regression technique. In: Artificial Intelligence and Applications, vol. 2, pp. 358–365 (2024)
2. Boudreau, J.W., Boswell, W.R., Judge, T.A.: Effects of personality on executive career success in the united states and Europe. J. Vocat. Behav. **58**(1), 53–81 (2001)
3. Das, S., Barik, R., Mukherjee, A.: Salary prediction using regression techniques. In: Proceedings of Industry Interactive Innovations in Science, Engineering Technology (I3SET2K19) (2020)
4. De Haro, J.M., Castejon, J.L., Gilar, R.: Personality and salary at early career: the mediating effect of emotional intelligence. Inter. J. Human Resource Manag. **31**(14), 1844–1862 (2020)

5. Dilchert, S., Ones, D.S.: Personality and extrinsic career success: predicting managerial salary at different organizational levels. Zeitschrift für Personalpsychologie **7**(1), 1–23 (2008)
6. Fernández-Berrocal, P., Extremera, N., Ramos, N.: Validity and reliability of the spanish modified version of the trait meta-mood scale. Psychol. Rep. **94**(3), 751–755 (2004)
7. Kablaoui, R., Salman, A.: Machine learning models for salary prediction dataset using python. In: 2022 International Conference on Electrical and Computing Technologies and Applications (ICECTA), pp. 143–147. IEEE (2022)
8. Matbouli, Y.T., Alghamdi, S.M.: Statistical machine learning regression models for salary prediction featuring economy wide activities and occupations. Information **13**(10), 495 (2022)
9. Nguyen, N., Cripps, A.: Predicting housing value: a comparison of multiple regression analysis and artificial neural networks. J. Real Estate Res. **22**(3), 313–336 (2001)
10. Rasmussen, C.E., Williams, C.K.: Gaussian processes for machine learning cambridge. MA: the MIT Press.[Google Scholar] (2006)
11. Rasmussen, C.E., Nickisch, H.: Gaussian processes for machine learning (gpml) toolbox. J. Mach. Learn. Res. **11**, 3011–3015 (2010)
12. Specht, D.F., et al.: A general regression neural network. IEEE Trans. Neural Netw. **2**(6), 568–576 (1991)
13. Spurk, D., Abele, A.E.: Who earns more and why? a multiple mediation model from personality to salary. J. Bus. Psychol. **26**, 87–103 (2011)
14. Uypatchawong, S., Chanamarn, N.: Enhancing surface water quality prediction efficiency in northeastern Thailand using machine learning. Indonesian J. Electr. Eng. Comput. Sci. **36**(2), 1189–1198 (2024)

Optimizing Escape Routes in Emergency Scenarios: A Comparative Study of Pathfinding Algorithms

Apisan Janwangphom(✉), Surasit Uypatchawong, and Pokpong Songmuang

Faculty of Science and Technology, Thammasat University, Bangkok, Thailand
apisan.jan@dome.tu.ac.th

Abstract. This research focuses on optimizing escape routes in emergency scenarios involving active threats to minimize risks to lives and property. We evaluate the effectiveness of four algorithms Ant Colony Optimization (ACO), Bellman-Ford, Dijkstra, and A* in determining the most efficient escape routes across 50 maps. The primary objective is to identify paths that not only provide the shortest escape route but also reduce potential exposure to the threat. Our results demonstrate that the ACO algorithm consistently delivers the best performance, offering optimized escape routes that meet these criteria more effectively than the other algorithms. By prioritizing safety and minimizing exposure, this approach contributes valuable insights to emergency response planning in high-risk situations, potentially mitigating harm to individuals and property. The comparison and analysis of these algorithms provide a foundation for future advancements in intelligent navigation systems for crisis management.

Keywords: Ant Colony Optimization · Bellman-Ford Algorithm · Dijkstra Algorithm · A* Algorithm

1 Introduction

Responding to critical events such as active threats in public spaces is highly complex and requires urgent attention, necessitating the use of advanced technology to enable rapid and effective responses. This project focuses on implementing algorithms to calculate the shortest and most efficient escape routes, providing a tool to assist individuals in navigating high-risk areas safely and quickly. Between 2022 and 2024, the U.S. experienced fluctuations in firearm-related incidents. While active threat cases decreased by 18% in 2022 compared to 2021, the overall five-year trend indicated a 66.7% increase. In 2023, firearm-related fatalities, excluding self-harm, dropped to 18,874, representing a 7% reduction from the previous year, and firearm injuries also saw a 6% decrease. Despite these positive trends, incidents involving children and teenagers remain a concern, with 6,192 minors affected in 2023, resulting in over 1,600 fatalities. Since 2020, firearms have remained a significant cause of fatality among children, underscoring the need for ongoing efforts to address safety challenges [11].

J. Kertesz et al. (Eds.): CSoNet 2024, LNCS 15417, pp. 466–475, 2025.
https://doi.org/10.1007/978-981-96-6389-7_43

The literature review of this paper should explore the current state of re-search on escape route planning in emergency situations, particularly in volatile environments like forest fires. Previous studies have widely employed algorithms like A*, Dijkstra, and Ant Colony Optimization for pathfinding, with A* often favored for its balance between computational efficiency and accuracy. However, the traditional A* algorithm's effectiveness in real-time, dynamic environments such as forest fires is limited, as it doesn't account for continuously changing risk factors. Recent efforts have focused on improving A* by integrating external data sources like remote sensing and by adjusting heuristic functions to enhance adaptability to dynamic conditions. Additionally, multi-criteria decision-making techniques, such as FAHP and CRITIC, have been increasingly utilized to weigh the importance of various environmental and safety factors affecting route planning. This study builds upon these advancements by incorporating real-time data from satellite imagery to optimize escape route planning, demonstrating significant improvements in safety and risk reduction over traditional methods. Furthermore, the integration of a dynamic escape window method with the improved A* algorithm is a novel contribution, providing a more responsive and accurate escape planning solution in life-threatening scenarios.

The literature review for this paper should explore advancements in evacuation route planning in fire emergencies, focusing on the limitations of traditional fixed-route evacuation diagrams. Earlier studies have shown that conventional diagrams fail to adapt to dynamic fire conditions, such as changes in temperature, smoke, and toxic gases, often leading to suboptimal or unsafe evacuations. Ant Colony Optimization (ACO) has been widely applied to evacuation planning due to its efficiency in solving complex pathfinding problems. However, standard ACO algorithms are limited in their ability to account for real-time environmental factors during emergencies. Recent research has introduced improvements to ACO by incorporating real-time data from monitoring systems, such as temperature and CO concentration, to adjust pheromone levels and heuristic functions. Simulation tools like PyroSim and evacuation software such as Pathfinder have also been employed to model fire scenarios, but they often lack the flexibility to adapt routes in real-time. This paper builds upon these efforts by proposing an Improved ACO (IACO) that integrates real-time fire product data to optimize evacuation routes. The IACO's ability to dynamically avoid dangerous areas and reduce evacuation casualties offers a significant improvement over both traditional ACO and existing commercial solutions, contributing to safer evacuation strategies in fire emergencies.

The objective of this project is to enhance safety and reduce risks to individuals and property during critical situations that require swift and effective responses.

2 Related Literature and Research

Research on Escape Route Planning Analysis in Forest Fire Scenes Based on the Improved A* Algorithm. This research is particularly valuable for our project as it demonstrates how the A* algorithm can be improved to manage emergency situations more effectively through the use of real-time data and multi-criteria decision-making frameworks. Our work, which evaluates various escape route planning algorithms in dynamic environments, can build on these findings by integrating similar techniques to enhance algorithmic performance. The dynamic escape window method proposed in this study offers a promising model for optimizing real-time route planning in critical, life-threatening situations, making it highly relevant to our approach [9].

Intelligent Planning of Fire Evacuation Routes Using an Improved ant Colony Optimization Algorithm. In our project, which employs Ant Colony Optimization (ACO) for planning escape routes in emergency scenarios, we draw inspiration from the Intelligent Ant Colony Optimization (IACO) algorithm used in fire evacuation planning. The IACO algorithm demonstrates the advantages of incorporating real-time data to adjust routes dynamically based on changing conditions. Similarly, by integrating real-time situational data, such as the location of the active threat, our approach can continuously refine and update escape routes. This improvement enhances the adaptability of the algorithm, making it more effective in handling unpredictable emergency situations [10].

2.1 Decision System for Recommending Escape Routes

First Case: The condition checks if the weight from the START Node to the DANGER Node exceeds 5, indicating that the user is at a safe distance from the potential threat. If this condition is met, the system proceeds to calculate and recommend an optimal escape route. This approach is informed by research on emergency response planning, particularly within the context of Mahidol University Salaya, where understanding spatial relationships between individuals and potential risks is crucial for effective evacuation strategies [13].

Second Case: The condition checks if the weight from the START Node to the DANGER Node is less than 5, suggesting that the user is within close proximity to the potential threat. In this case, the system prioritizes safety by recommending the user find a secure location to stay instead of attempting to escape. A warning message will be displayed to alert the user of the situation. This approach aligns with emergency response research, emphasizing situational awareness and adaptive strategies, especially in high-density environments like university campuses [13].

2.2 Theoretical Concepts

2.2.1 Ant Colony Optimization (ACO)

Ant Colony Optimization (ACO), introduced by Marco Dorigo in the 1990s, is a pathfinding algorithm inspired by ants' foraging behavior. Ants communicate by depositing pheromones, which guide others toward efficient routes, with pheromones evaporating over time on less optimal paths [1]. ACO represents problems as a graph where pheromone levels influence route selection. Enhanced versions like MAX-MIN Ant System (MMAS) and Ant Colony System (ACS) improve efficiency. ACO is widely applied in fields like travel planning, network management, and circuit design due to its flexibility and effectiveness in solving complex problems [2].

Parameters

ALPHA: Controls the importance of pheromone levels on the paths. Higher values prioritize paths with higher pheromone concentration.

BETA: Determines the importance of visibility (inverse of distance). Higher values favor shorter paths.

EVAPORATION_RATE: Specifies the rate at which pheromone evaporates, preventing excessive accumulation on a single path.

Q: A constant used to calculate the amount of pheromone deposited by ants based on the path length.

NUM_ANTS: The number of ants per iteration, influencing the exploration of possible routes.

NUM_ITERATIONS: The number of iterations, balancing computational cost with solution accuracy.

2.2.2 A* Algorithm

The A* Algorithm is an informed pathfinding technique that searches for the optimal route between a starting point and a destination in a graph or grid. It combines heuristic estimates of the remaining distance with the distance already traveled to calculate the total cost of a path [3]. The algorithm operates by maintaining open and closed lists to track unexplored and explored nodes, respectively, selecting nodes based on the lowest estimated cost. Widely used in applications like vehicle navigation and game development, A* is known for its efficiency in handling large graphs [4].

2.2.3 Bellman-Ford Algorithm

The Bellman-Ford Algorithm is a pathfinding algorithm that handles graphs with negative weights. It initializes distances from the starting point and iteratively updates them to find the shortest paths. It also checks for negative-weight cycles, which indicate potential issues in the graph. Although its time complexity is $O(v \cdot E)$, making it slower than other algorithms, it is well-suited for large graphs and those containing negative edge weights [8].

2.2.4 Dijkstra's Algorithm

Dijkstra's Algorithm is a pathfinding method that identifies the shortest path from a starting point to other nodes in a graph using a Greedy approach [5]. It initializes distances, selects the unvisited node with the shortest distance, and updates neighboring nodes accordingly [6]. The algorithm continues until the shortest path to the target node is determined. With a time complexity of O(v2) or $O((V + E) \log V)$, Dijkstra's Algorithm is efficient for large graphs without loops, making it suitable for a variety of shortest path applications [7].

2.3 Objective Function Overview

2.3.1 Objective Function for A* Algorithm, Ant Colony Optimization (ACO) Algorithm, Dijkstra Algorithm, Bellman-Ford Algorithm

$$Minimize \sum_{(u,v)\in P} w(u, v) \tag{1}$$

The objective function in ACO algorithm, Bellman-Ford algorithm, and Dijkstra algorithm minimizes the total distance along a path P, which is the set of edges connecting the start node s to the exit node, while avoiding the danger node. In this equation, $w(u, v)$ represents the weight (or distance) of each edge (u, v) along the path P, where u is the starting node of the edge and v is the ending node. The goal is to find the path that results in the smallest sum of edge weights.

The ACO algorithm iteratively improves this solution by updating pheromone levels, though these parameters are not part of the objective function itself.

In the Bellman-Ford algorithm, the constraint ensures that no edges in the path P include the danger node, i.e., $d \notin \{u, v\}$. This ensures the algorithm finds the shortest path from the start node to the exit node without passing through the danger node. If the graph contains a negative-weight cycle that does not involve the danger node, the algorithm raises an error. The final solution yields both the shortest path and its corresponding distance, subject to the danger-avoidance constraint.

In the Dijkstra algorithm, the method ensures that the path does not pass through the danger node. By iteratively updating the distances from the source node to its neighboring nodes, the algorithm guarantees that the shortest possible path is found while maintaining the constraint of avoiding the danger node. This method efficiently computes optimal escape routes in environments with hazardous zones (see Fig. 5).

2.3.2 Objective Function for A* Algorithm

The objective function for the A* algorithm in this scenario aims to find the shortest path from the start node s to the exit node t while avoiding the danger node d and its nearby nodes within a specified proximity threshold. The function can be expressed as

$$Minimize f(n) = g(n) + h(n) \tag{2}$$

where $f(n)$ is the total estimated cost of the path through node $n$which is a common node in a graph, $g(n)$ is the actual cost of the path from s to n (the sum of edge weights from s to n, and $h(n)$ is the heuristic function, representing the estimated cost from n to t. The heuristic $h(n)$ is calculated as the Euclidean distance between node n and the exit node. The algorithm iteratively selects nodes with the lowest$f(n)$ value, ensuring the path avoids the danger node and its proximity, and terminates once the exit node is reached. This method efficiently computes optimal paths in environments where safety and hazard avoidance are critical (see Fig. 6).

The workflow illustrates the process of optimizing escape routes through graph construction, key location identification, and algorithm execution, and also serves to compare algorithmic performance. It begins with Graph Construction, where a network of nodes and edges is defined to represent possible paths. Then, the Key Location Data

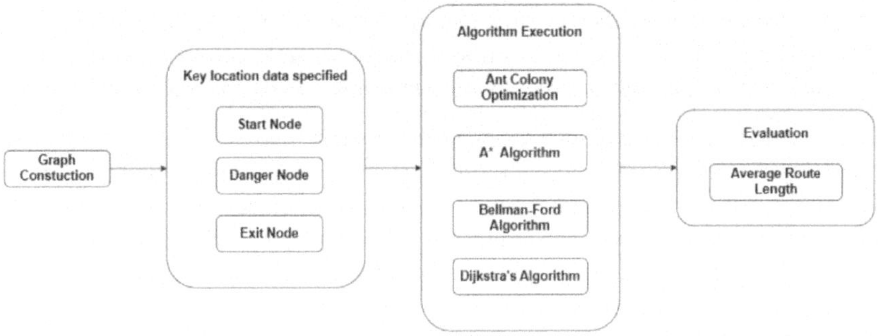

Fig. 1. Work Flow

Specification step identifies the Start Node (representing the initial position), Danger Node (indicating hazardous areas to avoid), and Exit Node (the target for escape). Once the key nodes are specified, Algorithm Execution is performed using four different algorithms: Ant Colony Optimization, A* Algorithm, Bellman-Ford Algorithm, and Dijkstra's Algorithm. These algorithms compute potential paths through the graph to find optimal escape routes while avoiding the danger nodes. The performance of these algorithms is compared based on factors such as path length with the goal of determining the most efficient algorithm for ensuring safe and effective escape route planning (see Fig. 1).

3 Experiment

The experiment aims to evaluate the efficiency of different algorithms in finding optimal escape routes under varying conditions. For this purpose, maps with three distinct route densities 1, 0.5, and 0.3 will be created. In each testing round, the positions of both the user and the threat actor will be randomly selected, while the exit point will remain fixed across all rounds.

Each density level will be tested over 50 rounds to measure the performance of escape route algorithms under different conditions. The experiment will simulate a variety of real-world scenarios, ensuring that the evaluation reflects how well the algorithms adapt to changes in route density.

3.1 Experiment Setting

- Hardware: NVIDIA T4 GPU
- Ram: 16 GB

3.2 Creating a Node Graph Representing the Map for Escaping the Threat Actor

The process begins with creating a node graph that represents the map used for calculating escape routes from the threat actor. A total of fifty different maps are created as examples for implementing the algorithms. These maps are represented as graphs, where:

- Nodes represent key locations on the map (e.g., rooms, exits, or checkpoints).
- Edges represent the paths or connections between these locations.
- Each map varies in layout complexity to test the algorithms under different scenarios.

The fifty maps are meticulously designed to simulate real-world environments with varying levels of complexity, incorporating obstacles, danger zones, and multiple exit points. These features are essential for assessing the efficiency of various algorithms in emergency scenarios. Each map comprises 20 nodes, representing individual rooms within a building. Pre-assigned weights are used to calculate the optimal escape route, reflecting real-world constraints.

In density 1, the escape route is relatively straightforward due to the abundance of available paths, which provides multiple options for avoiding the threat actor and finding an optimal way to reach safety (see Fig. 2).

In density 0.5, the maps become more complex since the number of available paths is reduced, making it more challenging for escapees to navigate and find an optimal route to avoid the threat actor and finding an optimal way to reach safety (see Fig. 3).

In Density 0.3, the maps are the most complex, as there are very few escape routes available, which makes it more challenging to navigate but allows for efficient testing of each algorithm (see Fig. 4).

To ensure variability in testing, the Start and Danger nodes are randomly assigned across the fifty maps, adding an element of unpredictability to each scenario. This approach allows for a comprehensive evaluation of the algorithms' performance under different configurations. The figures below provide visual representations of the node structure and layout for each test scenario.

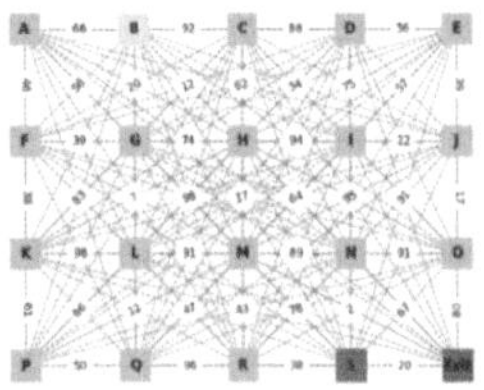

Fig. 2. Density 1

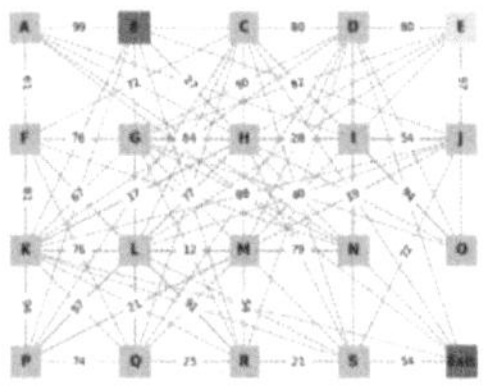

Fig. 3. Density 0.5

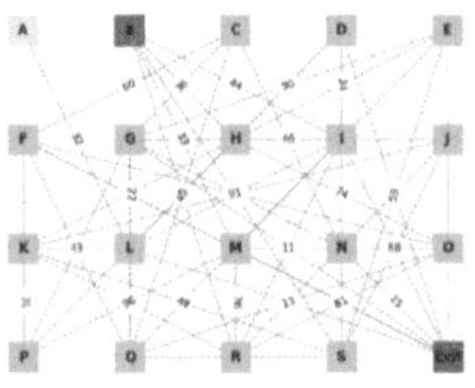

Fig. 4. Density 0.3

1. **START Node:** Represents the current position of the user, visually distinguished by a yellow node to indicate the starting point.
2. **EXIT Node:** Represents the safe exit from the building, marked in green to signify safety and the target destination.
3. **DANGER Node:** Represents the danger point, such as the location of the perpetrator, highlighted in red to indicate a high-risk area.

The evaluation criteria are based on minimizing both the total distance traveled and the time taken by the algorithm to find the optimal path. These metrics ensure the algorithm's efficiency in identifying the shortest and fastest route while avoiding danger node (Table 1).

Table 1. The result of experiment.

Algorithm	Density 1		Density 0.5		Density 0.3	
	Average Route Length	Required Time (second)	Average Route Length	Required Time (second)	Average Route Length	Required Time (second)
Ant Colony Optimization (Ant 100, Numitreration 100)	22.56	15.00	44.14	7.95	72.86	5.48
Ant Colony Optimization (Ant 500, Numitreration 100)	21.20	108.44	42.26	57.87	68.20	41.08
Ant Colony Optimization (Ant 3000, Numitreration 200)	19.60	2,037.49	38.93	853.46	65.82	549.71
A* Algorithm	20.98	0.001	39.72	0.002	67.0	0.003
Bellmanford Algorithm	20.90	0.006	39.72	0.003	67.0	0.002
Dijkstra Algorithm	21.38	0.231	40.38	0.06	67.0	0.002

3.3 Results

The table highlights the performance differences among four algorithms ACO algorithm, A* algorithm, Bellman-Ford algorithm, and Dijkstra algorithm across varying route densities. ACO, particularly with higher parameters (e.g., 3000 ants, 200 iterations), finds slightly shorter paths but requires significantly more computation time, especially in lower density environments, revealing a trade-off between path accuracy and processing time. This makes ACO suitable for scenarios where path optimization is prioritized and longer computation times are acceptable. In contrast, the A* algorithm consistently achieves near optimal route lengths with minimal computation time, even as density decreases, making it highly efficient and well-suited for quick decision making is essential. Bellman-Ford and Dijkstra offer reliable performance with route lengths comparable to A* but slightly higher computation times, particularly in denser networks, with Dijkstra showing a slight increase in time as density decreases. Overall, while A* is the most practical choice for scenarios requiring rapid response, ACO remains advantageous where a small improvement in path length justifies the additional processing time.

4 Summary of Experiment Results

The experimental results highlight the distinct strengths and trade-offs of each algorithm Ant Colony Optimization (ACO), A*, Bellman-Ford, and Dijkstra in navigating various route densities, showcasing their suitability for different application scenarios. ACO stands out in its ability to optimize path length, particularly in high-density environments, where it consistently finds shorter routes. This effectiveness can be further enhanced by adjusting parameters, such as the number of ants and iterations, making ACO a flexible choice for path optimization. However, these fine-tunings often come at the expense of computation time, especially in lower density networks, emphasizing a trade-off between path accuracy and processing speed. In contrast, A* and Bellman-Ford algorithms achieve an ideal balance of route accuracy and exceptionally low computation times, making them highly efficient for real-time or emergency applications that demand quick decision making. Their consistency across different densities underscores their adaptability and efficiency, providing reliable performance without significant computation delays. Dijkstra's algorithm also performs comparably well, offering similar route lengths to A* and Bellman-Ford, although with slightly longer computation times, especially as route density changes. Overall, while ACO is highly effective for precise path optimization, A* and Bellman-Ford prove more practical for scenarios requiring a balance between accuracy and efficiency, with A* being particularly suitable for situations where speed is paramount.

5 Future of Work

Future developments of this research aim to enhance the system's adaptability by incorporating real-time updates on the location of potential threats. This improvement would greatly increase the practicality of the algorithms in real-world applications, offering more responsive and accurate escape route recommendations. However, this remains a current limitation of the study and will require further exploration.

Additionally, the proposed approach has the potential to be adapted for a wider range of emergency scenarios beyond those involving active threats. For instance, it could be utilized in evacuations during natural disasters such as floods, hurricanes, or earthquakes. These applications would necessitate further studies to address the specific challenges and constraints unique to each type of emergency. Such advancements would significantly contribute to the development of comprehensive systems for emergency response and safety planning.

References

1. Dorigo, M., Stützle, T.: Ant colony optimization: overview and recent advances, pp. 311–351. Springer (2019)
2. Dorigo, M., Birattari, M., Stutzle, T.: Ant colony optimization. IEEE Comput. Intell. Mag. **1**(4), 28–39 (2006)
3. Howden, W.E.: The sofa problem. Comput. J. **11**(3), 299–301 (1968). https://doi.org/10.1093/comjnl/11.3.299

4. Tang, G., Tang, C., Claramunt, C., Hu, X., Zhou, P.: Geometric a-star algorithm: an improved a-star algorithm for AGV path planning in a port environment. IEEE Access **9**, 59196–59210 (2021). https://doi.org/10.1109/ACCESS.2021.3070054
5. Javaid, M.A.: Understanding Dijkstra's Algorithm (2013). SSRN. https://ssrn.com/abstract=2340905 or https://doi.org/10.2139/ssrn.2340905
6. Gunawan, R.D., Napianto, R., Borman, R.I., Hanifah, I.: Implementation of Dijkstra's algorithm in determining the shortest path (case study: specialist doctor search in Bandar Lampung). Int. J. Inf. Syst. Comput. Sci. **3**(3), 98–106 (2019)
7. Khakzad, N.: A methodology based on Dijkstra's algorithm and mathematical programming for optimal evacuation in process plants in the event of major tank fires. Reliab. Eng. Syst. Saf. **236**, 109291 (2023)
8. Arnau, R., Calabuig, J.M., García-Raffi, L.M., Sánchez Pérez, E.A., Sanjuan, S.: A bellman-ford algorithm for the path-length-weighted distance in graphs. Mathematics **12**(16), 2590 (2024)
9. Zhou, J., Jiang, Y., Li, M., Li, G.: Research on escape route planning analysis in forest fire scenes based on the improved A* algorithm. Ecol. Ind. **152**, 112683 (2024). https://doi.org/10.1016/j.ecolind.2024.112683
10. Li, X., Zhu, W., Zhang, X.: Intelligent planning of fire evacuation routes using an improved ant colony optimization algorithm. Saf. Sci. **157**, 105977 (2024). https://doi.org/10.1016/j.ssci.2024.105977
11. CNN. Gun violence is remaking America's classrooms. CNN (2023). https://edition.cnn.com/interactive/2023/us/changing-classrooms-shooting-safety-dg/
12. Smith, J., Doe, A.: States with the most school shootings. U.S. News & World Report (2024). https://www.usnews.com/news/best-states/articles/states-with-the-most-school-shootings
13. Department of Homeland Security. Active Shooter: How to Respond Booklet (2024). https://www.dhs.gov/xlibrary/assets/active_shooter_booklet.pdf

Features Analysis of Respiratory Disease in Thailand

Kunanon Kongchatree, Ongon Suriyo(✉), Natvara Pichedpan, Rachada Kongkachandra, and Pokpong Songmuang

Thammasat University, Khlong Nueng 12121, Pathum Thani, Thailand
ongon.sur@dome.tu.ac.th

Abstract. This research aims to explore the key features influencing the number of respiratory disease cases in Thailand. We analyzed various features to identify their correlation with respiratory disease rates per 100,000 people. By utilizing clustering techniques, we grouped provinces with similar characteristics to better visualize the relationships between these features and respiratory health outcomes. This method provides insights into the types of urban and environmental characteristics that contribute to the incidence of respiratory diseases.

Our findings reveal that air quality, influenced by urban expansion and agricultural activities, is the most significant feature associated with high respiratory disease rates. Following this are severe environmental conditions, while local environmental features and employment practices shaped by provincial development policies also play a crucial role.

Keywords: Respiratory Disease · Air pollution features · Clustering Techniques

1 Introduction

The health situation in Thailand has worsened in recent years, especially in terms of respiratory diseases. This issue is driven by several interconnected features, such as public health policies that do not effectively promote healthy living and changing environmental conditions like unpredictable weather and global warming. According to the Thai Asthma Council, these shifts have led to increased levels of pollen and mold spores in the air, resulting in a 15% rise in respiratory-related disease cases.

Several research studies have examined the relationship between air pollution and respiratory diseases. For example, Jing Yang et al. (2023) studied the impact of meteorological features and air pollution on respiratory disease hospital visits in Linyi, China, using Support Vector Regression (SVR). The study shows how pollutants like NO2, PM2.5, and PM10, along with weather conditions, influence the occurrence of diseases like pneumonia.

Zhang and Yang. (2022) studied PM2.5 pollution data in China using clustering methods to analyze patterns between cities and identify clusters of co-occurring pollution.

J. Kertesz et al. (Eds.): CSoNet 2024, LNCS 15417, pp. 476–485, 2025.
https://doi.org/10.1007/978-981-96-6389-7_44

Jagadeesh Puvvula et al. (2023) studied the impact of social features, such as income, education, and access to healthcare, on children's health in Douglas County, Nebraska, USA, showing how these features affect exposure to disease and the likelihood of child hood asthma.

This data shows that health problems today are complex and influenced by many different aspects, including environmental, economic, and social features.

This research aims to determine what features are related in Thailand. We believe that there are features beyond just smog that contribute to the impact. So we explored various features from several government databases and conducted literature reviews, which led us to identify 28 features across 6 categories. We categorized the data of the province into high disease number and low disease number clusters and analyzed the relationships between these features and respiratory disease rates. After normalizing the dataset, we used Principal Component Analysis (PCA) to reduce it to two dimensions. We then applied k-means clustering to organize provinces with similar characteristics, particularly focusing on those with high disease rates.

Our analysis showed that we could classify the provinces into three main clusters, indicating similar environmental conditions and patient profiles. We also broke the data down into subgroups that addressed the environmental, economic, and social aspects of each region.

The purpose of this study is to enhance understanding of the factors influencing respiratory diseases and to assist the government in developing policies to address these issues.

2 Literature Review

All three research studies discussed focus on the impact of air pollution on health, particularly respiratory diseases, using different methods and contexts.

Jing Yang et al. (2023) applied Support Vector Regression (SVR) to analyze the effects of meteorological factors and air pollutants (NO2, PM2.5, PM10) on respiratory disease hospital visits in Linyi, China. By modeling the complex relationships between weather, pollution, and disease occurrence, the study provided more precise predictions of diseases like pneumonia, aiding in healthcare resource management and environ mental policy planning.

Liankui Zhang and Guangfei Yang (2022) analyzed PM2.5 pollution patterns in China using a novel frequent itemset clustering method, comparing it to the traditional correlation coefficient approach. Their method identified complex relationships between cities, leading to more precise grouping and pattern identification, which is particularly useful when dealing with nonlinear or outlier-heavy data. For example, cities with many features often experience high levels of PM2.5 and noise pollution simultaneously, which can aid in regional pollution management and policy planning while optimizing government budgets.

Jagadeesh Puvvula et al. (2023) that social features, such as income, education, and access to healthcare, significantly affect children's health, particularly concerning respiratory diseases. Using a regression model, they accounted for various variables that might influence the relationship between social determinants and respiratory health.

Their findings revealed that Black and Latino children living near industrial facilities and high vehicle emissions are at greater risk of developing asthma. This highlights the impact of social features on respiratory diseases.

Air pollution significantly contributes to respiratory diseases like asthma and chronic obstructive pulmonary disease (COPD) in areas such as China, and Douglas County. Major pollutants, including industrial emissions, vehicle use, and PM2.5, pose serious health risks, especially for children, the elderly, and those with chronic conditions. This highlights the urgent need to address air pollution and protect public health. This study will analyze features influencing respiratory diseases in Thailand to support policy development and health interventions.

3 Methodology

This study focuses on identifying the features of provinces that impact respiratory health. We collected data from multiple sources, considering 27 features related to air pollution and respiratory disease rates per 100,000 people. These features are categorized into three clusters, as summarized in the "Provincial Data Overview" tables below (Table 1).

Table 1. Table Provincial Data Overview.

	Features Name	Data Description	Reference
Economic	1. Total Registered Vehicles	indicating transportation and economic activity	8
	2. Number of Tourists	reflecting tourism impact	7
	3. Tourism Revenue (Million Baht)	Income from tourism, showing its economic contribution	7
	4. Population	Total number of residents	10
	5. Employed	indicating job availability	5
	6. Not in Labor Force	People not working or seeking jobs, reflecting demographics	5
	7. Provincial Budget	Financial resources are allocated to the province	13
	8. Number of MPs	Several parliamentary representatives from the province	10
	9. Number of Industries	Total industries, indicating industrial activity	17
	10. Agricultural Land Area (rai)	Land used for agriculture	21
Environmental	11. Water Consumption (cubic meters)	Total water usage	20

(*continued*)

Table 1. *(continued)*

	Features Name	Data Description	Reference
	12. Burned Area (rai)	Area affected by wildfires	12
	13. Waste Generation (tons/day)	Daily waste production	20
	14. Unmanaged Waste (tons)	Waste not properly disposed of	20
	15. Green Space Area (rai)	Total green space area	19
	16. Number of Wildfire Extinguishments	Several fires were extinguished	12
	17. Average Temperature	Average yearly temperature	4
	18. Area of Mulberry Cultivation (rai)	Area for mulberry farming	18
Social	19. Population with Higher Education	Number of residents with higher education	10
	20. Population without Education	Number of uneducated residents	10
	21. Number of Schools	Total schools in the province	14
	22. Number of Medical Personnel	Total healthcare workers	16
	23. Number of Temples	Total Buddhist temples	9
	24. Birth Rate	Number of births per year	6
	25. Death Rate	Number of deaths per year	6
	26. Number of Airports	Total airports in the province	15
	27. Number of Houses	Total residential buildings	10

We analyzed the relationship between various features and the number of respiratory disease patients. To ensure the data was in a usable format, we performed thorough data cleaning. This process included verifying data accuracy through data visualization, ad dressing missing data, and identifying outliers. We normalized the data and applied Principal Component Analysis (PCA) to reduce its dimensions for 2D visualization. This approach simplifies the data, making it easier to identify clusters with K-means clustering, which does not handle many features well. Our focus was on identifying similar provinces in terms of features related to respiratory diseases. We chose k-means because it's popular and simple, making it suitable for our data. We visualized the results using PCA scatter plots to explore the relationship between the number of patients and other features. The scatter plots display the distribution of data points, representing a high number of patients and a low number of patients. This approach helps to visually identify patterns and clusters in the data.

4 Results and Discussion

Our analysis of 27 features that might influence the number of respiratory disease patients in Thailand (calculated as the number of cases per 100,000 people) reveals several interesting relationships between environmental conditions and urban features. These results are visualized using the heatmap below.

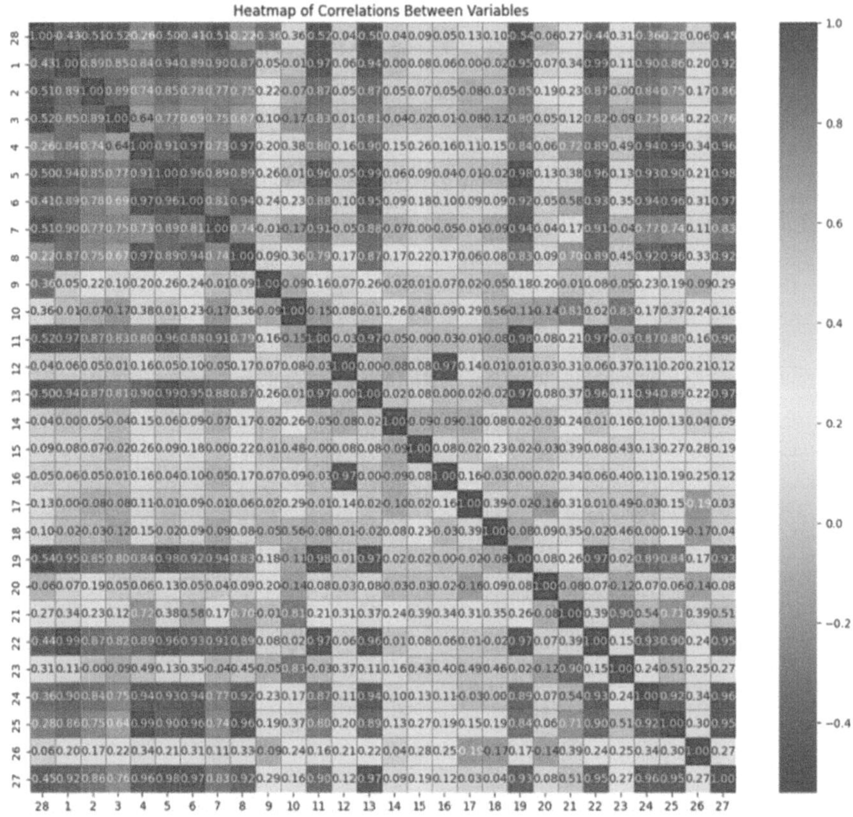

Fig. 1. Heatmap Showing Feature Relationships with the Number of Cases per 100,000 People. (A value of 28 is designated as the number of cases per 100,000 people.)

Based on the heatmap in Fig. 1, we identified the top five features that correlate most strongly with the number of respiratory disease cases: Number of Wildfire Extinguishments, Burned Areas(rai), Number of Airports, Tourism Revenue(Million Baht), and Number of Industries. However, these correlations are not immediately clear due to the complex interactions between many variables. To better visualize and understand these relationships, we used Principal Component Analysis (PCA) to reduce the data dimensions, enabling us to identify clearer patterns.

$$\mu_j = \frac{1}{|C_j|} \sum_{x_i \in C_j} x_i$$

where μ_j denotes the centroid of cluster C_j, xi refers to the data points within cluster C_j and $|c_j|$ represents the number of data points in that cluster.

$$C_j = \left\{ x_i : \left\| x_i - \mu_j \right\|^2 \leq \| x_i - \mu_k \|^2, \forall k \right\}$$

where cluster C_j, is defined as the set of data points x_i for which the squared distance to the centroid μ_j is less than or equal to the squared distance to any other centroid μ'_k for all k (Figs. 2 and 3).

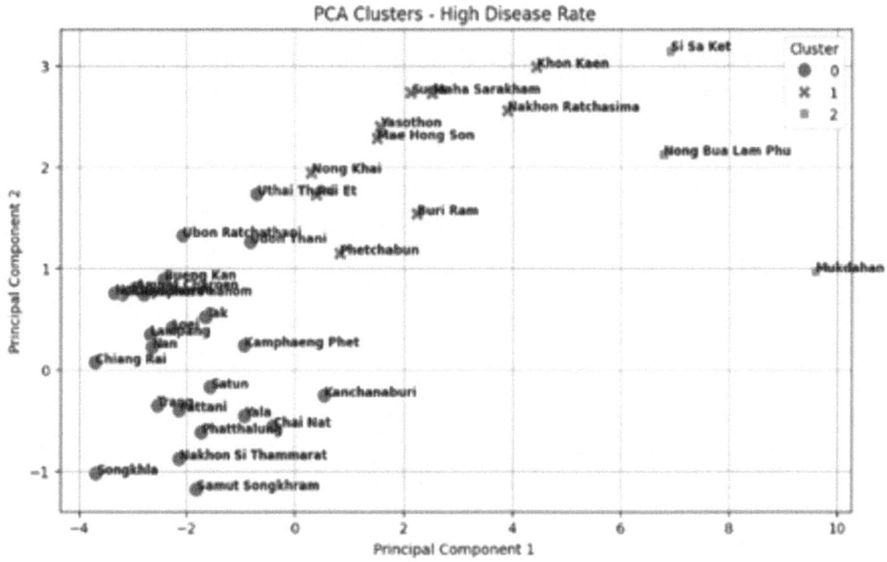

Fig. 2. PCA Clusters with High Disease Rate

- Cluster H0: This cluster is associated with economic activities and resource use, such as agricultural land, the number of Members of Parliament, waste generation, vehicle usage, and water consumption.
  - Hypothesis: Provinces in this cluster are predominantly agricultural areas with a high level of urban expansion and population density, leading to high pollution levels.
- Cluster H1: This cluster focuses on environmental conditions and features affecting environmental quality, such as the number of uneducated people, burned forest areas, wildfire incidents, tourism revenue, and average temperature.

Cluster	Province
H 0	Si Sa Ket, Nong Bua Lamphu, and Mukdahan.
H 1	Khon Kaen, Maha Sarakham, Surin, Nakhon Ratchasima, Yasothon, Mae Hong Son, Nong Khai, Roi Et, Buri Ram, and Phetchabun.
H 2	Uthai Thani, Ubon Ratchathani, Udon Thani, Bueng Kan, Amnat Charoen, Tak, Loei, Lampang, Nan, Kamphaeng Phet, Chiang Rai, Satun, etc.

Fig. 3. The provinces included in H0, H1, and H2 clusters.

  - Hypothesis: Uncontrolled burning in forests and agricultural fields, driven by a lack of awareness and increased tourism activities, results in elevated pollution levels and serious air quality concerns.

- Cluster H2: This cluster relates to social infrastructure, such as the number of factories, the uneducated population, tourism revenue, and water consumption.
  - Hypothesis: Due to limited education, a large proportion of the population works in factories and tourism, leading to lower health awareness and limited access to healthcare services

The clustering results reflect the relationship between different environmental conditions and respiratory disease rates, showing that certain clusters have similar characteristics. We used the standard deviation (SD) of each feature to identify the shared characteristics of each cluster, sorted the SD values, and selected the top five to describe the defining attributes of each cluster.

The provinces within these clusters have varying relationships with respiratory disease rates. Cluster H0, associated with economic activities, includes provinces like Sisaket, Nong Bua Lam Phu, and Mukdahan, which face air quality issues due to urban expansion and agricultural activities. Cluster H1, linked to environmental features, includes Khon Kaen, Maha Sarakham, and Surin, where forest fires and tourism play major roles in air pollution. Cluster H2, related to social infrastructure, includes Uthai Thani, Ubon Ratchathani, and Chiang Rai, which face challenges due to industrial emissions and limited educational resources (Figs. 4 and 5).

For Low Disease Rate clusters, we divided the data into three clusters: L0, L1, and L2.

- Cluster L0: Associated with a variety of environmental and economic features, such as the number of wildfire incidents, number of industries, burned areas, tourism revenue, and number of airports.

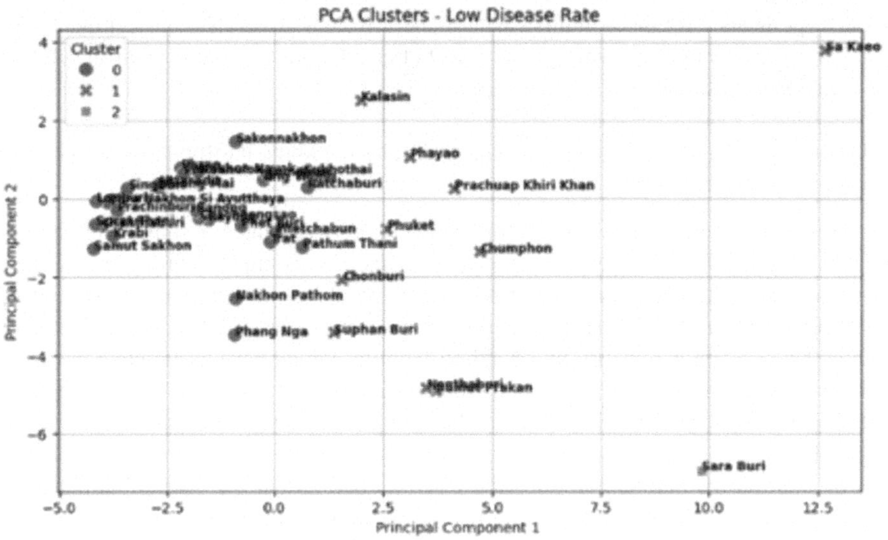

Fig. 4. PCA Clusters with Low Disease Rate

Cluster	Province
L 0	Sakon Nakhon, Chiang Mai, Krabi, Trat, Ratchaburi, Phetchaburi, Nakhon Pathom, Phang Nga, etc.
L 1	Khon Kaen, Sa Kaeo, Kalasin, Phayao, Prachuap Khiri Khan, Phuket, Chumphon, Chonburi, Suphan Buri, Nonthaburi, and Samut Prakan.
L 2	Only Saraburi province is included, so it's still not possible to identify the group's key characteristics.

Fig. 5. The provinces included in L0, L1, and L2 clusters.

  - Hypothesis: Provinces in this cluster have fewer pollution sources, leading to lower respiratory disease rates.

- Cluster L1: Focuses on government investment and education level, with features such as provincial budget, tourism revenue, number of industries, and high education levels.

  – Hypothesis: Provinces in this cluster benefit from high levels of government support and awareness, which results in better air quality management and lower disease rates.

- Cluster L2: Consists of a single province, Saraburi, making it difficult to analyze this cluster's characteristics.

Overall, these findings highlight the clear link between the environmental characteristics of a province and respiratory disease rates. For example, Cluster L0 includes provinces like Sakon Nakhon, Chiang Mai, Krabi, and Ratchaburi, which have low air pollution due to limited industrial and tourism activities. Cluster L1 includes provinces such as Khon Kaen, Chonburi, and Nakhon Pathom, which have sustainable development plans, high investment in environmental initiatives, and strong public participation. The single-province L2 cluster (Saraburi) has unique characteristics that require further investigation.

An example of practical application can be observed in the case of Suphanburi Province, which exhibits a lower number of respiratory disease cases. This can be attributed to its features, such as the Number of Wildfire Extinguishments (44 instances) and Burned Area (1,082 rai), both of which are significantly lower compared to Chiang Rai Province. In contrast, Chiang Rai has a Number of Wildfire Extinguishments of 163 and a Burned Area of 4,361.76 rai.

5 Conclusion

In summary, this study identified key features that influence the number of respiratory disease cases in Thailand. The highest contributing features are air quality issues caused by urban expansion and agricultural activities. This is followed by severe environmental challenges, such as forest fires, and finally, environmental and occupational features related to economic activities.

To reduce the number of respiratory disease cases, we recommend the following policy actions for high-risk provinces:

1. Promote the use of organic fertilizers and support eco-friendly agricultural practices to reduce pollution.
2. Encourage sustainable tourism to minimize environmental impacts in popular destinations.
3. Implement efficient water management and support local product processing to reduce transportation needs and emissions.
4. Increase green spaces to absorb pollutants and control climate change.
5. Promote clean energy use, such as solar or wind energy, to reduce dependency on fossil fuels.
6. Enhance educational opportunities and improve access to basic healthcare services, particularly in rural areas.

For provinces with low respiratory disease rates, the key success feature is balancing environmental and economic development. Supporting government investment to increase provincial income and encouraging public participation in environmental conservation are also crucial strategies.

Creating a healthy city requires sustainable policy planning that balances economic growth and environmental protection, along with promoting healthcare access and educational opportunities, especially in rural and urban areas.

References

Yang, J.: Application of machine learning to predict hospital visits for respiratory diseases using meteorological and air pollution factors in Linyi, China (2023)
Zhang, L .: Cluster analysis of PM2.5 pollution in China using the frequent itemset clustering approach (2022)
Puvvula, J.: Role of social determinants of health in differential respiratory exposure and health outcomes among children (2023)
Average Monthly Temperature by Province. e-report.energy.go.th/weather.html. Accessed 19 Sept 2024
Labor Demand Statistics. https://www.doe.go.th/prd/assets/upload/files/lmia_th/. Accessed 19 Sept 2024
International Statistical Indicators. https://www.nso.go.th/nsoweb/nso/statistics_and_indicators. Accessed 19 Sept 2024
Tourism. https://view.officeapps.live.com/op/view.aspx?src=/. Accessed 19 Sept 2024
Transport Statistics Group. https://web.dlt.go.th/statistics/. Accessed 19 Sept 2024
Summary of the Number of Temples. https://web.onab.go.th. Accessed 19 Sept 2024
Population Statistics from Civil Registration. https://web.dopa.go.th. Accessed 23 Sept 2024
Municipal Solid Waste Management Information System. https://pcd.go.th. Accessed 23 Sept 2024
Forest Fire Control Division, Department of National Parks, Wildlife and Plant Conservation. https://dnp.go.th. Accessed 24 Sept 2024
Budget Allocation by Province for the Fiscal Year 2023. https://bb.go.th. Accessed 24 Sept 2024
Educational Institutions. https://GDCatalog.go.th. Accessed 24 Sept 2024
List of Airports in Thailand (Codes). https://www.easy-travelworld. Accessed 24 Sept 2024
Annual Health Workforce Report 2023. https://moph.go.th. Accessed 24 Sept 2024
Industrial Factory Statistics – Department of Industrial Works. https://diw.go.th. Accessed 24 Sept 2024
Sugarcane Plantation and Production Report. https://www.ocsb.go.th/. Accessed 24 Sept 2024

Author Index

J. Kertesz et al. (Eds.): CSoNet 2024, LNCS 15417, pp. 487–489, 2025.
https://doi.org/10.1007/978-981-96-6389-7

The manufacturer's authorised representative in the EU is Springer Nature Customer Service Centre GmbH, Europaplatz 3, 69115 Heidelberg, Germany. If you have any concerns regarding our products, please contact ProductSafety@springernature.com

Printed and bound by CPI Group (UK) Ltd, Croydon, CR0 4YY

01/10/2026

02225834-0019